This Elusive Land

Edited By Melody Hessing,
Rebecca Raglon, and Catriona Sandilands

This Elusive Land:
Women and the Canadian
Environment

UBCPress · Vancouver · Toronto

15 14 13 12 11 10 09 08 07 06 05   5 4 3 2 1

Printed in Canada on acid-free paper that is 100% post-consumer recycled, processed chlorine-free, and printed with vegetable-based, low-VOC inks.

Library and Archives Canada Cataloguing in Publication

This elusive land : women and the Canadian environment / edited by Melody Hessing, Rebecca Raglon and Catriona Sandilands.

Includes bibliographical references and index.
ISBN 0-7748-1106-4

1. Women and the environment – Canada. I. Hessing, Melody II. Raglon, Rebecca Sue, 1950- III. Sandilands, Catriona Alison Hayward, 1964-

HQ1453.T48 2004   333.7'082'0971   C2004-904486-9

Canadä

UBC Press gratefully acknowledges the financial support for our publishing program of the Government of Canada through the Book Publishing Industry Development Program (BPIDP), and of the Canada Council for the Arts, and the British Columbia Arts Council.

This book has been published with the help of a grant from the Canadian Federation for the Humanities and Social Sciences, through the Aid to Scholarly Publications Programme, using funds provided by the Social Sciences and Humanities Research Council of Canada, and with the help of the K.D. Srivastava Fund.

The editors gratefully acknowledge both the Social Sciences and Humanities Research Council of Canada and Douglas College for grants in support of the completion of the index.

UBC Press
The University of British Columbia
2029 West Mall
Vancouver, BC V6T 1Z2
604-822-5959 / Fax: 604-822-6083
www.ubcpress.ca

HQ
1453
T55
2005

Contents

Introduction:
Women and Environment

(precede me into this elusive country)
always this place, this latitude escapes me
— Gwendolyn MacEwen[1]

This Elusive Land: Women and the Canadian Environment is a multidisciplinary anthology exploring a feminist approach to the Canadian environment. A number of factors have coalesced to form a foundation for rethinking how gender influences our perspectives of the Canadian landscape. These include new academic research, especially feminist studies; conflicts in resource use; the articulation of new interests and stakeholders in the development of environmental policy; the increased profile of land claims by First Nations; the creation of a new territory, Nunavut; additional understanding of the global significance of Canadian resources; and decreases in biodiversity and biological integrity. All of these factors have generated increased attention to the Canadian environment. Yet we felt that the topic of gender had been developed only incidentally – for instance, as a chapter on resource management or as a topic developed sporadically in the context of women's writing. Given the increasing recognition of the importance of gender to environmental history, literature, economics, and politics, it seemed the right moment for a book to examine how Canada, too, is a particular site of feminist interaction with the environment.

This collection of essays, drawn from a variety of academic backgrounds, is meant to fill a gap in our knowledge of women and the environment in Canada. As editors, we wanted to develop a multifaceted look at the topic of women and the environment that would collectively address the still powerful, gendered reality of Canadian experiences of the land. In addition, we wanted to build on (1) feminist scholarship on women's relations to the Canadian landscape and (2) ecofeminist scholarship theorizing women's relations to natural environments, and to critique both if necessary. In

particular, we wanted to make links between and among disciplinary perspectives by including a variety of views from both the humanities and
social sciences (which merge in some chapters). In this way we hoped that
a fuller picture of women's experiences would emerge, one that would provide a useful basis for reassessing gendered human relationships to nature.
We proceeded on the assumption that women's experiences and positions
in society have given us and continue to give us different sets of lenses
through which to observe the natural world. Sometimes this gaze is critical,
and sometimes it underscores the interests of patriarchal society. At all times,
gender is also unavoidably located in historically, geographically, and culturally specific relations of race, colonialism, and class.

While gender is significant to our understanding of all facets of Canadian
society, it is especially so in how we confront, depend on, and interact with
the natural world. Why this might be so has been the topic of endless and
often confusing debate. Is woman really associated with nature as man is
with culture, as some feminists claim? Or are women the caretakers of
culture, while men are associated with the wild (which is often considered
the experience of nineteenth-century women settlers in North America)?
Despite the blurring that has occurred in other professions and other aspects of society, association with the environment – in terms of resource-
intensive jobs, exploration, or leisure activities – remains largely a man's
game. Yet paradoxically, women outnumber men as members of environmental organizations and have been a significant source of environmental
activism and leadership. What is to account for these apparent contradictions? Are women still so strongly associated with domesticity that even
environmentalism confines them to the role of cleaning up the mess, while
men go out and heroically save (or exploit) the wild?

Among the questions this volume explores, then, is how gender influences perspectives and experiences of the environment, how women's relations to the environment embody and reflect the experiences and the
perspectives of "others," and how physical environments influence social
and political relations. In addition, contributors to this volume ask: How
are women's positions in the family, the community, and the labour force
mediated by the environment? How are women politically active in developing environmental/resource policy? What would a feminist environmental
perspective look like, especially in the Canadian context? And finally, and
perhaps most important, does a feminist perspective enable us to better
know, understand, and value the Canadian environment, and if so, how?

The contributors to this book have all focused on how women's lives are
the product of biophysical places as well as social and institutional factors.
What emerges is a nuanced picture of the constant interplay between social
factors and the biophysical context of the Canadian environment, one

that is dynamic and varied, reflecting an array of ecological systems, political and biological regions, historical and cultural variables, and theoretical views. This interplay expands both the way the environment is portrayed and notions of what constitutes a problem or crisis. Consequently, this book contributes to women's studies through its environmental focus, it informs environmental studies with a range of feminist perspectives, and it complements Canadian studies by integrating a variety of disciplinary perspectives of the Canadian experience from the humanities and social sciences.

Gendered Accounts of Canada

The familiar facts about the place we call Canada found in its history, economics, and literature are based primarily on the gendered accounts provided by its white settlers, from the first European explorers to workers in today's resource-based economy. Men such as Jacques Cartier, Henry Hudson, Samuel de Champlain, and John Cabot charted Canada's extensive coastline; Alexander Mackenzie, Samuel Hearne, and John Franklin explored the Arctic and interior reaches of the country. Collectively, they described a country that was both harsh and unsuitable for farming: Jacques Cartier is reported to have said, as he navigated the Saint Lawrence River in 1534, that the Gaspé area was "the land God gave to Cain."[2] Germaine Warkentin points out that even though early exploration accounts are filled with descriptions of the lives of Native inhabitants, much of the interior of Canada during the seventeenth and eighteenth centuries was depicted primarily as a storehouse of resources that existed outside the civilized fold.[3] Traditional accounts of the fur trade tend to suggest that this was exclusively men's work, performed by First Nations hunters, French Canadian voyageurs, and Hudson's Bay administrators. Yet even the fur trade was often contingent on women's contributions. As Sylvia Van Kirk has documented extensively, without First Nations women as guides, many of the hunters, voyageurs, and traders would have found themselves hopelessly lost and, in all likelihood, starving or facing death.[4]

The historian W.L. Morton argues that during the nineteenth century, the "rural myth" took hold in Canada: the belief that the basis of "welfare and virtue was the land and its cultivation."[5] Accompanying this "rural myth" was the understanding that women immigrants from England, Ireland, Scotland, and Europe typically suffered greater hardships than men when it came to backwoods life. However, in the context of the demise of the fur trade and the rise of a settler society, women were also understood to *embody and transport* necessary "civilization" to colonial landscapes. On top of their sustaining (and largely unrecognized) contributions to frontier economies, these women were thought to bring domestic stability and social conservatism to the "wild." Men could thus trap, hunt, explore; women were confined to the cabin or to some middle ground of garden or field, where their virtues could, literally, be planted in the national soil.

Immigrant women often longed for the homes they had left behind. In the early nineteenth century, Anna Jameson stated, "I have never met with so many repining and discontented women as in Canada. I have never met with one woman recently settled here, who considered herself happy in her new home and country."[6] Apart from missing the support of family and friends and the landscapes of previous homelands, women were often confined by domestic responsibility to isolated cabins and woodlots. The "adventure" of settling in a new country was not necessarily undertaken of their own initiative. A hundred years later, the novelist Frederick Philip Grove continued to echo these sentiments as he portrayed the desire to possess and transform land as a masculine obsession in which women were often unhappy accomplices. In his 1923 novel, *The Turn of the Year,* he writes of a man and a wife growing apart as the woman finds employment in the city and begins to enjoy life there. One summer, when the work in the fields took all his time, the duties of milking the cows, feeding the pigs, and tending the garden fell to the woman. "But while he worked his vision was of the farm; her vision was a comparison between this slavery and the city. Man and wife found themselves estranged."[7]

In the mid-twentieth century, Northrop Frye, surveying Canadian fiction and poetry, theorized that Canadians had a "garrison mentality" in relation to nature. Unlike Americans, who marched confidently forward, intent on converting their wilderness into a New Jerusalem, according to Frye, Canadians were appalled by the brooding forests and enormous spaces around their settlements. As a consequence, they huddled indoors, looked inward, and sought comfort from one another. Furthermore, while Americans could regard their wilderness with certain affection, Canadians viewed theirs with ambivalence, even terror: "I have long been impressed in Canadian poetry by a tone of deep terror in regard to nature ... It is not a terror of the dangers or discomforts or even the mysteries of nature, but a terror of soul at something that these things manifest. The human mind has nothing but human and moral values to cling to if it is to preserve its integrity or even its sanity, yet the vast unconsciousness of nature in front of it seems an unanswerable denial of those values."[8]

Once again, however, women's relations to this mentality suggest a more nuanced story. While, on the one hand, such writers as Susanna Moodie indicate that women's sense of "homelessness" in the New World actually intensified their terror, others – including her sister, Catharine Parr Traill – clearly sought to create a dwelling in the wilderness by crafting a complex intimacy with the wild nature around them. Diana Relke's ecocritical reading of some of Canada's most prominent women poets suggests that women have long been "redrawing the map" of nature by consulting the contexts of their own experiences.[9] This redrawing of the map continues in the work of contemporary authors such as Dionne Brand, who views the brooding forests of the Canadian North through the context of nontemperate landscape experiences and histories. For Brand, November "is when missing plumes";[10] its rain brings memories of tropics and tamarinds and not the pastoral England of Moodie's particular nostalgia. Again, in contrast, Mohawk author Beth Brant finds solace in the natural world; it is in her identification with the wild, not her protective retreat from it, that she discovers safety and personal resolution to crisis and tragedy.[11] In Bernice Morgan's *Random Passage*, Mary Bundle's adept criminality finds an odd welcome in a bleak Newfoundland outport.[12] These women's writings speak of a landscape tradition with roots and branches that extend well beyond the walls of Frye's garrison. Often garrisoned by domestic responsibilities, women may find a kind of solace or relief in the ambiguities and diversities of wild nature.

Economic expansion adds another layer to the experience of the Canadian environment. While First Nations for centuries lived in diverse subsistence and gift economies, contemporary capitalist livelihoods are largely wrested from the resources we exploit. Indeed, what we now perceive as the "environment," the biophysical systems that support this country, is still reduced by conventional economics to the utilitarian notion of "resource." Resources are sold in an increasingly global, if still American-dominated, marketplace. Today the Canadian economy is based on the exploitation of resources in sectors such as forestry, mining, fishing, energy, and agriculture, which account for almost one-third of the value of all exports. Canada is still a country dependent both materially and symbolically on natural resources, although diversification and technological innovation have reduced jobs in resource sectors. Resource economies, involving the direct exploitation of the environment for human use, have been overwhelmingly characterized by a male workforce, although employment has decreased in recent decades. Nonetheless, resource processing (e.g., pulp and paper production or food processing) and related transportation, construction, and service activities, as well as indirect employment in retail, wholesale, and government sectors, provide opportunities for many women in rural communities.

Here again, gender complicates the picture. Although well-paid jobs in the resource sector go to men, women have played – and continue to play – important roles in resource communities. Meg Luxton points out in *More than a Labour of Love* that women are reproductive labourers in resource communities;[13] in addition, women have played significant productive roles in particular resource industries. They have salted, dried, packed, and canned fish; they have picked fruit among families of migrant labourers (legal and illegal); they have transformed billions of potatoes into French fries and tomatoes into ketchup. In addition, as particular resource industries feel the pressures of globalization, patterns of resource exhaustion and technological change disrupt long-established gender and family patterns, a significant issue for resource communities. Women's employment outside the home ironically becomes the basis for staying on the land and holding on to the farm. As tourist-industry jobs replace logging, and as lands once occupied by family farms are taken over by agribusiness or residential development, gendered relations to landscape cannot help but shift, reflecting changes occurring in labour patterns.

Finally, a gendered account of Canadian environments must include a sense of how women and men are affected and politicized in different ways by environmental degradation. The environmental-justice movement in the United States has increasingly recognized that we live in a global as well as a local environment. People are not equally affected by toxic wastes, industrial agricultural discharges, chemical spills, and air-quality alerts.[14] Race and class are important factors in determining who gets what in their ecological backyards. It is thus frequently low-income women and women of colour who must respond to the task of recognizing the effects of environmental contamination on their families and communities. These women are then charged with the task of pursuing justice in the face of unresponsive bureaucracies and reluctant industrial polluters. In Canada major urban centres are increasingly faced with significant pollution problems. The more children develop severe asthma and other respiratory problems, and the more the safety of the food and water systems is called into question, the more women will be called upon to politicize the ecological conditions of their families' illnesses. In places like Whitney Pier, Nova Scotia, residents are still seeking justice in the face of years of irresponsible contamination and cover-up. For many First Nations women, toxic politics are compounded by isolation and social problems. Labrador Innu are fighting environmental battles against low-level NATO flights at the same time as they are struggling to preserve and vivify their traditional land-based culture in the face of alcoholism and abuse.

In past male-authored accounts of Canadian exploration and exploitation, the rougher and tougher the landscape, the more heroic are the men who seek to discover its secrets, tame it, and wrestle the wealth from it. Yet women's labour – invisible, marginalized, devalued – enables men's adventures. These same labours, of course, alert women to environmental change. In the midst of an environmentalist critique of resource exploitation and toxic imperialism, then, feminists have an important role to play in issuing a reminder about the complex gendered dimensions of Canadian environmental history, literature, and economics. An understanding of the complex and diverse relationship between women and the natural environment will contribute to a deeper understanding of the environmental challenges facing Canada.

Feminist Scholarship on Environment and Gender

Feminist scholars, confronting these gendered relations, have reacted in a variety of ways. Helen Buss, noting some of the shades of women's responses to their newfound lands, suggests that far from communicating the kind of "terror" that Frye discovered in his reading of primarily masculine works, women's accounts convey a different ethos. According to Buss, "All the women autobiographers ... react to the strangeness of the Canadian landscape by merging their own identity, in some imaginative way, with the new land." This feminine merging is certainly considerably different from the terrified recoiling detected by Frye. Buss believes that such moments of intimacy are arrived at in two ways: "through a relationship with significant others and through some creative activity that discovers each woman's unique relation to the land." She urges literary critics to begin to see through "ungarrisoned eyes" and suggests that the "interconnection of self, other, and land" is a "female vision of the land."[15] Annis Pratt goes even further in her discernment of difference between the male and female experiences of nature, suggesting that Canadian experiences with nature generally, compared with the American experience, have certain "feminine" attributes. According to Pratt, this femininity can be characterized by a kind of "animistic reciprocity between being of woman and being of rock, tree, and beast."[16]

Interpretations such as Pratt's and Buss's tended to coincide with the evolution of ecofeminist writings in the 1980s and seemed to suggest that women had – or have – a more evolved connection to the natural world than men. Although ecofeminist thinkers have generally eschewed biologically determinist arguments about women's inborn proclivities to "nature-nurturance," they have also emphasized strong connections between the oppression of women and the domination of nature. For some ecofeminists, Western philosophical systems of hierarchical dualism have organized a world in which women are subordinated to men, emotion to reason, body to mind, and nature to culture. In this broad conceptual frame, women share a degraded social position with nonhuman nature; both are "resources" for male exploitation, overused, undervalued, and denied full subject status in patriarchal thought. For others, it is more the case that women's social position in patriarchal societies shapes a particular consciousness of natural environments. As indicated earlier, women are often alerted to particular conditions of ecological degradation in the course of their everyday work as caregivers for families and communities. In addition, it is often women's work that is most adversely affected when ecological systems are devastated. In subsistence economies, women have to work harder to feed their families when their community resource base is depleted – for example, in favour of cash crops for export. In both cases, ecofeminists have suggested that it is not so much that women have an innate connection to nature as it is that women occupy a social position that allows them epistemic privilege in relation to nature and, especially, to processes of environmental degradation.

Ecofeminist analyses of this kind have been hotly criticized by feminists such as Janet Biehl, who speak of the political dangers of creating essentialized connections between women and nature, even in the act of opposing male-dominated agendas.[17] In recent years, however, ecofeminist scholarship has become increasingly more complex than this idea of essential connection allows. In some instances, writers such as Noël Sturgeon have argued in favour of a strategic essentialism, in which women activists are able to mobilize around problematic understandings of gender and nature in order to make crucial points about the effects of these essentialist ideas.[18] In other cases, writers such as Lee Quinby argue for a more interrogative political form, in which the deep specificities of local struggles are not and cannot be located in singular, overarching conceptions of gender or nature (or race, class, sexuality, or nation). In contrast to Biehl, for whom ecofeminism is to be rejected partly as a result of its conceptual "incoherence," Quinby embraces it for its intellectual and political diversity.[19]

Still, some feminist ecologists, including Bina Agarwal, remain deeply critical of ecofeminism, indicating the ease with which international institutions have picked up languages of gender difference and planetary nurturance.[20] They suggest that any political stance that relies on notions of women's "difference" to carve out an ecological politics runs into the danger of reinforcing, rather than challenging, patriarchal and colonialist ideas of gender and nature. It is also important to recognize that ecofeminist ideas about labour, history, and even the nature of oppression do not exhaust the theoretical possibilities for feminist/environmental inquiry. In this context, ecofeminist scholarship could continue to benefit from a more thoroughgoing understanding of the intense particularities of gender and nature in specific places and how these are organized by complex intersections of power based on both physical and cultural environments.

Organization of This Book

In addressing some of these questions, the book encompasses a range of perspectives, topics, and issues investigating women's experiences of the Canadian environment. The chapters range from literary and historical discussion to investigations of socio-economic and political issues. They reflect the experiences of women in different provinces and bioregions across the country, from Newfoundland to British Columbia. In order to organize this very wide-ranging inquiry, we chose four broad areas to examine: the cultural and historical representation of the natural world found in women's writing; the roles of women in environmental and resource work, especially logging, fishing, agriculture, and tourism; the roles of women in both local and global environmental politics; and finally, the possibilities for reframing and reimagining the gendered experience of wilderness, nature, and the environment.

Part 1, "Explorers and Settlers," deals with the literary and historical record of women's relations to the Canadian environment. This part asks whether women were in fact as alienated from the settlement experience as past writers and recent feminist scholarship have claimed. Does an ecofeminist viewpoint reveal an alternative story to the one of women's alienation? Do women have a "special" relationship with the natural world? In this part we find two sets of ideas. On the one hand, there are examples of adventurous women (who negate the idea that exploration is a man's activity); on the other hand, many women were incapable of meeting the rigours of life in the bush. This part contains examples of women who endorse what we now understand as patriarchal social structure or who were enthusiastic supporters of what we now perceive as imperialistic projects of settlement and colonization. Certainly, evidence also points to situations in which women's work, for example, gave them the ability to develop apparently "caring" relations with the natural environment and to develop autonomy and competence, even if involuntarily.

Catharine Parr Traill is well known to many Canadians, yet she is usually viewed as the "less interesting" of the two Strickland sisters. Rebecca Raglon provides an ecocritical reading of Traill that places her work in a more congenial context and in the process suggests that Traill's early feminine viewpoint offers new insights that challenge the genre of nature writing. Daniel O'Leary looks at a neglected Canadian writer, Agnes Deans Cameron, who travelled in the far North in the early part of the twentieth century. One has to be impressed with her energy, independence, and spirit, but O'Leary does not engage in feminist hagiography. Rather, he develops a critical approach that allows him to acknowledge Deans Cameron's imperialistic mode and missionary zeal and sets it within the context of the missionary magazines that were popular reading among the Canadian public. Randall Roorda plays with the term "wilderness wives," wondering why so many accounts of wilderness travel, exploration, and adventure were written by "wives" in the twentieth century and why these "wives" clung so fiercely to their gender roles, finding them so difficult to abandon. Finally, Jo-Anne Fiske brings readers up to date on the present-day North, with all of its contradictions, revealed by the irony of her chapter's title, "And the Young Man Did Go North (Unfortunately)." Fiske, an anthropologist, sees the North not as a land that is "true and free" and filled with brave and stalwart men, but as a place almost hallucinogenic in its cognitive dissonance. According to Fiske, while some residents still cling to old myths, they do so while plugged into satellite TVs or imagining pure wilderness adventure from the cab of an oversized pick-up truck.

Part 2, "Making a Living: Making a Life," examines the diverse ways that women engage with the natural environment not only as a means of economic survival, but as the basis for their connection to family and community. Women's labour, both paid and unpaid, constructs the frame(work) in which they weave their lives – where women spend time, learn skills, meet other people, and earn wages (in some kinds of work). This part challenges several common assumptions about the male character of employment in the resource sector, extending our ideas about the nature of work and who should be doing it. Men's work has, and continues to be, directly associated with resource economies; however, declines in traditional male employment have created increased demand for women's contributions to household incomes. While technology, resource supplies, and resistance to women's labour have historically curtailed women's paid work, the emergence of new technologies additionally spur women's participation in the labour force.

This part examines a Canadian resource economy in transition by exploring women's contributions to the fishery, forestry, agriculture, and tourism, which is a growing force in environmental employment. Barbara Neis and Brenda Grzetic focus on the impacts of economic and environmental restructuring on women's work and, in turn, their health. They discuss the economic, social, and personal costs of environmental restructuring due to overfishing. They argue that restructuring is not gender neutral but threatens women's health by eroding and transforming opportunities for work and by reducing household incomes. Restructuring is not merely macroeconomic; rather, it intrudes into women's lives, reshaping health and households just as it transforms canneries and mills. Maureen G. Reed explores the role of women in forestry by discussing women's experiences of paid work within the forestry industry and in communities. By adopting women's perspectives on their work, we understand how their location in households and communities informs their life choices and opportunities for work. Martha McMahon explores how farming is a gendered experience. She describes how small-scale women farmers resist marginalization through the generation of an alternative ecological agriculture, one that rejects and disrupts conventional understandings about food and our relationship to the land. Finally, Catriona Sandilands' chapter demonstrates how gender informs environmental politics in the "nonconsumptive" sector of tourism. Discussion of how gender infiltrates parks interpretation and wilderness tourism in Banff National Park and others reveals the continuing primacy of male definitions of what it is to be a park warden, and also of the role of national parks in Canadian nationalism. Here, a lesbian treatment of this work challenges the conventional separation between rock-and-ice machismo and cabin domesticity.

Part 3 deals with "Environmental Politics: Issues at Home and Away." While politics are often thought of in terms of formal institutions such as Parliament, individuals also engage in political activity and experience the consequences of political actions in all facets of their lives. Environmental politics refers to how power is mobilized, decisions are made, and policy is formulated and implemented with respect to our physical and social surroundings. Politics, then, refers to the processes by which humans decide how to live on this earth – how they should distribute wealth, whether to recycle goods, and where (and if) to situate an industrial dumpsite. It includes the allocation of household tasks and the kitchen-table discussion of neighborhood traffic control, in addition to traditional municipal, provincial, and federal decision-making. International tribunals and agencies are increasingly relevant to environmental governance due to the extent and fluidity of ecological systems and the global dimensions of contemporary society. Women have been significantly underrepresented in formal political processes at the provincial and federal levels in Canada but have been especially visible and active in environmental and municipal politics. Women's political activity often interprets the personal as political, and it also understands the importance of every stage of political struggle, from the local to the global.

The chapters in this part show how women integrate household, community, and society through their political activity. Sherilyn MacGregor's chapter, "The Public, the Private, the Planet, and the Province: Women's Quality-of-Life Activism in Urban Southern Ontario," describes how women activists politicize personal and local environmental issues. MacGregor discusses the burden of "caring" and household support that women have absorbed in the face of government cutbacks. First-hand accounts explain how women personally accommodate the additional responsibility of political work, their perceptions of their own contributions to society, and their views about the relationship between sustainability, society, and political citizenship.

On the global stage, Canadian development agencies have been widely recognized within the international community for their work on two major concerns: gender and the environment. Leonora C. Angeles, Layla Saad, and Rebecca Tarbotton's chapter, "Desperately Seeking Sisterhood and Sustainability: Creating Transnational Social Learning Spaces for Sustainable Agriculture and Environmental Advocacy," describes how women have mobilized around environmental issues in less developed countries, specifically India, the Philippines, and Brazil. These examples of local political organization are significant not only for Canadian women, but for hinterland communities, where resources are also under pressure from global markets.

The politics of reproduction, family, and industrial production are addressed in the next chapter, "Too Close to Home: Dioxin Contamination of Breast Milk and the Political Agenda." Kathryn Harrison discusses how breast milk reflects environmental quality, demonstrating how the personal – the breast milk mothers provide their babies – becomes political. Economic and political actions – the character of industrial production, the implementation of regulatory policies – are not usually associated so closely with our personal health and intimate relations. Finally, Katherine Dunster's chapter, "Acting Locally," demonstrates how mapping can be used as a means of community mobilization by putting environments and issues on the political map. The process of mapping politicizes participants, while the map as a product is a visual manifestation of environment, integrating individuals not only into community but into the larger physical context of region, province, nation, and planet.

Living in the twenty-first century involves living in that uncomfortable zone known as the "environmental crisis." If this crisis has come about because of a nexus of historical, economic, and political forces, then it seems vital that we try to find new ways of thinking about human relationships with the natural world. Part of this process involves identifying the gendered reality of many activities, histories, and cultural engagements with the Canadian land. In Part 4, however, the authors have gone beyond identifying the attitudes and activities that have enmeshed women within a reality increasingly perceived as an ongoing "environmental crisis." In this final part of the book, the authors tackle the idea of "rethinking," or "remapping," the environment as they break free from the contexts that have garrisoned women in domestic quarters or in the roles of helper and enabler of environmental destruction.

Anne Kaufman looks across the border in her comparison of Willa Cather and Aritha van Herk in a chapter that examines a different form of "Canadian western," one that opens up a new scale of authenticity and revivifies familiar Prairie territory by examining it through the experience of feminine eroticism. Kaufman concludes in "Tracing Amorous Journeys from the Sweetwater to Watson Lake" that Canadian writers are less confined by nation-building issues such as Manifest Destiny and thus more open to parodying the myth of the West. In "A Vision of Transformation: Ecofeminist Spiritualities in Canada," Heather Eaton examines the transformative possibilities of spirituality and the importance of the sacred in any reassessment of human interaction with the land. Eaton points out that spirituality often underscores what communities consider to be most profound in their lives and examines how ecofeminism and spirituality have intersected in Canada.

The theme of rethinking the human relationship to the Canadian environment by discussing the physical wilderness, which still exists as a defining characteristic of Canada, continues in "The Fall of the Wild? Feminist Perspectives of Canadian Wilderness Protection." According to Melody Hessing, despite the relative abundance of wild places in this country, Canada lags behind many other countries in terms of wilderness protection. Hessing's chapter is a call for continued recognition of the wilderness as a central aspect of the Canadian experience and identity. This recognition can be approached, however, only through a careful rethinking of the term wilderness and its various, often contradictory meanings. Finally, in "The Listening World: First Nations Women Writers and the Environment," Marian Scholtmeijer examines how many First Nations writers convey a sense of a nonhuman world that is very different from the natural world of Western literary tradition, which most often presents nature as a backdrop to a more absorbing human drama or as a storehouse of convenient metaphors and symbols to enhance human importance. In particular, the identification of human and animal can be very close in First Nations women's writing, which suggests yet another way of thinking about the world, a profound way that reaches beyond the identification of nonhuman nature as mere resource.

Together the chapters in this collection are meant to identify how gender has contributed to experiences of the land. Our hope is that such an examination, touching on many diverse places and issues, will highlight previously neglected issues concerning the environment, while also suggesting the many challenges lying ahead in developing a more meaningful, equitable, and enduring relationship to the natural world.

Notes

1 Gwendolyn MacEwen, "The Caravan," in *Modern Canadian Verse*, edited by A.J.M. Smith (Toronto: Oxford University Press, 1967), 415.

2 Jacques Cartier, *The Voyages of Jacques Cartier* (Toronto: University of Toronto Press, 1983), 10.

3 Germaine Warkentin, *Canadian Exploration Literature: An Anthology: 1660-1860* (Toronto: Oxford University Press, 1993).

4 Sylvia Van Kirk, *Many Tender Ties: Women in Fur-Trader Society, 1670-1870* (Winnipeg: Watson and Dwyer Publishing, 1980).

5 W.L. Morton, *The Shield of Achilles: Aspects of Canada in the Victorian Age* (Toronto: McClelland and Stewart, 1968), 312.

6 Anna Jameson, *Winter Studies and Summer Rambles in Canada* (1838; reprint, Toronto: McClelland and Stewart, 1923), 139.

7 Frederick Philip Grove, *The Turn of the Year* (Toronto: McClelland and Stewart, 1923), 60.

8 Northrop Frye, *The Bush Garden* (Toronto: House of Anansi, 1971), 250.

9 Diana Relke, *Greenwor(l)ds* (Calgary: University of Calgary Press, 1999), 323.

10 Dionne Brand, *In Another Place, Not Here* (Toronto: Alfred A. Knopf, 1996), 200.

11 Beth Brant, *Food and Spirits: Stories* (Vancouver: Press Gang, 1991).
12 Bernice Morgan, *Random Passage* (St. John's, NF: Breakwater, 1992).
13 Meg Luxton, *More Than a Labour of Love: Three Generations of Women's Work in the Home* (Toronto: The Women's Press, 1980).
14 Robert Bullard, *Dumping in Dixie* (Boulder, CO: Westview Press, 1990).
15 Helen Buss, "Women and the Garrison Mentality: Pioneer Women Autobiographers and their Relation to the Land," in *Re(dis)covering Our Foremothers,* edited by Lorraine McMullen (Ottawa: University of Ottawa Press, 1988), 123-36, 126.
16 Annis Pratt, "Affairs with Bears: Some Notes towards Feminist Archetypal Hypotheses for Canadian Literature," in *Gynocritics: Feminist Approaches to Writing by Canadian and Quebecoise Women,* edited by Barbara Godard (Toronto: ECW Press, 1987), 157-78, 162.
17 Janet Biehl, *Finding Our Way: Rethinking Ecofeminist Politics* (Montreal: Black Rose Books, 1991).
18 Noël Sturgeon, *Ecofeminist Natures: Race, Gender, Feminist Theory, and Political Action* (New York, NY: Routledge, 1997).
19 Lee Quinby, *Anti-Apocalypse: Exercises in Genealogical Criticism* (Minneapolis, MN: University of Minnesota Press, 1994).
20 Bina Agarwal, "A Challenge for Ecofeminism: Gender, Greening, and Community Forestry in India," *Women and Environments International Magazine* 52/53 (Fall 2001): 12-15.

Part 1
Explorers and Settlers

Much of how the Canadian environment is perceived is filtered through the written record that emerged during the nineteenth-century settlement of Canada. In this part this record is examined from both an environmental and feminist viewpoint. Catharine Parr Traill, often treated dismissively by literary scholars and historians, nevertheless provides an interesting example of a writer who confronts the experience of preserving feminine domestic life in a difficult situation without an associated hostility for the natural world. What is remarkable about Traill is that she viewed the natural world as a source of intellectual solace: The flowers and ferns she loved were a backwoods library, society, and cultural event all in one. Modelling her own work on that of the English naturalist Gilbert White, Traill found herself having to make adjustments to her botanizing and moralizing that took into account the very different conditions in which she lived. Gilbert White's village was stable, long-standing, and sustainable. The landscape Traill recorded was in upheaval. In part, she favoured this upheaval, knowing that it was necessary for her survival and her family's wellbeing. She believed, as did many women, in the benefits that British civilization was bringing to this land. But very early on, she suggested that the settlers of Upper Canada could go "too far" when she championed the rare woodland flowers that were disappearing as trees were felled and land was cleared for fields. The right of the rare and the beautiful to exist, and the suggestion that truly civilized behaviour would make room for appreciation of such life, are all part of an aesthetic that Traill cultivated over a lifetime.

Agnes Deans Cameron was one of a number of remarkable women who produced travel narratives about Canada throughout the late nineteenth and early twentieth centuries. Many accounts were semiautobiographical, and many were written by missionaries who enthusiastically shared in the progressive aims of British imperial civilization. Daniel O'Leary, drawing on extensive reading of missionary accounts of the Canadian North, concludes that imperialistic sentiments, including loyalty to the idea of the British Empire, in fact helped to protect the North from encroachments by American whalers and others intent on intensive exploitation of the resources of the Arctic. In addition, Cameron uses what O'Leary calls an androgynous narrative voice in order to appeal to both a male and female readership. Much of the success of both wilderness and missionary accounts thus depended upon a successful "double gendering" of the text – an interesting concept when contrasted with the preoccupations of twentieth-century writers who strove to achieve an authentic "female" voice in which to write "herstory." Nevertheless, even within the context of an imperial setting and a carefully modulated androgynous voice, Cameron's account of her travels through the far North provides a record of intense sensitivity to the land and its beauty.

Randall Roorda's chapter, "Wilderness Wives," probes a twentieth-century phenomenon: women writing as the *wives* of more experienced backwoodsmen. Here the androgynous voice O'Leary detects in writers like Cameron is replaced by a concept that rather uncomfortably joins the most domestic of roles for women – wife – with the wilderness. Roorda's work examines the odd interregnum that exists between the turn of the century, when Agnes Deans Cameron and scores of others wrote their own accounts of travel through the natural world, and the beginning of the environmental movement in the 1960s and 1970s. This period appears to be the age of the wilderness wife, who, rather than travelling on her own as Cameron did or finding her role as Traill did, is preeminently pictured as an accompaniment to the main course: a woman who goes along with the more knowledgeable, stronger husband into the wild. Wilderness wives, Roorda shrewdly notes, both embarrass feminism and at the same time flout the masculine imperative for a solitary wilderness experience. They seem to exist in their own category, yet this category, mildly ridiculous as it is, nevertheless deeply probes the domestic/wild split that has been one of the problems bedeviling cultural constructions of the natural world.

Finally, the anthropologist Jo-Anne Fiske brings the narrative up to date with her account of the present-day "settlement" of the North. This is a land where, stereotypically, the new wilderness man drives a pick-up truck plastered with bumper stickers deriding environmentalists and Natives alike. The "North," Fiske concludes, is an imaginary geography but one that still appeals and is used to represent a personal stereotypical masculinity and freedom. This myth of masculinity, however, emerges in opposition to the feminine and domestic. The fantastic and often violent culture that is produced through this opposition is not satisfying for communities that must deal with the rural realities of the North, including boom-bust economies, the importation of "southern" cultural artifacts like country and western music, and public policy that is often drafted in the south. Here, in an awesome land of great physical beauty, the borrowed cult of the rugged individual becomes fantastical, for it is grounded in a myth generated in the south. It is an import, and according to Fiske the wilderness man represents nothing if not a new kind of colonialism as he stalks through mining communities and other single-resource towns.

1
Little Goody Two-Shoes: Reassessing the Work of Catharine Parr Traill
Rebecca Raglon

Despite recent renewed interest, seen in the publication of her letters, a new biography, and new editions of *The Backwoods of Canada* and *Pearls and Pebbles,*[1] Catharine Parr Traill's work continues to be regarded by many as the less interesting and less "truthful" of the writing produced by the two Strickland sisters, who settled in Upper Canada in the nineteenth century. The popular biographer Charlotte Gray, while admiring the "sunny personality" of Traill, nevertheless finds her work less vivid than Susanna Moodie's, for Moodie is able to show the "dark underbelly of experiences" that Traill writes about with "gentle joy." To emphasize her point, Gray contrasts an account of a work bee that both sisters describe and points out that while Moodie wrote about riotous, drunken behaviour, Traill made her account of the event "sound like a dainty tea party."[2] According to Gray, Traill indulged in "upbeat pretense" to gloss over the inadequacies of her marriage and the hardships of pioneer life.[3]

Consequently, Susanna Moodie's *Roughing It in the Bush* is viewed by many scholars as not only more truthful, but also livelier, more dramatic, more problematic, and hence the more interesting of the accounts written by the two sisters. In part, this is because Moodie's work seemed like a fertile ground upon which to develop Canadian myths, "while practical, sensible Catharine Parr Traill did not attract analysts of Canada's psyche."[4] Moodie's work has inspired both creative and critical responses far beyond the attention given to her sister.[5] Among some critics at least, Traill's work suffers from "blandness"[6] and is still viewed as representing "the happy camper version of Canadian pioneer experience."[7] Although there are some exceptions,[8] as Michael Peterman shrewdly notes, there is a "tendency to be intellectually dismissive of Traill's work as a whole."[9]

This dismissive critical response to Traill's work arises in part from confusion about the literary genre in which she worked. As a reporter of pioneer experience, as a travel writer, and as a short-story writer or novelist, she might indeed suffer in comparison to her sister. Efforts on the part of scholars to place her within a tradition of early Canadian scientific activity, while more promising and surely more in line with Traill's own interests, nevertheless also tend to end with a sense of frustration and disappointment: If only she had known more opportunity, or had experienced less hardship in her life, or had been a different gender, or if the learned societies of the nineteenth century had been hospitable to women, then she might indeed have made her mark, if not on the literary world, then on the world of science.[10] As it stands, two of her books, *Canadian Wildflowers* (1867) and *Studies of Plant Life in Canada* (1885) are frequently viewed, when remarked upon at all, as merely interesting footnotes to nineteenth-century intellectual life in Canada.[11]

In fact, Traill worked very self-consciously within a clearly defined and specialized literary tradition of nature writing, and perceiving her as a contributor to that tradition allows for a much more appreciative view of her work and overall accomplishment.[12] Rather than being assessed either as a weak literary figure existing in Susanna Moodie's shadow or as a disadvantaged scientist, she should be placed within an eighteenth-century tradition of nature writing, which itself was a unique hybrid of both literary and scientific concerns. In such a setting, it is possible to view her work as a significant contribution to the growing field of environmental thought and ecocritical approaches to literature.

Naturalists and Natural History

Nineteenth-century reviewers of Traill's work, themselves familiar with the tradition of natural-history writing, frequently praised her work and suggested that she had succeeded in her desire to become a "sort of Canadian counterpart" to Gilbert White,[13] the eighteenth-century British writer widely held to be an originator of the tradition of outdoor natural-history writing. George Grant, the principal of Queen's University, noted that Traill had the ability to combine a "keen eye and trained powers of observation" with "fine poetic feeling and an intense appreciation of all that is beautiful and good,"[14] which were and continue to be hallmarks of the genre. Placing Traill within the context of a genre that blends science and literature, rationality and empathy, allows a different critical gaze to be cast upon her works, revealing that the case against Traill (bland, boring, a happy camper) has less to do with her work per se and more to do with a contemporary bias that deems writing about nature to be less interesting then work that deals with the human comedy.

The eclipse of Traill's reputation, however, also coincides with an eclipse of the idea of the amateur scientist and the importance of nature writing in the early twentieth century. That is, natural history at one time referred to an almost universal, generalized knowledge about the world.[15] It had an important social aspect, was practised by the highest levels of society in both Britain and her colonies, and flourished through letter writing, associations, dinners, and organized excursions. The study of natural history was considered not only intellectually stimulating, but also "wholesome" and "moral," for the notion that nature provided innumerable illustrations of God's beneficently ordered universe is at the core of much eighteenth- and nineteenth-century nature writing. This viewpoint, however, could not withstand Darwin's theory of evolution, and by the time Traill published *Pearls and Pebbles* in 1894, naturalists were already learning to rely on more specialized studies to supplement their own field observations. By the early twentieth century, the naturalist was no longer a cultural hero but had descended to the status of a well-meaning amateur who could even be accused of faking his or her observations.[16]

Thus learning once again to appreciate Traill's works coincides with coming to understand both natural history as a unique intellectual discipline and nature writing as a clearly defined literary endeavour. Natural history has had different meanings during different periods of its development, yet its methods, aims, history, and orientation are quite different from those of modern science, which aspires to a kind of value-free, neutral existence. Contemporary scientific activity is typically expressed in agentless rhetorical forms free of sensual and social elements, whereas eighteenth- and nineteenth-century writers concerned with natural history frequently indulged in both sentiment and sentimentality. Naturalists nevertheless are scientific in the sense that they employ observation, taxonomy, classification,[17] and the "sustained intensity" of dedicated observation.[18] But compared to twenty-first-century scientific activities, natural history is far more diffuse in its approach. Writing based on natural-history studies has aesthetic concerns, a moral dimension, and very frequently a nostalgic cast. While some aspects of natural history emphasized collection and classification, the more profound aspect tended to rely on observation of living things over a period of time. Writers such as Gilbert White, upon whom Traill modelled her own work, were able to reveal the complex relationships between organisms, or what is today known as the ecology of a place, through long contact with a particular location.[19] White's writings, for example, touched on people, folk beliefs, antiquities, religious sentiment, gardens, recipes, and pets – topics that are not in the modern sense strictly "scientific" yet fit comfortably within the fold of natural-history writing.

Catharine Parr Traill and the Natural-History Tradition

What has proved remarkable about this old-fashioned, proto-scientific endeavour, however, is that it has continued to flourish, even in the late twentieth and early twenty-first centuries. Even though science itself has changed, moving from the field into the laboratory, the insights emerging from ecology have reinvigorated both natural-history studies and nature writing, and during the twentieth century new ways of appreciating and evaluating older works of natural-history writing developed. According to the historian Donald Worster, for example, Gilbert White is responsible for an ecological view of nature that is still relevant today. According to Worster, White's vision offered an "Arcadian" approach to ecology, in contrast to a more imperial model. The Arcadian view seeks to understand, while the imperial view seeks to control and manipulate. In Worster's view, the Arcadian approach is organic, vital, and steeped in interrelationships, while the imperial approach tends to be reductionist and mechanistic.[20]

The best of Traill's writing, found in *The Backwoods of Canada*, *The Canadian Crusoes*, and *Pearls and Pebbles*, conveys an Arcadian sense of wholeness in her understanding of her new home, where plants, insects, storms, animals, and humans each play a role. The goal of such writing is to develop an understanding of this intricately related whole expressed through aesthetic admiration and wonder. Traill is also important, however, for bringing an early feminine viewpoint to her chosen genre and, in the process, challenging some of its conventions. Because Traill is confident in her abilities, sure of her literary place, and able to skilfully use her knowledge of natural history to help build a concept of home for herself in Upper Canada, her role as a wilderness wife and guardian of the domestic is modified considerably. There is little hostility toward wild nature in her work; in fact, a certain tension between the claims of the settler and the right of exquisite flowers or animals to exist opens up a very early version of the dialogue between the claims of civilization and those of wild nature that continues to engage Canadians. In addition, she frequently betrays an anxiety not about the presence of the wilderness, but about its disappearance due to ever-intensifying human activity – much of which was thoughtless and careless. Her position as a genteel bearer of class values is also challenged by conditions in the backwoods; the spirit of Mrs. Grundy, she notes, has little power there.[21] She quickly learns that she must come to terms with Canada: If she is to be the "Gilbert White" of this country, then she must produce something that conveys her home as forcefully as White's work conveys the meaning and reality of Selborne. In order to be a writer of the highest calibre, she must capture the particularity of place.

White's work, however, was the testament of a writer "at peace with the world and with himself, content with deepening his knowledge of his one small corner of the earth, a being suspended in a perfect mental balance."[22] Above all, White provided a picture of what might today be called a sustainable village: an agricultural enclave that had changed very little over the centuries. Indeed, the task facing Traill was very different, for while she, too, strove to be at peace with the world and with herself, she had to do so

while coping with rapid transformations. Traill, in fact, was facing ecological upheaval. The sense of calm and peace, which is thus one of the most
telling features of White's work, is achieved only occasionally in Traill's
letters. While White's letters record the familiar and unchanging, Traill is
clearly struggling to find what is familiar in her new home and to identify
what might be constant, what could and should be preserved. The letters
that form the basis of her book thus form a different kind of narrative than
the one White pioneered, for they inescapably describe not a settled village,
but an almost violent transformation – both of a place and of the mind of
the female settler.

Furthermore, it is to Traill's credit that there are moments of reflection
that suggest an alternative ethic to the propagandistic colonial rhetoric of
the time, which celebrated, among other things, the transformation of forest into farm. Even in the backwoods, she notes, there must be limits to the
seemingly endless claims of the European settler to absolute dominion over
the land. She also investigates the notion that Europeans, their plants, and
farm animals, are in fact "usurpers." For Traill, there is something about the
Canadian bush that is valuable in and of itself and that does not need "transformation." In a letter to the editor of the *Genesee Farmer*, Traill writes, in a
very Thoreauvian way,[23] that she wishes to "speak a few words on behalf of
the natives of the soil – I mean the lovely Wild Flowers."[24] Traill, who was at
pains to collect and record the flowers of Canada and who taught herself to
love them, notes that many flowers that she once admired are now gone.

> I am a great admirer of the indigenous flowers of the forest, and it is with a
> feeling strongly allied to regret, that I see them fading away from the face of
> the earth. Many families, containing blossoms of the greatest beauty and
> fragrance are fast disappearing before the destructive agency of the chopper's
> axe, fire and the plow. They flee from the face of men and are lost, like the
> aborigines of the country, and the place that knew them once, now knows
> them no more. I look for the lovely children of the forest, those flowers that
> first attracted my attention, but they have passed away, and I seek them in
> vain – another race of plants has filled their place. Man has altered the face
> of the soil – the mighty giants of the forest are gone, and the lowly shrub,
> the lovely flower, the ferns and mosses, that flourished beneath the shade,
> have departed with them. The ripening fields of grain, the stately planta-
> tions of Indian corn, with the coarser herbage of the potato and turnip,
> grasses and clover, have usurped their places, a new race of wild plants,
> suited to the new condition of the soil springs up, to dispute the possession
> of the ground with the foreign usurper. Where now are the lilies of the
> woods, the lovely and fragrant Pyrolas, the Blood-root, the delicate sweet
> scented Michella ripens, the spotless Monotrope, with Orchis of many
> colours, and a thousand other lovely flowers?[25]

Flowers, fireflies, cedar forests, ferns, and the antics of birds and other wild animals provide her with intellectual, emotional, and aesthetic sustenance even in the most difficult times. It is odd that such sustenance has somehow come to be viewed as unsophisticated or even untruthful: From a more informed point of view, a view conditioned by the ongoing environmental crisis of global modernity, her work shines, offering hints of how it might be possible to engage more honourably with the natural world than has been done in the past.

Traill and the Roles of Women and Nature in North America

As is well known, feminist scholars who have looked at the topic of women and nature in the North American context have found that women were firmly assigned to the home, while men were allowed the freedom of the outdoors. Wilderness thus quickly became a gendered concept that tended to magnify and exaggerate the differences between men and women. In addition, the cultural restrictions placed on women's access to nature became internalized in the wilderness setting. Particularly when children were involved, it seems that women struggled above all to civilize the environment. In *Frontier Women,* Julie Jeffrey agrees, pointing out that "frontier women gave many indications of their desire to hold on to the conventions of female culture no matter how unfavorable the circumstances seemed ... Women planted flowers and trees from seed they had brought with them and generally tried to maintain the standards of domesticity with which they had been familiar."[26] In their work on pioneer women, Elisabeth Hapstead and Lillian Schlissel found that women tended to focus on the threat that the environment posed to the home and agree that frontierswomen clung to their traditional roles – for example, by resisting modifications to dress that might have made life and work easier.[27] Women, unlike men, weren't free to enjoy the new landscape. One Wisconsin farmer recalled settling the land in 1839, when "the country was all open and free to roam over. We could roam and fish or hunt as we pleased amid the freshness and beauties of nature. With wives it was different. From all those bright and to us fascinating scenes and pastimes they were excluded. They were shut up with the children in the log cabins."[28] Annette Kolodny believes that unlike men, women came to North America with no prior fantasized attachment to the idea of the wild and that because they had no such attachment, because the adventure of settling the wilderness was not *theirs,* women could "with greater equanimity than men ... accept its disappearance."[29]

The same pattern is frequently noted in Traill's own work: "The men are in good spirits and say they shall in a few years have many comforts about them that they could never have got at home had they worked late and early; but they complain that their wives are always pining for home and lamenting that ever they crossed the seas. This seems to be the general complaint with all classes; the women are discontented and unhappy. Few enter with their whole heart into a settler's life. They miss the little comforts they had been used to enjoy; they regret the friends and relations they left in the old country, and they cannot endure the loneliness of the backwoods."[30] The reason for this is not hard to find, for "Young men soon become reconciled to this country, which offers to them that chief attraction to youth – great personal liberty. Their employments are of a cheerful and healthy nature; and their amusements, such as hunting, shooting, fishing and boating are peculiarly fascinating. But in none of these can their sisters share. The hardships and difficulties of the settler's life, therefore, are felt peculiarly by the female part of the family."[31]

It was for the purpose of ameliorating these felt hardships and limitations, however, that Traill wrote. If women were not expected to hunt, fish, and boat, they nevertheless could botanize, and Traill early in her work notes that "It is fortunate for me that my love of natural history enables me to draw amusement from objects that are deemed by many unworthy of attention. To me they present an inexhaustible fund of interest. The simplest weed that grows in my path or the fly that flutters about me, are subjects for reflection, admiration, and delight."[32] Thus the entrée for the female into the backwoods is not through strenuous and active adventure, but through a more patient and careful watching. What is discovered is thus more subtle: the rare, the interrelationships between organisms, the behaviour of animals, the place of the human. It would be presumptuous, I think, to "challenge" Traill's claim that natural history is for her an "inexhaustible fund of interest," for her accomplishments as a naturalist are too vivid and too real to question her sincerity or to label her a little Goody Two-Shoes.[33] Clearly, the flowers and animals she wrote about played a real and deeply felt role in both her intellectual and emotional wellbeing and were the basis for her being able to create a feeling of home in Canada.

In *Made from this Earth*, Vera Norwood finds that women interested in the natural world tend to express this interest through some domesticated "middle ground" – the rural setting, the garden next to the house. Norwood feels that women are concerned with making a home in nature rather than striking out into the unknown.[34] In a way, this is promising because it tends to challenge the paradigm that has insisted on pure nature as the necessary base for male adventuring. The desire for pure or pristine nature can lead to strange outcomes – as seen, for example, in the idea that humans have in essence *incarcerated* wilderness itself.[35] Yet the idea that "everything is home" has its dangers as well, putting the human handprint on everything.

What is significant about Traill's vision is that she retains a careful empathy and respect for other wild beings in her new home. Traill recognizes –

cannot help but recognize – the power of humans as agents of environmental change, but she also articulates the idea that other living things – particularly rare flowers and ferns – must be allowed to continue to exist. If, because of nineteenth-century social conventions, she is cut off from pursuit of the wild, she nevertheless records incidents whereby the wild contacts her. For example, in recounting a voyage down river she writes,

> Our attention was drawn to some small object in the water, moving very swiftly along; there were various opinions as to the swimmer, some thinking it to be a water-snake, others a squirrel or a muskrat, a few swift strokes of the paddles brought us up so as to intercept the passages of the little voyager; it proved to be a fine red squirrel, bound on a voyage of discovery from a neighbouring island. The little animal, with a courage and address that astonished his pursuers, instead of seeking safety in a different direction sprang lightly on the point of the uplifted paddle, and from thence with a bound to the head of my astonished baby, and having gained my shoulder, leaped again into the water and made direct for the shore, never having deviated a single point from the line he was swimming in when he first came in sight of our canoe.[36]

Traill was surprised and amused by the agility and courage displayed by the squirrel. This passage is not unlike one that myriad male wilderness writers might have written but with one very large difference: the presence of the baby. Traill, in other words, changes the paradigm here: The pre-eminent wilderness experience is not a man-alone experience, but an experience of a woman accompanied by husband and children. Interrelationships are a given in such a construct, and domestic arrangements and cares are necessarily a part of the picture. The most urgent question is no longer what is an individual position vis-à-vis the universe at large, as it was for Emerson, Thoreau, Muir, and many other wilderness writers up to the present day, but rather what is *our* relationship to the beings who constitute what we know as our home.

Augustan Aesthetics and Backwoods Realities

Wilderness, it is often argued, thrives in opposition to domesticity, which is why in the North American context it has been aggressively construed as male space. However, Gilbert White, who was preeminently interested in the community of relationships in Selborne, is the British writer upon whom Traill modelled her own work, and his is a model that proves to be far less dichotomous. White's work is engaging for a number of reasons, most notably – as David Elliston Allen suggests in *The Naturalist in Britain: A Social History* – for its empathy: "his ability to infuse deep feeling into what he described and recorded so carefully and soberly."[37] This is evident in the affection he felt for many of the nonhuman creatures he wrote about: his turtle, Timothy; the shrilling crickets; a seventeen-year-old hog. In a letter to Thomas Pennant, he wrote about a tame bat, a "wonderful quadruped" that took flies out of a person's hand. "If you gave it anything to eat, it brought its wings round before the mouth, hovering and hiding its head in the manner of birds of prey when they feed. The adroitness it showed in shearing off the wings of the flies, which were always rejected, was worthy of observation, and pleased me much."[38]

The same type of affection, even empathy, is discernable in Traill's work, when she writes: "I found a little family of woodpeckers last spring comfortably nested in an old pine, between the bark and the trunk of the tree, where the former had started away, and left a hollow space, in which the old birds had built a soft but careless sort of nest; the little creatures seemed very happy, poking their funny bare heads out to greet the old ones, who were knocking away at the old stumps in their neighbourhood."[39] White's style of natural-history writing is not to look at large scenic vistas, but rather at the close-up view. This is something that was also suited to women, like Traill, who were circumscribed by the customs and domestic duties of the nineteenth century. White's work showed that there is no object of nature so humble as not to contain its own interest and lesson. A mouse's nest, a "wonderful procreant cradle found in a wheat-field, suspended in the head of a thistle," is discovered to be "platted, and composed of the blades of wheat; perfectly round, and about the size of a cricket-ball" and containing eight little blind mice.[40] Traill, in a remarkably similar passage, carefully describes the workmanship displayed in a wasp's nest. "The nest was about the size and shape of a turkey's egg, and was composed of six paper cups inserted one within the other ... of the most exquisite neatness."[41]

Why was there such interest in describing fairly commonplace and humble things? While both White and Traill were claiming scientific merits for their observations, there is also a clear sense that the careful workmanship of even such humble creatures as mice and wasps is an example of God's careful plan and care for His creation. Observing nature thus becomes a way of witnessing God's goodness. While such conceits may seem curious to post-Darwinian investigators of nature, compared to either Traill or White, contemporary attitudes to nature frequently seem blunted. Furthermore, the casual interrelationships between species recorded by White and Traill are simply not available for the average urban dweller to witness. Ecology had not yet been invented, yet both Traill and White, living within natural settings, are able to trace out the complex interrelations between species, often in the process correcting popularly held beliefs. White notes the usefulness of earthworms at a time when they were routinely destroyed by farmers because it was believed that they ate green corn. He points out the cycle of life that occurs as cows wallow in a pond during the day, dropping dung, "in which insects nestle; and so supply food for fish, which would be poorly subsisted but from this contingency. Thus nature, who is a great economist, converts the recreation of one animal to the support of another!"[42] Similarly, Traill notes that settlers in their new log houses are disturbed by a continual creaking sound produced by insect larvae. "You would be surprised at the heap of fine saw-dust that is to be seen below the hole they have been working in all night. These sawyers form a fine feast for the woodpeckers, and jointly they assist in promoting the rapid decomposition of the gigantic forest-trees, that would otherwise encumber the earth from age to age! How often do we see great events brought about by seemingly insignificant agents! Yet are they servants of the Most High, working his will, and fulfilling his behests."[43]

Finally, this tradition also frequently conveys expressions of wonder over miraculous occurrences in nature. Only the patient watching over the course of a lifetime could make sights such as the shower of cobwebs that White witnessed falling out of the sky seem credible. White reports that "on this day the flakes hung in the trees and hedges so thick, that a diligent person sent out might have gathered baskets full."[44] Similar prodigies of nature are noted by Traill, particularly at the end of *The Backwoods of Canada,* where she recounts having seen in the sky at Christmas a "splendid pillar of pale greenish light in the west." Traill remarks that she was grieved when it vanished and seems uncertain whether it was the robe of some bright visitor from another and better world, but then she very practically adds that perhaps it might have been a phosphoric exhalation from the swamps or in some way connected with the aurora frequently seen in the skies.[45]

For all these similarities – in values, observations, vocabulary, preferences, form, and sentiment – and despite Traill's desire to become for Canada what Gilbert White was for England,[46] her portrait of life in Upper Canada ultimately traces out a very different kind of life than the one described by White. White's letters reveal a social and ecological stability that points toward sustainability. The parish he knows so well has changed over the years but at such a slow pace that the cause of change is not always clearly ascertained and is often discerned only through the written historical record. White remarks that certain birds and deer once common to the region are no longer seen but doesn't speculate on the reasons for their "disappearance." For Traill, however, the rapidity of change makes the cause of the disappearance of rare flowers and ferns readily apparent. This is the colonies' contribution to natural-history studies: a strong new thesis pointing to humans themselves as agents of ecological, even geological, change – brought about by such practices as creating canals and burning off vast tracts of forests. Furthermore, because such change often occurred within a single lifetime, it is also a revelation to see that this change, if pushed too far, is undesirable. Only someone entering a mysterious woods at the beginning of her journey to her new home, as Traill did, someone trained to carefully note the flowers, birds, and wildlife of that home, as Traill was, would have the skill and knowledge to make this kind of assessment: "On first coming to this country nothing surprised me more than the total absence of trees about the dwelling-houses and cleared lands; the axe of the chopper relentlessly levels all before him. Man appears to contend with the trees of the forest as though they were his most obnoxious enemies."[47] Traill clearly longs for the landscape of England, with its parklike aspect and large graceful trees standing alone. Yet the large forest trees that she tries to save are easily uprooted in storms, a danger to householders and cattle alike. Traill learns that rather than "hedge-rows and trees," it would be better to "leave several acres of forest in a convenient situation, and chop and draw out the old timbers for fire-wood, leaving the younger growth for ornament." A new aesthetic is thus forged that combines both necessity and desire.

It is through the poignancy of Traill's struggles with conflicting values that her greatest significance is revealed. White was born into his home; Traill had to make a home for herself by painfully creating it, layer by layer. There were neither familiar faces nor stories, ghosts, or history with which to stimulate the imagination or orient herself. For White even the ash trees of his home have a history: The scars upon them are left from ancient folk rituals performed by anxious parents, and during every walk in his parish he passes by innumerable stories collected over centuries. Traill's first impression of home is forever governed by her experience of walking through a dense woods at night: "Every few yards our path was obstructed by fallen trees, mostly hemlock, spruce or cedar, the branches of which are so thickly interwoven that it is scarcely possible to separate them, or force a passage through the tangled thicket which they form."[48] She longs for the variety of clearings, the charm of a varied vista, impressions of a natural world formed by England. The monotony of the unbroken forest, she finds, "insensibly inspires a feeling of gloom almost touching on sadness."[49]

In *This Incomperable Lande*, Thomas Lyon suggests that naturalists and nature writers made up a "distinctly nonconforming, even heretical minority" among the settlers of North America. The chief heresy of the naturalist, whether English, Canadian, or American, is that of a widened vision, a moving outward from the self, and even from society, toward the lives of other species and other lands. "A radical proposal follows on the widened vision: that the environment, nature, is the ground of a positive and sufficient human joy."[50] I believe that this is indeed a supposition that is confirmed by Traill's work. The critical heritage that has often been so impatient with her seems to deny this possibility, yet it is one that Traill took to heart. If the natural world she confronted in Upper Canada challenged her, it also brought her solace. In the same passage where she remarks on the "sadness" of the Canadian forest, she also notes that "still there are objects to charm and delight the close observer of nature." It is the "close observer" who is rewarded: The distant vista is too large and too stern. Yet an appreciative reading of Traill will allow that this passion for the small wild things is as consuming and "real" as Mrs. Moodie's most unhappy, frantic social moments, that Traill's admiration for flowers, vines, ferns, insects, and animals was as great as her sister's antipathy for the "trap" that became her backwoods home. It is churlish to deny the reality or sincerity of a concept like "sufficient joy" in passages like the one describing the fireflies in Traill's backwoods home: "They are often seen during warm June evenings after dark, sporting among the cedars at the edge of the wood, and especially near swamps, when the air is illuminated with their brilliant dancing light. Sometimes they may be seen in groups, glancing like falling stars in mid-air, or descending so low as to enter your dwelling and flit about among the draperies of your bed or window-curtains."[51] The small wild things sustained Traill through incredible hardship because for her they were indeed a source of "sufficient joy."

Conclusion

In *A Border Within*, Ian Angus suggests that Canadians must learn to "read" the idea of the garrison mentality in a way that will allow us to "found a civilizing project in the wilderness that is not simply a garrison, an outpost of a civilization whose centre is back in Europe."[52] Can Canadians find a different kind of relationship than the "headlong American race through the domination of nature to homogeneity, universality, and the reduction of desires to their satisfaction by commodities?"[53] If so, such a relationship redefines the meaning of the various "borders" that have confirmed Canadian identity – the border with the United States, the border between Quebec and Ontario, the border been our "garrisons" and wilderness lands. In its most profound sense, however, the border is not there to keep out the "other." Rather, it can be a statement that creates limits and goals for ourselves, that proclaims a middle ground, a mutual place of respect where we say that beyond this border we will not go, that here we have drawn a limit. Such a border is erected not to keep the wilderness out, but to keep *ourselves* from trespassing too deeply, or too far, into wilderness territory.

Such a moment of not going too far, or trespassing too deeply, is found near the end of *The Backwoods of Canada,* where Traill recounts trying to deal with the squirrels that carried off great quantities of grain from both her fields and her house. Traill discovered that they also enjoyed sunflower seeds, which she saved for her flock of chickens. One day she caught two squirrels conveying "away whole heads at once." Traill cut the heads off the remaining sunflowers, put them in a basket, and put the basket on a block in the garden. Soon she saw the same pair looking at her with "imploring gestures." "I was too much amused by their perplexity to help them, but turning away my head to speak to the child, they darted forward, and in another minute had taken possession of one of the largest of the heads, which they conveyed away, first one carrying it a few yards, then the other, it being too bulky for one alone ... In short, I was so well amused by watching their maneuvers that I suffered them to rob me off all my store."[54]

It is in the tension between her English model and her backwoods realities that Traill's real stature is to be found. She longed to remain humane and empathetic in a forest that often confused her and threatened to swallow her up. That she nevertheless found great beauty and grace in the backwoods is to her eternal credit; that she was able to teach Canadians to see that beauty should have been her legacy.

Notes

1 Carl Ballstadt, Elizabeth Hopkins, and Michael Peterman, eds., *I Bless You in My Heart: Selected Correspondence of Catharine Parr Traill* (Toronto: University of Toronto Press, 1996); Charlotte Gray, *Sisters in the Wilderness: The Lives of Susanna Moodie and Catharine Parr Traill* (Toronto: Penguin Books, 1999); Catharine Parr Traill, *The Backwoods of Canada*, edited by Michael Peterman (Ottawa: Carleton University Press, 1997); Catharine Parr Trail, *Pearls and Pebbles*, edited by Elizabeth Thompson (Toronto: Natural Heritage Books, 1999).

2 Gray, *Sisters in the Wilderness*, 206.

3 Ibid., 115.

4 John Thurston, *The Work of Words: The Writing of Susanna Strickland Moodie* (Montreal and Kingston: McGill-Queen's University Press, 1996), 6.

5 Margaret Atwood, *The Journals of Susanna Moodie* (Toronto: Oxford University Press, 1970); Carol Shields, *Voice and Vision* (Ottawa: Borealis Press, 1977); Lorraine McMullen, ed., *Re(dis)covering Our Foremothers* (Ottawa: University of Ottawa Press, 1990). The latter volume contains three articles on Moodie but only one on Traill and thus seems fairly representative of a critical interest that favours Moodie's work.

6 Clara Thomas, "Journeys To Freedom," *Canadian Literature* 51 (1972): 19.

7 Carol Gerson, "Catharine Parr Traill: *The Backwoods of Canada*," *University of Toronto Quarterly* 69, 1 (1999-2000): 256-59.

8 Elizabeth Thompson, *The Pioneer Woman: A Canadian Character Type* (Montreal and Kingston: McGill-Queen's University Press, 1991); William Gairdner, "Traill and Moodie: The Two Realities," *Journal of Canadian Fiction* 2, 2 (1973): 75-81; David Jackel, "Mrs. Moodie and Mrs. Traill, and the Fabrication of a Canadian Tradition," *Compass* 6 (1979): 1-22. Thompson, in particular, has worked to revive Traill's reputation and makes the point that Traill's work, both fiction and nonfiction, should be read as an innovative attempt to convey a type of Canadian pioneer far removed from the sentimental view of the nineteenth-century English lady.

9 Michael Peterman, "'Splendid Anachronism': The Record of Catharine Parr Traill's Struggles as an Amateur Botanist in Nineteenth-Century Canada," in *Re(Dis)covering Our Foremothers*, edited by Lorraine McMullen (Ottawa: University of Ottawa Press, 1990), 173-97.

10 Ibid.; Marianne Ainley, "Science in Canada's Backwoods," in *Natural Eloquence: Women Reinscribe Science*, edited by Barbara Gates and Ann Shteir (Madison, WI: University of Wisconsin Press, 1997), 79-97.

11 Suzanne Zeller, *Inventing Canada: Early Victorian Science and the Idea of a Transcontinental Nation* (Toronto: University of Toronto Press, 1987). Zeller points out that Traill collected botanical specimens for a professor at the University of Edinburgh and suggests that the lack of a good botanical guide to consult led her to model her own work on the more accessible Gilbert White.

12 It is also interesting to note, however, that her status as both a "Canadian" writer and a woman writer has also meant that she has not received the wider attention she deserves. Lorraine Anderson's wide-ranging 1991 collection of women's nature writing, *Sisters' of the Earth*, has no mention of Traill. *The Norton Anthology of Nature Writing* and other standard collections of nature writing have not used Traill's work, although Canadian collections do feature her. See, for example, Andrea Lebowitz, *Living in Harmony: Nature Writing by Women in Canada* (Vancouver: Orca Books, 1996).

13 Peterman, "'Splendid Anachronism,'" 177.

14 *Week*, 1 February 1895; in Peterman, "'Splendid Anachronism,'" 267.

15 William Martin Smallwood, *Natural History and the American Mind* (New York: Columbia University Press, 1941), 4.

16 John Burroughs, "Real and Sham Natural History," *Atlantic Monthly* 91 (1903): 301.

17 Marston Bates is one writer who has attempted to defend natural history as a legitimate branch of scientific endeavour against claims that it is nothing more than a "popular and superficial" study of plants and animals. Bates is generous in his assessment that natural history is a discipline and that its methods, attitudes, and goals are the same as those of any other science, but he is in a minority in holding this opinion. Marston Bates, *The Nature of Natural History* (New York: Charles Scribner's Sons, 1954), 3-7.

18 Raymond Williams, *The Country and the City* (London, UK: Hogarth Press, 1985), 118.

19 For example, Mary Bedford, an eighteenth-century entomologist, discovered that every species of butterfly and moth has its own special food plant. David Elliston Allen, *The Naturalist in Britain: A Social History* (London, UK: Allen Lane, 1976), 28.

20 Donald Worster, *Nature's Economy: A History of Ecological Ideas* (Cambridge: Cambridge University Press, 1985), 3-25.

21 Traill, *The Backwoods of Canada*, 194.

22 Allen, *The Naturalist in Britain*, 51.

23 "I wish to speak a word for Nature." Henry David Thoreau, "Walking," in *The Natural History Essays* (Salt Lake City: Peregrine Smith Books, 1980), 93.

24 Ballstadt, Hopkins, and Peterman, eds. *I Bless You in My Heart*, 75.

25 Ballstadt, Hopkins, and Peterman, eds., *I Bless You in My Heart*, 75.

26 Julie Jeffrey, *Frontier Women* (New York: Hill and Wang, 1979).

27 Elisabeth Hapstead and Lillian Schlissel, *Women's Diaries of the Westward Journey* (New York: Schocken, 1982).

28 Annette Kolodny, *The Land before Her: Fantasy and Experience of the American Frontiers, 1630-1860* (Chapel Hill: University of North Carolina Press, 1975), 9.

29 Ibid., 7.

30 Traill, *The Backwoods of Canada*, 4.

31 Ibid., 4.

32 Ibid., 14.

33 The term originated with a nursery tale that first appeared in 1765. The heroine of the tale owned only one shoe, and when given a pair she was so pleased that she showed them to everyone, saying "Two Shoes!" Adrian Room and John Ayto, *Brewer's Dictionary of Phrase and Fable* (London, UK: Cassell and Co., 1999 [1870]). Traill's cheerfulness in view of her family's extreme poverty is often viewed with condescension in critical assessments of her work.

34 Vera Norwood, *Made from this Earth: American Women and Nature* (Chapel Hill: University of North Carolina Press, 1993).

35 Thomas Birch, "The Incarceration of Wildness: Wilderness Areas as Prisons," *Environmental Ethics* 12 (1990): 3-26.

36 Traill, *The Backwoods of Canada*, 189.

37 Allen, *The Naturalist in Britain*, 50.

38 Gilbert White, *The Natural History of Selborne*, edited by Richard Mabey (Harmondsworth: Penguin Books, 1977), 35.

39 Traill, *The Backwoods of Canada*, 164.

40 White, *The Natural History of Selborne*, 37.

41 Traill, *The Backwoods of Canada*, 215.

42 White, *The Natural History of Selborne*, 27.

43   Traill, *The Backwoods of Canada*, 222.
44   White, *The Natural History of Selborne*, 176.
45   Traill, *The Backwoods of Canada*, 228.
46   Catharine Parr Traill, *Studies of Plant Life in Canada* (Ottawa: A.S. Woodburn, 1885).
47   Traill, *The Backwoods of Canada*, 144.
48   Ibid., 59.
49   Ibid., 53.
50   Thomas Lyon, *This Incomperable Lande* (Boston: Houghton Mifflin, 1989), 19.
51   Traill, *The Backwoods of Canada*, 214.
52   Ian Angus, *A Border Within: National Identity, Cultural Plurality, and Wilderness* (Montreal and Kingston: McGill-Queen's University Press, 1997), 127.
53   Ibid., 126.
54   Traill, *The Backwoods of Canada*, 191.

2
Environmentalism, Hermeneutics, and Canadian Imperialism in Agnes Deans Cameron's *The New North*
Daniel O'Leary

It is useful to begin an analysis of Agnes Deans Cameron's work with provisional remarks on methodology. For the great German hermeneuticist Johann Augustus Ernesti (1707-81), the key to all interpretation lay in the discovery of a quantity he termed the "usus loquendi."[1] The *usus loquendi* consisted of two aspects of interpretation: the "grammatical," or what can be described as the semantic, and the "historical," the use of knowledge based on a range of printed and written documents from a wide variety of discourses. Recent works on print culture and book history by scholars like Robert Darnton have advanced the sophistication of hermeneutical categories with a fuller analysis of the varieties of phenomena related to the circulation of written materials.[2] But although Ernesti's European and British fame has receded from its nineteenth-century height, his work remains very suggestive. In the following analysis, in order to achieve a more precise reappraisal of the life and work of the late-Victorian Canadian environmentalist, suffragist, educational pioneer, and British-immigration propagandist Agnes Deans Cameron (1863-1912), I will explore her book *The New North* from an Ernestian point of view. According to Ernesti's doctrine, philological study – including what in our own time may be described as the study of print culture or book history – contributes an enriched perception of the *usus loquendi*, a complex understanding based upon knowledge of "time [historical context], religion, sect, education, common life, and civil affairs."[3] In Moses Stuart's fourth edition of Ernesti's *Elementary Principles of Interpretation* (1842), Stuart, the editor and translator, adds a note from the once-famous German hermeneuticist and commentator on Ernesti, S.F.N. Morus (1736-92), explaining that in order to arrive at a valid reading of a historical text, a reader must realize that the "ancient and modern sense of many words differs."[4]

Hermeneutical questions of this kind are germane to the study of early-twentieth-century works, particularly when questions of collusion or complicity with the British imperial project arise in connection with Canadian figures whose surviving utterance shows much evidence of imperialist sentiment. The determination of the *usus loquendi* involves an attempt at situating a subject text within its own historical and semantic conditions so that a more valid judgment of the merits and demerits of an author's thought might be made. In order to consider Agnes Deans Cameron's importance as an early Canadian environmentalist, and to offer critical judgment of her historically significant work, *The New North* (1909), I will place the text in the several contexts suggested by the features of Ernesti's *usus loquendi,* considering the Victorian use of several key imperialist, patriotic, and raciological terms that are obscured for the contemporary reader by use subsequent to the ontological reordering that followed the First World War.[5] I will begin with a discussion of three popular Victorian and Edwardian genres that contributed elements to the form of *The New North.*

The New North as a Wilderness Journal

Although *The New North* fits the genre of works now often characterized as "travel literature," it is clear from the text that problems of narrative technique preoccupy its author and that Agnes Deans Cameron shapes her account in order to exploit several existing discourses or genres. Knowledge of these textual matrices illuminates our reading of her text. That these genres include discourses dominated by both male and female authors is especially worthy of notice and casts light on the androgynous character of Cameron's work. In creating her characteristic late example of the wilderness journal, Cameron borrows narrative elements from a tradition including Sir W.F. Butler (1838-1910), George M. Grant (1835-1902), J.W. Tyrrell (1863-1945), Albert P. Low (1861-1942), and Charles R. Tuttle (b. 1848), among numerous others who contributed to the wide Victorian taste for authentic British and British Canadian accounts of extreme northern adventure. Cameron's narrative procedures also resemble many near-contemporary women's accounts of Canadian travel, both autobiographical and semifictional, written by British and British Canadian women like Hariot Georgina Hamilton-Temple-Blackwood (1843-1936), Lady Dufferin (d. 1936), Isabel Aberdeen (1857-1939), Jane Phillipps-Wolley (1863-1921), and Mary Agnes Fitzgibbon (1851-1915), again among numerous others. The autobiographical accounts of Protestant missionaries in the North and Northwest, another widely popular literature in late-Victorian Britain and post-Confederation Canada, is another genre that shares many features with Cameron's work, including an articulate enthusiasm for the progressive aims of British imperial civilization. As James Woodsworth, superintendent of the North-West Missions of the Methodist Church, writes of Canada in his *Thirty Years in the Canadian North-West* (1917):

On her soil all phases of thought and life meet and intermingle. As a part of the British Empire, Canada must share in the responsibilities of the Empire on whose dominions the sun never sets. To her sons, Imperialism should mean more than the consolidation of her several units into a national whole. Imperialism should mean the improvement of the greatest opportunity the world has ever presented for the application of those principles which alone can truly exalt any people and cause God's glory to dwell in the land.[6]

The Canadian missionary literature of the Victorian period has been given insufficient attention since the Canadian (and British) public taste gave way to amusements of a less spiritual cast, and most of the once widely read Victorian biographical and autobiographical accounts of pioneer and First Nations evangelism – works that would have been known to a Canadian educator of Cameron's period – have come to be ignored or censured. The Christian denominations all contributed to this literature, and some of the most interesting accounts of life in Canada during the Victorian and early-Edwardian periods are to be found in works like those of Egerton Ryerson Young (1840-1909), John Maclean (1851-1928), Charles Gordon (1860-1937), Charlotte Selina Bompas (1830-1917), George Bryce (1844-1931), James Woodsworth (d. 1917), Thomas Crosby (1840-1914), and John McDougall (1842-1917), to name but several of the prominent.

This genre of Canadian Christian writing is Victorian Canadian, rather than Victorian, in the sense that provincial or colonial characteristics, including a more-or-less explicit anti-Americanism, are often apparent even in its most imperialist moods. And Victorian Canadian imperialist usage generally finds a ready sympathy in the works of British-born missionaries as well as in Canadian works of this kind. Although the imperialist vocabulary of these authors is shared by imperialists in Great Britain, and by those elsewhere in the British Empire, the *usus loquendi* of the terms differs in the Canadian context and is modified by a history of tension with the burgeoning empire on the Canadian border. The history of American incursions against Canadian sovereignty ensured that Canadian imperialist rhetoric was encoded with anti-American connotations much more specific in nature than the detached sense of English superiority to be found in England and elsewhere in the British Empire. Perhaps not surprisingly, British authors in Canada quickly naturalized their own usage and adapted their imperial rhetoric to new Canadian conditions. Many evangelical works with northern Canadian wilderness settings were written by native British, Scottish, and Irish clergy, and their accounts, like those written by British Canadians generally, use strongly loyalist language in their expressions of Canadian nationality.[7]

Imperialism and Conservation in *The New North*

From an environmental perspective, the question of Canadian imperialism is particularly germane to the case of Agnes Deans Cameron. Reconciling the pioneering naturalist travelling into the unexplored North with the British-immigration booster and racial nationalist is a vexing task without a clear understanding that Cameron's imperialism was important to the preservation of the North from American encroachment. And readers who rely on the only modern reprint of Cameron's work – an abridged edition by David Richeson published in 1986 that lacks both a full chapter and most of the wonderful photographs of the original edition – could overlook this aspect of her thought.[8] In the chapter that Richeson omits, Cameron considers the state of the whaling industry in the Canadian North, presenting statistics and anecdotes to argue in favour of both preservation of whale populations and of Canadian economic development and sovereignty over northern Canadian waters.[9] Cameron writes: "Off the Mackenzie mouth is Herschel Island anchorage. Here, since 1889, the American whaling-fleet, setting out from San Francisco, has made its summer stand, its winter waiting quarters. One whale to one boat in a season covers the cost of outfitting and maintenance, and more than one spells substantial profit. In 1887, one of the Arctic whalers, the steamer *Orca*, captured twenty-eight whales. The *Jeanette* in 1905 got ten whales and a calf, the *Karluk* got seven whales, the *Alexander* eight, the *Bowhead* seven."[10]

After providing a list of figures to illustrate the substantial profits of the American whalers in Canada, Cameron adds: "A trade in fur also makes out by this Pacific-Arctic, Arctic-Pacific route. We estimate that total products to the value of a million and a half find their way each year out of Canada in the ships of the whaling-fleet. 'The farther north the finer fur' is a recognized law. The American ship brings flour, provisions, Krag-Jorgensen guns, ammunition, tea, trinkets to the Eskimo, and receive for these the choicest furs this continent produces."[11]

Cameron equates Canadian control of the whale fishery with conservation of whale populations and calls for regulation of the hunt: "Off the delta of the Mackenzie, the Circumpolar or Arctic Bowhead whale *(Balaena mysticetus)* is making his last stand. Unless a close season is enforced, this cetacean carrying round his ten thousand dollar mouthful of baleen will soon fold his fluked fins like the Arab and swing that huge body of his into line with the Great Auk, the Sea-Otter, the Plains Buffalo, and all the melancholy procession of Canadian Has-beens."[12] With extensive analysis of the northern whale fishery, Cameron also emphasizes the need for Canadian sovereignty over northern waters as an important element in conservation:

Unless the Circumpolar Bowhead is to become extinct within a decade, the thinking world should strengthen the hands of the Canadian authorities in an effort to put a close season for four or five years on the great Arctic Baleen Whale. At their rate of reproduction it is not so easy to restock a whale pasture as a salmon stream. Cutting down a whale which has taken ten centuries to grow is like cutting down an oak tree with a thousand concentric rings. You cannot in one or two or twenty scant generations of man grow another to take its place.[13]

The official Canadian position on the whale fisheries at this time was not far removed from that of Cameron. In November 1915 Edward E. Prince, Dominion commissioner of fisheries, made substantially the same arguments before the Commission of Conservation Canada Committee on Fisheries, Game and Fur-Bearing Animals:

The question of the utilization of whales, porpoises, sea-lions, etc., is an important one. We have too long allowed our American friends to go into our northern waters and utilize these valuable products. Considerable fortunes have been made from Canadian whales and walruses by enterprising intruders. I remember many years ago some American boats coming into Hudson Bay and carrying off many tons of valuable walrus ivory and I noticed the other day that a boat came into Seattle from Nome, Alaska, after two very successful cruises in our northern waters. She reported that on her first cruise she secured 837 walruses, and on her second, 516. I am quite satisfied that these fisheries are carried on in our own Canadian waters and that they probably centre at Herschel island and make trips from there just as on the east they make excursions from someplace like Marble island in Hudson bay. I often think we might have listened to the advice of Sir John Schultz who, thirty years ago, said our Arctic waters would yet prove to be the last habitat of those most valuable Arctic animals, the right whale and the walrus, and that some effort should be made to prevent their being entirely destroyed.[14]

Part of Cameron's objection to the American whaling industry is also related to racial preoccupations. Cameron worries that "Eskimo" identity will be erased by the "miscegenation" that ensues from whaling-industry traffic, although she expresses no similar qualms about Scottish influence on First Nations identity.[15]

Although the logic of Richeson's excision of Cameron's "The Tale of a Whale" from his edition of *The New North* is clear enough – as the account forms the only lengthy digression in the journey narrative – the chapter is nevertheless essential to a proper understanding of the depth of Cameron's commitment to conservation. Perhaps otherwise mindful of the sensitivities of her American publisher, Cameron's thoughts on America are also expressed here in a manner not found elsewhere in the work. More generally,

Cameron's imperialism and Canadian nationalism take the form of extolling the British Empire rather than criticizing the United States, and she emphasizes the British identity of what she refers to as the "outer vedette of the British Empire."[16] References to the empire, and to things British in Canada, are very frequent in the work, and it is clear that Cameron's Mackenzie and Hay Rivers are, for her, as British as the Thames.[17] That Cameron had written briefly for a Chicago newspaper after leaving Victoria is not a sign of any wavering of her commitment to imperial Canadian nationality. In fact, Cameron's journalism can be taken as evidence of the Canadian contribution to British influence on early-twentieth-century America. Cameron does comment on the feared "Americanization" of Canada but believes that Canadian independence is secure and that Canadian institutions are superior: "As Canadians we believe that our national institutions, though far from perfect, are in some respects superior to those of the United States. We believe they are at once more elastic, more responsive to the popular will, and more stable because more elastic."[18] Cameron distinguishes, however, between loyalty to England and loyalty to the British Empire: "'Is Canada loyal to England?' is a question that sometimes meets us. No, Canada is loyal to the British Empire of which she forms a part. Let England see to it that she, too, is loyal."[19]

This point is important to understanding the *usus loquendi* of Cameron's deployment of "British," which in her usage is an inclusive term signifying a relationship with the civilization of the British Empire rather than a narrowly defined ethnological identity. In treaty negotiations with the Native peoples of the Northwest in the 1870s, for example, Alexander Morris (1826-1889), the lieutenant-governor of Manitoba, the Northwest Territories, and Kee-wa-tin, uses the term "British Indians" to distinguish them from the refugees from the genocide being carried out in American territory during this period.[20] For Cameron, and for many if not most Canadians, the term "British" suggested law and order, an advancing civilization, and freedom from the social problems of the republican democracy over the line. Consequently, the connotations of the term differ from those associated with it in Britain itself, where usage was either ethnological, referring to the Celtic element of the British islands, or political, referring to the citizens of the United Kingdom.[21] This does not preclude the widespread application of the term "Briton" to Canadians as a synonym for "British subject" in the same manner that it was applied in England, although this use of the term was problematic when applied to French Canadians, for example, because of its ethnological connotations. The use of terms like "Canadian-Britons," "West Britons," or "North Britons" is very widespread in nationalist writings of the Victorian and Edwardian periods and is a central feature of the rhetoric of nationalist writings by the members of the Canada First movement and by others like the influential Alexander Morris, whose 1858 essay

Nova Britannia has been credited with inspiring a belief in Confederation in both D'Arcy McGee and Sir John A. Macdonald.[22]

Before non-British immigration had made the doctrine untenable, racial nationalists believed that the French Canadian and Native populations of the country would be absorbed into the British population, that Canadians would gradually become a racially homogenous variety of Briton, and that Canada would be transformed into a nation in the sense that France or Germany were taken to be nations – that is, with a single raciological identity.[23] By Cameron's time, there was much anxiety about the changing ethnological composition of the country, and Cameron's own efforts to encourage British immigration may be seen in this light. In *The New North,* Cameron is careful to insist upon the racial "homogeneity" of the Canadian Prairies despite the presence of other immigrants: "While seventy-five per cent of Canada's wheat farmers are either Canadian, American, or British born, and of the class that preserves the homogeneity of the race, every country on the map pays tribute to the plains."[24] Edwardian Canadian exertions to encourage British immigration in order to preserve the British character of the country were quite successful, if only temporarily, as the founder and first president of the Canadian Federation of University Women, Margaret May McWilliams, points out in her history *Manitoba Milestones* (1928):

> Once the tide of American immigration began to move into Western Canada, Clifford Sifton turned his attention to the United Kingdom and from that to the countries of Europe. To arouse interest there was easier since the remarkable fact that Americans were actually preferring to find homes in Canada had attracted the attention of the entire European world, which up to that time had had its interest focused upon the United States so far as emigration was concerned. The same methods of advertising and exhibits and lectures were employed. To these were added now in Great Britain a play upon the motive of patriotism. "Settlement should be kept within the Empire," "Keep Canada British," were the cries. British immigration to Canada, which in 1900 stood at 10,000, had seven years later risen to the astonishing yearly total of 132,000.[25]

Cameron herself was part of the efforts that McWilliams refers to here and gave lectures in Britain on the subject of British emigration to Canada.[26] Fear of American immigration during this period was intensified by a long tradition of resistance to American cultural domination, a common theme in Victorian Canada, as has been demonstrated, for instance, in Colin Coates and Cecilia Morgan's historiographic study of Laura Secord in *Heroines and History* (2002).[27] The Americanization of Canada through American control of Canadian print culture has often been asserted, frequently in the editorial pages of struggling Victorian Canadian periodicals. And evidence, very extensive in the form of both pirated and legal American editions of British authors, points to widespread penetration of the American book trade. But two factors militate against the expected result of such a situation (i.e., cultural domination): The Canadian population's demand for reading material was largely urban and hence comparatively limited, and more important, America itself was so heavily interpenetrated with Victorian intellectual culture that its book trade simply facilitated the circulation of British imperial culture in Canada.

For what it's worth, the residue of the sales of these books, which remains in the form of stock in the Canadian used-book trade, can be taken as an indication of the preponderance of British, Irish, and Scottish titles in American imprints (long considered worthless from a commercial point of view in the used-book trade, as it happens) in Victorian Canada. Not only Dickens, the Brownings, and Tennyson, but the entire range of British intellectual culture, found a ready audience through the presses of America. This did not contribute to the Americanization of Canada in nearly so direct a way as has often been assumed. Although these books were not printed in Great Britain or Canada, they did not interfere with the circulation of the dominant national themes of Great Britain during this period, and in all probability there was no more reading of American authors in Canada than in Great Britain itself. The contribution of American authors like Emerson to Victorian British culture is a subject too far removed from the present one to invite close analysis here. But the crucial point is that the overlap of Canadian and British discourse in large measure resembled that of Ireland, Scotland, and Wales, and American printings of British texts did not alter these national cultural tendencies. An exception that might be raised is the magazine trade. In the *Victorian* in the 1840s, in the *Canadian Magazine* in the 1890s, and in most secular Canadian periodicals published in the interim, one can find ample proof of editorial displeasure at the domination of the popular-magazine trade by American periodicals. Again, without going into the question of British influence on nineteenth-century American culture, it should be noted that the Canadian religious periodicals were by far the most circulated reading material in Victorian Canada. The *Canadian Methodist Magazine*, for example, printed 50,000 copies at a time when the popular American magazines did not circulate much more than half of this number to Canada. At a time when reading materials were much recycled, this gave an enormous Canadian audience to authors like W.H. Withrow (1839-1908) and Albert Carman (1865-1939), two of the many Canadian Methodist imperialists at the turn of the twentieth century.

Agnes Deans Cameron, Naturalism, and Missionary Writing

A feature that marks *The New North* is the precision and exhaustiveness of the author's descriptions of nature and natural phenomena. The work includes catalogues of plants (especially flowers), birds, and animals, and Cameron describes a collection of wild flowers that she gathers along the way.[28] Cameron even uses analogies from nature – light-heartedly – to explain ethnological questions and to comment on women's rights:

> The Chipewyan wife is the New Red Woman. We see in her the essential head of the household. No fur is sold to the trader, no yard or pound of goods bought, without her expressed consent. Indeed, the traders refuse to make a bargain of any kind with a Chipewyan man without the active approbation of the wife. When a Chipewyan family moves camp, it is Mrs. Chipewyan who directs the line of march. How did she happen to break away from the bonds that limit and restrain most Red brides? This is the question that has troubled ethnologists since the North was first invaded by the scientific. We think we have found the answer. Along the shores of Fond du Lac we descry a long-legged wader, the phalarope. This is the militant suffragette of all bird-dom. Madame Phalarope lays her own eggs, but in this culminates and terminates all her responsibilities connubial and maternal, "this, no more." Father Phalarope builds the house, the one hen-pecked husband of all feathered families who does. He alone incubates the eggs, and when little phalaropes are ushered into the vale, it is Papa who tucks their bibs under their chins and teaches them to peep their morning grace and to eat nicely. Mamma, meanwhile, contrary to all laws of the game, wears the brilliant plumage. When evening shadows fall where rolls Athabasca, she struts long-leggedly with other female phalaropes, and together they discuss the upward struggles toward freedom of their unfeathered prototypes.[29]

Several of Cameron's concerns are humourously alluded to here, including her interest in ornithology, anthropology, and feminism. And it should be noted that one of the virtues that Cameron saw in the spread of British civilization was that it would ameliorate the condition of Native women, which frequently had been woeful.[30]

A usual critique of Victorian Canadian missionary literature, insofar as it is considered at all, premises a long history of injustices committed by Protestant and Catholic Christians alike against First Nations peoples.[31] Nonetheless, historically instructive and important descriptions of episodes in nineteenth-century Canada, and work that quite often rises to a literary standard, are to be discovered in surprising profusion in this largely forgotten literature. Roughly speaking, and aside from the obvious denominational and gender divisions that might be noted, these works fall naturally into two categories: works dealing with the progress of the Christian churches in the European settlement of Canada and works dealing with the evangelizing and *civilizing* of First Nations peoples. The missionary literature shares

much with other Victorian travel literature, with a good deal of close attention to environmental particulars, often in the service of a narrative mimeti-
cism, but also in frequent lyrical passages that serve to capture the moment
of the wilderness epiphany or the celebration of or lament for Canadian
flora and fauna. At such moments, the works of John McDougall, Egerton
Ryerson Young, and Thomas Crosby, like that of Agnes Deans Cameron, all
resort to a conventional high-Victorian style that, however pleasingly mel-
lifluous, may tax the endurance of the unsympathetic reader. But such a
reader is unlikely to have a very elaborate understanding of the nuances, or
the *usus loquendi*, of Victorian Canadian culture. In any case, Cameron places
a high value on missionary activity, and her work shows much evidence of
her familiarity with the Canadian missionary literature:

> We have had occasion to speak of the splendid service rendered to North-
> ern and Western Canada by the Hudson's Bay Company and by the Royal
> Northwest Mounted Police. A third factor through the years has been build-
> ing Empire with these. Are we not as a people too prone to minimize the
> great nation-building work performed by the scattered missionaries in the
> lone lands beyond the railway? Ostensibly engaged in the work of saving
> souls, Canadian missionaries, both Roman and English, have opened the
> gates of commerce, prosecuted geographical discovery, tried to correct so-
> cial evils, and added materially to our store of exact science. Through their
> influence, orphanages have been founded, schools established, and hospi-
> tals opened.[32]

This passage touches upon several dominant themes in Cameron's work,
and the congruence of "nation-building" and imperialism, the progressivism of the imperial and national project, and the centrality of Christian
activity in the spread of civilization are all explicit here. In the same passage, Cameron also claims that "Scottish blood" runs "through the veins of
nine-tenths of the people of this North," again stressing the familiar and
British character of the North for potential British emigrants. Her allusion
to the classic travel account *The Great Lone Land* (1872) by Sir William Francis
Butler in this context is also significant.

Recent scholarship tends to overlook that in Britain and Canada many of
the most popular of the accounts of Canadian adventure and wilderness
travel were missionary narratives, and in the Victorian and Edwardian public consciousness missionaries like James Robertson (1839-1902), John
McDougall, Bishop William Carpenter Bompas (1834-1906), and Egerton
Ryerson Young were widely known and associated with frontier life in both
Canada and Great Britain.[33] Catherine Cavanaugh and Jeremy Mouat's
"Western Canadian History: A Selected Bibliography" is a typical example
of this kind of limitation of critical perspective, one that tacitly downplays

the central role of missionaries in the integration of the Northwest into Confederation.[34] In this otherwise very useful outline of works relating to western Canadian history, mention is made neither of the large and once-popular missionary literature nor of the scholarly literature that has dealt sympathetically with this aspect of early Canadian culture.[35] Cavanaugh and Mouat refer laconically to "'Imperial dreams' [that] stimulated the creation of new institutions," but Doug Owram's *Promise of Eden: The Canadian Expansionist Movement and the Idea of the West, 1856-1900* is one of the few works of the many they list that deals at any length with these forces in Victorian Canada.[36] Canadian missionary literature forms an important adjunct to the mainstream of Victorian and Victorian Canadian literature and deserves the same kind of scholarly attention that has recently been given to Victorian travel literature by geographers like Derek Gregory.[37] Secular travel accounts, such as Butler's *Great Lone Land* (1872), and Canadian adventure fiction also contribute to a fuller recovery of the *usus loquendi* of Cameron's work. The projection of anachronistic strictures on imperial, Canadian-nationalist, and evangelical vocabulary obscures the progressive nature of Cameron's thought and undermines her position as a pioneer British Canadian environmentalist. The creation of a distinct Canadian ontology, or national identity, was the product of a half-century of scientistic propaganda of racial nationhood, a myth that harmonized with the romance of an expanding Confederation. British imperialism in Canada consolidated an identity made uneasy by the stress of asserting a national unity that was essentially fictive. The British Canadian of the pre–First World War period has become a casualty of the multicultural, multiethnic ethos that of necessity supplanted the earlier notion of British Canadian nationality.

The Androgynous Pilgrim: Agnes Deans Cameron and the Men of England

Since her death soon after the publication of *The New North*, Agnes Deans Cameron has received little critical attention, and her work as a pioneer in British Columbian education, as a executive member of the Society for the Prevention of Cruelty to Animals, as vice president of the Canadian Women's Press Club, and as an early member of the British Columbia Women's Council has been mostly overlooked in historical surveys of the period.[38] An element to be recalled in reconsidering the place of women in Edwardian Canada is the then-recent date of Canada's deliverance from the semibarbarism and licence of second- and third-generation pioneers in nineteenth-century British North America.[39] In effect, women's use of British racial and imperial discourses served to facilitate the institution of Victorian norms, such as temperance, self-control, duty, and domestic harmony, which were fostered by a raciological connection with British civilization. Agnes Deans Cameron's enthusiasm and her active service to the imperial and *national*

– in the Victorian and Edwardian usage – aligned her with forces of progress and melioration. It is clear that the raciological perspective, derived, directly or indirectly, from Victorian philology and anthropology, was distorted into xenophobia by the ignorance of some Canadians. Nonetheless, evidence of widespread acceptance of these quasi-scientific doctrines of Canadian racial identity can be seen in the genuine and widely dispersed Canadian enthusiasm for patriotic and imperialist organizations that assumed the British identity of Canadians.[40] The Orange Lodges, the societies of the several British patron saints, the patriotic bands that formed such a large part of early Canadian social life, and even the Methodist, Presbyterian, and Anglican Churches all reinforced the idea of a Canadian nation racially aligned with the Mother Country as well as bound by law, sovereign, and custom. These raciological notions were further inscribed on the Canadian consciousness by the later forms of the Canadian Red Ensign – which on its shield represented the arms of the four founding peoples over a branch with three maple leaves, presumably a symbol of the three nations of the United Kingdom, from which Canadian institutions and law had been transplanted – and by the general official use of the Union Jack until 1945.[41] There was no dissonance in Cameron's earnest environmentalism, progressivism, and suffragettism or in her emotional attachment to British nationality and civilization. It would be incorrect to overlook the potentially distorting effect that Cameron's beliefs had upon her opinions of peoples and things. But it would be equally incorrect to use her acceptance of the raciological convictions of her nationality and culture to dismiss her contribution, as she saw it, to a more elevated and enlightened public feeling.

One of Cameron's most interesting achievements in her memorable account of subarctic travel is her success in emphasizing the unspoiled remoteness of the Mackenzie Basin and the difficulties of life there, while at the same time conveying the fitness of the area for British settlement and the British character of the existing backwoods culture. She does this in two ways. First, using Hudson's Bay Company journals preserved at remote posts, she presents the challenges of life in the region in a narratological form that amplifies the romance associated with European experience of the North as propagated in popular and missionary accounts widely circulated in late-Victorian Britain and Canada. And again her eye for detail intensifies the effect. "A pressed mosquito of the vintage of 1790 is very suggestive," she writes, in describing the pages of one such journal.[42] Her second strategy involves a comparison of the wilderness of the Mackenzie Basin with the prosperousness and industry of Vermillion-on-the-Peace:

> Everything on a Vermillion dinner-table is produced in the country, with the exception only of tea, coffee, sugar, and pepper. The country furnishes beef, pork, and fowl all locally matured; home-cured ham and bacon; every

known variety of hardy and tender vegetables; home-made butter; bread made from flour grown and ground on the premises; pies whose four constituents – flour, lard, butter, and fruit – are products of the country; home-made cheese; wild honey; home-made wines; splendid fish caught from the Peace, and a bewildering variety of wild game – moose, caribou, venison, grouse, brant, wild geese, canvas-backs, and mallards.[43]

After a further display of her penchant for the naturalistic catalogue, she continues: "The farm of Sheridan Lawrence, exhibiting its wide-stretching wheat-fields, some heads of which counted seventy-one kernels, with its patches of one-pound potatoes, twelve-foot sunflowers, and its quiverful of happy, tow-headed children, gives as sweet a picture of Canadian thrift and happiness as one would wish to see."[44] It is probably unnecessary to point out the British character of her example. Other remote northern frontier areas are also noted for their British or loyal-French character.[45] Nonetheless, the romance of the alien, or non-European, elements in the author's surroundings is not neglected, and Cameron's eye for acute anthropological and sociological detail is apparent throughout the work. For instance, in describing Fort Providence, she writes:

Beyond Great Slave Lake, forty-five miles down the Mackenzie, we reach Fort Providence, as strongly French in its atmosphere as Hay River is British. Our coming is a gala day. The hamlet flies three flags, the free trader sports his own initials "H.N.," the Hudson's Bay Company loyally runs the Union Jack to the masthead, over the convent flies the tri-colour of France. We walk to the convent and are hospitably received by the nuns. They call their Red flock together for us to inspect and show us marvelous handwork of silk embroidery on white deerskin. The daintiest of dainty slippers calls forth the question, "Where are you going to find the Cinderella for these?" A blank look is my answer, for no one in Providence Convent has ever heard of Cinderella![46]

One function of this passage is to insinuate that the loyalty of the Catholic Church is questionable, a common theme in Protestant Canadian writing of the time, while at the same time the anecdote makes these Republican French pretensions ridiculous by revealing the remoteness of the convent's inmates from European culture.

The already-noted androgyny of the narrative voice of *The New North* also deserves consideration in analysis of the rhetorical strategies Cameron employs to ensure the proper framing of her chronicle in order to appeal to an Edwardian male readership at least as misogynist as their Victorian fathers. The effectiveness of following the textual architecture of the closely related wilderness and missionary texts depends upon a successful *double-gendering* of the text that creates a narrative which sustains both male and female readings. Details of the kinds of game to be hunted and fish to be caught, as well as an account of Cameron's own hunt for a moose, lent the book appeal for the large British audience for Canadian hunting narratives.[47] In one sense, this androgynous quality of the text is, perhaps, an emancipatory mood to be found in much humanistic writing; but in the case of *The New North*, this quality also suits the purpose of encouraging the immigration of British men capable of imagining a wealthy and industrious Mackenzie Delta and understanding the romance of hunting moose in Not-in-a-gu Seepee.[48] A comparison of Cameron's book to a more exclusively feminine text is illustrative of this point. In 1929 S.A. Archer edited *A Heroine of the North*, the memoirs of Charlotte Selina Bompas (1830-1917), which contain interspersed biographical passages. In some respects the work resembles that of Cameron. It describes Charlotte Bompas's journeys into the same territory and presents many details of life in the North (in fact, Cameron discusses Bishop Bompas's wife in her own work).[49] But unlike Cameron, Mrs. Bompas focuses almost exclusively on the women she meets, the fostering of children, and the details of domestic life in the wilderness. In many respects, Cameron's book more resembles the memoirs of the peripatetic scholar Bishop Bompas himself (published four years earlier than her own) than those of his wife.[50]

This analysis began with remarks about Ernesti's principles of interpretation. One of the central tenets of Ernesti's thought was his belief that the meaning of all words is "conventional" and, therefore, that "language can be properly interpreted only in a philological way."[51] Although contemporary scholarship has learned to be wary of unqualified faith in the detachment and objectivity of philologists (and of scholars generally), Ernesti's remarks continue to be worthy of consideration. There are numerous approaches by which an attack on the thought of Agnes Deans Cameron might be prosecuted convincingly by a hostile critic. She uses language and displays attitudes toward non-British people that an enlightened contemporary reader cannot but find regrettable, and her faith in British imperialism is no longer widely shared, to say the least. But a *philological*, or Ernestian, reading of Cameron's text reveals that the attitudes she espouses were ontological for a European Canadian of her period and that from her perspective these beliefs were identified with progressive values of civilization, such as the amelioration of the suffering of women and the disadvantaged and the preservation of the Canadian environment in its fullest sense. Given the tremendous devastation that took place during Cameron's lifetime, her efforts toward conservation and environmentalism demand at least as much notice as her Eurocentrism, and no historical study of Canadian women of her period can be complete without some reference to her contribution to ecology and social progress.

Notes
1 Johann Augustus Ernesti, *Elementary Principles of Interpretation* (Andover: Allen, Morrill, and Wardwell, 1842), 19-43.
2 Robert Darnton, *The Kiss of Lamourette: Reflections in Cultural History* (New York: Norton, 1990); David Nicholas and Maureen Ritchie, *Literature and Bibliometrics* (London, UK: C. Bingley, 1978); Harold Adams Innis, *Empire and Communications* (Oxford: Clarendon Press, 1950).
3 Ernesti, *Elementary Principles,* 25-26.
4 Ibid., 25.
5 By "raciological" I mean thought informed by the scientific study of race.
6 James Woodsworth, *Thirty Years in the Canadian North-West* (Toronto: McClelland, Goodchild, and Stewart, 1917), xv.
7 W.S. MacTavish, ed., *Missionary Pathfinders: Presbyterian Laborers at Home and Abroad* (Toronto: Musson, 1907); Archer Wallace, *Blazing New Trails* (Toronto: Musson, 1928); William T. Gunn, *His Dominion* (Toronto: Canadian Council of the Missionary Education Movement, 1917); R.G. MacBeth, *Our Task in Canada* (Toronto: Westminster, 1917); L. Norman Tucker, *Western Canada: Handbooks of English Church Expansion* (London, UK: A.R. Mowbray, 1908).
8 The importance of the photographs in the original edition of Cameron's book should not be overlooked. There well over a hundred, a great many of them candid photographs of Native people whose lives are not well documented. The lack of them in the modern abridged edition of the work certainly detracts from the reader's understanding of the text.
9 Agnes Deans Cameron, *The New North: Being Some Account of a Woman's Journey through Canada to the Arctic* (New York: D. Appleton, 1909), 281-302.
10 Ibid., 285-86.
11 Ibid., 287-88.
12 Ibid., 281-82.
13 Ibid., 301-2.
14 Edward E. Prince, "Unutilized Fisheries Resources of Canada," in *Conservation of Fish, Birds and Game: Proceedings at a Meeting of the Committee on Fisheries, Game and Fur-Bearing Animals, Commission of Conservation Canada, November 1 and 2, 1915,* edited by James White (Toronto: Methodist Book and Publishing House, 1916), 47-64.
15 Cameron, *The New North,* 226.
16 Ibid., 179.
17 Ibid., 172, 194-211.
18 Ibid., 389-90.
19 Ibid., 390.
20 Alexander Morris, *The Treaties of Canada with the Indians of Manitoba and the North-West Territories, Including the Negotiations on Which They Were Based, and Other Information Relating Thereto* (Toronto: Belfords, Clark and Co., 1880), 50, 69.
21 Katie Trumpener, *Bardic Nationalism: The Romantic Novel and the British Empire* (Princeton, NJ: Princeton University Press, 1997).
22 In fact, the North British Society was founded in Halifax as early as 1768. See James S. MacDonald, *Annals of the North British Society of Halifax, Nova Scotia, 1768-1893* (Halifax: John Bowes, 1894).
23 W. Stewart Wallace, *The Growth of Canadian National Feeling* (Toronto: Macmillan, 1927), 43-56; Alexander Morris, *Nova Britannia, or Our New Canadian Dominion Foreshadowed* (Toronto: Hunter, Rose and Co., 1884), 3-51.
24 Cameron, *The New North,* 386.
25 Margaret McWilliams, *Manitoba Milestones* (Toronto: J.M. Dent, 1928), 175.
26 For a typical and widely circulated example of British-emigration propaganda, see Emily P. Weaver, *Canada and the British Immigrant* (London, UK: Religious Tract Society, 1914).
27 Colin M. Coates and Cecilia Morgan, *Heroines and History: Representations of Madeleine de Verchères and Laura Secord* (Toronto: University of Toronto Press, 2002), 119-255.
28 Cameron, *The New North,* 58, 108, 122, 129-33.
29 Ibid., 132-33.

30   If Cameron is right about the position of Chipewyan women, Diamond Jenness exagger-
     ates when he claims that in "the opinion of every Indian tribe in the Dominion ... the
     female sex as a whole was considered definitely inferior to the male." Diamond Jenness,
     The Indians of Canada, 6th ed. (Ottawa: National Museum of Canada, 1963), 137.

31   Setting aside the question of Christian culpability, and despite any weaknesses in the fac-
     tual histories of the times, places, and events described therein, the study of these works
     remains valuable for the light they throw on Canadian thought of the period.

32   Cameron, *The New North*, 184-85.

33   Charles W. Gordon (Ralph Connor), *The Life of James Robertson, D.D.* (Toronto: Westminster,
     1909). Two notable exceptions to this tendency in recent scholarship include: Neil Semple,
     The Lord's Dominion (Montreal and Kingston: McGill-Queen's University Press, 1996); and
     Phyllis D. Airhart, *Serving the Present Age: Revivalism, Progressivism, and the Methodist Tradi-
     tion in Canada* (Montreal and Kingston: McGill-Queen's University Press, 1992).

34   Catherine Cavanaugh and Jeremy Mouat, "Western Canadian History: A Selected Bibliog-
     raphy," in *Making Western Canada*, edited by Catherine Cavanaugh and Jeremy Mouat
     (Toronto: Garamond, 1996), 267-82.

35   Another example of this tendency can be found in the otherwise illuminating bibliographical
     essay of Kerry Abel, "The Northwest and the North," in *Canadian History: A Reader's Guide*,
     edited by M. Brook Taylor (Toronto: University of Toronto Press, 1994), 335-55.

36   Cavanaugh and Mouat, "Western Canadian History," 273.

37   Derek Gregory, *Writes of Passage: Reading Travel Writing* (New York: Routledge, 1999).

38   One of the few articles to discuss Cameron's role as a feminist is Roberta J. Pazdro, "Agnes
     Deans Cameron: Against the Current," in *In Her Own Right: Selected Essays on Women's
     History in British Columbia,* edited by Barbara Latham and Cathy Kess (Victoria, BC: Camosun
     College, 1980), 101-23.

39   Edwin Guillet, *The Pioneer Farmer and Backwoodsman*, 2 vols. (Toronto: University of Toronto
     Press, 1962), 1:125, 150-52.

40   W. Stewart Wallace, *The Growth of Canadian National Feeling;* Carl Berger, *The Sense of Power:
     Studies in the Ideas of Canadian Imperialism* (Toronto: University of Toronto Press, 1970),
     78-108.

41   In order to appreciate this symbolism more fully, it is perhaps useful to know that earlier
     forms of the Canadian Red Ensign, used after 1870, entwined oak leaves with the maple
     leaves on the rondel.

42   Cameron, *The New North*, 97-100, 189-93.

43   Ibid., 261-62.

44   Ibid., 335-54.

45   Ibid., 171-74.

46   Ibid., 172.

47   Ibid., 346-49.

48   Ibid., 346.

49   Ibid., 186-89.

50   H.A. Cody, *An Apostle of the North: Memoirs of the Right Reverend William Carpenter Bompas,
     D.D.* (Toronto: Musson, 1908).

51   Ernesti, *Elementary Principles*, 20, 27.

3
Wilderness Wives: Domestic Economy and Women's Participation in Nature
Randall Roorda

Most of us, I suppose, at one time or another experience a longing
for another way of life. Suddenly our days and our energies seem
to be expended on trivia. We are overcome by a sense of being alien,
of not belonging in the world in which we find ourselves, of being
out of step with the times and out of sympathy with the attitudes
that we encounter. We are hungry for the fundamentals – for the
satisfaction of wresting food from the stubborn earth, of raising
our own rooftrees with our own hands, of combating successfully
man's implacable, hereditary foes, the wind and the weather. We
suffer a great nostalgia, which means a sickness to return home.
— Louise Dickinson Rich[1]

"It was the kind of day for cooking moose muzzle," she mused,
and plucked the thick hair from the animal's severed snout.
— Bradford and Vena Angier[2]

"Wilderness Wife" – catchy, isn't it? I can't take credit (or blame) for the
expression, which leapt out at me from the stacks near some other title I
was after. The sing-songiness of the phrase reinforced its wry twist – the way
this most domestic of titles, the "wife," was joined to an entity that might
seem antithetical to it. "Wilderness," one might think, would reject "wife"
the way the bloodstream shucks off a pathogen. Yet the words cleave as though
joined at some Sanskrit root. In fusing them, the expression sloganizes anti-
pathies key to nature-retreat narratives, as regards the presence or absence
of women therein – charmingly so.

To see that this is the case, consider that the expression entitles not just
the book I ran across in the stacks. So far I've found three books entitled
Wilderness Wife, which considered together nicely triangulate a territory
the phrase conveys. One of these books is a children's biography of Rebecca

Boone, Daniel Boone's spouse and the quintessential pioneer wife[3] – a figure imaged as striding through Cumberland Gap, babe in arms, in the vanguard of settlers set to subdue the wilderness. This wife follows the explorer husband into a territory made not yet fully safe for a civilization he embraces ambivalently, she less so, as successor to a wilderness that is pristine, breathtaking, yet rightly doomed. Much discussed by the likes of Annette Kolodny[4] and Julie Roy Jeffrey,[5] this figure is more commonly dubbed the pioneer woman, associated with wilderness intensely yet only in passing, her role to soften, chasten, domesticate the unkempt space her husband has broken and cleared.

This first book contrasts with and sets off the Wilderness Wives I have in mind. The other two are emblems of the type. The earliest *Wilderness Wife*, the one I stumbled upon, was written by Kathrene Pinkerton and published in 1939.[6] Pinkerton herself is the wife in question, her book a narrative of retreat in nature, a charming nonfiction account of homesteading in the bush of Ontario. It is an early instance of a genre that its title might as well name: the Wilderness Wife narrative, in which a married couple settles in wilderness, with the wife writing their story. A later instance, appearing in 1976 in the wake of the back-to-the-land rage, is the *Wilderness Wife* of Bradford and Vena Angier. The genre in some ways culminates and in others hits bottom in this potboiler of a how-to manual cum heaving-breast romance saga of homesteading in British Columbia, the first-person narratorial voice of wife Vena belied by the pride of place given her co- or ghost- (or boast-) writing husband Bradford, longtime champ of the woodcraft-manual business. A further twist in titles bears out how these identically named books rope off a genre. The Angiers' *Wilderness Wife* constitutes a sequel to their 1951 book, which first recounted their retreat to British Columbia, *At Home in the Woods*. In 1976, when this sequel appeared, the *Wilderness Wife* of Pinkerton was reissued (posthumously) under an altered, less impolitic title: *A Home in the Wilds*.[7] The watchword slides between "wife" and "home" in these still-near-synonymous titles. The half-century or so bracketed by these books can be read as a loosely strung epoch in relations between home, woods/wilds, and womanhood, one related to the unfolding of nature writing at large, to the role of women writers in that development, and to the standing of the Canadian environment, the far North, in the designs of these writers, who mostly hail from the urbanized States. This chapter explores these relations in the figure and genre of the Wilderness Wife.

The Wilderness Wife, for starters, *is* a genre, a set of texts enacting common conditions and sharing a generic prehistory – a genre, in the broad sense some recent writers have explored, at once derived from and constitutive of recurring social situations.[8] It is a genre not confined to books bearing this title, yet neither does it encompass all books concerning or written by women living in wilderness. In particular, it is a genre situated in the mid-twentieth century, one distinct from the sorts of women's wilderness or nature writing typical of the nineteenth century. When writers such as Susanna Moodie in Canada and Caroline Kirkland in the United States re-counted their moves to wilderness,[9] they did so as literate successors to Rebecca Boone, as part of a larger saga of settlement. What appreciation they express toward their wild environs is subordinated to their main pur-pose: that of establishing households and communities to supplant the wild-ness they confront. They may have moments of rapturous encounter with nature, but they aren't nature writers in the common sense of the term. Nor are women nature writers of the time writers of wilderness, but rather gar-den, rural, and bird-life enthusiasts of the sort Vera Norwood describes.[10] Both the pioneer woman and the lady nature lover are figures, broadly speak-ing, who refute nature writing's generic master narrative, which is Thoreauvian in essence: that of the individual's solitary retreat into a wild nature devoid of human presence, to be recognized and experienced for precisely this quality. This is mainly male turf – experience of a sort that women were not much privy to and were unlikely to recount in such terms. As scholars like Jeffrey have had to concede, we search mostly in vain for equivalents of the Thoreauvian attitude toward wild nature and solitary retreat among women of that era.[11] Thus even readers powerfully motivated to find evidence of transformed attitudes toward wilderness, such as the latter-day Thoreauvian Anne LaBastille, have reluctantly reached this con-clusion.[12] What prevails in writing of pioneer wives is a conventional do-mesticity, versions of the belief in women as foes to wilderness, as bearers of civilized virtue among wild men and wilder beasts.

But toward the middle years of the twentieth century, with the passing of the frontier famously declared, with the era of homesteading mostly con-cluded in areas where agriculture is practicable, and with both the roles of women and attitudes toward nature in continued flux, another sort of women's wilderness book appeared. Books of this sort recount a married couple's settlement in wilderness, undertaken with Thoreauvian motives of self-sufficiency and retreat, the object being to escape the orbit of industrial civilization rather than to serve as its vanguard. Against the background of the classic retreat narratives of single males like Thoreau, John Muir, and Henry Beston, the married couple's retreat may be instigated by men but is typically narrated by women – by Wilderness Wives. With these narratives, it's as though Henry Beston's fiancée, instead of packing him off to the cabin on Cape Cod and telling him they could not be married till he'd written up his solitary retreat in *The Outermost House*, had instead gotten hitched to him forthwith, gone along on the rustic interlude, and written the book herself.[13]

Who are these women? Early on, as noted, there is Kathrene Pinkerton, whose retreat to the Ontario bush, not recounted till 1939, in fact took place much earlier, before the Great War.[14] There is Louise Dickinson Rich, author of *We Took to the Woods* (1942), an account of married life in the backwoods of Maine's far north – widely reviewed (by the prominent mid-century nature writer Donald Culross Peattie, among others)[15] and serialized in the *Atlantic Monthly* and *Reader's Digest.* Somewhat later, there are Margaret Murie, author of *Two in the Far North* (1962), which recounts adventures with her naturalist husband, Olaus, in Alaska, and Helen Hoover, whose mid-century books of cabin life at the boundary waters of Ontario and Minnesota, such as *A Place in the Woods* (1969), were illustrated by her husband Adrian. There are Lois Crisler (*Arctic Wild*, 1958) and Billie Wright (*Four Seasons North*, 1973, also set in Alaska, which has served as a sort of naturalized Canada for a nation that has lots of west but is largely short on its own far North).[16] And there are several others, more obscure. An important early instance of the type, and a landmark in women's writing on the Canadian environment, is *Driftwood Valley* (1946) by Theodora C. Stanwell-Fletcher.[17] This was the first book written solely by a woman to win the prestigious Burroughs Award in nature writing and remained for years one of very few books by women to be so honoured. *Driftwood Valley* and Pinkerton's *Wilderness Wife*, as works set in Canadian wilderness, will serve as primary examplars of the type for this chapter, along with a third, later narrative of retreat in north-central British Columbia, *Island Sojourn* (1980) by Elizabeth Arthur, a post-1960s back-to-the-land narrative,[18] to which they'll be counterposed.

If as some contend, there is a perceived interregnum in women's nature writing between the turn-of-the-century cult of nature and the apotheosis of Rachel Carson – between the reappropriation of nature study by male scientists and the resurgence of nature writing with the rise of modern environmentalism – then the writing of Wilderness Wives is a key place in which to seek to fill this gap. Even the second edition of *The Norton Book of Nature Writing*, for instance – revised to address a reputed bias toward white male writers – includes but three women writers active between Mary Austin and Carson, none of them (Virginia Woolf, Isak Dinesen, Meridel LeSueur) primarily a writer on nature.[19] Vera Norwood, the scholar most assiduous in moving to fill the gap, cites Peter J. Schmitt (in the preface to his revision of *Back to Nature*) as bemoaning the notion that women's nature writing is a recent phenomenon.[20] Schmitt drops some names as examples of neglected writers, one being that of Kathrene Pinkerton, yet her name doesn't even make his index, and Norwood misspells it (as Katherine) in transcribing the quotation. Stanwell-Fletcher and Crisler warrant discussion by Norwood, but as examples of women's bonding with wild animals, not with their spouses. Since what's at issue for Norwood and others is largely women's circumscription within conventions of domesticity, it is not surprising to find marriage overlooked as a condition and signal aspect of these writers' engagement with wilderness. The Wilderness Wife embarrasses feminism while flouting the masculine imperative to solitude in retreat. Yet for women between the wars seeking models for participation in nature – women like Phyllis Rose, who, growing up, "wanted wild women,"[21] if not women in the wild – Wilderness Wives were about the only game in (or out of) town.

Their interest, then, is historical, but not only so. As a genre, they pose an overarching question to the larger genre formations of nature writing in which they figure. What happens to the Thoreauvian project of solitary retreat in nature when, updated by a century or more, it is undertaken not alone but with another person, situated within a marriage, and represented by a woman writer? Thoreau's pugnacious bachelorhood, his disaffection from most companions and especially women, remains a sticking point to many readers of *Walden*, for all its influence. Hightailing to a cabin is well and good for him (the objections go), but not for anyone with a family or with any ties to other people. Thoreau invites objections on such terms, for the enduring appeal of his account, as of subsequent books in its image, resides largely in the way it lays out a model domestic economy: a set of practical, material arrangements to effect experiential, spiritual ends. Thoreau advises that we not abandon our castles in the air but rather put foundations under them,[22] yet he holds forth on the construction and provisioning of the castle as well. This melding of devotional literature and how-to manual has continued to mark books in this vein ever since, with sometimes the instructional and sometimes the experiential (or for that matter, "literary") element predominating. This is why the Angiers' *Wilderness Wife*, as dimwitted, antiliterary a tome as can be conceived, can quote and evoke the subtle Thoreau at every turn, between recipes for moose snout and tips on homesteading the Yukon, the next refuge from civilized encroachments once the bulldozers hit British Columbia. The practical creation of a domestic economy, Bradford Angier's stock in trade, enables and manifests everything Thoreau is after; it's at the centre of every account of living in wilderness that goes beyond the scope of a day hike. Every backpacking, camping, or woodcraft guide details the crafting of a domestic economy. One of the most astonishing things about *Walden*, considered from a certain perspective, is how Thoreau reports having cooked for and cleaned up after himself. In his economy of one, he reports doing the work of a wife.

Marriage, of course, remains par excellence the basis for the domestic economy, however ideologically freighted its arrangement, its categories of husbandry and wifery neatly apportioning the work that economy demands. The Wilderness Wife narrative recounts such arrangements being imported to and transformed in the wilderness place. That the arrangements are more imported than transformed is the burden these narratives bear for current readers, the conventionality of their gender-based division of labour a vestige of bad old days when a woman's place was in the home, albeit "a home in the wilds." In terms of work, the Wilderness Wife is very much a wife. Stanwell-Fletcher, arriving at the lake called Tetana in the late 1930s, finds herself plunged with but meager preparation into the role of cook and house (or tent) keeper for her husband and the First Nations men he hires to help him build. Mildly resentful, she nonetheless acknowledges the justice of the situation, given as how, in both expertise and brute strength, he is so obviously needed elsewhere.[23] Pinkerton, a thoroughgoing city dweller, can't cook a lick when the couple first shoves off; she defers to her bush-savvy husband in this as in tent pitching, paddling, and every other aspect of campcraft. Yet she soon asserts herself in this feminine realm, taking the initiative to cook a fish over the fire using a method surpassing her spouse's rough and ready one, at which point she is vouchsafed this duty for good.[24] It is common in these books to find accounts of comically botched first forays into one or another cooking feat or other domestic chore – rock-hard yeast breads, laundry that takes all day – succeeded by expertise. The Wilderness Wife may be humble and self-deprecating, but she proves to be intrepid.

Her intrepid character is not a function of adaptation to conditions foisted upon her, for the Wilderness Wife is a willing participant in the couple's relocation, not someone dragged along to clean and cook for her man – no Ma Ingalls to a footloose, ever-migrating Pa. She is a full partner in the Thoreauvian design. Her willingness to engage the design may in part be a function of her marriage to her husband (as seems the case with Pinkerton), or her attraction to her husband may stem partly from his character as the sort of man harbouring such designs (as is clearly so with Stanwell-Fletcher). It is not always easy to tell and may not even make sense to ask. In the typical Wilderness Wife narrative (excepting full-life memoirs like Murie's), the couple's life before departure for wilderness is foreshortened or soft-pedalled – not being pertinent to the business at hand. In this, too, the narrative is Thoreauvian, an instance of nature writing more generally, which tends not to feature personal history incidental to nature retreat. Pinkerton notes briefly that the couple left their jobs and made for the bush when the husband left his newspaper job on doctor's orders, yet she does not divulge the nature of his supposed infirmity, the type of job she herself held down, the manner of their meeting, the specific grounds for his wilderness expertise (which, typically, proves considerable), or much else. Stanwell-Fletcher is more forthcoming in prefacing the diary entries that comprise her book, yet here, too, the couple's pasts are encapsulated in a paragraph, with no word on the circumstances of their meeting, only remarks to the effect that they had long harboured tastes and dreams in parallel, separately before they met, together thereafter.[25] It is this togetherness, a present unity of purpose and resolve, that the Wilderness Wife stresses, both partners doing their part in realms they deem proper, to the best of their ability.

As their parts are not the same, so their abilities are not equal. The wife is intrepid, but she is dependent, at times abjectly so. She may have outdoor and travel experience – may even, like Stanwell-Fletcher, be a widely travelled, doctorate-holding naturalist – but her preparation for wilderness living, especially under far-North conditions, is typically scant. Her husband, by contrast, is a man of almost preternatural experience and prowess. It seems he can do anything, especially get by in a country where, left to her own devices, the wife would rapidly perish. Pinkerton's husband, Robert, she notes, "had worked in logging camps and in a fur trading post and had cruised in a canoe," whereas she is a rank greenhorn, who "had never been off a sidewalk" and who knows him only as a man who can order well in restaurants.[26] Once on the lakes, Robert performs so manfully, one wonders what sort of ailment might misfit a person for newspaper service while permitting him to build cabins, haul sledges, track moose, and lug home their parts. Stanwell-Fletcher's spouse, whom she refers to by the monolithic-sounding initial J., is even more daunting. A former British army officer, a world traveller and arctic explorer who has tracked wolves on tundra and wintered with "Eskimos," J. seems omnicompetent, his strength, speed, and endurance in wilderness travel rivalled only by his ability to build or jury-rig devices for every contingency. He is both protective and reproving toward his wife, whose nickname, Teddy, emphasizes her initially diminutive, even toylike, aspect. Elizabeth Arthur, writing decades later in the wake of the liberatory sixties, is more jocularly addressed as "Arthur" by her husband Bob – the mock male moniker revealing, for one thing, that she's retained her own surname and suggesting moreover a sort of equivalence in preparation and role. It's true that Arthur reveals a hiking and climbing background more comparable to her husband's, befitting the greater range of opportunities and role models she's enjoyed. Yet Bob, too, is a pillar of a husband, an accomplished outdoorsman, professional mountaineering instructor, crack builder and mechanic. For all these women, the greater strength and competence of the male is a recurring concern and source of mixed feelings: awe and gratitude for how their husbands conduct them through the wild; shame and frustration over their own incompetence and dependency, their inability to lift the same objects, carry the same loads, handle boats, track game, fire guns.

This is nothing new. Disparities in competence and strength are certainly cultural residue – in large part, an outgrowth of how the outdoors has been coded as male terrain, the indoors as female. True to type, these women writers lavish attention on interior spaces they've created; they are avid decorators as well as laundresses and cooks, within the limitations of their rustic sites ("Was there ever a man who didn't love curtains!" enthuses Stanwell-Fletcher).[27] And they expound warmly on the sensation of returning to their wilderness domiciles after an absence; they are well enculturated in these as in other ways. Yet male physical strength remains a recalcitrant presence, even an embarrassment for feminist-inflected understandings of such accounts. The gender problem for the livelihood these women seek compares with those concerning women's roles in firefighting or military service: No outright dichotomy, no essentialized divide, need separate gender roles, yet a propensity to contrast persists, with marked material consequences. When in mid-winter, during a time of depleted food supplies, J. butchers a dead moose, he, Teddy, and their two pack dogs tote loads of the frozen flesh miles back to the cabin. Nearly twice her size, he carries exactly twice what she does; the bigger of the dogs also exceeds her load.[28] Arthur and her husband both tote building supplies, but while she carries lumber, he handles plywood, two sheets at a time – the sheets too wide for her to get her arms across. All these women see fit to report such details, almost compulsively so, since they so materially affect their sense of how they get by in a fundamentally inhospitable terrain. They are crucial to grounding the narratives in what Arthur calls "the stubborn indifferences of the inanimate world," to calibrating one's standing in a place where, as Stanwell-Fletcher notes, nearly all talk concerns "necessary elements of daily life."[29]

Given the relative incompetence and dependence these women report of themselves, it is no surprise that their progress toward expertise and self-reliance in the wilderness economy should be a prime source of drama in their accounts. It is not the plot but the wife that develops – in strength, skill, fortitude, and comfort. Her development accompanies the usual retreat-narrative plot of movement toward recognition and fulfillment within nonhuman nature: In fact, the wife's progress is indispensable to this plot, as the dual character of the Thoreauvian scenario, both how-to guide and experiential manifesto, reinforces. As the wife develops at maintaining the domestic economy, she develops at apprehending and taking pleasure in relations to place that the economy enables. She develops in several ways. As noted, she progresses as a "domestic," at housekeeping in the wild – partly (as in camp cookery) under her husband's tutelage, largely by hook or by crook, making her way in this sphere as the husband moves inexorably through his. She develops, further, at the work of men in an almost exclusively male domain. She moves material (although less than the husband); she helps build the house (in ways ancillary to his efforts); she paddles the canoe (although feebly at first and generally from the bow). Says Stanwell-Fletcher, "A woman here performs any job of which she is physically capable, including many of which she may suppose herself incapable." The narrative charts this movement toward first envisioning and then achieving capability, even as her labours remain supplemental to his: "The man's whole time and energy are consumed in performing those deeds which only his strength and skill make possible."[30]

Certain stages in this movement are so common to the genre that they can be predicted as aspects of encountering and subsisting in the place. The writers whose books I am working with all report such incidents. There are always places where the woman must come to terms with the husband's absence, as he leaves to track game, bring in supplies, or indulge an impulse to explore; she must deal with her solitude and the prospect that he might not return, stranding her in a place she is ill-equipped to survive in or escape from on her own. There are incidents in which she proves her mettle during an extended spell alone, even (in Stanwell-Fletcher's case) undertaking a solo camping excursion to demonstrate her ability to survive. There are points at which the couple takes on animal companions – pack or sled dogs, mostly, in pre-snowmobile accounts – which the wife forms a relationship with and learns to handle. Crucially, there are encounters with hunting, trapping, killing – which are pervasive because the taking of animals underwrites every mode of far-North subsistence, in both the proximate, daily-meal economy and the extended realm of monetary exchange. For daily meals, the husband blasts moose, and the wife peppers grouse and rabbits: Both put meat on the table. With agriculture mostly a nonstarter (the Stanwell-Fletchers' garden nets a few meager lettuce heads; the Pinkertons do better, effusing over their radishes, but two years in a row must replant when their seedlings freeze),[31] meat is the mainstay. As Stanwell-Fletcher cheerily exclaims, "In the northern wilderness, no greeting sounds pleasanter to the ears than the one which says fresh meat is at hand."[32] Pinkerton becomes quite an avid butcher, wading with relish into the work of cleaving up moose.[33] For money, she goes further, electing to set herself up as a trapper, taking mink and ermine of the sort she once sported on city streets to augment the couple's scarce cash reserves. The Stanwell-Fletchers also hunt for cash indirectly: They trap and shoot specimens in their role as collectors for a museum, this activity paying the expenses for their wilderness idyll. Here again a division of labour obtains: Teddy takes birds with a shotgun, freeing J. to focus on large mammals.[34] The division may be broached, sometimes near-ritually: It is a rite of passage for the wife to take on bigger game. Yet normally this is an episode, not a shift in the dispensation of the domestic economy. Arthur, for instance, brings down a moose, but it's her husband who locates it and hands her the gun.[35]

The singular nature of Arthur's foray into big game – a token bagging that Stanwell-Fletcher, with respect to the trophy hunting prevalent among men, declines to take part in (she thinks she's "the only white woman" to go big-game hunting "without 'getting her bear.' *And I am proud of it!*")[36] – underscores the qualified nature of the wife's growth into competence. This growth is pronounced enough, and the contemporary reader's desire to detect it sharp enough, that one may be led to discredit ways in which the wife continues to discount her own efforts. In her insightful article "Women

and the Great Canadian Wilderness," for instance, Rebecca Raglon charts
some episodes in Stanwell-Fletcher's progress toward greater independence.
Raglon notes how this writer grows increasingly fit at coping with extremes
of cold and privation, how she undertakes to camp out in winter by herself,
and how in one case, she tweaks gender roles by compelling some men in
camp to pare onions and potatoes for their dinner in twenty-six-degree-
below weather, inwardly exulting at their incompetence in so doing. These
are indeed milestones in her development, yet it is not as clear that the
"poor little woman" persona that Raglon notes toward the book's beginning does indeed, as she remarks, "finally subside" at this point.[37] Both
before and after this episode, Stanwell-Fletcher disparages not just her lapses
in competence, but her own increasingly frequent feats of independence.
During her solo winter camp, she mainly laments her inability to perform
camp chores as expeditiously as J., obsessing at once romantically and
practically about missing not only "J.'s warm body ... to snuggle against,"
but also "the extra bedding which he is able to carry." When her long-
anticipated spell of living alone in the cabin is done, she remarks that her
"little adventure," once over, "didn't seem very big or important at all." On
their last long collecting expedition in the mountains, she is still limning
her impressions in terms of her husband's, observing that, "For almost the
first time on a trip in this country, J. has been comfortable and carefree, and
consequently, so have I." In some ways, despite all she has accomplished,
she remains, as she says near the book's end, "his wife, that weak and silly
creature," as if by a sort of congenital condition.[38]

Neither Pinkerton nor Arthur appears quite so dependent, although their
situations are less extreme: a day's round trip without portage by boat or
snowshoe for each, as opposed to a trek of several days or a bush-plane ride
for Stanwell-Fletcher.[39] As for Arthur, she writes in a time of changing expectations for women as well, such that there is less at the outset of which
she's prone to believe herself incapable. She is also the most artful, reflec-
tive writer of the lot (workshop-trained and a successful novelist since);
thus her trials over her own capacities find more deliberate, sustained expression. A key instance of this occurs in her account of learning to manage
the boats by which they move on and off their island retreat. Recounting
how she took on the strenuous operations necessary to run their first boat,
Arthur tropes on notions of power and absorption in the waves the craft
traverses, expressing her relation to these in terms of alternating alienation
and embrace, the external conditions figuring the internal. When the couple
finally relinquishes the flat-bottom power boats they've used and acquires a
canoe, Arthur feels freed to a relation of response to the waves. She even
persuades her normally more adventurous husband into braving a strong
headwind toward home rather than sitting it out on shore, and exults in

her power to move the craft through the water.[40] In this respect, she comes into a condition that Pinkerton reports early on in her narrative, when in the weeks preceding the couple's settling on a cabin site, they head out on an extended backcountry canoe trek to acquaint Kathrene with the country. From her initial feeble, intermittent stroke, which forces constant adjustments on frustrated hubbie, she makes a breakthrough into an avid, voracious paddler, so bent on moving water that her spouse nicknames her "map-eater."[41] Yet both women remain in the bow, the subordinate spot, although their growing expertise might better suit them for stern, where control and dexterity, not brute strength, are what's called for.

A negotiation between convention and capacity, then, dictates how labour is divided in the domestic economy of these couples, with the wife performing habitual housework largely but not only because this is what's expected of her. It should be noted that these arrangements are flexible enough, sufficiently open to circumstances, to run against type in some cases. Sometimes the wife proves more adept than her husband at tasks one would expect the man to perform. Stanwell-Fletcher tries snowshoes for the first time, and in no time is outstripping her husband, the arctic explorer: She is lighter and more lithe, better fitted to the devices.[42] Arthur takes over for her spouse when he gets frustrated trying to place rafters that have been sawed in a pattern just a bit off line; she has the patience to adjust them, to fit individual pieces to different locations, that is lacking in a man who, as a friend had remarked, "has two speeds – Off and High."[43] And Pinkerton, as noted, undertakes to set up a trapline, working at this during the mornings that her husband is parked at the typewriter. All do work they are "physically capable" of – and capability does not reduce to brute strength.

However, dwelling on the wife's growing powers and the ways labour is apportioned between partners can distract from the fact that the domestic economy is based on mutual reliance. Less important than what wife or husband can do is what the couple does together. Indeed, the degree of mutuality, sharing, cooperation, solicitation, and such demonstrated in these books is truly notable. Pinkerton especially enjoys an exemplary marriage, to all appearances, with the couple's every move seeming to crystallize from unspoken consensus, each discovering they're thinking what the other's been thinking all along ("we knew we had reached the same decision").[44] Still, the couple's joint enterprise does raise a point of tension when considered in light of the Thoreauvian scenario of retreat. The problem, simply, is that of being alone together. The imperatives of solitude and companionship, of seeking the nonhuman while cultivating human relations, do not always sit easily together. This tension has consequences for the genre. Since these books, like nature writing in general, take relations with place as their primary focus, relations with the spouse may get dealt with only diffusely.

In a man's account, of course, they are liable to be effaced altogether, as when Ed Abbey omits his spouse from *Desert Solitaire*, very likely to the benefit of the book, certainly to that of his image and career. These women's books are not nearly so extreme, yet even here the figure of the husband is not exactly a developed character but more a presence or foil or condition. No full-fledged picture of J. or Robert emerges from these books – more so for Bob since Arthur is more a novelist, but even there the portrait is episodic, incidental, not sustained. Signs of the husband's character and hints of spousal relations emerge largely in snippets and asides – brief flushes of intimacy, flashes of irritation and anger. Considering the likes of Abbey's omissions and Thoreau's much-remarked acts of filtering, one wonders what might have been selected for exclusion from these accounts.[45] There are moments in Stanwell-Fletcher, especially, where I sense that she is putting a lid on things, on features of marital relations embarrassing to recount and peripheral to her focus on place. She has a penchant for what seem to me unwitting parallels, in which some hint of an irruption on the domestic scene is succeeded with a natural-history episode that seems somehow consonant. Especially intriguing are hints of sexual jealousy displaced onto animals, as when, immediately following a line about J. "strutting like a turkey gobbler" after catching a trout, Teddy observes a grouse appearing to court her, till she sees in a nearby tree a female grouse, who "eyed me very coldly!"[46] Pinkerton, for her part, is comically histrionic in denouncing a female dog, an "artful wench" named Belle, who refuses to work, flaunts her pedigree and good looks, and clearly favours the company of males over that of Kathrene and their female cat – a collie whose "cream colored panties" make a "constant display of pulchritude" that she pretends will tempt her husband.[47] Not only wedded bliss – as with Stanwell-Fletcher's admired wolves, which in their trait of monogamy stand in contrast to the domestic dog and "a certain percentage of human beings"[48] – but insecurity and annoyance in marriage are diffused through natural-history observation.

Isolation is a special pitfall to the couple in wilderness. Key to the domestic economy, as crucial as loading in firewood, are measures the couple takes to avoid crowding each other, rubbing up against each other to the point of irritation. Stanwell-Fletcher remarks how "seemingly unimportant little customs and habits ... are vital in relationships of people thrown together in a lonely wilderness" and reports on how her husband "decreed that we take short walks separately" so that after brief separation, "each has something new to tell, and we're happy to be together again."[49] Pinkerton's trapping routine is part of this couple's measures: She gets out of the house in the morning while he writes; he vacates to get firewood during the afternoons while she works in the house. Their arrangement appears to work well (at least no irruption is reported), even during winter, particularly perilous for its short, dark days and long periods of enforced cabin time. The danger is acute, then, of becoming "bushed" – drifting into a condition of paranoia, hypersensitivity, aversion to touch and contact, active disgust of the partner. Stories of becoming bushed are part of the lore of the bush. Stanwell-Fletcher remarks how "certain highly respectable citizens of the North" have turned into "uncontrolled murderous creatures" under such conditions and how this couple, too, might have succumbed to such if not for "J.'s years of experience (not to mention the fact that he has a wise wife)." Since their success is not entire – they "have plenty of lapses" during which they're "scarcely on speaking terms" – one suspects her "wisdom" to consist not least in keeping her trap shut when her husband's flirting with rage.[50] Even so, one notes that she credits them both with the capacity to turn "murderous," as with the capacity for the tact or acumen and the concrete strategies to avoid this.

Arthur, for her part, is as versed as any in the lore of the "bushed." In her more artful and recent account, she draws out the dynamic of the couple's isolation in ways that Pinkerton seems rarely concerned with and that Stanwell-Fletcher only in passing admits. In her more sustained attention to experiential aspects of solitary wilderness life, Arthur presents the tensions of companionship in isolation as something integral to the endeavour. The most intense episode in her book – the narrative's climax, in effect, despite its diarylike form – explores this tension in ways that point up a contrast between earlier and later instances of this genre. Weeks into winter, housebound by storms for days on end, Arthur is becoming bushed and sees Bob getting there, too. The fascinating thing is that Arthur recognizes her condition, could even be said to be scripted in it, generically speaking, since she spends hours reading the many accounts of wilderness living and exploration they've brought along, the sort that feature narratives of arctic travel, in which accounts of cabin fever abound – the sort that have inspired their retreat in the first place, including, as we learn elsewhere, works by Bradford Angier. One account she reads has a special resonance for her: It concerns two Yukon gold seekers, friends since boyhood, who in a mutual rage split up their shared possessions right down the middle, even sawing bags of flour in half, thereby assuring perfect equity and certain death for both. Arthur is piqued by this perverse Solomon's solution to a domestic economy gone bust. Yet diagnosing it does nothing to help her remedy a condition she likens to an itch she can't help scratching, despite the harm this does. Inevitably, the couple blows up. Bob slugs her in the stomach, then storms out into the snow. Left gasping for breath on the floor, Arthur is somehow relieved: She is free to hate him without reservation now. Even so, after a day and a half of silence, the couple reconciles, after having gone through their respective and gender-specific rites of solitary passage: Bob goes out on snowshoes and faces a great moose without shooting; Arthur repaints the sooted kitchen ceiling.[51]

The difference in these accounts, then, is that while Arthur's text clearly takes after ones like Stanwell-Fletcher's, hers is less idyllic, more conflicted and equivocal. While hardly renouncing husband or marriage or home, it more directly fronts the dark side of male prowess and the woman's compensatory angers and initiatives. It more explicitly situates silence and solitude in the gendered domestic economy, along with interdependence and intimacy. Though the conditions it reports are less extreme and the privation less acute than in Stanwell-Fletcher's *Driftwood Valley,* it might even be regarded as more "Canadian" than that honorary landmark of Canadian women's writing in its musings on the psychic terrain of survival in a harsh country and its mingled antipathy and attraction toward the prospect of absorption by an immense, indifferent landscape. Arthur figures this as the "rock" of the island they live on, at once their prison and refuge. Her portrayal of Bob, both intimate and remote, echoes this character, reminding me sometimes of how Margaret Atwood imagines the husband of Susanna Moodie as a shadowy figure receding into the trees.[52] Something of Arthur's attitude toward her surroundings is captured in a quip that Stanwell-Fletcher reports from a Vancouver man traversing this difficult land: "This, said he, was a 'wonderful country, wonderful country, but my God, let me get out of here!'"[53]

These couples all *do* get out of there, ultimately. In Arthur's *Island Sojourn,* however, their blowup is not the proximate cause of their departure: The episode of violence makes the couple's departure seem inevitable, confirming the conclusion that the title has presaged all along. Hardship and isolation draw them away – poverty, too. For a further difference marks the later from the earlier books, one crucial to the terms of the wilderness domestic economy. This difference concerns a sense of enterprise and purpose. As post-1960s back-to-the-landers, Arthur and spouse seek a home in wilderness as an escape from city ills and a metropolitan sense of desperation and incipient collapse. They are drawn back to the land but not forward into some enterprise, some basis for subsistence and exchange beyond what they can scrounge up in a hard place. Like all these couples, they drag in tons of stuff from "outside"; they need money for this. When broke, they must go to town and take jobs for day wages, he at a sawmill, she as a bank clerk. They don't even get to stay at their place during the summer, but rather head back south to work as wilderness instructors, missing their island's best season in the process of scraping up money to stay. The arrangement proves untenable at last. It's no wonder they become bushed, with nothing special to do but read, keep a diary, and stew through long evenings following short, stormy days.

The other, earlier wives are different. They and their husbands go to work each day. The Stanwell-Fletchers are naturalists in the wilderness on a mission to observe and collect for a museum; they have their specimens to stuff and their notes, reports, and articles to write. The Pinkertons turn to writing to finance their wilderness retreat: first, to fiction that Robert sweats over mornings, crafting tales brainstormed with Kathrene, and when that doesn't pan out sufficiently, to outdoor articles, photo-illustrated. They step into a loop of participation in genre, peddling "how-to" advice to readers dreaming of wilderness living, drawing proceeds that enable them to persist in that very life. Kathrene contributes her share of these pieces, angling them toward women in the bush – partly by including cooking tips she's created, as it were, from scratch – and comes increasingly to secure typewriter time of her own.[54] The point is that the Wilderness Wife *writes*, her domestic economy is maintained in writing, and her domicile is a scene of writing. She subsists through literacy. This differentiates her both from pioneer women, whose testaments are famously scattered and sparse, and from others in the lightly populated region, including Native people.[55] Her book is a testament to her character as a writer. *She* writes it; the husband doesn't. Whatever his role in motivating or instituting their move to the wilderness, it falls to her to recount it, which she does in ways he would not. This is a job she is "physically capable" of – one for which there's a market as well.

If these women are going to work, making their way, solidifying the grounds for a domestic economy that enables their wilderness experience, then why after all do they leave this experience behind? Not through any diminution in their pleasure with their place, certainly. Pleasure, interest, satisfaction, wellbeing, peace: These are the prevailing notes in all these accounts, rarely mitigated at all. Expressions thereof are so frequent as to baffle sampling; I'll let a few by Stanwell-Fletcher sketch patterns for the lot. Despite physical exertion and hardship sometimes to the point of tears, she reports, "we are deeply content. I can't think of anyone in the world with whom I'd change places. This must be what is meant by perfect happiness." She feels not just content, but completed, living "the fulfillment of my childhood dreams, the strong determination of adolescence, something that has always been meant for me." She relates the satisfaction she feels to the condition of the creatures around her, speculating, for instance, that "Much of an animal's time must be spent in the sheer joy of living, the sheer pleasure of physical sensations." This sense of relationship, resulting from pleasure, deepens into a wilderness ethic, "a kind of kinship with it all. There *is* a secure way of life, and all manner of help and care for us, if we use the wilderness rightly, study it, work with it, not against it." Finally, these sensations, these realizations, emerge not despite but because of the solitary character of the couple's retreat, which she reaffirms: "Furthermore,

J. and I *don't want any other companions!* One of our chief objects is to see it through alone and discover just what it means to be alone."[56] The Thoreauvian prospect has rarely been so entirely ratified.

The Stanwell-Fletchers leave Tetana finally because of the war – so that J., an officer, can rejoin the military. The Pinkertons leave because their wilderness enterprise has grown to the point where maintaining it threatens to consume them in ways contrary to their motives for retreating. But in both cases, these final departures have been prefaced, made nearly inevitable, by another departure. Both wives leave to bear children. In a mild irony, that aspect of women's existence supposedly anchoring them to nature, coding them as such in a patriarchal dispensation, is responsible for these women's separation from direct nature experience. When the Stanwell-Fletchers return for a last year, they do so without their daughter, left with Teddy's parents in milder suburban climes. The Pinkertons bring their daughter back, over the protests of *their* parents, but discover, over their own protestations, that indeed (as a late chapter proclaims), "A Baby Does Change Things." It doesn't help that they're saddled with then-modern baby-care appurtenances or that they refuse to use the baby-board a Cree friend has given them, thus condemning Kathrene to full hands and eternal vigilance. Even beyond the tender, preambulatory stage, the offspring bodes to pose difficulties. There's the question of schools, for one thing, which a hyperliterate pair will require to be exemplary. (Louise Dickinson Rich, who stayed put longer than these others, also came to this point.) The child will need to be socialized in a manner analogous to her parents' upbringing. So an old dilemma rears up predictably, one incipient but suppressed in the domestic economy all along. Metropolitan culture: Can't live with it, can't live without it. To the extent that nature retreat is pursued and disseminated in writing, it always ends up in these straits.

That's one lesson I draw from this genre, from these Wilderness Wives. I will conclude with some others pertinent to the Thoreauvian retreat motif the genre pursues and transforms. First, and most obvious, is its provenance as male. Some recent discussions of nature writing have been wont to characterize wilderness retreat as a male fantasy, sheer escapism, a doomed impulse toward flight from a social realm that is political through and through, riven with divisions of race, class, and gender that seem perversely most in force when ostensibly most eluded. Yet it seems clear from these narratives that while wilderness experience, like fixation on nature in general, may indeed be a male fantasy, it is not necessarily so. It is not necessarily male since women participate in the undertaking in ways not reducible to the terms and experiences of men, although of course in ways often kindred to them. And it is not necessarily a fantasy but often an accomplished fact, a recurrent element in human experience, although not inevitable, invariable, or reducible to a single description. It is not a fantasy, or need not be, not unless we believe that expressions of pleasure, satisfaction, health, and wellbeing are ipso facto expressions of fantasy, mere projections, or textual effects. Such is the stuff of fantasy, to be sure, but the substance of politics as well. It is disrespectful, to say the least, to presume to know better than these women what it is they've experienced in wilderness simply from having parsed the terms in which this experience is expressed. These women are wives, but they will not be condescended to.

What is deemed most fantastic about wilderness retreat in a masculinist vein is the appeal to individualism, the presumption to rugged independence, manifested in a solitude bespeaking ostensible self-sufficiency. This criticism has force: It seems indeed the case that a life of rugged independence – at least in extreme, absolute terms – is a fantasy. No person is an island; all are implicated in relations of codependence with others, not least those who produce and read books. But codependence and self-sufficiency are not absolutes, as gardeners, bioregionalists, globalization enthusiasts, and grown-ups in general can attest. A *relative* independence, the sort attained in relation to spouse, family, neighbours, community, and *place*, is no fantasy but an accomplished fact. In both her movement toward competence and her continuing and productive state of dependence on spouse, stray neighbours, and wild place, the Wilderness Wife dramatizes such a condition – call it rugged interdependence.

Interdependence entails division of labour, which we have always with us. This, in turn, spells domesticity on *some* terms or other. Contempt for domesticity is cosmopolitanism of the most suspect sort, predicated on specialization and surplus of the most thoroughgoing order. The woman writer with a room of her own, like the man, has more servants than she'll take notice of. Dispensations of domesticity are not essential, not invariable, generally asymmetrical (as the expression goes), but they needn't be arbitrary or capricious either. It is not writ in the stars or the genome that the woman does the cooking – but *someone* cooks, and this imperative isn't settled by flipping a coin. Such matters, and attitudes attending them, are more complex and interesting than that, even in straightforward accounts like Pinkerton's, certainly in more nuanced ones like Arthur's. It is indisputable that as these matters have been coded, domesticity and women have been opposed in a binary structure to wildness and men. How women writers have disrupted and undermined this binary has been demonstrated by Stacy Alaimo, who posits wilderness as an "undomesticated space" that women can construct in lieu of recapitulating the domestic sphere. Alaimo's premises are stimulating and her readings resourceful; she's deft, for instance, at analyzing feminism's difficult engagements with the "transhistorical tenacity" of the nature-culture divide underpinning the domesticity question.[57] But as the Wilderness Wife genre shows, there are alternatives to deeming a woman *either* relegated to a domesticity opposed to wildness, reproducing terms of oppression dictated by men, *or* pitched in an agonistic struggle to stake out in wilderness a space not scribbled on by patriarchy. There may be undomesticated *space* in wilderness, but there is no undomesticated *place*, not if anyone *lives* there, even in passing (as we all live in passing). Where there's dwelling, there's domestic economy. Wilderness Wives dramatize how the domestic and the wild may interpenetrate: a sort of etiquette of freedom, in Gary Snyder's phrase.[58]

However, given these affirmations of the wife's wild condition, does it follow that any of us should seek to recapitulate her state? For the most part, I think we should not, not least because we *can't*. One thing we can gather from these books is that such lives as these women led are mostly over. Not only changing gender constructions rule them out, rendering quaint the cheery Erma Bombeck-meets-the-bush tone of Pinkerton and Rich, especially. A host of environmental developments and ills make ever more manifest that the regress involved in wilderness retreat is not infinite. As long ago as the 1970s, Bradford and Vena Angier were looking to the Yukon (or claiming to from their home in California, if Arthur's informant is to be believed) – a radically difficult place for humans, its carrying capacity practically nil. The critters that the wilderness couple blows away, the swaths of turf they deforest for firewood – none of this can be sustained. Worse, there's corporate and governmental rapacity, which has brought a logging road and train tracks to the very fringes of Tetana, the Stanwell-Fletchers' remote, pristine lake.[59] Even the Cree have snowmobiles now. What's a white, book-making, wilderness-loving couple to do with their nostalgia – their sickness for home?

They might do as the Pinkertons did: load their typewriters and kid into the car and keep moving, deferring their vision of home until it was clear they'd been homemaking all along.[60] They might breathe a deep sigh and remain in suburb or city, the way most are obliged to, those lacking the relative leeway a successful life of letters can enable. Or they might remake the dream of wilderness retreat on altered terms, in acts of reclamation, reinhabitation. This is what happens in what I construe as a latter-day instance of the Wilderness Wife genre: *A Handmade Wilderness*, by Don Schueler. Rather than a white married couple, Schueler's book recounts the retreat experience of a pair of gay men, one white, the other African American. Rather than focusing on strike out for the far North, the couple heads to the deep South.[61] They settle on a degraded rural tract and set about restoring its health and wildness. They lead a life of rugged interdependence, relatively speaking, until AIDS takes Schueler's "spouse." If it is true, as William Cronon has claimed, that there is a "trouble with wilderness"[62] – that the prizing of pristine land tacitly authorizes the trashing of places not untouched – it may be that the solution lies not in debunking wilderness as a category, but rather in extending it, hand-making more of it. Making things by hand; there's a domestic virtue worthy of marriage. Both domestic and wild are served thereby.

Notes

1 Louise Dickinson Rich, *The Peninsula* (Philadelphia: J.B. Lippincott, 1958), 13.
2 From the dust jacket of Bradford and Vena Angier, *Wilderness Wife* (Radnor, PA: Chilton, 1976).
3 Etta B. DeGering, *Wilderness Wife: The Story of Rebecca Bryan Boone* (New York: McKay, 1966).
4 Annette Kolodny, *The Land before Her: Fantasy and Experience of the American Frontiers, 1630-1860* (Chapel Hill: University of North Carolina Press, 1984).
5 Julie Roy Jeffrey, *Frontier Women: The Trans-Mississippi West, 1840-1880,* rev. ed. (New York: Hill and Wang, 1998).
6 Kathrene Pinkerton, *Wilderness Wife* (New York: Carrick and Evans, 1939).
7 Vena and Bradford Angier, *At Home in the Woods* (New York: Sheridan House, 1951); Kathrene Pinkerton, *A Home in the Wilds* (Marlboro, NJ: Taplinger Publishing Co., 1976). This is a reissue of *Wilderness Wife.*
8 For an overview of recent genre theory in both literary and rhetorical studies, see Amy J. Devitt, "Integrating Rhetorical and Literary Theories of Genre," *College English* 62, 6 (2000): 696-718. For remarks on genre theory as pertaining to nature writing, see Randall Roorda, *Dramas of Solitude: Narratives of Retreat in American Nature Writing* (Albany: State University of New York Press, 1998), 3-12.
9 Susanna Moodie, *Roughing It in the Bush; or, Forest Life in Canada* (New York: Dodge, 1913); Caroline Kirkland, *A New Home – Who'll Follow? or, Glimpses of Western Life,* by Mrs. Mary Clavers [pseud.] (New York: C.S. Francis, 1839).
10 Vera Norwood, *Made from This Earth: American Women and Nature* (Chapel Hill: University of North Carolina Press, 1993).
11 Summarizing the thrust of her discussion, Jeffrey finds that the writing of pioneer women "Shows an acceptance of social norms of domesticity and expectation, or hope, that the norms could function on the frontier," despite conditions militating against them. Jeffrey, *Frontier Women,* 33.
12 See Anne LaBastille, *Women and Wilderness* (San Francisco: Sierra Club Books, 1980), especially her overview of frontier women's antipathy toward wilderness, 5-6.
13 Henry Beston, *The Outermost House: A Year of Life on the Great Beach of Cape Cod* (1928; reprint, New York: Penguin, 1988). The marriage anecdote is related in Robert Finch's introduction to the reprint edition (x-xi).
14 In her book, Pinkerton discloses neither the specific time nor the specific locale of the couple's wilderness residence. She is more forthcoming in a book published two years later, *Two Ends to Our Shoestring* (New York: Harcourt Brace, 1941), a sort of autobiography of the marriage, recounting the couple's wilderness homesteading and such later exploits as their numerous transcontinental peregrinations by auto – they were, for instance, the first to cross the Pigeon River bridge from Minnesota into Port Arthur, Ontario (now, with Fort Williams, part of Thunder Bay), doing so over loose planks several days before its official opening – and their years of residence on a boat sailing the Pacific Coast off Puget Sound, British Columbia, and southeastern Alaska.
15 Donald Culross Peattie, "They Refused to Go Home," *Saturday Review of Literature,* 21 November 1942, 7. Peattie praises Rich's book for its humour, wisdom, and attention to backwoods social relations, while remarking on its relative inattention to particulars of "living Nature."
16 Alaska's problematic character as a site of conquest by and a putative nature repository for the United States is the subject of Susan Kollin, *Nature's State: Imagining Alaska as the Last Frontier* (Chapel Hill: University of North Carolina Press, 2001). As Kollin notes, national

formation of Canada and of a United States including Alaska unfolded in relation to each other, with Canada's formation as a Dominion occurring simultaneously with and in reaction to the US's purchase of Alaska in 1867, which presaged its imperial designs upon the entire far North (180). Kollin's chapter "Domestic Ecologies and the Making of Wilderness: White Women, Nature Writing, and Alaska" (91-126), featuring examinations of Lois Crisler and Margaret Murie, relates especially to the subject of this chapter, although the temper of her discussion contrasts with my own.

17 Theodora C. Stanwell-Fletcher, *Driftwood Valley* (1946; reprinted as *Driftwood Valley: A Woman Naturalist in the Far North,* New York: Penguin, 1989). Now out of print in the Penguin edition, the book has subsequently been issued in a new edition (Corvallis: Oregon State University, 1999). The new edition includes an introduction by Wendell Berry, featured in the Penguin reprint, and includes as well an afterword and bibliography by Rhoda M. Love; it also restores an appendix from the original edition, listing species found in the Driftwood region. Also restored are black-and-white sketches of animals by husband J. (John F., a.k.a. Jack). I will note in passing how often books by Wilderness Wives are illustrated by their husbands, in sketches or photos. This practice, also that of filming wildlife for scientific and/or entertainment purposes (as engaged in by the husbands of Stanwell-Fletcher and Crisler, as famously by Martin Johnson, whose wife, Osa, author of *I Married Adventure*, became in effect a star of his films), is susceptible to analysis as a masculinist spectatorial practice – a line of speculation I won't here pursue. See Donna Haraway, *Gender, Race, and Nature in the World of Modern Science* (New York, NY: Routledge, 1989), 44-45, for a discussion of the Johnsons framed in such terms.

18 Elizabeth Arthur, *Island Sojourn: A Memoir* (1980; reprint, Saint Paul: Greywolf Press, 1991).

19 Robert Finch and John Elder, eds., *The Norton Book of Nature Writing,* college edition (New York: Norton, 2002). See the introduction (16-20) for remarks on how the collection was reshaped since its first edition (1990). The college edition goes under the title of the original edition; the revised trade version of the anthology is now called *Nature Writing: The Tradition in English.*

20 Vera Norwood, *Made from This Earth: American Women and Nature* (Chapel Hill: University of North Carolina Press, 1993), xiv; Peter J. Schmitt, *Back to Nature: The Arcadian Myth in Urban America* (1969; reprint, Baltimore: Johns Hopkins University Press, 1990), xiii.

21 Phyllis Rose, introduction to *The Norton Book of Women's Lives,* edited by Phyllis Rose (New York: Norton, 1993), 11-37, 12.

22 "If you have built castles in the air, your work need not be lost; that is where they should be. Now put the foundations under them." Henry David Thoreau, *Walden* (1854; reprint, Princeton, NJ: Princeton University Press, 1971), 324.

23 Stanwell-Fletcher, *Driftwood Valley*, 28.

24 Pinkerton, *Wilderness Wife*, 29-30, 32-33.

25 Ibid., 14; Stanwell-Fletcher, *Driftwood Valley*, xv-xvi.

26 Pinkerton, *Wilderness Wife*, 14.

27 Stanwell-Fletcher, *Driftwood Valley*, 52.

28 Ibid., 244.

29 Arthur, *Island Sojourn*, 12; Stanwell-Fletcher, *Driftwood Valley*, 29.

30 Ibid., 28.

31 Ibid., 216; Pinkerton, *Wilderness Wife*, 151-52, 251.

32 Ibid., 267.

33 See, for instance, her glee over preparing a carcass for winter freezing: "a field day for a meat enthusiast like me," an "ecstatic onslaught," the enthusiasm of which she attributes to "'the cave woman coming out in me.'" Pinkerton, *Wilderness Wife*, 200.

34 Stanwell-Fletcher, *Driftwood Valley*, 193.

35 Arthur, *Island Sojourn*, 189-90.

36 Stanwell-Fletcher, *Driftwood Valley*, 355, emphasis in the original.

37 Rebecca Raglon, "Women and the Great Canadian Wilderness: Reconsidering the Wild," *Women's Studies* 25 (1996): 526.

38 Stanwell-Fletcher, *Driftwood Valley*, 246, 327, 343, 347.

39 A further factor in relative dependence and self-image may be physical size. Stanwell-Fletcher was small – barely over five feet and weighing a hundred pounds. I find nothing on the statures of Pinkerton or Arthur but doubt they were this diminutive: Photos of Pinkerton in her book, although hard to gauge, make her appear of average size and hardly slight; Louise Rich, as her photos show, was strapping.

40 Arthur, *Island Sojourn*, 137-39.

41 Pinkerton, *Wilderness Wife*, 40.

42 Stanwell-Fletcher, *Driftwood Valley*, 287.

43 Arthur, *Island Sojourn*, 9.

44 Pinkerton, *Wilderness Wife*, 92.

45 Sex, for instance. The older books, those by Pinkerton and Stanwell-Fletcher, are quite chaste even though, as will be remarked, theirs are the marriages that produced children. Arthur's postsexual-revolution book reports intimacy more forthrightly but still nothing explicit or extended. The raciest book in the genre is that by the Angiers: It is full of deep sighs, strong arms encircling and quelling wifely shudders – cheesy stuff, attributable to the fact that the book, although in Vena's voice, was likely scripted by Bradford.

46 Stanwell-Fletcher, *Driftwood Valley*, 181.

47 Pinkerton, *Wilderness Wife*, 197.

48 Stanwell-Fletcher, *Driftwood Valley*, 136.

49 Ibid., 238.

50 Ibid., 238-39.

51 Arthur, *Island Sojourn*, 161-76.

52 Margaret Atwood, *The Journals of Susanna Moodie* (Toronto: Oxford University Press, 1970).

53 Stanwell-Fletcher, *Driftwood Valley*, 332.

54 Pinkerton ultimately became a more widely published writer than her husband, if it is reliable to go by the number of titles turned up in a web search for used books. She co-authored some works with her husband, but *Wilderness Wife* was her first book published under her name alone – this a quarter-century after the end of the epoch recounted, with the author having already turned forty. She was prolific thereafter till her death in 1967, mainly as a writer of children's novels about families in wild places. In the description of her papers, housed at the University of Oregon, she is categorized as a children's author. Her marriage, evidently, was ended by death – whose, I don't know.

As for Stanwell-Fletcher, she wrote two more books, including one in which she re-counts in veiled terms the circumstances of meeting husband Jack: *This Tundra World* (Boston: Little Brown, 1952), a fictionalized, diary-form account of her graduate-student field experience at Hudson Bay. Jack divorced her before the book was published. She married twice more and died in 2000, at age 94. For details, see Rhoda M. Love's afterword to Oregon State University Press's recent reprint edition of *Driftwood Valley*. I wish to acknowledge Rhoda's support for my work on Stanwell-Fletcher and commend her for her efforts to keep this fine writer's work and life available for new readers.

Of Elizabeth Arthur, I know only that she has published several novels since this wilderness memoir, her first book – all with premises placing women in wilderness situations, all critically well received, and the most recent one, set in Antarctica, a bestseller as well. In one of these novels, at issue is the protagonist's marriage to a strong, difficult man. I don't know if her own marriage has lasted.

55 For all these writers, as for anyone writing of the far North, the presence, character, and company of First Nations peoples is an issue. The couple's relations with and the wife's responses to Native people – the mingled condescension, admiration, typecasting, and close, detailed engagement – would provide grounds for a discussion in itself, one that this chapter's scope prevents my undertaking.

56 Stanwell-Fletcher, *Driftwood Valley*, 81, 273, 144, 184, 158, emphasis in the original.

57 Stacy Alaimo, *Undomesticated Ground: Recasting Nature as Feminist Space* (Ithaca, NY: Cornell University Press, 2000), 13. See her discussion of "The Nature of Feminist Theory," 2-13.

58 This phrase is the title of the lead essay in Gary Snyder, *The Practice of the Wild: Essays* (San Francisco: North Point Press, 1990).

59 This is reported in Rhoda Love's afterword to the new edition of *Driftwood Valley*, cited above.
60 Their saga is related in Pinkerton, *Two Ends to Our Shoestring*, with pursuit, deferral, and recognition of home a motif therein.
61 Not an option for Canadians, of course. As the US is short on far North, so Canada lacks a true South, with Upper Canada, perversely, as close as it gets.
62 William Cronon, "The Trouble with Wilderness; or, Getting Back to the Wrong Nature," *Uncommon Ground: Rethinking the Human Place in Nature*, edited by Cronon (New York: Norton, 1996), 69-90.

4

And the Young Man Did Go North (Unfortunately): Reflections on Issues in Gender and the Academy

Jo-Anne Fiske

Ellie Peters slings the 35-pound beaver over her back and smiles at the camera. She is in her late teens and has trapped the beaver herself. A young, newly married Carrier woman of Central British Columbia, she has captured the beaver on reserve land belonging to the Red Bluff First Nation. It is not the first beaver she has trapped; in fact, Ellie had been trapping successfully since 1965, when she left the residential school at age thirteen. As the second eldest of twelve children, she often was responsible for snaring and trapping sufficient food for them while her parents, Lashaway and Janet Alec, worked away at railroad tie camps. Thus by the time this picture was taken, Ellie had had several years of trapping and had already earned the respect of her family and community for her trapping expertise.

With these words, Caroline Mufford and I opened our paper presented at the Seventh North American Fur Trade Conference. Entitled "Hard Times and Everything Like That: Carrier Women's Tales of Life on the Trapline," this paper drew together stories we had gathered of Carrier women's routine lives as trappers.[1] Our purpose in presenting these narratives of Aboriginal women trappers to an academic audience was twofold. On the one hand, we wanted to add empirical accounts of women's lives on the trapline to the historic and ethnographic literature on Athapaskan cultures (the Carrier being the Athapaskan peoples of central British Columbia) and to the fur trade literature. On the other hand, we wished to challenge the established genre of ethnographic narrative on Athapaskan trapping cultures and to question the biases of fur trade history with respect to a continuing neglect of gendered history. Our intent was to address what Fentress and Wickham identify as problems in understanding feminine historical consciousness, among which they include "the as yet unresolved issue of how far women's separate consciousness depends on a diversity of experience from men's rather than on something innate in gender ... [and] the fact that, despite all the work in the field of women studies in recent years, very little has yet been done on the specific nature of female perceptions of the past."[2] Specifically, we asked: How does an understanding of female narratives alter our perceptions of the lives of the narrators and deepen our understanding of the construction of academic knowledge?

In reply to our own question, we argued that patriarchy and colonialism have muted Aboriginal women's voices. We pointed out that in the narratives that the trappers had related to us, the women spoke about their work from a common perspective, one that takes their own trapping for granted as a tale of family survival and nurture rather than as drama or heroics. We then turned to our quest to understand more fully how meaning is produced by Aboriginal women and by ethnographic narrators. We contrasted the Aboriginal image of trapper as woman and mother with the prevailing image of trapper as the lone male provider (as it had been produced by ethnographers and historians) in order to challenge knowledge construction in the academy. We argued that trapping narratives project European motifs of masculinity onto trapper and narrator. Both emerge from the page as the European archetypal male hero, an intrepid loner engaged in a transformative quest. From the pursuit of the medieval Holy Grail to managing the modern trapline, male heroes combat nature in order to create culture. Allowing female images to intrude upon (indeed, to subvert) male heroics has far-reaching consequences. Feminine intrusion not only disrupts inequality of gender, but unsettles racial identity as well.[3]

Upon examining some theoretical assumptions regarding women's public voice, we were led to contend that the genre of women's narrative differs in ways that others often do not recognize. These others seek accounts of bravery and self-reliance, which impedes their ability to appreciate women's narratives. Deconstruction of dominant masculine motifs, we continued, is critical to comprehending the persistence of the illusion of male drama and heroics. We concluded by refuting Fentress and Wickham's assumption regarding the nature of feminine historical consciousness. We had found that women's historical consciousness does emerge in the absence of a gendered culture. Gender inclusion, not sexual difference and exclusion, had given rise to a distinct feminine genre that celebrates women's historical consciousness without condescension to the male "other."

Very few female narratives have been incorporated into fur trade history. Indeed, fur trade studies have been criticized for remaining outside the mainstream of historiography, paying scant attention to the rich insights revealed in the fields of gender and social histories. Ray indicts fur trade historians on several grounds: "The lack of any systematic examination of the gendered dimension of the fur trade or of the differential impact of the industry on the lives of aboriginal men and women is a prime example of the general failure to connect to mainstream currents in other academic fields. This omission is particularly remarkable given the popularity and innovative nature of gender studies in history today."[4] Indeed, the investigative directions pointed to by the ovarian works of Jennifer Brown and Sylvia Van Kirk with respect to gender and the fur trade, which opened new spaces for social history, have been neglected.[5] Fur trade history constitutes a place where men can still talk about being men.

Given the constraints of this subfield of North American history, we were aware that our work might not receive a warm reception from scholars with long-standing interests in the fur trade. Therefore, we were neither surprised nor particularly upset when we were chastised for not having included male views of these trappers' stories. Given that ours was the only paper to discuss women's trapping, the "equal air time" argument had little to offer. We were, however, somewhat more distressed by later comments, which came in response to the manuscript we had revised for publication. We were particularly troubled by the assumptions that women would trap for dependent kin (elders, grandchildren, siblings, children, nieces, or nephews) only in the absolute absence of a male alternative. "You did not interview men who as the eldest in the family would have been responsible for the family when the parents left to work," accused our reviewer. It was clear that our reviewer could not conceive of family relations in which women might routinely provide for men. Given the manner in which this allegation was levelled at us, we wondered whether he had chosen to ignore our concluding argument or whether we had indeed scored a point. For we had written that "male heroics cannot be sustained if women too wrest their living from a harsh world. If women routinely butcher and kill wherein lies the glamour the male narrator has appropriated for himself? More compelling a threat, if women of a subordinated race/ethnic group provide for others free from male company whom will men protect? ... To accept the ungendered reality of life on the trapline is to destroy a male identity constructed to span ethnic divisions and to render male heroics universal."[6]

Questions of male identity and individual heroics by academics have, of course, been the subject of academic discourse for some time. Susan Sontag's "The Anthropologist as Hero" is one of the earliest essays to speak to the appropriation of the "other" by the self-exiled compulsive traveller. "Europe seeks itself in the exotic – in Asia, in the Middle East, among preliterate peoples, in a mythic America ... The 'other' is experienced as a harsh purification of 'self.' But at the same time the 'self' is busily colonizing all strange domains of experience."[7] Her concentration, however, lies with extolling the sad, spiritual beauty of the contrary positions the hero faces as he "submits himself to the exotic to confirm his own inner alienation as an urban intellectual"[8] rather than with the gendered consequences of heroics in academia, to which I now wish to turn. I will do so by reconsidering my own encounters with self-acclaimed heroism – as I recorded them in twenty years of erratic journal entries – in the light of contemporary theories of the politics and construction of academic knowledge. In so doing, I make no claim to offer a systematic or representative study of multiple masculinities nor of masculine academic practices that fall outside of my construction of the hero. Rather, I wish to confine my discussion to a singular focus in order to foreground a particular discursive relation of power and knowledge, one that emerges as male voices frame their heroic endeavours within a discourse of danger and endurance within the "wilderness" that unites them with a masculine "other." Simultaneously, I wish to locate these heroics within discourses that allow them to incite the pleasure of speaking on behalf of the marginalized dwellers of that wilderness, with whom they claim to identify.[9] I am not alone in considering these issues; rather, I seek to add my voice to the works of Dorothy Smith, Caplan, Behar and Gordon, Newton and Stacey, and Lutz, who among others have struggled to deconstruct the psychodynamic relations of masculinity and knowledge.[10] Building on the broader scope of these discussions, and of current theoretical trends, I locate my subject in my experiences in central British Columbia. In writing this chapter, I am aware a caveat is in order. These experiences do not (indeed, cannot) be read as a statement on academic men in general. Nor should they be construed as representative or stereotypical of "men of the north." For, indeed, there is no one masculine identity or narrative that can embrace the diversity of northern male subjectivity, which ranges from macho industrial worker to the back-to-the-lander, the environmentalist, and the poet. My aim is more deliberate: to consider how a particular form of masculinized heroics that emerges in an imaginary geography is imbricated in gendered politics of intellectual production.

The Phalleolithic

The politics of academic knowledge, as others have pointed out, evolves as a circle of those present build on the work of the past to create a distinct style of knowledge with its own questions, evolutions, and standards. Insofar as women have been absent in this construction of the past, they are marginalized in the present, for there exists no past work to be invoked as intellectual precedent. The inner circle appropriates unto itself the power to label challenges to its authority as vulgar or impolite, as reverse sexism or reverse racism, or as male bashing. In this manner, the circle comes back unto itself, for women are continuously forced outside of it, their work dismissed as unworthy.[11] Exiled into subordination, women's intellectual production is positioned within the discursive terrain either as rejoinder or as imitative and is threatened continuously with obscurity. Unusual courage is required to challenge this reception, as efforts to do so are jeopardized by possibilities of being disqualified for an "in-your-face attitude." Behar and Gordon, for example, adopted a stance that deliberately challenged the politics of academic exclusion of feminist anthropologists by entitling their edited volume *Women Writing Culture,* thereby accepting the "risk of having [their] book dismissed (by men) as derivative"[12] – that is, as a self-aware imitation of Clifford and Marcus's *Writing Culture: The Poetics and Politics of Ethnography.* By attaching the label "phalleolithic discourse" to this particular masculine academic politics, I hope to take this insight regarding construction of knowledge both a step further and a step backward to the putative Palaeolithic evolutionary origins of the masculine that are interwoven with romanticism of the perpetual masculine quest.[13]

I first used the term "phalleolithic" in 1994 at a reading by feminist poet Betsy Warland. Attending a conference at the University of Northern British Columbia, Betsy read her poetry as an opening strategy to a talk about the meaning of feminism. The first response from the audience came from a man, who immediately sought to locate her work in a genealogy of "poetic fathers." Betsy protested that she had not read the poets mentioned and therefore resisted this location of her work, only to be informed that she needed to recognize that such placement relative to these male poets was nonetheless a "correct reading." Sensing the inflexible male resistance of the audience to Betsy's protests, I suggested that we were living in the age of the stone phallus, in the realm of the phalleolithic discourse. As Gilbert and Gubar state, "in patriarchal Western culture, therefore, the text's author is a father, a progenitor, an aesthetic patriarch whose pen is an instrument of generative power like his penis. More, his pen's power like his penis's power, is not just the ability to generate life but the power to create a posterity to which he lays claim ... As the author of an enduring text the writer engages the attention of the future in exactly the same way that a king (or father) 'owns' the language of the present."[14]

Phalleolithic discourse offers an easy myth of intellectual origins, invested with a rigid identification of masculinity with authenticity and truth. It establishes its authority in a range of now-familiar and easily identified ways within the academy: course curricula that purport to cover the history or "state of the art" of a discipline yet exclude women's writing; self-serving justifications for conscious exclusions of feminist writing on the grounds that it fails to be "textually innovative,"[15] an excuse that follows earlier condemnations that women's writing failed to meet standards of analysis and realism; privileging male subjectivity; citation of a closed circle of male colleagues who may refer to women's work but neglect to name them in doing so;[16] and the self-asserted stance of intellectual superiority of the male circle that claims its "advanced" status.

Phalleolithic discourse is, as is any discourse, multivocal and contains within it many strands. Masculine discourses that establish gendered boundaries to truth by glossing over women's distinct contributions constitute one strand of the phalleolithic.[17] The heroic quest by the urban academic, played out in multiple tales and dramas of adventures with the exotic, is another. Subordination of women's knowledge, therefore, should not be considered without reflection on the foundations of masculine subjectivity.

Within social sciences, the assumptions of socio-biological and evolutionary theories built upon images of "man the hunter," male bonding, and the male capacity to develop language are perhaps the most glaring examples of confusing human development with male subjectivity. As Sally Slocum states, "The theory of man the hunter is not only unbalanced; it leads to the conclusion that basic human adaptation was the desire of males to hunt and kill ... *it derives culture from killing.*"[18] This construction of (hu)man evolution not only allows the contemporary nonessential hunting by men to be perceived as having inevitably risen from evolutionary/cultural survival, but also grounds individual heroics within an essential masculinity. Anthropology and geography in particular are rife with examples of the appropriation of male subjectivity and its heroics. One needs only to consider the popularity of Colin Turnbull's account of the Ik, "the mountain people," or of Napoleon Chagnon's heroic exploits among "the fierce people," a text reproduced over two decades primarily for students of introductory ethnography courses to ponder the myriad ways that geographers constitute nonurban spaces as the field in which the hero locates his feats of virile endurance.[19]

The alienated self of the hero appropriates the periphery as the enduring frontier and uses it to project his purified self onto the metropolis. The frontier emerges as the space in which the young man proves his manhood and the older man reclaims his youth. This frontier, existing in fantastical masculinity, has no temporality. It lies outside of society and exists in the discursive construction of the confrontation between strangers. Whether it be by worshipping on the altar of the past – as, for example, in George Bowering's *B.C.: A Swashbuckling History* – or by the assumption of a rugged individualism in distant places, heroics give rise to a particular form of discursive colonialism, for the hero achieves distance from his society by the celebration of strangeness. Within the discursive space he has created for himself, the hero can "model the world according to his own image without any interference."[20]

Phalleolithic discourse is necessarily a discourse of modernity rooted in the Enlightenment's vision of progress. As Sontag avers, "Modern sensibility moves between two seemingly contradictory but actually related impulses: surrender to the exotic, the strange, the other; and the domestication of the exotic, chiefly through science."[21] The hero must articulate his sense of identity within the Palaeolithic, surrendering to the exotic like the frontier man embarking on a dark voyage. The ivory tower is stage for the Dark Tower narrative.[22] To be hero is to reclaim a frontier within one's own yearning for the authentic masculine self, to hold forth the phalleolithic as the "real": the real sexuality, the real history. ("One day [George Bowering's] editor told him to get off the pot and write a real history of the place [British Columbia]." He did and was immediately heralded for his engaging tales of the "swashbucklers of the western frontier," the "strange characters" who shaped our province.)[23]

The hero's subject formation arises from modernity, and binary oppositions are the semiotics by which the hero sustains his identity and asserts his power on the frontier. The hero positions himself in shifting oppositions of good/evil, inferior/superior, frontier/civilization. Variously placed as paternal protector of the colonized, he articulates a morality on their behalf. The hero's "surrender to the exotic, the strange, the other," is celebrated by those who desire the frontier for themselves. The academic hero who positions himself as the urban maverick ever desires the opposition of the inferior and superior.[24] He must act on behalf of the former in order to valorize himself within the latter. As self-appointed critic of the corrupted metropolis, the hero appears to act in the interests of a subjugated frontier population. He appropriates their struggles in the quest for his own redemption. He transports the exotic onto the academic stage. Even while he extols their haunting beauty, he stands above them, for his heroic dimensions require their diminishment. As it was for the anthropologist Lévi-Strauss, who sought to inscribe living culture within the formal dualisms of structural theory,[25] so it is for the paternal hero: "The man who submits himself to the exotic to confirm his own inner alienation as an urban intellectual ends by aiming to vanquish his subject."[26]

Self-imposed alienation makes it impossible for the hero to be the good citizen at home. The hero of the frontier must be known for his own alienation. He must stand in opposition to domesticated conformity. Thus he cannot seek political power at home but must repudiate it to stand as a critical dissenting voice, comfortable only within the circles of veracity authorized by phalleolithic precedent. He positions himself against the metropolis by his appropriation of the frontier. It is no accident that when the academic hero emerges from the frontier, he rejects the postmodern and postcolonial discourses, for modernity, as Rey Chow reminds us, "needs to be understood as a force of cultural expansionism whose foundations are not only emancipatory but also Eurocentric and patriarchal."[27]

The Northern Frontier

The "north" has emerged on the culturalscape as the last North American frontier, a site of expansion and modernity. "Go west, young man, go west," was the rallying cry of American frontiersmen, a cry later replaced in western Canada by the call of the north. In British Columbia, the central interior – industrial spaces of the margins, the timber towns, the mining communities of contemporary industrial growth, their small, hinterland, single-resource communities and sprawling ranch lands – has been inscribed with the hallmarks of frontier society. The harsh winter climate, expansive forests, rushing rivers, and snow-capped mountains create an ominous tract: a natural space to be tamed; a social space in which to be wild; a space where rivers are dammed against all odds in the name of the collective southern interests and where women's liberation is damned in the name of frontier individualism; a space in which to surrender to the exotic, to "go native." "The north," as Shields observes, "is less a real region signified by a name and more a name, a signifier, with a historically-variable, socially-defined content."[28]

Politics of the boom-bust economy based on extraction of rich natural resources and modern progress capture the heroic imagination in a series of rich oppositions: northern development versus the southern investment, forest harvesting versus environmentalism, fishery versus logging, First Nations versus settlers. Central British Columbia offers a montage of heroic possibilities – trapper, cowboy, logger, trucker, lone prospector, isolated rancher – each etched with loneliness, courage, love of adventure, and physical hardiness. Each, too, is captured in historic icons: Alexander Mackenzie and Simon Fraser, the first fur trade adventurers; James Douglas, a trader who became colonial governor; Adrien Morice, a nineteenth-century missionary/linguist/ethnologist/cartographer; Rich Hobson, a rancher/writer ...

On the cultural edge of the "northern" frontier, the urban hero emulates his paperback heroes and embraces their symbols of exaggerated individualism. The safe life of class privilege is repudiated. Like the historic frontier of the encroaching colonial settlement, the contemporary space is populated by and subjected to the exoticized, often by brash posturing of self-created dangers. "If it doesn't kill you, it will make you strong," the hero proclaims by baring his chest to subzero temperatures.

To conceptualize the industrial periphery of central British Columbia as the "north" is to embrace an individualism that vehemently defends a sense of purpose as being against the metropolis (against the state, against bureaucracy, against institutional conformity). Discourses of frontier justice protest a "southern" judiciary. The symbol of "northern" justice is slung in truck cabs, the spectre of death invoking a John Wayne cynicism about law and government. The noose marks the meaning of the now-empty gun racks, silent protest against big government's interference into private life. American rhetoric on the right to bear arms appears as if an afterthought on the dusty truck bumper. Hands are raised and horns tooted as the drivers passing through the back roads acknowledge their sense of community, and a new bumper sticker appears: "Hug a logger and you will never hug a tree again."[29]

"One law for all": Fading billboards of the past election proclaim the ever-felt threat of multiculturalism, the growing resistance to Aboriginal resource rights, and scorn for the bleeding hearts who seek reconciliation through the newly founded British Columbia Treaty Commission.[30] Journalists' by-lines and pub philosophers share the view that "we" are "giving" too much away. How can "we" save "our" lands from the communal desires of First Nations peoples? What would they do with it anyway? Why can't they get a truck, or fishing boat, or perhaps a feller buncher and make a living like "we" do? Why can't they buy their own homes, invest in private property? And by the way, why the heck didn't Mulroney put private property into the Constitution? And he wonders why we went Reform?

While these symbols of culture represent immediate issues for the people of central British Columbia, their tone, semantics, and purpose vary little from a cultural politics of rural and resource-based communities (not unfamiliar elsewhere in the Canadian North) that is infused with an "us" versus "them" mentality encoded in masculine values of self-reliance and rugged individualism. In this culture the heroic intellectual finds fertile ground in which to establish himself, as these observations from my journals and field notes, written erratically over the past twenty years, affirm. The excerpts below represent notations in which I have at the times of writing explicitly combined statements and observed actions of heroics with later statements and actions that address the narrative construction of an idealized masculinity and romanticized "other."[31] They are selected to illustrate how the north of an imaginary geography comes to stand for a personal masculinity. As the north emerges in opposition to the feminine and the domestic, it proves to be a "state of mind as well as certain material conditions ... The North is not found along a line. It is a space with depth."[32] The state of mind, as these excerpts illustrate, deracinates material reality from specificities of the geographic and economic relations of the British Columbian resource towns in which they take place.

February, Mid-1970s

A miscellanea of notes taken in a college class during a visit to the isolated ranch of the instructor for a course exercise that required "fieldwork" with a rural/ranching family living beyond city or town boundaries.

Like many of my colleagues in the public school profession, I take night classes as a routine part of my social life. This term I go on Thursday and can choose between Spanish or anthropology. I take anthropology. In other years I join classes in geography, sociology, or education. My notebook is a kaleidoscope of notes, lists, and asides to whomever was sitting next to me. On one page, my list reads, "to do: 1) participant observation in rural household, 2) collect folklore, 3) Lévi-Strauss TT [Tristes Tropiques]." A cross-referencing scrawl directs me to the page in my "field notes" needed for the assignment. In part they read:

The baby hasn't stopped whimpering and [she] doesn't pick him up. If you touch him he screams. I think he's in pain. The kitchen is really hot now, and we have several more lots of jam to put up before we are through. She's taken last year's fruit out of the freezer to make room for a jacked moose. Glass jars are steaming and paraffin wax melts on the stove. She moves silently and quickly, surprised that I know what I am doing. "School teacher huh? What's a school teacher going to college for? Don't you know enough already?"

At 4:30 she starts making dinner, and I clean up as quickly as I can. "The old man" eats at six, sharp, in a clean kitchen. Steam and sweat mingle on our faces; she wipes hers and I move my eyes away. I pretend I don't notice the fading blues and yellows on the cheek bones. I don't look at the crying baby.

At the bottom of the "field notes," I find a dismal grade and the caution "keep your mind on culture, you are doing anthropology not sociology." Tucked in with these notes, I find some insights into my former instructor, who has presented a cogent, detached structural analysis of "origin myths of frontier farmers." Still further scattered through my class notes, I find summations of his anthropological project, which entails many hours in the "bush" in the winter with a lone trapper or logger, and his descriptions of life on an isolated ranch to which he retreats in solitude, beyond the amenities of electric power, running water, and the like.

Women are erased from his account. In my growing awareness of gendered relations of power, this erasure has taken on greater significance. The battered women's movement and endless feminist struggles for legal and social reform have emerged as central issues for feminist scholars. My own growing feminist consciousness turned to questions of knowledge construction in my student years and erupted in frustrated anger at the intellectual distance between anthropological theory and the reality of empirical violence. Below this, several years after the class, I have howled in an angry scrawl, "What the fuck did Lévi-Strauss know about battered babies?"

Summer, Several Years Later

Field notes/journal from research concerning a First Nation and a proposed development project that would potentially have devastating effects on their fish resources.

I am working with two First Nations women in a small community, studying traditional land use. On this day we have been sent to a regional public conference on land-claims research along with other researchers: anthropologists, archaeologists, and geographers. We are the only women, we three. My two coworkers are the only First Nations representatives who are not elected chiefs or senior administrators. In part my notes read:

We had prepared our presentation very carefully. Their work had been on the go for months, and while it had been the first time we had done work together of this specific nature, we were confident of the quality of our work. Everything that could be done twice, had been. We were excited and proud to be part of this important work.

At lunch break I approached another anthropologist who was working for another community in the region.

The **** [this is actually how I wrote it]. He wouldn't talk to us. In the afternoon I found out he had had lunch with the lawyer. Asked him to check on me. Could I be trusted? Why hadn't _____ [the community we worked for] sent the chief? We won't be included in the conference field trips that include an aerial survey of the land.

Sometime later I listened to him at a southern conference. He spoke of that work and drew from the research data collected at that time. The references cited made no mention of my work nor of the work of several other female graduate students who combined their graduate research with land-claims work commissioned by other First Nations. Nor did his work, which included some social-impact statements respecting economic "development" and the centralization of the forest industry, include any mention of the lives of women: women who trapped while their male kin were at the mills, who bore babies in the wilderness, who endured hardship in the brutal cold, and who confronted violence, conflict, and impoverishment on an almost daily basis.

His report did, however, describe with jocular humour and self-satisfaction the thrills of surveying the country from the small airplane, the several land trips taken into remote traplines, and the dangers and obstacles faced "in the bush." In retrospect, I understand that this encounter exemplifies, as Dorothy Smith has articulated, the exclusion of women from men's culture. The exclusion is twofold: the erasure of women's scholarly contributions and the erasure of women's routine economic and political contributions to community life.

More Recently

Notes taken from my private journal reveal a narrative strand of male heroics imbricated with colonial posturing that seeks to claim Native identity.

We drive with his usual caution, the truck rattling with tapes, empty pop bottles, books and outdoor equipment. In the cassette tray lie bullets, displayed to me with boyish excitement. On the dashboard is a bullet belt, empty. At his knee, rising from the leather case, a large hunting knife menaces the air. He takes it and flails it through the air and boasts he can pick up a hitchhiker any time. I can borrow his car. I can be safe. Behind me, hidden under a mound of laundry, snack bars, and outdoor clothing, his high powered hunting rifle lies in its locked box, locked by protest. I don't say anything. Won't go there ... Can't take the uselessness of the argument. He doesn't understand, won't accept restrictions on his "civil rights."

I know better than to comment on the music. A whining western singer excusing himself for bashing his woman: "I'm just a jealous kind of guy," the psychotic laments, whimpering of his need to lash out because his woman has attracted the eye of another man. I want to scream, to shut the sound off, but I don't. I don't want to hear it: "If it doesn't kill you, it will make you strong." Not today. Not today. We are going to a funeral. An elder, a leader. I have known her for 20 years. I try not to think.

But I hear him anyway. He's one of "them" now. "When they say 'we' they mean 'me' too," he tosses at me with adolescent fervour. "I'm part of it, all of it. I was in _____ this weekend. Did a bunch of work. Land claims. Went to the party. R_____, he's talking about throwing all the white guys out. Upsets the community when they hang around."

So, I ask quietly as I can, "How does that feel? Will you be angry when they throw you out?" A shocked silence is followed by an impatient outburst. "Not me, I'm one of them now. I belong."

I know about that party. I know who they brought into the transition house the next day, a two-hour ride over the logging roads and highways, dodging loaded trucks, trying not to look to see if she was being followed. I saw the kid they took to the hospital. So I ask, "Didn't that party get kind of wild, bunch of white guys crashed in drunk?" I deliberately adopt the local way of speaking. And I wait. "Yeah, but I left early. I don't hang around to watch it."

I'm staring out the side window now, trying not to curse this Lawrence of the North. I don't worry about my tears, I'm going to a funeral.

Identification with the "Native" continues to resonate with the male desires of colonialism, which is underscored by the privilege of white maleness: the privilege to ignore violence against women and children and the privilege of assumed identity with the male oppressed. Just as the famous Kim of Kipling's tale is able to acquire the stature of knowing more about the "other" than they can know about themselves, so the male academic may be similarly "inducted into a deep and structured tradition of male dreaming and male visions, of European exploration and adventure." The need to assume membership within the community of the oppressed sets the alienated hero against others who also seek to speak for the oppressed. Like adolescents who seek their freedom in random acts of minor violence or rebellion, the alienated urban maverick seeks his in rebellion against the institution and colleagues, only to find, "when the adrenaline ha[s] stopped pumping, that nothing ha[s] changed."[33] Another entry in my journal records one such conflict, which was never resolved by the players but ran, with the tone of soap operas, from moments of anger to skirmishes of one-upmanship.

He's pacing in front of me while I eat. He's trying to keep his voice low, doesn't want anyone else to hear. He's angry with his fellow workers, his employer, with a lot of people. (Me too? Perhaps not yet?) He wants some help. The others are wrong. They can't be trusted. They don't get it. A list of complaints is catapulted at me. What do I think? Should he go to the elected leaders? Give them a list of names to bar from the community? What do I think? How do I respond? I ask, "Seen any John Wayne movies lately?" He doesn't get it.

The fusion of a self-constructed identity as the "other" with a sense of the lone hero emerged in this encounter as permission for the lone hero to speak and act as "their" defender against institutional interests.

The Present
Journal notes that reflect some anger and frustration, a sense that I can neither escape nor alter social constructions of wilderness and hero.

I am seated in a quiet gathering, a reception preceding a lecture at an urban university. I am feeling far away from home at the present and glance at the soft well-kept hands clutching long stemmed glasses and delicate nibbles of cheese and fruit. My mind wanders and I try to recall who had written ruefully of similar gatherings among the "white" settler community of Anaheim Lake, where such posturing marks the neophyte from the south as urban and pretentious. I am about to share these thoughts with a friend, a man who indeed lives in a small community of central B.C. and whose own hands mark his life as a tradesman, a stark contrast to those around him, when I am interrupted. I describe this in my journal a few hours later:

Black vest and bare arms thrust before me followed by an intrusive voice mouthing intense claims. The young man says he is excited to find someone he can "talk to" to "speak about it."

His excitement and flailing arms shatter the academic quietude. It takes him only a moment to catch his breath and then to say, "I was up north." I feel myself withdrawing, sensing an internal conflict between curiosity as to what will follow and an unwillingness to listen. But I listen. He spent several years in volunteer service to youth. Worked in "wilderness" cultural camps. Spent days even weeks in a remote camp. Went back there after everyone else had gone. Just him and some European kid. Two nights they stayed there by themselves.

And there is more. He has an "adopted family" in a First Nations community. His own speaker. Held his own feast. Moved to another First Nation.

Taught them "cultural" songs because their own culture doesn't allow them to sing their own songs outside of spiritual and social gatherings. He adds, abruptly, anticipating empathy, that he embraces eco-feminism which is "dangerous," which can turn around the entire forest/resource management regime.

I disengage myself from his excitement, murmur assent that we know people in common, beg the need for another glass of wine and the responsibility to move along in polite cocktail party mingling manners.

I see this young man frequently: Our shared paths crossing the campus lock us in our common past of known faces and places of the north. His bared arms and slightly covered chest convey his "otherness" to the urban campus dwellers. He approaches me occasionally, sometimes to tell me of gossip he has heard from the north: First Nations discontent with my university, a failed First Nations community project by an unnamed church group, the reception of his own achievements in cross-cultural education, and sundry remarks on his alternative life, his original views, his commitment to changing the academy. (All of which makes me wonder: Does he, too, challenge his coworkers, incite his right over theirs, to speak – with satisfaction – for the "other"?)[34]

His mission, it seems, is to undo the missionaries, to restore Aboriginal culture, the north's salvation from civilization. He asks me if I have time to listen to him. He is out of sorts here in the city and needs, he says, someone who can understand what it means to live in the wilderness, where he would live if he could be in the north.

Implications

The discourses embraced by categorizing the forests and forest towns of British Columbia as the "north" can offer only a partial picture of the culturalscape. Embedded in the mytho-poetic subjectivity of the masculine quest, these discourses cannot retain their appeal *and* account for the material conditions of women's lives in remote single-resource communities or in even more remote First Nations communities, where everyone, women and men alike, must confront their socio-economic marginalization. Hayden White has argued that "in the past, when men were uncertain as to the precise quality of their sensed humanity, they appealed to the concept of wildness to designate an area of subhumanity that was characterized by everything they hoped they were not."[35]

While many of the "space-myths" of the north affirm White's view, I would argue that these are not universal. In fact, by appealing to wildness, the academic hero can fantasize that he is a member of that subhumanity – indeed, he can assert himself as its very symbol by embracing solitary heroism within it. What he cannot do, however, is confer upon himself, or his audience, a fully sensed humanity. For the mythic space in which the young man proves his manhood does not allow woman to prove her womanhood with the same freedom. Confronted by the violence inherent in the rugged individualism that serves as a marker for northern masculinity, she must perforce construct her own strength in terms of the stoic individual, becoming a self-sustaining woman who eschews the "dainty" femininity of the metropolis in favour of self-reliance, physical strength, and dispassionate endurance. Character is reflected in facing danger, a stance that risks complicity with the very ruggedness against which she must protect herself. Her very strength demands that she be erased from the northern fantasy, for she has no need for heroic protection and offers no foil to assured masculinity.

Her stance as stoic individual, moreover, overlaps with masculine heroism, and just as the narrators of trapping accounts mentioned above link culture and killing to men, so the narrators of contemporary heroism link male endurance and solitude with culture. Women have no place within these fantasies as northern actors in their own right. No mention is made of female ranchers, farmers, or resort keepers who live in relative isolation while male kin work and dwell in urban areas. We see no pictures of her killing a bull moose or with her fallen bear. No understanding is offered of women who seek so-called nontraditional jobs that require physical strength and endurance.

Rather, women appear only as audience beyond the frontier. Within the academy, heroic fantasies constitute a "hidden curriculum" whereby action and bravado of the heroic individual unsettle science-based critiques that have exposed the flawed basis of the 1960s man-the-hunter theory and the popular culture based upon it. Tantalizing tales reflecting the hidden curriculum doubly exile women: They not only erase women's lived reality in the resource regions, but also offer no opportunity for academic rejoinder.

Moreover, appropriation of the Palaeolithic man through semiotics of a claimed wildness depoliticizes gender relations and excuses sexual violence and excesses. In discourses of lone heroics and exaggerated masculinity, the symbols of male power constitute discursive and lived subjugation of women. The north emerges only as opposed to female. "This 'True North' is a masculine-gendered liminal zone of *rites de passage* and recreational freedom and escape."[36] It is not a domestic arena but a region hostile to domesticity. Female occupants, insofar as they are acknowledged, are sexualized – romanticized and eroticized. In this way male heroics simultaneously uphold and disallow the male/culture-female/nature dichotomy. In appropriating the wild for themselves, male heroes displace women into the scorned civilization of the south, into domesticity that threatens male essence.

The implications of male heroics reverberate beyond gender. Heroic postures that are located in mythic wildness do not extend to appropriating the dangers and endurance of industrial jobs by taking on an alternative masculinity as the tough worker among comrades (as other academics have done in a rush of ethnographic fieldwork), for to do so violates the lone hero's sense of social class. In constructions of the self-acclaimed hero, superiority as an individual is positioned against the collectivism of the working class. To acknowledge industrial workers as class members is to acknowledge the domestic, for the wildness fantastically represented rarely exists materially beyond a domesticated site, whether that be the cultural camp in which women cook and clean or the resource village in which men dwell with their families.

In conclusion, it is unfortunate that the young man comes "north" rather than to an urbanized industrial centre struggling to establish its own identity in the postcolonial, postnational crises of contemporary Canada. His "arrival" is signalled by articulations of subjectivity within a frame that conflates north with the enduring frontier of Palaeolithic man. He emerges with a double identity: as the northerner of determined individualism ever opposed to the faceless, amoral civilization of the south, with its indifference to and exploitation of the northern communities, and as the hero of that very civilization upon whose paternalism others must rely. The young man of the north reproduces the dualism of colonialism and imperial history. These oppositions provide the space in which he weaves his drama of mystification.

Appropriation of frontier identity stabilizes colonial relations, for romanticization of the "other" has meaning only to an audience beyond the frontier. The academy undergirths the phalleolithic construction of this identity. Built on an ethos of competition and individualism, the elite group sustains itself by exclusionary claims to legitimacy through precedence and by staging its intellectual alienation as privileged knowledge. Placed at the centre of the academic mode of production, it perpetuates an incomplete knowledge by invalidating women's experiences and scholarship. Thus the hero brings the frontier back into the circle.

Recognition of phalleolithic discourses calls for a feminist rethinking from the margins. Feminist narratives emerge from a critique and have less invested in the culturalscape of the frontier. They are not rigid but flexible. Feminist narratives are open to shifts, sensitive to theories. They reject the impossibilities of the frontier for the possibilities of a postcolonial and postnational periphery.

Acknowledgments
I would like to thank Lisa Young, Nikki Strong-Boag, and Ann Clark for their comments on earlier drafts of this chapter. SSHRC funded the research projects in central British Columbia that led me to the material for this chapter. An earlier version was produced as a working paper by the University of British Columbia Centre for Research in Women's Studies and Gender Relations, Occasional Papers 6, 3 (1997).

Notes

1 Jo-Anne Fiske and Caroline Mufford, "Hard Times and Everything like That: Carrier Women's Tales of Life on the Trapline," in *New Faces of the Fur Trade: Selected Papers of the Seventh North American Conference on the Fur Trade*, edited by Jo-Anne Fiske, Susan Sleeper Smith, and William Wicken (East Lansing: Michigan State University Press, 1997), 13-30.

2 James Fentress and Chris Wickham, *Social Memory* (Oxford: Blackwell Press, 1992), 138.

3 This point had already been made by Lilianne Ernestine Krosenbrink-Gelissen, *Sexual Equality as an Aboriginal Right: The Native Women's Association of Canada and the Constitutional Process on Aboriginal Matters, 1982-1987* (Saarbrucken, Germany: Verlag, 1991).

4 Arthur Ray, "Review of *The Fur Trade Revisited: Selected Papers of the Sixth North American Fur Trade Conference*," *William and Mary Quarterly*, 3rd series, 52, 4 (1995): 740.

5 Jennifer Brown, *Strangers in Blood: Fur Trade Company Families in Indian Country* (Vancouver: UBC Press, 1980); Sylvia Van Kirk, *"Many Tender Ties": Women in Fur Trade Society in Western Canada, 1670-1870* (Winnipeg: Watson and Dwyer, 1980).

6 This was not the first time I had raised this issue. Ten years earlier, I had written on the issues of gender and ethnographic biases in Jo-Anne Fiske, "'Ask My Wife': A Feminist Interpretation of Fieldwork Where the Women Are Strong but the Men Are Tough," *Atlantis* 11, 2 (Spring 1986): 59-69.

7 Susan Sontag, "The Anthropologist as Hero," in *Against Interpretation and Other Essays* (New York: Dell, 1969), 69-81.

8 Ibid., 77.

9 Here I am adapting Homi Bhabha's concept of colonial discourse and the satisfaction of speaking for the oppressed. "The Other Question: The Stereotype and Colonial Discourse," *Screen* 24, 6 (1983): 18-36.

10 Dorothy Smith, "A Peculiar Eclipsing: Women's Exclusion from Men's Culture," *Women's Studies International Quarterly* 1, 4 (1978): 281-95; Pat Caplan, "Engendering Knowledge: The Politics of Ethnography," in *Persons and Powers of Women in Diverse Cultures: Essays in Commemoration of Audrey I. Richards, Phyllis Kaberry and Barbara E. Ward*, edited by Shirley Ardener (New York: Berg, 1992), 65-87; Ruth Behar and Deborah Gordon, eds., *Women Writing Culture* (Berkeley: University of California Press, 1995); Catherine Lutz, "The Erasure of Women's Writing in Sociocultural Anthropology," *American Ethnologist* 17 (1990): 611-25, and "The Gender of Theory," in Behar and Gordon, eds., *Women Writing Culture*, 249-66; and Judith Newton and Judith Stacey, "Ms. Representations: Reflections on Studying Academic Men," in Behar and Gordon, eds., *Women Writing Culture*, 287-305.

11 Caplan, "Engendering Knowledge," 85. Caplan is drawing on the much earlier work of Dorothy Smith, "A Peculiar Eclipsing."

12 Ruth Behar and Deborah Gordon, eds., *Women Writing Culture* (Berkeley: University of California Press, 1995), 5.

13 James Clifford and George Marcus, eds., *Writing Culture: The Poetics and Politics of Ethnography* (Berkeley: University of California Press, 1986). Behar and Gordon are not the first to appropriate male semantics in order to further feminist knowledge. Sally Slocum deliberately sought to upset biases by juxtaposing "Woman the Gatherer" to "Man the Hunter"; see "Woman the Gatherer: Male Bias in Anthropology," in *Toward an Anthropology of Women*, edited by Rayna Reiter (New York: The Monthly Press, 1975), 36-50. Michelle Zimbalist Rosaldo and Louise Lamphere succeeded with the same tactic when they transformed Harry Shapiro's *Man, Culture and Society* by writing the path-breaking, now-classical *Woman, Culture and Society* (Stanford: Stanford University Press, 1974).

14 Sandra Gilbert and Susan M. Gubar, *The Madwoman in the Attic: The Woman Writer and the Nineteenth-Century Literary Imagination* (New Haven: Yale University Press, 1979), 6-7.

15 This was the reason given by James Clifford for not including feminist experimental writing in the controversial anthology that marked the turn toward the postmodern in anthropology. Clifford and Marcus, eds., *Writing Culture*.

16 Many examples come to mind. One glaring instance is found in R. Jon McGee and Richard L. Warms, eds., *Anthropological Theory: An Introductory History* (Mountain View, CA: Mayfield Press, 1996), 393: "This essay [Sally Slocum's 'Woman the Gatherer,' cited above] is taken

from *Toward an Anthropology of Women,* edited by Rayna Reiter, one of several groundbreaking anthologies of feminist anthropology to appear in the 1970s." Notably this "ground-breaking" work is not identified, and the authors go on to locate feminist anthropology as a secondary voice within a male scholarship critical of humanism and in so doing identify the male scholars.

17   Caplan, "Engendering Knowledge," 85-86.

18   Sally Slocum, "Woman the Gatherei," 39, emphasis added.

19   Colin Turnbull, *The Mountain People* (New York: Simon and Schuster, 1972); Napoleon Chagnon, *Yanomamo, the Fierce People,* 3rd ed. (New York: Holt, Rinehart, and Winston, 1983).

20   I have drawn this from Marx but employ it with parallel intent to the original, which directed our attention to "the Christian colonial system," which ought to be studied in detail to "see what the bourgeois makes of himself and the worker when he can model the world according to his own image without any interference." Quoted in Laura E. Donaldson, *Decolonizing Feminisms: Race, Gender and Empire Building* (Chapel Hill: University of Northern Carolina Press, 1992), 77.

21   Sontag, "The Anthropologist as Hero," 70.

22   It is perhaps fitting that as I prepare this manuscript for publication, I am drawn to the sound of the television in the room above, where an invisible male narrator intones authoritatively on the doomed Scott expedition to Antarctica, which he romanticizes as "the holy grail of Antarctica exploration."

23   Saturday Review, *Weekend Sun* (Vancouver), 21 September 1996.

24   Laurent Dubois, "'Man's Darkest Hours': Maleness, Travel and Anthropology," in Behar and Gordon, eds., *Women Writing Culture,* 308. As Michael Kowalewski has noted of contemporary travel writing, "The vestiges of imperialism continue to linger ... in a more ingrained and nebulous confidence about being culturally and racially superior" ("Introduction," in *Temperamental Journeys: Essays on the Modern Literature of Travel* [Athens: Univeristy of Georgia Press, 1992], 12).

25   Claude Lévi-Strauss, *Structural Anthropology* (New York, NY: Basic, 1976).

26   Sontag, "The Anthropologist as Hero," 77.

27   Quoted in Kamala Visweswaran, *Fictions of Feminist Ethnography* (Minneapolis: University of Minnesota Press, 1994), 88.

28   Robert Shields, *Places on the Margin: Alternative Geographies of Modernity* (London, UK: Routledge, 1991), 163.

29   The perception of polarized positions on environmental protection versus commercial logging was dramatically represented in a 1997 act by a solitary protester against "extreme" viewpoints. Driven by a sense of outrage against the growing powers of Aboriginal nations and environmentalist groups to influence cutting practices, he travelled to the islands of Haida Gwaii (Queen Charlotte Islands), where he felled an ancient and rare golden spruce protected from cutting because it held spiritual significance for the Haida Nation.

30   In 1990 the Canadian and British Columbian governments entered into an agreement with the First Nations Summit regarding the processes and goals for trilateral negotiations leading to settlement of Aboriginal rights, establishment of new resource-management regimes, and conditions of greater local authority for First Nations governments in British Columbia. Forty-three First Nations accepted this challenge in 1993, most of whom continue to work within this new intergovernment structure.

31   The notations in this journal and the "field notes" transcribed in the first entry have been edited and ambiguously dated in order to protect identities. My journal observations were not originally intended as "data" for academic publications, and most were compiled prior to new ethics standards requiring informed consent. Practically speaking, it is doubtful that this material could now be collected and published. Although Paul Rabinow and others have suggested that what is needed in order to achieve true reflexivity is an ethnography of hall gossip among our colleagues, such an enterprise is fraught with difficulties. Judith Newton and Judith Stacey attempted a much narrower and more clearly defined project of this nature with colleagues identified as supportive of feminism. The mixed and discouraging results are presented in "Ms. Representations," cited above. Paul Rabinow,

"Representations Are Social Facts: Modernity and Post Modernity in Anthropology," in Clifford and Marcus, eds., *Writing Culture*, 234-61. For a discussion of Rabinow's position, see Caplan, "Engendering Knowledge," 85.

32 Shields, *Places on the Margin*, 170, citing Bruce W. Hodgins and Margaret Hobbs, *Nastawgan: The Canadian North by Canoe and Snowshoe, A Collection of Historical Essays* (Toronto: Betelgeuse Books, 1985), 1-2.

33 Dubois, "'Man's Darkest Hours,'" 311.

34 Bhabha, "The Other Question." For an example of this discourse, see Ed Struzik, "Blackrobes: Across the Tundra and Forest, the Oblates Have Left a Quixotic Legacy," *Equinox* 9, 51 (June 1990): 42-55.

35 Quoted in Robert Shields, *Places on the Margin*, 163.

36 Ibid.

Part 2
Making a Living: Making a Life

The Canadian environment encompasses a variety of biophysical systems from which humans and other species derive their sustenance. Economics and ecology are usually discussed independently even though they are drawn from the same root, *ecos*, which means "home." In contemporary society, economic issues such as employment conditions and globalization are considered to be separate from the very environment that supports them and of which they are a part. While "making a living" is basic to human survival, its embeddedness in and dependence on the environment is overlooked. The ecological basis of economic activity – the fish that are caught or the trees that are logged – is disaggregated, or "externalized," from concerns with income and consumption. Indeed, for the majority of urban dwellers, who comprise 80 percent of the Canadian population, economic success is measured by distance from the natural environment: residence and employment in high-rise urban towers, food imported from tropical plantations, and clothing manufactured in offshore free-trade zones.

Economic and ecological systems are in fact not separate spheres but interconnected. They are also dynamic. Canada's population has more than doubled in the last fifty years, and economic output has increased nearly seven times,[1] drawing on the natural environment as the source of resources as well as jobs. Canada's history as a staples economy, based on the exploitation of natural resources as exports, underscores the primary relevance of our natural environment as a source of resources (commodities to be sold in the market). Yet resource industries are diminishing in economic significance due to overharvesting, technological innovation, global markets, and other factors; service sector employment has become our economic mainstay although its relations to the natural environment are more diffused and indirect. Whereas traditional resource-based industries represented two-thirds of Canada's exports in 1961, these industries represented only one-third of 1995 exports.[2] The change in the work people do reflects changes in the physical environment. The work done by women has evolved from its location in the resource sector (as farmers, in the timber industry, or as fishery workers) to the tertiary, or service-and-information, sector (as health care workers, teachers, and retail or administrative support staff). The economic and ecological "restructuring" occurring both locally and globally reflects changes that continue to reshape perceptions of the work that is done and the impact it will have on the way Canadians live.

A gendered analysis of work parallels an ecologically grounded analysis. Like the pervasive but devalued productivity of ecological systems, what is known as "women's work" in both the household and the labour force supports society, although it also remains invisible and undervalued. In Canada the juncture between women's work and the environment is especially significant, given the pivotal role of the natural environment as a resource base and the gendered character of resource work. Canada's rich endowment of natural "resources," staples economy (based on the export of raw goods), restricted economic diversification (relative to other industrialized nations), continuing economic dependency (especially on the United States) for trade and commerce, and continuing difficulties in the face of economic globalization attest to the primacy of the natural environment for the nation.

The Canadian environment as a "resource sector" is significant not only as the source of employment and material goods, but also as an enduring symbolic basis for settlement. Gender figures strongly in the characterization of the Canadian environment as a place of sustenance, a place of work. In the context of resource industries, women have generally been portrayed as domestic creatures: wives and mothers, homebodies whose "menfolk" have worked the mines, fished the seas, and logged the forests. Women have been less associated with the rigours of the Canadian landscape than their male peers, although as contributors to this book note, they too have settled this land – building homes, cooking, teaching children, farming and provisioning, fishing, and conducting a wide range of other outdoor activities. The land, in turn, has been portrayed as a gendered construct – its wild and rugged character depicted as male, its civilized and urban counterpart feminized.

Canada represents over one-tenth of the world's forests, and half of the country is forested;[3] Canada continues to be the largest exporter of forest products.[4] We have valued forests primarily in terms of timber and board feet rather than for their ecological contributions, such as providing habitat for other species, soil stabilization, and carbon sequestration. If our vision of the environment has been economically reductionist, it is also socially limited, especially in terms of gender. The economic perception of the Canadian environment as a resource reflects not only a biophysical place identified by forests, fish, and farms, but also a society marked by divisions of gender as well as class, race, ethnicity, and age. Women's (as well as other minorities's) contributions to the economy in both the household and the labour force have been devalued and ignored. This in turn has reinforced the narrow association of environment with resources, deflecting consideration of the environmental consequences of development, such as pollution and compromised human health and wellbeing.

As chapters in this part illustrate, women's association with the Canadian resource economy has been significantly underrepresented with respect to both their paid and unpaid work. Forestry, the fishery, and agriculture remain significant Canadian industries, although they employ fewer and fewer people. In Canada that part of the economy generating/extracting raw materials from the natural environment accounted for 41.2 percent of jobs in 1870 but only 4.8 percent of jobs in 1996; in contrast, the service economy, which employed only 36 percent of the 1870 population, now employs 73 percent of Canadians.[5] This economic transition provides an opportunity to re-examine the potential roles of women in their relations with the Canadian environment. Women's increased financial household responsibility, access to childcare, changes in employment due to technology, restructuring and resource shortfalls, as well as the development of new employment possibilities, such as ecotourism, all indicate new ways of understanding women's potential in terms of the natural environment. We have not yet examined nor anticipated the combined implications of these transitions in work, environment, and gender.

This part of the book describes how women are marginalized within and by resource industries and other environmental/outdoor work, in the context of both their households and their paid labour. Women are underrepresented in resource employment as well as devalued and underreported in the jobs they do occupy. The work that women do, and the gendered character of resource industries, continues to shape their lives and those of their families. Three resource sectors – the fishery, the logging industry, and agriculture – are discussed in this part. Each has been impacted by a number of factors. They have all been marked by "overshoot," the overexploitation of resources, whether it be the "falldown" effect in the timber industry, overfishing, or overuse of pesticides and monocultures in agriculture. Each sector has also experienced technological innovation, which has decreased jobs in communities but shifted opportunities for women. Each has been significantly impacted by globalization and has responded with different forms of economic restructuring.

Barbara Neis and Brenda Grzetic discuss the health consequences for women of economic and environmental restructuring in the Maritime fishery. They describe the significance of environmental (e.g., declines in biodiversity) as well as economic restructuring. Neis and Grzetic argue that gender influences relations to the physical environment as well as both environmental and industrial restructuring. Women's work in the Newfoundland and Labrador fish-processing sector has been reduced and become more insecure. Decreased income is correlated with the lack of access to childcare and increased household responsibilities. While lower levels of employment could potentially result in decreased exposure to occupational disease, underreporting of disease and lack of adequate health care services increase occupational risk. Inadequate retraining programs for women, as well as insufficient access to education and health care services, exacerbate women's situations. Moreover, this chapter points to the larger implications of the environment and work. Making a living means much more than "staying alive" and requires health, community, and other factors often overlooked in market concerns with the economic bottom line. This analysis of the consequences of both environmental and industrial restructuring reveals the difficult situation of women and families in hinterland communities and the inadequate response of governments to this reality.

Maureen G. Reed discusses women's employment in the forestry industry and how gender roles are being shaped by the global economy. Reed observes that gender has long been a primary basis for the division of labour in resource industries. Patricia Marchak reports that in the late 1970s between 63 and 87 percent of the men in forestry communities worked in the forest sector, compared to 3 to 7 percent of women.[6] Statistics Canada reports that in 2003 the forestry, fishing, mining, oil, and gas industries employed less than 3 percent of all men and only 0.6 percent of all women.[7] Reed argues that the marginalized position of women in the paid labour force in forestry communities remains overlooked, both descriptively and theoretically. She explores the contradictory nature of women's roles in forestry, in terms of their marginalized employment, integration of household and forestry communities, and relations to a shifting global economy. Reed argues that there are increasing opportunities for women in forestry occupations but that the restructuring of the industry is also affecting their employment.

While much of the literature on the south deals explicitly with women's agricultural work, studies of the farm crisis in Canada rarely make gender an issue. In response, Martha McMahon discusses how gender is (re)produced in Canadian agriculture. McMahon describes women's initiatives in small-scale farming on Vancouver Island. The "ecological agriculture" that she describes reveals by contrast the gendered, class-based, and racial assumptions of mainstream Canadian agriculture. It also reveals the potential for alternative approaches to the production of food as well as innovative ways of living with the land.

Catriona Sandilands focuses on the environment as a locus of employment: for park wardens in the public sphere and for the domestic workers who sustain these services. Sandilands begins by exploring the national parks, especially Banff, as a construct of nationhood, a source of national identity, and a means of symbolically linking the human presence to the wild. Her discussion of the "men for these mountains" demonstrates how a male lexicon of traits – physical strength, austerity, and authority – has endowed our view of the mountain landscape. In turn, the work of wardens' wives is domesticated, devalued, and made invisible. This chapter not only validates household work, but includes it as both a dimension of national parks' presence and a component of the parks-and-wilderness experience. Nature and the wild thus expand beyond the male heroic to include a fuller embrace of the earth as household, challenging our assumptions about wilderness and domesticity. Finally, Sandilands questions our assumptions about sexuality, both human and, ultimately, environmental. Her description of "Lesbian Rangers" not only reveals the heterosexism and gendered assumptions associated with park wardens' work and, by extension, resource-sector employment, but also challenges our assumptions about how we know and experience the wild.

Economic relations are not peripheral to one's life, but rather constitute its essence, determining life choices, the work we do, and the communities in which we live. The Canadian environment has traditionally been the lifeblood of a resource economy in which women's paid work was marginalized. Today, job losses and new employment trends due to technological innovation, overharvesting, and globalization, as well as to cultural changes in gender roles, are slowly changing the gendered character of resource production. Women's changing economic roles, the decline in resource employment, and the growth of employment opportunities in the service sector reflect changes as well to the environment. We have moved from a nation of seemingly unlimited resources to a paradigm of more extensive demands and decreased supplies of resources. As the physical environment has shaped the lives of Canadians, the landscape of this country in turn has been, and will continue to be, influenced by gender.

Notes

1 Statistics Canada, "Human Activity and the Environment," report (Government of Canada, catalogue #CS11-509-/2000E), Population.
2 Statistics Canada, "Human Activity and the Environment," report (Government of Canada, catalogue #CS11-509-/2000E), Economy, International Trade.
3 Statistics Canada, "Human Activity and the Environment," report (Government of Canada, catalogue #CS11-509-/2000E), Forest Industries.
4 National Forest Strategy Coalition, <http://nfsc.forest.ca/strategies/nfs5.pdf>, National Forest Strategy (2003-2008), *A Sustainable Forest: The Canadian Commitment* (Ottawa: National Forest Congress, 2003), 9.
5 John J. Macionis and Linda M. Gerber, *Sociology*, 4th Canadian ed. (Toronto: Prentice Hall, 2002), 398 (Figure 16-2).
6 M. Patricia Marchak, *Green Gold: the Forest Industry in British Columbia* (Vancouver: UBC Press, 1983).
7 Statistics Canada, <http://www.statcan.ca/english/Pgdb/labor10a.htm>, *Employment by Industry and Sex*, 19 August 2002, 1.

5
Environmental, Industrial, and Political Restructuring and the Health of Women Processing Workers in Newfoundland's Fishery-Dependent Communities
Barbara Neis and Brenda Grzetic

Canadian society is experiencing the effects of extensive environmental, industrial, political, and social restructuring. Overharvesting, reduced biodiversity, and pollution are examples of environmental restructuring. Industrial restructuring processes include work reorganization (deskilling and reskilling), downsizing, outsourcing, and capital flight. Political restructuring processes include trade liberalization, privatization, deregulation, and changes to public services and social programs. Social restructuring refers to such processes as urbanization, demographic change, and changes to community and household dynamics.

Existing research on the relationship between restructuring and health has primarily focused on industrial and political restructuring in heartland areas and on urban service-sector and manufacturing employment.[1] Relatively little research has examined the relationship between restructuring and health, particularly women's health in resource-dependent regions. In many such areas, environmental restructuring is interacting with industrial, political, and social restructuring to influence such health determinants as income, employment, education, physical and work environments, gender, and health services. Restructuring processes of particular importance to such regions include those associated with resource degradation, changing resource-management regimes, and regional shifts between resource sectors, such as the shift from fisheries to oil-and-gas production in Atlantic Canada. Remote locations, single-industry communities, high unemployment rates, and seasonal jobs with associated heavy dependence on shrinking social services, such as those related to education and employment, link political restructuring to vulnerabilities to unemployment, to underemployment, and to reduced incomes in rural areas.[2]

Differences in men's and women's relationships to natural resources, their differing educational backgrounds, the gender division of labour at work and at home, and the persistence of a male-breadwinner model in resource-dependent areas ensure that the relationship between health and restructuring is mediated by gender. Leach and Winson's gender-informed research on industrial restructuring in rural Ontario communities found that affected workers experienced "occupational skidding" (i.e., reduced incomes, less secure work, higher unemployment, and longer commutes). They found that women and men who had worked in similar work environments with limited wage differences prior to plant closures subsequently had different options.[3] Because of their responsibility for caring labour and related rural cultural assumptions and ideologies, and because their rural location meant that comparable industrial jobs were not available locally, women were more likely than men to opt for local, more precarious, and poorly paid work or to end up unemployed.[4] As a result, women suffered greater losses in income and employment than men. Impacts of plant closures on employment and income were particularly great in households where both husband and wife lost their employment; older workers were particularly likely to be facing long-term unemployment. Young people were doubly impacted.[5] Leach's research reminds us that restructuring outcomes are mediated by "the particular cultural forms taken by gender relations in household and community in rural areas."[6]

Leach and Winson did not explore the health impacts of restructuring for women and men in rural communities.[7] With a focus on women's health, our reports to the National Network on Environments and Women's Health used a case study of restructuring in a fisheries-dependent region of Newfoundland in the wake of the 1990s collapse of Atlantic Canadian groundfish stocks to explore these relationships. Treating the collapse of the groundfish stocks as a case of environmental restructuring, the study explored interactions between women's health and environmental, industrial, and political restructuring in fishery-dependent areas. The remainder of this chapter summarizes some of the findings from this research.[8] This is part of a larger body of research on the relationship between health determinants, the fisheries restructuring, and health outcomes for fisheries workers in the region. The research links the closure of the groundfish fisheries to short- and longer-term mental and physical health issues,[9] including work-related health risks among male and female processing workers and harvesters.[10]

The Context

The period between 1985 and 1998 has been one of substantial downsizing and reorganization within the Newfoundland and Labrador fishing industry. These changes were linked to the collapse of Atlantic-cod and other groundfish stocks in the early 1990s and the resulting moratoria on groundfish harvesting introduced by the federal government starting in 1992. In 1988 groundfish catches in the province totalled 400,000 metric tonnes. In

1994 they were less than 30,000 metric tonnes, a 90 percent drop. Despite the moratoria, groundfish landings remained well below 100,000 metric tonnes in 2000.[11]

Groundfish processing provided a major source of paid employment for women in hundreds of single-industry fishery communities in Newfoundland in the 1980s. Just over 50 percent of fish-processing workers and 10 to 12 percent of fish harvesters were women. Women and men in the industry tended to have relatively low levels of formal education. Women were more likely than men to work in seasonal and nonunionized plants and experienced substantially lower incomes than their male counterparts.[12] Within their paid work, women and men processing workers encountered all five categories of occupational health risks: physical, chemical, biological, ergonomic, and psychosocial.[13] Outside of their paid work, these women grappled with primary responsibility for childcare and domestic labour in the context of shift work, uncertain working hours, low and uncertain incomes, and limited access to childcare.

With the closure of the groundfish fisheries in the 1990s, roughly twelve thousand Newfoundland and Labrador women lost their jobs.[14] Between 1992 and 1999, the federal government responded to the collapse of the groundfish stocks in Atlantic Canada with a series of moratoria and adjustment programs. The latter included the Northern Cod Adjustment and Recovery Program (NCARP), the Atlantic Groundfish Strategy (TAGS), and the Post-TAGS program. The TAGS program was the largest and most sustained of these. It had a budget of $1.9 billion for a population of 40,025 in four Atlantic provinces, 27,934 of these in Newfoundland.[15] Those eligible included fishers, plant workers, and trawler men. The TAGS program had several components, including income support, counselling, training, mobility assistance, employment supports, early-retirement programs, and a limited range of job-creation initiatives.[16] It ended in 1998, but the Post-TAGS program extended it for four months, providing lump-sum payments for those with the longest duration of TAGS eligibility.

In 2000 the abundance of most of Newfoundland and Labrador's groundfish stocks remained at or near historic lows, and the volume of overall landings was approximately half that of 1989. However, production value more than doubled between 1993 and 2000 to reach approximately $1 billion, exceeding the 1988 value of $800 million.[17] Northern-shrimp and snow-crab landings have increased substantially in the past seven years, reflecting, many believe, an ecosystem shift caused by the removal of groundfish predators. Snow crab has replaced Atlantic cod as the most commonly processed and highest revenue-producing species in the industry, with a landed value of $270 million in 2000 compared to $22 million in 1988.

The period of environmental and industrial restructuring in the fishery during the 1990s was accompanied by a process of political restructuring associated with changes in some support programs of critical importance to these largely rural, seasonal workers. Changes to unemployment-insurance regulations enacted in 1996 renamed the program Employment Insurance (EI), made it more difficult for seasonal workers to qualify for benefits, and reduced the level of benefits that eligible seasonal workers could receive. These changes also made it more difficult for unemployed workers to qualify for retraining and educational support.[18] In addition, postsecondary education became more costly for their children.

The Study
The research for this study was undertaken between 1998 and 2000, just as the TAGS program was coming to an end. We decided to focus on the relationship between employment, income, work environments, and education as determinants in the health of current and displaced women processing workers. Tracking the relationships between restructuring, gender, and health can be challenging, particularly when different types of restructuring are taking place simultaneously, as in Newfoundland in the 1990s. For this exploratory study, our methodology combined in-depth interviews with thirty-eight women affected by the fisheries restructuring, key-informant interviews with educators and health professionals, and analysis of existing statistical data. We interviewed two groups of women. The first included twenty-three women who had been crab processors prior to the moratoria and continued this work after the groundfish fishery closed or who had shifted from processing groundfish to processing crab and shrimp in the 1990s. The second group included fifteen women who did skills-based training in an attempt to find work in other sectors of the economy after the closure of the groundfish fisheries. Most interviewees had spouses. Of the twenty-eight who told us their spouses' employment, twelve had husbands currently employed in the fishery. The spouses of eleven women worked full time, one part time, and twelve seasonally. One was unemployed, one retired, one on disability, and one self-employed. Only four out of thirty-four of these respondents had children under the age of five at home. Seventeen had one child of school age, and five had two children of school age in their households. Interview data were contextualized using key-informant interviews with health professionals and educators, an analysis of Workplace Health Safety and Compensation Commission (WHSCC) claims data for fish processing workers, and an analysis of data on TAGS-funded training programs introduced in response to the fishery crisis.

The study area was the Conception-Trinity Bay area on the northeast coast of Newfoundland. We chose this area because it has a large number of fish- and shellfish-processing plants, some of which closed in the 1990s. Others converted from groundfish to crab and shrimp processing or increased their concentration on processing crab and shrimp. The area also includes a number of private and public colleges where a significant amount of training directed at fishery workers displaced by the collapse of Newfoundland's groundfish stocks took place.

Findings

The sample of current and former processing workers we interviewed was weighted toward older women and women who continued working during the moratoria. Eighteen were forty-five or older, and only one was younger than thirty. Five women had some trade-school or college training, eighteen had completed high school or high school equivalents (ABE), and the educational level of the remaining fifteen was between Grades 8 and 11. Younger women (aged thirty-nine and under) were more likely than older women to have high school equivalents and postsecondary training.

General Health

When asked to rate their overall health, three out of twenty-nine respondents to this question rated their health as excellent, eleven as very good, nine as good, five as fair, and only one as poor. Closer questioning suggested that responses to this question reflect a general tendency to downplay health issues when asked about them in this way. In response to other questions, sixteen out of thirty-six reported having been diagnosed with arthritis or rheumatism, eleven out of thirty-six had been diagnosed with asthma, and three reported that they had "crab lung" (occupational asthmatic reaction to snow crab). Four out of thirty-six had been diagnosed with emphysema or chronic bronchitis, two with hay fever, and twelve with other allergies. Eight had been diagnosed with skin rash, three bursitis, two tendonitis, six tennis elbow, ten stomach ulcers, and four other digestive problems. Six said they had been diagnosed with high blood cholesterol and five, high blood pressure. Three had been told they were diabetics and three had been diagnosed with cancer. Eight had been diagnosed with recurring migraine headaches and eight with depression.

When asked how stressful they found their lives at present, twenty-one out of thirty-six respondents said they found it either very stressful (3) or somewhat stressful (18). Twenty-two out of thirty-five said they found their stress levels at the time of the interview compared to six years earlier either much higher (9) or somewhat higher (13). Eleven out of thirty-two respondents said they had been depressed either most of the time (4) or some of the time (7) in the past six years. The main sources of stress in their lives included income shortages and lack of income security, lack of work, work uncertainty and worry about the future, personal health problems, health problems of family members, worry about their children, their access to postsecondary education, and out-migration of children and grandchildren.

Twelve out of thirty-one respondents were either rarely (3) or never (9) able to relax. More were able to enjoy normal day-to-day activities and to keep busy and occupied, indicating satisfaction with the way they did things most of the time or some of the time. Almost all had one or more people they could really count on when they were under stress (25/26). Walking and talking with friends and family members were the stress-reduction activities most commonly identified.

When asked to specify any of their health problems that they believed could be attributed to the moratoria, they identified worry and depression, migraine headaches, digestive problems, and ulcers. Respiratory and skin problems that they associated with processing crab were linked to the closure of fish-processing lines, which had forced them into crab processing (see below). In addition to the moratoria on groundfish fishing, workplace exposures and heredity were also identified as responsible for some of their health conditions (thyroid ailments, allergies).

These women were asked to select items from a list of changes that they thought would improve their health. The items most commonly selected included: a more secure income (29/35); caring more for themselves (26/35); relaxing more and worrying less (26/36); spending more time with their families (18/28); spending more time with friends (18/28); change in job or business (18/34); and others taking more responsibility (11/25). They were often pessimistic about the likelihood of these changes happening in the near future. Those changes that they saw as most likely were changes related to their own behaviour, such as relaxing more, caring more for themselves, and spending more time with friends and family. They tended to identify the following barriers to change: not enough money (10/19); uncertainty about the future (9/19); fish stocks are not recovering (5/19); government won't listen (5/19); don't know how to get started (4/19); can't get the training needed (4/19); fear of the unknown (4/19); lack of self-confidence (4/19). Six out of nineteen said they did not know what was stopping them from changing. Other barriers identified included: "the employer doesn't want to know, doesn't care to find out"; "no jobs"; and "people who have worked in the fishery have a bad reputation, like they are illiterate."

Restructuring, Employment, and Health

At the time of the interviews, twenty-two of these women were shellfish-processing workers, eleven were unemployed, four were employed outside of fish processing, and one was working on a grant/retraining. Younger women with lower seniority and women who had attempted to leave the industry were most likely to be unemployed or underemployed. Unemployment, underemployment, employment uncertainty, and low and uncertain incomes are all health determinants.[19] Physical and psychological health problems are also associated with women's efforts to balance unpaid and paid work.

Statistics on employment trends and trends in seasonality in fish processing suggest that the unemployment and less secure employment experienced by a majority of the interviewees are indications of larger trends in the industry. In 1992 Newfoundland and Labrador had 193 licensed primary processing plants and 11 secondary processing plants. By 2000 the number of licensed plants had been reduced to 126 active licensed primary plants and 9 secondary processing plants.[20] Reductions in employment occurred both in fish harvesting and in processing. However, reductions were greater within fish processing, where women's employment has been concentrated, than within fishing, which, despite some significant changes, remains male-dominated.[21] Between 1987 and 1997, average monthly employment in fish processing in Newfoundland and Labrador peaked at 13.3 thousand in 1989, declined to a low of 3.7 thousand in 1994, and increased again to 6.2 thousand in 1998 (46.62 percent of the 1989 figure).[22] In the case of fishing, during the same period, average monthly employment declined from a high of 12.7 thousand in 1987 to a low of 8.8 thousand in 1995, increasing again to 10.5 thousand in 1998 (82.68 percent of the 1987 figure). During the same period, the ratio of highest to lowest employment per month in fish processing (one index of seasonality) almost doubled, increasing from an average of 2:3 between 1987 and 1991 to an average of 5:59 between 1993 and 1998. The 1992 ratio was 2:9.

Overall trends in employment within fish processing in Newfoundland and Labrador partly reflect the effects of environmental restructuring, moratoria associated with the collapse of the groundfish stocks, and the related overall reduction in the volume of landings in Newfoundland and Labrador since 1990. However, the trends also reflect the effects of tighter limits on access to processing licences, reduced state regulation of snow-crab processing so that companies are now able to export most of their crab products in semiprocessed form, and the lower labour requirements associated with crab and shrimp relative to groundfish processing. Overall, person years of employment in processing declined from a peak of over 14,000 in 1988 to just over 6,000 in 2000.[23]

The problems with depression and stress identified by many of the women interviewed probably partly reflect the health effects of increased unemployment, employment uncertainty, and reduced incomes. Their access to social support is evident from their answers and may have helped protect their health from these threats. However, the pessimism of many regarding their capacity to introduce positive changes into their lives in the near future, particularly into their work, income, and community environments, points to an environment characterized by low control.

During the period of the TAGS program, the interview data suggest that the effects of employment loss and income uncertainty were offset in the short term by the availability of adjustment payments for those who were eligible. Some workers who were eligible for TAGS for the full duration – and who either had very low incomes from processing prior to the moratoria or were able to access processing or other work during the moratoria and had TAGS support – were somewhat better off and enjoyed more secure incomes while on TAGS. Some women took training while they were on TAGS: twenty-one out of thirty-eight did skills training since the moratoria. Only five of the thirty-eight received career counselling after the groundfish moratoria, and fifteen of the thirty-eight did upgrading (ABE training) in that period.

Women processing workers who were not eligible for TAGS or whose eligibility was of shorter duration and those who had worked in unionized, year-round plants prior to the closure and did not work while on TAGS experienced reduced incomes during the moratoria and found it harder to make ends meet.

Since the end of the TAGS program, uncertainty about employment and income has increased due not only to the failure of the groundfish stocks to return to earlier levels, but also to restructuring of the industry toward shellfish and the restructuring of the Employment Insurance Program during the 1990s. Income support for all those entitled had either ended by 1998 or would end in the next several months, particularly for those unable to work due to illness and those with relatively low seniority. Those with low seniority tended to be younger and to have young children. For these workers and for those who had lost their employment due to plant closures, anxiety about future employment and about Employment Insurance eligibility was evident. Those with processing work described difficulty matching home responsibilities with irregular hours of work during the processing season.

Restructuring, Work Environment, and Women's Health
Work environment is another important health determinant. The relationship between work environment and health is mediated by gender, income-support programs, and organizational, regulatory, and compensation environments. The fisheries restructuring has been associated with both physical and social changes in work environments that have implications for the occupational health of women and men processing workers and fish harvesters. The shift from groundfish to shellfish, driven by the restructuring of the marine ecosystem due to overfishing, means more workers are processing shrimp and crab than in the past. The occupational health risks associated with crab and shrimp processing are somewhat different from those associated with groundfish processing. Some physicians we interviewed

pointed to these changes in occupational health risks among processing workers over time and to gender differences in exposures and related problems. One said that in the mid- to late 1980s, local plants were seasonally busy processing crab and groundfish. For those working at the plant, "the spectrum of problems I saw at that time was ... a lot of RSI [Repetitive Strain Injury], accidental injuries, slips, falls, tripped up, dropped a pan of fish on their foot, etc." More recently, the expansion of crab processing and the introduction of some other shellfish species in one of the plants have produced the following pattern of musculoskeletal problems: "There are a lot of RSI, especially associated with the crab plant. A lot of women are scrubbing crab shells by hand. In the last couple of years the location of RSI has been in the upper arms, neck, shoulders."

Other changes in the occupational health risks confronting processing workers include an increase in work-related allergies and occupational asthma and possible increases in work-related stress due to the increased vulnerability of workers associated with reduced employment alternatives and increased seasonality. A rural-health physician commented, "Yes, more problems with allergies, asthma than before." When asked about respiratory problems among crab-processing workers, he said that he was "getting all of them, sinusitis, asthma, crab lung, eczema (not respiratory but common) ... Also, probably a fair amount of stress may affect them as well. They are driven to the limit, in a state of fright, panic. That's not true of all the bosses, but a fair number want to get what they can from you ... There is a lot more stress in the crab plant."

In the interviews, twenty-two workers were asked questions related to skin, eye, and respiratory problems.[24] Eight out of twenty-one said they had had eczema at some point in their lives, and two said it was worse at work. Thirteen had experienced burning eyes, and eleven said this was worse at work. Nine had experienced itching eyes, and all said this was worse at work. Eight had experienced running eyes, and six said this was worse at work. Eleven said they usually had a cough, and the period of time that they reported having this cough varied, ranging from less than one year, to four to six years (7), to more than six years (3). Eight out of nine respondents said the cough improved on days off; six out of seven said it improved during the off-season. Thirteen out of twenty-three respondents said they had experienced trouble breathing, five continuously, and six repeatedly. Eight found that their breathing was worse at work. Seven said they had shortness of breath when hurrying, and five said they walked slower than those their own age. The period of time during which they reported experiencing shortness of breath varied, ranging from one to ten years. Six had been woken by an attack of shortness of breath at night, and eleven had experienced such attacks at work. Nine said they had experienced chest tightness or difficulty breathing. Eleven said their chest sounded wheezy and that the wheeze had been present for between one and eleven years; eight said the wheeziness improved during the off-season and on days off. Five said their symptoms had been worse over the past three years, one better, and four the same. Twelve said they had periods when their chest felt tight; of these, eleven said this would come in attacks and be associated with difficult breathing. Five said their chest tightness occurred most at work. Twelve had seen a doctor for breathing problems or shortness of breath, and ten were currently taking medicine for breathing problems. Five had visited the emergency room after hours because of breathing problems. Five had seen a specialist about their breathing problems.

Between 1985 and 1998, a total of 27,154 accidents were reported to the Newfoundland Workers Compensation Commission (now the Workplace Health Safety and Compensation Commission/WHSCC) by shellfish- and fish-processing workers. Annual reported accidents declined five-fold between the period 1985-88 and the period 1993-98. Incidence rates (accidents/average number of workers/month) declined from a high of 30/100 workers in 1987 to a low of 12/100 in 1993. These changes correlated with the cuts to and eventual closure of provincial groundfish fisheries between 1990 and 1994. As industry employment has expanded in recent years due to the expansion of the crab and shrimp fisheries, the number and incidence of reported accidents has begun to increase again, with incidence rates for male and female workers combined at 17/100 in 1998. A gender-based analysis of claims data shows that overall, although women workers made up slightly over 50 percent of processing workers for the period under study, they made up only 28.6 percent of all WHSCC accident claims between 1985 and 1998. The average ratio of females to males reporting accidents was 0:27 for the period 1985-88, 0:29 for the period 1989-92, and 0:35 for the period 1993-98, suggesting that reported female accidents have increased in importance relative to male accidents in recent years.

Incidence rates for males and females for the period between 1992 and 1998, the only period for which such data were available, place female incidence rates at about 50 percent of those of men. We know that, as in other industries,[25] women and men do different jobs in fish and shellfish processing.[26] Do lower frequency and incidence rates mean that women's jobs are safer than men's?[27] This is unlikely. As Messing has argued, there are a lot of pitfalls in comparing women's and men's accident rates.[28] The lower incidence of reported female accidents in Newfoundland and Labrador WHSCC data probably partly reflects the impact of gender differences in hours of exposure resulting from gender differences in the seasonality of work and in access to full-time work, particularly during the 1980s.[29] Gendered patterns in frequencies and in incidence rates related to WHSCC claims could also reflect access to sources of income support other than WHSCC benefits as well as the influences of seasonality and uncertain work on reporting.

Workers eligible for TAGS may have resorted to this type of income support rather than workers' compensation benefits in the early to mid-1990s. Increased seasonality and uncertainty about access to work may have encouraged underreporting because of the risks that time away from work can pose for access to Employment Insurance (time off work on WHSCC benefits is not included in the calculation of hours worked for EI purposes) and, possibly, by increasing the vulnerability of workers to layoff and replacement by employers, thus indirectly reducing their willingness to report accidents and to take time off work. Seasonality may also contribute to underreporting by making it easier for workers to work in pain and cope with respiratory symptoms because they know that the season will be over and that they will get a break from the job. As our interview data show, and as suggested in earlier research,[30] many women workers are working in pain and appear to have been underreporting musculoskeletal health problems that may well be work-related.

Finally, lower incidence rates for female workers may reflect greater problems with the fit between the types of workplace injuries and industrial diseases associated with women's jobs in fish and shellfish processing. The training of health-and-safety committee personnel, the training of rural health professionals, and recognized diseases and injuries within the WHSCC system may also influence the incidence of accident claims by women and men processing workers. A gender-based analysis of WHSCC claims points to a disturbing upward trend between 1985 and 1998 for both male and female accident claims in the classification accident type "unspecified, nec [not elsewhere classified], unknown." For males and females, some of the most common accident types in the early years had largely disappeared by the late 1990s. These trends may reflect the development of a poorer fit between WHSCC categories and actual events related to industry restructuring, but this possibility requires further research. Although these are well-documented occupational risks to health for shellfish-processing workers, there was no code for shellfish occupational asthma or shellfish allergies in the WHSCC data for the period examined. Allergic responses can vary but in their most extreme form include shellfish occupational asthma.[31]

Our interviews with twenty-two crab-processing workers in three areas found that eleven reported having sufficiently serious breathing problems to require them to use inhalers, but none of these had reported these respiratory problems to the WHSCC. Of these workers, three could no longer work with crabs.

Restructuring, Education, Training, and Health
The 1999 *Second Report on the Health of Canadians* describes the interrelatedness of social and economic conditions, noting that our health is

greatly affected by adequate learning opportunities, meaningful work and working conditions, income, and physical safety.[32] Education is an important determinant of health. Employment earnings and health increase with the number of years of education. While education levels are often credited with improving people's health by improving social supports and participation, the greatest impact of education on health results from the ways it mediates access to meaningful employment experiences.[33] People who are well educated have more options and greater access to better jobs with higher incomes.

Changes in employment opportunities associated with environmental, industrial, and social restructuring point to the ways restructuring can alter the fit between employment opportunities and the training/education and work experience of women and men workers. Opportunities to retrain or to return to school and upgrade are very important for workers displaced during restructuring and tend to differ for women and men. Because of physical isolation, the preponderance of single-industry towns, and the structure of labour markets in resource-dependent areas, the adjustment challenges for workers negatively affected by restructuring tend to be particularly great.

Training, like any other form of education, has the potential to be a powerful and positive determinant of health and wellbeing for women and men but only if it is of good quality. It must be affordable, provide fair and equitable access, and be connected to meaningful, accessible work done under decent working conditions. During periods of restructuring, opportunities for training/education may change, gender ideologies may limit the training opportunities available to women, and gender segregation within education and training programs can be challenged or reinforced depending on the willingness of governments and social institutions to take responsibility for addressing barriers to women's full participation.

We explored the relationship between restructuring, education, and health for women fish processors during the moratoria, using results from in-depth interviews with fifteen women displaced from fish processing who opted to do skills-based training funded through TAGS, a gender-based analysis of TAGS-related training data, and interviews with educational-service providers.

Analysis of TAGS training data for our study area indicates that although women made up roughly one-third of displaced fisheries workers in Newfoundland and Labrador, they comprised only 20 percent of those receiving TAGS-funded training. Women's training was concentrated in programs related to fisheries, business, computers, and the service industry. They did virtually no training related to the development of emerging resource industries, such as minerals and petroleum, or to male-dominated apprenticeable trades. Women were also underrepresented in fisheries training. The median duration of men's training was greater than women's for technology, computers, business, farming, arts/crafts, and the fishery. Some of the greatest differences were in the technology category, where the median duration of training was forty-nine weeks for men but only twenty-eight weeks for women. In the business category, the median duration of training was sixty-seven weeks for men but only forty-two weeks for women.

Of the fifteen women interviewed in depth about training, four took business programs and five completed technology programs that were two years or longer. Three of these five women trained in traditionally female occupational areas, and two chose male-dominated areas. Three women said they discussed studying/working in a nontraditional trade with someone close to them, such as a spouse, and two women went on to complete trades programs while on TAGS. Two women chose an arts/crafts training program. Two other women decided not to pursue skills training after ABE: one for financial reasons (because TAGS ran out of money for training) and the other for health reasons. In all, nine women trained in what would be considered female-dominated occupational areas, and four completed programs in male-dominated areas. Male-dominated areas are occupations in which women make up less than 33 percent of the workforce in Canada. The women who took trades and technology programs were among the youngest in the group.

Among this group of fifteen women, some jumped at the opportunity to train for work outside the fishery, but others needed more time to deal with losing the work they had done for most of their lives. Despite these differences, most said they enjoyed the time spent in their training programs, the support they received and gave to each other as classmates, and the excitement of learning something new. While a bit intimidating at first, having the opportunity to retrain helped some of the women to see that they were capable of doing other things besides working in the fish plant: "When I was first laid off, all I could think about was work in the fish plant. Now after being away from it for a while and going back to school to study computers, I can't ever see myself going back. At first I had a real fear of using computers but I got over it."

Interviewees identified a broad range of shortcomings in their training programs. Most said they were basically left on their own to figure out what training program to take. Only one attended a career-counselling program. As one woman said: "You were encouraged to figure out for yourself what you wanted to do. There was no aptitude testing or anything like that. I found out about my program from two men who attended a public meeting about it." Women criticized the limited availability of training programs in their areas and the quality of the ones they enrolled in. Many of their comments echoed those of women across Canada who have been complaining for years about the problems they confront when they try to build/rebuild an attachment to the workforce through education/training: the lack of institutional or political commitment to women's education; harassment in trades programs; lack of finances for education; discrimination in access to training; poorly designed training programs; lack of support for women in trades and technology programs; lack of recognition of prior learning, especially skills acquired in the home; inadequate career counselling or "mainstream" counselling programs that inadvertently stream women into low-paid, low-status occupations; lack of employment opportunities after training; discrimination in hiring; and lack of ties with economic-development plans.[34]

The women in the study understood training to be part of an employment strategy, and in the interviews they did not really separate training from its expected outcome: employment. However, none were able to find stable employment after training. Only one woman was working, temporarily, in her area of training, and a second woman who completed a technology program had done contractual work with occasional layoffs. Three women got temporary work on community projects, two returned to work in fish plants, and the others were unemployed at the time of the interviews.

Women attributed stress-related health problems to the moratoria period and to their inability to secure work and make an income after training. Ten of the fifteen women said their lives at present were stressful; of these, two said their lives were very stressful, and eight somewhat stressful. When asked to compare this with their lives six years ago, when the moratoria were announced, three said their lives were much more stressful at present, and seven somewhat more stressful. The health problems they linked to this stress included ulcers and other digestive problems, migraines, rashes, depression, high blood pressure, and weight gain. A number of women reported changes in their diets during the moratoria, and subsequent problems with high cholesterol.

Depression was a particularly common and persistent health problem among the displaced women who opted for skills-based training. Ten out of fifteen said they had experienced depression during the moratoria, whereas only one woman said she had experienced depression prior to the moratoria. Seven said they felt depressed some of the time, and three said they were depressed most of the time. Two women were taking medication for depression at the time of the interviews. One woman said: "In January I was depressed [for] about three weeks worrying about work. I'm not content at all when I'm not working. Being at home drove me out of my mind. When I get work, the depression goes away."

When asked to list their greatest source(s) of stress and worry, seven women said "uncertainty of work," seven said "lack of finances and fear that they may have to go on welfare," three said "worrying about the children and their education," two said "having to move away/sell their home," two said "feeling like there is no future," and two said "minor health problems." Ten women said they felt tired a lot during the day, and seven said they felt anxious a lot of the time. Six women said they felt unable to relax. Nine women reported disturbed sleep patterns: eight said they wake up often in the early hours of the morning, five said they worry about things before getting out of bed, and five said that more than once a week they have trouble sleeping. Not surprisingly, feelings of tiredness and depression as well as dietary changes were causing excessive weight gain for some women in the study: "I would exercise more and lose weight if I only knew what was making me so tired."

Women living in the more rural areas covered by our study were more critical of the quality of training provided than those living in larger communities. They talked about having instructors who were not qualified and who had no practical experience in the area they were teaching, the high turnover of instructors, and a self-paced approach that did not provide a good environment for adult students who had been out of the school system for many years. Other concerns about the quality of training focused on the short duration of programs and on program developers who tried to do too much too quickly, which meant that women did not get an appropriate level of training in particular areas. Others said their programs were inappropriate for the local job market or not respected by employers and that on-the-job training was not provided. Two women reported being confronted with sexual harassment in the classroom.

Programs seemed to have been designed and funded without any follow-up supports that would have increased the likelihood of women's re-employment. Many women said they initially wanted to start small businesses, but there were few or no institutionalized links to provide the entrepreneurial support and funding these women needed in order to get small businesses off the ground.

All of the above shortcomings in TAGS-related training appear to have contributed to the general underrepresentation of women in this training. In addition, apart from feeling the stress caused by displacement and uncertainty due to the moratoria, women who did pursue training appear to have experienced frustration, disappointment, and stress linked to the gap between their training-related hopes and investments and actual outcomes. These women were very critical of government spending on such haphazard training programs. One said a factory should have been built in their community instead of handing all that money over to "private trainers who had no commitment to the community." Many of those interviewed are still angry about the government's lack of support for good quality training and about the lack of work after training: "I used to do volunteer work for politicians but now I don't care if I even vote anymore."

Women talked about the impacts of the moratoria and about their futures in rural Newfoundland. One woman went back to work in the fish plant after completing a technology program. She said, "My personal expectations have gone down a lot. I feel like I am stuck in a job that I despise and I'm angry about not getting work after training. I can't dwell on it and I can't think about working in the plant for another ten years. It's too depressing."

Conclusion

Different types of restructuring can undermine or enhance the health of women and men by influencing such health determinants as physical and work environments, employment, incomes, social equality (including gender equality), health systems, social programs, and educational services and requirements. Restructuring is not gender neutral. As argued by Jenson, "it is only by understanding the extent to which a new set of gendered employment relations is at the heart of the restructured economies that we can begin to comprehend the restructuring, as well as the space available within it for generating equality."[35] Because women's and men's relationships to physical environments and natural resources differ, and due to the gender division of labour, women and men tend to be differently affected by environmental restructuring and industrial restructuring.

Environmental restructuring can threaten health by eroding and transforming regional employment opportunities and reducing incomes. Environmental degradation and transformation, coupled with government and industry efforts to downsize the industry, have resulted in fewer jobs and less certain work, particularly in the processing sector of the Newfoundland and Labrador fishery.[36] As has been the case in other sectors of the economy,[37] in the 1990s processing jobs became more like women's processing jobs of the past. Jobs became scarcer and work more uncertain and more seasonal, as had been more typical of the seasonal, inshore sector in the late 1980s, in which female workers were overrepresented. When combined with changes in Employment Insurance regulations and changes in licensing policies, environmental and industrial restructuring have contributed to reduced incomes and to increased insecurity about employment and income for many processing workers. This pattern of "occupational skidding" is similar to that identified among women and men affected by restructuring in rural Ontario.[38] In the short term, workers eligible for TAGS often availed themselves of this alternative type of income support if they lost time at work or were ineligible for EI. However, this alternative was not available to all workers and disappeared after 1999. For many processing workers, restructuring appears to have eroded the fit between Employment Insurance regulations, available work, and household strategies to protect incomes.[39] Many women workers experience a lack of access to affordable, high-quality childcare, related heavy responsibilities for childrearing and household work, and vulnerability to gender ideologies. Restructuring can exacerbate these problems.[40]

Women's occupational health problems tend to be poorly understood and women poorly served by occupational health regimes and services.[41] Restructuring can exacerbate these problems by changing work-related exposures and eroding the effectiveness of regulatory regimes.[42] Our analysis of WHSCC claims for the period between 1985 and 1998 found that environmental, industrial, and political restructuring reduced the number of processing workers exposed and the overall hours of exposure to occupational health risks in processing-work environments. However, restructuring may also have contributed to greater reluctance on the part of both men and women to report accidents in the 1990s, particularly lost-time accidents. Lower numbers of reported accidents may also be linked to increased problems with the fit between WHSCC categories and the types of accidents and occupational diseases associated with processing shellfish. A case study of the problem of shellfish occupational asthma that was central to this project suggests that processing workers' vulnerabilities to this type of illness and related socio-economic costs to those with respiratory problems at work have been aggravated by gaps in regional research, in existing regulations for licensing processing plants, in health services and health-professional education, and in the workplace compensation regime.[43]

Environmental, industrial, and political restructuring can erode the fit between the education and training background of workers, work and labour-market requirements, and available educational services.[44] This study found that some women who attempted to leave fish processing in the 1990s encountered inadequacies with the retraining options and services provided under the federal government's adjustment programs. These programs failed to offset the risks to these women's health caused by the fisheries crisis and failed to give them the skills and supports they needed to find employment outside fish processing. Unemployment, poverty, and unfulfilled expectations have been associated with depression and stress in the lives of these women. Political restructuring has "hollowed out" the welfare state, upon which poor and working-class women depend. In the 1990s, such restructuring was also associated with a retreat from social commitments and the related shift toward "targeted" programs that deny access to many women and men, and establish strict constraints on access to others.[45] Political restructuring has also reduced access to publicly funded training programs, postsecondary education, and health services through privatization, increased "user fees," and the geographical concentration of services.

Acknowledgments

This chapter is based on research partially funded by the National Network on Environments and Women's Health (NNEWH), the Health Promotions Branch of Health Canada, and the Institute for Social and Economic Research at Memorial University, St. John's, Newfoundland. NNEWH is financially supported by the Centres of Excellence for Women's

Health Program, the Women's Health Bureau, and Health Canada. The views expressed herein do not necessarily represent the views of NNEWH or official policy of Health Canada.

Notes

1 See, for example, S.W.J. Kozlowski, G.T. Chao, E.M. Smith, and J. Hedland, "Organizational Downsizing: Strategies, Interventions, and Research Implications," *International Review of Industrial and Organizational Psychology* 8 (1993): 263-332; Sheila M. Neysmith, "Networking across Difference: Connecting Restructuring and Caring Labour," in *Restructuring Caring Labour: Discourse, State Practice, and Everyday Life,* edited by Sheila M. Neysmith (Toronto: Oxford University Press, 2000), 1-28; Claire Mayhew, Michael Quinlan, and Rande Ferris, "The Effects of Subcontracting/Outsourcing on Occupational Health and Safety: Survey Evidence from Four Australian Industries," *Safety Science* 25, 1 (1997): 163-78.
2 Belinda Leach, "Transforming Rural Livelihoods: Gender, Work, and Restructuring in Three Ontario Communities," in *Restructuring Caring Labour,* ed., Neysmith, 209-25.
3 Belinda Leach and A. Winson, "Bringing Globalization down to Earth: Restructuring and Labour in Rural Communities," *The Canadian Review of Sociology and Anthropology* 32, 3 (1995): 341-64.
4 Leach, "Transforming Rural Livelihoods."
5 Leach and Winson, "Bringing Globalization down to Earth."
6 Leach, "Transforming Rural Livelihoods," 219.
7 Leach and Winson, "Bringing Globalization down to Earth."
8 A more detailed discussion of the research and findings can be found in Neis et al., "From Fishplant to Nickel Smelter: Health Determinants and the Health of Newfoundland's Women Fish and Shellfish Processors in an Environment of Restructuring," research report (Toronto: National Network on Environments and Women's Health, 2001).
9 See Lillian Benham, "Shelburne Fishnet Addresses Women's Health Issues," *Coastal Community News Magazine* 5, 1 (1999): n.p.; Marion Binkley, "Lost Moorings: Offshore Fishing Families Coping with a Fisheries Crisis," *Dalhousie Law Journal* 18, 1 (1995): 84-95; Linda Christiansen-Ruffman and Stella Lord, "Under Stress," *Yemaya,* International Collective in Support of Fishworkers' (ICSF) newsletter on gender and fisheries, August 2000, 16-17; Michael Murray, D. Fitzpatrick, and C. O'Connell, "Fishermen's Blues: Factors Related to Accidents and Safety among Newfoundland Fishermen," *Work and Stress* 11, 3 (1997): 292-97; Neis and Grzetic, "From Fishplant to Nickel Smelter"; Susan Williams and Barbara Neis, *Stress, Repetitive Strain Injuries and Fishplant Workers in Newfoundland* (St. John's, NF: Institute of Social and Economic Research, Memorial University, 1993).
10 Brenda Grzetic, "Between Life and Death: Women Fish Harvesters in Newfoundland and Labrador" (MA thesis in women's studies, Memorial University, St. John's, NF, 2002); Murray, Fitzpatrick, and O'Connell, "Fishermen's Blues"; Barbara Neis, "Can't Get My Breath: Occupational Asthma and Women Snow Crab Processing Workers," in *Invisible: Issues in Women's Occupational Health,* edited by K. Messing, B. Neis, and L. Dumais (Charlottetown: Gynergy, 1995), 3-28; Neis et al., "From Fishplant to Nickel Smelter."
11 Alastair O'Reilly, "Politics, Demographics and the Potential Demise of Newfoundland's Seafood Processing Industry," paper presented to "Stemming the Tide: Keeping Our Workforce Strong," St. John's, NF, 15 November 2001.
12 Rowe Consulting Economists, *Effect of the Crisis in the Newfoundland Fishery on Women Who Work in the Industry* (St. John's, NF: Women's Policy Office, Government of Newfoundland and Labrador, 1991).
13 Barbara Neis, "Female Fish Processing Workers: Occupational Health and the Fishery Crises in Newfoundland and Labrador," *Chronic Diseases in Canada* 15, 1 (1994): 12-16.
14 Susan Williams, *Our Lives Are at Stake: Women and the Fishery Crisis in Newfoundland and Labrador,* ISER Report No. 11. St. John's, NF: Institute of Social and Economic Research, Memorial University, 1996.
15 Human Resources Development Canada, *Evaluation of the Atlantic Groundfish Strategy (TAGS): TAGS/HRDC Final Evaluation Report* (Ottawa: Human Resources Development Canada, 1998), 14.

16 Ibid., 1.

17 O'Reilly, "Politics, Demographics."

18 Payne in Neis et al., "From Fishplant to Nickel Smelter: Health Determinants and the Health of Newfoundland's Women Fish and Shellfish Processors in an Environment of Restructuring" (Toronto: National Network on Environments and Women's Health, 2001), 34-5; Martha MacDonald, "Gender and Social Security Policy: Pitfalls and Possibilities," *Feminist Economics* 4, 1 (1998): 1-25; James Overton, "The Politics of Sustainability and Privatization: The Example of Newfoundland's Cod Crisis," unpublished paper, Department of Sociology, Memorial University, St. John's, NF, 1998.

19 Health Canada, *Towards a Common Understanding: Clarifying the Core Concepts of Population Health* (Ottawa: Ministry of Supply and Services, 2000); Rhonda Love, L. Jackson, R. Edwards, and A. Pederson, with the Critical Social Science and Health Group, "Gender and Its Inter-Relationship with Other Determinants of Health," paper presented to the Fifth National Health Promotion Research Conference, "From Research to Policy: Gender and Health Conference," Dalhousie University, Halifax, NS, 4-5 July 1997.

20 Newfoundland and Labrador, Department of Fisheries and Aquaculture, *The Newfoundland and Labrador Fishery: A Perspective* (St. John's, NF: Fisheries Forum 2000, 14-15 March 2000), 2.

21 Grzetic, *Women Fishes These Days* (Halifax: Fernwood Books, 2004).

22 As reported in "The Economic Review," report, Economics and Statistics Branch, Provincial Department of Finance, Government of Newfoundland and Labrador, November 2003.

23 O'Reilly, "Politics, Demographics."

24 This was not a random sample of workers and was biased, to some degree, toward women considered to have respiratory problems associated with crab processing.

25 Karen Messing, "Don't Use a Wrench to Peel Potatoes: Biological Science Constructed on Male Model Systems Is a Risk to Women Workers," in *Changing Methods: Feminists Transforming Practice,* edited by Sandra Burt and Lorraine Code (Scarborough, ON: Broadview Press, 1995), 217-63.

26 Fishery Research Group, "The Social Impact of Technological Change in Newfoundland's Deepsea Fishery," Labour Canada Technology Impact Research Fund Report, 1986; Williams and Neis, *Stress.*

27 Karen Messing, *One-Eyed Science: Occupational Health and Women Workers* (Philadelphia: Temple University Press, 1998).

28 Ibid., 13.

29 Rowe Consulting Economists, *Effect of the Crisis.*

30 Williams and Neis, *Stress.*

31 J.L. Malo, P. Chrétien, M. McCants, and S.B. Lehrer, "Detection of Snow-Crab Antigens by Air Sampling of a Snow-Crab Production Plant," *Clinical and Experimental Allergy* 27, 1 (1997): 75-78; Neis, "Can't Get My Breath"; K.A. Weytjens, A. Cartier, J.L. Malo, P. Chrétien, F. Essiembre, S.B. Lehrer et al., "Aerosolized Snow-Crab Allergens in a Processing Facility," *Allergy* 54, 8 (1999): 892-93; A. Cartier, J.L. Malo, H. Ghezzo, M. McCants, and S.B. Lehrer, "IgE Sensitization in Snow-Crab-Processing Workers," *Journal of Allergy and Clinical Immunology* 78 (1986): 344-48.

32 Canada, the Federal, Provincial, Territorial Advisory Committee on Population Health, *Toward a Healthy Future: Second Report on the Health of Canadians* (Ottawa: Ministry of Supply and Services, 1999).

33 Catherine Ross and Marieke Van Willigen, "Education and the Subjective Quality of Life," *Journal of Health and Social Behaviour* 38 (September 1997): 291.

34 Barbara Cameron, "From Equal Opportunity to Symbolic Equity: Three Decades of Federal Training Policy for Women," in *Rethinking Restructuring: Gender and Change in Canada,* edited by Isabella Bakker (Toronto: University of Toronto Press, 1996), 55-81.

35 Jane Jenson, "Part-Time Employment and Women: A Range of Strategies," in Bakker, ed., *Rethinking Restructuring,* 92-110, 92; see also Pat Connelly and Martha MacDonald, "The Labour Market, the State, and the Reorganization of Work: Policy Impacts," in Bakker, ed., *Rethinking Restructuring,* 82-91.

36 O'Reilly, "Politics, Demographics."

37 Pat Armstrong, "The Feminization of the Labour Force: Harmonizing Down in a Global Economy," in Messing, Neis, and Dumais, eds., *Invisible*, 368-92.
38 Leach and Winson, "Bringing Globalization down to Earth."
39 Connelly and MacDonald, "The Labour Market"; MacDonald, "Gender and Social Security Policy."
40 Belinda Leach, "Behind Closed Doors: Homework Policy and Lost Possibilities for Change," in Bakker, ed., *Rethinking Restructuring*, 203-16; Leach, "Transforming Rural Livelihoods."
41 Messing, "Don't Use a Wrench"; *One-Eyed Science*.
42 Mayhew, et al., "The Effects."
43 Neis et al., "From Fishplant to Nickel Smelter."
44 Thomas Dunk, Stephen McBride, and Randle Nelsen, eds., *The Training Trap: Ideology, Training, and the Labour Market* (Halifax: Fernwood, 1996).
45 Sheila M. Neysmith, "Networking across Difference," 4.

6
Working at the Margins of Forestry: The Gender of Labour Practices on British Columbia's West Coast
Maureen G. Reed

> Women are not viewed as equals. It's a man's community.
> — Interviewee on northern Vancouver Island, 1997

How do we explain women's paid work in forestry communities? Forestry communities, where loggers and mill workers toil hard and long, are built upon a celebration of masculine culture. Forestry work is frequently represented by reference to the physical labour, the hard work, the danger, and the drama associated with logging.[1] Indeed, one of the most enduring empirical characteristics of forestry towns is that gender remains a fundamental determining factor in the distribution of jobs, status, and income.[2]

Yet there is relatively little theoretical research that explains the gendered labour practices of rural places, particularly in forestry.[3] Egan and Klausen's literature review focused on gender and the restructuring of British Columbia's forest industry, noting that while some investigations used a gender-sensitive approach,[4] "the bulk of recent research ... neglects gender as a central category of analysis ... overlooks the marginalized position of women in the paid labour force and forest-sector unions and, moreover, ignores the broader issue of the sexual division of paid and unpaid labour in forest-dependent communities."[5] Reliance on Census data, combined with the lack of theoretical attention to gendered divisions of labour in resource communities, has lead to an incomplete and inaccurate assessment of the importance of forestry as an employer in forestry-dependent regions and as an employer of women and men.

In this chapter, I begin to address this research gap by focusing on women's experiences of paid work in forestry communities.[6] While forestry-town women have frequently been classified as dependent on men's income, women in fact support forestry both directly by their employment within the industry and within the governance of forestry and indirectly by their broader employment within forestry communities. With respect to forestry occupations, evidence from the 1990s suggests increasing opportunities for women based on their entry into traditional forestry occupations (e.g., as mill workers[7] or as registered professional foresters)[8] and into new forestry occupations that have opened up as a result of changing regulatory require-ments (e.g., in planning, regulation, and enforcement). Although women are still underrepresented in positions of decision-making authority in gov-ernment agencies, in companies, and in unions, they have begun to acquire informed work experiences in other kinds of forestry occupations. Thus, in contrast to academics and policy makers who continue to point to the rela-tive insignificance of women in the paid work of forestry, I argue that women have a significant role to play. Furthermore, I suggest that women have become part of, and affected by, the restructuring of the industry because of their employment both in the forest industry and in forestry communities more broadly.

I develop my discussion in two ways. First, I draw on Census data and other public information to provide an empirical description of women's forestry-related work. By doing so, I try to make visible the experiences of women in order to redress the imbalance I see in the dominant his-stories of forestry and forestry-town development on British Columbia's west coast. Second, I weave throughout the chapter three theoretical explanations of women's work: labour-segmentation theory, spatial entrapment, and social embeddedness. None of these theories in isolation explains women's work choices. However, I favour social embeddedness as an explanation for women's employment choices in forestry communities because it can in-clude a consideration of how the local culture of forestry shapes women's choices for employment, both enabling and constraining their decisions to enter paid work. I believe this is a critical element for explaining labour practices in rural places that has not been captured by other theoretical explanations.

The study I describe here took place on northern Vancouver Island be-tween 1996 and 1999. This region is described by local residents as "the North Island" and defined here by interviewees as all areas north of Woss (Figure 1). The North Island is sparsely populated and had only 15,441 resi-dents in the Mount Waddington Regional District (MWRD) in 1996.[9] Local women view the communities as isolated from the rest of the island and the province; it is approximately 235 kilometres to the nearest movie theatre and full-scale hospital in Campbell River and 500 kilometres to the province's capital city, Victoria. While mining and fishing have also been important for employment and income, forestry continues to dominate the regional economy. At the time of the research, six major forestry companies and a district office of the Ministry of Forests operated in the region. Tourism and outdoor recreation promotion are increasingly important economic gen-erators but remain small in terms of employment and income.

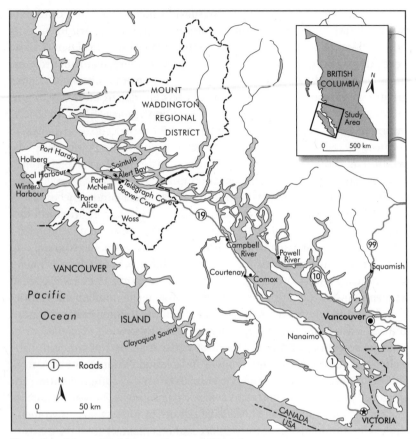

Figure 6.1   Mount Waddington Regional District

To conduct this research, I combined analysis of public policy initiatives, program documents, and Census data with feminist participatory and case-study methodologies outlined by Reinharz[10] and McDowell[11] and in particular by Gibson-Graham.[12] Women from Port Hardy (1996 population 5,470), Port McNeill (1996 population 3,014), Port Alice (1996 population 1,626), and Alert Bay (on Cormorant Island; 1996 population 697) were interviewed as well as women from the unincorporated places of Sointula (on Malcolm Island), Holberg, Winter Harbour, Coal Harbour, and Woss. Initially, thirty-two in-depth interviews were conducted by myself and my research assistants with women who had varying connections to forestry. From this group, ten women were selected to be community researchers who would discuss local issues and be trained to conduct in-depth interviews. In total, fifty interviews were completed for analysis.[13] Upon undertaking preliminary analysis, I conducted three focus groups with local women who had not been previously interviewed. The focus groups served a dual function: They provided an opportunity for me to give direct feedback to the local communities about the nature and status of the research, and they assisted directly in corroborating and refining emerging themes and social categories I had established. After conducting the focus groups, I undertook further analysis and then held a workshop with the community researchers, in which I again presented my results. The community researchers offered more suggestions for refining the analysis and for undertaking extension work in their communities.

Women as Woods Workers

It is still rare to find a woman logger on northern Vancouver Island. Nevertheless, women in this study worked in the woods as forestry technicians, scalers, front-end loaders, enforcement officers, stream-restoration workers, and camp cooks. In addition, they worked in the industry as administrative officers in the Ministry of Forests or for companies. For some women, economic transition meant new job opportunities, particularly in forestry. For example, while jobs in logging have declined, opportunities have opened up in silviculture, planning, engineering, enforcement, and administration. Women also worked as private consultants, accountants, public educators, and administrators – all related to the forest industry.

The Census interpretation is that just under 4 percent of women in the region are found in a category entitled "jobs unique to primary industries." This definition, although popular, proved to be an exceedingly narrow view of women in forestry. Women openly challenged Census definitions, arguing that many jobs conventionally classified in other ways are jobs that are directly reliant on forestry. As forestry occupations move beyond the physical work related to tree harvesting to include other forms of work, opportunities to employ women continue to diversify. Notwithstanding these observations, women's paid work has been almost invisible in forestry communities. Theoretical explanations, interpretation of empirical evidence, and ultimately, public-policy formulation about labour, training, and "economic transition" have largely omitted women's contributions.

Theoretical Exclusions

In labour-segmentation theory as advanced by Doeringer and Piore, the primary segment is characterized by "high wages, good working conditions, employment stability, chances of advancement, equity, and due process in the administration of work rules."[14] In contrast, jobs in the secondary segment tend to have "low wages and fringe benefits, poor conditions, high labour turnover, little chance of advancement, and often arbitrary and capricious supervision."[15] Workers in the secondary sector are more likely to be nonunionized and female and to belong to a visible minority. According to feminist geographers Hanson and Pratt, women's exclusions from the primary segment "build on the sexist practices of male employers and employees. Male employers may be reluctant to hire women for the most prized jobs because of gender stereotypes, worries about complaints from male employees, and their more general fears about losing male advantage ... White, male employees also have organized through unions and professional organizations to shelter jobs for themselves."[16]

According to Roger Hayter, labour-segmentation theory is an effective representation of labour-market conditions in BC's forest economy in the post–Second World War era.[17] Hayter focused on small and medium-sized enterprises at a regional or provincial level as forming the secondary segment. Yet one might also view segmentation in terms of a local labour force. In this context, the secondary segment is composed of nonunionized peripheral workers whose wage levels and employment stability are typically less structured than those in the primary sector.

Labour-market theory attempts to classify empirical observations. It may help to organize the observations, but it does not explain the structures or processes that give rise to them. As the quotation above from Hanson and Pratt illustrates, feminist geographers have developed explanations that point to unequal practices associated with hiring and retention of workers. However, feminist geographers have yet to highlight the particularities of local culture. For rural-labour theory, the culture of local places is an important element of the explanation of women's marginal location within predominant labour practices. The male-dominated nature of occupations within resource-based communities has created and elevated the importance of a working man's culture.[18] Institutional factors, local practices, and sexist attitudes form part of the culture of forestry towns, rendering less important – and, in come cases, invisible – the nature and extent of women's employment within forestry communities. In this light, the classification "primary" denotes not only occupations based on the extraction of raw materials, but also occupations that hold primary importance in the local culture and economy. In short, jobs in "primary" (extraction) industries have "primary" importance to local communities and policy makers. Women's employment within these communities is viewed as secondary or tertiary not only because it is more likely to be in manufacturing and service sectors, but also because it is seen as being of second- and third-order importance to the overall workings of the forestry community.

This rendering of women's paid work in forestry towns as "secondary" does not merely relegate women to secondary and tertiary sectors. Even women who figure within conventional counts of forestry-related occupations are subject to limitations and erasure. Women employed in forestry jobs discussed restrictions in hiring and promotion practices and the lack of recognition for the contributions they made directly to the industry. These observations will be discussed later in the chapter. The bias that focuses all attention on male wage earners is part of the local culture of these places. This bias is also evident in databases and academic work that might otherwise provide accurate empirical descriptions of employment. In combination, these sources shape policy debates and public programs that are proposed during times of economic and social transition.

Empirical Exclusions: Counting Women "in" Forestry

Reliable, valid, current, complete, and commensurable data on gender and employment in forestry are not readily available from government agencies or private companies. Company records typically do not distinguish between women in nontraditional jobs (e.g., planers) and those employed in traditional jobs (e.g., secretaries) within the firm. Employment counts by resource sector, location, and gender in combination are not routinely made available by either Statistics Canada, other government agencies, researchers, or even industrial employers. In a special tabulation of the 1991 Census, approximately 10 percent of the provincial workforce in logging industries comprised women, and 28 percent of jobs were related to forest services.[19] These numbers are higher than those of academic studies, but they are still derived from an unnecessarily narrow definition of forestry employment, thereby underestimating the number of women who work in forestry occupations. For example, the workers in forest services counted by the Census do not include those with jobs in management, information, or administrative services.

These "other" positions are likely significant for both the number of women they employ and the quality of the jobs they provide. For example, the Ministry of Forests' district office in Port McNeill had a workforce of eighty-nine in 1997, thirty of whom were women. Sixteen of eighteen administrative jobs were held by women, while eleven of fifty-three people with occupations as technicians, foresters, and planners were women.[20] None of these jobs were classified as forestry jobs by the Census.

Academic work reinforces and is shaped by biases in the availability of data. Empirical studies that use standard Census categories continue to report the very limited participation of women in forestry occupations.[21] Other studies about work in forestry towns focus on worker mobility[22] and displacement.[23] Like other studies in the forest industry, these research efforts tend to favour consideration of men's employment. Some researchers have attempted to address this bias by undertaking employment counts within specific firms,[24] but these data, collected for other purposes, are incomplete from a regional perspective.

In one study, Eric Grass and Roger Hayter collected data from a random sample of sixty-three plants during 1981 and 1985 to determine the employment characteristics of workers in those plants who experienced layoffs during a widespread recession in the industry.[25] They noted that with the exception of women middle managers (who were few in number), women lost their jobs more rapidly than men. This was particularly evident in clerical and production jobs. Yet their data also revealed that women occupied only 3 to 4 percent of industry jobs, including jobs in administration, trades, and production work. Women comprised more than 50 percent of the clerical workforce. While their analysis revealed a higher vulnerability of women workers to job loss, for the purposes of this study, their data do not provide a very complete picture of women's paid work in forestry for at least two reasons. First, the data are now quite dated. Second, by the authors' own admission, the study omitted employment in other sectors of the industry, most notably in head offices of firms, in woods work (e.g., loggers, camp cooks), in research and development, and in regulatory and planning positions with the Ministry of Forests. All of these sites are important components of the industry and increasingly important places of paid employment for women. Given the limitations of the existing research, it is not surprising that policy debates reflect and reinforce the same biases.

Policy Debates

In policy debates, forestry is considered a primary industry in terms of its reliance on the extraction of "natural resources"[26] and its economic importance to both local communities and the provincial economy. For example, while forestry employs only 5 percent of the province's total workforce,[27] the forest sector accounted for more than half the value of all manufacturing shipments in the province in 1993.[28] Individual rural communities across the province still rely heavily on forestry to anchor their economies.[29] Clearly, forestry remains a large social and economic element of rural BC.

During times of economic transition, there is a distinct policy preference for protecting only those jobs that directly depend on forestry. Government programs have focused on retention, retraining, or retirement packages aimed at the male wage earner in forestry occupations – specifically woods workers and those employed in sawmills and pulp and paper mills. For example, the Commission on Resources and Environment (CORE) was established in BC in the 1990s to determine a land use strategy. In 1994 CORE made recommendations for new land allocations on Vancouver Island. In its final report, CORE predicted that at least as many jobs in secondary and tertiary sectors would be lost as in the primary sector, yet it made no recommendations to support these second- and third-order workers. Instead, new governmental programs were put in place for those who qualified for (un)employment insurance.[30] Most of these programs targeted male workers. In contrast, CORE provided a brief catalogue of employment prospects and social impacts affecting women, suggesting that the information it presented about women might be useful in designing "social services support to better respond to the needs and roles of women in communities affected during economic change."[31] The information provided to CORE did not form part of its recommended transition strategy, nor did it signal the need for specific policies or programs to address the impacts of job loss. Indeed, social-service provisions were reduced, restructured, and regionalized at the same time as forestry was experiencing employment losses.

To summarize, women's work has been largely "invisible" to researchers, to policy practitioners, and to residents themselves because it intersects less obviously with male employment. Women's employment (whether on the "main stage" of forestry jobs or in "supporting roles") is viewed as secondary, both in terms of its relation to the primary industry and in terms of its importance to the overall workings of the community. In the following section, I turn to women's overall employment status on northern Vancouver Island before examining their employment experiences within forestry more specifically.

Gender at Work on the North Island

Employment is key to living on northern Vancouver Island. In 1996, 85 percent of all income was derived from employment, as opposed to 70 percent for the province as a whole. These levels rise to 92 percent for Port Alice, where the pulp mill is the major employer, and to 88 percent in Port McNeill, where private forest companies and the Ministry of Forests have regional offices. Less than 3 percent of all income in the region came from pensions, as opposed to almost 25 percent for the province as a whole. These data indicate that as people attain retirement age, they leave the region – possibly for better medical and social services and perhaps also to escape the isolation. This is also illustrated by a demographic structure in which only 8 percent of the population is sixty-five or older, compared to 23 percent of the population of the province. Using Census data, the BC Ministry of Finance calculated that 51 percent of after-tax income in 1996 came from forestry in the region. This number was even higher for particular communities. For example, in Port McNeill 58 percent of employment incomes were derived from forestry, and in Port Alice 84 percent.[32]

Labour-force participation, occupational status, and wages provide an initial indication of the gendered dimensions of paid work in the study region. Both women and men living in the region participated in the workforce at rates about 10 percent higher than those for their counterparts across the province (Table 6.1). These data were surprising, contradicting the long-held stereotype that women in forestry towns are less likely to be employed in the paid workforce.[33] However, these data supported another important dimension of women's paid work in forestry towns: It is hard to get a well-paid, full-time job, and the impact of this reality on women's income is severe.

Table 6.1

BC and Mount Waddington Regional District (MWRD): Male/female participation in industries, 1996

	BC				MWRD			
	Total		Male	Female	Total		Male	Female
Industry type	(No.)	(%)	(%)	(%)	(No.)	(%)	(%)	(%)
Management occupations	60,200	1.9	2.1	1.9	565	6.9	7.5	6.0
Business, finance, administration	230,600	7.4	7.0	1.5	985	12.0	1.9	25.6
Natural and applied sciences	106,200	3.4	4.0	3.0	470	5.7	8.4	2.1
Health occupations	183,400	5.9	2.3	10.2	195	2.4	1.0	4.3
Social science, education, government, service, religion	117,600	3.8	2.8	5.1	505	6.1	2.9	10.6
Art, culture, recreation, sport	84,800	2.7	2.9	2.8	125	1.5	1.1	2.1
Sales and services	1,645,800	52.9	49.7	59.9	1,840	22.4	11.5	37.0
Trades, transport and equipment operators	393,400	12.6	14.8	11.8	1,620	19.7	31.4	3.9
Occupations unique to primary industries	84,800	2.7	4.2	1.3	1,310	15.9	25.0	3.7
Processing, manufacturing, utilities	205,800	6.6	10.2	3.2	605	7.4	9.5	4.4
Experienced labour force (in numbers)	3,112,600				8,220			
Male	1,557,900				4,725			
Female	1,454,800				3,500			
%	N/A	100	100	100	N/A	100	100	100

Note: Proportions may not add up to 100 due to rounding.
Source: Statistics Canada, 1999, 24 and 474-75.

As shown in Table 6.1, women dominated in sales and services as well as in business and financial occupations while men were overwhelmingly slotted into trades and occupations unique to primary industries. Women were more than three times more likely than men to enter service occupations, while men were more than six times more likely than women to be found in primary industries. One result of this job segregation is a large differential in wages. In 1996 the average earnings of women in the region were the equivalent of 87 percent of women's average incomes for the province as a whole. Those earnings represented 54 percent of men's average incomes across the province. Table 6.2 reveals that men in the region earned 23 percent more than their provincial counterparts. Women were not so lucky. Women's income in the region was only 48 percent of men's. Part-time income is important both for women generally and for men in forestry occupations. Women on the North Island are more likely than women elsewhere or men generally to work part time, with the wage differential most marked in this classification. Women's part-time incomes for both BC and the region were virtually the same and represented 66 percent of men's part-time incomes for the province as a whole. However, in the Mount Waddington Regional District, women's part-time incomes were the equivalent of only 46 percent of men's part-time incomes. These "factual" data illustrate a strong divide between women and men. As the next section illustrates, the women involved in paid work also document these differences in a more personal way.

Table 6.2

Mount Waddington Regional District (MWRD): Income levels for males and females, fifteen years and older, 1996

Employment type	MWRD Income			BC Income		
	All persons	Male	Female	All persons	Male	Female
Full-year, full-time:						
Average income[a]	41,589	48,439	28,758	39,414	44,784	31,218
Part-year or part-time:						
Average income[b]	22,370	30,207	13,912	17,379	21,071	14,034
Average income[c]	29,161	37,702	18,077	27,480	33,366	20,722

a Full-time work of thirty hours or more per week in 1995, as reported in 1996.
b A part-time job for part of the year or a full-time job for another part of the year.
c Total incomes during the1995 calendar year from wages and salaries (before deductions), net incomes from unincorporated businesses, professional fees, and net farm self-employment incomes, as reported in 1996.
Source: Statistics Canada, 1999, 28 and 478-79.

Fitting into the Local Employment Structure

The [forest] industry is why we're here. Like you've seen, you've gone to one-horse towns and when the company leaves it, people are upset, but eventually the town dies unless something else comes in to replace it. Now this is not entirely a one-horse town, but it comes pretty close.

This community, this area [is] male oriented – forestry, fisheries – it's really hard to get in, even if you are smart. I think it's even harder if you're Native.

The quotations above were taken from different women who were employed at the time of the research. Despite holding paid jobs, women were virtually unanimous in describing the limitations placed on them in both finding and retaining work. Only two of the fifty women interviewed refused to acknowledge specific barriers for women in seeking and retaining employment. For all the others, the towns were not simply one-horse towns; they were also uniform in terms of gendered opportunities for paid employment. Women's attempts to attain paid work and to be valued within paid occupations were constrained by practical limitations of opportunity, such as infrastructure and services that might support their employment. Importantly, however, the culture of forestry reinforced women's employment as secondary to the primary goal of timber production. This culture had multiple effects on the women who lived there.

Women believed that employment opportunities for women were in extremely short supply or simply did not exist. In the smaller communities such as Holberg, Woss, Port Alice, and Winter Harbour, women again and again stated that they simply wanted jobs, any jobs at all. They perceived that their options were severely restricted compared to those available in "larger" centres such as Port Hardy and Port McNeill. Yet, even there, jobs for women were scarce, and most paid the provincial minimum wage of $7.50 per hour.

There is a lot of challenge here because, number one, there's not the jobs ... Women in Port McNeill do not have the opportunity to get a job, number one; it's really a battle for a woman to get a job. And it doesn't matter, any kind of job. I mean, like, in Vancouver they might think waitressing is a low-paid, bottom of the line job, where in Port McNeill you're darn happy to get it.

Women in this study argued that forestry directly affected the wage prospects for women. One woman who was holding down four part-time jobs was asked why. In her words:

Why do I have that many jobs? Because a woman in this area cannot get a one full-time, forty-hour-a-week job that pays properly to support a family ... Women are still making seven-fifty an hour. I can't get full-time work in town *because it's a logging industry town* and a fishing industry town. There's not that many jobs to go round for women. If you're not self-employed, it's very likely you'll just continue to make seven-fifty an hour. (Emphasis added.)

While it could be argued that these low-paying jobs were available to both men and women, interviewees suggested that there was a pervasive perception among employers that women, particularly married women, do not require the same salary or benefits that men enjoy. One woman who was self-employed at the time of the interview had previously worked for many years in a position within the local public service. She had been part of several hiring procedures. She explained sex-typing like this:

The minute a man applies for a job, the [employer] thinks, oh, this is a person who has to look after a family. They don't consider that a woman looks after a family until she's a single mother, then they'll look after that, and consider that that's different, and they'll pay her more money than they would a married woman.

Women who participated in focus groups confirmed that women who held positions that were not protected by union contracts frequently got paid "as little as possible." Consequently, for women living in two-adult households, labour-market participation may depend on a process of social negotiation about their home and outside work obligations not solely with their partners and families, but also with their prospective employers.[34]

The spatial entrapment of women who try to juggle domestic and paid-work responsibilities is also evident in forestry communities. The spatial-entrapment thesis was first promoted by feminist geographers almost two decades ago with reference to urban labour markets.[35] It linked the empirical observation that white, middle-class women had smaller labour-market areas than men because they preferred shorter journeys to work so that they could fulfill their domestic responsibilities. Their employment opportunities were accordingly more limited. Rural and urban women who seek paid employment share similar problems, including a lack of affordable, convenient, and safe childcare, an inadequate public-transportation infrastructure, and limited training opportunities. Women in the paid workforce require supportive partners and/or other family or social networks to assist in meeting the multiple demands of home and paid work.

In small forestry towns, these requirements are often more challenging than in urban localities. For example, there was no institutional group daycare located on northern Vancouver Island. There were only a few "family daycare" operations and many informal arrangements made between family and friends. For those doing shiftwork outside of a nine-to-five schedule, daycare was a major and ongoing source of frustration and anxiety. One woman described her experiences in this way:

> For me, who works shiftwork, there's been times I've had to have a baby-sitter until midnight, and I'm at work from four-thirty or four o'clock on, sometimes from twelve o'clock ... trying to find people that would stay there until midnight ... it's hard for single parents ... but, for the most part, childcare, for me, is a big concern.

This is made more acute by the lack of extended family living in forestry communities who might otherwise be able to provide informal childcare services. Provincial legislation passed during the study period required that childcare providers over the age of sixteen be paid minimum wage. This new law meant that for women slotted into low-paid employment who did not have additional family members to assist them, paid childcare was impractical financially. For many women, particularly those with children, the lack of a basic social infrastructure and/or family networks limited their possibilities for work and discouraged them from seeking paid employment, especially since the monetary rewards were minimal.

Transportation to and from work sites was also a significant barrier for some women. From an urban perspective, several communities are located within commuting range. For example, Port Alice, Sointula, Port McNeill, Port Hardy, and Coal Harbour are all within fifty-five kilometres of each other. However, the roads that connect these places are not urban highways and are not linked by regular public transit. Some roads are active logging roads, and some are paved while others are not. Many of the roads were considered by women to be treacherous, particularly during winter, when days are short, roads may be covered in snow or ice, and logging trucks may continue to roam. Many women refused to drive regularly under these conditions, and those who did described their commute like this:

> It's a long drive over here. I drive it every day. It's forty-five minutes, and in the winter it takes often twice as long. And it's not fun to drive a twisty mountain road at thirty kilometres an hour when you're afraid of sliding into a four-hundred-foot chasm.

A lack of education was another hurdle women saw to their employment prospects. Women, both in the workforce and those wanting paid employment, saw themselves as undereducated. Local institutions for further education provided uneven availability of educational programs for women living across the scattered communities of the North Island. However, in the vicious circle of limited infrastructure, simply acquiring "more skills" does not necessarily lead to more opportunities.

In order to get a higher-paid job in this town, of course, you have to further educate yourself, and that wasn't possible here, until the last few years ... Since then I have further educated myself to the point where, now that I'm educated, and I have five years into my accounting, I can't get a job because the town doesn't service that. It doesn't have the population mass that you need for these jobs that are going around, that you want to be able to survive on. There's one accounting office, two accounting offices, and it employs two people ... and every year, [North Island College] puts on this course for office training ... Do you know how many people, how many women take that course every year? At least twelve. So every three years twelve people are coming out of there with these qualifications, with no jobs, because there's none here for that ... So they're being educated for jobs that aren't here. It's stupid. It's a waste of money.

One woman who was dissatisfied with her current occupation in forestry considered how several of these issues constrained her mobility in searching out alternative employment. She identified the barriers in these words:

The fact that I'm female. The fact that I'm undereducated. The fact that I have four children. I'm not free to move around ... I'm the only, sole support of my children, too. So it's not just a matter of taking a few months off ... I can't afford that luxury. Economically, I can't afford to indulge myself. I have to be very careful in what I decide to do. I don't have a lot of skills. I have marketing skills, sales skills, but I don't have the background that companies would want.

Family considerations are rooted in geographical communities because they influence the training options that may be deemed acceptable. Even (or perhaps especially) for families that have separated, women's "choices" about training and employment may be confined to those opportunities that support family unity. In other words:

Let's put it this way. Families have split up. The women go on welfare, and then they're encouraged to retrain, and then they basically leave the community because the only [way] they can get retraining is to attend North Island College full time in Port Hardy or Port McNeill or down island or somewhere, and then they don't have the family support, and then the fathers lose contact with their children, and it puts tremendous pressure on the families to have the women have to leave. I've seen that happen over and over. Also, in small communities, especially one-industry towns, they only employ males in the jobs that can support a family ... There's very few jobs for women, then that means that women leave to find jobs ... And it's hard. It's hard on the families. And it's not fair to the kids.

These challenges are ideological as well as practical. Power relations within the household influence decisions concerning employment. These are particularly significant when considering the effect of financial control within the household on the employment participation of women. In a reversal of the "traditional stereotype" that places women in the home, one woman described how she felt compelled to contribute to her partner's desire to lead the high life despite her own wishes to scale down their consumption and allow herself more time to pursue personal interests. In her words:

My husband decided he wanted to build this great big beautiful forty-six-hundred-square-foot home. And I said, I don't want a home that big, you know. We [family of four] were living in nine hundred square feet. That was just adequate, you know. I could do anything. I didn't have to work anymore. And I started going back to school then. Now all of sudden we had this great big home that I have to maintain because he has chosen to build this big home. He has chosen to own a big boat. He has chosen to own a big truck. He has chosen this lifestyle, and I have kind of fit into it, and I'm part of his way of paying for it. And I'm quite angry about it ... but in order to do that, I think he had this concept in the back of his mind, well, he has one job. He makes thirty bucks an hour. I can go out and find the same thing. But it doesn't happen that way, sweetie. I have to have five jobs to accommodate the lifestyle that he has chosen for us. But I've allowed him to do that ... I was angry. I'm still angry about it. But I allowed him to do it. I just allowed him to do it to me. I did ... It's my own fault. I have created this mess.

In this case, his much larger contribution to the household income allowed him to make decisions about the lifestyle they would lead. However, his income was not quite sufficient to provide all the components. Thus the interviewee felt compelled to "go to work" against her wishes, working several low-paying, part-time jobs to meet the demands of her partner and, increasingly, her children as well. In the end, she blamed her predicament on her own inability to assert herself.

For women in forestry communities, logistical and ideological factors often combine to create conflict about paid employment and domestic duties. The limited availability of childcare, for example, reinforces the attitude that women "should be" in the home. However, as some women in this study suggested, they chose not to risk affecting the "manliness" of their partner by taking a job. In the smallest and/or least diversified localities (e.g., Port Alice, Holberg), where a forestry company may account for more than 80 percent of paid jobs, company policies sometimes preclude the employment of more than one member of the family. Men, therefore, whose jobs almost invariably accounted for the larger economic benefit, are more likely to come first. This bias was sometimes acknowledged by women residents themselves. As one woman explained, "I understand why the logging companies aren't hiring women over the men, for the simple fact that they don't have enough jobs for the men, let alone the women."

Last, it should be noted that for some women, disengagement from paid employment was a deliberate and desirable choice. For example, some women valued the opportunity to stay at home and engage in the full-time "reproductive" work of maintaining the household and raising children. This perspective was adopted by a small group of the women interviewed. Perhaps surprisingly, this decision did not always correlate with women's educational or previous employment status. For example, one woman who was university-educated and had several years of work experience as a professional forester decided not to return to her previous job once her second child was born. She explained her decision in this way:

> I'm lucky. I have an option in a small community. I think you'll find most of the women in the Lower Mainland [in which Vancouver is located] don't have the option I have to stay [at home], you know ... I'm lucky that ... my husband is in the forest industry. And I think you'll find that there's a lot more women that stay home in the smaller communities.

Here, we see how elements of forestry culture not only *constrain* women in the home but also in some cases, *contain* women by *allowing* them, both practically and ideologically, to remain in the home. Where families are supported by the higher wages of forestry, women may find opportunities for well-paid employment limited and limiting; however, they may also find that the decision to stay at home to raise a family is a choice that is validated and affirmed. These choices form part of the very definition of forestry communities located on Vancouver Island. Notwithstanding practical and local cultural constraints to paid work, women did undertake work within the industry. Their stories illustrate their marginal position within the forestry workforce as well.

Working at the Margins of Forestry

At the time of my research, forty-three of the fifty women interviewed were in the paid workforce, sixteen of these in forestry occupations. Thirty-three of the fifty women (including eight of the sixteen forestry employees) were in relationships with men in forestry.[36] Of the thirteen women who participated in focus groups, eight were employed, four in forestry occupations. In addition, of the cohort of fifty women, many had been previously employed in the forest industry.

Women's marginality in jobs within the forest industry was a dominant theme for most women in this study. For those working in unionized jobs, salaries were standardized along the scale for training, work experience, and seniority. Women reported being able to earn additional income through overtime. However, sexist practices within the union and within the jobs were subtle. They related to women being (in)visible for new training and promotion opportunities, having to prove over and over again that they were capable of undertaking new tasks, and simply being heard in union meetings. Those women working in nonunionized positions believed that hiring, wage setting, and promotion practices were extremely irregular. Women in all job classifications experienced sexism within their daily work lives.

Table 6.3 illustrates five forms of sexism identified by women working in forestry. This situation was pervasive partly because of the strong link between forestry occupations and masculine identities.[37] These masculine identities, in part, have been built on the notion that forestry jobs, from logging to manufacturing, require hard, dangerous, physical work that often entails long hours and adherence to the rough-and-tumble ethos found in logging camps. Women who attempt to enter nontraditional occupations in forestry challenge this gender ideology directly. Some whom I interviewed did so without success. One woman was told during a job interview that she wouldn't be hired as a logger because she couldn't handle the language. She viewed this excuse as a metaphor for other activities that might be expected during work in the woods and the logging camps. Another woman who was a professional forester and seeking an engineering position to match her training said, "[The company] wouldn't hire me and I'm pretty sure it's because I was female. And they've hired less, people with less experience than I had, that couldn't even read a compass. You know, so it was kind of upsetting to find that they'd do that and not hire me."

Table 6.3

Forms of sexism expressed by women in forestry occupations

Form of sexism	Quotation	Job classification
Stereotyping	There's a tendency for a lot of the guys that may not really know you, especially if they're new, to call you the secretary. You know, if you're a woman, and you work, then you must be the secretary.	Accountant in a private company

►

◄   *Table 6.3*

Form of sexism	Quotation	Job classification
	There was a lot of camp work, a lot of guys. They wouldn't allow me to go into that situation. They had problems with a female sleeping out there, so they figured all females are the same. So I was sort of stuck ... in silviculture.	Registered professional forester
Limited promotion	I haven't heard of anyone from up here [scaling] ever being promoted to any position like [quality control].	Scaler
Not being taken seriously	Basically, you don't get anything unless you bang on your hands and feet. They won't give you a promotion or a raise because you're doing such a great job or you've exceeded their expectations. The only way you'll get a raise is by begging or threatening to leave.	Registered professional forester
	I swear, if I was six-foot-four, had a big hairy chest, I probably could be a lot more persuasive, but as a woman it's really hard because they look at you as not serious.	Scaler
Underestimating	Even when I first applied for the job, even though I'd worked with the guys for twenty years ... They still have this closed mentality that they don't really want a woman in that position, you know? And I really had to prove myself, that I could do the job. And that I could learn. And that I could take the risks, and that I could do it.	Front-end loader
Lack of networks	Men are perceived as being more competent in a lot of cases. And there's a lot of mentorship that goes along with men. Like men will promote men under the buddy system, but they won't do the same for women necessarily. Like men have an edge. I'm not saying that women can't get where they want to go to, but it's usually they have to work harder, be smarter, and they have to be lucky.	Scaler

The other types of woods work for which women were hired on the North Island included cone picking and log scaling and grading. Scalers are responsible for assessing the volume of timber and the quality of wood that is derived from each tree brought to the sorting area. Although women did not have to climb hill slopes, some found that their bodies became worn out over time, as explained below:

> When I worked in that industry, after nine, ten years, you know, I got really bored because it's a treadmill job. You're doing the same thing hour after hour. The hours are long. You know, here I work seven and a half hours a day. In that industry I was working ten hours a day. And that's sort of a regular shift. And it's physical work. So you're walking eight miles a day. You're up on the logs jumping all the time. By the time I hit forty-five, I kept thinking, is this all there is? ... There's no opportunity to go anywhere else with this. I'm just going to be doing this until I'm sixty-five, another twenty years of treadmill. You know. It was good money, but I was just very bored. So when my physical body started to break down, that was my excuse to get out.

As documented earlier in the chapter, the numbers of women in professional forestry are increasing slowly across the province.[38] When the Forest Practices Code was first introduced, demand for registered professional foresters in both government and private industry increased. Unable to meet demand locally, companies and government sought qualified students enrolled in forestry programs across the province. One woman said:

> [In Ontario] I competed in woodsmen's and lumberjack competition[s] all through university, and I came second out of fifty. I came out here and it's, "Oh my God, don't touch that, oh you might hurt yourself," so that is quite different. So it's harder for me, like even though when I graduated, I wanted sort of to be an engineer, like [in] logging, I couldn't get a job ... I had interviews where they wouldn't, basically, it's because there was a lot of camp work, a lot of guys. They wouldn't allow me to go into that situation. They had problems with a female sleeping out there, so they figured all females are the same. So I was sort of stuck into being something in silviculture.

In the manufacturing jobs, the challenges were similar. Another woman described them in this way:

> The pulp mill doesn't hire women into the general population. The pulp mill hires women for clerical positions or cleaning positions, but the wider progression through the pulp mill is through the finishing room, where

you have these great bales of, rolls of pulp that you're heaving around, and you have to be of a certain physical build to handle the job, and that excludes women ... There's lots of jobs in there women could do, but they don't hire them. So, ah. I understand that somebody's brought a suit before the Labour Relations Board or something, they've taken it to the next level, but in the past it's been you don't fight it because if you scream about not getting your job in there, then that jeopardizes your husband's position.[39]

Women applying to work for the provincial government in the Ministry of Forests reported the lowest incidence of overt sexism. Union contracts, clear job classifications, regular work hours (including flexible time), and an administration that provided logistical and moral support for women employees had established conditions that were favourable to women's employment. For women in office jobs, the salaries paid by the ministry were comparable to or better than administrative positions in private companies. However, the ministry did not match the salary possibilities provided in private companies for unionized or professional workers.

Nevertheless, new administrative positions created openings for women. Ministry positions increased jobs in compliance and enforcement. Existing jobs became more complex, and women moved from clerical positions to more administrative and regulatory ones requiring more advanced computing skills, regulatory knowledge, and "customer" service. The ministry itself provided training for its employees. In part, this training was provided to women as part of general provisions to keep staff abreast of new regulations and to ensure that the local workforce met changing regulatory needs. In part, the promotion of women through the administrative ranks was due to the forward thinking of the manager of corporate services at the district office. She worked very hard to ensure that women were able to improve their job skills as changes took place in the regulation of forestry and as new demands were subsequently made of ministry personnel. One woman who began doing data entry and secretarial work explained her experience:

So [my job has] expanded and just grown, and now I'm being trained again. We're getting a lot into the Forest Practices Code for contravention with the companies whoever they are. And that has opened a whole new area where I have to sit in on the hearings, do the minutes, prepare the packages. I'm now going down to learn this tracking system so that I can come back as a trainer to the district and train all the technical staff.

Consequently, for some women, changes in government regulation opened opportunities for employment not only in terms of numbers of positions, but also in terms of chances for enrichment and advancement.

But the most pervasive and formidable challenges were ideological. It appears that old attitudes about women's (in)abilities die hard. Women from all occupational groups expressed their frustration with the constant and consistent belief that they were inadequately suited to work in forestry. This affected the perceptions men had of women's duties while on the job (e.g., only female professional foresters were required to make the coffee and clean up after meetings), the opportunities for promotion (women were passed over), and ultimately, the size of the pay cheques they brought home each month. Once in jobs, women believed that the need to prove themselves was constant. Women who had been employed for more than twenty years still believed they had to prove their worth; women who had been employed for only two years believed they would never be able to do so. Instead, many women stated that recognition of their abilities on the job would require a new generation of managers to replace the "dinosaurs" who were currently in positions of prestige and power. Prospects for improvement appear bleak in the near future at least. Women believed that sexism was endemic, pervasive, and enduring.

Women who moved into positions considered to be male jobs have met with considerable resistance both from management and from male workers. Women identified sexism at the worksite, at union meetings, from their coworkers, and from management. Female jobs still dominate in secretarial and administrative positions,[40] which are the lowest-paid work. Data for 2002 from the records of the Association of BC Professional Foresters reveal that only 22 percent of women registered as foresters work in the industry, in contrast to 36 percent of male registrants. Of women foresters, slightly more women are obtaining jobs in government, consulting, and academia, although, based on current numbers, this observation is tenuous. Women are also underrepresented in leadership roles in unions and other decision-making bodies. Indeed, in 1995 only 4 percent of the International Woodworkers of America (IWA) – the dominant union representing loggers – was composed of women, while about 8 percent of the Pulp and Paper Workers Union was composed of women.[41]

Changes in the structure of forestry will affect women as well as men, both as workers and as residents of forestry communities. Both face uncertain futures. Evidence from restructuring in other rural contexts suggests that experiences of restructuring for women and men are quite different. Women's re-employment prospects are more tenuous, and they are more likely to take a larger drop in income on a sustained basis after job loss.[42] Some of these findings were evident when the Commission on Resources and Environment developed its recommendations; however, the final report contained no recommendations that would address differential circumstances faced by male and female workers.[43]

Conclusion

The most intensive periods of macroeconomic and social restructuring in forestry began in the 1970s and 1980s. For example, economic restructuring of the industry occurred in the late 1970s and early 1980s,[44] reorganization of the welfare state began in the 1980s, and restructuring of forest policy began in BC in the early 1990s. Yet the concomitant *social* restructuring of the attendant forestry culture has only now become a reality. Located within generational social networks and historical practices, social reorganization of forestry communities will be a long-term enterprise. While government policies attempt to "soften the blow" through job training and transition measures that may provide short-term relief, the alteration to the foundation and culture of forestry will be profound and long-standing, requiring a shift that may take generations to be absorbed. While economic aspects of forestry work can be addressed in the short term, the social and cultural dimensions of changes in the paid work of forestry will take much longer to overcome. Women who support conventional forestry through their labour practices are embedded within social relations of production in the workplace, family dynamics at home, and cultural or socialized expectations within their broader communities.

Women's relationship to paid work is contradictory. For forestry communities on northern Vancouver Island, the incomes of women and men illustrate greater polarization than that found in the "national average" across Canada. Women and men have played different roles in the economic relations of forestry communities, so waged work has taken on different meanings for men and women. Women recognized how paid work for men reinforced men's contribution to forestry communities and to the masculine identity that pervades forestry communities. In their paid work, men learned the value of hard work and hard play, the rewards of physical work in the bush, and how to deal with occupational hazards. They were rewarded with high incomes and a promise of "the good life." Women, in large part, also became part of these community ideals. In their support of forestry jobs, they were part of the struggle to maintain the family wage. They had a clear understanding of the culture of forestry work, which is associated with characteristics such as danger and physical strength. However, in their own paid employment, women have become marginalized both within the industry and within the community at large. Thus women's identity is marked by marginality. Women are placed at the edge of forestry culture despite their central importance in maintaining its foundations.

Women's paid work in forestry communities is part of a complex network of household and regional economies, social restructuring of communities, and local cultural identity that determines women's choices and experiences of paid work. My own research revealed that local cultural practices embedded within the notion of a "forestry community" may also be important in understanding how and why women adopt particular employment strategies. Labour-segmentation theory provides some explanation of the macroeconomic conditions but does not develop an understanding of the social relations (household and region) of work. Feminist scholars have tried to fill these gaps by describing these social relations and by posing an alternative theory of spatial entrapment. This theory illustrates how household social relations and the provision of services locally (e.g., transportation, childcare) affect employment choices for women. But spatial entrapment does not provide any observations about cultural identity. Economic, social, and cultural practices and meanings in forestry communities place women's paid work in a marginal position in relation to the paid work of men. As a result of gendered divisions of labour within forestry communities and because of local cultural norms, women's direct attachment to the industry is a contradictory one: Women want in, but they are simultaneously repelled by structural and patriarchal norms within the industry and within the communities. Consequently, their support of the labour process is partial. Most women interviewed were quite open about the sexism they encountered in their everyday lives at their places of work. Nonetheless, they shared interests in, and support for, forestry.

My use of "social embeddedness" is consistent with that of other feminist scholars (including geographers and sociologists) who have explained women's employment choices and circumstances within their broader social and geographical contexts.[45] Like other elements of social life, paid employment illustrates how women's experiences are embedded in multiple layerings of "community" and in concrete, ongoing systems of social relations that link economic and noneconomic goals.[46] Within a framework of social embeddedness, workplace, family, and community dynamics can be considered important elements in an analysis of paid work in forestry communities. Future research and policy must tackle the multiple ways in which these elements intersect, offering employment options that allow for a progressive balance among workplace, family, and community needs while eschewing those elements of local culture that do not serve women or men particularly well.

Acknowledgments

This chapter is adapted from Chapter 4 of Maureen Reed, *Taking Stands: Gender and the Sustainability of Rural Communities* (Vancouver: UBC Press, 2003).

Notes

1 For a lovely example in poetry, see P. Trower, *Chainsaws in the Cathedral: Collected Woods Poems, 1964-1998* (Victoria, BC: Ekstasis Editions Canada, 1999).
2 B. Egan and S. Klausen, "Female in a Forest Town: The Marginalization of Women in Port Alberni's Economy," *BC Studies* 118 (1998): 5-40.

3 See G. Halseth, "We Came for the Work: Situating Employment Migration in BC's Small, Resource-Based Communities," *Canadian Geographer* 43 (1999): 363-81; C. Sachs, *Gendered Fields: Rural Women, Agriculture and Environment* (Boulder, CO: Westview Press, 1996); J. Little, *Gender and Rural Geography: Identity, Sexuality and Power in the Countryside* (Harlow, Essex: Pearson, 2002).

4 Egan and Klausen cite the following as examples of a gender-sensitive approach: S. Mackenzie, "Neglected Spaces in Peripheral Places: Homeworkers and the Creation of a New Economic Center," *Cahiers de Geographie du Quebec* 31, 83 (1987): 247-60; E. Grass, "Employment Changes during Recession: The Case of the British Columbia Forest Products Manufacturing Industries" (MA thesis, Simon Fraser University, 1987); E. Grass and R. Hayter, "Employment Change during Recession: The Experience of Forest Product Manufacturing Plants in British Columbia, 1981-1985," *Canadian Geographer* 33, 3 (1989): 240-52; M. Stanton, "Social and Economic Restructuring in the Forest Products Industry: A Case Study of Chemainus" (MA thesis, University of British Columbia, 1989); R. Hayter and T.J. Barnes, "Labour Market Segmentation, Flexibility, and Recession: A British Columbian Case Study," *Environment and Planning* 10 (1992): 333-53; E. Hay, "Recession and Restructuring in Port Alberni: Corporate, Community and Household Coping Strategies" (MA thesis, Simon Fraser University, 1993).

5 Egan and Klausen, "Female in a Forest Town." The authors cite the following as examples of neglecting gender: K. Drushka, *Stumped: The Forest Industry in Transition* (Vancouver: Douglas and McIntyre, 1985); N. Ettlinger, "Worker Displacement and Corporate Restructuring: A Policy-Conscious Appraisal," *Economic Geography* 66, 1 (1990): 67-82; T.J. Barnes and R. Hayter, eds., *Troubles in the Rainforest: British Columbia's Forest Economy in Transition,* Canadian Western Geographical Series No. 33 (Victoria, BC: Western Geographical Press, 1994); R. Hayter and T.J. Barnes, "The Restructuring of British Columbia's Coastal Forest Sector: Flexibility Perspectives," in Barnes and Hayter, eds., *Troubles in the Rainforest,* 181-202.

6 Unpaid work is also an important contribution of women and men in forestry communities. Contributions of women in unpaid work in forestry communities is specifically addressed in Sachs, *Gendered Fields;* Maureen G. Reed, "Taking Stands: A Feminist Perspective on 'Other' Women's Activism in Forestry Communities of Northern Vancouver Island," *Gender, Place and Culture* 7, 4 (2000): 363-87; and Maureen G. Reed, *Taking Stands: Gender and the Sustainability of Rural Communities* (Vancouver: UBC Press, 2003).

7 V. Preston, D. Rose, G. Norcliffe, and J. Holmes, "Shifts and the Division of Labour in Childcare and Domestic Labour in Three Paper Mill Communities," *Gender, Place and Culture* 7, 1 (2000): 5-19.

8 P. Tripp-Knowles, "The Feminine Face of Forestry in Canada," in *Challenging Professions: Historical and Contemporary Perspectives on Women's Work,* edited by E. Smyth, E. Acker, and P. Bourne (Toronto: University of Toronto Press, 1999), 194-211.

9 In local jargon, "the North Island" refers to the northern portion of Vancouver Island. It sometimes includes Woss and sometimes does not. Women who participated in the study argued very strongly that Woss exhibited all the characteristics of a northern town and should be included in any description. All population figures are from the Census of Canada, 1996. The Mount Waddington Regional District is the Census division that most closely describes the region. Although some of this district is located on the mainland of British Columbia, over 80 percent of the population is based on the North Island.

10 S. Reinharz, *Feminist Methods in Social Research* (New York and Oxford: Oxford University Press, 1992).

11 L. McDowell, "Space, Place and Gender Relations," part 1, "Feminist Empiricism and the Geography of Social Relations," *Progress in Human Geography* 17 (1993): 157-79; part 2, "Identity, Difference, Feminist Geometries and Geographies," *Progress in Human Geography* 17 (1993): 305-18.

12 J.K. Gibson-Graham, "Stuffed If I Know! Reflections on Post-Modern Feminist Social Research," *Gender, Place and Culture* 1, 2, (1994): 205-24.

13 Among the interviewees, five identified themselves as First Nations. I have not highlighted First Nations women because some women asked not to discuss their ethnicity, leaving numbers too small to retain confidentiality.

14 P. Doeringer and M. Piore, *Internal Labour Markets and Manpower Analysis* (Lexington: D.C. Heath, 1971).

15 Ibid., 165.

16 S. Hanson and G. Pratt, *Gender, Work, and Space* (London, UK, and New York: Routledge, 1995), 6.

17 R. Hayter, *Flexible Crossroads: The Restructuring of British Columbia's Forest Economy* (Vancouver: UBC Press, 2000).

18 Thomas Dunk, *It's a Working Man's Town: Male Working-class Culture in Northwestern Ontario* (Montreal and Kingston: McGill-Queen's University Press, 1991).

19 CS/RESORS Consulting Limited, "Women and the Forest Industry," report to the Policy Development Division, Ministry of Employment and Investment (Victoria, BC: Ministry of Employment and Investment, 1997).

20 Ministry of Forests, Port McNeill District, 1998.

21 J.E. Randall and R.G. Ironside, "Communities on the Edge: An Economic Geography of Resource-Dependent Communities in Canada," *The Canadian Geographer* 40 (1996): 17-35; Halseth, "We Came for the Work."

22 Ibid.

23 See, for instance, M.S. Carroll, S.E. Daniels, and J. Kusel, "Employment and Displacement among Northwestern Forest Products Workers," *Society and Natural Resources* 13 (2000): 151-56.

24 For instance, Grass and Hayter, "Employment Change during Recession"; Hayter and Barnes, "The Restructuring."

25 Grass and Hayter, "Employment Change during Recession."

26 Although this term remains in common usage, the association of nature with "resources" that are made valuable through economic production processes is highly contested by environmental organizations, ecofeminists, and philosophers of environment.

27 M.P. Marchak, S.L. Aycock, and D.M. Herbert, *Falldown: Forest Policy in British Columbia* (Vancouver: David Suzuki Foundation and Ecotrust Canada, 1999).

28 O. Forgacs, "The British Columbia Forest Industry: Transition or Decline," in Barnes and Hayter, eds., *Troubles in the Rainforest,* 167-80.

29 G. Horne, *British Columbia Local Area Economic Dependencies and Impact Ratios 1996* (Victoria, BC: Business and Economic Statistics, 1999).

30 During the course of this study, the federal government changed the terminology of worker insurance from unemployment insurance (UI) to employment insurance (EI). This insurance program is managed by the federal government but is paid for by employers and employees. Upon job loss (temporary or permanent), insurance benefits are generally available only to those workers who receive income from an employer. This plan omits many self-employed and/or contract workers.

31 Commission on Resources and Environment (CORE), *Vancouver Island Land Use Plan,* vol. 1 (Victoria, BC: Commission on Resources and Environment, 1994), 205.

32 Horne, *British Columbia.*

33 J. Parr, *The Gender of Breadwinners: Women, Men, and Change in Two Industrial Towns, 1880-1950* (Toronto: University of Toronto Press, 1990); M.P. Marchak, *Green Gold: The Forest Industry in British Columbia* (Vancouver: UBC Press, 1983).

34 Y. Smith, "The Household, Women's Employment and Social Exclusion," *Urban Studies* 34, 8 (1997): 1159-78.

35 S. Hanson and I. Johnston, "Gender Differences in Work-trip Length: Explanation and Implications," *Urban Geography* 6 (1985): 193-219.

36 Some women were single, and others had previously been married to loggers. There were no known lesbian women in the sample.

37 V. Brandth and M. Haugen, "Breaking into a Masculine Discourse: Women and Farm Forestry," *Sociologia Ruralis* 38 (1998): 427-42.

38 Data provided from the British Columbia Association of Professional Foresters indicate that the proportion of women members increased from 10 percent in 1995 to 14 percent in 2000 and to almost 15 percent in 2002. It is striking that almost 8 percent of the 4,048 members are retired, but only one of them is a woman (representing 0.02 percent). Statistics

Canada estimates that women accounted for 36.5 percent of management positions across all jobs in Canada in 1999; see E. Teske and B. Beedle, "Journey to the Top: Breaking through the Canopy: Canadian Experiences," unpublished report for the Canadian Forest Service and British Columbia Ministry of Forests, 2001.

39 The woman discussed in this interview was successful in the claim she raised with the Labour Relations Board.

40 Grass and Hayter, "Employment Change during Recession."

41 CS/RESORS Consulting Limited, "Women and the Forest Industry."

42 Belinda Leach, "Transforming Rural Livelihoods: Gender, Work, and Restructuring in Three Ontario Communities," in *Restructuring Caring Labour: Discourse, State Practice and Everyday Life*, edited by Sheila M. Neysmith (Toronto: Oxford University Press, 2000), 209-25; S. Whatmore, T. Marsden, and P. Lowe, "Feminist Perspectives in Rural Studies," in *Gender and Rurality*, edited by S. Whatmore, T. Marsden, and P. Lowe (London, UK: David Fulton, 1994), 1-10; Ontario Ministry of Labour, "The Displaced Workers of Ontario: How Do They Fare?" unpublished report prepared by Economic and Labour Market Research, Ontario Ministry of Labour, n.d., reprinted in Commission on Resources and Environment (CORE), *Vancouver Island Land Use Plan*, vol. 2, Appendices (Victoria, BC: Commission on Resources and Environment, 1994); M. Wright, "Women in the Newfoundland Fishery," in *Framing Our Past: Canadian Women's History in the Twentieth Century*, edited by S.A. Cook, L.R. McLean, and K. O'Rourke (Toronto: Oxford University Press, 2001), 343-46.

43 This gap is true of other resource sectors such as fishing; see Wright, "Women in the Newfoundland Fishery."

44 Hayter, *Flexible Crossroads.*

45 K. England, "Suburban Pink Collar Ghettos: The Spatial Entrapment of Women?" *Annals of the Association of American Geographers* 83 (1993): 225-42; Hanson and Pratt, *Gender;* Parr, *The Gender of Breadwinners;* M.S. Carroll, *Community and the Northwestern Logger* (Boulder, CO: University of Colorado Press, 1995); Carroll, Daniels, and Kusel, "Employment and Displacement"; L.M. Tigges, A. Ziebarth, and J. Farnham, "Social Relationships in Locality and Livelihood: The Embeddedness of Rural Economic Restructuring," *Journal of Rural Studies* 14 (1998): 203-19; A. DeBruin and A. Dupuis, "Towards a Synthesis of Transaction Cost Economics and a Feminist Oriented Network Analysis: An Application to Women's Street Commerce," *American Journal of Economics and Sociology* 58 (1999): 807-27.

46 M. Granovetter, "Economic Action and Social Structure: The Problem of Embeddedness," *American Journal of Sociology* 91 (1985): 481-510.

7
People for Pigs in Pleasant-Land: Small-Scale Women Farmers
Martha McMahon

> Writers imagine that they cull stories from the world. I am begin-
> ning to believe that vanity makes them think so. That it's actually
> the other way around. Stories cull from the world. Stories reveal
> themselves to us. The public narrative, the private narrative – they
> commission us. They insist on being told. Fiction and nonfiction
> are only different techniques of story telling.
> — Arundhati Roy[1]

Sociologists like me usually say our stories are "culled" from the world, not
that stories find us. Most of us distinguish science from narrative and say
our work is subject to quite different standards.[2] Some use words like "rigour"
and "systematic" to convey the serious character of this work of culling
from the empirical world and words like "validity" and "reliability" to express the trustworthiness of their accounts. Many would be offended by
having their sociological accounts called "stories" and be uncomfortable with
the blurring of the identities of the knower and his or her object, as well as
with the attribution of subjectlike agency, be it coyote or trickster, to the
world.[3] Few would see stories seeking them out, insisting to be told. But perhaps Arundhati Roy is right. My account of small-scale women farmers' activism is not so self-important that it *insists* on being told, but bits and pieces
of a something that is like a story both refuse to go away and at the same
time refuse to metamorphose into a coherent narrative. This is a boundary-
transgressing, fragmented tale that is neither fact nor fiction but still bound
by very old-fashioned notions of fidelity and loyalty that can thrive in postmodernist spaces and places.[4]

On southern Vancouver Island[5] and on the Gulf Islands, where I have lived
for ten years, I have observed that women small-scale organic farmers provide what I believe to be a disproportionately large amount of the leadership
and energy associated with the development of locally oriented, ecological

or organic agriculture. In the academic literature, this is also sometimes called alternative agriculture because, to those concerned about the environment, it represents an alternative to the environmental destructiveness of industrial agriculture. As has been noted about much feminist organizing and many new social-movement groups, the term leadership and even the term group are inadequate to capture the nonhierarchical, consensus-oriented, flexibly organized, diverse nature of collectivities such as the women farmers about whom I am writing.[6] Women farmers have set up, managed, or provided the initiative for farmers' markets, Community Supported Agriculture (CSA) projects, and other box-programs, organic-farming education groups, on-farm work parties, farmer-chef initiatives, an organic café, public-education initiatives on sustainable agriculture and the value of local food, an organic-certifying group (which operates at arm's length), an apprenticeship program, programs to acquire land for landless farmers, an agricultural-tool lending "library," and coalitions for political lobbying, to mention just some of their activities. Local women-led farmer groups or networks have been involved in partnerships with other groups on food and social-justice initiatives and involved in international collaborations with other small-farmer groups. The observation about women's central role in community-supported agriculture is not unique to southern Vancouver Island. Research by DeLind and Ferguson and by Abbott Cone and Myhre found that women formed the majority of the active members involved in the CSA projects that these authors studied in the US.[7]

The data for this chapter are drawn from several recent struggles over agricultural land use in which local small-scale women farmers were centrally involved. I use this opportunity to explore how an ecological feminist might begin to understand this apparent phenomenon of small-scale women farmers' activism (for want of a better term).

Marked but Not-Essentialized Identities: The Local and Gender
Modern agriculture in the US, Feldman and Welsh argue, has been shaped by a scientifically based, universalizing epistemology that has both facilitated the exclusion of women from farming and made the contributions of those who remain largely invisible.[8] The adoption of this particular form of positivistic agricultural science in the US, they note, coincided closely with the rapid capitalization of agriculture. Whereas agriculture before the Second World War can be understood to have also been gendered, the rapid capitalization and intense mechanization of farming established new forms of engendering. Capitalization and the associated move to specialization and mechanization, and not simply male control, meant that the accounting logic of investment, debt repayment, and profit replaced more traditional models of husbandry in which a certain form of care for the land was more central. Not surprisingly, critics of the modern agri-industrial food

system increasingly look to local knowledge to ground alternative agriculture systems. Unfortunately, however, few turn to an analysis of gender. Yet, as explained by Feldman and Welsh, who use feminist epistemological insights to reflect on the possibilities of a successor science for alternative agriculture, gender analysis is essential to reclaiming local knowledge about farming.

In *Bringing the Food Economy Home: Local Alternatives to Global Agribusiness,* Helena Norberg-Hodge, Todd Merrifield, and Steven Gorelick document the potential contribution of local-food economies to a host of ecological, social, health, local-revitalization, and economic benefits to communities.[9] It is clear, however, that the focus in this work is not exclusively on the local, but also on the local as a way of resisting some of the more pernicious consequences of global agribusiness. Similarly, this research has shown me that the notion of local as used among small-scale women farmers on Vancouver Island should not be interpreted literally or exclusively as one of spatialized relationships. The idea of the local has become a political (and, I argue below, a cultural) project.

Contemporary sociological literature tends to conceptualize agricultural change, including the emergence of alternative and organic agriculture, in a context of global agrifood restructuring. The factors identified as determining this restructuring, and hence the future of farming, include the demise of Fordist production strategies, the emergence of niche markets, global regulation, the new international division of labour, new social movements, and transnational corporations. But as Lyons and Buttel emphasize, this perspective risks exaggerating the power of global forces. It also homogenizes the paths of social change by not recognizing the importance of the local in the process of social change and by underestimating the possibilities of farmers' agency.[10] While we may recognize the value of a "turn toward the local," the idea of the local needs to be used carefully. Lessons from past ecological feminist analysis caution us to avoid the problems of romanticizing and essentializing that are characteristic of ecofeminist approaches. Rather than being a fixed place, the local is seen by Feldman and Welsh as a complex, contested, heterogeneous domain. One of the central lessons of the ecofeminist and environmental-justice movements is that relations with nature (such as agriculture) are organized by power relations such as gender, race, and class.[11] This is true at the local as well as the global level. Jolly, who calls for more adequate conceptualizations of gender than are conventionally used in analyses of social change, for some captured by the term "queering," emphasizes that gender shapes our access to economic resources and our ability to participate in social and political activities – including access to land and food.[12] It also shapes the subjectivities of political actors and the strategies they use. The shift to the local does not allow us to ignore the gendered, racialized, and economic relations that may organize food production even at the local level.

Whereas the idea of the local is undertheorized in research on alternative agriculture, gender is very commonly theorized. Conceptualizations of the role of gender in sociological analyses of alternative agriculture, however, are generally limited to the use of gender as a variable, or "gender" is used interchangeably with "women." Gender is better addressed in the literature on agriculture in "developing" countries. Research on agriculture in Canada and the US typically operates with a concept of the farmer as male, with women appearing primarily as farm wives. One of the challenges, as shown in Reimar's study of Canadian farm women, has been to recognize women's direct involvement in farm labour as well as to make visible the value to the farm of their so-called reproductive labour.[13] Departing from the usual use of gender as a variable, Lyons uses an ecofeminist lens to analyze the different and gendered understandings of organic farming held among her sample of primarily male organic farmers in Australia and New Zealand and to reflect on their contrasting motivations for farming organically.[14] Gender, in Lyons's analysis, becomes a way of looking. It allows her to investigate both the potential of organic farming to become an alternative social and ecological food system and the potential for its conventionalization, as many of those adopting a global agrifood-systems perspective gloomily predict will be the future of organic farming.

An Aside on Methodology

Because this story found me, the usual accounts of a realist methodology do not fit.[15] This chapter draws on my first-hand knowledge of efforts by rural women to preserve the capacity for local, small-scale farming in their British Columbia communities. It also draws on the accounts of several farmers who were actively involved. I have woven bits and pieces from several stories into a single composite story set in a fictitious district called Pleasant-Land. The reality of the parts that make up the story is to be found in their insights, but events are paraphrased, speeches are rearranged in time and space,[16] and I make no claim to their "realness" as correspondence in the conventional sense of the word. Dates, places, names, and other details are changed. This is done partly to observe responsibilities about privacy and anonymity (though the data could be said to have been available in public space) and also to avoid making claims to be representing the truth about events in which many people participated. Of equal concern to issues of voice are issues of representation. The representation of the social world here does not rely on a notion of the validity of the correspondence portrayed but is faithful to a deeper commitment to making more visible the subtle workings of power and also the possibilities for resistance. This is not an ethnographic study of local resistance or women's organizing. I am not trying to capture and represent the lived experience and complexity of any one or all of these struggles. The story here is a collage, not a case study.

Pleasant-Land, 2001
Phone calls that went something like this:

Pam, this is Nellie. Have you seen the draft of the new bylaws? I know, I know, who hasn't better things to do, being in the middle of lambing. But this is entirely crazy. Those new local councillors want to stop us farming. This is "officially" a rural area, isn't it? But now they are telling us that if you don't have at least three acres of land you are no longer allowed to keep livestock? Not even one single sheep on three acres. What have they got against sheep, for God's sake? And pigs – well pigs are to be banned entirely. There's only two pigs in the entire district. But it seems it is two pigs too many. This is to become "a pig-free zone."

Calm down Nellie. Stop being paranoid. You must be delirious from lack of sleep being up with the ewes every night. Look, nobody told us there were going to be restrictions to agriculture in the new bylaws. Surely they would have consulted with the farm groups in the area. Let me check it out. What you are saying makes no sense at all. Why would anyone want to stop us farming in a rural area? And most of us small-scale people are organic farmers; surely the planners at least would be trying to encourage us.

I talked to our local councillor. You're right. There is to be no livestock on holdings of less than three acres, and we can no longer graze our livestock on other people's land as we have up to now. One member of the land-use committee called us "itinerant farmers" because we move our animals from one neighbour's pasture to another's. And no pigs at all. And you'll never believe it, but our councillor told me that these were *not* restrictions on agriculture because small-scale farming is not agriculture. It was doubly not agriculture, I was told, not just because it was small-scale but because no one was making a full living from it. I suppose growing food to eat doesn't count either. Anyway, he talked of Walkerton and the contamination of drinking water and of animal manure as a toxic waste. Didn't he know that it was *industrial* agriculture that created those water risks? You would think he would be more concerned about the human septic systems. He made our farm animals sound dangerous to the public good and the environment. Imagine telling a small-scale organic farmer that she was a threat to the environment. What does he think the environmental impact of his supermarket food is – benign? But he was very clear Nellie; he insisted small-scale farming is not real farming. Apparently, the whole committee and planners agree with him.

What follows is excerpted from a formal submission by a rural women's organization in Pleasant-Land. It attempts to articulate the invisible or discounted ecological and community value of small-scale farming. It also points to the class and gender biases of the proposed bylaw and challenges both dominant notions of economic value and the definition of real work as full-time, income-generating employment.

On _____, 2001 Pleasant-Land's [women's group] _____ unanimously voted to write a letter outlining our strong opposition to the proposed new bylaws that will restrict small-lot agriculture in our area. We are particularly concerned about:
- the increase in lot size required for livestock keeping from one acre to three acres;
- the total prohibition on even small-scale pig keeping in the area;
- the prohibition of an established Pleasant-Land tradition of allowing farmers to graze their livestock on their neighbours' land within rural residential areas if invited to do so;
- the gender bias of the proposed bylaws (small-scale farmers are more likely to be women);
- the devaluation of the economic value of small-lot agriculture;
- the depreciation of the ecological and social benefits of small-lot agriculture for our community;
- the lack of justifiable and defensible grounds for the proposed changes;
- the implicit lack of awareness that livestock manure is vital to chemical-free horticultural practices and considered integral to organic farming;
- the proposed bylaws violate the mandate of Pleasant-Land local authority (to keep the local area rural and protect the environment).

These bylaws will place unwarranted and harmful restrictions on small-lot farming in Pleasant-Land. While some people may not consider small-scale farming real or valuable farming, we would remind you that (a) much of the farming in the general region is small-lot agriculture and that (b) local and international research repeatedly points to the economic, community, and ecological benefits of small-scale farming. Increasingly, research internationally shows that small-scale agriculture is more efficient than large-scale farming on a per acre output and when full social and ecological accounting is considered in the evaluation. Many of our small farms here are ecologically farmed, and research shows that such small-scale farming typically encourages greater biodiversity than large-scale farming. We do not understand why neither available research findings nor local expertise were considered worth consulting in drafting these bylaws.

We would like to point out that women farmers in particular will be affected by barriers to small-scale farming, as they are more likely to be small-scale farmers. We reject the idea implicit in these bylaws that part-time farming is of little or no value ... What are the reasons for making some long-standing agricultural practices illegal? Some families on the island use their small lots to feed their families and to share healthy local food with their neighbours. Why is this to be made illegal?

As a rural women's organization, we are deeply offended by the barriers to community sharing and cooperation and to the ability to feed our families and our neighbours good, wholesome, local food that these bylaws propose to introduce. We would remind you that farming is about producing food and also about living sustainably with nature and building healthy communities. These bylaws undermine our capacity to achieve all three here in Pleasant-Land.

Sturgeon developed the concept of direct theory to analyze women's involvement in peace activism and antimilitarism during the 1980s.[17] Direct theory represents a kind of theory that exists in or is implicit in action. Direct theory, she explains, typically involves the articulation of an oppositional political theory that speaks a silenced politics and connects various forms on inequality and injustice to concrete practices of the state. In such cases, she continues, culture cannot be separated from politics, theory from practice, or everyday life from history. It is a useful conceptual tool for understanding women farmers' actions in Pleasant-Land.

People for Pigs (and People) in Pleasant-Land

Over the weeks following Nellie and Pam's phone call, it was learned that the proposed bylaws would restrict farming on smaller acreages. A small core of women, not all of whom were farmers, started to organize to oppose the bylaw changes. It is important not to essentialize the identities of actors in these events. The rural women and small-scale farmers who were involved typically had multiple identities (and sophisticated social resources), which were strategically employed in representing themselves, whether it be as small-scale women farmers or as citizens denied opportunity to participate.

To councillors and planners whose thinking or training is shaped by modernist notions of urban planning, food issues are far less visible than issues like transportation, housing, employment, or the environment.[18] Like women's unpaid work, food systems are taken for granted. The reasons for this, according to Pothukuchi and Kaufman, include such historic developments as the spread of refrigeration, improvements in transportation, and the introduction of cheap energy, all of which allowed food production to be distanced and farmland around cities to be lost without concern. To this list one must add the cultural separation of the natural and the social, which ecofeminism has made the centre of much analysis.

The modernist separations of the social from the natural and the urban from the rural are disrupted in the kind of farmer organizing I witnessed.

Despite the association of the urban with culture, civilization, and sophistication and the corresponding association of the rural with nature and tradition,[19] the organizing undertaken by women farmers exhibited many of the characteristics of new social movements and postmodernist cultural politics. The internet became a crucial tool in information gathering, communication, organizing, and mobilizing support from remote but strategic allies. Engaging in what theorists of new social movements call "politics-as-spectacle," organizers playfully dramatized the issue as one of "Pleasant-Land People for Pigs." Someone came up with the idea of "campaign buttons" and had a friend arrange for them to be made in Vancouver and hand-delivered by another friend to Pleasant-Land within a week. A woman whose occupational identity required that she not be visible in the political organizing designed the buttons, and the final caption was worked out through email networking. The political "Pig Buttons" (worn on jackets and hats) bore the image of a rather cute pink pig with a caption in which the pig said, *"What do you mean I can't live here any more?"*

The attribution of political subjectivity to a pig in the women's organizing further disrupted the modernist separation of culture and nature. While pandas, whales, or dolphins are often symbolically centred in political-ecological struggles over (pure) "wild nature," the pig is ecologically impure, a boundary-transgressing creature – a domesticated animal – part cultural construct, part animal. Although often valued in many peasant societies, it is now more often seen as unclean nature.

Why was the pig the focus of political exclusion and resistance to exclusion in Pleasant-Land? That the pig was the subject/object of symbolic contestation is clear: There were in fact no more than two pigs in all of Pleasant-Land at the time, and existing bylaws and zoning would have made large-scale pig farming in the area illegal. Culturally drawn boundaries, as Mary Douglas reminds us, are about purity and danger; they represent efforts to contain the social world by maintaining the separation of things that should not be mixed. Dirt, she continues, is matter out of place.[20] Pigs in modern society have come to represent dirt. Because the pig was the object of total exclusion in the proposed bylaws, it was chosen as the symbol of farm women's resistance. "Pleasant-Land People for Pigs," read the political button. In nineteenth- and early-twentieth-century Montreal, Bradbury's historical research shows, the pig became the focus of a series of new laws that systematically restructured modern urban spaces and introduced, in the name of health and sanitation, new forms of surveillance of the poor, while severely curtailing the proletariat's access to means of supplementing their wages or engaging in nonwage subsistence.[21] It was the "poor man's pig" (and the Irish poor, in particular) rather than cows or horses (associated with higher social strata) that was first targeted for exclusion in the removal of farm animals from the city. Human struggles over the proper places for animals expressed broader social and class struggles. Bradbury notes that "as the divisions between workers, the middle classes, and the capitalists became clearer, an assault on animals began."[22]

Testifying to the diffuse and productivist nature of power and regulation in late capitalism, neither the local councillors nor the planners involved in drafting the bylaws could provide a coherent public account of why the bylaw changes were being introduced. Those who inquired were told that there was no concrete problem that the new restrictions were addressing. Small-scale farmers had apparently become entangled in their local authority's enactment of regulatory solutions for a problem the authorities could neither identify nor articulate.

(Agri)culture as Politics

It is hard to tell a story about women's activism in support of small-scale farming on southern Vancouver Island. Before I even start, my story is framed by a "bad" history of the essentializing of women in (some) ecofeminist work (from which some readers may want me to now take the time and space to distance myself); by (equally, albeit differently) essentializing treatments of gender as a variable in nonfeminist work on women and agriculture (and the work of critiquing and reconceptualizing gender, which other readers may insist should be done before going on); and by the typecasting of women farmers as either the real victims of global agribusiness or the new hero(ine)s of sustainable agriculture. A lot of baggage. The complexity of writing about women farmers is deepened because it is partly gender itself, I argue, that is being reconfigured, theoretically and politically, in the struggles over local food and farming about which I write.[23] And of course, although gender may be an analytic category and a lens for inquiry, it is embedded with other social relations and does not operate alone.

On southern Vancouver Island, as in many other places in North America and Europe, in particular social spaces, food and farming have become the site of a variety of cultural struggles that are profoundly political, ecological, and for some, aesthetic and spiritual.[24] For example, in the US last year Eric Schlosser's book *Fast Food Nation: The Dark Side of the All-American Meal* quickly became a best-seller, and in Europe French organic farmer Jose Bove, co-author of *This World Is Not for Sale: Farmers against Junk Food*, has become an important political figure.[25] The commodification of agriculture and food in advanced capitalism, Lamb argues, destroys agriculture as a cultural activity.[26] There are, of course, international differences in the politics of food and farming as cultural struggles. The movement against genetically modified produce has been far more politically powerful in Europe than in North America. In ways not disconnected from the antiglobalization movement's targeting of McDonald's (although the actors are drawn from very different segments of the population), the growing interest in the "slow food" movement exemplifies how "culture" is deployed to symbolically resist the dominance of the economic, which is iconographically represented in this case by fast food. For Abbott Cone and Myhre, the Community Supported Agriculture movement is represented by its leaders as a radical attempt to resist industrial agriculture.[27] The movement, they continue, is also an attempt to counter many of the problematic aspects of modernity, such as the fragmentation of self and the experiences of disembeddedness in time and space. Abbott Cone and Myhre found that the success of such alternative (agri)cultural projects largely depended on women as consumers initiating and maintaining farm membership. Unlike the women in Abbot Cone and Myhre's study, who are engaged in cultural resistance as consumers, the women in this study are farmers. As I argued earlier, local women farmers' involvement in ecological agriculture and their engagement of issues related to preserving agricultural land and promoting small-scale farming and local food on southern Vancouver Island can be read as forms of what Noël Sturgeon calls "direct theory," that is, a lived analysis of contemporary domination by industrial agriculture.[28]

It would be easy to overlook the political and cultural significance of the revitalization of small-scale local agriculture by the women farmers on southern Vancouver Island. The diminutive sizes of many of their farms, often between one and five acres, seem almost trivial compared to the thousand-acre farms of the Prairies so emblematic of "real" Canadian farmers. In private conversations and at public meetings around land use, southern Vancouver Island's small-scale women farmers are told that they are not real farmers, that what they are doing is not agriculture, and that given the financial difficulties of even very large farms, tiny holdings such as theirs cannot possibly be economically viable. Small-scale women farmers are actively challenging these repressively gendered and classed notions of what real farming is.

Salvatore Engel-Di Mauro provides an insightful analysis of the roles of soil science, gender, and economics in explaining the development of environmentally destructive industrial agriculture under state socialism in Hungary.

In practice, soil science was dictated by an androcentric market-oriented farming system in a context of global capitalism in which the socialist state not only participated but also contributed to effectively foreclose alternative forms of agriculture ... gender relations were central to the ensuing commodification process in agriculture through the reproduction of the pre-socialist externalization of primarily women's subsistence use of soils. For instance, soil scientists ignored women-controlled subsistence plots until they and women's unpaid labor were integrated into lucrative male-controlled, small-scale farming ventures.[29]

Images of men in feedcaps driving powerful tractors across open landscapes make women farmers who handweed garlic in fields that look like gardens appear romantic and artisanlike, but not agricultural. In contrast to the functional physical organization of many conventional farms and the apparent lack of concern with aesthetics, the farms of local women organic farmers on southern Vancouver Island will typically intersperse crops, flowering herbs, and cut flowers in the same area.

By comparison, the harsh reality of contemporary farming is reinforced in the public mind by a background of enormous bank debt, loan foreclosures, and drought.[30] Apparently, even a valued tradition of Canadian masculine toughness grounded in integrity, hard work, and a family farm can no longer survive in a globalized environment of urban-based financial institutions and unpredictable weather that seems like a physical metaphor for an unpredictable global economy. Small-scale women farmers in their flowery gardens seem like lightweights in these massive upheavals. Pretty but not serious. What is seldom made clear in public discourse on the demise of the Canadian family farm is that it is a particular gendered form of "productivist"[31] agriculture (and a particular historical form of masculinity) that is being "lost" and that the demise of the family farm is an inevitable part of what Engel-Di Mauro describes as androcentric market-oriented farming that is rooted in the context of global capitalism. Canadian agriculture is represented as determined by the laws of nature, economic efficiency, and global competitiveness. Small-scale women farmers in Pleasant-Land can be understood as attempting to reclaim farming as local culture.

Paralleling the focus on culture as politics by new social movements, the local (agri)culture movement that provides the background to my story embodies cultural resistance. It is theory in action, and like new social movements, it is both oppositional and prefigurative,[32] often as much performative as instrumental. The orientation of Pleasant-Land's women farmers to community and locality, like that of the organic farmers studied by Abbott Cone and Myhre, "prefigures" an alternative food system based on reconnecting people and the land and the food that sustains them. And, as many new social movements destabilize such traditional identity categories as gender, understanding local women farmers' struggles with land issues will require us to conceptualize gender in ways that are quite different from those available in much of the contemporary writing on gender and alternative agriculture.

The impact of the efforts of local small-scale farmers is difficult to capture. The impulse in new social movements, Sturgeon explains, is not to form a successful interest group, to have a marginalized section of the population included, or to get a larger share of the pie. The conventional understanding of gender and social movements leads DeLind and Ferguson to conclude that women's participation in Community Supported Agriculture is more "feminine" than feminist.[33] They argue that the participants they studied did not use their participation to raise issues having to do with gender relations or women's subordination, nor did they profess a feminist identity. But this suggestion implies a narrow approach both to gender and to social movements that connect gender, agriculture, and ecology. In asking "is this a women's movement?" DeLind and Ferguson pursue the wrong question. Melucci emphasizes that new social movements must not be assessed by success that is measured only in terms of political effectiveness and institutional modernization. Rather, a major part of their importance is their contribution to internal change, to the transformation of "biological, emotional, and cognitive structures on which we base the construction of our experience and relationships."[34]

The small-scale women farmers whose story is told here were using their socially constructed identities as women and their orientation to community food provisioning to disrupt dominant, classed, and masculinist taken-for-granted ideas about farming – ideas that can also be seen to rely on racialized relations of international trade. Their resistance rested as much on who the actors were not, and on the harm their farming was not doing, as on any essentialized notion of women, women farmers, or conventional liberal-feminist notions of equality. To understand new social movements, Sturgeon argues, one must attend to how new meanings and new cultural codes are produced within submerged networks and recognize the production of complex, new, and varied kinds of political subjectivities.[35] Movement politics, Sturgeon adds, are not about the inclusion of excluded individuals (many of the participants in the "People for Pigs" campaign had socio-economic privilege); rather, they are about "excluded politics." Here the excluded politics involved claiming food and farming as sites for the production of new ways of living in the complex and changing intersections of nature and culture. Too often, as Sturgeon suggests, academics have misread women's ecological activism in terms of claims about women's closeness to a romanticized and essentialized nature in order to dismiss the potential of ecological feminism.[36] The story of Pleasant-Land's "People for Pigs" campaign should challenge any such easy misreading.

Notes

1 From a talk entitled "Come September" given by Arundhati Roy at the Lensic Performing Arts Centre, 29 September 2002.
2 But see Joseph Gusfield, "The Literary Rhetoric of Science," *American Sociological Review* 4 (1976): 16-34; and Laurel Richardson, "Writing: A Mode of Inquiry," in *Handbook of Qualitative Research,* edited by Norman Denzin and Yvonne Lincoln (Thousand Oaks, CA: Sage, 1994), 516-19.

3   Donna Haraway, "Situated Knowledges: The Science Question in Feminism as the Site of Discourse on the Privilege of Partial Perspective," *Feminist Studies* 14, 3 (1988): 575-99.
4   Arundhati Roy's claim would make inappropriate or meaningless many methodological conventions that social scientists practise in order to be able to claim scientific authority. It does not, however, mean that anything goes but raises new questions about how one tells stories about social and natural worlds.
5   I am talking particularly about the area in and around Victoria. Because of the proximity to fairly dense populations, small-scale farming in this area could be considered almost peri-urban, even in rural locations.
6   Noël Sturgeon, "Theorizing Movements: Direct Action and Direct Theory," in *Cultural Politics and Social Movements*, edited by Marcy Darnovsky, Barbara Epstein, and Richard Flacks (Philadelphia: Temple University Press, 1995), 35-51.
7   Laura DeLind and Anne Ferguson, "Is This a Women's Movement? The Relationship of Gender to Community-Supported Agriculture in Michigan," *Human Organization* 58, 2 (1999): 190-200; and Cynthia Abbott Cone and Andrea Myhre, "Community Supported Agriculture: A Sustainable Alternative to Industrial Agriculture?" *Human Organization* 59, 2 (2000): 187-97.
8   Shelly Feldman and Rick Welsh, "Feminist Knowledge Claims, Local Knowledge, and Gender Division of Agricultural Labor: Constructing a Successor Science," *Rural Sociology* 60 (1995): 23-43.
9   Helena Norberg-Hodge, Todd Merrifield, and Steven Gorelick, *Bringing The Food Economy Home: Local Alternatives to Global Agribusiness* (London, UK: Zed Books, 2002).
10   Kirsten Lyons, "Understanding Organic Farm Practices: Contributions for Ecofeminism," in *Australasian Food and Farming in a Globalised Economy*, edited by D. Burch et al. (Melbourne: Monash, 1998), 57-67; and Fred Buttel, "Theoretical Issues in Global Agri-Food Restructuring," in *Globalization and Agri-Food Restructuring: Perspectives from the Australasia Region*, edited by D. Burch, R. Rickson, and G. Lawrence (Aldershot, UK: Avebury, 1996).
11   Catriona Sandilands, "From Unnatural Passion to Queer Nature," *Alternatives Journal* 27, 3 (2001): 31.
12   Susie Jolly, "'Queering' Development: Exploring the Links between Same-Sex Sexualities, Gender, and Development," *Gender and Development* 8, 1 (2000): 79.
13   William Reimar, "Women as Farm Labor," *Rural Sociology* 15 (1986): 143-55.
14   Lyons, "Understanding Organic Farm Practices."
15   I have, however, been involved in a more conventional study of local women organic farmers over the last several years, and no doubt my ideas in this chapter have been shaped by that research. Norman Denzin, *Interpretive Ethnography* (Thousand Oaks, CA: Sage, 1997).
16   This approach also helps address ethical issues of consent, anonymity, and confidentiality even though the events described here happened in the public sphere. The story as told represents no place and no one.
17   Sturgeon, "Theorizing Movements."
18   Kameshwari Pothukuchi and Jerome Kaufman, "Placing the Food System on the Urban Agenda: The Role of Municipal Institutions in Food System Planning," *Agriculture and Human Values* 16 (1999): 213-24.
19   Sandilands, "From Unnatural Passion," 31.
20   Mary Douglas, *Natural Symbols* (London, UK: Barrie and Rockliff, Crest Press, 1970).
21   Bettina Bradbury, "Pigs and Cows and Boarders: Non-wage Forms of Survival among Montréal Families, 1861-91," in *The Challenge of Modernity: A Reader on Post-Confederation Canada*, edited by Ian McKay (Toronto: McGraw-Hill Ryerson, 1992), 65-91.
22   Ibid., 76.
23   Barbara Marshall, *Reconfiguring Gender: Explorations in Theory and Politics* (Toronto: Broadview Press, 2000).
24   French sheep farmer and co-author of *This World Is Not for Sale,* Jose Bove has captured the public imagination not just for his role in dismantling a McDonald's Restaurant in Millau in the southwest of France in 1999, but for seeming to embody a commitment to good food as a socio-political as well as nutritional and culturally specific aesthetic concept.

25 Eric Schlosser, *Fast Food Nation: The Dark Side of the All-American Meal* (Boston and New York: Houghton Mifflin, 2001); Jose Bove and Francois Dufour, *This World Is Not for Sale: Farmers against Junk Food* (London, UK: Verso, 2001).
26 Gary Lamb, "Community Supported Agriculture: Can It Become the Basis of a New Associative Economy?" *Threefold Review* 11 (1994): 39-44.
27 Abbott Cone and Myhre, "Community Supported Agriculture."
28 Sturgeon, "Theorizing Movements," 36.
29 Salvatore Engel-Di Mauro, "Gender Relations, Political Economy, and the Ecological Consequences of State-Socialist Soil Science," *Capitalism, Nature, Socialism* 13, 3 (2002): 95.
30 Ingeborg Boyens, *Another Season's Promise: Hope and Despair in Canada's Farm Country* (Toronto: Penguin, 2001).
31 Hilary Tovey, "Food, Environment and Rural Sociology: The Organic Farming Movement in Ireland," *Sociologica Ruralis* 37, 1 (1997): 21-37.
32 Sturgeon, "Theorizing Movements," 36.
33 DeLind and Ferguson, "Is This a Women's Movement?"
34 Alberto Melucci, "The Global Planet and the Internal Planet: New Frontiers," in Darnovsky, Epstein, and Richard, eds., *Cultural Politics,* 287-98, 288.
35 Sturgeon, "Theorizing Movements."
36 Noël Sturgeon, *Ecofeminist Natures: Race, Gender, Feminist Theory and Political Action* (New York: Routledge, 1997).

8
Where the Mountain Men Meet the Lesbian Rangers: Gender, Nation, and Nature in the Rocky Mountain National Parks

Catriona Sandilands

Tell about the women. Them that was tough enough to live out here in the high lonesome with us. Now there's a real story.
— Sid Marty[1]

I suppose I should have been lonely. Maybe I was but I was so busy I didn't have time to give it much thought. We always had a comfortable well-kept home which we were just as proud of as though it had been our personal property. When I look back I am amazed at how productive I was and still had time to sew and read and write letters.
— May Tocher[2]

So if you're hankering to wear a uniform and find your true orientation, remember the Lesbian National Parks and Services wants you!
— Margot Francis[3]

Banff and Beginnings: (Re)discovering Nature, Nation, and Gender
In 1883, during a winter lull in the construction of the Canadian Pacific Railway (CPR), three young men hiked into the mountains to prospect near the unfinished end of the rail line, just east of the Great Divide. William McCardell, his brother Thomas, and Frank McCabe thought that Sulphur Mountain (then Terrace Mountain) looked minerally promising and began to bushwhack up the slope. As Sid Marty puts it, "a strong smell of sulphur greeted them, and there, at the base of a small cliff, lay a large basin of steaming water, partly blocked with fallen timber."[4] Dreaming of profits from the wealthy tourists about to be carried by the CPR into the Rockies, McCabe and the McCardells toiled through everything from sordid personal relations to an unresponsive federal bureaucracy to try to claim the

rights to the Cave and Basin Hot Springs. CPR general manager William Cornelius Van Horne was, at the same time, anxious to establish a reservation in the mountains as a destination for rail travellers and had made his desires well known to Superintendent of Mines William Pearce. The profit potential of (and resulting controversy over) the hot springs finally drew the Macdonald government's concerted attention to the park question, and Pearce eventually presided over the inquiry that paid off McCabe and the McCardells in favour of the 1885 establishment of a twenty-six-square-kilometre reserve around the Cave and Basin Hot Springs. In 1887, after the completion of the railway – and after Van Horne had already begun to erect luxurious hotels in the mountains at Field, BC, and Rogers Pass – Rocky Mountains Park (RMP) was given royal assent, "reserved and set apart as a public park and pleasure ground for the benefit, advantage, and enjoyment of the people of Canada."[5]

Although Leslie Bella, among others, has emphasized the tension between profit and preservation inherent in these rather unceremonious beginnings to the Canadian national-park system,[6] I would like to begin by suggesting the importance of these events to an unfolding narrative of parks in relation to Canadian *nationalist* discourse, by which I mean the movement of the post-Confederation collection of Dominion territories toward some form of national identity.[7] Here the park's establishment marked an influential confluence of two crucial processes. First, in the formal designation of a Dominion reserve, RMP imposed on the mountain landscape a monopoly of practice and vision enacted by the CPR but animated and legitimated by the state. The point of the park may have been rail tourism, but part of the tourist value of the park lay in its status as a *national* park, a post-Confederation cultural icon, a place to visit to discover the heart of the country. That representation was very particular; Van Horne was able to carve out and maintain, largely free from unsightly competition and alternative local production – including that of the Stoney people, who had lived in the area for generations – the image of an *empty* wilderness that had been "conquered" by the CPR and the federal government. And as a designated Dominion park, this emptied nature came increasingly to signify the wild origins and essence of the developing Canadian nation. As MP Donald Smith said to the House of Commons in 1886, "anyone who has gone to Banff ... and not felt himself elevated and proud of all that is part of the Dominion, cannot be a true Canadian."[8]

Second, the hot springs, subsumed into the CPR empire, marked a vital site of stable commercial development, as opposed (say) to the wild fortune-hunting aspirations of individuals such as McCabe and the McCardells. Lasting "improvements" to the wilderness were part of the westward expansion necessary to an effective economic and political confederation. In this project, the CPR had many roles. For one, resource extraction continued in

RMP until 1930, and the CPR town of Bankhead, only four kilometres west of the Banff townsite (but out of sight in a range of ways), flourished from 1903 to 1922.[9] For another, the CPR was in the business of courting immigration to the Prairies and actively campaigned in eastern Canada and western Europe to lure willing (preferably English-speaking and family-oriented) souls to turn the rich sod of land once deemed unfarmable.[10] The Banff Springs Hotel, however, offered a different *kind* of development along the same rail line; in its active copying of European spas and resorts, and also in its appeal to privileged world adventurers, it firmly established white upper- and middle-class life in the mountains. Thus Banff became a sort of elite border to the colonized and settled world, an exciting edge-space between the laboriously tilled Prairies and the awesomely uncultivable mountains.

In a powerful if contradictory combination, then, the CPR's luxury hotels and bourgeois tourist rituals promised a settled civility for a new nation *and* an iconic representation of the nation as an awesome and timeless place of wild beauty. More accurately, perhaps, the park offered Canadians and international tourists a set of increasingly nationalist recreation practices in a relatively new kind of national space.[11] White, bourgeois tourists went to the Rockies along with the legions of workers (guides, cooks, servants) needed to service them. While there, the elite climbed along the nation's mythic edge. In the soft light of the evening, they drank sherry and soaked in the hot, therapeutic mineral water of civilization, now piped conveniently to various bathhouses. In the full light of day, however, they sought out the mountains, reliving the original white explorers' awe of the undiscovered landscape. Erased from this picture was, of course, the vast infrastructure necessary to transport both tourists and provisions to this edge of empire and, particularly, the constitutive productive presence of the First Peoples, for whom the land was never really empty at all. These absences were the product of the active *emptying* of the land that the park performed; Banff was the core of a "new" nation, and visiting it – however luxuriously – was an act of colonial (re)discovery. As one 1887 CPR pamphlet put it:

> There will be no hardships to endure, no difficulties to overcome, and no dangers or annoyances whatsoever. You shall see mighty rivers, vast forests ... stupendous mountains and wonders innumerable; and you shall see all in comfort, nay in luxury. If you are a jaded tourist, sick of Old World scenes and smells, you will find everything fresh and novel ... If you are a mountain climber, you shall have cliffs and peaks and glaciers worthy of your alpenstock, and if you have lived in India, and tiger hunting has lost its zest, a Rocky Mountain grizzly bear will renew your interest in life.[12]

As is the case with many facets of nationalism and nation building, Banff's iconic nationalism was effected by clear gender and racialized dynamics. As

Anne McClintock puts it, white women were the boundary of the colonial nation; often denied direct agency as national citizens, white women represented the nation symbolically by being, among other things, the bearers of white families with which to fill colonial space.[13] In the case of Banff, white women represented the edge of the nation in their symbolization as bearers of the *domestic;* with white women's arrival in the mountains, Banff was able to achieve edge status by enabling *a gendered division of labour* between the sublime and the domestic nation. Specifically, the timeless nature of the romantic national origin could be cast as necessarily beyond and prior to the mundane domestic details of daily living; it was, ideally, a male-homosocial space in which feminine domestic pursuits were aberrant. This empty wilderness was, relatedly, represented as a space *before and beyond inhabitation*, thus displacing and delegitimating the views and desires of those people for whom it *was* home.[14] At the same time, of course, the park's move toward development required the *extension* of heterosexualized domestic relations into the wilderness; in order for the tourist town to appear safe, settled, and genteel, there had to be a significant white feminine presence, in contrast to Aboriginal women and to non-British and/or working-class women who were part of the resource communities in the region.[15] As Sarah Carter notes in her discussion of class and racialized representations of women in the late-nineteenth-century colonial Canadian West, such representations "were central to the new notions of spatial and social segregation that were taking shape"[16] at this time.

In this chapter, I would like to argue that these gendered and racialized dynamics do not simply pertain to Banff's origins in the period immediately following Confederation but persist in the ongoing representation and experience of nature and nation in Canada's national parks, particularly the Rocky Mountain parks. A tension remains in the parks between an *iconic* national nature (coded as wild, empty, cold, white, except for a romanticized view of Aboriginal peoples, and male-homosocial) and a *domestic* national nature (appearing civil, secure, warm, infrastructurally complex, and feminine/family-oriented).[17] Parks serve both nationalisms. In their mandate of preservation, education, and recreation (in that order since the 1980s), there is an enormous contradiction between a view that would keep the landscape as empty of humans as possible for the sake of "future generations" (thus preserving its timeless and sublime qualities) and one that would encourage Canadians en masse to learn about, and relax healthfully in, the nature that signifies the nation (thus making us good domestic citizens).[18] Banff, as Canada's first, probably most iconic, and certainly most developed park, is the poster-child both for these ongoing mandate and use contradictions (as framed and described, for example, by the federally appointed Panel on Ecological Integrity) and for the ongoing rearticulation of discourses of nature and nation. I would, however, argue that all of Canada's national parks, and especially its four (northern) Rocky Mountain parks – Banff, Jasper, Yoho, and Kootenay – share, along with topography, these tensions.[19]

Wardens: Gender Policing the Wild?

With that sketch in place, I would like to turn to the National Park Warden Service as a particular, historical, and embodied site for enactments of – and resistances to – these articulations of nature, gender, race, and nation. Although there are many categories of park actors in whose lives, bodies, and park experiences lie complex dimensions of nature and nationalism – such as residents of former and current resource towns in and around the parks, hotel and other service employees, Aboriginal peoples denied resource access and/or artifactualized in museums, and contemporary park and wilderness activists[20] – I choose the Warden Service for two primary reasons. First, wardens, from their earliest incarnations as fire and game guardians to their currently diverse roles as law enforcement officers, safety monitors, and resource managers, embody the official and contradictory mandate of the national parks. Even as they may, as individuals, rail against various branches of the park bureaucracy of which they are a part – many did and do – they still represent and reproduce, in the actual spaces of the parks, the changing nature-nation discourses of the federal state. Wardens enact (in a wide variety of ways and in both adherence and resistance to federal mandates) the nation's changing desires for its park-natures. Second and relatedly, wardens embody precisely the tension with which this chapter is concerned: the gendered and racialized organization of the line between the iconic and the domestic nation. In fact, their job is, in many respects, visibly concerned with the *policing and management* of the boundary between these two nationalisms. As game guardians, part of their job was to keep wild herds safe from poachers (a category that included Aboriginal hunters, a source of ongoing tension), many of whom were interested in the "domestic" benefits of the animal (for food, for clothing, for sale). As safety officers, part of their job was (and is) to keep people away from natures that are, it seems, too wild – avalanche slopes and grizzly bears – and that threaten the security of, for example, vacationing families and backpackers. Most recently, as resource managers, their job is to devise short- and long-term park strategies to keep the lines between domestic and wild space secure and sustainable.

The first fire and game guardians in the Dominion parks were stationed at Rocky Mountains Park in 1909; with the establishment of the National Parks Branch in 1911, these often seasonal and casual employees were increasingly institutionalized into a full-time Warden Service reaching all of Canada's (then) seven national parks. As Robert J. Burns makes clear, the role of the game guardian was ideally constructed according to a particular kind of masculinity, one that straddled the boundary between the wild or lawless and the settled or orderly. Guardians needed to be "mountain men," but according to the federal government, not any mountain man would do. The appropriate recruit, as the bearer of federal presence in the wild, needed also to be on at least speaking terms with the sort of Canadian lawfulness – even civility – in which the federal government liked to cloak its western colonial expansion (and for which the Royal Northwest Mounted Police already stood, ideologically, in the Canadian public eye). Ideally, then, wardens had to be "bicultural": deeply familiar with the mountain wilderness, but also approaching a certain level of civility appropriate to federal employment. The latter, of course, also meant "white"; the Stoneys were undisputed experts on mountain terrain and survival, but it would have been both legally impossible and culturally unthinkable for them to represent the state of which they were, following Treaty 7, effectively wards. As Burns writes: "The official criteria called for an individual who 'shall be sober, industrious and orderly, and shall be engaged in no other employment than his official duties.' Superintendents were directed that recruits be 'used in operations in the woods, able to organize and manage a crew of fire fighters, and shall have education enough to report intelligently to the Department.'"[21]

Burns also notes that the practice differed fairly significantly from the ideal well into mid-century. "In practice, game guardians were to be chosen from among those who were familiar with life and survival in the mountains. This meant in most cases the choice of [white] men who had served as outfitters, guides and packers in the Rockies. The delicate task here was to pick individuals who had not been too blatant in their violation of existing poaching and weapons regulations."[22] Simply, guardians were effective only when they knew the terrain from a poacher's perspective. Thus the choice to hire guides and outfitters, most of whom had supported themselves on the side with a little bit of now-illegal game, was quite intelligent, but it did not suggest men of the kind of sobriety and respectful relationship to centralized power that the federal government deemed ideal. As Sid Marty describes one early warden, "Public relations was not Bill [Peyto's] long suit ... but in his district, he was omniscient."[23]

What we see here is an interesting masculine confluence of the warden and the outlaw, an entente cordiale between the rules of the nation-state and the laws of nature survival.[24] Wardens walked the line between formal federal mandate and local wilderness skill, taking seriously their tasks of fire suppression, game protection, and tourist monitoring (and, often, rescue) but largely doing so as they saw fit from their own experiences in the bush. Early wardens had little education, little formal training, few colleagues, little communication with park headquarters, and very isolated living and working conditions. Ottawa certainly imposed criteria and constraints –

everything from the design of wardens' cabins to so-called predator-control policies – but guardians were mostly on their own in their interpretation and enactment. By and large, the early years of the Warden Service in the Rocky Mountain parks involved white men patrolling large, often hazardous territories from remote warden stations, often year-round. In the period preceding the Second World War, even as the warden's mandate expanded to encompass a broader range of duties – including a great deal of tourist infrastructural development, meaning increased training in techniques and technologies[25] – wardens were generally "men for the mountains" far more than they were respectable civil servants. For example, in the fall and winter, writes Burns, "the wardens toured their districts for perhaps a week at a time, returning to their cabin to make the telephone link with park headquarters, then embarking on the next trip."[26]

Men for the Mountains

What particularly interests me here is that Burns, Marty, and others consider this period the *glory years* of the Warden Service. "In the [post–Second World War] world," writes Burns, "the Warden Service would encounter twentieth century labour relations in the form of established hours and overtime pay. In the interim, the so-called 'golden age,' the wardens remained tied to their districts but free of close supervision."[27] Beginning in this period and continuing well into the present, the figure of the warden has come to be *idealized* as a rugged, white male individual whose work takes him deep into the dangerous wild for weeks and months. What had been a practical consideration in early recruitment came to signify the essence of wardendom, even as (or perhaps because) the warden's job came to require a broader range of skills, from resource management to public relations. In 1940 Parks Commissioner J.B. Harkin argued (upon losing a highly educated forester) that a warden should have "a rugged constitution, good physique, [and be] self-reliant and able to do hard manual labour to efficiently patrol outlying districts and properly maintain trails and telephone lines."[28] And in 1973, in what can only be called an act of lament for the golden age of rugged men, Sid Marty invoked the spirit of Bill Peyto to introduce and, I think, masculinize his own book about the Warden Service.

I would like to dwell on Marty's book *Men for the Mountains* at some length because it demonstrates with particular clarity the gendered stakes of Warden Service that concern me in this chapter.[29] Published in 1978, *Men for the Mountains* is clearly located in a different Warden Service than the one that hired Bill Peyto (if, in fact, we are to entirely believe Marty's characterization, as Peyto's second marriage included two children, and he was as a result posted to the relatively populated Banff district so that his family could be near a school).[30] The post–Second World War period saw a distinct professionalization and bureaucratization of the Warden Service with the addition of resource (and, later, ecosystem) management to the warden's repertoire, with the increased centralization of living quarters in townsites, and especially with the rapid rise in tourist visitation following the mass introduction of automobile-based tourism. In particular, in 1968 the Sime-Schuler Report[31] noted the vastly increased breadth of wardens' duties, especially in the areas of resource management, public relations, and visitor policing. Sime and Schuler argued for the delegation of many of the labouring jobs that had once been a clear part of a warden's daily activities, recommended raising education requirements for wardens to university graduation, and argued for a six-month formal training period to weed out unsuitable recruits.[32] The early 1970s also saw women's formal entry into the warden service, a large increase (under Trudeau) in the number and type of parks in the national-park system, an attempt to work with Aboriginal peoples (in some parks) on issues of representation and management, and a greater emphasis on nature education and visitation as part of the park mandate.

Marty, who entered the Warden Service just as these changes were being implemented, clearly shares many longer-serving wardens' hostility to them (he doesn't mention women wardens at all). More than most, however, he is a bit of a class traitor and in fact was hired into the Warden Service as a very recent university graduate. He is clearly *not* a "mountain man" at the time of his own hiring. Indeed, he spends the first chapters of the book laughing, from the safety of the future, at his own clear ineptness as a raw recruit, a "boy" as opposed to the "man" he eventually became while serving in Yoho, Jasper, and Banff. The veteran wardens play tricks on him to rid him of the idea that anything useful about, say, horses can be learned from books. Even more tellingly, nature herself teaches Marty that his Montreal education does him no good above the treeline in Yoho. He needs to realign his senses in order to see, and to hear, the apparently real world that lies beyond urban artifice, must purge himself of modernity in order to be part of nature. Thus he prescribes, trying to appear duly unphilosophical, such a self-transformation as precisely a cure for the ills of modernity that so threaten the parks: "If the modern ear is an auditory appendix, there is still hope of restoration, but first the jammed switches have to be freed. There's only one way to do this. You have to dunk the head in a bucket of icy mountain water, drawn from as close to the toe of a glacier as possible, just before sunrise. The war-whoop emitted when you try this will create the back pressure needed to clear those smog-bound circuits."[33]

Marty clearly understands the professionalization of the Warden Service as part of a broader and unwanted incursion of modernity into nature. In particular, he sees these modernizations as impositions of an outsider's view of wardens, nature, and parks onto "real" men, who, having local tradition, know better. The context here is important: The 1960s and 1970s, which

Marty had clearly experienced in his student days as an English major in Montreal, saw the rise of countercultural, political, sexual, and feminist movements that were radically different from the ones officially associated with national parks. In addition, 1973 saw a very different wilderness in the northern Rocky Mountain parks than the one patrolled by Harkin's rugged men; although there were still backcountry areas in all four parks, it was no longer the case that these areas were largely inaccessible. For Marty, all of these modernizations are related, and all are negative.

Although his stories derive primarily from his own experiences as a warden in the late 1960s and early 1970s, Marty wishes to draw a direct connection between his own activities and those of the idealized "men for the mountains" who haunt his campsite in the opening chapter. And he carves out his tradition of manly wilderness policing specifically *against* the modern Warden Service, an organization of "bureau-craps and windbags"[34] oriented to the *domesticated* park. Thus his stories involve a clear bifurcation of national parks into a "good-old" masculinity and an urbane effeminacy (tourist, bureaucratic) that not only threatens the old-time warden tradition but negatively affects the health and wellbeing of the natural world itself. The dualities are rather overpowering. His wardens are grizzled heroes who know nature; his Ottawa superiors are completely out to lunch, having spent their lives looking at books. His large carnivores (and horses) are wilful, intelligent individuals; his tourists are an indistinct class of idiots, notable only as accident victims in need of rescue ("my hero," says one warden to another "with a fake female trill" as they simulate an alpine rescue).[35] His hunters are either honourable woodsmen passing wilderness respect from father to son or greedy and incompetent urban interlopers in a nature that they constitutionally misunderstand. In short, Marty's parks are composed of a bad and feminine/domesticated modernity and a mythic and hypermasculinized nature.

The idea that nature is a space for real men and that domestic traces are unwelcome therein is not a new story. Authors such as Anne LaBastille have, for example, constructed a counternarrative to this one emphasizing women's ongoing presence in the wild as naturalists, as explorers, and even as guides, outfitters, and outlaws (although not as park rangers or wardens until recently).[36] What I find particularly interesting about Marty's account is that he so clearly considers the Rocky Mountain parks to be a staging ground for a battle between an unwholesome modernity and a virtuous nature, with wardens as the footsoldiers of the *good* even though their presence, whether he likes it or not, represents a *domestic* state presence. Fuelled by his tendency to romanticize the golden years of the Warden Service, he displays clearly the idea that parks are perched on a line between the wild and the domestic, and that urban, effeminate, tourist/bureaucratic sensibilities need to be kept at bay for the parks' sake. Here the rugged masculine virtues personified and performed by old-time wardens (however idealized a picture this may be) are crucial to the effective policing of the line between the two; the heart of the "real" park, for Marty, is male. ("'Women!' Peyto interjected. 'To hell with that. One of them tried to poison me once. Leave 'em out.'")[37]

Perhaps even more so than at Banff's origins, we can also see displayed in Marty's radical bifurcation the national-park tension raised earlier between *iconic* and *domestic* nature-nationalisms. On the one hand, Marty's distaste for the domestic nation is abundantly clear; represented by ideas of economic expansion (greed), settlement (tourist development), and civil order (bureaucratic rationality), the nation of the colonially expanding CPR becomes the nation of the federally centralized nation-state. Despite the paradoxical reality that Trudeau both expanded *and* rationalized the national-park system (expropriating a fair bit of previously settled land along the way in the interests of preserving a nature "unspoiled"), and although wardens are, by design, representatives of exactly the government he so loathes, Marty sees in the modern federal state all of the qualities he wishes to subtract from the nation. His nation is, here, sublime. For Marty, the parks represent the lifeblood of the nation in their testament to a collective origin and memory. In fact, his vision of the national parks echoes the idea that their nature directly offers the essence of the *timeless* nation, from the mythic past to the glorious future (if only the tourists and bureaucrats could just see it for what it really is). Simply, the good part of the park is that which escapes history, and the essence of the park-nation rushes us from a geologic time that shaped our origins to a glorious future for our children. As he writes in his book commemorating the centennial of the national parks, the careful visitor *can* re-experience the timeless national essence, the sensation (like the warden's) of encountering a pristine, white, and original national landscape, so long as she or he leaves behind the domestic park:

> These mountains, with their hearts of stone, are no less subject to time's transforming tides. Wind, water, and ice are working everywhere to level them under gravity's invisible hand. But once you leave the highway, the process slows down. Behind the evergreen curtain, you become a time traveler moving into the past. Stare at the compacted earth under your boots. These are the tracks of ancient inhabitants, coyotes, deer, and rarely, the naked five-toed track of a bear. Sometimes you forget that you are not the first human to come this way; the naked foot of man [sic] stepped here thousands of years before you ... To take these journeys backward in time is to search for a new future, still connected to the great chain of life, life unbroken.[38]

Wardens' Wives and Domestic Spaces

What is, I think, perhaps most striking in Marty's *Men for the Mountains* is its almost-complete erasure of women from the space of nature. This exclusion is apparent, of course, in the book's linking of (antinature) modernization with effeminacy, but it is equally striking in its almost-complete excision of the lives of actual women from the Rocky Mountain naturescape. To be sure, Marty has a wife (Myrna); he also has a child (Paul), and they appear in some of his later stories as an indication of a sort of domestic, nuclear-family *refuge* from the wilderness (although they do accompany him on a few risky excursions into remote areas). Myrna is clearly no slouch in the pioneer department and braves bears in the kitchen with exactly the sort of no-nonsense determination that Marty finds admirable in his male colleagues. But Marty figures her spaces as, primarily, domestic; she is a "city girl" who, out of devotion, learns to love a mountain-nature that is really quite foreign to her (as Marty makes clear repeatedly, emphasizing her kitchen and her garden). She makes a home; he is sustained by her domestic and emotional labour so that he can be in his *true* home, on the range. Indeed, Marty is clear that it is *he* who speaks for nature when he chastises Myrna, jokingly, for her illicit raspberry collection on park property. She "wins" because she rules the domestic sphere (and Marty will, after all, eat any ensuing jam), but he has still made his point about the wilderness.[39]

Marty's placement of women on the domestic margins of the Warden Service is hardly unusual. Even Burns's four-hundred-page history (written twenty-eight years after Marty's stories) only briefly mentions that wardens were often married men and that "wardens' wives" were actually regular unpaid members of the park labour force. Throughout much of its history, it appears that the National Parks Branch had a rather ambivalent view of women. On the one hand, allowing a wife to accompany her husband to remote district cabins was a good way to combat the risky isolation and phenomenal loneliness experienced by many of the men (especially in the long winter months); her presence was, among other things, a way of avoiding having to pay two men to share a remote patrol. On the other hand, a wife (probably) meant a family, and a family meant a need, at the very least, for schooling for the children (having a family did not suggest that a warden be given extra pay, however). Thus, in practice, many wardens' families lived in relatively larger settlements such as Banff, joining husbands and fathers in remote cabins in the relatively less isolated summer months.

Here again, one sees a tension – now institutionalized in the Warden Service – between a highly prized frontier masculinity and an also valued (if unpaid) familial/feminine domesticity. Single men were prized for their independence, individualism, and mobility, whereas families, and especially white women, were prized for their ability to bring a certain level of comfort and civilization to the park-frontier (of course, wardens' wives were not the only women in the national parks). That domesticity was increasingly a *white* women's task is very clear; the more settled the West became, the more emphasis was placed on the more domestic elements of wardens' lives. Compare two examples. Some of the earliest wardens' wives were Aboriginal and Métis women; for example, Suzette Swift, a Métis, was married to Lewis Swift, Jasper's first game and fire guardian. The family, including four children, was completely self-sufficient, and Suzette also made, and occasionally sold, finely embroidered buckskin clothing from her isolated homestead near Pyramid Mountain.[40] By the 1930s, however, the National Parks Branch was clearly interested in making sure that the children of wardens were appropriately "civilized" (read: assimilated and white) members of western settler society. The following passage was written by Banff Superintendent Jennings in 1934, who was trying to persuade Parks Commissioner J.B. Harkin to transfer one warden, J.W. Gladstone, to a posting that would allow his children to attend school: "These young boys are growing up in absolute ignorance. This family, as you know, are half-breeds and in my opinion we are creating a dangerous situation by not taking some steps at this time to see that these children are given at least a modicum of education."[41]

It is, then, quite interesting (if probably not all that surprising) to note that the official history of the Warden Service gives enormous credit to its solitary old-timers for their mountain hardships in policing the wild. In reality, however, women were a relatively common and significant presence in wardens' lives *even in the so-called golden age;* they were also key workers in the parks even though their labours were seldom formally recognized. On a more ideological level, as the Warden Service evolved into a more institutionalized force, white women came to be increasingly valued because they brought domestic stability, not just "frontier" culture, to the parks. As one report from the 1950s summed it up:

> It is also noticed that there are some fairly large gardens at one or two of our warden stations. However, it is rather difficult to make a hard and fast rule as it is the warden's wife who usually works the garden and cans the fruit and vegetables. The warden of course also works in the garden to some extent but there is no objection to this if it is done in his own time. It is certainly preferable to see a nicely laid out garden, even if it is large, rather than an area full of weeds and rank grass.[42]

Tellingly, then, Anne Dixon entitles her 1985 collection of memoirs from wardens' wives *Silent Partners*. The work is a labour of love – it is individually researched, self-published, and partly autobiographical – and is aimed at recollecting "the tremendous role those women played in the National Parks of Canada."[43] Although it does not aim to provide a single historical account of the transformation of the roles and conditions of wardens' wives, it is particularly interesting because it provides an account of the development of the national parks that is almost entirely focused on the project of making a home in the wilderness – in other words, on the unfolding of the *domestic* portion of the warden story. The women tell similar and sometimes overlapping stories about how they cooked family meals on camp stoves, how they coped with sick children miles away from formal medical attention, how they put out forest fires alongside their husbands on the sorely understaffed fire lines. But they also tell about how they made curtains for the tiny warden cabins and how they rescued their sewing machines from fires.

Let me offer three (of many) examples of the wardens' wives' pride in their frontier homemaking:

> The warden's house was built about a mile and a half from the station [at Leanchoil, in Yoho]. The house consisted of five rooms: a kitchen, living room, two bedrooms and a utility room. However, there were no conveniences such as running water or plumbing, and lighting was by kerosene or gas lamps. We spent the winter here, and by spring had had a carpenter build cupboards in the kitchen with a sink for which my husband dug a septic tank. Every drop of water was used for flushing it.[44]

> Days were so full the worrying [about her children leaving for and returning from school in the dark] had to be done on the run, for there were barns to clean, cows to milk, clothes to wash by hand and bread baking for four hungry lunchers, plus the usual housework. Mother even canned the cow's milk to have on hand for the children when the cows went dry.[45]

> In the winter we made our own fun. Most women were good cooks and the Christmas feasts were amazing. They lasted into February.[46]

Taken as a group, the women narrating Dixon's stories thus contest "national"-park narratives in two linked ways. First, *Silent Partners* places women and domesticity directly at the *centre* of national-park development. Women's domestic stories of making a home in the wilderness are not banished to the settled margins of the real nature of the national parks (compare to Marty, but also to Burns). Rather, the whole history of the Warden Service comes to resemble a rather fragile story about families' ability to thrive *inside* the parks. As a Canadian story, this one is not especially unusual; Dixon draws from a long and rich tradition of local historical writing to craft her collage of personal reminiscences of daily life and ends up producing a patchwork story about the extension of settlement in the mountains, about the expansion of the heterosexual nuclear family into unlikely places. Certainly, this is a colonial story, and the accounts of early Métis and Aboriginal women are blended uncritically into an overarching narrative about colonial progress and modernization on the frontier. As a *national-park* narrative, however, Dixon's book is very rare, indeed. In the context of a history of the Warden Service – and indeed, of parks generally – focused intensively on lonely male pursuits in the sublime and "unpenetrated" wilderness, a story about homemaking is quite a dramatic departure. Simply put, Dixon places the extension of the *domestic* nation at the centre of the story of national-park development, which is (one might argue) where it belongs.

What we have in Dixon's book is a series of settler narratives located *inside* the park, crossing and intersecting with some of the more (male-homosocial) traditional accounts of living in the parks. This emphasis has the effect of displacing the more mythic national nature that national parks tend to embrace and represent; a nature that includes laundering dirty diapers can hardly be sublime. In the perpetuation of a mythic and empty park-nature, narratives such as Marty's *hide* the fact that parks are an extension of colonial relations, an active emptying of the landscape of traditional, productive, and reproductive activities. Dixon, rather than hiding the parks' representation of colonial expansion behind this masculinized narrative of the unbroken wild-warden tradition, demonstrates that the extension of settlement has, since the very early years of the Warden Service (at least), been a clear part of the national parks. Indeed, she demonstrates effectively (if unintentionally) that the mythic idea of the wild warden has, since the arrival of the very first warden's wife (or maybe lover?) in the Rocky Mountain national parks, been *contingent* on someone else doing the domestic tasks necessary to a warden's work.

Lesbian Rangers: Contesting the Gendered Nation

Dixon's stories leave out a great deal, of course. For one thing, in its predominant focus on *some* women's domestic roles, many other aspects of women's experiences are left out. Women have had a stunning variety of relations to Rocky Mountain park-natures, both historically and in the present. Aboriginal and Métis women such as Suzette Swift were crucial to the early years of development in the Rocky Mountain region in a whole host of roles. Colonial white women alpinists and adventurers such as Mary Schäffer played an important role in exploring and mapping the terrain for future recreational travellers. Women naturalists and other "amateur" scientists and collectors such as Mary de la Beach-Nichol were among the region's earliest tourists; accompanied or single, they entered the region and brought back to eastern Canada and Europe many examples of hitherto apparently undiscovered flora and fauna. Women lived and worked at Silver City and, later, Bankhead as shopkeepers, miners' wives, teachers, prostitutes. Women have been paid park workers: wardens, naturalists, service workers in hotels and restaurants. Women have struggled to pre-serve the parks against resource development; women have struggled to *open* the parks to Aboriginal harvesting and land negotiation.

Thus, even as the thread is important, I happily concede that the history of gender in the Rocky Mountain national parks cannot be written along a single dimension of wilderness and domesticity. In this chapter, therefore, which concerns how the domestic-wild tension works in the parks toward the production of a certain gendered *nationalism*, I would like to include at least one overt *challenge* to the discourses I have thus far outlined. That challenge arrives in the works of performance artists Lorri Millan and Shawna Dempsey, who in 1997 staged a site-specific work in Banff National Park called "Lesbian National Parks and Services" (LNPS). In their resistances to *both* the domestic and wilderness narratives operating in the parks, one can see that this division of nationalist labour is both foundationally gendered and, in fact, heterosexually inscribed.

In their summer-long performance, Dempsey and Millan, both young white women, looked very official in their short-sleeved, beige uniforms crested with "Lesbian National Parks and Services" and with "Rangers" patches on the left arms. In various locations around the Banff townsite, they handed out brochures to visitors, responded to requests for informa-tion and directions, and were highly visible interlopers in the day-to-day workings of a tourist town in the middle of a national park. Clearly, mem-bers of the public mistook them, however temporarily, for "real" wardens, and this misrecognition was a crucial part of the point of their performance. Once engaged – trapped in an interaction clearly based on the Rangers' performance of official park knowledge and authority – visitors gradually came to recognize that something was wrong. The word "Lesbian" was emblazoned in red letters on Dempsey and Millan's hats. The supposedly official brochures, while covering accurate directions to some "official" sights, also included such destinations as the "Invisible Lesbian Heritage House and Gardens." In an interview with Margot Francis, Millan commented that "during the course of answering these questions the fact that the frame was hanging a bit crooked on the wall would dawn on them. I used to think it would be nice if we had a little video camera on those pamphlets to see what happened when they opened them and read it."[47]

Even more strikingly, Dempsey said of one man, "when he got up to us he read the label of my shirt insignia out loud. L E S B I A N National Parks and Services. Realizing that he didn't know (or couldn't acknowledge) what he was dealing with, he suddenly had to improvise. His conclusion: 'Now that must be Federal, isn't it!'"[48]

Dempsey and Millan argue that the LNPS performance is largely about contesting the hegemony of heterosexuality, both by challenging the vast unspoken assumption that the world is straight and, more specifically, by "naturalizing" the presence of lesbians in it. "The assumption of hetero-sexuality," they note, "really does mask everything we do. It's about time we're seen as a normal part of an ecosystem rather than an exceptional part ... or an aberrant part."[49] In this task, the LNPS performance in Banff National Park is crucial. First, Dempsey and Millan take on the authority and knowledge of the national park, *including* the nature knowledge presumed to be attached to the position.[50] The conflict between this nature authority – which is clearly coded as heterosexual and male – and the big red letters "L E S B I A N" is, in fact, a large source of the dissonance that drives the humour of the whole piece. This conflict, however, is not the only source; given that Banff is a resort, wilderness is only part of the visitor's attraction to the place. Indeed, although Dempsey and Millan pose as LNPS wardens, they do much of their work in the Banff townsite, which is, like most recreational spaces, framed and organized by heterosexual conventions. Here, then, the LNPS's critique is not only of the presumed heterosexuality of *nature*, but also of the pervasive heterosexuality of *domestic* (commercial) space. As they specifically argue, Banff "is a place where people come to shop, maybe see a little nature, and then do some more shopping. It's about a certain sort of heterosexual commercial activity, and people are caught off guard – we look like something that fits, we make them laugh, hopefully, but the strategy is that by engaging people's sense of humour and humanity, maybe they'll open up a bit and think about something they haven't thought of before."[51]

I would like to argue that the LNPS, in its exposure of the heterosexism of both wilderness and domestic space in Banff National Park, also takes aim at its national significance. At the most obvious level, Dempsey and Millan are parodying wardens; they are taking in and spitting out the mandated authority of the federal state. But they are also, as pseudo-wardens, populating the parks with lesbians who aspire to official inclusion and recognition. Thus, if wardens are positioned as the speakers for iconic park-nature, as boundary police between the wild and the domestic, then it is highly significant that the hypermasculine *homosocial* version is challenged and replaced by a gender-bending female *homosexual* one; Dempsey and Millan are, in fact, highlighting the ongoing, pervasive, and invisible presence of queers in nature, in the domestic, and throughout narratives of the Canadian nation.

Peter Dickinson argues that Canadian national narratives are filled with male homosociality; following Eve Sedgwick, he contends that male homosociality and homosexuality are part of the same phenomenon of male-male attraction but that homophobic panic refracts male homosocial desire through "the passive positioning of women as displaced objects of nominal/patrimonial heterosexual desire."[52] Briefly, he notes that the hypermasculinized homosociality of wilderness stories, for example, plays with the fact that heterosexual conventions have not been formally established in the outlaw wild of the frontier. In Major John Richardson's 1832 *Wacousta,* for example (a novel that Gaile McGregor considers a crucial origin of the linkage of Canadian nationalism with wilderness),[53] men thrive on their intense friendships and circles of same-sex admiration. In such texts, however, the inclusion of women and the domestic tend to function to guarantee heterosexuality in the midst of this rather passionate homosociality; the story of the nation in the wilderness, then, requires the looming presence of domestic order so that the hypermasculine admiration of the frontier cannot be mistaken for anything else.[54] Women are, here, both the bearers of the future nation in the form of the heterosexual family and the guarantors against the degeneracy of the frontier in its homosocial wildness.

The LNPS asserts the visibility of a counternarrative of specifically *lesbian* desire in both the wild and the domestic nation-spaces of national parks and, in so doing, highlights the fact that neither the masculinity of nation nor the heterosexuality of the domestic – and thus the heterosexuality of the nation – is guaranteed. Here we can see that the dominant national-park nation-narrative represented by the Warden Service, as apparent in Marty's enthusiastic embrace of the masculine homosocial ideal, is not only *physically* enabled by the "silent" presence of wardens' wives but *sexually* legitimated by their heterosexual and familial presence. In response, Dempsey and Millan "queer" the Warden Service and the national parks along with it. They raise the possibility of a homosexual presence in official national-park culture; they make same-sex desire – and especially same-sex desire among women – a reality in the iconic space of the masculine wilderness-nation; and they call into question the assumption of women's heterosexuality and, along with it, their heterosexualizing role as bearers of the domestic nation.[55] The LNPS, then, queers the "national"-park story rather strikingly.

Conclusion: Home on the Range?

In the conclusion to *A Border Within,* Ian Angus argues that English Canadian identity rests on a tension between a history of building a home in the wilderness and "a moment of wildness, of loss, and of absence, for wilderness is precisely what cannot be captured. In the same moment that we reflect on our construction of a home, the ineradicability of the wilderness must be brought inside as an acceptance of the locality of all belonging."[56] I have argued throughout this chapter that the national significance of Canadian national parks (and especially of the four northern Rocky Mountain parks) rests, more or less, on exactly this tension. They straddle a border between a narrative of nation building via settlement, domestication, economic expansion, and assimilation and a narrative of wildness and *sublime* nationality, of a colonially derived iconic nature-space presented as before and beyond any human homes.

With Angus looking critically over my shoulder, then, I wish to reiterate that this identity tension is a very risky one and that there are complex and problematic power relations behind both national stories involved. First, we have a strongly *racialized* dynamic in which wilderness "becomes" wilderness via the violent and systematic erasure of peoples from particular landscapes. In the case of national parks, which one can (arguably) consider as federally instituted attempts toward the national (English Canadian) identity Angus describes, the trouble with wilderness (to use Cronon's phrase)[57] is that it wasn't. Wilderness is, in the parks, achieved via the violent *imposition* of emptiness on the land, with "homemaking" in the now-empty land thus becoming, ideally and primarily, white. Second, we have a historically articulated gender division of labour between the masculinized narrative of wilderness and the feminized expansion of homemaking. As is particularly clear in the case of the Warden Service, the discursive border between the wild and the domestic is enabled by the *erasure* of women's homemaking labour; their contributions are systematically excluded from depictions of the history of the parks, which allows the parks to continue to be portrayed as wild and masculine spaces. Third, of course, the apparent bifurcation of wilderness from domesticity in the parks rests on a strongly heterosexual assumption that, although women are the "silent partners," they are *wives*. If national parks require *both* nature-nations in order to play out their organizing tension between wild and domestic currents, and if there is a gender division of labour between the two, then parks are inscribed as fundamentally organized by a sort of heterosexual complementarity. Wild spaces are homosocially risky; their iconic nationality is, in fact, performed and justified by their attachment to the feminine, even as their ideology of wilderness would seem to exclude any such domesticating presence.

To be sure, I think there are significant differences between Angus's call for an English Canadian philosophy of belonging and abjection (which I think ends up as a very interesting environmental philosophy) and my analysis of parks as highly problematic sites of racial and gender politics. But the question remains: If there *is* something to this idea that Canadian national identity rests in a tension between wilderness and domesticity, then what is narratively erased, displaced, and/or reified along this border? While I would be among the last people to suggest that the parks should simply embrace the domestic – especially if the domestic means shopping malls – I would also argue that national parks must be understood as sites of gendered, racialized, and sexualized negotiations among national discourses. Thus any environmental philosophy attached to such a family of negotiations – and any set of federal policies aimed at "preserving" or "restoring" national parks as sites of Canadian heritage – should be very careful about where they are stepping.

Notes

1 Sid Marty, *Men for the Mountains* (Toronto: McClelland and Stewart, 1978), 11.
2 May Tocher, interviewed in Anne Dixon, *Silent Partners: Wives of National Park Wardens* (Pincher Creek, AB: Dixon and Dixon Publishers, 1985), 59.
3 Margot Francis, "Wild Kingdom: There's No Life Like It," *XTRA!* 16 May 2002, 6.
4 Sid Marty, *A Grand and Fabulous Notion: The First Century of Canada's Parks* (Toronto: NC Press and Ministry of Supply and Services, 1984), 34. Marty also notes that McCabe and the McCardells were hardly the first to "discover" the springs, including centuries of use by the Stoney people (a fact they wisely kept secret from such early travellers as the Earl of Southesk). For histories of Banff, see also W.F. Lothian, *A History of Canada's National Parks*, vol. 1 (Ottawa: Parks Canada, 1976); and Eleanor Luxton, *Banff: Canada's First National Park: A History and a Memory of Rocky Mountains Park* (Banff, AB: Summerthought, 1975).
5 *Statutes of Canada*, 1887, 50-51 Victoria, c. 32.
6 Leslie Bella, *Parks for Profit* (Montreal: Harvest House, 1987).
7 I recognize that my use of the terms "nation" and "nationalism" in the first section of the chapter is historically contentious and that the emergence of Canadian nationalist rhetoric per se might be more accurately dated to the period immediately following the First World War. I use the terms in order to suggest that the parks played a role very soon after Confederation in *shaping* nationalist discourse. Although the parks are clearly steeped in the rhetoric of empire (as remnants of the "wild lands" civilized by Britain), they are also grounded in a desire to highlight the natural *difference* between Canada and Britain.
8 Donald Smith, cited in W.F. Lothian, *A Brief History of Canada's National Parks* (Ottawa: Ministry of the Environment, 1987), 22.
9 Ben Gadd, *Bankhead: The Twenty Year Town* (Banff, AB: Canadian Parks Service, 1989).
10 The Dominion Lands Act of 1860 promised 160 acres to any man willing to stake ten dollars on his ability to cultivate 40 acres. This Act excluded women from holding independent title, but clearly encouraged men with families to settle the Prairies. As Cecilia Danysk notes, although there was space for bachelor farmers on the Prairies, small family farms offered economic, social, and political benefits to the expanding nation; women's nation-building labour was completely hidden, but their interest in their property served as a conservative force. See "'A Bachelor's Paradise': Homesteaders, Hired Hands, and the Construction of Masculinity, 1880-1930," in *Making Western Canada: Essays on European Colonization and Settlement*, edited by Catherine Cavanaugh and Jeremy Mouat (Toronto: Garamond, 1996), 154-85.
11 RMP was only the world's third national park, following the United States' Yellowstone Park and Australia's Royal National Park.
12 *The Canadian Pacific: The New Highway to the East across the Mountains, Prairies and Rivers of Canada* (Canadian Pacific Railway, 1887), cited in E.J. Hart, *The Selling of Canada: The CPR and the Beginnings of Canadian Tourism* (Banff, AB: Altitude, 1983), 25.
13 Anne McClintock, *Imperial Leather: Race, Gender and Sexuality in the Colonial Contest* (New York: Routledge, 1995), 354-55.
14 In this analysis, I am, of course, indebted to William Cronon's now (in)famous essay, "The Trouble with Wilderness, or Getting Back to the Wrong Nature," in *Uncommon Ground: Toward Reinventing Nature*, edited by William Cronon (New York: Norton, 1995), 69-90.
15 Bankhead, for example, was ethnically diverse, with a population that included Italian, Polish, Czech, German, and French Canadian families, in addition to a number of single Chinese men (Gadd, *Bankhead*, 39). There was, clearly, a racialized and class division between Banff as a site of CPR nature consumption and Bankhead as a site of CPR coal production.
16 Sarah Carter, *Capturing Women: The Manipulation of Cultural Images in Canada's Prairie West* (Montreal and Kingston: McGill-Queen's University Press, 1997), 9.
17 I would argue that the domestic ideal of the national park is, in its more contemporary form, assimilationist, whereas the wilderness ideal is exclusively white. National-park recreation facilities are supposed to invite diverse people to "become" part of the nation; the nation that they are to become is already stamped with colonial whiteness.

18 The idea of parks as preserved "unimpaired for future generations" is an interesting twist on Homi Bhabha's description of nationalism as a temporal move that takes the nation from a timeless past to a future glory, rushing us past the messiness of the present; see *The Location of Culture* (London, UK: Routledge, 1994). Here the parks specifically deny the messy present – which appears in discourses of ecological integrity as "impairment" – in a desire to move park-nature, as unchanged as possible, from pre-Columbian past to glorious future. The idea of ecosystems as *including* human beings, and as dynamic sites for human-nature interaction, threatens to render nature historical (full of people doing things either carefully or wantonly) rather than national (timeless and empty).

19 Yoho was established in 1895, Jasper was reserved in 1907, and Kootenay was established in 1920. I do not include Waterton Lakes in this group because it is historically, culturally, ecologically, and geographically quite distinct from the four northern Rocky Mountain parks (which are now World Heritage sites). All four parks were "railway" parks, serviced by the CPR (CNR in Jasper's case although the Jasper Park Lodge was a CPR Hotel), and all four parks were – and are – caught between the scenic nationalism of the Rockies (complete with stories of the nation-building railways that run through them) and the incursion of settlement and infrastructure brought by tourism. Other parks in other landscapes – including Waterton – bear different inflections of nationalist tension. On this topic, see Catriona Sandilands, "Cross-Border Natures: Nationalism and Tourism in Waterton-Glacier International Peace Park," in *The American and Canadian Wests: Essays on the History of the Border-lands of the Western United States and Canada*, edited by Sterling Evans (Albuquerque, NM: University of New Mexico Press, forthcoming).

20 On these actors, respectively, see Gadd, *Bankhead;* Gail Guthrie Valaskasis, "Postcards of My Past: Indians and Academics," in *Between Views,* edited by Daina Augaitis and Sylvie Gilbert (Banff, AB: Banff Centre for the Arts, 1991), 31-35; Sheila J. McHugh, *Give My Regards to the Beanery: Reflections of a Summer Staff Person at Banff Springs Hotel* (Lethbridge, AB: n.p., 1987); Bart Robinson, *Banff Springs: The Story of a Hotel* (Banff, AB: Summerthought, 1973); and Rick Searle, *Phantom Parks: The Struggle to Save Canada's National Parks* (Toronto: Key Porter, 2000).

21 Robert J. Burns, with Mike Schintz, *Guardians of the Wild: A History of the Warden Service of Canada's National Parks* (Calgary: University of Calgary Press, 2000), 8.

22 Burns, *Guardians,* 7.

23 Marty, *Grand and Fabulous Notion,* 101. Bill Peyto, who, according to Marty, "loathed the government with a passion," was hired as a part-time deputy warden in 1912 and came to be one of the archetypal "old-timers" of the Warden Service.

24 Game guardians came to be known as "wardens" in 1914. Parks Commissioner J.B. Harkin had been in the midst of a heated power struggle with the Forestry Branch and is reputed to have chosen the term "warden" specifically as a contrast to the forest-service "ranger." See Burns, *Guardians,* 13.

25 A 1925 list of topics for training suggested by Parks Commissioner J.B. Harkin implies that wardens were being forced, even here, to dip their toes into public relations. Alongside "care and repair of hose" and "driving and running of Ford trucks," Harkin saw the need for wardens to consider "education of public in regard to care in use of fire." Burns, *Guardians,* 162.

26 Ibid., 149.

27 Ibid., 169-70.

28 Cited in ibid., 167.

29 My thanks to Melody Hessing for suggesting this text.

30 Burns, *Guardians,* 172.

31 J.A. Sime and D.E. Schuler, "The Park Warden Function in the National Parks Service," (Hull, QC: Parks Canada, National Parks Documentation Centre, 1968).

32 Sime and Schuler, "The Park Warden Function," cited in Burns, *Guardians,* 263-65.

33 Marty, *Men for the Mountains,* 39.

34 Marty puts this phrase in the mouth of the ghost of George Busby, who was an early warden of Jasper National Park (ibid., 11).

35   Ibid., 161.
36   Anne LaBastille, *Women and Wilderness* (San Francisco: Sierra Club Books, 1980).
37   Marty, *Men for the Mountains*, 11.
38   Marty, *Grand and Fabulous Notion*, 145. In this passage, Marty also demonstrates a common dehistoricization of Aboriginal peoples, in which their *past* presence is highly visible but not their present struggles. Daniel Francis (among others) argues that this erasure is a form of genocide. See *The Imaginary Indian: The Image of the Indian in Canadian Culture* (Vancouver: Arsenal Pulp Press, 1992).
39   Despite his clear distaste for Parks Canada bureaucracy, Marty apparently adheres to prohibitions like these with some devotion.
40   Dixon, *Silent Partners*, 31-32.
41   Cited in Burns, *Guardians*, 173.
42   Superintendent Mitchell to Chief Park Warden Allan, 1956, cited in Burns, *Guardians*, 228. The gardens described are actually in Riding Mountain National Park (Manitoba), but there were also gardens in the Rocky Mountain parks, grown and officially tolerated for much the same reasons.
43   Dixon, *Silent Partners*, 3.
44   Rhoda Nicholson, in Dixon, *Silent Partners*, 67.
45   Dean Allen (about Theresa Allen), in Dixon, *Silent Partners*, 63-64.
46   Ellen Giddie, in Dixon, *Silent Partners*, 71.
47   Lorri Millan, interview with Margot Francis, cited in "The Lesbian National Parks and Services: Reading Sex, Race and the Nation in Artistic Performance," *Canadian Woman Studies/ les cahiers de la femme* 20, 2 (2000): 134.
48   Shawna Dempsey, interview with Margot Francis, in "Lesbian National," 143.
49   Shawna Dempsey and Lorri Millan, "Lesbian National Parks and Services," video clip, in *Live Decade: 1989-1999*, directed by Shawna Dempsey and Lorri Millan (Winnipeg: Finger in the Dyke Productions, 1999), film.
50   In a more recent video – Dempsey and Millan have, in fact, continued the LNPS performance in a variety of ways, including a "world tour" that got them interesting coverage in the *Sydney Morning Herald* – the two transform their performance into a parody of a nature documentary. As Margot Francis notes, this act "sends up the heterosexist bias of [nature] shows, when they focus on the bizarre mating behaviours and drive toward reproduction that supposedly characterize the natural world" ("Wild Kingdom," 6). This critique has been extended in their recent work, *Lesbian National Parks and Services Field Guide to North America: Flora, Fauna, and Survival Skills* (Toronto: Pedlar Press, 2002).
51   Dempsey and Millan, "Lesbian National," film.
52   Peter Dickinson, *Here is Queer: Nationalisms, Sexualities and the Literatures of Canada* (Toronto: University of Toronto Press, 1999), 11.
53   Gaile McGregor, *The Wacousta Syndrome: Explorations in the Canadian Langscape* (Toronto: University of Toronto Press, 1985).
54   Dickinson argues that Richardson does *not* eventually guarantee the legitimating presence feminine virtue: Domestic harmony is "not allowed to triumph amid a chaotic wilderness setting where national, social and sexual conventions have not yet been stabilized" (*Here is Queer*, 15).
55   Much as I think Millan and Dempsey's work is intelligent and courageous, I should point out that their work leaves the *whiteness* of both the iconic and the domestic nation intact. As Margot Francis also notes, their ability to "pass" as wardens hinges on the fact that they are white (and, of course, on the fact that women wardens are no longer as uncommon as they were in Sid Marty's day); it is only because of the moment of passing as wardens that the performance "works" ("Lesbian National," 135). Parks Canada has almost no people of colour in its Warden Service; one exception is Pukaskwa National Park, which includes a number of Aboriginal wardens.
56   Ian Angus, *A Border Within: National Identity, Cultural Plurality, and Wilderness* (Montreal and Kingston: McGill-Queen's University Press, 1997), 202.
57   William Cronon, *Uncommon Ground: Toward Reinventing Nature*, edited by William Cronon (New York: Norton, 1995).

Part 3
Environmental Politics:
Issues at Home and Away

For Canadians, the phrase "environmental politics" conjures up a variety of images. One of the more dramatic ones from recent history is probably that of Clayoquot Sound, where in 1994 eight hundred people were arrested for blockading a logging road at Kennedy Lake. This protest was the largest instance of civil disobedience in Canadian history. Individuals from many walks of life felt compelled to say "no" to Interfor and MacMillan Bloedel, who wanted to clearcut a large swath of old-growth forest in a region of Vancouver Island increasingly bereft of any forest at all. That this area was also contested by the Nuu-chah-nulth Nation added a layer of tension and complication to the picture, with members of First Nations communities occupying a range of positions between and among the bifurcated "loggers versus environmentalists" depiction so dear to the media.

The Clayoquot protests – and the negotiations preceding and following them – politicized and transformed the local logging industry. They also affected gender relations: in the environmental community participating in the protests, in the logging community of Ucluelet, the tourism town of Tofino, where the landscape is an attraction, and among the Nuu-chah-nulth, who were also affected in diverse ways by both the industry and the protests. For example, Greenpeace activist Tzeporah Berman, one of the most prominent actors in the Clayoquot protests (who later wrote a master's thesis theorizing from her experiences, on which many of the present observations rest),[1] made a conscious effort to organize the "Peace Camp" tent-city of protesters along ecofeminist principles: consensus decision-making, collective labour (cooking and site maintenance), and nonviolence at all times. In so doing, she drew attention to some of the issues plaguing gender relations of wilderness activism: Although women make up the majority of members of preservationist organizations, men had tended to take on the most high-profile roles, those often associated with "heroic" acts of individual bravery. Berman thus helped open the door to a differently gendered

environmental activism, one in which a greater variety of forms of participation was valued.

Behind this positive change, however, the picture of gender relations in
Clayoquot Sound is more complicated. Anecdotal evidence suggests that
the incidence of violence against women in both white and First Nations
communities in the Clayoquot region rose noticeably during the protests.
Particularly given the visible feminist presence among the environmentalist actors in the conflict, the gender composition of the logging industry
came into sharp relief. High-wage, unionized jobs typically performed by
men were under attack, and most of the environmental groups involved in
the protests did not have many concrete alternatives. Ecotourism, the much-
touted economic future for the region, promised a raft of low-wage, nonunionized service jobs: women's work. Indeed, even among Nuu-chah-nulth
communities, some women ran into a considerable gender barrier as they
moved to take advantage of Clayoquot's vault into international prominence as an ecotourist destination. Here the displacement of industrial logging involved the disruption of some fairly entrenched gender relations,
and environmentalists, in failing to fully address the profound social consequences of the economic and ecological changes for which they were fighting, lit a gender firecracker.

Of course, MacMillan Bloedel has hardly been a paragon of feminist virtue, providing few job opportunities for women in forest-resource communities and even fewer supports for women and families in the increasingly
isolated regions in which forest operations are concentrated. When MacBlo
pulled out of the Clayoquot region, it hardly demonstrated significant care
and attention to the domestic instability and uncertainty it caused in doing
so. Yet the company was more than happy during the Clayoquot protests to
exploit ecofeminism in its quest for good public relations. In a blatant attempt to contest the protesters' presumed claim to a feminine moral high
ground, the company took out a television advertisement that prominently
featured a very pregnant MacBlo vice president speaking in glowing maternal terms about the company's benevolent forest practices.

Not surprisingly, what the Clayoquot example suggests is that environmental issues are strongly gendered and that these gender relations are deeply
embedded in the particular social and ecological relations of the place(s) in
question. Thus participants in environmental politics need to take gender
into consideration both inside their operations *and* in terms of the larger
communities affected by environmental change. Environmental politics
derive *from* gendered relations and also contribute *to* them in a variety of
ways both intentional and unintentional.

To argue that environmental politics are gendered is not to suggest that
there is a single "women's" standpoint on environmental degradation, nor
is it to argue that women have a special responsibility to "clean up" the planet

located in some presumably greater connection to natural processes. It is, rather, to argue that gender relations – among and in intersection with other power relations – shape people's experiences of, and desires for, the natural world. Hence they shape politics. Women, for example, are often at the forefront of struggles for community environmental health. At one level, women's often primary or sole responsibility for their families' daily well-being may condition a particular alertness to family illnesses; at another level, women's communication networks may further alert them to unusual health-related events in the larger community. Women are also the primary consumers of household goods and often have a much more sophisticated awareness of nutrition and food standards as a result. In addition, men in health-impacted communities are often employed by precisely the industry that is causing the problem and may be reluctant to act as "whistle-blowers." And finally, of course, community epidemiology is not a very glamorous occupation; climbing a skyscraper to hang an anticorporate banner is far sexier than trudging from door to door asking about family incidents of cancer or birth defects.

That said, not all women are equally affected by environmental degradation, nor are they equally involved in environmental politics. For example, working-class women and women of colour are far more likely than white, middle-class women to live in close proximity to toxic environments or to be displaced as a result of environmental change. Lesbian couples are more likely than heterosexual women to feel unsafe in rural and wilderness environments. At another level, one should point out that some women engage in environmental politics for reasons that have nothing to do with their families; these women are motivated directly by a general concern with abstract principles of justice or value or responsibility. Of course, some women are also actively antienvironmental for reasons that have everything to do with their families, such as many women who have been involved in the so-called Wise Use movement (promoting "resource sharing" as opposed to conservation). So the relationship between women and environmental politics is hardly simple.

As the chapters in this part demonstrate, however, there remain important commonalities to consider. Women's labour, perhaps especially in a neoliberal era of downsizing and downloading, increasingly involves a difficult negotiation of realms of life that affect, and are affected by, environmental issues. Women's subsistence activities, so often left out of environmental development and planning activities in both North American and overseas contexts, form a rich bed of knowledges from which to formulate policies and politics alternative to current paths of management and destruction. Women's bodies are the subject of considerable environmental controversy, being constituted in very particular ways in the public eye for deeply gendered political reasons. And women are often politically active

in specific, often local grassroots milieux; although many consider themselves active environmental citizens alongside men, it is also the case that
women's environmental activism is shaped by their particular skills, conflicts, relationships, responsibilities, and exclusions.

Sherilyn MacGregor tackles this complex nexus of issues head-on. Drawing from interviews with women "quality-of-life" activists from the Toronto
area, she notes that women are both particularly enabled and particularly
constrained by existing gendered environmental relations. On the one hand,
women activists are deeply involved, in a range of ways, in struggling to
improve environmental health and social justice in southern Ontario. Their
political activities are often shaped and enriched by their intimate and expert understandings of quality-of-life issues in their households, neighbourhoods, and communities. On the other hand, women activists often face
enormous obstacles to their political involvement, ranging from heavy care-
giving responsibilities to conflicts between paid and unpaid work. Especially in the midst of a New Right atmosphere of public unloading of social
and environmental responsibility, women activists find that their political
labour is both more important and more difficult. Women are tackling air-
quality issues, protesting urban sprawl, campaigning to ban pesticide use,
and struggling to clean up industrially contaminated soils. Women are also
struggling to find the time to be activists in the middle of a general decline
in social services in Ontario and to implement in their households the kinds
of green values they see as crucial in other political spaces. Despite these
conflicts – which are particularly acute for women who are racially marked
and economically disadvantaged – women understand their activism as a
significant practice of environmental citizenship.

Moving from local to transnational politics, Leonora C. Angeles, Layla
Saad, and Rebecca Tarbotton argue that international discourses of
"sustainability" need to be viewed with a strategic, critical, feminist eye. In
particular, development practices and policies grounded in northern agendas are deeply problematic and often cover over the need for a thoroughgoing critique of globalization, including its economic, environmental, and
social – gendered, racialized, colonial – effects. As an alternative, the authors
present a political "path of knowledge production and social learning that
privileges the knowledge learned from the experiences of oppressed and
marginal communities," particularly those of women from the global South.
Women's organizations are on the front lines of criticizing development
policies that serve capitalist markets at the expense of the rural poor and
the natural environments on which subsistence practices depend. For example, the Women's Alliance of Ladakh (WAL) is based on a combination of
ecological awareness and gendered cultural resistance to the incursions of
global-market relations; it explicitly links the preservation of Ladakhi traditional rural culture with the reinvigoration of resistant agricultural prac-

tices. In a more urban setting, the MAKAKABUS women's organization in Bukidnon initiated a series of cooperative ventures to support organic agriculture in this peri-urban region of Mindanao, Philippines. It has successfully created a diverse range of revenue-generating activities for poor communities, from rice production and marketing to microcredit loans and farm-equipment rental. Finally, in Santo Andre, Brazil, women have been instrumental in community-based watershed management, using oral histories from community members as a way of documenting and promoting locally based, sustainable water practices. Globalization is, in all three contexts, something of a double-edged sword. At the same time as capitalist expansion impoverishes local environments and livelihoods, it also enables a North-South feminist ecological politics based on a "strategic sisterhood" of transnational dialogues and interactions.

Moving out from these hopeful and generative projects, Kathryn Harrison draws our attention back to the disturbing fact of the widespread dioxin contamination of breast milk in North America. In a 1990 report by the Canadian federal government, it was estimated that breast-fed infants receive 16.5 times the "tolerable daily intake" of dioxins set by that same government. Despite the sustained attention given to dioxins by environmental groups, as well as the cultural significance of breasts as symbols of the continuity of life, almost no political attention has been paid to this fact in either Canada or the United States. Harrison's chapter asks "why?" in a thoroughgoing way. First, she locates this loaded question in a larger theoretical discussion of risk perception and political agenda setting, discussing both psychological and political dimensions of risk. Second, she offers detailed and substantial evidence for the tremendous hazard of breast-milk exposure to dioxins: The US Environmental Protection Agency estimates that breast-fed infants receive 4 to 12 percent of their lifetime exposure to dioxins in the first year of life, and all evidence points to dramatic impacts. Harrison then moves into a more focused discussion of breast milk on the public agenda, documenting a staggering absence of attention and, finally, comparing a series of different explanations for such a silence. The reason for this inattention is certainly not that the problem is not potentially severe: Other issues, such as the presence of Alar in apples, are probably less risky in actuality but have received far more notice. Nor is it the case that there have been no focusing "events" to prompt a public questioning; environmental organizations concerned with particular hazards seldom have difficulty orchestrating such events. Harrison also rejects, on the balance of evidence, explanations based on institutional factors and on agenda denial by such actors as physicians and breast-feeding advocates. Disturbingly, Harrison concludes that "the media have seldom focused on the questions of dioxins in breast milk largely because environmentalists themselves have made relatively few efforts to date to draw attention to the issue." Particularly among women environmental activists, the issue has been described as "too close to home." Harrison calls into question the idea that women's environmental activism stems, transparently, from personal issues; this one, it seems, might be *too* personal.

Finally, Katherine Dunster draws our political attention to "what we do where we live." In the post-Rio context of globalizing capital – and, despite Rio, of continuing environmental devastation – it is often difficult for individual women to feel they are making a difference in world events. Community activism and everyday changes are, however, significant. Although there are many forms that such "local" activism can take, Dunster points particularly to making *maps* – literally – as engendering alternative meanings and relations to one's places, lands, and local relations. Community mapping is a way of reclaiming the language and skills of map making for people to investigate and record the significant events and sites of their home-places. It involves sorting through various sources of available textual information, listening to and recording stories from elders, and not least walking the land itself and learning to recognize its subtle changes, shapes, and variations. In Dunster's home-place, a region she calls the "Islands in the Salish Sea," a well-developed community mapping project stands as a grassroots bioregional attempt to help develop sustainable ecological and social relations. Mapping here is a tool for both community self-knowledge and community transformation; as she writes, "when a map is created that counters prevailing knowledge, it can be used to help frame questions and challenge decision makers to change politics and practices." And it is not technically difficult to do, even as it requires energy and commitment for tasks beginning with the development of basic community awareness through education, continuing with data collection and coalition building, and extending to the use of newly found local knowledges in order to challenge government structures and processes.

Here, echoing observations made by the other contributors to this part, Dunster notes that a deeper understanding of women's experiences of particular landscapes, and a deeper understanding of a landscape's particular effects on gender relations, shapes a rich and, ultimately, more ecological politics.

Note
1 Tzeporah Berman, "Standing for Our Lives: Ecofeminism and Lessons from Clayoquot Sound" (Master's thesis, Faculty of Environmental Studies, York University, 1995).

9
The Public, the Private, the Planet, and the Province: Women's Quality-of-Life Activism in Urban Southern Ontario

Sherilyn MacGregor

> It's time to take responsibility and to take action. Environmental citizens must become better informed and get involved. How? By learning more about the environment and taking actions that show we care about planet Earth – our air, land, water, wildlife, fisheries and forests. Individuals, communities, organizations and governments must think about the environmental rights and responsibilities we all have as residents of planet Earth. We all have to become part of the solution – in our schools, in our communities, at work and in our own backyards. Individual efforts taken together can be powerful forces for environmental change. In fact they can make all the difference in the world!
> — Environment Canada[1]

Women do a disproportionate amount of unpaid community and environmental work in Canada. As those who are still primarily responsible for childcare and household management, many women appear to be more "in tune" than most men with quality-of-life issues, such as healthy air, soil and water quality, access to housing and green space, and the availability of safe and nourishing food. It is no surprise, then, that they tend to listen more carefully when called upon – by governments and greens alike – to act as good environmental citizens by buying the right products, refraining from the wrong behaviours, and teaching their children well. It is also because of these gender norms that women are expected to "pick up the slack" when New Right governments (such as the one under Ontario premiers Mike Harris and Ernie Eves from 1995 to 2003) erode the social and environmental safety net. The implications of this conjuncture for women activists who attempt to juggle the work of caring for people and the planet are the focus of this chapter.

Drawing on interviews I conducted with thirty women activists from the Toronto area at the height of the Harris government's tenure in the late 1990s, I discuss relationships between women's caring and household labour and their activism aimed at improving the quality of life in their neighbourhoods (and on the planet as a whole). I present excerpts from their stories in order not only to highlight their contributions to the struggle for environmental health and social justice in Ontario, but also to examine the costs and obstacles they experience in the process. In my conversations with women working on urban environmental issues ranging from lead contamination to pesticide use to police violence, I asked them about how they manage to juggle their various roles and what their experiences have taught them about the concepts of sustainability and "environmental citizenship." What I highlight here is the finding that these women sustain their green commitments and activist projects at significant cost to themselves. In so doing, I hope to expose an oft-overlooked paradox of a sustainability agenda that has become mainstream in Canadian life.

The Sustainability Agenda Meets Harris's New Right: Ontario in the 1990s

Interest in "sustainability" grew rapidly in Canada in the early 1990s, when popular concern for the environment was at its height and when governments at all levels were compelled to incorporate green strategies into their policy initiatives.[2] At the federal level, a five-year Green Plan was unveiled in 1990 that set out an ambitious list of goals for improving Canada's environmental record. Among the central priorities was to encourage environmentally responsible decision-making within all social strata and at all levels of government. Along with this move came the introduction of the concept of environmental citizenship as a way for individual Canadians to take an active role in moving toward sustainability. This role includes doing one's bit at home to implement the three Rs (reduce, reuse, recycle) as well as becoming knowledgeable about and actively participating in environmental issues. There was also a great push for local communities to take the lead on environmental stewardship programs, along the lines espoused in United Nations Local Agenda 21 (established at the Rio Earth Summit in 1992). Unique to Ontario, the Environmental Bill of Rights took effect in 1994, giving citizens of the province "formal rights to play a more effective role" in environmental protection.[3] Municipal blue-box programs and composter give-aways, such as those provided by the City of Toronto, were expanded, making environmental practices more convenient for the conscientious household. Nongovernmental environmental groups were also active throughout the early 1990s, promoting individual responsibility and green lifestyle changes. Popular guidebooks for green living and consuming (such as Pollution Probe's *Canadian Green Consumer Guide*, published in 1991) became best-sellers. Given all of this attention, it is not surprising that businesses started to capitalize on the ecofriendly trend. Ontario's Loblaws grocery stores launched a line of green products (some of which were publicly endorsed by environmental groups like Pollution Probe), and the availability of green services such as diaper laundering, organic-food delivery, and chemical-free lawn care increased dramatically (for those who could afford it).

By the mid-1990s, the social and political climate in parts of Canada started to undergo some drastic changes (alongside the climate change that citizens were beginning to realize was really happening). Ontario was particularly hard hit by a turn to the right after the election of the Progressive Conservative Party, led by Premier Mike Harris, in 1995. (He was succeeded by former finance minister Ernie Eves in 2002, who was defeated by Liberal candidate Dalton McGuinty in 2003. As it is too soon to say how or if policies have changed, I shall refer to them and their results in the present tense.) Soon after its election, the Ontario government – like other governments around the world – proceeded to adopt a host of neoliberal economic policies and socially conservative social policies that together form a New Right agenda (a.k.a. the Common Sense Revolution in Ontario). As part of this agenda, the Tory government cut funding to many of its ministries and social programs and downloaded the responsibility for a variety of public services to the local level. In an effort to reduce the unwieldy "burden" of responsibility of the local government, many of these services, particularly care and support services, were in turn contracted out to private companies or downloaded to the volunteer sector and to private individuals in families. The provincial government attempted to justify these policies, at times, by a socially conservative vision of community self-reliance and the duty of the family to take care of its own. This created a dangerous parallel between the ecoresponsibility espoused by the green Left and the neoconservative call for a return to ostensibly "traditional" methods of social provisioning (e.g., through churches, charities, and community volunteerism) as a way to cut costs and thus taxes.

Feminist political economists and policy researchers have explained the overall effects of New Right economic policies on women and have argued that policies such as Harris's take for granted that households (and the women who do unpaid caring labour in households) will be able to absorb the costs of restructuring and a diminished state role in the provision of basic services to citizens. In Ontario, while there were no explicit policies for forcing women to "take up the slack," there is evidence to suggest that this is what has happened. From helping to reduce the impacts of cuts to education through home-school committees to taking care of disabled or ailing family members at home, women all over Canada are shouldering a greater share of unpaid work than men.[4] Just under half of the thirty women I interviewed are working on improving conditions relating to the *social* environment, such as immigrant settlement, "neighbourhoodism," affordable housing and homelessness, and community-police relations. Their particular concerns demonstrate that "environment" means something broader for urban women than it tends to mean to those who move and think in so-called green or "environmentalist" circles.

At the same time as there are more people to take care of, there is a growing need for attention to the impacts of New Right policies on the *physical* environment in the city. The reality of a growing population, combined with pro-development policies, has led to an urban sprawl problem that places tremendous strain on the public infrastructure as well as on the physical (including the "natural") environment in and around Toronto. Local governments struggle to cope with the need to provide housing, jobs, and socio-economic support to the unemployed as well as to provide basic public services like transportation, waste disposal, and water and sewage treatment. Air quality is fast approaching a crisis situation as a car-dependent population with a need for heat in winter months consumes ever-higher quantities of nuclear and fossil-fuel energy.[5] Environmental organizations in Toronto, such as the Toronto Environmental Alliance (TEA), have named air quality one of their top priorities for political action. Asthma continues to grow at alarming rates; smog is said to kill more than eighteen hundred people in Ontario each year. Programs to reduce car use are popular, including increasing the use of public transit and other modes of transportation, such as bicycles. Another major issue for environmental groups is waste management. In an effort to curb the growing quantities of garbage produced by a large population, the local government charges dumping fees to industries and provides a household curb-side recycling program (called the blue-box program), but Toronto's waste-reduction efforts pale in comparison to those of other cities in Canada, like Halifax and Edmonton. Many western-European countries that once looked to Canadians for examples of effective municipal recycling schemes, but now the trend toward deregulation of business means that consumers (optionally) shoulder a greater responsibility for the three Rs than do producers. Other pressing local environmental issues include preserving important wetland areas (the Don River Valley and the Oak Ridges Moraine), banning residential and parkland pesticide use, and cleaning up lead- and chemical-contaminated soil that is a toxic legacy of Toronto's industrial past.

On the topic of environmental policies and politics in Ontario, it should be noted that the Harris government also revoked many environmental regulations and cut funding to the Ministry of the Environment by approximately 40 percent. These changes resulted in a reduced ministry capacity to monitor environmentally risky activities, so local governments and private citizens are now on their own in taking responsibility for the quality of their environments. Several environmental disasters occurred in Ontario during the Harris reign (e.g., the Plastimet fire in Hamilton and the E. coli water contamination in Walkerton), some would say as a direct result of the weakening of environmental regulations.[6] There is a large number of groups and organizations in Toronto dedicated to either resisting environmental deregulation, or pressing for environmental regulation and clean-up, or of course, doing both at once. Many of the women who took part in my study are actively involved in these kinds of local environmental issues. In fact, sixteen of the women I interviewed are involved in antipesticides organizations. Others are involved in lead remediation in deindustrialized areas, safe sewage and waste management, and green community programs like the walking school bus and community gardening. Much of this work is done with little or no funding from government sources, and the majority of women run their activist groups out of their homes. As I discuss in the next section, these facts make the intersection of private caring work, active citizenship in the public domain, and the values of "living green" all the more challenging.

Environmental Citizenship in Public and Private: Sustainable for Whom?

According to most definitions on offer, an important aspect of environmental citizenship is responsibility: Simply put, good green citizens take part in the affairs of the polis while making ecologically responsible choices at home. Ecopolitical theorist John Barry provides a particularly concise definition to add to the one given by Environment Canada cited above:

> Citizenship, as viewed by green democratic theory, emphasizes the duty of citizens to take responsibility for their actions and choices, and also an obligation to "do one's bit" in the collective enterprise of achieving [environmental] sustainability. There is thus a notion of "civic virtue" within a green conception of citizenship. This implies that the duties of being a citizen go beyond [active participation in] the formal political realm, including, for example, such activities as recycling and energy conservation.[7]

What are the implications of this notion of citizenship for women's everyday lives? It is well known than women in general already find it challenging to juggle a heavy load of private household responsibilities and caring work with paid employment, so how might they manage to add a third or even fourth layer by taking on the care of the planet? And what might this be like in the context of Harris's or Eves's (or McGuinty's) Ontario? What I found in my conversations with women who are attempting to perform this juggling act is that women activists face significant obstacles to their community work, many of which have been erected by New Right policies. I also found that, at home, their efforts to live green are more complicated than proponents of environmental citizenship (mostly male, it is worth noting) seem to acknowledge.

A quick word about the women activists I interviewed. All live in or around the city of Toronto, including the small suburban cities of Thornhill and Newmarket and two larger cities slightly farther away: Burlington and Hamilton. It is a diverse group that consists of sixteen Anglo-Canadian women, five Jewish women, and nine women of colour (including two African women, two Caribbean women, two Latin American women, one East Indian woman, and two "biracial" women). This is not representative of the diversity of cultural groups that live in the region (people from well over eighty ethnocultural groups live in Toronto). Nine of the women are relatively recent immigrants. With respect to socio-economic status, thirteen describe themselves as "working-class" (including six who say they live in poverty and/or on welfare), and seventeen describe themselves as "middle-class" (which includes both "lower"- and "upper"-middle-class). The women range in age from thirty to sixty-eight. All have been involved in activist work for a prolonged period of time, ranging from a minimum of three years (for one woman) to "all my adult life" (for ten women). All but three of the women report being involved in more than one organization or project, and several are involved in more than four each. The amount of time that the women say they spend on their unpaid activist work each week ranges from two to forty hours, with an average of about fifteen hours per week. Twenty-one women have paid employment (of these, eleven work part time or less than thirty hours per week), six are self-employed, six have contract or temporary employment, and four have more than one job. Nine women do not have a paid job; of these, four have chosen not to be in the paid labour force (as full-time mothers), two are looking for paid employment, one is on disability leave, one is a graduate student, and one receives social assistance. All but two of the thirty women have a university or college education. All of the women have caring responsibilities: All are mothers. Of the thirty women interviewed, the majority (twenty women) live with a husband and one or more children (the average number of children is three). One woman is in a same-sex partnership and lives with her children from a previous relationship. Nine of the women are living independently (a.k.a. "single mothers"), and of these, eight are raising children, two with the help of their mothers, who live with them. Children range in age from infant (under one year old) to adult (in their thirties); most of these adult children live at home because they are disabled and thus remain dependants. Four women have parents living with them, three have disabled adults living with them, seven have unrelated household members living with them (friends of their children or lodgers), and one lives with her husband and child in a communal home with four other adults. Only one of the thirty women is not now living with her children; she is living with an elderly friend who requires as much, if not more, care than a child.

Women and Local Quality-of-Life Activism in the Toronto Area

As noted, there is a broad range of concerns among the women activists I interviewed, such that "quality-of-life" activism is a more fitting term than "environmentalism" to describe their work (all of the women agree with this assertion). Most of the thirty women are involved in small grassroots groups that try to lobby governments and the public (most often neighbours) to change their actions and priorities. Their affiliations range from provincewide networks that involve cooperation among many diverse environmental groups (e.g., Campaign for Pesticide Reduction) to small groups of parents concerned with conditions at their neighbourhood schools (e.g., Parents' Environmental Network). Several have established their own groups and run them from home, while others became members of an already-existing group (or groups) when they learned of an issue or problem affecting their community. For many, this awareness is linked to their maternal concerns for children's health and wellbeing, but this is not true for all, nor is it experienced in the same way by all women. As ought to be expected, there is a diversity of motivating reasons among this diverse group of women. There is also a range of strategies the women use to act on their chosen issues. This includes: organizing petitions and public awareness campaigns, running an Earth Day poster competition, making deputations at City Hall, writing letters to councillors and newspaper editors, sitting on municipal, tenants', and home-school committees, doing research, and organizing and participating in strikes, demonstrations, and lawsuits. Many have found these strategies effective, but the degrees of success vary. Some women have enjoyed minor victories (e.g., having pesticides banned in local parks), while many others keep plugging along year after year with a mix of anger, frustration, and dogged determination to effect some kind of appreciable change.

Recognizing that being an unpaid activist at this point in time cannot be easy, I asked the women about what kinds of obstacles they face and how their social location and situation as citizen activists in Ontario influence their ability to participate in their communities. The overwhelming response was "time scarcity": Well over half of the women said that "lack of time" is a significant obstacle to their activist work and that they subsidize their activism by depriving themselves of time for themselves. This claim is not out of line with a Statistics Canada finding that in 1998 at least one in three married mothers aged twenty-five to forty-four who are employed full time are severely "time-stressed."[8] Many of the women have school-aged children and can therefore be expected to have the highest burden of unpaid work among all categories of parents.[9] Responsibilities for the care of children and elders were a concern for most of these women, who said they constantly struggled to find ways to juggle these with their activist commitments. New Right governments seem to assume that families can take up the slack when public services are cut, but the negative consequences of this assumption for individual women are seldom recognized.

The majority of the women reported that because of this time scarcity, their involvement in activist work has led to burn-out. The most common cause they gave was stress, which included mental, physical, and financial stress. Many of the women told burn-out stories that highlighted the emotional exhaustion, including frustration and anger, that comes with engaging in activities that are controversial and that are oftentimes met with little or no success. Especially when they are fighting to change the immediate conditions of their lives, like cleaning up a contaminated site in their backyard or trying to stop an expressway from being built through their neighbourhood, there is an understandable level of anxiety. Some others, who have dedicated their professional and personal lives to making changes in "the system," said they feel "devastated" when they see the erosion of public services at the hands of the government. Many said that this frustration leaves them tired and ready to give up; a few described their burn-outs as minor "mental breakdowns." Several had no choice but to cut back or give up their activism for a time, raising the question of how sustainable activism is in the context of an inhospitable social, economic, and political environment.

With regard to their roles as volunteer (i.e., unpaid) activists, a significant number of the women – more affluent women included – said that "lack of support" is an obstacle to doing their political work. For most this means lack of financial and organizational support for their groups and campaigns. Six of the women are trying to run organizations on limited or no budgets. Even though their work often amounts to a full-time job, they receive no pay and minimal (if any) official recognition (through funding) from the government. This lack of support dramatically restricts what they are able to accomplish.[10] Two of the women told me, and this may be true of others who describe themselves as middle-class, that they have used their family's money to support the organizations with which they are involved. When I asked one of the pair to describe the most significant obstacle she faces as an activist, she replied, "I think money is the biggest obstacle. And I think the government knows that, and that's one of the reasons why they've cut back on funding us."

This comment resonates with feminist analyses of neoliberal economic restructuring and the concomitant downloading of public services to volunteers in communities that I noted above.[11] A few of the women had strong criticisms of the economic marginalization and exploitation of unpaid activist and volunteer work. For example, echoing what many feminist political economists have said, one woman commented:

I think there needs to be a balance: Volunteering is a good thing to do and we should do it at younger ages so that we do help other people who are less fortunate. But I don't think we should use it as an excuse like this government is, to do all of the good work. You know "well those people can go to the church for help, they will fix it up." That's not going to work; there has to be a balance and an organization like [mine] should be paid something – whether it's from the government or whatever, because the work that we're doing is important.

Nonprofit and volunteer organizations run by women may be disproportionately disadvantaged economically because the work they do is assumed to be a natural extension of what they already do as caregivers. Calling this situation "re-privatization," Janine Brodie argues that shifting more responsibility onto women's groups at the same time as funding is reduced is part of a New Right attempt to redefine (and perhaps limit) practices of citizenship.[12] On the other hand, when women's participation is encouraged, even invited, it can lead to the exploitation of their volunteer time as a means of lending credibility to public processes. As a woman who leads a community action group in a working-class Hamilton neighbourhood observed, the processes involved in local community planning benefit a range of people (most of whom are white and male) who make good money being professional planners, lawyers, politicians, academics, and health-policy consultants. Yet they increasingly rely on the time and labour of citizen volunteers (many of whom are women) to monitor the health of their own communities and to fill the seats at the public consultations needed to validate their progressive-sounding plans. This situation brings to mind Sherry Arnstein's argument that "participation without redistribution of power is an empty and frustrating process for the powerless."[13] Arnstein suggested in 1969 that a distinction be drawn between participation that leads to citizen control and the kind of participation that can be coopted and manipulated to support the desires of the power elite. This kind of critical analysis, it seems to me, along with analysis based in women's interpretations of the way local politics work, is needed in discussions of the merits of women's active participation in quality-of-life struggles today.

Many of the women I interviewed offered their interpretations of relationships between their class locations and their ability to engage in activism. For example, several women noted that their middle-class status facilitates their activist work, acknowledging that activist work can be a luxury that is not an equal option for everyone. For example, one recognized that the women she works with in antipesticides organizations are "not poor." She said, "it helps if you can afford to do it." In contrast, another suggested that there are both pros and cons to being a (relatively privileged) white middle-class woman activist. She made the following comment: "As a white, middle-aged, middle-class woman, I find I blend in and am not taken very seriously by people in power. I am not considered a threat. So I am able to, almost invisibly, continue to work on one issue after another, providing information to my community."

It is not surprising that several women commented that their working-class status can be a significant obstacle to activist work. One woman named "being poor" and not having a car as the two biggest obstacles. Women with relatively modest incomes and women living in poverty report that it is sometimes difficult to justify devoting time to unpaid community work when they are not able to make ends meet. A lack of access to affordable childcare has a limiting effect on women's ability to engage in activism. In addition to not having the resources to engage in active participation, those living in poverty lead stressful lives that are not conducive to community engagement. Even though they have at times considered themselves part of the "middle class," two women said they have had to cut back or stop their activist involvements altogether when household finances are stretched too thin to support them.

Many of the women activists offered important analyses of the relative ability of women and other marginalized people to engage in effective activist work. In the process of talking about their activist work, I found the women eager to explain the things that frustrate them as activists and the systemic and structural obstacles that make it more difficult to achieve success. Most acknowledged that some people are more able to be activists than others. Some of the women (both working-class and middle-class) said that social attitudes and stereotypes, especially on the part of public officials, can hinder or impede their ability to do effective activist work. This resonates with an observation made by feminist theorist Iris Marion Young, who writes that, for the disadvantaged in particular, "their appearance in the world has a peculiar paradoxical quality; they are at once made invisible yet marked out by stereotypes."[14] Being white and middle-class might make it easier for some women to blend into established organizations and be taken more seriously than working-class women of colour when they act in the political domain. However, for other women, being invisible and/or having their identities reduced to stereotypes hinders the possibility of being listened to as citizens. Two of the women said that racism plays a significant part in the way they are treated as activists. One commented: "As a woman of African descent, I am hindered in my activist work and volunteer work. I find that I have to prove myself repeatedly." This comment provides an important reminder that social justice is a precondition for bringing about the kind of sustainable society in which environmental citizenship may be commonly and widely practised.

Greening the Household: Women's Work?

Activism is typically associated with activities in the public domain. It can be argued, however, that activism transcends the public-private divide when people attempt to live consistently with their political commitments. Most of the women indicated in their questionnaires and interviews that they regard green household practices as "very important." While this finding may appear congruent with environmentalists' call for citizens to "do their bit" at home in addition to taking an active role in local politics, the women presented some interesting challenges to this position. The association of activism and publicity (and the concomitant depoliticization of the private sphere) is challenged when women choose to regard household issues as political issues and thereby make their homes a focus of their activist engagement. Their homes are both the base for their public activism (i.e., "command central") and a place where political action and conversation take place. An exchange I had with one of the women helps to illustrate this point:

You were saying ... that a lot of your activist work gets done in your own home. Those types of choices – consumer choices and parenting choices – are a form of activism?
I didn't always think like that; I thought that consumer change at the household level was somehow less political or less important than doing it at the macro level. Mind you, I don't think that one can come without the other. But at certain times in our lives, we have to follow the open spaces we have and to start from where we are and not from where an external person tells us we should be at ... I make political choices all the time. At the household level, it used to be seen as the three Rs, but as you start learning more, [you ask] how do you live without buying PVC plastics? What furniture should I buy for my house or what carpet? ... [Or you] talk about the possibility of solar panels or alternative technologies. Those are things I'm interested in and try to bring more and more into my household level. And I get lots of comments from other people about making my house a scent-free zone and about perfumes. Yeah, it can be a courageous thing to make your household a political [space] when often you just want to make it invisible and just do it at an organizational level ... It takes courage to show your politics at the household level when you have people walking in and out of your household who may not share your perspective.

This comment offers a counterpoint to those green theorists who present the household only as a place of consumption at the same time as they restrict their discussions of politics to the *formal* public sphere.

When asked, all but one of the women said that green household practices, such as recycling and composting, are either very or somewhat important to them. However, none referred to these actions as an expression of citizenship. Responses to a questionnaire and to interview questions indicate the following: Twenty-eight recycle, nineteen compost, four women are "master composters," having taken a government-sponsored composting course, eighteen buy organic food, twenty clean without chemicals, twenty try to substitute homemade for store-bought foods, twenty-three conserve energy, sixteen buy in bulk, and ten grow some of their own food. Other green household practices mentioned include: buying nongenetically modified foods, awareness/avoidance of electromagnetic fields, not driving a car, using water filters, not using pesticides or toxic pest control, water conservation, and buying second-hand items, especially clothes.

My conversations with the women included a discussion of who takes responsibility for living green at home and whether the women see it as another layer of work to add to their already substantial list of domestic duties. Several themes emerged. First, most of the women said they are the ones who initiate and maintain green practices at home, while significantly fewer said that the work of living green is shared more or less equally among family members. Although they did not necessarily complain, about half felt that they do not get as much cooperation from family members as they would like; some expressed frustration at the need to constantly manage their families' participation in green household practices. Second, in a discussion that brought out expressions of guilt from some of the women, about two-thirds said they are unsatisfied with the success rate of their efforts to live sustainably: A common response can be paraphrased as, "although we try, we could always do more!" The conversations tended to become confessional at this point. Not surprisingly, several women said that time scarcity leads to tensions between, and trade-offs among, their environmental values and their consumer choices. (The same point emerged about the conflict between social-justice commitments and the need to save time: twelve of the thirty women said they hire cleaning ladies.) I admitted that while conducting my research, I had made good use of microwave dinners and overpackaged take-away food in order to save time. Like me, some women said they use prepackaged foods and other convenience items when life gets too hectic; some said they drive their cars too much. This, too, may cause feelings of guilt, demonstrating that environmentalism is highly disciplinary (i.e., people must police their own behaviour to ensure that it complies with particular normative rules), as some theorists have explained.[15]

Because we're busy, we tend to use some of the things that are not environmentally friendly to make our life a little easier and more comfortable.

I order in food, and I do feel badly when I do because there is so much packaging and plastic.

A third theme emerged from the issue of environmental values creating more housework. Many women said that living green is not difficult and had few complaints about ecofriendliness adding another layer of things to be responsible for at home. In fact, a few challenged my assumption that trying to "do one's bit" for the environment at home intensifies women's burden of domestic labour:

The amount of time that some people I know spend shopping and buying things that they don't need or things that match ... these are things I've never particularly cared about. So in a way I have a whole lot more time; we have more time because we're not obsessive about pretension ... Of course, I can't have just anybody into my house as a result!

I think it's a myth that living in your household in a sustainable fashion takes a lot of time; in actual fact this whole issue of time and convenience is something that we've been sold by manufacturers who want us to buy their products.

For many of the women, green practices have become a part of their daily routines. They seem not to mind the extra layer of responsibilities if it is seen as an extension of their activism:

Doesn't that add another layer of things to be responsible for?
Only if you haven't patterned yourself into it. You see I think I've patterned myself into the recycling since my kids were very small. I got into the habit of recycling way back before there were any municipal projects for it. I'm a packrat, and so I don't throw things out, I tend to pass them along. Even my activism brings me into the job of finding homes for things and finding ways for people to trade things. It is part of my activism – I hadn't thought of that – and it's what we call stewarding the earth's resources, and it helps other people. Why should something go in the garbage if it's reusable?

But, when I asked them to reflect on the concept of environmental citizenship, there were a number of women who claimed that green household practices do indeed add a layer of work and expense to their lives. Specifically, I asked the women to read and comment on Barry's definition of environmental citizenship. Not unexpectedly, many of the women agreed that citizens ought to take responsibility for their actions vis-à-vis the environment. What I find interesting, however, is that Barry's definition prompted some women to reflect critically upon the assumptions and expectations underlying the notion of being a good green citizen. Several women wondered whether Barry's concept of citizenship was "realistic." They suggested that he overlooks the fact that "real people" with busy lives may find it difficult to live up to such high standards. An exchange with one of the activist women (who has five young children, a part-time job, and an antipesticides campaign to codirect) offers a direct challenge to theorists who fail to consider the exigencies of everyday life:

> *Some of the environmental principles for living sustainably have been thought up*
> *by people like Barry who perhaps are not in the position to have to do it all.*
> They've been thought about by people writing a dissertation or living in an
> ivory tower; they're not living life with kids who have to be taken for physio-
> therapy and an aging parent, whose house is accumulating dirt, whose kids
> have homework or who are getting into big fights with their friends, who
> has a car pool that's falling apart, who has to get ready to teach or go to
> work. Life is a dynamic process.

Some women said that because it is often frustrating being the ones to take care of the green household practices, with insufficient help from family members, the idea of spreading the duty around is a good one even though it may not happen in practice. One woman said:

> Well, I certainly agree that you have to do your bit at home, in terms of the
> community, [but] what does [Barry] mean?
> *To be active and to inform yourself to participate.*
> I think that's a nice ideal but I don't think it's realistic. I think if everybody
> could just do it at home, the things that are expected – or what should be
> done – that would be great and we would have a huge improvement.

For others, the quotation prompted a discussion of the obstacles to living green. In keeping with their commentary on the difficulties involved in trying to live consistently with one's green values, several women said that Barry's idea of citizenship for sustainability would be difficult for them to live up to. For example:

> [He] is saying that civic virtue includes personal responsibility for the envi-
> ronment ... For me that's true; however ... it's really hard to do. It's really
> hard to keep that woven through my life. I get in my car way too often. I do
> all sorts of things that are problematic if I were a "green" activist.

Further, with regard to the ideal of incorporating environmentally friendly activities into their practice of citizenship, several of the women activists wondered how they should be expected to accomplish this in light of some significant obstacles, such as a lack of time, space, support, and money. Their analyses raise the significant point that it is important to address the conditions of environmental citizenship if visions like Barry's are to be extended to a broader population. For instance, some women wondered how they could be expected to be ecofriendly when they live in inner-city neighbourhoods that do not have recycling programs (as is the case for women who live in public housing) and provide insufficient space for a composter. In areas like Hamilton, where the soil is contaminated, it is unsafe to eat home-grown produce from a backyard garden.[16] A couple of women said that physical constraints inhibit their green practices: They have disabilities that render impossible a number of labour-intensive activities. Some women also commented that green consumer choices can be significantly more expensive than nongreen choices and thus are out of the question for lower-income people. For example, several felt that although they would like to give their families organic food, making this a habit would be too expensive. Many of the middle-class women reported that they buy organics, but the working-class women either cannot afford them at all or purchase organics only once in a while.

There were also some interesting critiques of recycling and precycling[17] from a few of the immigrant women I interviewed. While they did not, in principle, object to the practices, they pointed out that there is an obvious cultural specificity to the kinds of things I have been calling "green household practices." Their comments implied that using such a specialized phrase should not be necessary to describe activities that are just common sense:

Where I came from [in Eritrea], my mother never threw away any cans; she kept them and we recycled. With clothes, we never threw away clothes partly because she was giving birth every year, but the other part was the environment; you don't dump on the environment. And the spiritual part; it's a sin – to me, dumping this and that into the garbage is a sin. So they have to find a way of reusing it in a different way.

Many women in Peru are very into the work of the environment even though they don't say it. They save everything, they recycle there, and it's not because they are conscious; it is because they need it. My sister saves the paper from tea bag wrappers and uses [it] for her shopping lists. They separate everything in their garbage, and it is recycled inside the kitchen – this is for the dog, this is for the person down the street who keeps chickens. And there are no piles of garbage like here.

And sometimes you find that back in China some of these practices were just normal. Because things are less developed there – like they don't use as many plastic bags or they've always ridden a bicycle, for example, so they might just do some of these things normally – and mostly out of economic reasons.

Some women's critical responses to Barry's definition resonate with ecofeminist critiques of "environmental privatization." Catriona Sandilands, for example, expresses concern that an emphasis on green household practices like recycling and green consumerism effectively downloads ecological duty to the private sphere, to those most involved in unpaid domestic labour (i.e., women).[18] Echoing this critique, one woman said that by focusing on the responsibility of individual citizens, Barry's definition lacks a broader analysis of structural issues that contribute to environmental problems. She said:

> I took a course in my undergrad in political science on the discourse of the environment, and I did a paper on the discourse of environmentalism in Toronto, you know the blue box. And at the time I was doing it, it was a really hot topic, and people were thinking that they were doing so much by recycling. And I just was disgusted! Feeling like they were good citizens by doing their part, like the [Barry] quote says. But for me that was such a way to take people's attention from the big issues ... It takes attention away from the big issues of who is polluting and who's benefiting and why are we just being content with a garden or a blue box when we should be lobbying governments to stop the transnationals and corporations from polluting our environment. That's the big thing, right?

Finally, for some women, Barry's definition of environmental citizenship inspired the kind of gender analysis and politicization of sustainability discourse that I have been trying to develop. The following comment illustrates the resistance of women activists to the gendering of environmental responsibility.

> As people working in environmental justice, we've really got to put the burden back where it belongs. It does not belong on the backs of women. And for us, right now living in downtown Toronto, to tell a woman like myself who owns this meagre home to go green 100 percent, I can't. I can't even get green energy to come into my home. I've been trying for months now to switch to natural gas, but it's a whole thing that is involved. So I think we need to bring back the burden and place it where it belongs. And that whole big burden really does belong with the people who have the power. And as people who have the education and the knowledge and people who have the opportunity to carry that information, people like you who are at university and doing the research really need to be instrumental in

taking the burden off the women, because really and truly, the women have enough to carry.

Conclusion

Over the past several decades, feminist research in Canada has yielded vivid pictures of women's experience with juggling multiple roles. Much of this work looks at the so-called "double burden" or "second shift" – the dual role played by women employed in the labour market while performing the typical load of domestic provisioning and care-giving work at home.[19] Feminist analyses of women's double and triple role in a variety of cultural and economic contexts are important in highlighting the persistently unfair and unsustainable gender division of labour in capitalist society. My research contributes more and different things to that discussion. First, it investigates the implications for women of adding a third or fourth role – that of "earth caring" – to their already busy lives. It considers these implications in light of theoretical and popular understandings not just of the division of environmental labour, but also of the kind of active citizenship that is promoted in green visions of a sustainable society. One implication requiring further consideration and research is that doing one's bit for the environment in private may not always be compatible with engaging actively in the public sphere in a way that can be comfortably sustained over time. I would suggest that for any vision of an alternative society to work, and to be an improvement on current arrangements, it must address issues of equity, access, and the conditions of everyday life that are needed to foster democratic participation in the political domain. Women's own stories, such as those upon which I have drawn herein, provide important insight into these and many other issues.

Second, by focusing on urban women's activities and concerns, this discussion provides a more complex picture of environmentalism than is typically presented in the mass media and green political texts. Government efforts to turn us all into good green citizens notwithstanding, in Canada popular images of green activism are still more likely to include angry and unkempt students canvassing door-to-door for Greenpeace or ecofreaks blockading logging roads "up North" and "out West" than suburb-dwelling, minivan-driving women who work for environmental-political change in their kitchens and back gardens. In green literature, ecofeminist texts included, very little attention is paid to the environmental concerns of Western women living in urban places, Canadian or otherwise. I would argue that most ecofeminists tend to focus on peasant struggles in developing countries (such as the Chipko movement in India or the Greenbelt movement in Kenya) while avoiding the experiences of middle-class women in overdeveloped countries. This unfortunate avoidance implies that only a particular kind of activism and resistance by women marginalized by class or racialized status is of interest to ecofeminists and that only poor women and women of colour can be authentic ecofeminists. My research with thirty women from diverse socio-economic backgrounds who live and work in the largest urban region of Canada (a country that the United Nations has repeatedly identified as having the highest quality of life in the world) disrupts this exclusionary and selective focus. Although I do not claim that the women with whom I had conversations are ecofeminists or that their work in some way demonstrates ecofeminism in action, by including them in my study, I am broadening the scope of women who are relevant to ecofeminist research, politics, and theorizing.

Notes

1 Environment Canada, Ontario Region, 2000 *Great Art for the Great Lakes: A "Virtual" Classroom Resource for Environmental Information,* <http://www.on.ec.gc.ca/water/greatlakes/classroom/chapter-3/understanding-e.html>.

2 By most accounts, the ascendance of environmental concern was initiated by the release of the World Commission on Environment and Development report *Our Common Future* in 1987. For more information on the history of the Canadian environmental agenda, see B. Dalal-Clayton, *Getting to Grips with Green Plans: National-Level Experience in Industrial Countries* (London, UK: Earthscan, 1996),

3 Ministry of Environment, Government of Ontario, Environmental Bill of Rights Homepage, <http://www.ene.gov.on.ca/envision/env_reg/ebr/english.htm>.

4 Statistics Canada, *Women in Canada 2000: A Gender-Based Statistical Report* (Ottawa: Ministry of Industry, 2000).

5 Toronto is one of the most energy-intensive regions in the world, according to the Royal Commission on the Future of Toronto's Waterfront, *Regeneration: Toronto's Waterfront and the Sustainable City: Final Report,* Honourable David Crombie, commissioner (Toronto: Minister of Supply and Services, 1992).

6 During the spring and summer of 2000, Walkerton, Ontario, made international headlines when E. coli bacteria contaminated its water supply, resulting in widespread illness and the death of at least seven residents. Most environmentalists contend that this disaster was the result of the Harris government's policy to allow intensification of the commercial livestock industry and the downloading of environmental monitoring to the municipal level.

7 John Barry, *Rethinking Green Politics* (London, UK: Sage, 1999), 126.

8 In comparison, 26 percent of married fathers with full-time employment report being time-stressed (Statistics Canada, *Women in Canada,* 111).

9 Judith A. Frederickson, *As Time Goes By ... Time Use of Canadians: General Social Survey.* Statistics Canada: Housing, Family, and Social Statistics Division (Ottawa: Minister of Industry, 1995).

10 A few women said that although it is a challenge to run an organization with no funding, accepting funds from the state would compromise their credibility in the community, so they prefer not to do so.

11 See Janine Brodie, *Politics on the Margins: Restructuring and the Canadian Women's Movement* (Halifax: Fernwood, 1995).

12 Janine Brodie, "Restructuring and the New Citizenship," in *Rethinking Restructuring: Gender and Change in Canada,* edited by Isabella Bakker (Toronto: University of Toronto Press, 1996), 126-40.

13 Sherry Arnstein, "A Ladder of Citizen Participation," *Journal of the American Institute of Planners* 35, 4: 216-24.

14 Iris Marion Young, *Justice and the Politics of Difference* (Princeton, NJ: Princeton University Press, 1990), 59.

15 See, for example, Éric Darier, "Environmental Governmentality: The Case of Canada's Green Plan," *Environmental Politics* 5, 4 (1996): 585-606; and Catriona Sandilands, "On 'Green Consumerism': Environmental Privatization and 'Family Values,'" *Canadian Women's Studies/Les Cahiers de la Femme* 13, 3 (Spring 1993): 45-47.
16 Temma Kaplan notes that the women who lived in the Love Canal neighbourhood became suspicious of the safety of their garden produce and eventually stopped gardening altogether; see *Crazy for Democracy: Women in Grassroots Movements* (New York: Routledge, 1997).
17 Precycling refers to the practice of purchasing goods that will create minimal or no waste – for example, unpackaged bulk items and fresh produce. See Irmgaard Schultz, "Women and Waste," *Capitalism, Nature, Socialism* 4, 2 (1993): 51-63.
18 Sandilands, "On 'Green Consumerism.'"
19 See, for example, Meg Luxton, "Two Hands for the Clock: Changing Patterns in the Gendered Division of Labour," in *Through the Kitchen Window: The Politics of Home and Family,* edited by M. Luxton, H. Rosenberg, and S. Arat-Koc (Toronto: Garamond, 1990), 17-36; Ann Duffy and Noreen Pupo, *Part-Time Paradox: Connecting Gender, Work and Family* (Toronto: McClelland and Stewart, 1992); Pat Armstrong and Hugh Armstrong, *The Double Ghetto: Canadian Women and Their Segregated Work* (Toronto: McClelland and Stewart, 1994).

10

Desperately Seeking Sisterhood and Sustainability: Creating Transnational Social Learning Spaces for Sustainable Agriculture and Environmental Advocacy

Leonora C. Angeles, Layla Saad, and Rebecca Tarbotton

Canadian development agencies have been widely recognized within the international donor community as champions of two major concerns: gender and the environment – particularly through the work of the Canadian International Development Agency (CIDA) and the International Development Research Centre (IDRC) within the Organisation for Economic Co-operation for Development (OECD).[1] That Canadian donor agencies should position their gender-equity and environmental-protection work in the contexts of both developed and developing countries is a clear indication that they view "Canadian environments" and concerns about sustainable development in transnational terms. Such identification with environmental and gender politics that stretch over transnational geographic space also provides "social space,"[2] or a transnational social space, for social learning, networking, and collaboration across nation-state boundaries. As an analytical perspective, transnationalism proposes more complicated and contingent analyses of historical and geographic linkages in the global circulation of ideas, goods, people, and services,[3] including ideas, cultures, and politics on feminism and sustainable development circulating between and among the countries in the North and South. Closely linked to transnationalism are perspectives on globalization, which has removed geographic constraints on mobility and linkages, making us realize that we live on one planet and that our most pressing environmental problems are global in scope and require global interventions. Globalization also creates transnational civil societies that include regional and global networks of women and environmental groups.

The ecological and sustainable-development movements that started in the 1970s have relied on the active role of women who combine "strategic sisterhood" with sustainability principles. Like feminism and sisterhood, sustainability is a highly contested concept that has been the subject of heated debates. The mantra of sustainable development promoted by United Nations agencies has been understood in many different ways. Its original formulation as the ability to meet current needs without sacrificing the welfare of future generations[4] and its propagation by Western institutions have been criticized for lacking self-reflexivity and for preaching to the rest of the world what these institutions have not been able to accomplish within their own backyards. Such criticisms parallel Third World women's critique of Orientalist tendencies within Western feminism, particularly its lack of awareness of its own positionality and (self) representations.[5] To some feminist and postdevelopment thinkers, the term "sustainable development" is almost an *oxymoron* – how can we have a sustainable future in the face of "development" that subjugates women and promotes higher productivity based on cheap female labour, profit orientation, rising incomes, expanding markets, and sprawling industries and megacities? At the same time, some feminist circles have modified the term "sustainable development" to include the variations promoted by nonstate intermediaries, nongovernmental organizations (NGOs), and proponents of participatory development/alternative development approaches.[6] Thus the term that stirs more controversy is not sustainability per se but the concept of development. In many developing countries, for instance, the term "human development" is much more commonly used than "sustainable development." *Human development* to them captures the ultimate goal of development, which is to expand people's capabilities, increase their ability to lead long and healthy lives, develop their talents and interests, and allow them to live in dignity and with self-respect.[7]

Both sustainability and feminist studies, therefore, have tackled head-on the challenges to contemporary development posed by globalization and its various dimensions – economic, financial, military, political, social, cultural, environmental, technological – including trends associated with the globalization of communication, networks, poverty, terrorism, and global warming. Thus the North-South divide is just as compelling to consider as gender, race, and class dimensions when discussing differences in environmental impacts and ecological footprints. The consumption-driven lifestyle in the North that many southern countries want to emulate is ecologically destructive and unsustainable. Moreover, marginalized social groups such as the poor, indigenous peoples, ethnic minority groups, and disadvantaged women do not equally participate in the globalization practices being pushed by transnational agents, such as multinational corporations and financial institutions. Worse, some of these practices exploit their labour and indigenous knowledge or are harmful to their wellbeing, cultural traditions, and natural environments.

Consistent with a transnational analytical perspective, we avoid in this chapter the use of locational dichotomies and polarities such as "North and South" and "global and local" to emphasize their interpenetrating dynamics and overlapping characteristics. There are of course "southern" pockets of poor, marginal areas (e.g., low-income urban neighbourhoods, Aboriginal reserves, declining rural communities) in industrialized countries. From the time human slaves became a commodity essential to capital accumulation in/from the colonies, one might argue that the "North" has existed within the "South" and the "South" within the "North." And because of the contemporary migration, immigration, and resettlements of colonized people, this is increasingly the case. However, this discussion is postponed here in order to examine the unity and coherence, amidst contradictions, of global economic practices and policies that are functional to the workings of capitalism. Here we are unashamedly guilty of using "strategic essentialism," typical of some postcolonial and socialist writings, to argue for the analytical distinction between a "global North" and a "global South." The divide is not along gender, nation, race, or ethnic lines, but along those of class, property, power, and privilege. We therefore argue for a path of knowledge production and social learning that privileges the knowledge learned from the experiences of oppressed and marginal communities and social groups within the "global South." This argument also specifies that it is more precisely women from the "global South," particularly those who belong to democratic social and environmental movements, who have the most valuable lessons to teach Canadian and other northern societies about justice, peace, and sustainability. Thus we are equally guilty of a parallel "strategic gender essentialism" in arguing for alliance building among women in the "global South," and among allies in both the North and South, to approximate what Agarwal calls "strategic sisterhood" based on cross-class and cross-cultural alliances.[8] Such strategic alliances begin from creating transnational socio-political spaces for enriched dialogues and interactions between progressive women and men in the North and South so that they can share their experiences, strategies, and development alternatives.

This chapter examines some of the valuable lessons that Canadian and other northern environmental movements and institutions, including donor agencies, have already been learning from the South. Three social and environmental organizations and their projects led by women in the South are used here as case studies to provide local, empirical grounding for the transnational insights generated. These are the Women's Alliance of Ladakh (WAL) in India, the MAKAKABUS (Pro-Poor) women's organization in Bukidnon, Philippines, and the Community-Based Watershed Management (CBWM) project in Santo André, Brazil.[9] These three cases have Canadian transnational connections: WAL has Canadian program officers, and the MAKAKABUS and CBWM projects are both funded by CIDA. These cases point to some important lessons relevant to Canadian institutions and agencies working on women and environmental issues. When Canadian agencies are working in developing-country contexts, they often make clear the links between gender, development, and environmental issues, while ignoring their relevance to Canadian environments. "Development" work is often seen as something that Canadians do "elsewhere" and as being badly needed "out there" but "not here." The association of development with poor countries in the South often leads to the erroneous assumptions that domestic-development problems do not exist in Canada's inner cities, resource communities, and Aboriginal reserves, and that local environmental concerns can be tightly contained geographically. While knowledge transfer from the "South" to the "North," and vice versa, is already taking place, there is still very little interaction between and among local communities in the "global South." Thus it is important for Canadian and other international development agencies, academics, and researchers to bring these lessons to North-based contexts and to support avenues for "South-South" and "global-South" interactions. These avenues for interactions could create new transnational political and social learning spaces for social justice, women's-rights advocacy, environmental sustainability, and natural-resource management. Women's local knowledge and understandings of their biophysical, socio-economic, political, and cultural environments are critical to ensuring that development interventions are not inimical to their strategic gender interests. These lessons are relevant to Canadian women and men working within different geographic locations (urban, rural, peri-urban), topographic conditions (tropical, temperate, etc.), environmental-resource bases (coastal, water, upland, forest, etc.), or economic sectors (agricultural farming and forestry, light or heavy manufacturing, service, etc.). Relevant to this discussion is the condition of environmental-resource and agrofood systems that affect women producers, consumers, and stakeholders, providing the context for the examination of the three case studies highlighted in this chapter.

Women's Critique of Global Impacts on Agriculture and Environment

Women's organizations are at the forefront of criticizing development policies that support capitalist growth and the global pursuit of market-oriented, neoliberal economic strategies. Supported by international agencies such as the International Monetary Fund (IMF), World Bank, and World Trade Organization (WTO), these policies have served capitalist markets whose goals are perpetuating growth and increasing incomes but not improving the quality of life. In the process, these policies and goals have dispossessed the rural and urban poor of their lands or tenurial rights, marginalized traditional agricultural systems, conditioned the steady flow of migrants to urban cities, thereby creating squatter settlements, and degraded natural environments. Monetarized market relations and increasing global consumerism channel resources into urban services and industries and dampen the demand for locally grown products, especially in the face of cheaper food imports, thus making self-reliant food systems noncompetitive and nonviable. The horizontal and vertical integration of production systems and markets subsumes women farmers, workers, and consumers in "global commodity chains" and, in the process, marginalizes other women who are trying to maintain their traditional agrofood production systems.[10] Thus these diverse groups of women suffer similar adverse consequences of their capitalist-market integration and degraded environments, either as cheap-wage producers, marginal subsistence farmers, consumers of genetically modified crops, or carriers of diseases from toxic chemicals and pollutants.

The globalization of agrofood systems has intensified women's reproductive and productive labour and devalued traditional farm practices and indigenous knowledge of women and tribal minorities.[11] In the process, their local knowledge, genetic materials, and traditional crops become attractive to biopiracy, biopatenting, and other profit-oriented commercial interests.[12] Thus power differentials and capitalist motives combine, further exploiting the knowledge of women farmers and their local communities and relegating them to the margins of the market economy. In the case of India, this has taken the form of piracy and threats to women's knowledge and biodiversity rights, best symbolized by the neem tree and the worldwide campaign against its patenting by corporate interests.[13]

To make matters worse, local and national government planners often rely heavily on top-down-planning rituals and master plans that do not incorporate meaningful forms of public participation and avenues for including local knowledge and inputs in policies and plans. Since the 1970s, social activists and NGOs have been influenced by the works of Paolo Freire[14] and by proponents of participatory action research.[15] More recently, governments and international development agencies,[16] including CIDA and the IDRC, have taken an interest in local capacity building and community participation. This interest stemmed from years of failed interventions and projects that repeatedly used top-down-planning processes and prescriptive methodologies to achieve an ethnocentric, imposed form of development that was "prepackaged" in donor countries. The realization on the part of Canadian and other donor agencies that project success was contingent on more inclusive forms of development has launched discursive development practices related to participation, partnerships, and capacity building.[17] Both the discourse and practice concerning participation involve the gendered dynamics and context of participation[18] and the interpretations and subsequent meanings that different cultures, communities, and ideological traditions attach to participation.[19] Governments and organizations have readily incorporated participation, having accepted that it is a critical element of development initiatives, but this general acceptance has caused the neglect of deeper discussion on the objectives for adopting participatory development methods.[20]

Thus translocal and transnational contributions to these debates, as well as forms of organized resistance to the globalization of agrofood systems, have emerged. Many local (especially indigenous, or Aboriginal) communities and environmentally aware urban and rural populations in industrialized countries in the North, such as Canada, Japan, Britain, New Zealand, and Australia, are regenerating sustainable-farming and resource-management practices. In many "Third World" countries, like India, Brazil, and the Philippines, resistance to global corporate interests takes the form of maintaining and rediscovering cultural traditions, especially in upland areas and tribal communities. At the political level, various local and international campaigns resist the new regulations on intellectual-property rights imposed by the WTO and its corporate sponsors. However, these campaigns, often led by intellectual elites in both developed and developing countries, have not led to active interaction and mutual social learning between diverse grassroots movements in the South. Despite the popularity of the Internet, many new information and communication technologies are not accessible to many poor people, especially those living in remote rural areas. This is most telling in the case of the Philippines, where a full 51 percent of total Internet users are women, or more specifically elite women, and less than 1 percent of the population have Internet access. The following case studies are notable not so much for their innovative combination of traditional and nontraditional forms of communication, but for their skilled leaderships, creative use of cultural expressions, and creation of translocal and transnational spaces for social learning and mutual knowledge transfer between North and South partners.

Case 1: The Women's Alliance of Ladakh and the Ladakh Farm Project

Ladakh's first women's organization, the Women's Alliance of Ladakh (WAL), was formed in 1991, based on the lessons learned from the mainstream ecological and alternative-development movement in Ladakh. This wider ecological movement has helped to raise environmental awareness among women, especially the small group of Ladakhi women who founded WAL. It was founded with help from the UK-based International Society for Ecology and Culture (ISEC), which was connected to Ladakh's ecological and alternative-development movement, which started in the 1970s. Founded upon assumptions about the relationship between women, culture, environment, and development, WAL posits that development and modernization in Ladakh have not affected women as much as men and that, for the most part, women remain impervious to the temptations of consumerist culture. As indicated by WAL's direct translation into the vernacular as "Mothers' Alliance of Ladakh," the organization's members and leaders share with

Canadian and other northern women's groups ecofeminist values and environmental activism.[21]

WAL sees women's closer ties to traditional culture, and their serving as the "natural caretakers of culture and nature," as the main reason why women are also the first "victims" of "progress." Citing studies by Ladakhi historians and other scholars, WAL asserts that traditional relations between women and men in Ladakh were equal, evidenced by the strong position of women within the household as the centre of economic life. Modernization, however, has caused the household economy to be decentred from family and community decision-making.[22] The dislocation of women from the traditional household arrangement marginalized them both psychologically, as Western-style education made younger women even less self-confident than their outspoken, less educated elders and peers, and economically, as women's workloads inside the household and within cash-based agricultural systems increased. Given that the decline in women's status has been traced to modernization and the erosion of culture, WAL exalts women's local knowledge, celebrates Ladakhi culture, and asserts the role of agriculture and farmers in sustainable development. It seeks to raise the awareness of Ladakhi people about the value of women, particularly their important role in agriculture, as the basis for their active participation in community decision-making. Toward this goal, WAL focuses heavily on environmental awareness and consciousness raising about women's role in sustainable agriculture and the preservation of Ladakhi culture.[23] WAL promotes the use of traditional agricultural practices, sells organic agricultural produce in the markets, campaigns against the use of polythene plastic to reduce trash in urban areas, and holds annual fairs to demonstrate women's skills in spinning and cooking.[24]

By 1999 WAL's membership had grown to 3,500 members. WAL is mainly concerned with preserving Ladakhi traditional culture and agricultural practices. Its regular activities range from village-level educational meetings on traditional and modern farming to participation in cultural festivals, the presentation of women's popular educational theatre, and environmental clean-up campaigns. It also oversees several projects, such as seed banks, a weaving exchange, writing a Ladakhi cookbook, and the Ladakh Farm Project (LFP), which was initiated in the summer of 1995 when two European volunteers were partnered with WAL-affiliated Ladakhi families to live and work on their farms for three months. The project proved so valuable for both the volunteers and their host families that it was continued, expanding to five volunteers in 1995, then to fifty-two in 1998. Most volunteers come from Germany, Canada, the United Kingdom, the United States, and Switzerland and have worked with families in fifteen remote and isolated villages.

Both WAL and ISEC run the project, and host families do not have to be WAL members to participate. Its focus is not on harnessing the labour power of volunteers to assist farm women, but on promoting the educational experience gained by volunteers and their hosts. WAL's goals fit with the project's overarching aim, which is to support traditional Ladakhi agriculture and culture while fostering positive local changes in the Western communities where the volunteers live. In other words, the project uses global North-South connections to foster translocal transformation for a more sustainable agriculture. The project hopes to achieve this goal in several ways:

1 Western volunteers' desire to learn from farming families counteracts the image of both declining agriculture and the "typical Western tourist" in the eyes of Ladakhis.
2 The volunteers help out with farm work at a time when the tradition of cooperative and communal work is breaking down.
3 Through daily interaction and limited conversation, volunteers are able to give Ladakhis a more accurate image of life in the West.
4 Lastly, the experience of living and working in a traditional sustainable but "modernizing" culture gives volunteers valuable insights that will inform their own community-based activism in their home countries.[25]

The creation of a transnational space for social learning in the Ladakh Farm Project is complicated by legacies of colonialism, contemporary impacts of global capitalism, translocally imagined polarities, including "modern and traditional" and "Third World and Western," and concepts of "white/ whiteness," "native," "indigenous," and "other." Angeles and Tarbotton have questioned the Ladakh Farm Project's underlying assumptions:

What are the real transformative potentials of such education based on a "real, traditional Third World experience," promoted by organizations fostering North-South partnerships in the face of undisturbed "business-as-usual" structures and unequal relations? The obvious benefits of the Project to volunteers are not readily matched by similar benefits to host families, many of whom may not have the chance to gain a parallel "real First World experience" to deflate their assumed unrealistic views of life in the West. The idea of traveling thousands of miles to a remote area to "learn" about another culture is inherently based on class privilege, as evidenced by the socio-economic background of volunteers. This idea is not imagined easily by many poor and less educated youth from the West, particularly those with non-white immigrant backgrounds, although it is probably the presence of this group that would likely be more effective in shattering the Ladakhis' imagination of the West. How different is the Farm Project really from a unique tourist experience for any Westerner who can afford the price?[26]

Feminists advocating postdevelopment perspectives criticize WAL and ISEC for "promoting a selective interpretation of indigenous knowledge where indigenous has meant Buddhist, even though half of the population is Buddhist"; they decry this interpretation's "lack of historical and class analysis," leading to the depoliticization of Ladakhis and misrepresentation of their demand for development.[27] Following this line of analysis, Aggarwal asserts that although ISEC (and, by implication, WAL) provides meaningful insights about the links between globalization and the marginalization of local agricultural economies, "it is based on the assumption that an authentic Ladakhi past can be recuperated, and that when this recovery takes place, it will result in a society more egalitarian in terms of gender."[28] This issue is shaped by the largely contextual nature of participation, which is influenced by cultural and gender considerations, in that "agricultural initiatives by Southern women have a naturalized spirit of collectivity, when legitimate means of community participation are not available to all women."[29]

As will be shown in the second case study, we cannot assume that control over land and property are equal and gender neutral, even when cultural, religious, and ethnic identities seem homogenous on the surface. In this case from the Philippines, women's cooperative and agricultural initiatives to assist poorer women agricultural workers were able to find legitimate avenues when challenged by their male-dominated parent cooperative's attempts to reinforce local gender hierarchies and identities.

Case 2: The MAKAKABUS Women's Organization in Bukidnon

Sustainable local livelihoods can be developed not just in rural settings like Ladakh, but also in urban city spaces where agricultural production may be promoted. Urban agriculture, however, is likely to be unsustainable if urban farmers get trapped in the cycle of dependency on expensive commercial fertilizer, pesticides, and other chemical farm inputs experienced by many rural farmers. This realization has led to the promotion of organic farming by local community-based organizations supported by a regional nongovernmental organization in a peri-urban area in Mindanao, Philippines. The local organizations in this case study are the Bukidnon MASIPAG Farmers' Multipurpose Cooperative and the MAKAKABUS women's organization, both based in peri-urban villages in the city of Valencia, a newly chartered city in Bukidnon, northern Mindanao. They promote organic agriculture with support from the Bukidnon Centre for Sustainable Agriculture (BCSA) and the College of Agriculture at Xavier University in Cagayan de Oro City. Xavier University researchers and the BCSA have been part of the MASIPAG,[30] a national network of Filipino scientists, farmers' groups, and development practitioners that opposes the spread of genetically modified seedlings and promotes sustainable farm practices. The BCSA works with other grassroots organizations, such as the Upland Development Farmers, using funds from CIDA's Partnership Branch, which oversees the Philippine Development Assistance Program, a partnership and institutional-strengthening program involving Philippine and Canadian organizations.

The Farmers' Multipurpose Cooperative was established in 1997, initially with sixty farmer members: fifty men and ten women, most of whom were wives and daughters of the male members. The BSCA channelled CIDA funds to the co-op to build a small rice mill and an organic fertilizer plant and to purchase a rice thresher, a farm tractor, and a six-wheeled truck for marketing organic rice and fertilizer. However, the co-op suffered drastic capital erosion when it faced problems with marketing and organizational consolidation. The co-op's organic products did not sell well, as the members lacked marketing skills, a problem that BCSA and Xavier University supporters were not readily able to address. The marketing of organic farm produce has always been a problem because of narrow domestic markets, the low purchasing power of the population, and poor distribution outlets. Due to low-scale production, organic-food producers often have to sell their products at higher prices than those charged for non-organic produce. This is compounded by the landlocked geographic location of their peri-urban town, which is three to four hours by land transportation from the nearest major distribution outlets.

Women members of the co-op wanted to assist the male leadership in getting the organization in shape. However, there was much resistance from the predominantly male members, who underestimated women's capacities and abilities and were averse to displaying discord and admitting their limitations in public. The women proposed venturing into pig raising, a backyard enterprise they considered not too labour-intensive that could be combined with their home gardens and domestic responsibilities to supplement incomes from rice and fertilizer production. However, the male members resisted the idea since raising pigs would mean using feed grown with commercial fertilizer, a practice contrary to organic farming. The women argued that using commercial feed, a step made necessary due to the long growth period of organic feed, would only be temporary. Challenged by the men's intransigence, the women decided to form a new affiliate organization called MAKAKABUS.[31]

MAKAKABUS membership expanded quickly, as though creating a new organizational identity, independent of the parent cooperative, suddenly unleashed women's interests in community-development issues. Women in the community were now joining MAKAKABUS instead of the Farmers'

Multipurpose Cooperative.[32] The women's cooperative also earned profits and in three months raised new capital equivalent to what the male-dominated cooperative had been able to generate in three years! Its highly dynamic and flexible organizational-management strategies have contributed much to its success.[33] Women's organizational capabilities were overlooked even by their NGO and university partners, whose program officers are usually men. Realizing women's organizational skills, these outside partners have supported MAKAKABUS by providing accounting and financial training. Unlike the parent co-op, which accepts mainly farmer owner-cultivators as members, MAKAKABUS has many members from landless families in Valencia. Since many women do not have access to land or do not own land titles, MAKAKABUS leaders realize that the parent co-op's membership restriction discriminates mostly against poor women agricultural workers.

While the parent co-op was mainly involved in rice and fertilizer production, MAKAKABUS knew that farm diversification and innovative marketing strategies would lead to more and denser social partnerships. "We do not concentrate only on one thing; we are into everything," the president of MAKAKABUS said about its diversified activities, which range from rice production and marketing to organic-fertilizer sales, mixed rice and duck farming, pig dispersal, providing microcredit as production loans, farm-equipment rental, and catering.[34] It takes good managerial skills to make money from rental farm equipment, especially given its seasonal use, competition from other rent capitalists in the area, and potentially conflicting schedules due to high usage rates during a limited period of time.[35] Following exposure trips to other areas in Mindanao doing organic farming, MAKAKABUS thought of the idea of demonstration farms to market its products to other cooperatives. The strategy enabled it to attract a contract for the sale of 2,600 bags of organic fertilizer to a huge marketing cooperative. This deal connected MAKAKABUS to the College of Agriculture at the nearby Central Mindanao University in Musuan, which saw potential in linking the college's teaching and research programs, particularly students doing their undergraduate and graduate theses on sustainable agriculture, with a local organization engaged in organic-farming practices. This new partnership made sense to MAKAKABUS, given their greater geographic proximity to Musuan than to Xavier University in Cagayan de Oro City.

The story of MAKAKABUS tells how women members, through gender-based solidarity, or sisterhood, organized themselves independently of the male-dominated cooperative and in the process became more prosperous and successful than their parent organization. It also tells the story of how development aid can be effective in promoting sustainable agricultural practices and in assisting the poor when local community members own and control the direction and use of aid and other resources. More important, it shows that women are highly effective agents in local resource mobilization and in harnessing social cohesion to achieve community-development goals.

MAKAKABUS has clearly used vertical social linkages in enabling the relatively better-off community members to assist the poor and less privileged. While highly politicized and democratic in its organizational practices, it continuously has to resist the temptation of local patronage politics encouraged by the party and electoral systems. Unlike the cases in Ladakh and Brazil, the organization has also neglected to tap more systematically into women's local knowledge about their community and development demands. The organizational and financial sustainability of the organization might also be in jeopardy in light of the precarious state of foreign-development assistance from CIDA and other agencies.

Case 3: Women and Culture in Community-Based Watershed Management in Santo André

The Community-Based Watershed Management (CBWM) project stemmed from a four-year partnership (1998-2002) between the Municipality of Santo André in São Paulo City and the Centre for Human Settlements (CHS) at the University of British Columbia (UBC), Canada. Santo André has long struggled with participatory planning and watershed management in addressing problems that arise from informal settlements in environmentally sensitive areas. Since watershed management in Brazilian cities has traditionally been dominated by top-down master plans that rely heavily on restrictive laws, an alternative CBWM strategy must be accompanied by new methods and operational tools that form part of a distinct type of participatory management. Municipal capacity building that addresses and incorporates socio-economic, biophysical, and institutional elements into planning for watershed management may include three main elements. These deal with (1) the collection and processing of data to provide the knowledge that is useful in making informed decisions, (2) how various stakeholders participate in ongoing watershed management, and (3) revealing ways to manage conflict among stakeholders regarding their interests in and use of the watershed. By setting up and institutionalizing a participatory framework, the CBWM project aims to make watershed management in Santo André "more effective, participatory and responsive to the needs of informal settlements."[36] The project has selected three pilot areas, among them Parque Andreense, one of the most populated and underserviced neighbourhoods in the watershed area. It was the first pilot study selected, so the insights and lessons learned here would serve to inform participatory watershed management in other Brazilian municipalities with similar settlement problems.[37] The CBWM project is expected to disseminate CBWM methods used in watershed-protection areas to other communities and municipalities in Brazil and, through a participatory approach to management, to improve the quality and availability of information necessary for municipal decision-making related to watershed management.[38] The focus is on locally "involving people in the development process as stewards of the environment."[39]

Poor and low-income Parque Andreense residents express a deep sense of isolation and alienation from the socio-political processes of Santo André. This makes them feel marginalized from the social life of the city. The feeling of alienation shared by many residents is nourished by a lack of citizen rights in terms of access to transportation, education, health, infrastructure, and employment. Such conditions have inevitably led to disenchantment with community life and a profound lack of self-esteem, especially among the women and youth. In recognition of the valuable and distinct knowledge held by local communities, the CBWM process seeks to encourage participation from a wide range of stakeholder groups, particularly the women and youth who are usually excluded from decision-making procedures. Many residents of Parque Andreense express the perception that their community is a place "at the end of the world" in terms of distance to the "formal" city, where commercial, industrial, and other urban services are concentrated. As a result, they resent the poor infrastructure and services in their community and therefore project a future for the area that is integrated and assimilated into the urban centre.[40]

Recognizing the importance of addressing social-justice issues in environmental management, the CBWM project incorporated gender analysis as one of its main themes, stimulating women's participation in the various stages of the development process. Many women describe *uma vida muito sofrida* (a life filled with suffering) in relation to fulfilling their daily domestic role, a point directly associated with the lack of roads, piped water, and urban services that complicates their domestic chores, such as child rearing. Thus the section of the CBWM project concerned with social and economic development, coordinated by the Gender Planning Office, initiated a number of activities in the pilot-project area. These activities included systematizing socio-economic indicators, creating socio-educational materials, experiential exchanges, capacity building and education for citizenship, and stimulating income-generation and employment initiatives.[41] In addition, a significant amount of social learning was produced via the dialogue between municipal planners and local community residents. Many of these activities provided the forum in which residents' local knowledge was expressed and often documented, supplying relevant information that nourished appropriate and informed decisions.

In February 2000 the Assesoria dos Direitos da Mulher (Women's Rights Bureau) and the Departamento de Desenvolvimento Urbano (Urban Development Department) initiated oral-history documentation as part of the CBWM project's attempt to incorporate cultural and creative expressions of local knowledge. This initiative reconstitutes the oral expression, visions, and perceptions of Parque Andreense residents regarding their daily experiences dealing with the limits and potentialities of living in a watershed-protection area and explores the watershed's link to their locale and its relationship with the city of Santo André. The oral-history project seeks to provide poor residents, generally excluded from "official history," the possibility of being heard by documenting their own visions of the world. This project's methodology presents an innovative way of approaching history through individual and collective memories.[42]

The project to document oral history sought to meet the larger objective of involving community residents in watershed management. The stories reveal valuable insights into the factors that trigger migration and informal settlements, the diversity of these communities, the process of change experienced over time (why, what, and how), the challenges and daily realities of living in the watershed, and the knowledge and skills of local residents. This project provides an interesting example of an innovative form of community participation that could serve as a forum for mutual learning and potentially support the municipal project of constructing active citizenship. The full potential of oral-history documentation as an interactive participatory planning tool is of course contingent on how it is designed, applied, and analyzed. If its objectives include fostering citizenship, then the project could for example elaborate on the rich content of the stories to raise discussion concerning social, economic, and environmental conditions, thus locating possible avenues for activism and community organizing.

Women's oral histories reflect the diversity of informal settlements that are formed by people who migrate from other regions of the country, both far and near, in search of a better life and an affordable place to live. Diversity can often pose an obstacle to collective participation and community action, and it is therefore essential to devise participatory strategies that cater to as many residents as possible. The following quotations capture the variety of origins, beliefs, practices, and distinct and diverse ethnic races in Parque Andreense.

"My name is Maria de Lourdes Barbosa. I am naturally from Pernambuco," a northeastern state of Brazil. "My name is Terumi Fuzita Kikuiri" of Japanese origin but "naturally from the city of Ituverava in the interior of Sao Paulo." "I was born in Parana," a state south of São Paulo. "I came from the interior but lived many years in a nun school in Belo Horizonte, Minas Gerais." "Here we have a mixture of everything! We have a diversity of interesting religions. There are the Pentecostals, evangelical, the 'batuques' and candomble. I am Adventist, next to my house the woman is Catholic.

In front of my house there is an 'umbanda' centre and this other woman is a Jehovah witness."[43]

Using oral histories as a participatory process provides a method of identifying talents existing in the community that may not have been "discovered." The richness of women's skills and local knowledge about the community can serve as potential sources of intracommunity organization and informal linkages. Being aware of who has what skills/knowledge that are useful to the community can trigger ideas for various community projects and opens the possibility for the implementation of partnerships between the community and the municipality.

Lourdes, for example, is an experienced and quite talented writer who has created more than three theatre pieces. Originally from Pernambuco, she knows the northern *literatura de cordel*, a "form of storytelling using simple text, verses and simple drawings on cheap paper, that is hung in public areas such as market places."[44] The use of this culture to informally discuss social issues and political struggles is slowly disappearing, and finding people with this knowledge is not so common anymore. Lourdes dreams of organizing youth to perform her plays, particularly one piece called *Coracao de Mae nao se Engana* (A mother's heart can't be fooled), which depicts the life of youth today and the struggles they face with drugs. She wants to organize a local theatre group to mount performances with acting, singing, and dancing. "Opportunities for youth here are few and difficult ... there are no activities for them. They are seventeen and eighteen year old kids that just sit around because they have nothing to do. Life for them here is really difficult. I believe that through theatre and poetry I can work with youth and insert them in cultural activities."[45]

Julia's family always worked on the farm, so she knows a lot about gardening and herbs. The introduction of a local garden has given Julia the opportunity to use some of her skills. When they have problems with plagues that destroy the vegetables, Tarciso (a community resident) makes "a homemade poison that does not harm" to be used on the garden. He is also creating a drip-irrigation system in order to save water and the time of those taking care of the plants. "We have planted herbs in the garden. Thank God we don't always need them, but if anyone does, they come to my house looking for herbs. I know that I feel very useful when people look for me to get herbs ... It's the best to mess around with earth, we nourish ourselves and we sleep better ... Having vegetables we don't think of money. Those fresh vegetables, healthy ... its economic for us, we don't have to go out and buy and we know where it comes from."[46]

Interviews with members of the women's collective reflected their possession of specific knowledge that is shaped by the gendered division of roles within the community. As collectors of water, women are familiar with the issues regarding water supply, such as its sources, locations, and the difficulties in obtaining it. It was stated, for example, that the people who live higher up run out of water because wells located on high streets cannot hold very much, whereas the wells on the lower streets can hold much more. This information may be useful in determining where to locate municipal water outlets. The women said that there used to be a little dam and a lake where the "unofficial" garbage deposit is presently located. The men would fish there, and the women would wash clothes. Then people started to build, cut the trees, and cover the area with grass and *lodo* (mud). This area now gets flooded when it rains, the water rising to as high as one metre inside the homes. Information on the existence, location, and previous use of this little lake was incorporated into the urban upgrading portion of the CBWM project, and the municipal planners proposed to rehabilitate and restore the site. This exemplifies the direct use of local knowledge in the design of public works, information that planners probably would have overlooked had it not been expressed during the interviews. Projects to document oral history are often conducted with groups from excluded, forgotten, and/or marginalized sectors of society. Due to their alienated status, these people's histories, perspectives, and insights are rarely known, heard, or appreciated as an integral part of the larger picture. Cultural expression through oral history and storytelling provides a rich account of people's lives and is indispensable to a deeper understanding of the social, psychological, emotional, and constructed realities to which they belong.

Women are also aware of the living conditions of other women, thus providing some insights into obstacles to women's participation in community development: "I know women who are abused, their husbands lock them in the house and do not let her talk to us ... so sometimes we try to give out pamphlets and/or talk about something that is going on and 'No!' the husband screams from inside the house, that she can't ... the woman becomes pale white like the colour of sulfate because she is locked in the house. He does not let her go anywhere."[47]

Contrary to common views, people who live in informal settlements in the watershed area have a deep understanding of and appreciation for environmental issues.

I would like for people to become more conscious, because the environmental problem is not just a problem of Parque Andreense. It's the whole world's problem. If people do not address environmental issues our Billings Reservoir will finish. With the way that people are invading lands and agglomerating houses it becomes more difficult to remove people, particularly without the conscientisation of public power. We have both sides. On one side we have people who do not have anywhere to live. But the fish also need clean water to live. So, when we see on television tons of food that the population is killing, (because of contamination) we perceive that we really need to raise people's consciousness regarding preservation.[48]

Thus the oral-history project within CBWM has made public and collective the local and private individual views of women and men living in the informal settlements. In particular, women's oral histories and collective forms of action have been instrumental in revitalizing and strengthening women's organizations that are now becoming involved in recycling, sanitation campaigns, and herbal gardens. This translocal social learning, initiated and supported by transnational partnership between Canadian academics, planners, and Brazilian municipal government, provides the foundation for the success and sustainability of CBWM.

As shown in the Ladakh case, the documentation of women's local knowledge and oral histories can be interpreted in varying ways. On one level (depending, of course, on how stories are used), the involvement of residents via the expression and documentation of their histories presents a creative form of consultative participation. On another level, this more extractive and rather pragmatic use of oral histories can provide a significant amount of information and insight into a local community's past, present, and future. The content provides valuable socio-cultural, economic, and environmental baseline information that serves to guide future actions within the planning process. This information fosters an understanding of (1) community diversity, (2) women's local knowledge and personal skills, and (3) the processes of change that the community has experienced over the years. Still, a skilful and meaningful handling of cultural expressions and documented local knowledge in the community must rely on local ownership rather than on sound organizational management and intervention from the outside. Two years after the project to document oral history began, many local residents, eager to see the results of their work in print, were still waiting for the promised output from the city planners and Canadian partner agencies. Here trust, accountability structures, and timely dissemination of results need to accompany local ownership and participation in order for cultural and artistic avenues of public engagement to generate greater community enthusiasm and sustainable results.

Conclusion: Lessons on Canadian Environments from Women in the Global South

Canadian organizations working in the area of women and environments can draw a number of valuable lessons from these three cases involving women's attempts to forge community-based sisterhood and political solidarity in order to achieve environmental sustainability. They demonstrate that women's rights and environmental advocacy cannot be isolated issues and must be addressed within the context of wider social-justice concerns for the poor and other marginal groups. Meeting basic needs of poor communities must be accompanied by confidence building among the poor, particularly poor women, in order to ensure their trust. In these three cases, women's material assets in terms of resources, and nonmaterial assets such as human capital, traditional ecological knowledge, relations of trust, social networks, and cultural capital are powerful elements for social transformation, especially when translated into environmental organizing.[49] The women's organizations examined above have strategic rather than practical goals, thus debunking the common assumption that "Third World" women are mainly interested in survival rather than in political action. Through their focus on education, empowerment, and support of traditional culture, these organizations reaffirm and utilize women's *nonmaterial assets* to achieve their goals and create spaces for social learning that are conducive to sustainable agricultural and environmental practices.

Sustainability or sustainable development in the Canadian context must not only be associated with environmental issues, but also be clearly linked to economic, political, social, and cultural concerns, particularly those of the most vulnerable and marginal social groups. As seen in the case studies, women's organizations have learned immensely from local southern experiences, which has led to recent shifts in development aid and international cooperation based on sound sustainable-livelihood analysis. This analysis is "the process of identifying the resources and strategies of the poor, the context in which they operate, the institutions and organisations with which they interact and the sustainability of the livelihood outcomes, which they achieve."[50]

In celebrating women's sisterhood, the cases also demonstrate that environmental sustainability rests upon the fundamental reorientation of expectations and values and upon cultural and behavioural change. Among low-income populations in "Third World" countries, the use of local culture and subculture has been instrumental in fostering self-esteem, identity, access, and solidarity,[51] which are often important stepping stones for effective participation. In the India and Brazil cases, in particular, the use of culture and women's oral histories became an important mechanism for community engagement, offering effective tools that have the capacity to reach and interest diverse segments of society. To be successful, the planning processes that seek to integrate community perspectives and knowledge, especially when applied in the northern context, must be planned carefully and often require that local organizations and/or government have the necessary skills, mechanisms, and attitude to be proactive in this regard. Often people, especially women, who participate in processes that use culture create a new self-awareness and start to critically observe their social situation. In many cases, this leads them to take the initiative in the transformation of a society that has often denied them the opportunity to participate.[52] Awareness of the opportunities and constraints involved in adopting innovative forms of participation that foster knowledge sharing and learning is important for planning practice. Such awareness may provide insights into how participatory planning processes can be designed for the larger objectives of social learning and social transformation through active citizenship.

Canadian environmental groups need to place ecological concerns squarely within class, race, and gender perspectives, as these perspectives simultaneously question the underlying power relations in any form of partnership with communities, both local and overseas. In other countries, as in many Canadian localities, poor and ethnic minority women's deep sense of nonbelonging and eroded sense of self makes it challenging to attract their effective participation in planning processes and stimulate an increased environmental awareness and stewardship. This requires a special approach as well as an institutional framework that is prepared to listen to and accommodate distinct forms of participation. Thus many Canadian activists and planners have already been experimenting with cultural and artistic mechanisms and avenues for engaging people in community-development initiatives while simultaneously providing a space for expression. The forum afforded by community participation through cultural expression can serve as an incubator for the expression/formation of critical consciousness and social responsibility. As a result, culture can be utilized to influence collective action by engaging people in processes that are transformative to them on a personal level.

The case studies also provide important lessons for Canadian public agencies, nongovernmental organizations, and private enterprises that engage in various forms of social partnerships to address feminist and ecological concerns. As shown in the three cases, the quality of local knowledge, social cohesion, and density of local social networks are the key to building effective organizations and translocal/transnational social partnerships. Women's local knowledge and perspectives are significantly shaped by the complex factors that underpin lived experience, which could be the legitimate focus of sociological action research.[53] The oral expression of individual and collective experience/knowledge in the Ladakh and Santo André projects, for example, is a valuable form of preserving culture and traditional practices, creating and fortifying identities and self-esteem, teaching and raising awareness, and excavating memories that provide stimulus for future action in community development. In the context of participatory planning with disadvantaged groups, context-specific realities are critical to the success or failure of community interventions and can form part of the essential baseline information with which planners often work. Gender planners and specialists must therefore link and adapt their universalized analytical tool kits to local conditions and local knowledge.[54] The documentation of local residents' oral histories is a mechanism for revealing local knowledge and raising awareness. This ultimately aims to increase local participation and to improve social networks and the exercise of citizenship rights and responsibilities in environmental management.

The WAL, MAKAKABUS, and CBWM experiences show the importance of democratic participation, organizational autonomy, and good leadership skills, which could be harnessed by strong social partnerships between international donor agencies, universities, local NGOs, and community organizations. Canadian and other donor agencies are commendable for their current efforts to address the issue of financial accountability while giving full ownership and voice to local partners. As shown in all three cases, especially the ones in Brazil and the Philippines, intermediary organizations such as NGOs, academics, and universities have recognized the importance of gender analysis, organizational capacity building, and adaptation to local cultures and social relations. Therefore, Canadian universities engaged in collaborative development projects with both local and international communities need to be more systematic in documenting the knowledge they have been gaining about learning processes from their action research while working with their partners, both local and overseas.[55]

More important, the men and women in the three cases examined have demonstrated that open lines of communication, careful gender negotiations, and the value of sex-role complementarity, intrinsic in most local cultures, could be potential sources of organizational revitalization and new forms of institutional cooperation. As the MAKAKABUS case demonstrates, the women and men turned their initial conflict over approaches into a source of new opportunities without letting past history exacerbate gender conflict or disturb domestic or marital relations. Taking a pragmatic approach, the women's organizations in Bukidnon and Ladakh have shown that organizational strengthening and sustainability partly rest upon a healthy revenue base and a well-consolidated membership base, or a good combination of material resources, social cohesion, and human capital. Canadian women's and environmental groups, therefore, could learn how the promotion of sustainable livelihoods and environmental management by and for the poor would have to take into account not just local knowledge, participation, and ownership of program successes, but also the gender identities and relations that underpin local organizational dynamics.

Moreover, these women's organizations demonstrate a profound concern with fostering greater material as well as strategic self-reliance and with reclaiming their citizenship rights and public interests. In each case, there is a manifest desire on the part of southern women's organizations to liberate themselves in some way from the vagaries of the global economic system and foreign development aid, even as they attempt to reap some of their benefits. This makes a strong case for Canadian planners to take this desire seriously, especially in the face of the recent softwood-lumber accord with the United States and the signing away of Canadian water rights under trade agreements. The reclaiming of the "public," "public interest," and the "public realm" seems like a hard sell given intellectual cynicism about the so-called "phantom public,"[56] especially in the face of the recent tide of neoliberalism in Canada. The collapse of centralized communist states, the power of neoliberalism to reshape government social programs, and "the rhetoric of privatisation – that government can do no right" all destroy the creation of "democratic publics" by assuming that "all government, not just bad government, is the problem."[57] More needy and poor communities are created, and their social cohesion destroyed, when governments cut back and privatize social services. This erodes the idea of any form of public responsibility for health, education, housing, and pension, which are increasingly seen as market commodities rather than as public goods. Hence there is a need for *social movements working with planners, and for planners working in social movements,* to recognize the power of ideas. Ideas concerning gender equality and sustainability principles help to organize people to reclaim the public realm both as an "imagined idea" and as a "real place" where people are interconnected, have individual freedoms, and still take responsibility for each other.[58]

For those involved in development planning at the community, regional, and international levels, a serious reclaiming of the "public" must be accompanied by a rethinking of what global/regional cooperation and North-South partnerships may entail when informed by gender analysis and sustainability principles.[59] In most international-development circles, *organizational or institutional sustainability* is narrowly understood in terms of its "financial" or "fiscal" dimension, with the emphasis on bringing in new funding or additional revenues, or at best mobilizing local resources, in order to sustain local organizations. As shown in these case studies, sustainability, or sustainable development, entails supporting women's solidarity (read: sisterhood) and negotiating power relations within the household, the larger community, and donor agencies. It also means that alternative forms of community, regional, and global integration could address problems common to both northern and southern contexts that destroy the environment and people's welfare – for example, when multinational corporations (MNCs) move into low-cost areas. Sustainable and equitable trading mechanisms must be developed within these forms of cooperation so that the initial disparities or cleavages arising from comparative advantages and division of labour do not lead to permanent cleavages but instead enable the weaker trading communities to develop their internal capacities.[60] Such alternative visions of sustainable development will be realized and remain sustainable only if women's active participation and contributions are seriously considered.

Notes

1 Diana Rivington, CIDA Gender Equity Division Head, speech to the Centre for the Study of the Americas, Vancouver, BC, 12 March 2001.
2 Dorothy Massey, *Spatial Divisions of Labour: Social Structures and the Geography of Production* (London, UK: Macmillan, 1984), 333.
3 Jennifer Hyndman, *Managing Displacement: Refugees and the Politics of Humanitarianism* (Minneapolis: University of Minnesota Press, 2000), 84.
4 World Commission on Environment and Development (WCED), *Our Common Future* (New York: Oxford University Press, 1987).
5 Chandra Talpade Mohanty, "Under Western Eyes: Feminist Scholarship and Colonial Discourses," in *Third World Women and the Politics of Feminism,* edited by Chandra Talpade Mohanty, Ann Russo, and Lourdes Torres (Bloomington: Indiana University Press, 1991), 51-74; Arturo Escobar, *Encountering Development: The Making and Unmaking of the Third World* (Princeton, NJ: Princeton University Press, 1995); Joanna Liddle and Shirin M. Rai, "Between Feminism and Orientalism," in *Making Connections: Women's Studies, Women's Movements, Women's Lives,* edited by Mary Kennedy, Cathy Lubelska, and Val Walsh (Washington, DC: Taylor and Francis, 1993), 11-23.
6 Rosi Braidotti, Ewa Charkiewicz, Sabine Hausler, and Saskia Wieringa, *Women, the Environment and Sustainable Development: Towards a Theoretical Synthesis* (London, UK: Zed Press, 1994); Wendy Harcourt, ed., *Feminist Perspectives on Sustainable Development* (London, UK: Zed Press, 1994); Heleen van den Hombergh, *Gender, Environment and Development: A Guide to the Literature* (Utrecht, Netherlands: International Books, 1993).
7 Keith Griffin and A.R. Khan, *Globalization and the Developing World: An Essay on the International Dimensions of Development in the Post-Cold War Era* (Geneva: UNRISD, 1992), 2.
8 Bina Agarwal, "From Mexico 1975 to Beijing 1995," *Indian Journal of Gender Studies* 3, 1 (1996): 21-35.
9 The details of these case studies are discussed in the following: Rebecca Tarbotton, "Global Connections, Local Transformation: Women, Agriculture and Activism in Ladakh, India" (MA thesis, University of British Columbia, 2000); Leonora C. Angeles and Rebecca Tarbotton, "Local Transformation through Global Connection: Women's Assets and Environmental Activism for Sustainable Agriculture in Ladakh, India," *Women's Studies Quarterly* 29, 1-2 (2001): 99-115; Leonora C. Angeles, "Women Farmers and the Struggle for Sustainable Livelihoods and Organic Farming in a Peri-Urban City in Bukidnon, Philippines," *Urban Agriculture Magazine* (special issue on organic urban agriculture) 4, 1 (2002): 32-33; Layla Saad, "Cultivating Citizenship through Culture: The Use of Participatory Planning Approaches in Community-Based Watershed Management in Santo André, Brazil" (MSc thesis, University of British Columbia, 2002).
10 Deborah Brandt, ed., *Women Working the NAFTA Chain: Women, Food and Globalization* (Toronto: Second Story Press, 1999); Jane Collins, "Gender and Cheap Labour in Agriculture," in *Food and Agrarian Orders in the World Economy,* edited by Philip McMichael (Westport, CT: Greenwood Press, 1995), 217-32.
11 Maria Mies, *Indian Women in Subsistence and Agricultural Labor* (Geneva: International Labor Organization, 1986); Maria Mies and Vandana Shiva, *Ecofeminism* (London, UK: Zed Press, 1993); Vandana Shiva, *Staying Alive: Women, Ecology and Development* (London, UK: Zed Press, 1988); Vandana Shiva, *The Violence of the Green Revolution: Third World Agriculture, Ecology and Politics* (Atlantic Highlands, NJ: Zed Press; Penang, Malaysia: Third World Network, 1991); Vandana Shiva, ed., *Close to Home: Women Reconnect Ecology, Health and Development Worldwide* (Philadelphia and Gabriola Island, BC: New Society Publishers, 1994); Vandana Shiva, "Golden Rice and Neem: Biopatents and the Appropriation of Women's Environmental Knowledge," *Women's Studies Quarterly* 29, 1-2 (2001): 12-23.
12 Donna L. Doane, "Indigenous Knowledge, Technology Blending and Gender Implications," *Gender, Technology and Development* 3, 2 (1999): 235-57; Vandana Shiva, *Biopiracy: The Plunder of Nature and Knowledge* (Boston: South End Press, 1997); Shiva, "Golden Rice."
13 Shiva, "Golden Rice," 20-22.
14 Paolo Freire, *Pedagogy of the Oppressed* (New York: Seabury Press, 1970).
15 See Robert Chambers, *Whose Reality Counts? Putting the First Last* (London, UK: Intermediate Technology Publications, 1997).

16 See Bhuvan Bhatnagar and Aubrey Williams, eds., *Participatory Development and the World Bank: Potential Directions for Change* (Washington, DC: World Bank, 1992).

17 Leonora C. Angeles and Penny Gurstein, "Planning for Participatory Development: Challenges of Participation and North-South Partnerships in Capacity-Building Projects," *Canadian Journal of Development Studies* (special issue on participatory development) 21 (2000): 447-78; Jules Pretty, *Regenerating Agriculture: Policies and Practices for Sustainability and Self Reliance* (London, UK: Earthscan, 1995).

18 Irene Guijt and Meera Kaul Shah, eds., *The Myth of Community: Gender Issues in Participatory Development* (London, UK: Intermediate Technology Publications, 1998); Nici Nelson and Susan Wright, eds., *Power and Participatory Development: Theory and Practice* (London, UK: Intermediate Technology Publications, 1995).

19 David Mosse, "Authority, Gender and Knowledge: Theoretical Reflections on the Practice of Participatory Rural Appraisal," *Development and Change* 25 (1994): 497-526; Bill Cooke and Uma Kothari, *Participation: The New Tyranny?* (London, UK, and New York: Zed Books, 2001).

20 J. Plummer, *Municipalities and Community Participation* (London, UK: Earthscan, 2000).

21 Tarbotton, "Global Connections."

22 Helena Norberg-Hodge, *Ancient Features: Learning from Ladakh* (San Francisco: Sierra Club Books, 1991).

23 Angeles and Tarbotton, "Local Transformation," 106-7.

24 Ravina Aggarwal, "Trails of Turquoise: Feminist Inquiry and Counter-Development in Ladakh, India," in *Feminist Post-Development Thought: Rethinking Modernity, Postcolonialism and Representation,* edited by Kriemeld Saunders (New York: Zed Books, 2002), 78-79.

25 Ibid.; Tarbotton, "Global Connections."

26 Angeles and Tarbotton, "Local Transformation," 109.

27 Aggarwal, "Trails of Turquoise," 79.

28 Ibid.

29 Ibid.

30 MASIPAG literally means "industrious" or "hardworking" in the vernacular and stands for Magsasaka at Siyentipiko Para sa Siyentipikong Agrikultura, or Farmers and Scientists for Organic Agriculture.

31 MAKAKABUS means "pro-poor" and stands for Malahutayong Kahiusahan sa Kababayenan Bukidnon.

32 From a low of 45 women who had initially been members of the Farmers' Multipurpose Cooperative in late 1999, the organization was able to expand to 106 members in 2000 and to 200 members in June 2001.

33 MAKAKABUS created a highly functional organizational structure composed of core committees and departments and a group of ward chairs, one in each of the seven villages where MAKAKABUS currently has members, who meet bimonthly. The women practise flexibility and "learning-by-doing" in everything they undertake. When having a single treasurer for the whole organization no longer suited their needs, they created the position of secretary-treasurer to assist the person in charge in each of the four activity departments: Livelihood, Organic Fertilizer, Equipment, and Lending. The organization was able to face many trials through transparency, especially in all its financial transactions and record keeping, and by employing democratic processes in all organizational activities. It had clear guidelines for members and nonmembers, such as criteria for lending and borrowing, payment requirements, repayment schedules, and criteria for returning borrowed machines, especially in the tricky business of equipment rentals. To earn extra income, MAKAKABUS members would cook the food during large gatherings, such as capacity-building training workshops and meetings with foreign and local visitors. Money saved from this catering business goes into a "kitty fund" from which MAKAKABUS provides a fifty-peso "incentive pay" to ward village chairs who attend their bimonthly meetings.

34 A good business opportunity for MAKAKABUS came when the BCSA asked the Farmers' Multipurpose Cooperative to use its built-up capital to purchase the leased farm equipment (two mechanical threshers, two pieces of ploughing equipment, and one piece of hauling equipment called an *ancar-ancar*) or simply to return the equipment to BCSA.

After a three-year lease period, based on income sharing of 40 percent for the BCSA and 60 percent for the co-op, the latter was not able to raise the money needed. Thus the BCSA was forced to seek open bids on the next term of farm-equipment leasing. MAKAKABUS decided to put up a bid and produced a proposal within one month. Co-op members were initially upset that they had not been able to come up with a proposal before the deadline but were relieved to find out that MAKAKABUS was going to manage the farm-equipment rental program, which would be open to all, including nonco-op members.

35 Using two communal cellular phones, MAKAKABUS ward leaders make sure that all their customers are served on time and that trips are maximized so as to minimize operating costs, such as for crude oil and drivers' fees. To attract more customers, the organization rents its ploughing machines or hand tractors for the price of only crude oil but makes it a policy that if its machines are used to plough an area, the farmer will later rent its thresher and hauling machines come harvest season. MAKAKABUS charges farmers one *cavan* (approximately fifty kilograms of paddy rice) per twelve *cavans* threshed with its machines. The hauling machine can earn as much as ten pesos per bag hauled for longer distances and five pesos per bag for shorter distances.

36 Centre for Human Settlements (CHS), *Community Based Watershed Management in Santo Andre, Sao Paulo, Brazil*, revised project proposal, 1998, 2.

37 The Municipality of Santo André was slowly addressing the issues stemming from the watershed even prior to the adoption of the CBWM project. The Municipal Service of Environmental Sanitation of Santo André (SEMASA) began to address issues of basic infrastructure and environmental education after the 1997 adoption of the State Law of Recovery and Protection of Watersheds, which required an "emergency plan" to deal with the health of watersheds. Thus in January 2001 the Municipality of Santo André created the Sub-Prefeitura (Submunicipality) of Paranapiacaba and Parque Andreense (SPPPA) to establish a municipal structure that is more responsive and accountable to the needs of watershed residents. The creation of the submunicipality was accompanied by a devolution of power to administer watershed programs and projects on education, health, culture, infrastructure, transportation, environment, and information dissemination (interview with Jao Ricardo, 30 July 2001, cited in Saad, "Cultivating Citizenship").

38 CHS, *Community Based*.

39 Ibid.

40 Saad, "Cultivating Citizenship."

41 Ibid. The main objectives of these activities were: (1) to ensure community participation in all phases of the project; (2) to integrate gender analysis into the policies of the Parque Andreense region and to amplify and consolidate women's participation; and (3) to include youth and youth perspectives and consolidate their participation.

42 Ibid.

43 Saad, "Cultivating Citizenship."

44 CHS, *Community Based*.

45 Saad, "Cultivating Citizenship," 5-6.

46 Ibid., 2-3.

47 Ibid., 14.

48 Ibid., 16.

49 Angeles and Tarbotton, "Local Transformation," 100-1; Rae Lesser Blumberg, Cathy Rakowski, Irene Tinker, and Michael Monteon, eds., *Engendering Wealth and Well-Being: Empowerment for Global Change* (Boulder, CO: Westview Press, 1995).

50 Alex Shankland, "Analyzing Policy for Sustainable Livelihoods," in *IDS Research Report 49* (Sussex: Institute for Development Studies, September 2000), 2.

51 R. Hart, *Children's Participation: The Theory and Practice of Involving Young Citizens in Community Development and Environmental Care* (London, UK: Earthscan, 1997); C.D. Kleymeyer, "The Uses and Functions of Cultural Expression in Grassroots Development," in *Cultural Expression and Grassroots Development* (Boulder, CO: Lynne Rienner Publishers, 1994), 17-36.

52 Freire, *Pedagogy*.

53 Dorothy Smith, *The Everyday World as Problematic: A Feminist Sociology* (Boston: Northeastern University Press, 1997).

54   Veronica Vasquez Garcia, "Taking Gender into Account: Women and Sustainable Development Projects in Rural Mexico," *Women's Studies Quarterly* 29, 1-2 (2001): 85-98.
55   On this topic, see Peter Boothroyd and Leonora C. Angeles, eds., *Canadian Journal of Development Studies, Special Issue on Canadian Universities and International Development: A Critical Look* 24, 3 (2003).
56   Walter Lippmann, *The Phantom Public* (New York: Harcourt Brace, 1925).
57   Zillah Eisenstein, *Global Obscenities: Patriarchy, Capitalism and the Lure of Cyberfantasy* (New York and London, UK: New York University Press, 1998), 25.
58   Ibid., 5-6.
59   Braidotti, Charkiewicz, Hausler, and Wieringa, *Women;* Mirjam de Bruijn, Ineke van Halsema, and Heleen van den Hombergh, eds., *Gender and Land Use: Diversity in Environmental Practices* (Amsterdam: Thela, 1997); Caren Levy, "Gender and the Environment: The Challenge of Cross-Cutting Issues in Development Policy and Planning," *Environment and Urbanization* 4, 1 (1992): 134-49.
60   Walden Bello, "Fast-Track Capitalism, Geoeconomic Competition and the Sustainable Development Challenge in East Asia," in *Globalization and the South,* edited by Caroline Thomas and Peter Wilkin (London, UK: Macmillan, 1997; New York: St. Martin's Press, 1997), 158.

11

Too Close to Home: Dioxin Contamination of Breast Milk and the Political Agenda

Kathryn Harrison

In 1990 the Canadian federal government released a report declaring dioxins and structurally related furans to be toxic to human health and the environment as defined by the Canadian Environmental Protection Act. Although the fact was not emphasized in the accompanying press release, a table in the report estimated that breast-fed infants receive 16.5 times the "tolerable daily intake" of dioxins set by the Canadian government.[1] Four years later, the US Environmental Protection Agency (EPA) released its draft "dioxin reassessment," which offered a comparable estimate of the daily dose of dioxin received by breast-fed infants. However, since the EPA's virtually safe dose of dioxin is much lower than Canada's, this estimate was six thousand times greater than the level of exposure considered acceptable by the US agency.[2]

One might have expected these dramatic findings to receive widespread media and public attention for a number of reasons. Dioxin is arguably the ultimate "political chemical,"[3] thanks to a combination of its long-standing reputation as the "most toxic chemical known to humankind" and the sustained attention to dioxin from environmental groups on both sides of the border. Moreover, breast milk is laden with cultural significance as a symbol of purity and sustenance for the most vulnerable members of society. The connection between dioxin and breast milk might thus be expected to yield a combination of fear and outrage – and, at a minimum, interest.

Yet the potentially explosive government findings received little attention from government, environmental groups, the media, or the public in either country. Although industrial sources of dioxin and various sources of human exposure, particularly contaminated fish, have continued to receive public and governmental attention, the level of contamination of breast milk by dioxins has gone relatively unnoticed in both Canada and the United States. The purpose of this chapter is to explore the reasons for the absence of this issue from the political agenda in North America.

The chapter begins with an overview of the literature on risk perception and agenda setting, followed by consideration of the health risks of dioxins and the lack of attention to the issue of dioxins in breast milk compared to other environmental issues on the public agenda. Thereafter, several explanations are considered for the absence of breast-milk contamination from the political agenda. Although some documentary evidence and statements by interviewees identify the cause as agenda denial by actors who have sought to keep the issue off the political agenda,[4] the chapter finds strongest support for an alternative explanation: that environmentalists consciously chose not to press the issue of breast-milk contamination in the first place for a variety of reasons, including concern that breast-feeding mothers would discontinue breast-feeding and personal anxiety about an issue that fundamentally challenges women's conceptions of their own bodies and their relationships with their children. The case study of dioxins in breast milk suggests that the literature on agenda setting must look beyond active strategies of agenda denial by economically and politically powerful interests to the role of shared cultural values in shaping – and restricting – the political agenda.

Risk Perception and Political Agenda Setting

Two different scholarly literatures can be brought to bear on this question: those concerning risk perception and those focused on political-agenda setting. It has long been established in the psychological literature on risk perception that the lay public's risk assessments are often very different from experts' estimates of statistical risk. Most people tend to underestimate familiar risks, such as the likelihood of dying in a car accident, and to overestimate risks that are unfamiliar, involuntary, or associated with either delayed impacts or "dread."[5] Displaying all these characteristics, dioxin contamination of breast milk would seem ripe for overreaction. This is reinforced by studies on gender and risk perception, which find that, confronted with similar hazards, women tend to perceive greater risks than men (especially white men).[6] Gustafson notes that not only do women tend to worry more about the same risks than do men, but they also tend to worry about different risks, paying greater attention to accidental and health risks.[7] Davidson and Freudenburg find strongest support for two explanations for the differences between men's and women's risk perceptions: (1) that women are socialized to nurture and maintain life and are thus more concerned about health and safety; and (2) that women have less trust in institutions associated with science and technology.[8] Again, since the presence of dioxins in breast milk is both a scientifically sophisticated issue and a health concern intimately linked to women's role as nurturers, one might expect a particularly strong reaction from women.

However, as Douglas and Wildavsky have noted, an important drawback of the risk-perception literature is its exclusive focus on the individual.[9]

While the lay public, and women in particular, may well have been primed to react strongly to news of dioxins in breast milk, as discussed below they had few opportunities to obtain that information from the popular media. Thus the risk-perception literature alone cannot tell us why this issue received so little attention from environmental groups and the press. Douglas and Wildavsky begin from the perspective that risk is a collective, rather than individual, construct and offer a sociological analysis of why some environmental risks become the object of widespread concern and others do not. They argue that the environmental movement, as a result of its "sectarian" organizational structure and ideology, is inclined to selectively publicize risks that are involuntary, irreversible, and hidden and for which blame can be attributed and conspiracies alleged (ironically, quite similar to the conclusions drawn by the psychological literature on individual risk perception of which the authors are so critical). "Purity becomes a dominant motif," according to Douglas and Wildavsky.[10] Given the hidden and involuntary nature of dioxin contamination of breast milk, the irreversibility of cancer, which is the health impact most often associated with dioxin, and the significance of breast milk as a symbol of purity, a cultural analysis of risk would seem to predict considerable effort by environmentalists to provoke public alarm about dioxins in breast milk.

The political-science literature on agenda setting also seeks to explain the processes by which we collectively select some issues for governmental attention and ignore others. The foundational work on agenda setting by Cobb and Elder emphasizes the characteristics of societal problems, including their magnitude and the potential for disasters, or "focusing events."[11] Birkland emphasizes the importance of the nature and organization of policy communities, arguing that well-organized policy communities are better positioned to take advantage of focusing events to achieve policy change.[12] Kingdon's "garbage can model" of agenda setting also emphasizes the role of policy entrepreneurs in bringing developments in the "policy stream" to the public's and thus the government's agenda.[13] Applying Kingdon's model to agenda setting for environmental risks, Harrison and Hoberg note that the discovery of dioxins in pulp-mill effluents received public attention in the US only when Greenpeace brought to light the EPA's finding[14] and in Canada only when Greenpeace released its own analyses of sediments from the receiving environment of a Vancouver Island pulp mill. In addition to focusing on events and interest groups, other authors have emphasized the importance of institutions in constraining the political agenda and of changes in institutional venue as a strategy for agenda change.[15]

Much of the recent literature on agenda setting has adopted a constructivist approach, focusing on how problems are defined, or "framed," by political actors. Thus Stone focuses on the strategic representation of problems by policy entrepreneurs and, in particular, on how they use causal stories to reframe accepted societal "conditions" as political "problems."[16] Similarly, Schneider and Ingram consider how stereotypes about target populations can increase or decrease the likelihood that an issue affecting those communities will reach the political agenda.[17] Baumgartner and Jones offer a punctuated-equilibrium model, in which a stable policy network and problem definition can occasionally be disrupted through popularization of an alternative problem definition by actors seeking to focus public attention on the issue.[18] Reflecting on this literature, Rochefort and Cobb draw a link between the earlier pluralist literature on agenda setting and more recent constructivist literature.[19] Ideas, language, and perceptions are the currency with which interest groups eager to place new issues on the agenda, and their opponents seeking to constrain that agenda, engage in political struggle. Again, one might expect an issue such as dioxins in breast milk to be ripe for strategic representation and framing and that an audience inclined to fear unfamiliar risks would be receptive to the issue.

Of particular interest for this chapter is an emerging thread in the constructivist literature that seeks to explain why some issues do *not* reach the agenda. Cobb and Ross analyze various strategies adopted by actors who oppose reframing of an issue and its emergence on the political agenda, as well as when those strategies tend to succeed. They conclude that "agenda denial occurs not just because of the complicated mechanics of the policy process or the lack of governmental resources, but often because a proposed action challenges existing world-views and identities in unacceptable ways that opponents demonstrate effectively."[20] The implication for the breast-milk case is that one should look to the counteractivities, including strategic use of symbols and rhetoric, of those who stand to lose if widespread public concern about dioxins in breast milk is mobilized.

The foregoing suggests several alternative explanations for the absence of dioxin contamination of breast milk from the political agenda. First, although the risk of contaminated breast milk may well be characterized by unfamiliarity, delayed impacts, and dread, there may simply be other issues with similar characteristics that present greater health risks and thus have been more successful in capturing the attention of interest groups, governments, and the public. Second, the emergence of this issue on the political agenda may have been precluded by the absence of a focusing event. Third, the institutional venue may not have been conducive to successful reframing of the issue in either country. Fourth, consistent with Cobb and Ross's analysis of agenda-denial strategies, environmentalists' efforts to publicize the issue may have been rebuffed by political opponents. Finally, environmentalists may simply have declined to press the issue in the first place, a form of self-censorship examined in greater detail below. Before turning to these hypotheses, a brief review of what is known about the risks of dioxins in breast milk is in order.

Dioxin and Human Health

The chemical usually referred to as "dioxin" is 2,3,7,8-dibenzo-p-dioxin (2378 TCDD), which is the most toxic of a family of structurally similar chlorinated dioxins and furans. Most analyses measure toxicity of all dioxins and furans collectively in terms of toxic equivalents or "TEQs" of 2378 TCDD. Dioxins and furans are never intentionally manufactured but are released as unintended by-products of processes such as incineration of chlorinated compounds, manufacturing of certain chlorinated chemicals, and chlorination of naturally occurring compounds in wood during pulp and paper manufacturing. Dioxins have low solubility in water but high solubility in fat, and they are extremely stable, persisting in the environment in some cases for decades. As a result of these two characteristics, dioxins tend to bioaccumulate as one moves up the food chain. At the top of the food chain, humans receive most of their exposure through consumption of animal products – meat, fish, chicken, eggs, and dairy products – and from human breast milk. Since dioxin is metabolized very slowly by the human body, the accumulated "body burden" of dioxin stored in fat tends to increase over time.[21]

The extent of risk to human health from dioxins is highly controversial. The ever-present difficulties of demonstrating statistically significant effects among diverse human populations is exacerbated in the case of dioxins by the fact that they are unintended contaminants. As a result, levels of contamination were often not measured historically, and exposure is typically confounded by concurrent exposure to other toxic substances. However, several large epidemiological studies in the 1990s did provide evidence of carcinogenicity in humans, prompting the International Agency for Research on Cancer to declare 2378 TCDD to be a known human carcinogen in 1997.[22] Nonetheless, given the limited number of epidemiological studies as well as researchers' capacity to experimentally vary exposure among laboratory animals, most risk assessments for dioxins continue to be based on studies of animals. At extremely low doses, 2378 TCDD has been found to cause a variety of adverse health effects in test species.

Cancer risk has dominated regulatory decisions concerning dioxins to date and will thus be the focus of the discussion here. However, it is noteworthy that regulators are increasingly attentive to other end points, since evidence suggests that humans may be more sensitive to the immunological, reproductive, and developmental effects of exposure to dioxins. For some of these noncancer effects, the EPA's dioxin reassessment concludes that, for the average population, the margin of safety between doses that caused adverse effects in laboratory animals and current levels of exposure is less than a factor of ten. It also noted that populations receiving high-end exposures are approaching the levels at which adverse effects have been reported in laboratory animals.[23]

The Canadian and US governments have adopted very different approaches to cancer-risk assessment for dioxins.[24] The US approach yields a more cautious "virtually safe dose" of 0.01 picograms per kilogram of body weight per day (pg/kg/day),[25] which is 1,000 times less than Health Canada's "tolerable daily intake" of 10 pg/kg/day.[26] The divergence between the Canadian and US estimates of acceptable exposure might be expected to have significant policy implications since estimates of current exposure levels at 1 to 4 pg/kg/day fall squarely between the two.[27] However, the fact that highly exposed populations, including those that consume large quantities of fish, can be exposed to doses several times higher than the average has prompted similar regulatory action in both countries, for instance to control discharges from pulp mills and to restrict consumption of fish.

Dioxin was first detected in human milk samples from Germany in 1984, followed soon thereafter by confirmation of comparable levels of contamination in other industrialized countries. During lactation, a portion of a mother's body fat, and with it dioxins accumulated therein since birth, is transferred to her breast milk, "effectively putting babies one step higher on the food chain."[28] Although dioxin levels between the mother and fetus tend to be in equilibrium before birth, after birth there is a net transfer of dioxins from mother to infant during breast-feeding. Indeed, one of the most effective, if unintended, ways for a grown woman to reduce her body burden of dioxins is through lactation.[29]

Given that breast milk is relatively contaminated with dioxins compared to other foods, that many infants initially subsist entirely on breast milk, and that they consume a large quantity of food relative to body weight, breast-feeding infants can receive a higher dose of dioxins per unit of body weight than any other population. Exposure estimates range from the EPA's 60 pg TEQ/kg/day to Health Canada's 165 pg TEQ/kg/day, depending on the averaging time.[30] Even the EPA's lower estimate is thirty-five times higher than the typical background exposure for adults. The EPA estimates that a breast-fed infant receives 4 to 12 percent of its lifetime exposure to dioxin during the first year of life.

We know relatively little about the impacts of these levels of dioxin exposure on breast-feeding infants. However, several ongoing epidemiological studies offer the potential to advance our understanding of the developmental impacts of dioxins and other persistent toxic substances. The earliest of these studies found a developmental deficit among the children of women who consumed fish contaminated with PCBs and other toxic substances from the Great Lakes.[31] A subsequent study of breast-fed children in North Carolina found lower psychomotor skills during the first two years among children whose mothers had higher levels of various contaminants in their breast milk,[32] but these effects were no longer observable by age five.[33] A Dutch study comparing breast-fed and formula-fed infants similarly found negative effects of PCBs and dioxins in breast milk at only seven months of age, although the negative effects were outweighed by the benefits of breast-feeding. The researchers did, however, find a negative correlation between *prenatal* exposure to toxins and a variety of developmental effects in infants.[34] This led them to conclude that even though exposure from breast milk may be less problematic than prenatal exposure, to the extent that it represents a significant contribution to the body burden of the next generation of women of reproductive age, it could still have an important delayed impact.[35] A recent finding that breast-fed infants whose mothers' milk contains higher levels of dioxins are more likely to have tooth defects is consistent with hypothesized developmental impacts.[36] Using risk estimates from animal studies, Hoover estimates that dioxins contribute three-quarters of the lifetime cancer risk associated with some two dozen toxic substances in breast milk.[37]

It is noteworthy that despite pronounced differences between US and Canadian regulators' cancer-risk assessments, the exposure received by breast-fed infants greatly exceeds both the EPA and Health Canada estimates of the acceptable daily intake of dioxin (at 16.5 times the Canadian tolerable daily intake and 6,000 times the US virtually safe dose). The question remains, however, of how to interpret a relatively high exposure for a short period of time, when animal tests and the risk estimates derived from them are typically based on lifetime-averaged exposures. Consistent with its more risk-tolerant approach, the Canadian government's assessment notes that although the exposure received by breast-fed infants is "relatively high," "breast feeding only occurs for a short part of the life span ... and lower exposures throughout the remainder of the life span reduce lifetime exposure below [the 10 pg/kg/day] guideline."[38] In contrast, the EPA has expressed concern that reliance on lifetime-risk estimates may actually underestimate the risk to breast-feeding infants since they are exposed during a time of rapid cell division and growth. The EPA thus identifies breast-fed infants among the "highly exposed populations" of particular concern.[39]

Breast-Milk Contamination and the Popular Agenda

Of course, the impossibility of proving something's nonexistence presents a fundamental obstacle to studying why some issues fail to reach the political agenda. However, it is not asserted here that the presence of dioxins in breast milk was on *no one's* public-policy agenda. The issue was undoubtedly a concern for some members of the public and some actors within government. Rather, the focus here is the inattention to this issue *relative to* other environmental health risks that have received more widespread media, public, and governmental attention.

Cobb and Elder distinguish between the popular agenda and the governmental agenda. The primary focus of this chapter is the former, defined by Cobb and Elder as the set of "issues commonly perceived by members of the political community as meriting public attention and as involving matters within the legitimate jurisdiction of government authority."[40] In the absence of detailed public-opinion polls comparing attitudes toward different environmental health risks, newspaper coverage will be used as a surrogate for public attention. Although extensive media coverage of an issue does not ensure that it will be perceived by the public as warranting a public-policy response, given the technically complex nature of the issues that will be compared, it is highly unlikely that an issue could reach the public agenda in the *absence* of extensive media coverage.

How does media coverage of dioxins in breast milk compare to that of comparable environmental health risks? Table 11.1 compares the number of stories on various environmental and health issues in the *New York Times* and the *Canadian Newspaper Index* between January 1985 and May 1999. The absolute figures are not comparable between Canada and the US since the Canadian index includes multiple newspapers.[41] Rather, it is the relative attention to different issues within each index that is of interest here. The issues presented were selected because, like dioxins in breast milk, each involves either risks from food contamination or risks to children, or both.

Table 11.1

Canadian and US newspaper coverage of selected environmental health risks

News index[a]	Search topics	NYT	Canadian
Dioxin and breast milk	Dioxin*[b] and milk and (breast* or mother*)	18	13
Dioxin and cow's milk	Dioxin* and milk and (cow* or carton*)	18	4
Dioxin and fish	Dioxin* and (fish* or shellfish or fisher*)	139	45
Alar	Alar	161	29
Mad cow disease	(Mad and cow*) or (Creudtzfeldt)	> 1000	225
Phthalates and toys	(Phthalates* or toxin* or toxic* or vinyl) and (infant* or baby* or children*) and (teething or toy*)	275	25
Pesticides in children's food	Child* and pesticide* and (food* or diet)	425	41
Bovine growth hormone	(Bovine growth hormone*) or BGH or BST	110	161

a Searches were completed 13-15 May 1999. The *New York Times* was searched using Lexus-Nexus. The *Canadian News Index* was searched using Canadian Business and Current Affairs.
b The asterisk in the search strategies indicates a trunction wild card.

In both countries, there has been greater media attention to dioxins in fish than in breast milk. The former issue has also received greater attention from government regulators, who have responded to detection of dioxins in fish and shellfish with fisheries closures and advisories in both countries. The issue of dioxins leaching from paper milk cartons into cow's milk received comparable attention to dioxins in breast milk in the *New York Times,* although less in Canadian newspapers. However, it is noteworthy that unlike breast-milk contamination, contaminated cow's milk elicited a policy response in both countries.[42]

Coverage of dioxins in foods is minor in comparison to two other potential food risks – "mad cow" disease and bovine growth hormone – although the latter received proportionately greater attention in Canada. Children's exposure to pesticides in foods, Alar in apples, and phthalates in infant toys also received greater coverage than dioxins in breast milk, especially in the US, where each of these issues has been the focus of prominent campaigns by environmentalists.

The Canadian newspaper coverage of dioxins in breast milk reported in Table 11.1 largely reflects two wire-service stories, each of which was covered in multiple newspapers. The first was a report in April 1988 that dioxins had been detected in samples of breast milk from Quebec (the first samples to be analyzed in a national study), which was picked up by Quebec newspapers and the *Globe and Mail*.[43] Then, in October 1990, references to high levels of infant exposure to dioxins from breast milk in the federal government's dioxin assessment were publicized in a widely reprinted story by the Canadian Press wire service.[44] A leaked draft of the EPA's dioxin reassessment also received front-page coverage in the *New York Times* in May 1994, although that story gave less prominence to breast milk as a source of exposure.[45] In other stories, the *New York Times* focused on dioxins in cow's milk, bleached coffee filters, and contaminated fish but did not even mention breast milk.[46]

Interestingly, with the exception of a couple of follow-up articles in which experts and politicians sought to allay public concern, each of these stories quickly faded from public view.[47] In both Canada and the US, bureaucrats and politicians stressed that the benefits of breast-feeding outweigh any risks. However, Canadian bureaucrats tended to provide stronger reassurance of absolute safety, as when one Health and Welfare Canada official stated, "It has no relevance to human safety when you get down to these extremely low levels."[48]

There has been somewhat greater media coverage of PCB contamination of breast milk. However, the focus has not been on the general population but on elevated levels of PCBs in the breast milk of Inuit women, which has been the subject of an ongoing study by Quebec researchers.[49] As well, the question of dioxins in breast milk appears to have received greater public attention recently in Japan, suggesting an opportunity for future comparative research.[50]

In summary, there is no question that the chemical "dioxin" has received ample attention from the media, the public, and governments in both Canada and the United States. However, in light of the relatively high exposures associated with dioxin contamination of breast milk, and the cultural sensitivity to infant exposure and to breast milk as a symbol of purity, it is striking how little attention there has been to this particular issue. The absence of significant press coverage, and the relatively low profile of environmentalists in that coverage, suggests that environmentalists have not attempted to publicize this particular issue, whether as a concern in and of itself or as a way to mobilize public concern about persistent toxic substances more generally. Environmentalists' role in problem definition will be further discussed below.

Explaining the Absence of Breast-Milk Contamination from the Public Agenda

Severity of the Problem

The remainder of this chapter considers alternative hypotheses for the absence of breast-milk contamination from the public agenda. First, might the lower level of media and governmental attention to the issue of dioxins in breast milk relative to other environmental health risks simply be a reflection of the fact that those other risks are more serious? This section compares the risk assessment of dioxins in breast milk with four other environmental issues that have received greater media and/or governmental attention. In each case, the estimated risks from dioxins in breast milk are comparable or greater, suggesting that the magnitude of the risk alone does not explain the absence of breast-milk contamination from the political agenda.

As discussed above, the presence of dioxins in fish has received both greater media attention and greater governmental attention, the latter reflected in fisheries closures and advisories in both countries. The EPA estimates that the average person consumes 0.1 pg TEQ/kg/day of dioxins from fish, although subsistence fishers and ethnic populations that eat more fish can consume as much as 2 pg/kg/day.[51] In contrast, the EPA estimates that a breast-fed infant receives a daily dose of 60 pg TEQ/kg/day. However, it is true that one consumes fish for a higher proportion of one's life than breast milk. Taking this into account, estimates of the lifetime cancer risks are comparable: 6.6 percent of the background cancer risk from dioxins is from fish, compared to 4 to 12 percent from breast milk.[52] The greater public and governmental attention to dioxins in fish and shellfish cannot be explained by the severity of risks since the risks are of similar magnitude.

The revelation that dioxins had been seeping from bleached cardboard cartons into cow's milk (it was not present at the same levels in milk stored in plastic or glass containers) received media attention comparable to that occasioned by dioxins in breast milk in the US, although less attention in Canada. However, it did achieve greater prominence on the governmental agenda: US regulators and their counterparts in at least one Canadian province (Quebec) responded promptly even though the dairy and paper industries had committed to voluntarily eliminating the problem by switching to dioxin-free cartons. Moreover, even limited media coverage of dioxin contamination of cow's milk provoked a public reaction, with sales of milk in cartons declining in Canada in October 1988 and in the US in September 1989.[53] Yet levels of 2378 TCDD in cow's milk were detected at 0.02 to 0.07 ppt, compared to a typical concentration in breast milk of 17 ppt, over 100 times higher.[54] Again, that one consumes cow's milk for a longer proportion of one's life should be taken into account. However, even then, the US Food and Drug Administration (FDA) estimated a lifetime risk from consumption of milk in chlorine-bleached cartons of between 5 and 7 in a million, compared with a contribution to lifetime cancer risk from breast milk estimated by the EPA to be between 4 and 100 in a million, again suggesting comparable or greater risks from the latter.[55]

More recently, the discovery in June 1999 that animal feed given to cows and chickens in Belgium was contaminated with dioxins received international press coverage and prompted consumer alarm and bans of Belgian beef, chicken, and dairy products by governments around the world. The Belgian food scare is widely considered to have been a significant factor in the defeat of the governing party in national elections in Belgium that same month. Yet the World Health Organization estimates the daily intake of dioxins associated with a typical diet of contaminated Belgian food to be 8 to 10 pg/kg,[56] roughly ten times less than the same organization estimates is consumed by breast-fed infants around the world every day.

Finally, the case of Alar, a growth regulator that was used to promote a firm texture and unblemished appearance in apples, is similar in many respects to that of breast-milk contamination. Like dioxins in breast milk, Alar (or more accurately the chemical UDMH, which was formed when Alar-treated products were processed) was considered a particular risk to children since they consume much larger quantities of apples, especially in the form of apple juice, per unit of body weight. Alar was the subject of an extensive media campaign by US environmental groups in 1989, as reflected in greater media coverage in Table 11.1, and was ultimately banned in both Canada and the US. The EPA estimated an upper limit lifetime risk of 4.5×10^{-5} for Alar,[57] roughly at the midpoint of the EPA's range for dioxins in breast milk, as reported above.

The point of these four examples is not to provoke alarm about dioxins in breast milk. The EPA's risk-assessment methodology is intentionally conservative, yielding what the agency itself describes as upper-bound risk estimates. Actual risks may well be much lower in each of the above cases. However, the fact that risks estimated using the same methodology[58] to be comparable or even lower than those associated with dioxin contamination of breast milk have received greater public and/or governmental attention indicates that the magnitude of risk alone cannot explain the lack of attention to breast-milk contamination.

The breast-milk case may be unusual in one respect, however. There is strong evidence that breast-feeding offers physiological benefits to both mother and infant, the latter including protection against infection, immunological benefits, and protection against allergies.[59] The relevant comparison thus may be *net* risk (or benefit) rather than environmental risk alone. Indeed, despite the presence of contaminants, physicians, government spokespersons, breast-feeding advocates, and even environmentalists invariably stress that the benefits of breast-feeding outweigh the risks.[60] Although in the examples discussed above, apples, milk, and fish also have nutritional value, equally nutritious substitutes for these products are, at least in theory, available, which is not the case for breast milk.[61] As discussed below, the perceived benefits of breast-feeding relative to the risks were clearly a consideration for all players in the relevant policy network. However, for this to explain the lack of attention to dioxins in breast milk, one would have to assume that the only policy option available, or the inevitable consequence of even raising the issue, would be to discourage breast-feeding. Yet it is conceivable that one could express concern about the extent of contamination and emphasize the need for reduction of dioxin sources even while encouraging women to continue breast-feeding. Indeed, one might expect those most aware of the benefits of breast-feeding to be among those most outraged and thus most inclined to seek action to prevent further contamination of breast milk.

Absence of Focusing Events

From Cobb and Elder to Birkland,[62] students of agenda setting have emphasized the role of focusing events in bringing new issues to the political agenda. "Sudden, dramatic and often harmful, focusing events give pro-change groups significant advantages" in overcoming opposition from those who seek to keep an issue off the political agenda.[63] It is beyond question that if there had been an epidemic of babies becoming noticeably sick from drinking contaminated breast milk, this issue would have assumed dramatic proportions. However, while the absence of a focusing event would appear to be a factor contributing to the low profile of this issue, it cannot offer a

complete explanation since focusing events are neither necessary nor sufficient for agenda change.

Not only do many issues reach the political agenda without a focusing
event, but many focusing events are orchestrated by policy entrepreneurs.[64]
Environmental groups have held press conferences to release their own
studies (as Greenpeace did in releasing analyses of dioxins in sediments
near pulp mills), to publicize expert reports that they themselves have commissioned (as US environmentalists did in the case of Alar), and to bring
little-noticed government or academic studies to the media's and thus the
public's attention (as Greenpeace did in publicizing Health Canada's detection of dioxins in cow's milk).[65] "Discoveries" can thus become focusing
events with a little help from policy entrepreneurs. Yet, as discussed below,
environmentalists have made little effort to generate such attention to dioxins in breast milk. It is also noteworthy that even dioxin-related focusing
events apparently have not been sufficient to concentrate attention on this
issue. Although the discovery of widespread dioxin contamination of the
Belgian food supply was a high-profile issue not only in Belgium but throughout Europe in 1999, there appears to have been little attention to the question of breast-milk contamination as a result.

Institutional Factors
The low visibility of breast-milk contamination relative to other environmental health issues is thus not readily explained by risk assessments alone
or by the absence of focusing events. This section considers the influence of
political institutions on agenda setting. Elsewhere I have offered an institutional explanation for the divergent Canadian and US risk assessments for
dioxin noted above.[66] The more open regulatory process in the US has resulted in greater politicization of risk assessments, and this has encouraged
US regulators to rely on conservative, formal models, which, in the case of
dioxin, have yielded more cautious risk assessments than do informal safety
factors.[67] However, that neither the public nor regulators in either country
have shown much inclination to focus on dioxins in breast milk suggests
that institutional *differences* are not an important explanatory factor in this
case.

On the other hand, institutional *similarities* may have shaped the terms
of debate in ways that constrained this issue's access to the formal agenda
in both countries. Both Canada and the US have statutes authorizing regulation of contaminants in foods sold in commerce. In the minds of bureaucrats, this institutional venue may have framed the issue as one of safety of
the *commercial* food supply. That breast milk is not sold commercially may
have meant that its contamination was not top of mind for government
officials, even though, if breast milk were regulated like infant formula,

levels of dioxin contamination would in theory prohibit its sale in both countries.[68] While this institutional barrier may have thus been a contributing factor, the significance of this explanation is undermined by the fact that both Canadian and US regulators have issued nonbinding advisories concerning dioxins to recreational and subsistence fishers, who do not sell their catch. Moreover, with the exception of fish, violation of dioxin standards for commercial foods is routinely ignored in Canada in any case.[69]

Agenda Denial

Recent literature on political-agenda setting focuses on the critical role of problem definition in the political struggle between actors seeking to place an issue on the agenda and those who would deny that issue agenda status. Extrapolating from the recent work of Cobb and Ross,[70] one can hypothesize that "initiators," in this case environmentalists, could have tried to redefine an environmental problem (dioxins or persistent toxic substances more generally) by focusing on the powerful cultural symbol of breast milk but that they failed to do so because "opponents," those who stand to lose if the issue achieves agenda status, succeeded in reinforcing an alternative framing of the issue.

As discussed above, a handful of stories concerning dioxins in breast milk have emerged in Canadian and US newspapers over the last decade. In some cases, environmentalists played a role in alerting reporters to those stories, although in others, such as the *New York Times'* coverage of the EPA's dioxin reassessment, the media appear to have simply been reporting on the government's own studies.[71] Canadian newspaper coverage of the potential risks to breast-feeding infants discussed in the 1990 Canadian dioxin report emerged only several months after the report's release, when Greenpeace hand-picked a wire-service reporter considered sympathetic and provided him with extensive background research. However, the Greenpeace campaigner recalled, "We hadn't planned to focus on breast milk. It was supposed to be about dioxin and food. It was [the reporter] who chose to emphasize breast milk." In the US the Environmental Defense Fund held a press conference in 1987 to release the results of a university scientist's testing of breast milk for dioxins.[72] It is noteworthy that at this press conference – indeed, in almost all cases where environmentalists referred even in passing to contamination of breast milk – they invariably stressed that the benefits of breast-feeding are believed to outweigh any risks.[73] In fact, on one occasion in 1997, when Greenpeace held a press conference at which an association between PVC and dioxins in breast milk was expected to arise (although it was not the primary focus of the press conference), they invited representatives of the La Leche League to present their own press release simultaneously.[74]

The "opponents" in this case include politicians and government officials, breast-feeding advocates, and the media themselves, all of whom were effective in using the cultural symbolism of breast milk to their advantage in containing the issue. Although many of the studies suggesting cause for concern have been prepared by government officials, not only have politicians and bureaucrats chosen not to highlight the issue of dioxins in breast milk, but they have gone to considerable lengths to downplay it, using the strategies of placation, denial, and attack identified by Cobb and Ross.[75] When press coverage did occasionally arise, government officials responded with a standard set of arguments. First, they expressed shared concern but noted that various actions were already being taken to reduce dioxin discharges at the source. Second, they dismissed the quantities as "minute" and detectable only as a result of recent advances in analytical techniques. Third, they dismissed the risks to infants as insignificant or, in the case of Canadian bureaucrats' statements, nonexistent.[76] Their reassurances were picked up in headlines such as "Dioxin traces found in breast-milk samples from Quebec no cause for alarm: scientists" and "'No problem' for infants in short term: Dioxin traces found in human milk in Quebec."[77] Fourth, like environmentalists, politicians and government officials stressed that the benefits of breast-feeding outweigh any risks and encouraged women to continue breast-feeding.

Finally, officials and politicians occasionally resorted to accusations that those who raised the issue were fearmongering. The most extreme example of this strategy was in evidence when the Canadian minister of health, Perrin Beatty, responded to questions about his government's dioxin report from the Parliamentary opposition, who had also been provided with Greenpeace's background research on dioxins in foods,[78] by accusing them of "attempting to frighten nursing mothers into believing that they were poisoning their infants."[79] Interestingly, the minister's comments indicate that he had been briefed to anticipate that the opposition would focus on dioxins in breast milk. He appears to have followed through with his briefing notes even though the opposition had not even mentioned breast milk in their questions about the dioxin issue. Other examples of self-restraint by those who might have sought to publicize dioxins in breast milk to further their policy objectives are discussed in the next section.

In responding to questions about contamination of the food supply and the government's proposals to relax dioxin standards for foods, Beatty conveniently hid behind the breast-milk issue, raising the proposition that "If we were to take the position that no dioxins whatsoever could be allowed in any food used in Canada, we would have to ban breast milk, for example, and throw away literally hundreds of millions of dollars worth of good, nourishing, nutritious food in Canada each year."[80] The Government of

Canada thus used rhetoric to place itself squarely on the side of babies and mothers, arguing that anyone who would even question the purity of breast milk was out to harm children.

The second source of opposition came from the medical profession and breast-feeding advocates. This includes physicians specializing in breast-feeding, who are frequently quoted in newspaper stories about breast-milk contamination. As one reporter reflected about Dr. Jack Newman, from the Hospital for Sick Children in Toronto, "If you write anything suggesting that there might be anything in breast milk that would cause anyone to consider not nursing, he fires off a letter or calls you up." In light of the well-documented benefits of breast-feeding, environmentalists' would-be allies within the medical profession tended to see the issue in the first instance not in terms of contaminated versus pure breast milk, but rather as one of discouraging versus promoting breastfeeding (breast milk versus artificial formula). They thus placed the burden of proof on those who would suggest risks from contamination.[81]

Also included in this community are volunteer groups such as the La Leche League and the Infant Feeding Action Coalition (INFACT). One can imagine that organizations that passionately support breast-feeding might have quite different reactions to news of dioxin contamination of breast milk: outrage at the desecration of breast milk or denial should any hint of risk discourage women from breast-feeding. The overwhelming reaction, at least for public consumption, has been the latter.[82] Echoing government officials, breast-feeding advocates emphasized the benefits of breast-feeding and the "minute quantities" of contaminants detected. Building on previous political struggles with infant-formula manufacturers, some breast-feeding advocates also raised two other themes. First, they emphasized that cow's milk and formula are polluted, too. And, second, some authors have suggested that allegations of contamination of breast milk are the work of formula companies seeking to discourage breast-feeding.[83]

Interestingly, a third, although less consistent, source of opposition has been the press itself. There have been almost as many stories criticizing "alarmist" coverage of pollutants in breast milk as there have been stories criticizing the presence of pollutants.[84] One US environmentalist interviewed said that although her group does include occasional references to dioxins in breast milk in press releases, the press won't cover the issue: "Reporters say that their editors say it's too inflammatory, no one will believe you." However, on the other hand, another US environmentalist reported resisting encouragement by reporters to sensationalize stories by playing on the breast-milk angle, and, as noted above, it was the 1990 Canadian Press reporter who chose to focus on dioxins in breast milk based on a broader Greenpeace report on dioxins in foods.

One example of the powerful backlash that references to contamination of breast milk can elicit appeared when Theo Colborn – a scientist with the World Wildlife Fund who was central to the emergence of the issue of endocrine disrupters on the public agenda with her co-authored best-selling book, *Our Stolen Future*[85] – responded to a question about dioxins in breast milk in an interview in *Mother Jones* magazine. Although Colborn's response included the standard statement that the benefits of breast-feeding appear to outweigh the risks,[86] the fact that she suggested any uncertainty about this view elicited what the magazine's editorial staff described as an "enormous volume of mail – all negative," a sample of which was reprinted in the following issue.[87] The letters to the editor included not only the arguments cited thus far, but also at least one personal attack on Colborn's scientific credentials.

As noted above, although a handful of stories about dioxin contamination of breast milk were published in both countries, in no case did the issue "take off." With the exception of one or more stories the following day reassuring breast-feeding mothers, there would be no further coverage in the same newspaper for months or even years. Whatever efforts environmental activists may have made to focus public attention on the issue of dioxins in breast milk as a symbol of more widespread risks from persistent toxic substances were rebuffed by more dominant messages: that "breast-feeding is good" and that anyone who might hint otherwise is at best irresponsible and at worst malicious. In contrast, when Greenpeace alerted the public to a government study confirming the presence of dioxins in milk in paper cartons, their message was met with a more measured response from both government and the affected industry. Although government officials provided comparable reassurances that the risks were minimal and that they themselves were taking every action to eliminate them, there was no comparable defence of the wholesomeness of milk nor depiction of the bearers of the news as somehow antichildren.

The literature on agenda denial thus offers considerable insight into this case study. However, it falls short in two respects. First, it is noteworthy that, unlike in most of the case studies analyzed by Cobb and Ross,[88] there is no industry whose self-interest is immediately threatened by allegations of dioxins in breast milk.[89] None of the opponents had an interest in maintaining contamination of breast milk – quite the contrary. In each of the cases of dioxins in fish and milk and of Alar in apples, there was an industry selling those products that was materially threatened by public concern about impurities, whether as a result of intentional use of a product like Alar or unintentional contamination. (Despite the incentives for those industries to defend the reputations of their products, it is noteworthy that, in contrast to the breast-milk case, these issues did achieve agenda status, which in turn resulted in policy change.) In the breast-milk case, the "opponents" were not defending their economic self-interest.[90] The emergence of a pro-breast-feeding lobby in this case appears to have depended more on culture than on self-interested agenda denial. Second, although agenda denial can help to explain why the story of breast-milk contamination never "took off," what is more striking is just how seldom environmentalists even tried to make an issue of dioxins in breast milk, an issue considered in the next section.

Self-Restraint by the Environmental Community

The media have seldom focused on the question of dioxins in breast milk, largely because environmentalists themselves have made relatively few efforts to date to draw attention to the issue, whether as a strategy to press for action on dioxins or on toxic substances more generally. The one instance, discussed above, in which Greenpeace Canada prompted, albeit inadvertently, a story about dioxins in breast milk that was picked up nationwide in 1990 would appear to be the exception that proves the rule. Although an internal Greenpeace memorandum describes the media focus on breast-milk contamination as a "negative feature" of the dioxins-in-food initiative that Greenpeace was "not prepared for ... and did not adequately deal with," the campaigner responsible for the initiative nonetheless was encouraged by the response and developed a proposal for an ongoing campaign focused on the risks of dioxin and other toxic substances to children as "the most defenceless and vulnerable members of our society."[91] He later explained, "I know people get more concerned about damage to their children. They're willing to put up with a certain amount if it's their own bodies, but they get more concerned if it's a threat to their kids. So I thought this was a great environmental issue, because of that angle." However, for reasons discussed below, his colleagues within Greenpeace chose not to pursue the campaign, displaying uncharacteristic restraint for an organization that has made its name with publicity-seeking protests.[92]

It is noteworthy that environmental groups' self-restraint in this case is quite inconsistent with Douglas and Wildavsky's depiction of sectarian environmental organizations using any hint of conspiracy or catastrophe to further their agendas.[93] The environmental community has not always been so restrained, even with respect to health risks to children. Indeed, in its current "toxic toys" campaign, Greenpeace is using threats to infants and children as a focal point for a larger campaign against PVC plastics. Similarly, as noted above, Greenpeace emphasized risks to children in pressing Health Canada to address elevated levels of dioxins in cow's milk in cardboard cartons. Greenpeace USA also petitioned the US Department of Agriculture to prepare an environmental-impact statement for its school lunch program that would reflect the risks to children from dioxin-contaminated cow's milk.[94] Greenpeace's emphasis on cow's milk is particularly note-worthy since, at the time of these activities, Greenpeace activists already had a copy of a doctoral thesis showing much higher levels of dioxin in breast milk than in cow's milk and were thus well aware of the contrast.[95]

Alar offers another compelling counterexample. In 1989 US environmen-tal groups launched a very public campaign against Alar. The campaign was orchestrated by a public-relations firm and involved both the release of a scientific study commissioned by environmentalists estimating high can-cer risks to children and extensive reliance on a media-friendly group, Moth-ers and Others for Pesticides Limits, fronted by Meryl Streep, that was created for the purpose of the Alar campaign. The strategy was effective in large part because it combined the credibility of science with "two potent symbols: the apple – long mythologized as the quintessence of pure, healthy food – and the threat to infants and young children – the most innocent and vul-nerable members of the population."[96] The EPA subsequently banned Alar but not before the public reacted with alarm to the environmentalists' cam-paign. Sales of apples and apple products plummeted, and dozens of school boards stopped distributing apple products in cafeterias.

In contrast to these examples, interviews with Canadian and US environ-mentalists confirm that they made conscious decisions not to sensational-ize the breast-milk issue, although for different and, in some cases, multiple reasons. The rationales they offered are grouped here into three categories: anticipation of defeat and/or backlash, concern about unintended conse-quences, and personal discomfort with the whole issue.

With respect to the first of these rationales, it is significant that evidence concerning dioxins in breast milk emerged in the late 1980s. In the last three decades, breast-feeding has experienced something of a renaissance in North America, with rates of breast-feeding doubling from 25 percent in 1970 to roughly 50 percent in 1987 in the US.[97] Popular culture has shifted from hostility to breast-feeding, such that a woman would not even con-sider breast-feeding in a shopping mall, to much wider acceptance, such that numerous US states have passed laws affirming women's right to breast-feed in public places.[98] At the same time, there has been an international campaign against formula manufacturers, focused especially on their ef-forts to promote bottle feeding in developing countries. As a result of these factors, some environmentalists expressed concern about the potential back-lash if they questioned the healthfulness of breast milk. An environmental-ist active in dioxin campaigns in the late 1980s and early 1990s explained in frustration, "Everyone was 'shh, shh' because breast milk is better for you ... You have to remember, there was the whole WHO [World Health Organi-zation] campaign [to promote breast-feeding] and the Nestlé's boycott at the time." The presence of a well-organized and favourably constructed community of breast-feeding advocates was a factor for another environmentalist, who explained, "It's extremely dangerous territory for us to wade into as political activists. There's been a huge investment from the La Leche League, nurses, and midwives, telling us the very best thing to do is to breast-feed your baby." Yet another observed that any time she did mention breast milk, "the La Leche League immediately started coming on to me and saying 'you can't say that!'" In other words, the anticipated backlash from the "opponents" was sufficiently strong that the "initiators" conceded the battle before it had even begun.

However, in other cases, environmentalists expressed confidence that they could have "gotten mileage" from the breast-milk issue but that they chose not to for two different kinds of reasons. First, some environmentalists exercised self-restraint out of concern that news of contaminants in breast milk might cause undue alarm and prompt some women to discontinue breast-feeding. The unanticipated strength of the public's reaction to the Alar campaign – effectively withdrawing a nutritious staple from many children's diets – may have been a factor. One US environmentalist reflected that "Alar was not our finest hour" and explained that "we consciously chose *not* to try to make [dioxins in breast milk] an issue ... I've tried very deliberately to frame this not as 'good grief, there's dioxin in breast milk' ... Breast milk is not the enemy, dioxin is." She acknowledged that it was a difficult decision to forgo an opportunity to mobilize public concern using such a powerful symbol as breast milk but nonetheless felt comfortable that her organization had made the right decision. Other environmentalists explained that "there was incredible fear within Greenpeace. People always said you can't *not* breast-feed," and that "when we look at the data, it's really frightening. We are all very concerned that what we do doesn't turn into a massive marketing campaign for formula."

The desire not to provoke alarm was apparently a factor in Greenpeace Canada's decision not to follow up the 1991 story about dioxins in breast milk with a campaign focused on the risks of dioxin to women and children. The male staff member who had developed the campaign proposal explained, "I really hit a raw nerve. There was a big reaction [among Greenpeace staff, especially the women, who said] 'we don't want people to panic.' I hit the roof. That's paternalistic and condescending. If people's kids are at risk, they *should* get worried. I didn't expect the women in Greenpeace to be that blasé."

As this comment suggests, it is possible that women and men in the environmental movement reacted quite differently to this issue. It is noteworthy that the leading environmentalists on toxics issues in both Canada and the US tend to be women, many of them mothers.[99] Their comments indicate that their decisions not to focus on breast milk represented more than just strategic anticipation of backlash or self-restraint lest there be unintended consequences, but rather highly personal and emotional reactions to an issue that fundamentally challenges our conceptions of women's bodies and their relationships to their children. Female environmentalists described how they "agonized" with women colleagues over the issue of breast-milk contamination. Interview subjects often invoked their own experiences as mothers. As one noted, "Pregnant women have enough other things to worry about. We've all been there." Women environmentalists stressed how "unthinkable" it is that they and other women are passing on toxic substances from their own bodies to their babies. A US environmentalist acknowledged that the apparent risks from dioxins in breast milk are "much higher" than those associated with children's exposure to pesticides in foods, an issue on which her organization has actively campaigned, but explained that "people just block it out ... As a mother, I breast-fed two infants. I remember thinking 'there's nasty stuff in there.' But in the end, I just didn't want to know." Female environmentalists' self-restraint thus reflected very personal consideration of the impact such information can have on women like themselves. A US activist explained, "I say to myself, what would I tell a pregnant woman? What advice would I give? If I don't know the answer, I shouldn't raise the issue." As a former Greenpeace activist summed up, "It was just too close to home."

These reactions suggest that women environmentalists in particular had internalized many of the same cultural values reflected in a backlash against allegations of dioxins in breast milk. Indeed, for them, the challenges posed to their self-image and their relationships to their children by the issue of breast-milk contamination were both serious and profoundly personal. In considering dioxins in breast milk, women are forced to think of their own bodies not only as contaminated, but also as toxic to those they most love and seek to protect.[100] In the end, the idea of defiling a sacred relationship between mother and child and the realization that women's own bodies were contaminated may in some cases have been too powerful for environmentalists themselves.

Looking to the Future
Clearly, the presence of dioxins in breast milk has not been a prominent issue on either the public's or environmentalists' agendas. In the forgoing discussion, I have identified several forces that have suppressed emergence of the issue. One need not imply, however, that such forces are immutable. In this regard, it is noteworthy that greater attention to this issue by environmentalists began to emerge in the context of international negotiations of a treaty on Persistent Organic Pollutants (POPs). The women's caucus of the International POPs Elimination Network, in particular, called for greater emphasis on breast milk by environmentalists. A member of that

caucus explained that "It became clear to us that the breast-milk issue and reproductive issues will help win the elimination debate. It's a straightforward and very moral argument, and God is on our side, whoever she may be." Such a strategy is reflected in recent reports issued by both Greenpeace International and the World Wildlife Fund of the UK (WWF-UK).[101] It is striking that these reports emerged only after a substantial decline in the levels of dioxin over the last decade, although they remain far above international guidelines.

Environmentalists are proceeding with extreme caution. The question of whether to further pursue the breast-milk angle is being contested among World Wildlife Fund affiliates internationally. As explained by an environmentalist affiliated with another organization that is considering whether to pursue a breast-milk campaign, "We have to be sure – really sure – that when we talk about the breast-milk issue, we scope it out in a way that allows us to move ahead politically, rather than blow it. If we were to say levels of dioxin in breast milk are so alarming we have to question breast-feeding in some parts of the world, we would get annihilated."

How far environmentalists will proceed with this strategy of reframing the issue, and whether it will succeed in the face of anticipated opposition, remains to be seen. It is noteworthy that both the recent Greenpeace and World Wildlife Fund reports received minimal media coverage in North America, failing even to elicit backlash stories on subsequent days. However, if breast-milk contamination does eventually reach the popular agenda, the relative lack of attention to the issue by environmentalists, the public, and politicians for over a decade remains an important finding that can inform our understanding of agenda setting and cultural selection of risks.

Conclusion

The absence of a potentially explosive issue such as dioxin contamination of breast milk from the political agenda suggests a need to counterbalance recent constructivist studies of political agenda setting with greater attention to the difficulty in reframing some issues. While studies of issue construction have yielded important insights, one should not assume, on the basis of certain issues chosen for study specifically because they reached (or returned to) the political agenda after being reframed, that successfully reframing an issue is a simple matter.

The emphasis of this chapter on the absence of an issue from the political agenda is reminiscent of an older literature on "nondecision-making." However, that literature was concerned with questions of competing class or economic interests and political power. Indeed, Bachrach and Baratz argue that nondecision-making can occur only if there is a conflict of interests or values.[102] Similarly, in more recent work, Cobb and Ross focus on the way self-interested actors use rhetorical appeals to popular culture and symbols to prevail over their opponents.[103] Yet it is striking that the breast-milk case is not about self-interested politics. None of the participants were in favour of breast-milk contamination or opposed to breast-feeding. Rather, it reveals how shared conceptions of ourselves and of our relationships with each other can shape – and suppress – political debates.

Thus, although there were instances in which political opponents reinforced an alternative issue construction ("breast-feeding is good") to deny agenda access, and instances in which environmental groups chose not to press the issue in anticipation of such a strategy, in other cases environmentalists chose not to pursue the potentially sensational issue of dioxins in breast milk simply because they shared the same concerns about provoking undue alarm and the same cultural values regarding breast-feeding as their would-be opponents. As Bosso has observed, "Conflict over problem definition is not guaranteed. There are a great many times when prevailing values or the rules of the game simply screen out most (and sometimes all) alternative definitions of a problem."[104]

It is also noteworthy that environmentalists' self-restraint, reflecting a mix of social responsibility and personal discomfort, is inconsistent both with Douglas and Wildavsky's cultural theory of risk selection and with a simple translation to the societal level of psychological studies of individuals' risk perceptions.[105] Environmentalists may well have reacted with alarm to the hidden, irreversible, and dreaded characteristics of dioxin contamination of breast milk, but for the most part they elected to focus on other issues lest they provoke public alarm. This suggests that the environmental movement is not as marginal as Douglas and Wildavsky suggested but rather that it shares many cultural norms that shape, and limit, the range of issues environmental groups choose to pursue.[106] Moreover, the tendency revealed by some environmentalists to deny or disregard such a disturbing risk might not be discernable from surveys eliciting individuals' initial reactions to a list of risks. The psychological literature on denial and avoidance of information about risks such as HIV/AIDS and tobacco, as well as the anthropological literature on taboos and sacred totems, may yield insights for further research on nonagenda setting.

The broader cultural context is clearly important in understanding which problem redefinitions are likely to succeed or even, as in the breast-milk case, be attempted. The discovery of dioxins in breast milk happened to coincide with a rediscovery of breast-feeding in North America. Yet it was not intuitively obvious whether the increased popularity of breast-feeding would propel the issue of contaminants in breast milk onto the political agenda or, as turned out to be the case, repress it. That the latter construction prevailed suggests that some cultural values may be so sacred that any hint of defilement, even by those who raise the threat in order to oppose it, may just be too unthinkable.

Acknowledgments

Research for this paper was funded by the Social Sciences and Humanities Research Council of Canada. The author gratefully acknowledges the research assistance of Will Amos and helpful comments from Lynda Erickson and participants of the European Consortium for Political Research workshop, "The Politics of Food."

Notes

1 Government of Canada, *Canadian Environmental Protection Act, Priority Substances List Assessment Report No. 1: Polychlorinated Dibenzodioxins and Polychlorinated Dibenzofurans* (Ottawa: Minister of Supply and Services, 1990), 42.
2 United States Environmental Protection Agency (EPA), *Health Assessment Document for 2,3,7,8-Tetrachlorodibenzo-p-dioxin (TCDD) and Related Compounds*, external review draft, 1994.
3 Liora Salter, *Mandated Science: Science and Scientists in the Making of Standards* (Boston: Kluwer Academic Publishers, 1988), 98.
4 With respect to documentary evidence, I reviewed all newspaper stories in which dioxins and breast milk are mentioned in the *New York Times* and the *Canadian Newspaper Index* between January 1985 and May 1999, Canadian and US government reports on dioxins, scientific literature on breast-milk contamination, and publications, web pages, and newsletters of interest groups active on toxins and/or breast-feeding issues in either country. In addition, I conducted open-ended confidential interviews with the following: eleven representatives of national environmental groups active on toxins issues and/or environmental health risks to children (six Canadian, five US); one physician specializing in breast-feeding; two reporters; and three representatives of national organizations for breast-feeding advocacy (one Canadian, two US). Unless otherwise noted, all quotations in the text are drawn from these confidential interviews.
5 Paul Slovic, Baruch Fischoff, and Sarah Lichtenstein, "Rating the Risks," *Environment* 21 (1979): 14-20, 36-39.
6 James Flynn, Paul Slovic, and C.K. Mertz, "Gender, Race, and Perception of Environmental Health Risks," *Risk Analysis* 14 (1994): 1101-8.
7 Per E. Gustafson, "Gender Differences in Risk Perception: Theoretical and Methodological Perspectives," *Risk Analysis* 18 (1998): 805-11.
8 Debra Davidson and William R. Freudenburg, "Gender and Environmental Risk Concerns: A Review and Analysis of Available Literature," *Environment and Behaviour* 28 (1996): 302-29.
9 Mary Douglas and Aaron Wildavsky, *Risk and Culture: An Essay on the Selection of Technical and Environmental Dangers* (Berkeley: University of California Press, 1982).
10 Ibid., 124.
11 Roger W. Cobb and Charles D. Elder, *Participation in American Politics: The Dynamics of Agenda Building* (Boston: Allyn and Bacon, 1972).
12 Thomas Birkland, "Focusing Events, Mobilization, and Agenda Setting," *Journal of Public Policy* 18 (1998): 53-74.
13 John Kingdon, *Agendas, Alternatives, and Public Policies* (Boston: Little-Brown, 1984).
14 Kathryn Harrison and George Hoberg, "Setting the Environmental Agenda in Canada and the United States: The Cases of Dioxin and Radon," *Canadian Journal of Political Science* 24 (1991), 1-27. See also, Carol Van Strum and Paul Merrell, *No Margin of Safety: A Preliminary Report on Dioxin Pollution and the Need for Emergency Action in the Pulp and Paper Industry* (United States: Greenpeace, 1987).
15 Frank R. Baumgartner and Bryan D. Jones, *Agendas and Instability in American Politics* (Chicago: University of Chicago Press, 1993).
16 Deborah A. Stone, "Causal Stories and the Formation of Policy Agendas," *Political Science Quarterly* 104 (1988): 281-300; and *Policy Paradox: The Art of Political Decision Making* (New York: Norton, 1997).
17 Anne Schneider and Helen Ingram, "The Social Construction of Target Populations: Implications for Politics and Policy," *American Political Science Review* 87 (1993): 334-47.
18 Baumgartner and Jones, *Agendas and Instability*.

19   David A. Rochefort and Roger W. Cobb, eds., *The Politics of Problem Definition: Shaping the Policy Agenda* (Lawrence, KS: University Press of Kansas, 1994).

20   Roger W. Cobb and Marc Howard Ross, *Cultural Strategies of Agenda Denial: Avoidance, Attack, and Redefinition* (Lawrence, KS: University Press of Kansas, 1997), 219.

21   There are two exceptions to this. First, the body burden can decrease during childhood as the relatively high dose received during breast-feeding is diluted by growth; see P. Ayotte, G. Carrier, and E. Dewailly, "Health Risk Assessment for Inuit Newborns Exposed to Dioxin-Like Compounds through Breast Feeding," *Chemosphere* 32 (1996): 531-42. Second, an adult woman's body burden declines during breast-feeding as she transfers lifetime-accumulated contaminants to her infant through her breast milk.

22   International Agency for Research on Cancer (IARC), "Polychlorinated Dibenzo-para-Dioxins and Polychlorinated Dibenzofurans," *IARC Monographs on the Evaluation of Carcinogenic Risks to Humans*, vol. 69 (Lyon: IARC, 1997).

23   EPA, *Health Assessment*, 9-82.

24   See my previous analysis in Kathryn Harrison, "Between Science and Politics: Assessing the Risks of Dioxins in Canada and the United States," *Policy Sciences* 24 (1991): 367-88.

25   EPA, *Health Assessment*.

26   The Canadian approach applies a "margin of safety" of 1,000 to the lowest dose at which no excess tumours have been observed in test animals. This presumes that there is a threshold dose below which exposure presents no risk to human health. In contrast, the EPA assumes that there is a linear relationship between dose and cancer risk and thus relies on mathematical models to extrapolate from high-dose animal tests the lower doses relevant to regulatory goals of health protection and current human exposure. Although this approach assumes that there is always some residual risk at any nonzero dose, the EPA typically defines the "virtually safe dose" as corresponding to a risk of one in a million. It is noteworthy that the more open and contested risk-assessment process in the US prompted the EPA to prepare a draft dioxin reassessment several thousand pages in length, compared to the fifty-five-page dioxin assessment issued by the Canadian government.

27   Health Canada estimates average exposure to be 2 to 4 pg TEQ/kg/day (see Government of Canada, *Canadian Environmental*), while the EPA estimates background exposure to be 1 to 3 pg TEQ/kg/day and 3 to 6 if dioxinlike PCBs are included; see United States Environmental Protection Agency (EPA), *Estimating Exposure to Dioxin-Like Compounds*, vol. 1, *Executive Summary*, external review draft, 9-15.

28   Great Lakes Science Advisory Board, *1991 Report to the International Joint Commission* (Windsor: International Joint Commission, 1991), 38.

29   M.J. Sullivan, S.R. Custance, and C.J. Miller, "Infant Exposure to Dioxin in Mother's Milk Resulting from Maternal Ingestion of Contaminated Fish," *Chemosphere* 23 (1991): 1387-96; Arnold Shecter, John Jake Ryan, and Olaf Papke, "Decrease in Levels and Body Burden of Dioxins, Dibenzofurans, PCBs, DDE, and HCB in Blood and Milk in a Mother Nursing Twins over a Thirty-Eight Month Period," *Chemosphere* 37 (1998): 1807-16.

30   The daily dose per unit of body weight decreases over time as an infant grows and begins to consume other foods and because dioxin in breast milk declines over time as dioxin reserves are flushed from the mother's body. Since dairy cows are continuously lactating, this also explains why cow's milk tends to be much less contaminated than human milk.

31   J.L. Jacobson et al., "Prenatal Exposure to Polychlorinated Biphenyls and Dioxins and Its Effect on Neonatal Neurological Development," *Early Human Development* 41 (1984): 111-27; J.L. Jacobson and S.W. Jacobson, "Intellectual Impairment in Children Exposed to Polychlorinated Biphenyls in Utero," *New England Journal of Medicine* 335 (1996): 783-89.

32   W.J. Rogan and B.C. Gladen, "PCBs, DDE, and Child Development at 18 and 24 Months," *Annals of Epidemiology* 1 (1991): 407-13.

33   W.J. Rogan and B.C. Gladen, "Breast-Feeding and Cognitive Development," *Early Human Development* 31 (1993): 181-93.

34   Svati Patandin et al., "Effects of Environmental Exposure to Polychlorinated Biphenyls and Dioxins on Cognitive Abilities in Dutch Children at 42 Months of Age," *Journal of Pediatrics* 134 (1999): 33-41; Svati Patandin et al., "Effects of Environmental Exposure to Polychlorinated Biphenyls and Dioxins on Birth Size and Growth in Dutch Children," *Pediatric*

Research 44 (1998): 538-45. The authors did not have the capacity to measure prenatal exposures to dioxins but observed that because levels of PCBs and dioxins tended to be correlated in the subjects' breast milk, it is difficult to ascertain the extent to which the observed effects were caused by PCBs or dioxins, or both. See also Marcel Huisman et al., "Neurological Condition in 18-Month-Old Children Perinatally Exposed to Polychlorinated Biphenyls and Dioxins," *Early Human Development*, Vol. 43, (1995): 165-76; Corine Koopman-Esseboom et al., "Effects of Polychlorinated Biphenyl/Dioxin Exposure and Feeding Type on Infants' Mental and Psychomotor Development," *Pediatrics* 97 (1996): 700-6.

35 Svati Patandin et al., "Dietary Exposure to Polychlorinated Biphenyls and Dioxins from Infancy until Adulthood: A Comparison between Breast-Feeding, Toddler, and Long-Term Exposure," *Environmental Health Perspectives* 107 (1999): 45-51.

36 J. Raloff, "Dioxin Can Harm Tooth Development," *Science News Online*, 1999, <http://www.sciencenews.org> ; S. Alaluusua et al., "Developing Teeth as Biomarker of Dioxin Exposure," *Lancet* 353 (1999): 206.

37 Sara M. Hoover, "Exposure to Persistent Organochlorines in Canadian Breast Milk: A Probabilistic Assessment," *Risk Analysis* 4 (1999): 527-45.

38 Government of Canada, *Canadian Environmental*, 44. To the extent that the Canadian risk assessment is premised on the existence of a threshold, compared to the US reliance on a model that is insensitive to the distribution of exposure over time, one would expect *greater* concern in Canada about a high dose concentrated over a short period.

39 EPA, *Health Assessment*, 9-19. However, at the same time, the agency curiously omits breast milk in summarizing lifetime sources of exposure even though by the agency's own estimates it contributes 4 to 12 percent of exposure. This is particularly noteworthy since the EPA's summary of exposure sources includes soil ingestion by preschoolers as a route of exposure but not breast-feeding even though the former constitutes only one-tenth of the lifetime contribution of dioxin from breast milk.

40 Cobb and Elder, *Participation*, 85.

41 Although I would have preferred to compare indexes with comparable groupings of newspapers, or comparable individual newspapers, such as the *Toronto Globe and Mail* and the *New York Times*, the *New York Times* (via Lexus-Nexus) and the *Canadian Newspaper Index* were the only indexes to which I had access.

42 "Quebec first to ban furans and dioxins in milk cartons: Pagé," *Montreal Gazette*, 17 March 1989, A2. The US Food and Drug Administration (FDA) promised action in May 1990 (*New York Times*, 1 May 1990, A17).

43 "Dioxin traces found in breast-milk samples from Quebec no cause for alarm: scientists," *Montreal Gazette*, 3 April 1988, A5; and "'No problem' for infants in short term: Dioxin traces found in human milk in Quebec," *Globe and Mail*, 4 April 1988, A3.

44 Dennis Bueckert, "Dioxins poisoning mothers' milk: Study finds deadly chemicals exceed limits in nearly all foods," *Winnipeg Free Press*, 29 October 1990, A1; Dennis Bueckert, "Unacceptable levels of toxic chemicals found in breast milk," *Montreal Gazette*, 29 October 1990, A7; "Mothers' milk high in dioxins, study says," *Toronto Star*, 29 October 1990, A1; and Mary Lynn Young and CP, "Breast milk has high dioxin levels," *Vancouver Sun*, 29 October 1990, A1.

45 Keith Schneider, "Fetal harm is cited as primary hazard in dioxin exposure," *New York Times*, 11 May 1994, A1.

46 See, for instance, Philip Shabecoff, "Government says dioxin from paper mills poses no major danger," *New York Times*, 1 May 1990, A17.

47 In addition to the stories cited above, see Dennis Bueckert, "Nurse babies despite dioxin, Beatty advises," *Winnipeg Free Press*, 30 October 1990, 15; and "Breast milk is safe, Beatty tells mothers," *Montreal Gazette*, 30 October 1990, B1.

48 Young, "Breast milk has high dioxin levels."

49 Pascal Milly and William Leiss, "Mother's Milk: Communicating the Risk of PCBs in Canada and the Far North," in *Mad Cows and Mother's Milk*, edited by Douglas Powell and William Leiss (Montreal and Kingston: McGill-Queen's University Press, 1997), 182-209.

50 "Dioxin scare unsettles many Japanese," *Vancouver Sun*, 3 June 1998, A14.

51 Average exposure is summarized in EPA, *Estimating Exposure*, Table II-6. The EPA indicates that high-end exposure can be twenty times higher (*Estimating Exposure*, 9-20).

52 This is based on the proportion of the EPA's estimated lifetime exposure from each source and assumes a linear dose-response function and that age of exposure is irrelevant (i.e., that infants are no more sensitive to exposure than adults). The percentage of exposure from contaminated fish, based on Table II-6 (EPA, *Estimating Exposure*), is calculated without accounting for breast-milk exposure and would thus be somewhat less corrected. This comparison neglects both the fact that some individuals consume more fish than the average person and that some infants are breast-fed longer or receive milk with a higher fat content.

53 See, for example, "Dioxins discovered in milk cartons," *Vancouver Sun,* 26 October 1988, A1-2; and Philip J. Hilts, "Cartons found leaching dioxin to milk," *New York Times,* 2 September 1989, 8.

54 Hilts, "Cartons found leaching dioxin to milk." Data on levels of breast-milk contamination in industrialized countries can be found in World Health Organization (WHO), *Assessment of Health Risks in Infants Associated with Exposure to PCBs, PCDDs and PCDFs in Breast Milk* (Copenhagen: WHO, 1988).

55 The FDA's estimate is reported in Hilts, "Cartons found leaching dioxin to milk." The estimate of lifetime cancer risk from breast milk is based on 4 to 12 percent (i.e., the proportion of total lifetime exposure from breast milk) of the EPA's lifetime cancer risks from dioxin of 1E-3 to 1E-4. It is noteworthy that the FDA has historically adopted a potency estimate for 2378 TCDD that is a factor of nine less than the EPA's; in other respects, the two agencies' risk-assessment methodologies for dioxin are comparable. This would have the effect of rendering the upper bounds of these risk estimates comparable if they were conducted by the same agency.

56 World Health Organization (WHO), European Centre for Environment and Health, "Contamination with Dioxin of Some Belgian Food Products," 1999, <http://www.who.dk/envhlth/dioxin/dioxin.htm>.

57 Kathryn Harrison and George Hoberg, *Risk, Science, and Politics: Regulating Toxic Substances in Canada and the United States* (Montreal and Kingston: McGill-Queen's University Press, 1994), 69.

58 Not all risk estimates cited above were prepared by the same agency. However, an effort has been made in each pair-wise comparison (e.g., dioxin in milk versus dioxin in fish) to cite estimates from the same agency or methodology.

59 Canadian Paediatric Society and Health Canada, *Nutrition for Health Term Infants* (Ottawa: Minister of Public Works, 1988).

60 Rogan et al. compare breast milk (taking into account both benefits and risks associated with contamination) and formula and conclude that "there is no clear advantage to avoiding breast feeding; there may be a disadvantage." W.J. Rogan, Patricia J. Blanton, Christopher J. Portier, and Eric Stallard, "Should the Presence of Carcinogens in Breast Milk Discourage Breast Feeding?" *Regulatory Toxicology and Pharmacology* 13 (1991): 235. Similarly, Hoover ("Exposure") reports comparable risks and benefits of contaminated breast milk.

61 In practice, however, one cannot count on consumers substituting nutritious alternatives, suggesting that the breast-milk case may not be unique. This is especially true when a population is heavily reliant on a particular food, as in the case of children's high consumption of Alar-contaminated apple products and some Aboriginal communities' heavy reliance on dioxin-contaminated fish.

62 Cobb and Elder, *Participation;* Birkland, "Focusing Events."

63 Birkland, "Focusing Events," 56.

64 Kingdon, *Agendas;* Harrison and Hoberg, "Setting the Environmental Agenda in Canada and the United States."

65 The milk testing had been conducted by the federal government and reported at an international dioxin conference in August 1989, which was attended by Greenpeace staff. The report received no attention until Greenpeace held a press conference in October to publicize the government's findings.

66 Harrison, "Between Science and Politics."

67 See also Sheila Jasanoff, *Risk Management and Political Culture* (New York: Russell Sage Foundation, 1986).

68　Under the Food and Drugs Act, Canada has prohibited any level of chlorinated dioxins in any food sold commercially, with the one (quite illogical) exception of allowing up to 20 ppt of only the most toxic dioxin, 2378 TCDD, in fish. With respect to the US, Rogan has noted that "breast milk, if regulated like infant formula, would commonly violate [US] Food and Drug Administration action levels for poisonous or deleterious substances in food and could not be sold." W.J. Rogan, "Pollutants in Breast Milk," *Archives of Pediatric and Adolescent Medicine* 150 (1996): 981.

69　Indeed, as discussed in Harrison, "Between Science and Politics," the economic relevance of the commercial fishery arguably contributed to less, rather than more, stringent regulation of 2378 TCDD in fish.

70　Cobb and Ross, *Cultural Strategies*.

71　Similarly, a series of stories on PCBs in breast milk in the early 1990s was initiated by the International Joint Commission. See IJC, "Contaminant Levels in Mother's Milk among Indicators of Ecosystem Health Recommended by Great Lakes Science Advisory Board," media release, 3 September 1991; Martin Mittelstaedt, "Lakes report cites risk to infants: Mothers' milk causes concern," *Globe and Mail*, 31 August 1991, A1; Martin Mittelstaedt, "No need to stop nursing, MDs say: PCBs detected in human milk," *Globe and Mail*, 4 September 1991; Stephen Strauss, "How some politically compromised scientists soured scientific truth," *Globe and Mail*, 21 September 1991, D10.

72　Philip Shabecoff, "Dioxin in breast milk is evaluated in private study," *New York Times*, 18 December 1987, A17.

73　See also Lois Marie Gibbs, *Dying from Dioxin: A Citizen's Guide to Reclaiming Our Health and Rebuilding Democracy* (Boston: South End Press, 1995).

74　Greenpeace USA, "PVC/Vinyl the 'Worst Plastic' for Environment," media release, 22 April 1997; La Leche League, "Earth Day Statement," 21 April 1997, and "Earth Days News is that Breastfeeding Remains Best Choice in a Polluted World," April 1997.

75　Cobb and Ross, *Cultural Strategies*.

76　For instance, when dioxins were reported to have been detected in the breast milk of Canadian women for the first time, a Health and Welfare Canada official stated, "Certainly, for an infant in the short term, there is no problem in terms of toxicity."

77　*Montreal Gazette*, 3 April 1988, A5; *Globe and Mail*, 4 April 1988, A3.

78　Greenpeace campaigners met with staff from Jim Fulton's office before releasing their story to Canadian Press. Confidential interview.

79　House of Commons, Debates, 30 October 1990, 14882.

80　House of Commons, Debates, 29 October 1990, 14807. It is by no means clear what statutory authority the minister would have relied on to ban breast milk even if he had been serious.

81　One physician interviewed who specializes in breast-feeding stressed that "There is *zero* research to show even dioxin-laced breast milk is worse than formula ... Before we make any changes, we have to be sure the alternative is better."

82　See, for instance, Gabrielle Palmer, *The Politics of Breastfeeding* (London, UK: Pandora Press, 1988), 51; La Leche League, "Earth Day Statement," 21 April 1997; Nancy Mohrbacher, "Breastfeeding and Contaminants," *New Beginnings* 2 (1986): 128-30, <http://www.lalechleague.org/llleaderweb/LV/LVNBSeptOct86.text>.

83　See also Naomi Baumslag and Dia L. Michels, *Milk, Money, and Madness: The Culture and Politics of Breastfeeding* (Westport, CT: Bergin and Garvey, 1995), 96.

84　See, for example, Ken Pole, "Report of dioxins/furans in breast milk a media fiasco," *Medical Post*, 13 November 1990; and "Crying wolf once too often: Experts debunk Greenpeace's warning about contaminated mother's milk," *BC Report*, 19 November 1990, 24. Although focused on PCBs rather than dioxins, a similar story about breast-milk contamination prompted by an International Joint Commission report and press release elicited a scathing response from columnist Stephen Strauss, who accused the IJC scientific advisory board of "cynically manipulat[ing] [nursing mothers'] fears and feelings." Martin Mittelstaedt, "Lakes report cites risk to infants"; Strauss, "How some politically compromised scientists soured scientific truth."

85 Theo Colborn, Dianne Dumanoski, and John Peterson Myers, *Our Stolen Future* (New York: Dutton, 1996).

86 Colborn responded to a question about the EPA's estimate that a breast-fed infant receives 4 to 12 percent of its lifetime exposure to dioxins in its first year of life by saying, "We don't have enough evidence yet. But I'll tell you quite frankly that I would not want to have to make the decision myself today. It appears that breast-feeding strengthens a baby's immune system, but we also wonder how these chemicals might be interfering with immune competency in these children. So far, the benefits seem to outweigh the risks, but we just don't know." "Theo Colborn," *Mother Jones*, March/April 1998.

87 "Backtalk," *Mother Jones*, May/June 1998. See also Colborn, Dumanoski, and Myers, *Our Stolen Future*, 215.

88 Cobb and Ross, *Cultural Strategies*.

89 Although the pulp and paper industry, as the most significant and visible industrial source of dioxins, was indirectly threatened to the extent that concern about dioxins in breast milk might prompt more aggressive regulation of the industry, its voice was noticeably absent from any articles on dioxins in breast milk. Reporters covering the stories do not appear to have made the connection, and the pulp and paper industry presumably chose not to weigh in on a potentially explosive debate by dismissing the risks of dioxins, which they had already voluntarily committed to reducing to nondetectable levels.

90 One might argue, however, that politicians were defending their political self-interest by deflecting attention from an issue that might have reflected badly on their performance in protecting the environment.

91 "A Proposal," Internal Greenpeace Memorandum, December 1990.

92 Three years later, when Greenpeace Canada tried to elicit interest in dioxin by holding a press conference to coincide with the release of the US's dioxin reassessment, the press release made only a passing and indirect reference to breast milk even though infants' exposure was arguably one of the most explosive findings in the EPA report.

93 Douglas and Wildavsky, *Risk and Culture*.

94 Kimberly M. Thompson and John D. Graham, "Producing Paper without Dioxin Pollution," in *The Greening of Industry: A Risk Management Approach*, edited by John D. Graham and Jennifer Kassalow Hartwell (Cambridge, MA: Harvard University Press, 1997), 203-68. The petition, based on Health Canada's test results, prompted the US Food and Drug Administration, at the Department of Agriculture's urging, to conduct its own testing of milk in cartons and subsequently to demand risk-reduction measures from the dairy industry.

95 Personal communication. See Gunilla Lindstrom, "Polychlorinated Dibenzo-p-Dioxins and Dibenzofurans: Analysis of and Occurrence in Milk" (PhD diss., Department of Organic Chemistry, Umea University, Umea, Sweden, 1988).

96 Harrison and Hoberg, *Risk, Science, and Politics*, 66.

97 However, Yalom notes quite disparate rates of breast-feeding among different racial groups in the US. Marilyn Yalom, *A History of the Breast* (New York: Ballantyne, 1997), 141.

98 Ibid., 142.

99 Although obviously a very small sample, the two male environmentalists interviewed were much more inclined to "go for it" and revealed frustration with the hesitation of their female colleagues. One US environmentalist seemed unaware of how gender-loaded his recounting was (in a sarcastic falsetto) of a meeting at which the female administrator of the EPA asked Theo Colborn, "But Theo, what should I tell nursing mothers?" He reported that, while Colborn hesitated, he interrupted with "Just tell them to write a letter to Congress!"

100 An analogy might be made to genetic testing for hereditary diseases.

101 Michelle Allsopp, Ruth Stringer, and Paul Johnston, *Unseen Poisons: Levels of Organochlorine Chemicals in Human Tissues* (Greenpeace International, 1998); Gwynne Lyons, *Chemical Trespass: A Toxic Legacy* (Godalming, Surrey, UK: WWF-UK, 1999). Interestingly, the Greenpeace Canada press release did not place much emphasis on breast milk in comparison to the report itself. However, press coverage of the Greenpeace report did focus on the breast-milk angle. Greenpeace Canada, "Greenpeace Report Shows Toxic Pollution Knows

No Boundaries," media release, 25 June 1998; "Breast Milk in Some Canadians among World's Most Toxic: Greenpeace," *Calgary Herald,* 26 June 1998, A21. In contrast, the WWF-UK's press release is the one example I have found of a rhetorical strategy that seeks to provoke outrage about contamination of breast milk (on the grounds that women have a right to breast-feed their infants with confidence) while simultaneously stressing the net benefits of breast-feeding. WWF-UK, "Government urged to tackle 'hand-me-down' poisons," 12 July 1999.

102   Peter Bachrach and Morton S. Baratz, *Power and Poverty: Theory and Practice* (Toronto: Oxford University Press, 1970), 49.
103   Cobb and Ross, *Cultural Strategies.*
104   Christopher Bosso, "The Contextual Bases of Problem Definition," in Rochefort and Cobb, eds., *The Politics of Problem Definition,* 199.
105   Douglas and Wildavsky, *Risk and Culture.*
106   Ibid.

12
Acting Locally: Mapping and Countermapping toward a Grassroots Feminist Cartography

Katherine Dunster

Being an activist means being aware of what's happening around you as well as being in touch with your feelings about it – your rage, your sadness, your excitement, your curiosity, your feeling of helplessness, and your refusal to surrender. Being an activist means owning your desire.

— Paula Allen and Eve Ensler[1]

The important message ... is that local problems and local solutions are of tremendous importance. No positive initiative and fruitful discovery should be lost. Whatever seems to be a local problem needs to become connected to the larger body politic, whether the city, the state or province, nation, region or world.

— Rosalie Bertell[2]

10...9...8...seven...six...5...4...three...2...one...and kerplooey. you're done. you're done for. you're done for good. so tell me. did you? did you do did you do all you could?

— ani difranco[3]

Still, I've learned enough from my years of activism not to argue that active citizenship is the only important issue facing progressive people. I have had too many arguments with those who told me that if the world blows up, feminism will mean nothing, or that if we poison the planet, wages and working conditions will make no difference.

— Judy Rebick[4]

I am an activist, not an academic. Sometimes I am a landscape architect, sometimes a geographer, and sometimes a biologist. Sometimes I juggle all three professions at once, but mostly I forget the labels and tap into whatever tools and knowledge I need to get the work done. I live and work from a small rural island, and much of my work is focused on protecting, managing, and studying island ecosystems and helping people learn what they can do to protect the ecosystems they inhabit. I live on a small farm, get my hands dirty every day, raise chickens, save seeds, and barter eggs for other food: I am one of the small-scale Gulf Islands organic farmers that Martha McMahon writes about in Chapter 7. I sometimes teach, usually working with multigenerational groups that want to expand their knowledge about the environment. So when we speak about "women and the Canadian environment," my contribution to the topic is personal, on the one hand, but driven by my education, career path, and life-long experience, on the other.

My activism is local because I have chosen to stay home and defend the local, and I have been doing this for over thirty years.[5] However, paying attention to the global is also very important in my line of work because many of the species I work with are migratory, and the ecosystems I study and protect are considered rare in the global context.[6] In my professional work, I have learned that few people are able to cope with the global environmental crises that we face as a species and often become overwhelmed when discussing them.[7] As an environmental educator, I have learned that the best way to work for global change is to place global issues in the local context and to work with people for incremental local change. In rural places, where there is a closer connection between people and the land, the problems are often "in your face." For instance, most islanders in the Salish Sea are very aware of the global water crisis because they deal with potable-water shortages and water-quality issues daily.[8]

These distinctions are important because I write from personal and practical experience rather than from purely academic theory or passive observation. This is not to say there is no theory attached to what I do but rather that theory does not necessarily drive the process. When it comes to defending the local, the process is very important to the participants because the conclusion will directly affect their lives and home-place.[9] Islanders in the Salish Sea are becoming quite adept at adapting formal or legal processes to meet specific local needs and circumstances, and one of my objectives in writing this chapter is to try to articulate some of the ways that this is being done. The stories in this chapter are my attempt to document, explain, and share some of the projects I have been involved in over the past few years and to place them in the context of some threads of feminist research.

This chapter also includes a section on how to make a map and use it to seek change. My purpose in providing a practical section is four-fold. First, I want to offer practical guidance for women who have never used map making, but may be inspired to do so, in their activist work. Second, because I have been testing my own maps in political and judicial spheres, I wanted to figure out where exactly my ideas on using maps for change have come from. This eventually led me to pull Saul Alinsky's classic guide for activists, *Rules for Radicals,* off the bookshelf and to my realization that map making for change can be framed in reference to the chapter titled "Tactics."[10] Third, I wanted to provide an example of how women can apply what they have learned by making maps to help bring about changes within the contexts of their own experiences. Finally, I wanted to reinforce the notion that map making is not restricted to the realm of "professional geographers or cartographers" and that a feminist can make a map without being a "feminist geographer."

When first published in 1971, *Rules for Radicals* created quite a stir and continues to do so. I've had a copy on my bookshelf since the early 1970s and was pleased to learn that it has remained in print since first published. The latest edition (1989) by the original publisher is easily obtained from Internet bookstores.[11] Scanning the reader reviews of *Rules for Radicals* published at Amazon.ca, I noted with interest that American readers generally write the book off as a 1970s leftist rant and that readers from countries like Brazil think it is brilliant. Why? Possibly because the activists in other countries have finally reached 1971 (in terms of the North American context) as they struggle for social and environmental justice in places where military tactics are regularly used against citizens.

It would be easy to dismiss *Rules for Radicals* as dated, aggressive, militaristic, simplistic, or clichéd.[12] However, anyone involved in community organizing and activism will find that the thirteen tactics posited by Alinsky still make good sense today. As I finish writing this preface, the antiwar movement is very much alive and is organizing for world peace in greater numbers and in more places than ever before.[13] Introducing my daughter to the spirit of collective activism at peace rallies and marches in the winter and spring of 2002 to 2003 was the best way to put our ongoing discussion of tactics into action. We marched in rallies, sang songs, were inspired by the Raging Grannies,[14] signed petitions, and wrote letters. We also sent instant electronic faxes to the prime minister and used the Internet to sign petitions and to connect with other groups and activists around the world.[15] We downloaded graphics that we could put on our protest signs and had a lot of fun during a time when the news was full of troublesome stories and sickening war images. As you read on, you will see that these are all tactics from the Alinsky era that have now been modernized.[16]

Praxis

There are many ways that activists in a community can help to bring about positive local change. Traditionalists protest, nag, write letters, and sign petitions.[17] Anyone with the wit to rewrite the words to popular songs, and the voice to sing them, can join the Raging Grannies.[18] Street theatre is fun but ephemeral. The truly motivated run for public office or spray walls with graffiti. When it comes to issues of the land or the heart, however, there is nothing better than making a map to make your point.[19]

Maps are a subtly seductive communications medium. Hang a map up anywhere, and people are drawn toward it to find out what it means and to see where they live. Surficially, colours are used to interpret and give meaning to the map data. The colours and graphics on a map help to seduce the eye and pull the mind into the map milieu. Map seduction is an interesting tactical phenomenon that has been used by map makers for centuries.[20] Because I am involved in the creation of community maps for positive change, I am interested in how map seduction can be used for positive societal purposes. A good map can change political opinions and influence decisions. A seductive map can make people love and care for a place even more.

Community Knowledge

Hand in hand with community map making comes the need to recognize, find, and record community knowledge. In the past, local knowledge was often handed down from generation to generation through storytelling.[21] Mothers told their daughters about the different and specific uses for apples from their orchards and used the kitchen as a school to transfer the technology of making apple jelly, cider, apple pies, and apple butter. The apple trees would survive as long as someone knew their names, remembered what their particular use was, and kept the traditional skills alive. Conservation was intertwined with need, desire, and local customs.

On the island where I live, there is an apple tree in one of the oldest surviving orchards. With some help from other heritage-apple enthusiasts, we learned that the apple is called "Porter." The Porter apple is interesting because it tastes terrible when it is picked ripe off the tree. So why ever would the pioneer farmer put it in his orchard? There are over ten thousand named apple varieties grown around the world, and the choice is deliciously diverse. It turns out that around the time that the orchard was planted, the first edition of the Fannie Farmer cookbook was published in 1896.[22] In the cookbook, only two apples are mentioned by name, the Porter and the Gravenstein, because they make excellent jelly.

While the Gravenstein also has a reputation for being a fine pie and dessert apple, the Porter has no such luck. We have the knowledge to restore the tree, and with gentle pruning it is doing just fine. We also have the skills to graft cuttings from the Porter onto new rootstocks; teaching people how to graft new apple trees was one of my first local-action projects. Making new trees from old will ensure that long after the original tree is gone, its genetic material will survive. There are now several new trees that have been given to volunteers, with the understanding that the day may come when someone may need to take cuttings to be sure there is always more than one Porter on the island.

Acting locally could end there, with the satisfaction of knowing we have preserved a fruit-tree variety. But unless we know how to make jelly, is there any point in keeping this variety alive? Of the thousands of apple varieties, approximately twenty were being grown commercially in apple-growing regions around the world at the beginning of the twentieth century. Most of these varieties did not store or ship well and were thus harvested and marketed in sequence, a few weeks apart, to ensure a steady supply of apples to the market. By the 1960s highly advanced cold-storage and shipping techniques, and the growing demand for juicy apples, allowed superior strains of the Red Delicious, Golden Delicious, and Spartan to be marketed year round. In these times of globalization, when an apple grown in Australia can end up in a West Coast kitchen, even the Red Delicious is being replaced by new, more tempting varieties bred for a world of changing tastes.[23]

Old apple varieties are forgotten and disappear from commercial production because they are unpopular or unprofitable to produce. This, in turn, inspires people into action – typically, direct action in the form of grafting old onto new and reviving old orchards. Heritage-apple activists remember what apples used to taste like, remember the names and the stories, and want to preserve fruit diversity for future generations.[24] Apples are believed to have originated in an area between the Caspian and Black Seas.[25] The earliest writings of Egypt, Babylon, and China mention the apple, and the breeding and selection of apples for various epicurean qualities have been practised for a long time. Cato, who lived in the third century B.C., mentions seven apple varieties in his writings, while a few hundred years later, Pliny, in the first century A.D., names thirty-six varieties. From their native origins, every named variety is inextricably linked to some human desire for the unique qualities of each kind of apple.[26] If you lose the desire, you lose the apple. Some may argue that this in itself is not terribly bad because with so many varieties, there's bound to be another one just as good. But it's another matter entirely when the variety about to become extinct is the one you remember from your grandmother's orchard or the one you raided from a neighbour's tree when you were a kid. Any given apple seed will grow into a tree, but that tree, if it produces apples, will be a new variety unto itself rather than the apple variety that the seed came from. With rare exceptions,[27] apples are not self-pollinating and require cross-pollination from one or two different varieties to create fruit. When grown from seed (or a pip),[28] the fruit of the new tree will be the unique genetic product of the parent trees. Without apple activists, the many centuries of apple breeding, and the inherent knowledge and biodiversity created through breeding, would be lost, as would the rich intertwining of nature and culture that has evolved from our historical relationship with the apple.

Thus truly acting locally means finding the elders in the community who know how to make apple jelly (and pie and cider) and will teach others, organizing a fruit-picking session, and hanging out in a kitchen helping and learning how to make apple jelly. It means mapping the locations of each tree and orchard, restoring the orchards, grafting new trees, sharing those new jelly-making skills, and teaching the importance of sharing knowledge with the next generation so that those skills will never again be lost. And lastly, it means becoming active locally to raise awareness that old orchards and the open spaces they occupy must be preserved if we want orchards for future generations to enjoy.

Leave the land, and the knowledge disappears. As our society became transient, so did local knowledge.[29] New people arrive in a community and have no idea of the preceding 100, 200, or 500 years of local history, culture, environment, and traditions that have come to define the local distinctiveness of their new home-place.[30] So most community map making has arisen from the need to help record and preserve those things that are important and should never be forgotten and to help people connect or reconnect to their home-places.

Community Mapping

Much of the historical and traditional knowledge about local places already exists within the individuals who live in a community. Tapping into this knowledge and giving it credibility has become one of the goals of community mapping.[31] Community mapping is thus a rich and inspiring process of reclaiming the language and skills of map making, long ago usurped by "experts," and then using those skills to make maps that can communicate in ways that resonate more quickly than words.[32]

Community mapping is a way for the people who share the same patch of this planet to come together to research, investigate, and record the special, significant, and valuable spaces in their home-places. Through participatory workshops, map-making skills are given back to the people of a community so that they can contribute their personal knowledge of their home-place.[33] Community mapping comes from the hearts, souls, and minds of community members. Sometimes the motivation is an external influence that introduces misunderstood or unwanted change into the community. Each individual and group identifies what is important and contributes to an inventory of community assets, be they environmental, cultural, social, or economic. Maps are created as a visual record of what is found and become a scientifically credible baseline against which all plans for the community can be measured and guided.

Community mapping involves collecting and sifting through diverse information sources, walking the land, listening to it, interpreting its messages, and working with others to come up with a shared picture of home. It brings community groups together: the elders who preserve the memories, the children, the scientists and planners, and the artists. It is a powerful process of seeing, learning, exchanging memories and experiences, and imagining both the past and the future. There are no limits to what can be mapped. A community of diverse individuals will create a collection of equally diverse maps.

Community Mapping on the Islands in the Salish Sea

The process of making maps can take many forms, especially when the goal is to record local knowledge about the environment at a specific point in time. Beautiful, artistically rendered maps such as those produced for the Islands in the Salish Sea Community Mapping Project (ISSCMP) have had such an immediate and immense impact on local island residents that the maps were returned to some of the islands for a second exhibit.[34]

The more than 470 islands in the Salish Sea are widely recognized as a region of national and international ecological and cultural significance. They are protected by a special Act of the Province of British Columbia and carefully administered as a Trust Area for all the people of British Columbia.[35] The waters surrounding some of the islands have been proposed as sites for some of the first national Marine Protected Areas in Canada, and lands on several of the southern Gulf Islands now form the nascent land base for the new Gulf Islands National Park Reserve.[36] Approximately twenty-five thousand people live and work on the eighteen largest and most populated islands. The islands have held on to their rural identities for the past hundred years but are now under increasing development pressure as more people arrive seeking a different way of life than can be found in cities or suburbia.

The ISSCMP is a grassroots response to the challenge of preserving the islands and helping to develop sustainable island communities within the Canadian waters of the Salish Sea. For the first time ever, individuals and island communities were linked together outside the political arena in a shared undertaking to identify, record, and map what remains of the original ecosystems, species, and habitats that have interacted over time with humans to shape the landscapes and cultures of the eighteen islands.

As the millennium turned, the project trained and supported people from the islands to research, record, and communicate their islands' distinct natural, economic, and cultural heritage. Local coordinators (mostly women) on each island organized public events, workshops, meetings, and interviews in order to bring their communities together to inventory their islands.[37] In a general sense, we have found that our methods closely resemble the pedagogies of participatory action research (PAR) and participatory rural appraisal (PRA), which are being used to involve local communities in community-development planning around the world.[38]

Artists interested in maps as a form of visual expression were chosen to work with each community group to turn the rough data into works of map art. All media forms were available to the artists, and the result is a rich assemblage of thirty paintings, woodcarvings, sculptures, collages, fabric art (quilts), and mixed media that in one way or another resemble "maps."[39]

From 2001 to 2003, the maps journeyed around the Salish Sea and were hung in eighteen galleries and community halls. One of the most rewarding outcomes for the artists and coordinators has been the unanticipated chance to sit in on the shows and watch how people "discover" the islands through the maps and learn new things about the islands that they think they know.[40] The guest book is full of beautiful stories and comments that capture the heart and soul of the islands and islanders. Our conclusion, which I elaborate on later in the section titled "Proof," is that the maps have made a difference in helping islanders to remember what is so important about their islands, and in motivating them to become activists if their communities or ecosystems are threatened.

The final stage of the project is to present the travelling map show in a more permanent and readily accessible format. Plans were underway in 2003 to create an atlas that, at its simplest level, will be a beautiful collection of map art to browse through, enjoy, and learn from.[41] The deeper intent is to render the book a learning tool by adding text describing the experiences that the islanders went through in creating the maps. By providing background information about the culture, environment, and economy of the islands, descriptions of the community-research and artistic processes, as well as details on the techniques and tools that were used, we hope that other artistic, community, and bioregional mapping projects will be initiated elsewhere. Sharing knowledge freely is perhaps the most powerful antidote to the trend toward corporate ownership of the global commons.[42]

Mapping as a Tool for Local Change

Along with the type of community mapping that records, preserves, and celebrates local knowledge about places comes the notion that maps can be created outside government for the specific purpose of informing the public and working toward political change. Maps can be the simplest and most easily understood medium for presenting research or information about a place. As long as the research has a place in time and space, it can be mapped.

In its simplest sense, map research can be described as an investigation or quest toward increasing the sum of knowledge about something by trying to understand it spatially. Over time the bits of knowledge acquired by individuals and groups contribute to the collective and greater body of knowledge shared by a community.[43] This collective knowledge leads to the placement of more dots on a map and to the testing of hypotheses that might explain distribution patterns. While a small community might never get to the hypothesis-testing stage, it will be better equipped to raise a ruckus when it feels threatened by inaction or proposals for change.

Without the contributions of community members, any studies supporting a development project that will have an impact on both the environment and a community will be superficial. By combining local knowledge, and newly armed with the technical skills of map making, community members can find and fill information gaps. The results can help to empower community groups to influence government decision-making in both political and bureaucratic arenas.

When a map is created that counters prevailing knowledge, it can be used to help frame questions and challenge decision makers to change policies and practices. Making maps can empower grassroots groups by placing them on equal footing with anyone who uses maps as power tools. The development of computerized geographic-information systems (GISs) has moved cartography into the digital realm. A GIS is expensive to obtain, requires specialized training to operate, and must have reliable sources of electricity to power the computers. These things are not always available to rural island communities on the West Coast of Canada. On the one hand, an island in this situation could be viewed as "disadvantaged."[44] However, on the other hand, a map is a map whether made with the simple tools of tape measure, compass, paper, and pencil or with the complex tools of a GIS. As explained in the "Proof" section below, a handmade map can sometimes have a lot of influence and, if necessary, can be transcribed into digital formats. Regardless of map format, the critical factors in community mapping are: (1) that the "community" is a full participant in the process of making the map; and (2) whether the map can be used to relocate the objects or themes at a later date.

Saul Alinsky succinctly enunciated the first rule of power tactics as: "Power is not only what you have but what the enemy thinks you have."[45] To this rule might also be added "and what the enemy thinks you don't have" because timing and the element of surprise are equally powerful. By using the same language – maps – grassroots activists will find it easier to challenge and subvert those who believe they are in the positions of "power" because they think they are the only ones who can make maps.

Publication and distribution of a map are oftentimes all that is needed to embarrass local government and motivate it to do something about a problem. Alinsky listed the fifth rule of power tactics for radicals as: "Ridicule is man's [sic] most potent weapon."[46] To this I would add that gentle or subtle ridicule is even more persuasive and helps to protect the group from being branded "anarchists," radicals, or bullies.[47] That being said, ridicule was possibly one of the most popular tools used by islanders actively involved in the successful Save Salt Spring Campaign, which became the subject of much local press and a production by the National Film Board of Canada.[48]

John Ralston Saul discusses the power of public language and of language that is corrupted to produce what he calls the "dialects of individual corporations." Dialects infused with jargon, babble, techno-speak, and acronyms are used by medicine, economics, the arts, science, social sciences, and government with the intent of building impenetrable complexity, elitism, and self-importance at the expense of open and understandable communication among people. Saul goes on to propose that "one of the signs of a healthy civilization is the existence of a relatively clear language in which everyone can participate in their own way."[49] I propose that the principal reason why people of all ages, abilities, and backgrounds react positively to maps is because maps are indeed one of those clear languages that can point accurately and succinctly in the direction of positive change.

Maps transcend barriers of language and literacy and translate complicated issues and matters of the world into visual comprehension.[50] Anyone making maps must enter into the process honestly. Maps can be deliberately made to mislead, suppress features or information, and emphasize facts out of proportion to reality. This was a well-used trick of the Fascist propaganda machine beginning in the 1930s and was countered by the Allies throughout the Second World War.[51] Good maps should tell their stories accurately and truthfully. If you question the reliability of others' maps, then keep in mind that it is fair game for someone to question yours.

How to Make a Map
The process of making a map varies in both time and energy. The variables include the number of people involved in the project, the number of people who have previous map-making experience or can contribute other useful skills, access to existing base maps and data, complexity of the data and the issues, preimposed and urgent deadlines, and the actual objectives for making the map. The geographic literature and Internet are sprinkled with excellent manuals and technical advice that can help you and your community make a map.[52]

The process I describe below is deliberately generic and intended for those who have never made maps before.[53] While the steps may seem simplistic, they have been tested with school children, teachers, elders, women, men, and numerous community groups, including delegates attending the 2002 International Children's Conference on the Environment.[54] The steps generally follow the techniques used by others working in the field of PAR.

I have avoided giving specific examples because they may inhibit inspiration, stifle local solutions and creative problem solving, and give away the element of surprise. However, it is useful to spend some time getting organized and making an action plan even if the path eventually diverges because of new information. Diversions can be fun and productive and relate directly to Alinsky's third rule, "Wherever possible go outside the experience of the enemy," keeping in mind the second rule, "Never go outside the experience of your people."[55]

1 Know what is happening in your community and what local government is doing in response. If it is doing nothing about an environmental issue, it obviously needs your help whether or not it asks for it. Strategically, it might be prudent to work in secrecy, but sometimes a public announcement of what you are up to may prod the other side into action – which is, after all, what you really want. This strategy is nicely put by Alinsky in his ninth rule: "The threat is usually more terrifying than the thing itself."[56]

2 Identify an issue that resonates within you. It may scare you or make you angry, but most important it will make you want to do something. Recruit others for the cause, especially those who might have specific skills, such as fundraising, public speaking and media relations, writing, cartography, and graphics. List the group's human assets and determine where there are gaps. The goal is to create a product that is professional in both appearance and content. If you are missing a particular skill, you may have to find a volunteer willing to learn how to do something new. Whether the issue is environmental, socio-cultural, or health-related, seek local experts who have professional and academic qualifications to add "weight" to your project. Expert opinions are difficult to argue against. Do not, however, allow the experts to take over the project.

3 Educate yourself about the issue. Even if the experts are not prepared to join your group in an advocacy or supporting role, they should be amenable to pointing you toward other experts and the information you need. Find creative, sustainable solutions. Determine what can be realistically accomplished by the decision makers' given budget and staff limitations. If this is an issue that should be made a priority, you need to examine, in the case of local government, the budget and lobby for reallocation of funds. At this stage, it is really helpful to have participants with budgeting, accounting, and financial analysis skills.

4 Create maps, graphics, and text that document the issue clearly. Keep in mind the notion that your map should seduce the viewer. Document your methods and back up your data. Develop a policy for local government to adopt. It is likely that your issue has already been an issue someplace else on the planet. The Internet is a good place to find examples from other locations that you can adapt to fit your situation. Use plain language so that everyone will understand the text. Policies are only

policies and can be forgotten or ignored. Develop best-management practices (BMPs) that take the policy into action. BMPs provide the practical steps, procedures, and techniques that should be followed to implement the policy properly. To create BMPs, find the best solutions, keeping in mind the people who will be doing the work. Where possible, provide choices that are equally acceptable. Remember Alinsky's twelfth rule: "The price of a successful attack is a constructive alternative."[57]

5 Inform your community. Make a formal presentation to a council meeting (or to other decision makers); make copies of the maps and post them everywhere; put a copy in your public library; write newspaper articles and issue press releases. If the issue affects a specific place, hold a press conference at the site. Use e-mail, street theatre, and other art forms to get your message out and about everywhere. Keep in mind Alinsky's tenth rule: "The major premise for tactics is the development of operations that will maintain a constant pressure upon the opposition."[58]

6 Persevere. Take Alinsky's eleventh rule to heart: "If you push a negative hard and deep enough it will break through into its counterside."[59] For instance, in Canada it is our democratic right to protect our democratic rights. Ignatieff explains that rights existed before government, that government must respect the rights we already possess, and that government must defend our rights when we believe they have been violated.[60] Our rights are entrenched in the Canadian Charter of Rights and Freedoms and in the 1948 United Nations Universal Declaration of Human Rights (UDHR).[61] Article 3 of the UDHR states that "everyone has the right to life, liberty and security of person." Polluters of air and water violate these basic human rights every day. The rights to clean drinking water are also entrenched in the United Nations Convention on the Rights of the Child, which clearly recognizes the dangers of environmental pollution and directs signatory states to pursue provision of clean drinking water to protect the health of children.[62] Making maps showing sites of water pollution and toxic waste can be a good place to begin talking about other issues that violate human rights.

7 Get other community groups involved. Focus on the positive reasons why change must happen. Help them to see their role and spread your knowledge to help empower them. The formation of coalitions of groups and individuals to fight an issue exemplifies the ecological concept of interconnectedness and the power of strength in numbers. The act of coming together over a common interest and sharing experiences is the fundamental reason for "community." The result can increase energy levels, add more credibility to the project, and help encourage others to support the call for change. For success, paying attention to this step is critical. Without enough help, it would be difficult to follow Alinsky's eighth rule: "Keep the pressure on."[63] Keeping the pressure on requires

sustained effort. This can only happen with high levels of enthusiasm and energy – all of which ultimately celebrate the essence of community. Keep in mind that only communities can make themselves. Local government is a community of politicians and bureaucrats unto itself, but it cannot "make" the community it governs.

8 Even in the darkest moments, enjoy yourself! Remember that you can do only your best. The sixth rule of Alinsky's power tactics is the one that bureaucrats and politicians never seem to comprehend: "A good tactic is one that your people enjoy."[64] When people are motivated to become involved because of concern for the common good, it is possible to have fun – so much fun, in fact, that the fun itself becomes an empowering tactic.

9 Perhaps most difficult for those involved in a map-making project is deciding when to end the project. Though a project may be a stage in a longer campaign, bear in mind Alinsky's seventh rule: "A tactic that drags on too long becomes a drag."[65] Maps are interesting artifacts because they capture specific pieces of information that have a place in space and time. When information and data are never-ending, a cut-off point must be decided upon. To return to an earlier point I made, ask whether you have learned something new and whether the project has increased the collective knowledge of the community. Can this new knowledge be used to spawn more projects, some of which may have nothing to do with maps? Choosing a cut-off point for data collection allows researchers a chance to begin anew, using the old map as a baseline and the new map for comparative purposes and further action. Collecting several time periods of data (seasonal, annual) allows you to look for interesting patterns or to monitor changes in the abundance and distribution of the entities you are mapping. Armed with your maps, you can then challenge government or industry to provide better explanations.

10 Even though your group may have accomplished more than any staff person or contracted-out consultant, do not expect government to be in much of a hurry to acknowledge or give credibility to your group, even if it is composed of well-educated professionals and has produced higher-quality work than anything the local government can afford. Why? Well, if nongovernmental organizations (NGOs) can do the work, usually operating under frugal conditions, this implies that communities can survive without government. The effort expended by the NGO might suggest that the NGO cares more about the community than does the local government. The local government does not want to support this impression because it questions government's priorities and existence. Beware of the seduction and flattery technique. Typically, an NGO will present its work at a local council meeting. Council members will say nice things about the work and are then faced with

several options. They can choose to ignore the work, giving excuses such as previous time commitments or their "heavy" agenda. They might see value in your work ("You did all this for only $1,000?") and will attempt to corrupt the group's integrity and independence by offering "grants" that detract from the real need to hire competent staff to do the work. Or the local government might recognize your independent and important role in environmental research, education, and local action and reallocate budgetary funds to assist your group in its work. In a perfect democratic world your group will then be invited to become part of an inclusive, participatory local-governance coalition based on respect, cooperation, consensus, and social justice.

Women and Maps

I have been able to find no body of literature specifically related to "feminist cartography" and only a few passing references within the subdiscipline of feminist geography.[66] In their separate texts, Kwan, Moss, and Pratt provide definitions and thorough and insightful reviews of the epistemology, methods, and practice of feminist geography, but they do so from the perspective of feminist geographers finding ways to rationalize their work, rather than as feminists seeking the answers to spatio-temporal questions through the use of geography.[67]

Writing from personal experience, I speculate that those women making maps with other women about issues of interest to women have been too busy making maps to write up their experiences, particularly in a scholarly context. While gender has not previously been the specific goal or instigator of community map-making projects on the West Coast, the potential for women's map-making projects that focus on women's issues is immense. I also would like to iterate along with Kwan that most environmental, sociocultural, and economic issues that affect women also affect men and that gender therefore may or may not be an issue.[68] I propose that the heart of a "feminist cartography" is based on the notion that maps are made by women for any audience they choose and in any map form they choose.

A women's map may be intended simply to make the point that there are differences in the way women experience and use a place, or that the names women have for some places are different than those that appear on other maps. The dots on the map may mark special places where women gather to pick berries, or other places that should never be forgotten because they are completely entwined with women's experience both of place and of community.

On the island where I live, many women supplied data to the two millennium maps that were contributed to the ISSCMP. As I gathered stories and information, we discussed a lot of things and talked about new maps we would like to make some day. By talking, we learned that there are some things affecting women on our island that are worth worrying about. Because we live on a small island that is tacked onto a larger urban census area for regional health statistics, my concern is that very local neighbourhood patterns may be lost in the larger data stewpot. The best way to find the patterns that we think we are seeing is to make some maps and then try to find the answers.

The first two maps being birthed deal with health issues. Globally, breast cancer is the most common cancer in women, and on my rural island breast cancer is becoming a fact of life.[69] Far too many women have been diagnosed with breast cancer, and too many friends have died from this disease.[70] Far too many partners of women have been diagnosed with other cancers, and too many of them have died, too.[71] This has worried and scared many people and, through informal discussions, has led to the collective conclusion that "we need to do something" (Step 2 above). The data for a map are slowly being gathered through word of mouth, discussions with the local doctor, and storytelling. As we colour the map, we are beginning to ask questions such as: Why are there so many cases of breast cancer? Why are there clusters of cancer? Is it something in the water? And is the industrial development on the nearby mainland a reason why there is so much cancer?

The process of making the cancer map began in 2000 and will likely go on for several more years. As a geographer and biologist, I have been trained to use statistics in various aspects of the work I do. Typically, in that work, phenomena are reduced to anonymous numbers, statistics, or datum points on a map. But this is not a typical research project, and the creation of this map is motivated by the rage and pain of knowing that the dots are not just numbers; they are friends and neighbours with names, lives, and experiences that have intertwined with our own. As survivors, we are making a map together that is deeply personal, meaningful, empowering, rewarding, and cathartic. This is a map that is evolving through process and progress. The data will eventually be transferred to a powerful GIS managed by a local NGO.[72] Then the task of trying to determine whether there are causal environmental links will begin.[73] Finally, a work of map art will be created that honours the victims and survivors who provided the data for the map.

The second map in the works was also spawned from a locally emerging health issue. *Blastocystis hominus* is a parasitic cyst that causes blastocystiasis, a persistent and often debilitating form of intestinal dysentery. While the geographic distribution of the cyst is cosmopolitan, it is quite prevalent in the tropics and developing countries because of poor sanitation and contaminated water. The cyst is transmitted between humans through contaminated food and water, personal contact, and poor hygiene, and is turning up in people of all ages on my island.[74] The map-making project was activated by several women who had noticed that the disease seemed to be found in one specific neighbourhood. Most of those infected have not been to tropical places, and the burning question is "why here?"

As we talk about this disease and discover that more people have been infected, the concern about one small cluster is expanding to concern that the distribution on the island is becoming ubiquitous. Suspicions and speculation are being formulated into hypotheses that can be tested once the map is completed and transferred into the GIS. One hypothesis relates to infill development and approval of septic systems that, although designed to health standards for the properties in question, may have been placed too close to wells and to potable-water sources for adjacent existing properties. The types of soil and other biophysical characteristics of the landscape may be contributing to the rapid leaching of sewage before it can be filtered and cleaned by the plants and microorganisms in the soil. A second hypothesis will test spatial relationships by asking whether the affected properties are downslope from infill properties. Using the GIS, we can explore these questions and test the hypotheses. The blastocystiasis health issue will likely become a political problem. If infill development is causing the health problem, then perhaps the island has reached its growth limits and no more subdivision and development should be allowed. On all the islands in the Salish Sea, finding the balance between either preserving and protecting the environment or developing the environment for larger human populations is the recurrent planning conundrum to which islanders dedicate great amounts of time and energy. It is the same conundrum that originally motivated a group of women to initiate the ISSCMP, some of whom continue to work with their communities by initiating new map-making projects.

Proof

One of the first practical tests of the ISSCMP came in 2002 when I was asked to help a coalition of island groups and regional NGOs (the GSX Marine Coalition) prepare scientific intervenor evidence to stop approval of a proposed natural-gas pipeline known as the GSX Canada Pipeline Project (GSXPL).[75] The GSXPL is a joint venture between BC Hydro, a publicly owned Crown corporation, and Williams, a private American energy company based in Tulsa, Oklahoma.[76] Islanders believe construction of the pipeline will directly affect their way of life, damage irreplaceable ecosystems, and harm a unique relationship between people and the hundreds of other species with which they coexist on the islands and waters of the Salish Sea.

During my technical review of the GSXPL documents, I found that data were missing from the "official" maps prepared by the proponent and decided that the best way to counter this was to provide the maps that had the missing information. Through my presentation of direct evidence to the joint review panel of the National Energy Board of Canada (NEB) and the Canadian Environmental Assessment Agency (CEAA), the maps of Saturna Island, Mayne Island, the Pender Islands, and the Islands Trust Fund were entered as legal exhibits. These maps portray the breadth of community knowledge that was never researched during the Environmental and Social Impact Assessment for the proposed project.

The formal NEB/CEAA public hearings were held in Sidney, BC, during March 2003. An ISSCMP art show was quickly booked into the foyer gallery in front of the hearing room, and over a two-week period, the full collection of thirty maps was on public display. The maps served as a visual reference for media interviews and provided opportunities for animated discussion among attendees at the hearing. Most important, the maps were a constant reminder to the presiding tribunal, agency staff, and GSXPL proponents that the places at risk are more than a few names on a map.

Final proof of the validity of the ISSCMP maps has come from the National Energy Board in their request to use the image of the transportation-and-energy map created for the ISSCMP on the cover of its *Reasons for Decision* in the matter of the GSXPL.[77] This also proves my case about the power of maps and their ability to seduce the viewer into making change. Up to this point, all NEB decisions, of which there are dozens, have been published with plain, pale-blue covers. Following discussion among the ISSCMP coordinating collective, the artist, and representatives of the Marine Coalition, a counterproposal was made to the NEB that the image could be used if the decision ruled against construction of the pipeline. The image was not used and despite overwhelming evidence of negative environmental impacts, David Anderson, Canada's minister of environment, recommended to the federal cabinet that the project proceed. Fortunately, the British Columbia Utilities Commission turned down the application to construct the power plant that would have been fuelled by gas from the GSX pipeline. GSXPL is currently considering other options.

Conclusion

Across Canada, talk about the need for change in local governance is slowly shifting to acting for change. While the previous two decades were spattered with protests and scarred by demonstrations, there is a new, slowly building trend toward working cooperatively with all parties involved in an issue. The success of recent mapping projects by West Coast communities is a positive indicator that community mapping can provide the common ground for this to happen. For this reason, and because of the hope it brings, I propose that Alinsky's thirteenth and last tactic is now an artifact of the last century: "Pick the target, freeze it, personalize it, and polarize it."[78] In its place, the new paradigm should be to pick the target and map it in the context of making positive local changes that have global consequences.

Kwan argues that feminist geographers using a GIS can help support GIS-based research in women's activism. However, she cautions that the technology can marginalize and eventually exclude the grassroots activist groups that conceived of the project because other participants may have better technical, political, or financial resources that become power tools.[79] For this reason, I would argue that if the grassroots group initiates the project and makes its maps by hand (or by GIS if it has the skills and technology), it will be better able to withstand power struggles because it already possesses the data. It can then invite other partners into the process and demand equitable participation as a project grows.

The notion of grassroots feminist groups making maps for their own purposes may be perceived by some as a threat to the formal subdiscipline of "feminist geography" as defined and practised by feminist geographers. In response to this, I pose a few questions to feminist geographers for their contemplation: Are feminist geographers the only ones qualified to make feminist maps? Is it ethical for feminist geographers to essentialize or objectify other women in order to conduct research from which these geographers benefit through publication, promotion, and tenure? Can the unpublished research and maps of grassroots feminist cartographers working outside academia and without academic qualifications in geography be recognized by feminist geographers as important contributions to feminist geography? Is feminist geography inclusive of all feminists using and making maps, or are feminist geographers creating an elite group of GIS experts that excludes feminist cartographers using other methods? At the beginning of this chapter, I explained that in community mapping, the process of making a map is as important as creating a map product. Understanding that this process is also a result is essential to answering these questions, as is the issue of who writes a paper about a feminist mapping project.

In their most literal sense, maps provide direction. Map making by community groups can bring focus to an issue and help to show the way toward the best locally made answers. As women form community map-making groups to make sense out of local issues affecting women, they will be making valuable contributions to local environmental issues from a feminist perspective. In the subtitle to this chapter, I have used the word "toward." What is now needed is a collection of mapping projects initiated entirely by grassroots women in other places in order to find common ground and to collectively craft a definition that explains the full meaning of "grassroots feminist cartography" to those outside the grassroots experience.

Notes

1   Paula Allen and Eve Ensler, "An Activist Love Story," in *The Feminist Memoir Project: Voices from Women's Liberation,* edited by Rachel Blau DuPlessis and Ann Snitow (New York: Three Rivers Press, 1998), 413-25.

2 Rosalie Bertell, *Planet Earth: The Latest Weapon of War* (Montreal: Black Rose Books, 2001), 223.

3 ani difranco, "Tamburitza Lingua," in *Revelling/Reckoning* [Sound recording] (Buffalo, NY: righteous babe records/BMI, 2001).

4 Judy Rebick, *Imagine Democracy* (Toronto: Stoddart, 2000), 229.

5 By local, I mean my home-place, the Canadian islands in the Salish Sea. The Salish Sea is located off the West Coast of Canada between Vancouver Island and the North American continent. The Salish Sea encompasses Puget Sound, Rosario Strait, and Admiralty Inlet in Washington State; the shared international waters of Haro Strait and Boundary Bay; and the Strait of Georgia, Howe Sound, Burrard Inlet, and Malaspina Strait on the Canadian side of the border.

6 I am speaking here of the globally scarce and threatened coastal temperate rainforests. Ecotrust, Pacific GIS, and Conservation International, *The Rainforests of Home: An Atlas of People and Place,* part 1, *Natural Forests and Native Languages of the Coastal Temperate Rain Forest* (Portland, OR: Ecotrust, Pacific GIS, and Conservation International, 1995).

7 United Nations Environment Programme, <http://www.unep.org/>.

8 On a global scale, the water issue is so serious that the United Nations designated 2003 the International Year of Fresh Water; see note 7.

9 Katherine Dunster, "Land Stewardship through Community Mapping: The Salish Sea Mapping Project," in *Caring for Our Land and Water: Stewardship and Conservation in Canada,* conference proceedings, vol. 5, *Traditional Knowledge, Partnerships and Organizations,* edited by S.G. Hilts, L. Milburn, and S. Mulley (Guelph: Centre for Land and Water Stewardship, University of Guelph, 2002), 31-37.

10 Saul Alinsky, "Tactics," in *Rules for Radicals* (New York: Vintage Books, 1971), 126-48.

11 For instance, try Advantage Book Exchange, <http://www.abebooks.com>.

12 The proof of its enduring utility rests with its use in academia as a text for required reading. I note, for example, that *Rules for Radicals* was a required text for a graduate course taught in the spring term of 2003 by Karen McGuinness in the Woodrow Wilson School of Public and International Affairs at Princeton University. The course was titled "Top Down and Bottom Up Approaches to Development: Persistent Poverty, Community Development and Asset Creation," <http://www.wws.princeton.edu/courses/syllabi_s03/wws572c.pdf>.

13 I am referring here to the "war on terrorism" (Afghanistan 2002 and Iraq 2003). In Canada coalitions of social- and environmental-justice groups were formed to hold rallies, send letters, and use various tactics to protest the wars. See, for example, the StopWar.ca Coalition, <http://www.stopwar.ca> and the Centre for Social Justice, <http://www.socialjustice. org>. The War Resisters League has published a handbook titled *Reviving Resistance: Tools for Anti-Nuclear Organizing in the Age of Terror* (New York: War Resisters League, 2002), <http://www.warresisters.org>.

14 The Raging Grannies are a truly inspiring made-in-Canada style of feminist activism. The original Raging Grannies were formed around 1986 in Victoria, BC, by a group of peace activists to protest nuclear proliferation and the use of Canadian waters by American nuclear submarines. Since then, similar-minded women have formed groups across the country. Working cooperatively, the Grannies change the words to popular songs. The recycled songs are satirical and timely. The Raging Grannies dress in stereotypical "granny" costumes and, in the finest street theatre tradition, perform at rallies, meetings, festivals, and demonstrations, where they sing their songs and raise awareness about issues related to peace, the environment, and social justice; see note 13. Their songbook, now out of print, provides information about their history, organizing tips, and songs. Jean McLaren and Heide Brown, eds., *The Raging Grannies Songbook* (Gabriola Island, BC: New Society, 1993).

15 For example, I was invited by e-mail, and signed the Berlin Declaration by e-mail, to oppose the "war on terrorism" and support the construction of a new global legal order to contain terrorism and preserve democracy; see International Peace Bureau, <http://www. ipb.org>, and the German Green Party (Die Grünen), <http://basis.gruene.de/bochum/pm-berliner-deklaration.htm>. Two long-established women's organizations that are actively using the Internet as a tool for global peace activism are Women's Action for New Directions, <http://www.wand.org>, and Women's International League for Peace and Freedom

(WILPF), <http://www.wilpf.org> and the WILPF disarmament project at <http://www. reachingcriticalwill.org>.

16 The use of the Internet for organizing activists at local, regional, and global levels is an emerging area of research. This has been addressed by Len Holmes of the University of North London, in "E-rules for Radicals? Community Organising in an E-world," paper prepared for the Ninth International Congress of Asia-Pacific Researchers in Organisation Studies, "Organization Theory in Transition: Transitional Societies, Transitional Theories," Hong Kong, 2001.

17 See, for example, the excellent guide by Virginia Coover, Ellen Deacon, Charles Esser, and Christopher Moore, *Resource Manual for a Living Revolution* (Philadelphia: New Society, 1985). Political activism across all disciplines is well covered in Randy Shaw, *The Activist's Handbook: A Primer for the 1990s and Beyond* (Berkeley: University of California Press, 1996).

18 See note 14.

19 Katherine Dunster, *Appendix C: Review of Benthic Flora Direct Evidence of the GSX Marine Coalition*, Canadian Environmental Assessment Agency/National Energy Board Joint Panel Review in the Matter of an Application by Georgia Strait Crossing Pipeline Limited (GSXPL), Hearing Order GH-4-2001, Board File No. 3200-G-49-1, 2002, <http://www.cpawsbc.org/action/gsx/>, and <http://www.neb.gc.ca/registry/gsx/pubreg_e.htm>.

20 Doug Aberley, ed., *Boundaries of Home: Mapping for Local Empowerment* (Gabriola Island, BC: New Society, 1993).

21 On the rural island where I live, this still goes on at the local schools. Elders (also known as "grandfriends") come into the classrooms to tell stories and share their knowledge and skills with the children.

22 The full and correct citation is, Fannie Merritt Farmer, *The Boston Cooking-School Cookbook* (Boston: Little-Brown, 1896). Numerous facsimile editions are still in circulation.

23 A few reference books that delve into apples are: Joan Morgan and Alison Richards, *The Book of Apples* (London, UK: Ebury Press, 1993); Roger Yepsen, *Apples* (New York: Norton, 1994); and Rosanne Sanders, *The English Apple* (London, UK: Phaidon Press, 1988).

24 One such organization that I belong to is the BC Fruit Testers Association, whose membership is devoted to perpetuating heritage orchards and fruits in British Columbia. They can be reached at: P.O. Box 48123, 3575 Douglas Street, Victoria, BC, Canada, V8Z 7H5.

25 While long out of print, the best reference is Ulysses P. Hedrick, *The Apples of New York*, 2 vols. (New York: Agricultural Experiment Station, 1905), which describes approximately one thousand varieties being grown in New York State and elsewhere in North America around 1900.

26 Hedrick *(The Apples)* and other horticultural experts recognized the need to classify apples in order to describe their qualities to growers and consumers, so they developed a system for categorizing apples by group, natural season, size, shape, and use. Groups are based on appearance (for example, smooth-skinned, green, and sour or smooth, flushed, and sweet). Natural season is based on ripening time: early (July to September), mid (October to November), or late (December onward). And use is divided into dessert (eating out of hand), culinary (cooking and cider), or dual purpose. See also Muriel W.G. Smith, *National Apple Register of the United Kingdom* (London, UK: Ministry of Agriculture, Fisheries and Food, 1971).

27 For example, the Wolf River was discovered as a seedling growing along the banks of the Wolf River in Wisconsin in 1875. This is one of the few apple varieties that can grow "relatively true" from seed.

28 A pip (seed) gives rise to the word "pippin." Hence a Cox's Orange Pippin originated from a seedling rather than from grafting a "sport," or genetic deviation, found on the branch of another tree.

29 The transfer of knowledge from place to place is one way we learn, and today it happens very quickly via the Internet. My concern here is with a keeper of knowledge leaving (or dying) without passing along her or his knowledge.

30 Local distinctiveness is a point of view pursued in England by the organization known as Common Ground; see <http://www.commonground.org.uk>. Two essential Canadian references to home-place are Sharon Butala, *The Perfection of Morning: An Apprenticeship in Nature* (Toronto: Harper Collins, 1994); and J. Stan Rowe, *Home Place* (Edmonton: NeWest, 1990).

31 Aberley, *Boundaries of Home.*
32 Experts will tell you that only trained cartographers can make maps, and the cartographic literature is rife with examples. A case in point is David Cuff and Mark Mattson, *Thematic Maps: Their Design and Production* (New York: Methuen, 1982), which states in the introduction that modern cartography can be divided into two groups: primary data collection by scientists that forms the basis for survey mapping and charting by large national agencies; and the use of government map data by professional cartographers to create other maps.
33 An excellent guide to the techniques of making a community map is Sheila Harrington, ed., *Giving the Land a Voice: Mapping Our Home Places* (Saltspring Island, BC: Land Trust Alliance of British Columbia, 1999). This text is available directly from the publisher.
34 For more information on the project, contact the Land Trust Alliance of British Columbia at <http://www.landtrustalliance.bc.ca>.
35 The Islands Trust Act was first enacted in 1974 in order to create a body known as the Islands Trust. The mandate of the Islands Trust is "to preserve and protect the trust area and its unique amenities and environment for the benefit of the residents of the trust area and of British Columbia generally, in cooperation with municipalities, regional districts, improvement districts, other persons and organizations and the government of British Columbia." See <http://www.islandstrust.bc.ca> for more information about the policies and programs of the Islands Trust and <http://www.islandstrustfund.bc.ca> for help regarding land conservation, stewardship, and protection tools.
36 The Gulf Islands National Park Reserve of Canada was formally established by the Governments of Canada and British Columbia on 9 May 2003.
37 Why so many of them were women has not yet been explored, although it has been noticed and discussed informally by a few coordinators and artists. The project is not a "feminist" project, but the vision for the project attracted a group of very interested, creative, and supportive women who have persevered and made it happen. They have since become good friends and colleagues and have collaborated on several other initiatives. As a member of the group, I have watched this happen with great interest because I have not been able to find any direct references in the literature to a "feminist cartography." There are, however, feminist geographers, and a good introduction to the theme of gender and geography is Mona Domosh and Joni Seager, *Putting Women in Place: Feminist Geographers Make Sense of the World* (New York: Guilford Press, 2001).
38 See, for instance, Aga Khan Rural Support Programme, *Rapid Participatory Rural Appraisal: Frontiers of Research* (London, UK: Aga Khan Foundation, 1991); P. Cormack, "Using Mapping in Ethiopia," *Footsteps* 17 (December 1993): 8-9; D. Davis Case, *The Communities Toolbox: The Idea, Methods and Tools for Participatory Assessment, Monitoring and Evaluation in Community Forestry* (Rome: FAO, 1990); and M. Robinson, T. Garvin, and G. Hodgson, *Mapping How We Use Our Land: Using Participatory Action Research,* 3rd ed. (Calgary: Arctic Institute of North America, 1994).
39 A few images of the maps are displayed on the website of the Land Trust Alliance of British Columbia; see note 34.
40 While the messages left in the guest book are written evidence of the direct impact of the maps, messages are also being scattered around the world via the Internet through electronic versions of the Gulf Islands' newspapers and various island bulletin boards. See, for example, Chris Corrigan's blog for 26 January 2003, <http://www.chriscorrigan.com/miscellany/bijournal/2003_01_01_archive.html>.
41 As of April 2004, the project coordinators were still looking for more publication funding. Contact the Land Trust Alliance of British Columbia at the website provided in note 34.
42 Vandana Shiva, *Biopiracy: The Plunder of Nature and Knowledge* (Boston: South End Press, 1997).
43 "Community" is defined here in its broadest sense. For various interpretations of "community," see Julian Dunster and Katherine Dunster, *Dictionary of Natural Resource Management* (Vancouver: UBC Press, 1996).
44 Balancing GIS use between those who have (money, power, human resources) and those who have not (NGOs, developing countries) has been a concern of the maker of the most successful and popular GISs on the planet. ESRI has had a long-standing corporate policy of donating GIS technology to the have-nots, which have included several NGOs located

on the islands in the Salish Sea; see Environmental Systems Research Institute, Inc. (ESRI), <http://www.esricanada.com/english/bottom/free.esp>.
45 Alinsky, "Tactics," 127.
46 Ibid., 128.
47 I am frequently on the receiving end of this type of labelling and speak here from experience.
48 While there are no "scholarly" publications about this community undertaking, a lot of maps were made by the community to demonstrate the need for conservation. There is documentation on the Internet at the Save Salt Spring Society, <http://savesaltspring.com>. Saving Saltspring was the subject of a 2001 National Film Board of Canada documentary directed by Mort Ransen and titled *Ah ... the Money, the Money, the Money: The Battle for Saltspring*. The film in itself was a tactic used to direct attention to the issue and to raise money for the Save Salt Spring Campaign.
49 John Ralston Saul, *The Unconscious Civilization* (Concord, ON: Anansi, 1995), 49, 57.
50 The use of map making and map reading in other cultures is extensively reviewed in Peter Poole, *Indigenous Peoples, Mapping, and Biodiversity Conservation: An Analysis of Current Activities and Opportunities for Applying Geomatics Technologies*, Peoples and Forests Program discussion paper (Washington, DC: Biodiversity Support Program, 1995); and Chandra Talpade Mohanty, "Cartographies of Struggle," in *Third World Women and the Politics of Feminism*, edited by Chandra Talpade Mohanty, Ann Russo, and Lourdes Torres (Bloomington: Indiana University Press, 1991), 28-47.
51 There are several good books that deal with this general subject and that can help you avoid falling into the propaganda trap. See, for example, Mark Monmonier and H.J. DeBlij, *How to Lie with Maps*, 2nd ed. (Chicago: University of Chicago Press, 1996); and Dennis Wood and John Fels, *The Power of Maps* (New York: Guilford Press, 1992).
52 Good places to start are the Land Trust Alliance of British Columbia (see note 34) and the Green Mapping Project, <http://www.greenmap.com>.
53 When someone says to me, "I'm a musician, but I want to make a map," this is where we start.
54 The International Children's Conference on the Environment (ICCE) was created by the United Nations Environment Programme (UNEP) to encourage greater involvement of children and youth in sustainable development. At the ICCE held in Victoria, BC, I attended as an adult delegate and presented a workshop for twenty adult delegates from around the world, titled "Making Maps to Make a Difference."
55 Alinsky, "Tactics," 127.
56 Ibid., 129.
57 Ibid., 130.
58 Ibid., 129.
59 Ibid., 129.
60 Michael Ignatieff, *The Rights Revolution* (Toronto: Anansi, 2000).
61 The Canadian Charter of Rights and Freedoms and other supporting educational materials are available at the Government of Canada, <http://www.canada.justice.gc.ca>, and the United Nations Universal Declaration of Human Rights is available at United Nations, <http://www.un.org>.
62 The United Nations Convention on the Rights of the Child can be obtained from the Human Rights Programme, Department of Canadian Heritage, Box 15-7-B, Hull, Quebec K1A 0M5, or at United Nations Children's Fund, <http://www.unicef.org/crc/crc.htm>.
63 Alinsky, "Tactics," 128.
64 Ibid., 128.
65 Ibid., 128.
66 N.H. Huffman, "Charting Other Maps: Cartography and Visual Methods in Feminist Research," in *Thresholds in Feminist Geography: Difference, Methodology, Representation*, edited by J.P. Jones III, H.J. Nast, and S.M. Roberts (Lanham, MD: Rowman and Littlefield, 1997), 255-83.
67 Mei-Po Kwan, "Feminist Visualization: Re-envisioning GIS as a Method in Feminist Geographic Research," *Annals of the Association of American Geographers* 92, 4 (2002): 645-61;

Pamela Moss, ed., *Feminist Geography in Practice: Research and Methods* (London, UK, and New York: Blackwell, 2002); Geraldine Pratt, "Feminist Geographies," in *The Dictionary of Human Geography*, edited by R.J. Johnston, D. Gregory, G. Pratt, and M. Watts (Oxford: Blackwell, 2000), 259-62.

68 Kwan, "Feminist Visualization."

69 D.M. Parkin, F.L. Bray, and S.S. Devesa, "Cancer Burden in the Year 2000: The Global Picture," *European Journal of Cancer* 37 (2001): S4-S66.

70 As I myself am one of the statistics, the creation of this particular map means a great deal to me.

71 A community member recently pointed out that an awful lot of pet dogs are dying of cancer, too, and wondered if we could make a map some time.

72 Our GIS gurus and partners are The Bowen Island Forest and Water Management Society.

73 Finding the links between breast cancer and the environment is the focus of a growing number of researchers. The Silent Spring Institute carries on the work of Rachel Carson; see <http://www.silentspring.org>. See also Julia G. Brody and Ruthann A. Rudel, "Environmental Pollutants and Breast Cancer," *Environmental Health Perspectives* 3, 8 (2003): 1007-19, <http://ehp.niehs.nih.gov.members/2003/6310/6310.pdf>. As I began looking for research on breast cancer and islands, I discovered that the Silent Spring Institute has been a pioneer on this subject. Two publications are invaluable: Silent Spring Institute, *The Cape Cod Breast Cancer and Environment Study: Results of the First Three Years of Study* (Newton, MA: Silent Spring Institute, 1998), <http://www.silentspring.org/newweb/publications/SilentSpring97report.pdf> ; and Silent Spring Institute, *Cape Cod Breast Cancer and Environment Atlas* (Newton, MA: Silent Spring Institute, 2000), <http://www.silentspring.org/newweb/atlas/index.html>.

74 As it turns out, this is a regional problem because the cyst is turning up on other islands too. Richard Moses, letter to the editor, *Gulf Islands Driftwood*, 7 May 2003, 9.

75 The Marine Coalition is comprised of the Saturna Community Club, Pender Islands Conservancy Association, Salt Spring Island Conservancy, Saanich Inlet Protection Society, Georgia Strait Alliance, and Canadian Parks and Wilderness Society, BC Chapter. The Gulf Crab Fishers Association was registered as a separate intervenor but participated with the Marine Coalition for the purposes of filing evidence. See note 19 and also GXS Canada Pipeline Project, <http://www.gsxreg.com>, for all documentation regarding the application to the National Energy Board of Canada for approval to construct a gas pipeline across the Salish Sea.

76 The GSXPL project website is <http://www.georgiastrait.twc.com>. The anti-GSXPL website is <www.sqwack.com/home.htm>.

77 Judith Stevenson, coordinator of the ISSCMP, personal communication, 26 May 2003.

78 Alinsky, "Tactics," 130.

79 Kwan, "Feminist Visualization."

Part 4
Rethinking the Environment

Canada, the top half of the North American continent, has been utilized, consumed, and abused in ways distressingly similar to the ways humans in industrial societies around the world have treated their environments. One theme of this book is the idea that some of this abuse originates in the inequalities and insecurities that exist within human societies, foremost among them perhaps the continued inequality between the sexes. The need for a place to "prove" one's manhood or, for women, to "escape" domestic tyranny has also undoubtedly had an impact on how the land is perceived and treated. In addition, historical and economic factors have also contributed to the "Canadian experience" of nature. When one compares the experiences of settlers in Australia, New Zealand, Canada, and the United States, for example, it becomes clear that no other English settlers faced a landscape quite as formidable as the Canadian landscape. Immigration rates to Canada were much lower than those to the United States, and as a consequence, the population on the northern half of the continent remained sparse. It is this relatively sparse population, combined with a very large landmass and the peculiar settlement of the bulk of the Canadian population along the border with the United States, that makes it possible for today's Canadians to imagine a different, more equitable relationship with their home. Canada has a vital role to play in environmental discourse because it still possesses significant wild areas. Consequently, a wide range of opportunities and possibilities exist here that are simply not available to more populated and developed countries.

In this final part, then, the authors explore the exceptional opportunity that Canada represents and, in the process, use the opportunity to "reimagine" a different kind of relationship to the natural world. This is necessary because, as Melody Hessing points out in her discussion of wilderness protection in Canada, "The Fall of the Wild?" women's expanded participation in resource extraction, while working to empower women, does so potentially at the cost of wild spaces. Nevertheless, Hessing believes that debates on development versus preservation that occur within Canada are both divisive and artificial. In a pluralist, multicultural society in which a great proportion of the land is Crown owned, democratic notions of "multiple stakeholders" – including First Nations land-claims issues – can help reshape more traditional ideas of both land ownership and stewardship. It is Hessing's contention that while wilderness is understood to be "gender neutral," its Canadian association with male employment and experiences tends to perpetuate an unattractive gender bias that may be responsible in part for restricting appeals for its protection. Here rethinking becomes a powerful tool for wilderness protection, for if wild areas can be viewed as ecologically diverse and abundant and can be portrayed as culturally resonant with an equally diverse Canadian society, wilderness protection has a much greater potential to attract public attention and political support.

Anne Kaufman also deals with the idea of rethinking and its importance to breaking old mythologies and stereotypes that have contributed to the harm done to both Canadian and American landscapes. Employing a close reading of both Willa Cather and Aritha van Herk, Kaufman concludes that there is a heavily encoded male discourse in the myth of the West that both authors parody, dismantle, and ultimately reconfigure. Arachne, van Herk's heroine in *No Fixed Address*, struggles with issues of leaving "home" (the domestic place) so that she might engage in a more free-wheeling exploration of the Canadian landscape. In a comic process, Arachne travels full circle when she realizes that rather than newly colonizing a place, she might instead ask: What does she have to offer to a place? While Cather's female characters live in a different and more difficult historical time, in which they find themselves constrained by economic and social factors, Kaufman believes that van Herk's postmodern imagery opens up opportunities: to cross tracks, remake lives, and create alternatives. Both authors use female eroticism to express their experiences of the land, experiences that are ultimately based on the idea of pleasure as a means of reconnecting with land.

Heather Eaton explores the possibilities of reigniting a sense of the sacred in the human relationship to the land. In doing so, she frankly addresses the fact that much ecofeminist discourse is utopic rather than a "functioning ideology." Nevertheless, her sense that the great *mysterium tremendum* was at the root of the human relationship to nature for much of human history and prehistory also reminds readers that the basis of any respectful treatment of the natural world must include some recognition of the sacred. As Eaton points out, recovery of the sacred is never a neat and tidy process, any more than ecofeminism is a neat and tidy theory. Nevertheless, she holds out hope that the recovery of the sacred – in a profound and deeply felt way – may have a role to play in future transformative activism.

Marian Scholtmeijer's chapter, "The Listening World: First Nations Women Writers and the Environment," discovers a feeling for nature that embodies the idea of "fellow creature" among First Nations poets. Although the Western Romantic tradition informs the beginnings of environmental thought, Scholtmeijer carefully points out that writers such as Lee Maracle push the felt relationship with the natural world even further than do poets such as Wordsworth. What Maracle perceives in a small, hardy dandelion is a fellow being struggling to survive; she feels, as Scholtmeijer suggests, "*with* rather than *for*" the flower. Canadian First Nations women writers frequently see the natural world as "peopled" and frequently and self-consciously seek to re-create the familiarity of natural environments in their writing. This familiarity is one that many environmentalists now see as an essential element in rethinking the human relationship to the natural world. In addition, however, Scholtmeijer points out that rethinking involves a further imaginative step: learning to see how humans might be perceived by the world itself. If humans imagine their actions as being viewed and heeded by the whole nonhuman world, the relationship that we might thus discern and long for may finally be one of reciprocity.

13

Tracing Amorous Journeys from the Sweetwater to Watson Lake: Environmental Ecstasies of Willa Cather and Aritha van Herk

Anne L. Kaufman

> Ultimately it comes down to: how do you manage?
> Simply: how do you manage? How do you tell the stories that
> need to be told? How do you look at yourself without flinching?
> How do you take care of your neighbour in a way that person
> needs? How do you give the world attention and care, and yet
> keep some attention and care for yourself? I think I'm talking
> about the grace of living.
>
> — Aritha van Herk[1]

Although her name does not necessarily leap to the lips of those most engaged in American ecocriticism, Willa Cather's powerful environmental
imagination is evident in her ability to find new axes of meaning for landscapes already heavily inscribed with a seemingly indestructible mythologi-
cal structure. Aritha van Herk exerts creative power through the landscape
in a similar way, using bodily experience as well as writerly strategy to produce a new vision of women's engagements with the land. Both writers use
negotiations with place to tell women's stories in new ways, allowing their
respective environmental visions to liberate such narratives from dominant,
confining structures. Also, concerns with the physical and literary health of
their respective environments pervade the work of Willa Cather and Aritha
van Herk. Cather, writing in the late nineteenth and early twentieth centuries, saw the coming of the railroads and the beginning of the technologically advanced industrial society of the present day. Although the Dust Bowl
years suggested that attention had better be paid to environmental issues,
contemporary concerns with pollution, land use, recycling, Earth Day, sustainable agriculture, and the like had not yet entered everyday discourse.

In his study *Coyote Country*, Arnold Davidson proposes that the structure
and conventions of the Canadian western afforded men and women writers more possibilities than did the American western – that it was, for

example, less fraught with issues of Manifest Destiny and therefore more open to possibilities. In a section on women writers, he notes that Aritha van Herk's early novels *Judith* (1978) and *The Tent Peg* (1981) make specific narrative choices that subvert the classic western. In doing so, he identifies an important aspect of van Herk's writerly process – her inclination to break down any and all established paradigms (narrative, the western, feminist revisionary myth making; the list goes on and on) in order to imagine and reimagine what a West created by/for/with women might look like, noting that this strategy allows van Herk to "insist that women can stake their claims ... in whatever realms they please."[2] A review of the now-considerable van Herk oeuvre[3] nearly a decade after Davidson's assessment makes it clear that her work does more than routinely subvert. Like Cather, van Herk writes familiar territory using a new scale of authenticity. As the graph of a mathematical function can be relocated by vertical or horizontal shifts, elongated or compressed by changes in periodicity, or reflected (as in a mirror) across a horizontal or vertical axis, so these writers present visions of women's western experience by shifting their narrative axes. Van Herk's process involves situating herself in a historical framework as well as a literary and cultural moment: She clearly sees her work as part of a continuum that includes, among others, Willa Cather and Margaret Laurence. She recognizes the pervasive presence of what one critic calls "the heavily encoded male discourse of the myth of the west,"[4] both parodying the myth and using it as a model to be dismantled. In the process she also dismantles a model of the reader as receptive, choosing instead to construct her texts in ways that make her readers (and listeners) work.

"Cather in Ecstasy," van Herk's plenary address at the 1995 International Cather Seminar in Quebec City, made her listeners work even as it entertained (or, in some cases, it must be noted, offended).[5] The piece begins by borrowing the epigraph to Cather's *A Lost Lady*[6] and adding to it three lines from Emily Dickinson:

Wild nights, wild nights ...
Were I with thee,
Wild nights should be our ecstasy ...[7]

Van Herk left those words reverberating in the air and proceeded to alter the imaginative axis on which Willa Cather, the writer, had been fixed for decades in the minds of her audience. Van Herk's Cather comments acerbically on her own characters as they wander, one by one or (as in the case of Niel Herbert and Marian Forrester) in pairs into the "marvellously dated period piece of a milliner's shop" that is her setting. And this is no ordinary milliner's shop: It is composed of layers, "a series of maze-like rooms, rather like hat-boxes within hat-boxes, or stories within stories."[8] This is as useful a description of van Herk's aesthetic as it is a commentary on Cather's narrative: Both writers, despite their desire to articulate new visions of story, invent a rich creative environment (at all levels), thickly mulched with allusion, literary conversation, and the memory of well-read texts.

Davidson says of van Herk's two early novels that each "playfully dismantles its quest plot into disparate sections the reader must fit together."[9] This dismantling process is equally evident in *No Fixed Address* (1986) and in her later works as well. In taking apart the structure of readerly (and critical) expectations, van Herk mixes genres, experiments with language, punctuation, and narrative form, and employs unusual protagonists. *No Fixed Address*, for example, has at its centre Arachne Manteia, a travelling underwear saleswoman who grows up essentially unparented (she refers to her childhood in Vancouver as "gasping" and "squalid")[10] and who moves to Calgary almost on a whim. She is an excellent sales rep, unrepentantly promiscuous, and, driving a 1959 Mercedes 300, filled with lust for travel: "How can she explain her inordinate lust to drive, to cover road miles, to use up gas? There is no map for longing."[11] Arachne first meets her lover Thomas when he leaves a map on the bus she's driving, and it is this object that initially draws her to him. His maps become her textbooks:

> From Calgary roads spider over the prairie. Arachne pores over Thomas' maps, the lines enticing her to quest beyond the city's radius. She gets into the car and sets the bonnet toward the sun. She is learning travel, the pace and progression of journey, the multifarious seduction of movement. She returns to Thomas vibrating at a pitch that he can take into his hands and drink. He is the author of those maps but he has never known their ultimate affirmation, the consummation of the pact between traveler and traveled. He only draws them; she traces them for him, leaving the pen-line of her passing.[12]

Arachne thinks over and over again that Thomas has saved her, but in fact she brings him a gift beyond price as well: the lived experience of his maps. The two of them are lovers literally under and over and through his maps, but it is only in leaving Thomas (however temporarily – this is another deliberately loose thread in the tapestry of the narrative) that Arachne can go beyond the map. In serving as textbook, the map (emblem of conquest and empire) empowers Arachne to create her own narrative: Arachne is not bound by the confines of the mapped landscape but enters a different, more flexible relationship with the terrain. She allows the landscape to become a player in her emotional life, both figuratively and quite literally; some of her deepest and most intimate moments come in physical connection with the land.

Arachne's prairie remaps that of Cather character Alexandra Bergson: While John Bergson, soon to be under the prairie himself, looks out the window and sees "the same land, the same lead-colored miles,"[13] his daughter Alexandra has a very different relationship with the land, a feeling that she and the land are connected in ways her less imaginative brothers cannot understand. This is what makes Alexandra's face radiant as she returns to the Divide from the river: "Even her talk with the boys had not taken away the feeling that had overwhelmed her when she drove back to the Divide that afternoon. She had never known before how much that country meant to her ... she had felt as if her heart were hiding down there somewhere."[14]

Here we see another Cather protagonist experiencing intense physical connection with the natural world, and the key to this moment is the language Cather uses to evoke Alexandra's emotional state. Unlike her brothers, Alexandra sees the land in more than financial terms. She is prosperous, but this prosperity is attributed to Alexandra's ability to respect the land. The typical male pioneer is thus differently gendered in this novel: While John Bergson and his sons, Lou and Oscar, engage the land and the new economy in various and variously unsatisfying ways, all connected with reaping financial benefit from land use, Alexandra, in her respect for and open-minded approach to the land and its needs, comes to both economic and spiritual rewards.

And the work of Alexandra's character extends beyond this vision of Cather's environmental awareness and beyond the usual "conflict ... around the situation of a woman assuming a male role, the criticism she must face when she does so, and the degree to which she can succeed under trying circumstances."[15] As I have already suggested, Alexandra does more than inhabit a male role: She creates a role the male characters in the novel lack the vision to imagine, never mind occupy. But she also sets the stage for what I am increasingly inclined to read as the complex construction of the character of Marie Shabata, yet another example of the ways Cather's environmental imagination advances her aesthetic project.

Carl Linstrum, on his first return visit to the old homestead, sees Emil and Marie from afar and knows they are looking for wild ducks. They do indeed find the ducks. Emil shoots five of them and drops them into Marie's apron: "As she stood looking down at them, her face changed. She took up one of the birds, a rumpled ball of feathers with the blood dripping slowly from its mouth, and looked at the live color that still burned on its plumage. As she let it fall, she cried in distress, 'Oh, Emil, why did you?'"[16]

Up to this point, the scene is a fairly standard one of belated regret at the transformation of wild things in death, but Marie reveals a more nuanced ability to be held accountable for her own actions when she continues: "Ivar's right about wild things. They're too happy to kill. You can tell just how they felt when they flew up. They were scared, but they didn't really think anything could hurt them. No, we won't do that anymore."[17]

This moment, significantly under the eye of an observer who cannot hear but rather feels "the import" of their conversation, both showcases Emil and Marie's growing intimacy and foreshadows their deaths. Carl Linstrum feels "unreasonably mournful" at the sight of them and, without being able to hear the words, feels for Emil and Marie the sadness that Marie feels for the now-silent ducks: that unthinking response to doomed creatures.

Later in the novel, after the news of Amédée's illness reaches her, Marie feels she cannot stay in the house and wanders through the orchard "like a white night-moth out of the fields."[18] She sits on the stile, considering what her life will be like now that she and Emil have acknowledged both their love and the impasse it produces, then walks across the pasture:

> She had scarce thought about where she was going when the pond glittered before her, where Emil had shot the ducks. She stopped and looked at it. Yes, there would be a dirty way out of life, if one chose to take it. But she did not want to die. She wanted to live and dream – a hundred years, forever! As long as this sweetness welled up in her heart, as long as her breast could hold this treasure of pain! She felt as the pond must feel when it held the moon like that; when it encircled and swelled with that image of gold.[19]

Marie has been, for the most part, a plaything for the various men who have taken an interest in her – a carefree and charming flirt even as a little girl, an ethnic beauty whose seemingly heedless behaviour has landed her in an unhappy marriage to the domineering, egotistical, and jealous Frank Shabata. Marie is also represented as Alexandra's only woman friend, another incongruous pairing. While she is described as "sincerely devout"[20] and attentive to elderly neighbours, up to this moment there has been hardly an inkling in the portrayal of Marie that she might be complex and thoughtful enough to look ahead to her future and consider the pros and cons of refusing to give in to her situation with Emil. It is not insignificant that Marie finds herself near the pond "where Emil had shot the ducks," the location of her own unprecedented empathy with them. The choice she is prepared to make preserves some sense of delight in life, a sense of respect for others, and the notion that she has significant agency in terms of her own future.

Marie has come to a place, both literal and figurative, where she can articulate her choice to give up romantic love in order to find a more "perfect love."[21] Her assertion that "we won't do that anymore" reflects back from the ill-fated sunrise expedition to shoot ducks to inform her resolution to live a full life without Emil, barely a day before Frank shoots them both. In her engagement with the water and the moon, Marie finds a truer voice than her earlier life has permitted, if only for a moment.[22]

Like some butterflies, Marie has a short time to live after discovering "the treasure of pain," but Cather allows her to "live a day of her new life."[23] The pond becomes window, mirror, mother – birthing a new and transformed Marie to live a life in a day. Susan Rosowski identifies this moment as part of Cather's process of "finding her way to her version of the West."[24] Water imagery is crucial to this vision, allowing a host of Cather's characters re-birth, revision, and the ability to reimagine the language of their storytelling. By the time Aritha van Herk comes along, enough has happened to narra-tive itself that this visionary work can look quite different.

The word "amorous" resonates from van Herk's subtitle in the picaresque novel *No Fixed Address,* back into that historical continuum I mentioned above, and toward (among others) Cather's *A Lost Lady,* suggesting that the strategy Cather uses in developing Marian Forrester as a character resur-faces, reimagined, in *No Fixed Address.* I focus on Marian because, of all Cather's women characters, Marian is the one imprisoned by economics, environ-ment, and the demands of her body in ways most similar, at least initially, to van Herk's Arachne. While Cather's characters in *A Lost Lady* are constrained by the very fact of the railroads – both economically and environmentally, as Sweetwater is a town created as a result of the railroad and "so much greyer today"[25] – van Herk can work with postmodern imagery of maps to give her characters an opportunity to try to cross tracks, remake lives, and create alternatives. Van Herk writes Arachne Manteia as a contrast to Marian Forrester.[26] In the process, the reader is drawn into a lecture on the history of women's underwear that continues for a page and a half, concluding:

> All that has changed and now, if we wear satin and lace we do so desirous of the proper consequences. We have forgotten our imprisonment, relegated underwear to the casual and unimportant ... No art, no novel, no catalogue of infamy has considered the effect of underwear on the lives of petty rogues.[27]

While few would describe Marian Forrester as a petty rogue, she has a lot in common with van Herk's protagonist. Arachne Manteia and Marian Forrester are both intensely sexual, sensual characters. Both have a man who keeps them tethered to a particular kind of respectable life of passable domesticity, with their reputations not *quite* free of smirch. Both characters have a novelistic companion who serves as interpretive lens: For Arachne, it is her only friend Thena, who speaks of Arachne's difference – to the reader? to the unknown researcher? – with pride and defiance; for Marian Forrester, it is Niel Herbert, who looks back on his first glimpse of her with pride "that at the first moment he had recognized her as belonging to a different world from any he had ever known."[28] In van Herk's novel, the maps work as alternative stories, windows of possibility for Arachne created by Thomas but brought to reality by her travels. It is only when she sees Thomas's maps that Arachne finds a way beyond both the constraints of the life she was born into and the artistic pain represented by the concert pianist Basilisk: "So Arachne is not wrong to credit Thomas with saving her. Only she knows how narrowly she has escaped, how closely the past treads on her heels, how with one stumble it can catch up with her."[29]

Van Herk's novel begins, then, with the fact of Arachne's absence, and the protagonist's first literal appearance is at a moment when she leaves the paved road for the marginal shoulder. She's thinking about her professional life, running comfortably through her knowledge of people and selling techniques and product – a product she refuses to use: "Although she might sell them, she cannot go around wearing bikini panties patterned with alligators. Ladies' Comfort cannot afford aberrance, so she must be dead ordinary. Still, it is fortunate no one ever checks. On principle, adamantly refusing to be her own best advertisement, Arachne wears nothing at all."[30]

Arachne is not a character willing to be contained in the way that Marian Forrester is contained: She will not be constrained by her clothes, and she will not live in a house like Marian's, "encircled by porches, too narrow for comfort."[31] Not only is Marian contained within the house, but it is not an easily accessible abode: "To approach Captain Forrester's property, you had first to get over a wide, sandy creek which flowed along the eastern edge of the town. Crossing this by the footbridge or the ford, you entered the Captain's private lane bordered by Lombardy poplars, with wide meadows lying on either side of it. Just at the foot of the hill on which the house sat, one crossed a second creek by the stout wooden road-bridge."[32]

(Sketch it; what does this map look like? Marian is trapped in this web, unlike other famous literary spiders, such as E.B. White's Charlotte, who create and dominate theirs. Also, unlike Charlotte, she is neither a good writer nor a good friend.) It's a process to get to the Forrester house and clearly a process to leave as well.[33] Arachne, on the other hand, begins her efforts to leave home by climbing fences at the age of three and continues in this mode throughout her adult life. She lives in Thomas's house without changing it at all: "He likes that, the way she took on his surroundings without rearranging one chair or cupboard."[34] Instead of making a home, infusing her surroundings with grace and charm, Arachne is able to reverse a feminine ideal, to live in Thomas's home without altering his domestic space.[35]

In a number of complexly evolved strategies, Willa Cather writes a woman's West in the way a mathematician shifts graphs of functions: She alters the axes of symmetry to reflect changes in the equation that defines the function. In Cather's work, the equation has changed the terms that define the value of the traditional male markers and mythology of the West and its land. Van Herk changes the terms of contemporary equations by hearing the conversations initiated by other writers. Her texts breathe air informed by a razor-sharp understanding of literary history; they exist in a kind of textual symbiosis, creating by their presence an environment conducive to multiple, evolving authenticities of understanding. Marlene Goldman notes that "when she enters the North, Arachne behaves like any other westerner. Searching for a frontier that can be colonized, she is both fearful and hopeful."[36] By the end of the novel (or the beginning since this has happened by the time the reader encounters the text), Arachne is looking for the edge of story, the place where the maps run out. She arrives in Calgary eager to belong to the land: "Field, Lake Louise, Banff, Canmore. As the mountains drop behind them and they level down, the sky fills with prairie, the immutable shape of the plain spread out like an embodied mirage. There is nothing Arachne can say, she is caught between her surprise and a sudden wrench to be part of this undulating plate of land ... Arachne is willing to acknowledge the truth, but she is unwilling to face the consequences."[37]

Yet it is the consequences of her relationship with the old artist Josef that push her north. Their initial encounter, over an exposed skull at Chief Crowfoot's grave, is full of hostility yet ends in amicable distrust. Still, it gives no hint of Josef's impact on Arachne's Calgary life. Their on-and-off relationship gets both of them in trouble with Josef's daughter; distrustful of Arachne, she cannot understand the other woman's desire to spend time with the old man. And it is when Arachne "springs" Josef from the nursing home and takes him on her sales route that she ends up in jail for kidnapping. When Thomas posts her bail, Arachne "gets into the Mercedes and drives west along the Trans-Canada highway."[38] As she gets further west, she begins to feel that she has made a mistake, should have headed east, but she keeps going.[39] For the first time, Arachne is making her own map: "This is the edge; not end but edge, the border, the brink, the selvage of the world. She can no longer go west. She is going north now but that will end soon; she has retraced her steps into this ultimate impasse and reached not frontier but ocean, only inevitable water."[40]

Although she thinks that "perhaps she will be able to find a place to settle in, to colonize," her next thought is not what it might mean to be the colonizer but instead "what has she to offer a raw place?"[41] The answer turns out to be underwear – as the unnamed researcher follows Arachne north in a rented truck:

A few miles up the road a flash of color makes you slam on your brakes. You slide out and step into the ditch, bend to retrieve it. The panties are gray with dust but their scarlet invitation has not faded, Ladies' Comfort. Another few miles and you find a peach pair, then a turquoise, then sunshine yellow. Each time you stop, shake the dust from their silky surface and toss them on the seat beside you. There is no end to the panties; there will be no end to this road.[42]

Strewing underwear like Hansel and Gretel scattered crumbs, Arachne is both divesting herself of the apparatus of the old life and making a different kind of story by adding those brilliant colours to the linear progression of the dusty road. Arachne keeps going, the underwear keeps going, the reader/ researcher keeps going. In an interview with Christl Verduyn in 1999, van Herk offered her own reading of the end of the novel: "At the end of *No Fixed Address,* when Arachne disappears off the edge of the mappable world, what she's doing is saying: the map cannot contain me; the rules, the way life is laid out, cannot keep me; the narrative isn't going to confine me. And she can come back when she chooses."[43] Cather imagines no such escape for Marian; she is bounded and confined by other people's stories about her. Niel Herbert sees the end of Marian's life in Sweetwater as a disappoint-ment: "Niel felt tonight that the right man could save her, even now. She was still her indomitable self, going through her old part, – but only the stagehands were left to listen to her."[44] In the end, he leaves "with weary contempt for her in his heart."[45] Mrs. Forrester goes south – not west, or north – when she leaves Sweetwater, ending her days in Buenos Aires, leav-ing behind a lifetime of attention for Captain Forrester's grave and the "warm wave of feeling"[46] that Niel Herbert and his boyhood acquaintance Ed Elliott share in their reminiscent discussion of her life and death. Both women leave their stories resonating among members of their communities: Al-though Marian Forrester is dead and Arachne Manteia, according to her friend Thena, certainly is not, their respective absences from their stories at the ends of both novels call particular attention to the way each is read by others – including the reader. Arachne had opportunities that Marian Forrester, written at a different historical time, could not have imagined. Both trace their amorous journeys across Wests (and Norths) bounded by railroads, convention, the edges of maps. Amorous: in their use of language, in their celebration of women's pleasure, in how their texts feel about the land. Even underwear can make an environmental statement.

Notes

1   Christl Verduyn, "The Grace of Living and Writing: An Interview with Aritha van Herk," in *Aritha van Herk: Essays on Her Works,* edited by Christl Verduyn (Toronto: Guernica, 2001), 15-30.

2   Arnold Davidson, *Coyote Country: Fictions of the Canadian West* (Durham: Duke University Press, 1994), 118.

3   The van Herk oeuvre must of course be seen as an *evolving* whole; she is only twenty-five or so years into what is certain to be a long writing career.

4   I have borrowed this phrase from Peter Mallios's comments on an early draft of this essay.

5 Van Herk's imagination of a scene in which Godfrey St. Peter is left alone in a room to masturbate took the notion of literary communion too far for some Cather aficionados.

6 "Come, my coach!
Good night, ladies; good night, sweet ladies,
Good night, good night."

7 Aritha van Herk, "Cather in Ecstasy," paper presented at the International Cather Seminar, Quebec City, Quebec, June 1995, unpaged.

8 Ibid.

9 Davidson, *Coyote Country*, 110.

10 Aritha van Herk, *No Fixed Address: An Amorous Journey* (Red Deer, AB: Red Deer College Press, 1986), 229.

11 Ibid., 138.

12 Ibid., 132.

13 Willa Cather, *O Pioneers* (New York: Houghton Mifflin, 1913), 8.

14 Ibid., 28.

15 Carol Fairbanks, *Prairie Women: Images in American and Canadian Fiction* (New Haven: Yale University Press, 1986), 171.

16 Cather, *O Pioneers*, 49.

17 Ibid., 50.

18 Ibid., 97.

19 Ibid., 98.

20 Ibid., 79.

21 Ibid., 102.

22 Within a larger context, the image of the moon in water recurs in *One of Ours*; Claude experiences a similar epiphany while bathing in the horse trough. These are, of course, only two in a series of important lunar images in Cather's work.

23 Cather, *O Pioneers*, 102.

24 Susan Rosowski, *Birthing a Nation: Gender, Creativity, and the West in American Literature* (Lincoln: University of Nebraska Press, 1999), 77.

25 Willa Cather, *A Lost Lady* (1923; reprint, New York: Vintage Press, 1971), 3.

26 We first meet Arachne Manteia, albeit indirectly, through an italicized, second-person address to an unnamed researcher (or the reader) following a title page inscribed "Notebook on a Missing Person": "*You discover in your search that the fashionable woman's shape has always been in a state of constant change*" (van Herk, *No Fixed Address*, 2). The researcher's distance is briefly reminiscent of Niel Herbert's effort to serve as narrator, but her investment in Arachne's story quickly mirrors Niel's emotional attachment to his vision of Mrs. Forrester.

27 Van Herk, *No Fixed Address*, 3.

28 Cather, *A Lost Lady*, 33.

29 Van Herk, *No Fixed Address*, 80.

30 Ibid., 6. The passage quoted above sets out some of the difficulty literary critics have had with van Herk: They would like her prose to be "dead ordinary," but even when she writes in an established genre form, her text wears no underwear; it is free of the staid conventions of literary propriety.

31 Cather, *A Lost Lady*, 4.

32 Ibid., 4-5.

33 Although Cather uses the web imagery here to emphasize the constraints of Marian's existence, she does use a similar image in *Shadows on the Rock* to cast a positive light on Cécile's place at the very heart of the new Canada: "Her mind roamed about the town and was dreamily conscious of its activities and of the lives of her friends; of the dripping grey roofs and spires, the lighted windows along the crooked streets, the great grey river choked with ice and frozen snow, the never-ending, merciless forest beyond. All these things seemed to her like layers and layers of shelter, with this shadowy, flickering room at the core." Willa Cather, *Shadows on the Rock* (New York: Alfred A. Knopf, 1931), 117-18. Van Herk responds to this in "Cather in Ecstasy" when she comments on the milliner's shop and its "maze-like rooms ... stories within stories."

34 Van Herk, *No Fixed Address*, 90.
35 Marlene Goldman argues that although "the text's subversive casting of a female picaresque character destabilizes certain narrative stereotypes ... this reversal does not prevent the text from maintaining significant links with traditional discourses." Marlene Goldman, "Go North Young Woman: Representations of the Arctic in the Writings of Aritha van Herk," in *Aritha van Herk: Essays on Her Works,* edited by Christl Verduyn (Toronto: Guernica, 2001), 35. I see this as fortunate: One of the traditional discourses with which van Herk maintains connections is the historical discourse of women writers writing the West, which lets us see Arachne as Marian's descendant.
36 Ibid., 35.
37 Van Herk, *No Fixed Address*, 80.
38 Ibid., 198.
39 Arachne keeps going even when it becomes increasingly clear that lived experience enhances mapped experience in unexpected ways: "Most cars turn back at Port Alberni. The highway changes, becomes tight and unnerving, vehicles are rammed against granite cliffs, plunged into depths of lakes; the road taunts and misleads deliberately" (ibid., 238). A mapped road cannot be read as possessing agency, but the lived road can.
40 Ibid., 239.
41 Ibid., 248.
42 Ibid., 260.
43 Verduyn, "The Grace," 22.
44 Van Herk, *No Fixed Address*, 143.
45 Ibid., 145.
46 Ibid., 150.

14
The Fall of the Wild? Feminist Perspectives of Canadian Wilderness Protection
Melody Hessing

Despite continuing efforts to protect Canada's heritage of undeveloped, "wild" areas, the decline of these "endangered spaces" challenges the potential for wilderness preservation.[1] The concept of "wilderness" reflects an evolving social, economic, and political context, and "wild" landscapes have long informed the Canadian sense of place and been a hallmark of this nation's identity.[2] Ideas about wilderness are at "the cutting edge of a conscious reconciliation with the origin of all things physical, biological, and cultural,"[3] but today Canada lags behind many other countries in the protection of "natural" and "endangered" areas. How can we explain the relative abundance but inadequate protection of wild areas in this country? This chapter argues that gender is a primary factor in the underprotection of Canadian wilderness. Conventional efforts to protect wilderness fail to resonate with the economic dynamics and cultural mosaic of contemporary Canadian society, especially as they are mediated by gender. The rhetoric, appeal, and implementation of wilderness protection do not acknowledge how social differences, especially gender, construct our perspectives of landscape. Gender remains unexplored as a potentially significant factor in the protection of the Canadian wilderness.

This chapter explores the potential of feminist approaches to understand and contribute to the issue of wilderness protection in Canada. It begins by examining the gendered character of conventional definitions of wilderness and then reviews the state of contemporary Canadian wilderness protection. A review of ecofeminist approaches considers both the connections and divisions between women and wilderness, providing a basis for exploring gendered strategies for the preservation of the Canadian wild. Canada's characterization as a staples economy in transition is discussed in terms of its restricted association of women with wilderness as well as its socioeconomic devaluation. The chapter argues that a gendered perspective provides a means to reconceptualize, revitalize, and extend contemporary efforts to protect Canadian wilderness.

Wilderness Preservation and Gender

Concepts about wilderness have evolved culturally and historically in response to a variety of material conditions and ideological forces.[4] Despite indigenous settlement and land claims and the impacts of contemporary technology, wilderness today is conventionally understood to be a place uninhabited by people and unaffected by human settlements and modification.[5] While greater harmony with the natural world may have been a guiding principle of prehistoric times, early agrarian societies viewed the wild as a "threat to human society; from the wilderness came barbarians to pillage and loot, beasts to prey on livestock, and pests to ruin the harvest."[6] By the nineteenth century, with increased recognition of resource limits in North America, wildlife conservation was directed to utilitarian ends in order to maintain habitat, wildlife, or other resources for future human use. Max Oehschlaeger notes that society has shifted "from viewing wild nature as merely a valuable resource (as a means to economic ends) and obstacle (wilderness must be conquered for a civilization to advance) toward a conception of wilderness as an end in its own right and an endangered species in need of preservation."[7] Escalating demographic growth, urbanization, and technological diffusion combine to package wilderness today as a commodity, an aesthetic and physical antidote to contemporary urban stress. The concept of "wilderness," then, has evolved from referencing the sacred to referencing a domesticated sublime, which in turn has represented a range of values from religious redemption, national renewal, and the passing of the frontier to the rejection of modernity and a rugged individualism.[8] Human ideas about wilderness are thus in transition, "intimately related to the evolving character of culture as human nature has articulated itself in particular places and times."[9]

Questions about the reasons for protecting wilderness, the character of wilderness, and the shifting relations between culture and nature permeate the wilderness discourse. Rationales for wilderness protection reflect diverse ethical, economic, and environmental objectives.[10] Ethical rationales for protection include the support of intrinsic values (all life has a right to exist for its own sake), heritage preservation, spiritual and aesthetic values, and cultural support. Economic reasons for the protection of watershed and soil underscore their significance for market transactions such as medicinal development and potential long-term resource use through tourism and job creation. The protection of wilderness also promotes the sustainability of ecological systems.[11] These support biodiversity and ecological integrity and in turn are the basis for the continuing support of all life systems on the planet.[12]

Yet, despite the diversity of reasons for wilderness protection, they have been predominantly anthropocentric and thus generated overwhelmingly on behalf of human interests. The interests of humans are seen as consistent with those of other species. While preservation objectives have increasingly included a biocentric perspective, they continue to emphasize human economic and recreational interests over those of other species and systems.[13] Moreover, although wilderness areas in Canada reflect considerable ecosystemic diversity, their distinguishing feature is the absence of human influence rather than their distinctive ecological attributes.

This anthropocentric and universalistic perspective on the wild also obscures an array of social differences – including those arising from gender, class, race, region, and nationality – that influence perceptions and experiences of wild places. Socio-economic disparities that may influence wilderness perspectives and use are glossed over by assumptions of wilderness as a collective good. Rationales for wilderness preservation tend to assume that all humans (and/or other species) share its benefits. Finally, the discourse on wilderness protection reflects a gender blindness; it fails to grasp how gender mediates perceptions and experiences of wild places.

Anthropocentrism and universalism obscure gender differences as well. An anthropocentric generic masculine pervades much of the canon of wilderness protection. The movement to celebrate wilderness has been developed, as Plumwood notes, from a white, middle-class, male perspective by writers such as Thoreau, Muir, Abbey, Leopold, and Snyder.[14] In the United States, the language of the Wilderness Act defines wilderness as a place "where the earth and its community of life are untrammeled by man, where man himself is a visitor who does not remain." As Eidsvik quotes Ian McTaggart-Cowan's justification for wilderness: "The maintenance of the best possible environment for future generations of men includes the maintenance of the entire gamut of variety in the living biota."[15] While the generic masculine is assumed to represent women, the notion of wilderness is not gender neutral.

Wilderness areas have been traditionally portrayed as an arena of male activity, whether through exploration, combat, or subjugation. As wilderness has "historically been construed as a man's world, a woman entering into that domain may feel that she is trespassing beyond the boundaries of her gender."[16] Women are underrepresented and unacknowledged in the context of wilderness. Gender is an unrecognized force in the protection of Canadian wilderness and thus invisible in the economic geography and cultural dynamics that have influenced this country's development.

Wilderness Protection in Canada

The existence of wild places is a defining characteristic of Canada not only in biophysical but also in cultural, social, and economic terms.[17] Canada's large mass, relatively small and concentrated human settlements, and limited industrial development have endowed this country with areas still relatively undisturbed. This nation's expansive size and proportionately small human population afford it an abundance of natural, undeveloped places.

Canada is the second largest country, with the longest coastline, of any nation on earth. Canada has a unique opportunity, as well as an obligation, to preserve its wilderness:

> Canada is a vast country in the enviable position of still having outstanding opportunities to conserve nature. Our country features the world's longest coastline, and encompasses an estimated 20 per cent of the world's remaining natural areas, 25 per cent of the world's wetlands, 20 per cent of the world's freshwater, and more than 10 per cent of its forests – including 30 per cent of the world's boreal forests.[18]

In Canada an ad hoc "preservation" of wild spaces has resulted from geographic inaccessibility and a recent history of colonization. Topographic ruggedness and a northern climate have restricted uniform settlement, while economic factors have also encouraged a concentration of population along transportation corridors and the southern border. Within a cultural tradition extolling human "survival" against the rigours of nature, 80 percent of Canadians today live in urban and primarily southern settings. Canada's potential for wilderness protection is also linked to the quantity and variety of large tracts of undeveloped areas and the high proportion of publicly owned land.

"Canadians face a particular challenge. The vast size of the country and of its resource endowment, particularly when measured on a per capita basis, has until recent times encouraged a sense of limitless potential."[19] Two centuries of extensive large-scale resource extraction have made "in-roads," both literally and metaphorically, on the natural landscape, fragmenting and degrading ecological systems. "Canada is ... home to widespread, natural resource-based industries and a growing population of more than 31 million people, heavily settled into a narrow band close to the U.S. border. Nature in Canada has changed in order to accommodate our presence and our needs."[20]

Canada hovers just above the global standard for the protection of wild areas, but its potential for protected areas far exceeds the norm in terms of the relative abundance and variety of natural features.[21] The World Commission on Environment and Development recommended in 1987 that 12 percent of a country's land be protected in natural areas.[22] Yet this 12 percent standard is inadequate and artificial, and fails to recognize the varied capacity and regional diversity of wild lands as well as ecological, cultural, and demographic variations. Globally, humans have already converted 29 percent of the planet's landmass to agriculture and urban use, and it is predicted that an additional one-third could be converted over the next century.[23] Projected increases in human populations and high standards of consumption pose a threat to remaining wild lands.

Although Canada is a country rich in natural areas, it is resistant to their protection.[24] While just over 11 percent of land in North America has been protected from development, only 9.6 percent of Canada has been designated as such.[25] The first Canadian national parks were established over a century ago[26] but today comprise less than 4 percent of the landmass.[27] There has been little protection of marine areas despite our rich and varied coastlines. In comparison, Costa Rica has protected 23.7 percent of its areas for conservation, the United States conserves 21.2 percent, and Australia has protected 13.6 percent of its land and marine areas.[28] In total, 8.83 percent of the earth's total area, including marine environments, has been protected.[29]

In Canada underrepresentation of the range of ecosystems and total land area, fragmentation of existing ecosystems, and inadequacy of the degree of protection remain problematic.[30] According to conservation biologists, protected areas should be as large as possible in order to retain ecological integrity, minimize species extinction, and promote biodiversity. Many Canadian ecosystems are endangered, while protection is unevenly implemented across regions and ecological features.[31] In British Columbia, 12.4 percent of the land base but only 7.2 percent of its grasslands are protected; most protected areas are smaller than ten square kilometres.[32] "Some areas of the province of British Columbia ... are more than 90 per cent fragmented by road access, with less than 1 per cent of their area protected in large parks or wilderness."[33]

The protection of wilderness not only means the preservation of physical biodiversity, but informs national identity. "The sine qua non of what we have chosen to identify as Canadian culture is the wilderness."[34] Widespread public support for wilderness protection in Canada indicates its significance as a public touchstone; in a 1999 poll, 91 percent of Canadians supported action to protect wilderness.[35] Stories ranging from historical accounts of settlement to fables of the early days of resource exploitation characterize this country as a wild place. Settlers have struggled to survive in this wildness and prosper from its resources. First Nations have claimed jurisdiction over many undeveloped areas although they do not necessarily identify unoccupied regions as "wild." While First Nations' perspectives of undeveloped areas may not necessarily be congruent with mainstream notions of "wildness," their resistance to pervasive regimes of resource extraction contributes to the diversity of definitions of the wild. In this country, ideas of "wilderness" have evolved from its association with the conquest of nature to concerns for its protection and have both "shaped our outlook and influenced our identity ... As we surrender our wild heritage, we surrender much of what distinguishes us as Canadians."[36]

Yet, as other chapters in this anthology indicate, the gendered bias of exploration and settlement has contributed to the invisibility of women's activity in the wild. The exploration and adventure of the Canadian wilderness is associated with a mythology of male adventure, extolling the exploits of Cartier, Franklin, Mackenzie, Fraser, Vancouver, and others. Descriptions of European settlement and the expansion of human activities into wild spaces have typically featured men's work in provisioning and resource extraction, while women have been associated with household labour. Hunting, fishing, and trapping have been characterized as predominantly male pursuits. Many recreational activities in wild areas, such as mountaineering, have traditionally been associated with men despite women's participation. How can we account for the lack of attention to women's association with Canadian wilderness? In what ways could a gendered analysis contribute to the protection of wilderness in this country?

Ecofeminist Approaches to the Environment

Ecological feminism, or "ecofeminism," explores the relations between women and the natural environment and provides a foundation from which to explore wilderness protection as a gendered construct. An ecofeminist exploration of the relations between human beings and the natural environment has the potential to explore gender as a feature of the struggle for wilderness protection in Canada. Carolyn Merchant observes that "women and nature have an age-old association – an affiliation that has persisted throughout culture, language, and history."[37] The oppression of women and the degradation of the natural world are seen by ecofeminists to be interconnected through the dynamics of patriarchal systems. Linkages between the biological, psychological, and spiritual characteristics of women and the character of the natural world have been explored by many ecofeminist writers.[38] Women's reproductive and nurturing activities are compared to those performed by ecological systems (such as biotic regeneration and habitat protection) for the survival of Gaia, the planet. Women's biology – sexuality, menstruation, birthing – is viewed as a source of empowerment.[39] The resuscitation of Goddess religions, and their celebration of the natural environment, is perceived as a source of women's authority.[40]

The linkage between wild landscapes and women is also explored by ecofeminists.[41] The wilderness "experience" is described as a gendered enterprise by one writer, who notes that in "subtle and significant ways women approach wilderness differently than men. On our own we usually walk slower and see more. When we are open to mystical thought we find extended meaning in natural objects."[42] A wilderness experience offers some women the opportunity to escape the domestic realm as well as the familial identity that entraps them. But the wild also offers a journey to potential and opportunity for women's empowerment, both physical and mental. A wilderness "experience" such as backpacking is identified by one writer as "a powerful tool in the quest for women's liberation."[43]

However, assertions that all women share physiological and psychological (as well as economic) characteristics are rejected by many contemporary ecofeminists as "essentialist."[44] Essentialism universalizes women's experience and attributes it to biological and genetic forces, reinforcing reproductive capacity and affective behaviour as a preferred natural order. While "strategic essentialism" is useful in promoting political change, it risks inaccuracy and backlash, such as the reinforcement of "natural" women. Women's nurturing character and spiritual longing are often viewed as intrinsic rather than the product of socialization and social organization. Women's closeness to nature and to animals is then understood as a natural predisposition rather than a learned trait. A selective anthropomorphism is reflected in parallels drawn between women's personalities and those attributed to animals, as illustrated by Clarissa Estés's *Women Who Run with the Wolves*.[45] Validation of the "feminine" reinforces and idealizes the biological characteristics of women.

Moreover, much of this literature points to individual rather than systemic solutions to environmental problems. The exploration of "the wild" in women becomes an exercise in personal growth, taking precedence over feminist and environmental political struggles. This not only reinforces an essentialist perspective, but also encourages an individualism that may deflect the political struggle for wilderness protection. The individual's search for personal fulfillment overrides an understanding of the biophysical wilderness and may both romanticize and appropriate the traditions that First Nations and other minority groups enact in their relations to wild spaces. This in turn ignores the perspectives of many women, ranging from First Nations women to ethnic minorities, who may entertain very different notions about the desirability of a wilderness experience. For instance, traditions of subsistence living in rural landscapes of developing countries may provide many Canadian immigrant women with a different sense of "the wild" than that shared by their Canadian-born counterparts. The commodification of wild spaces by culture, technology, and industry supports outdoor activity as a male-dominant activity, as a perusal of any *Outside* magazine confirms. Lack of attention to the significance of social and economic structure in the production of gender subordination and the emphasis on individual and psychological explanations encourage an "egofeminism" rather than an ecofeminism focused on the natural world.

Mainstream concepts of "wilderness" and the "wild" have been challenged by ecofeminists critical of the universalism and essentialism of these concepts.[46] Critics argue that concepts of the "wild" reflect a dualism through which the wild becomes the "other" of Western culture. Val Plumwood describes the domination of Western society over the wild, in which nature acts as a form of opposition to the "master identity."[47] Linda Vance argues that the protection of wilderness is connected to the larger political structure of domination and thus reflects the rationalist concept of controlling nature.[48]

The normative concept of wilderness as a place protected from human impacts thus becomes problematic. William Cronon argues that our contemporary vision of wilderness is flawed because "wilderness embodies a dualistic vision in which the human is entirely outside the natural. The place where we are is the place where nature is not."[49] Vance notes that the concept of wilderness as separate from human beings places humans at the centre of the definition of what is wild while homogenizing differences among wild areas. For her, the idea of wilderness "hyperseparates" the general Western conceptual division between culture and nature: "Idealizing wilderness as 'pure' or 'perfect' nature ensures two things: first, that a privileged few will always be able to shake off the yoke of civilization ... and revert to a temporary state of primal purity where they can be appropriately humbled in the presence of God's creation, then return restored and refreshed to the challenges of the human world; and second, that the inferiority of all other expressions of nature will be reinforced, thereby justifying continuing domination of them."[50]

Wilderness protection in this sense becomes a means of appropriating wild spaces for the use of the privileged and a means of subordinating the wild to human ends. The conservation of wilderness is pursued by and in the interests of those with power – the power of one group over another, of one place over another. Cronon argues that wilderness "tends to privilege some parts of nature at the expense of others"[51] and that the protection of certain areas as wild devalues those tainted by human contact

Furthermore, critics argue that cultural context produces varied concepts of nature. While the "otherness" of the wild – its exotic, complex, and unknown qualities – appeals increasingly in a world more homogeneous and technologically advanced, wilderness is not a universal good but one filtered through class, race, privilege, and culture. First Nations people, members of the working class, and people who live near toxic waste sites like the Sydney Tar Ponds do not necessarily benefit from wilderness protection. In the mainstream wilderness discourse, the ways that differences of social class, nationality, race, and ethnicity affect perspectives of the natural environment and wild spaces remain undifferentiated and generally unexamined.

While many contemporary ecofeminists advocate the preservation of wilderness as a feminist project, others challenge the dualism and elitism inherent in this issue. Potential solutions to a dualistic concept of the wild-human interface include the creation of an ecological feminist self that merges this dichotomy and fuses social alienation into a relation based on mutuality rather than domination.[52] Feminism's concern with the wellbeing of others, whether subordinated minorities, races, classes, or species, extends into a collective struggle for wilderness beyond the self. A feminist approach explores the source of dualism in the context of evolving economic relations with the land. How is it that "the wild" constitutes an "other" in Canadians' experience of landscape? How does gender mediate relations with wild spaces in Canada? How can we explain resistance to the conservation of wild areas? What are the material foundations of Canadians' connections to wildness, and how might these differ both among Canadians and within a global context?

Gender, Economics, and Wilderness Protection

Approaches to a Canadian wild landscape incorporate ecofeminist perspectives that reflect both its connection to and separation from society. The characterization of wilderness as both "home" and "other" is reflected in a Canadian political economy that orchestrates where we live and how we make a living. The tradition of a staples economy has characterized the Canadian wild as a resource (e.g, timber, fish, minerals, energy) valued primarily for extraction and export.[53] The manufacturing of resource-based commodities such as pulp and paper is based on resource exploitation as well.[54] Economic restructuring, globalization, and the development of a poststaples (e.g., knowledge- and service-based) economy[55] have implications for the relations between women and place as well as the concept of wilderness as protected area.

The connections between culture and nature are mediated by gender in large part due to the differences between women's and men's work. Wild spaces are portrayed as the traditional locus of work and "job site," as male terrain, surrendered to the conquest of men and male-operated technology. Resource exploitation is characterized as rugged, hazardous, tough, and dangerous, and those who have been associated with adventuring in it, surviving it – "taming" it – have been predominantly men. While Canadian employment in resource industries (logging, fishing, mining, and oil and gas) has diminished rapidly in recent decades, women are especially underrepresented. In 2002 only 1.8 percent of the Canadian labour force was directly employed in this sector, representing 2.8 percent of all men and 0.6 percent of all women.[56]

Women's historical underemployment in resource industries has contributed to their disassociation with the natural environment. It is not that women are simply missing from the picture. Rather, their marginalization in the terrain of wilderness conforms to a traditional model of female domestication. Women's household responsibilities, economic subordination, and social control limit their association with wild spaces. Women's continuing responsibility for domestic labour, and their unequal status in paid work, has contributed to a dual subordination in both households and the workplace.[57] Women have been restricted from direct experience of wild places by a cultural and physical "confinement," while their domestication benefits others socially and economically. The rewards for women's cheap and unpaid labour in households, schools, hospitals, and industry "trickle up" through the system to partners, employers, and society, as ecological systems support biological infrastructure. Much of the work that women do, whether in the factory or the household, involves the transformation of ecosystem products into socially consumable goods through the basic provision of food, shelter, and clothing. When women are employed in resource manufacturing, such as fish-processing plants, their work involves the conversion of wild "produce" into commodities distanced from the ecosystems that generate them.[58]

Market models devalue not only women's contributions, but also those of the wild. Natural environments are characterized as "resources" and in turn reduced to "natural capital" in an economic system predicated on growth and profit. The wild environment is a resource to be harvested and sold for the maximization of profits. Contemporary market paradigms result in "overshoot": the exploitation of resources beyond "carrying capacity."[59] Markets maximize profitability by externalizing the environmental costs of resource extraction. The value of wilderness in supporting ecological systems through water filtration, carbon absorption, and soil stabilization is invisible in market terms. The by-products of production – pollution, toxic dumps, resource shortages – are deflected to the public and to future generations in the form of health care costs related to illnesses such as asthma and cancer. Women in turn absorb the long-term costs of these environmental damages in the roles of nurse, mother, and caregiver.[60]

The economic and cultural roots of women's and nature's subordination are entwined in a global market system that supports the interests of capital and patriarchy while articulating women's association with the natural world. Economic globalization blankets the world in a market paradigm, under which the former "wild" is homogenized to market dimensions, as with timber or ecotourism on a global scale. High levels of foreign investment in the Canadian economy, in addition to the requirements of the North American Free Trade Agreement (NAFTA), make it difficult for this nation, like many others, to resist market imperatives. Increased markets, new technology, and the deregulation of standards have accelerated resource extraction over recent decades, leading to overfishing and the "falldown" effect in the timber industry.[61] With economic restructuring due to globalization and resource overshoot, women have become increasingly responsible for contributions to the financial support of the household. Unemployment has created economic stress and encouraged the depopulation of the hinterland as families move to urban areas, where they are further distanced from the natural environment.

The protection of wild spaces is thus hindered by the economic devaluation of women and natural environments in a global context of political and economic activity.[62] Within this universal context, however, there is considerable variation, reflecting differences of geography, race, and class as well as gender.[63] Women in wealthy countries benefit from the exploitation of ecological and social capital – that is, the resources and labour of women in less developed countries. Women in developed countries such as Canada are systemically linked to those in poor countries as exploiters of their environments – for example, as consumers of coffee or produce grown in these countries. The exploitation of global resources by wealthy countries also encourages the erosion of wild areas in poor countries as lands are brought into production for export markets. Ideas of "wilderness" and its protection are likely to be viewed by many as an initiative of Western culture and/or the expropriation of indigenous and traditional lands for Western consumption. Meanwhile, shifts in the global environment – including industrialization and urbanization, damages to the land due to poor agricultural practices, accelerating population growth, and an evolving commodification of nature through activities such as ecotourism – reshape the value of wild areas in less developed countries as well. Global development has "destroyed women's productivity both by removing land, water and forests from their management and control, as well as by the ecological destruction of soil, water and vegetation systems so that nature's productivity and renewability have been impaired."[64]

Women and wilderness are thus connected to the Canadian culture through a web of changing social and economic relations in which resource-market forces challenge wilderness protection. Multinational logging interests associate wilderness protection with the loss of timber licences, corporate profits, and household paycheques. To resist the allocation of the annual allowable cut in favour of greater protection of natural areas is to challenge an underlying patriarchal and capitalist economic structure. The maintenance of jobs and profits is bolstered by an ideology that justifies them as natural, eternal, and for the public good. Constructing wilderness protection as the primary source of unemployment ignores the larger, long-term context of the relations between humans and nature. These extend beyond corporate strategies for the short-term maximization of profit to include the long-term social, political, economic, and aesthetic relations of humans to the wild. The lack of value-added processing in the timber industry in British Columbia, inadequate silviculture, overharvesting, international-market competition, "free-trade" agreements, technological innovation, and dramatic increases in current logging practices bear responsibility for job loss, but the spectre of wilderness preservation is targeted as the "fall guy" for an economy in distress.[65]

In this context, the protection of wilderness challenges the continuing large-scale extraction of resources. Yet a perceived opposition between pro- and antiprotection groups is a constructed dualism that is not only divisive but simplistic and artificial. The preservation of wilderness is identified by resource interests as a white, urban, elitist pursuit that restricts already-scarce jobs and destroys resource communities, a "war in the woods" between environmentalists and loggers. Not only does this construction ignore class and power differences in communities and corporations, but it obscures gendered differences in employment and power. The characterization of the wilderness "debate" as a dualism also disregards the diverse and potentially cross-cutting interests of women, from environmental leaders to employees, wives, mothers, and community members. It neglects consideration of regional variation as well as a range of positions that remain invisible and unarticulated by other "multiple stakeholders" whose interests may oppose conventional land-use planning.

In a pluralist, multicultural society in which most land is publicly owned, democratic notions of multiple stakeholders assume the existence of a diversity of interests and perspectives on land-use issues. Considerable amounts of the Canadian land base remain undeveloped, but much of this area has been dedicated, both ideologically as well as contractually, to resource extraction. Although First Nations land claims challenge assumptions of corporate stewardship of the land, undeveloped areas have long been perceived as inherently exploitable for employment and profit. While over 90 percent of this country is publicly owned, the licensing of Crown lands to private industry for exploitation has resulted in a de facto privatization that obscures and hinders public access and stewardship.

The shift to a poststaples economy with greater economic diversification is also problematic for the preservation of wilderness. The transition to a value-added economy, the remediation of resource practices, and the internalization of environmental costs appear to be compatible with gendered and ecological benefits. Yet economic diversification does not contribute to the conservation of wild areas without larger structural changes. Economic diversity fails to alter women's continuing responsibility for domestic labour or the societal devaluation of this work. The devaluation of ecological systems continues to erode the value of the wild. Ecotourism, which would appear to sustain wild environments as its source of income, may also be responsible for their degradation. Ecotourist employment is seasonal and nonunionized, may degrade sensitive environments, and creates imbalances along class, ethnic, and racial lines as well as between local service workers and visiting tourists. Ecotourism is also problematic, as "wilderness becomes a special unit of property treated like a historic relic or ruin – a valuable remnant ... Wilderness as relic always converts places into commodities, because tourism, in its various manifestations, is a form of commerce."[66] As

Turner notes, both groups "exploit the wild, the first by consuming it, the second by converting it into a playpen and then consuming it."[67]

The addition of women to an economic equation that devalues and exceeds ecological carrying capacity further erodes the potential to conserve wilderness. Increased employment of women in resource regimes permeated by class, race, and gender inequalities also fails to address the inherent asymmetry of the underlying economic structure. Differential access to and perspectives of wilderness are not homogenized through the promotion of gender equity in existing regimes of resource extraction. Moreover, women's employment in resource sectors is not to be conflated with "wilderness experience." Moreover, those who are closer to nature "by view of geographic proximity to 'wilderness' may nonetheless be alienated from nature as the price of their survival in Western culture."[68] Ultimately, wild spaces represent potential market assets, and resource extraction is inconsistent with the preservation of the wild. It is only within the context of an economy directed to the sustainability of its biophysical systems that women's increased participation and the protection of wild spaces become potentially compatible. Indeed, women's increased participation in resource employment does not resolve, but may expedite, the demise of the wild.

A gendered legacy of resource extraction and the ideological prioritization of these interests continue to restrict the protection of wild areas as they have restricted women's association with the wild. In a poststaples economy, wilderness is still viewed as the repository of scarce jobs, its value utilitarian and anthropocentric within the context of a competitive global market. Although communities receive jobs and paycheques from resource extraction, foreign ownership and control alienate a large share of profits and economic benefits. Within communities, wealth is unevenly shared, with women and children likely to be economically dependent or subordinate. The association of wild spaces with universal economic gain through resource extraction makes protection a fiscal liability rather than a long-term asset. Furthermore, it obscures the differentiation of wealth along gendered lines. The portrayal of an either/or relationship between wilderness preservation and economic viability restricts support for wilderness and offers narrow, short-term responses to complex, long-term issues.

The Canadian landscape continues to be defined not only in anthropocentric and androcentric but also in market-based terms, reinforcing the dualistic character of our relations with the wild. While wilderness is understood to be gender neutral, its association with male exploration and employment perpetuates a gender bias that restricts appeals for its protection. A gendered remediation within the existing paradigm, such as the increased employment of women and the internalization of ecological costs, is not a sufficient foundation for protecting wild spaces. The economic determinism of market models understates the full array of social relations with the natural world. Markets fail to recognize the integrity, abundance, and complexity of life beyond the human scale. Ideas about wilderness resist and transcend a purely economic treatment. Wilderness embodies systems of essence, knowledge, and aesthetics not yet fully explored or embraced. Our humility[69] in the face of the complexity and diversity of wild systems potentially adds value, in the fullest sense. How might we forge a closer and more informed relationship with the biophysical world in which we live? This will require more than adding value to the wild in market terms, but rather the articulation and implementation of values beyond the market.

The Fall of the Wild? Gender and Wilderness Protection in Canada

In Canada the relative abundance of wild areas and the symbolic association of identity with natural landscapes have prompted renewed concern for the protection of natural areas. The shrinkage of potential "wild" areas, fragmentation of habitat, rapid population increase, escalating resource depletion, and encroachment of human activity on wild lands threaten the future of wild landscapes. But the protection of wilderness is constrained by numerous factors. The relative abundance of undeveloped space in this country diminishes the sense of urgency for its protection. Local struggles for the protection of specific areas may be strategically useful, but they are not necessarily linked to the larger national context of wilderness, which limits interprovincial and international comparison. While the wild may be romanticized as a cultural icon, increased urbanization and the depopulation of hinterland areas reduce direct experience with undeveloped spaces. A generalized wilderness advocacy may obscure the ecological and social uniqueness of specific places. While critical perspectives explore the inequities of power inherent in human-nature relations, concerns for ecological integrity are often overlooked. The diffuse appeal of wilderness protection and the lack of an ecologically specific perspective within a context of foreign media control and increased cultural homogenization also diminish a Canadian perspective. Inadequate management resources, overuse of already protected areas, and the "bureaucratization" of the wild in existing protected areas establish a negative precedent for protection.

Wilderness is endangered not only as a physical entity, but also as a symbolic reference. In Canada the term "protected area" has gained acceptance because of political sensitivity, ecological ambiguity, and pragmatism. A protected area is "an area of land and/or sea especially dedicated to the protection and maintenance of biological diversity, and of natural and associated cultural resources, and managed through legal or other effective means."[70] "Protected areas" incorporate a diversity of perspectives, such as those of First Nations, who do not traditionally perceive natural landscapes as "wild." The term incorporates a greater diversity of areas, including those already impacted by development, as well as a greater range of management regimes (including resource use). It encompasses urban landscapes as well as those already impacted by human activity. Recognition of the encroachment of humans on wild lands, the increase in developed and roaded landscapes, and the broad range of cultural values about wild lands have also encouraged the use of the term "protected area."

Yet the decline of the discourse on "wilderness," and its replacement by a focus on "protected areas," is more than a linguistic substitution. While "wilderness" points to the "otherness" of landscape, defined by its exclusion from or minimization of human impacts, "protection" assumes the presence of human beings as stewards of the land. Areas are to be "protected" from human interference or impact. While wilderness refers to a place set apart from human impact, protected areas are sheltered under a mantle of benevolent anthropocentrism. The designation "protected area" allows for flexibility in the preservation of natural features, but it also obscures the character and degree of protection of wild lands. "Protected areas" accommodates the demise, rather than the preservation, of the wild and further lulls us into complacency about the state of the natural environment.

Ecofeminist perspectives contribute to our concepts and strategies for the preservation for the wild. Women's traditional underrepresentation in the wild indicates the potential for identifying more complex and diverse understandings of a wilderness experience, derived from the experience of a variety of social locations – immigrants, First Nations, and other minorities. This social variation in wilderness experience already exists but remains unacknowledged, beneath the surface of a normative wilderness experience. As feminism informs our sense of the wild, and our reasons for its protection, so wilderness offers the potential to invigorate feminism. The investigation of diverse perspectives of wild spaces, including those of First Nations and other minority groups as well as women in rural and hinterland communities, addresses social and regional inequalities in Canadian development. Attention to the natural world – both its diversity and complexity – infuses feminism with the possibility of investigating a biophysical universe that we have largely subordinated to social projects. Many women have been compelled by wilderness, whether through their labour, settlement patterns, recreation, or spiritual affinity. Women such as Colleen McCrory, Vicky Husband, Elizabeth May, and Tzeporah Berman have been leaders in the campaign for wilderness protection. Their political organization, education, and vigilance promote a stewardship of wild places.

"Canadian wilderness" is a contradiction in that it is perceived as central to our national image yet is considered to be separate from human activity. Cronon argues that the central task is not the polarization of wild and civilized but the incorporation of both into the making of home. Canada has the potential to do just that. The reconstructive transformation of this wild "homeland" from an unlimited "re/source" into an ecologically differentiated and culturally diverse place is a necessary and significant project. This will require political will, public education, and the cultural and economic revaluation of the wild. But it will also require diligence. Adding women's voices to the existing array of stakeholders portends greater use of wilderness areas, more regulations and regulators, and a potentially diminished wild. Although the incorporation of diverse perspectives in a new wilderness ethic may appeal, it is also more than possible that they will further compromise conventional ideals of wilderness. Increased inclusion of difference may coopt wilderness, carving up endangered spaces into user-friendly areas with varying degrees of wildness. This variability may enhance human experience of the wild, but it may as easily dilute and tame its character.

Contemporary approaches to wilderness ask us to rethink our views regarding wilderness protection, especially in Canada, where "wilderness ceases to be an absolute and becomes a contingency, remarkable not for its separateness from human culture but for its connectedness to it."[71] Gender provides a lens to understand the alienation from wilderness experienced by many women as a product of social subordination, patriarchal control, and cultural domesticity. Conventional rationales for wilderness protection based on universality and inclusion may be restrictive in a social climate that celebrates diversity and that makes its "home" in a constellation of varied ecological systems. Ecofeminist approaches to wilderness hinge on both identification with and distance from "nature," embracing both the "otherness" of the wild and its familiarity as home. But ecofeminists are equally wary of the potential domestication of the "other" and support the integrity of other living things and other biotic systems that resist cohabitation.

The Canadian wilderness is already "home" to Canadians; it is the lack of acknowledgment and respect for this wild "homeland" that puts it at risk. Canada has the capacity for wilderness preservation unmatched by any nation. Possessing one-fifth of the total remaining wilderness on this planet, Canada has both the potential as well as a global responsibility to protect these "endangered spaces" for future generations.[72] A feminist perspective of wilderness understands its resonance for women and for others whose voices have not yet been heard. The revisioning of wild areas as abundant, ecologically rich, and culturally resonant with a diverse Canadian society has the potential to command public attention and political will. The protection of wilderness offers the opportunity to revision who we are and what our relations with the natural environment might be. Perhaps then we can begin to know and respect the integrity of the wild as Canada's greatest legacy.

Notes

1   See Monte Hummel, ed., *Endangered Spaces: The Future for Canada's Wilderness* (Toronto: Key Porter, 1989).

2 See John Wadland, "Wilderness and Culture," in *Consuming Canada: Readings in Environmental History,* edited by Chad Gaffield and Ann Gaffield (Toronto: Copp Clark, 1995), 12-15; Kevin McNamee, "From Wild Places to Endangered Spaces: A History of Canada's National Parks," in *Parks and Protected Areas in Canada: Planning and Management,* edited by Philip Dearden and Rick Rollins (Toronto: Oxford University Press, 1993), 17-54.

3 Max Oehschlaeger, *The Idea of Wilderness* (New Haven: Yale University Press, 1991), 349.

4 See especially ibid.; Jack Turner, *The Abstract Wild* (Tucson: University of Arizona Press, 1996); William Cronon, ed., *Uncommon Ground: Toward Reinventing Nature* (New York: Norton, 1995); David Rothenberg, ed., *Wild Ideas* (Minneapolis: University of Minnesota Press, 1995); David Rothenberg and Marta Ulvaeus, eds., *The World and the Wild* (Tucson: University of Arizona Press, 2001).

5 William Cronon, "The Trouble with Wilderness, or Getting Back to the Wrong Nature," in Cronon, ed., *Uncommon Ground,* 69-90.

6 Oehschlaeger, *Idea,* 347.

7 Ibid., 4.

8 Cronon, ed., *Uncommon Ground.*

9 Oehschlaeger, *Idea,* 5.

10 Harold Eidsvik, "Canada in a Global Context," in Hummel, ed., *Endangered Spaces,* 30-49.

11 See Bill Devall and George Sessions, *Deep Ecology: Living as If Nature Mattered* (Salt Lake City: Peregrine Smith, 1985).

12 John B. Theberge, "Ecology, Conservation, and Protected Areas in Canada," in *Parks and Protected Areas in Canada: Planning and Management,* edited by Philip Dearden and Rick Rollins (Toronto: Oxford University Press, 1993), 139.

13 Paul F.J. Eagles, "Parks Legislation in Canada," in Dearden and Rollins, eds., *Parks,* 57-74, 62.

14 Val Plumwood, *Feminism and the Mastery of Nature* (New York: Routledge, 1993).

15 Eidsvik, "Canada," 41.

16 Cheryll Glotfelty, "Femininity in the Wilderness: Reading Gender in Women's Guides to Backpacking," *Women's Studies* 25, 5 (September 1996): 447.

17 George Altmeyer, "Three Ideas of Nature in Canada, 1893-1914," in Gaffield and Gaffield, eds., *Consuming Canada,* 96-118.

18 World Wildlife Fund Canada, "Setting Conservation Priorities in the Twenty-First Century," in *The Nature Audit: Report No. 1-2003* (Toronto: World Wildlife Fund, 2003), <http://www.wwf.ca/>.

19 Iain Wallace, *A Geography of the Canadian Economy* (Toronto: Oxford University Press, 2002), 42.

20 World Wildlife Fund Canada, "Setting Canada's Conservation Agenda for the 21st Century." Available at <wwf.ca.AboutWWF/WhatWedo/TheNatureAudit/TheNatureAudit. asp?page=0.0>.

21 See Michael J.B. Green and James Paine, "State of the World's Protected Areas at the End of the Twentieth Century," paper presented at the symposium "Protected Areas in the 21st Century: From Islands to Networks," IUCN World Commission on Protected Areas, Albany, Australia, 24-29 November 1997.

22 World Commission on Environment and Development (WCED), *Our Common Future* (New York: Oxford University Press, 1987).

23 Gregory Mock, "Domesticating the World: Conversion of Natural Ecosystems," in *World Resources 2000-2001: People and Ecosystems: The Fraying Web of Life* (Washington, DC: World Resources Institute, 2000). See <http://earthtrends.wri.org/pdf_library/features/bio_feat_convert.pdf>.

24 Wadland, "Wilderness."

25 World Resources Institute, *World Resources 1992-93* (New York: Oxford University Press, 1992), 124.

26 McNamee, "From Wild Places."

27 In 1999, 3.8 percent of Canada was devoted to national parks, in comparison with a global ratio of 2.3 percent. World Conservation Monitoring Center (WCMC), *Protected Areas Database* (Cambridge, UK: WCMC, May 1999).

28 Ibid.
29 Green and Paine, "State of the World's," 7.
30 Dearden and Rollins, eds., *Parks;* Lee E. Harding and Emily McCullum, "Protected Areas in British Columbia: Maintaining Natural Diversity," in *Biodiversity in British Columbia: Our Changing Environment,* edited by Lee E. Harding and Emily McCullum (Ottawa: Environment Canada and the Canadian Wildlife Service, 1994), 355-74.
31 Theberge, "Ecology," 137; Harding and McCullum, "Protected Areas."
32 Harding and McCullum, "Protected Areas," 364.
33 Ibid., 237.
34 Wadland, "Wilderness," 14.
35 Federal Provincial Parks Council, "Protecting a Legacy for Canadians: Overview," <http://www.cd.gov.ab.ca/preserving parks/fppc/>, 1.
36 Bruce Littlejohn, "Wilderness and the Canadian Psyche," in Hummel, ed., *Endangered Spaces,* 13, 19.
37 Carolyn Merchant, *The Death of Nature: Women, Ecology and the Scientific Revolution* (London, UK: Harper and Row, 1983), xv.
38 See especially Irene Diamond and Gloria Feman Orenstein, eds., *Reweaving the World: The Emergence of Ecofeminism* (San Francisco: Sierra Club Books, 1990); Judith Plant, *Healing the Wounds: The Promise of Ecofeminism* (Toronto: Between the Lines, 1989).
39 Dolores Lachappelle, *Earth Wisdom* (Boulder, CO: Guild of Tutors Press, 1978).
40 Riane Eisler, *The Chalice and the Blade* (San Francisco: Harper Collins, 1987); Ynestra King, "Healing the Wounds: Feminism, Ecology and the Nature/Culture Dualism," in Diamond and Orenstein, eds., *Reweaving the World,* 106-21.
41 Susan Griffin, *Woman and Nature: The Roaring inside Her* (San Francisco: Harper and Row, 1978).
42 Maggie Nichols, *Wild, Wild Woman,* cited in Glotfelty, "Femininity," 441.
43 Ibid., 446.
44 See Catriona Sandilands, *The Good Natured Feminist: Ecofeminism and the Quest for Democracy* (Minneapolis: University of Minnesota Press, 1999).
45 Clarissa Pinkola Estés, *Women Who Run with the Wolves: Myths and Stories of the Wild Woman Archetype* (New York: Ballantine Books, 1992).
46 See Sandilands, *Good Natured;* Chris J. Cuomo, *Feminism and Ecological Communities: An Ethic of Flourishing* (New York: Routledge, 1998); Mary Mellor, *Feminism and Ecology* (New York: New York University Press, 1997).
47 See Plumwood, *Feminism.*
48 Linda Vance, "Ecofeminism and Wilderness," *National Women's Studies Association Journal* 9, 3 (1997): 60-77.
49 Cronon, ed., *Uncommon Ground,* 80-81.
50 Vance, "Ecofeminism," 3.
51 Cronon, ed., *Uncommon Ground,* 86.
52 See Plumwood, *Feminism.*
53 Wallace, *Geography.*
54 For a discussion of the character of the Canadian political economy, see Wallace, *Geography;* Melody Hessing and Michael Howlett, *Canadian Natural Resource and Environmental Policy: Political Economy and Public Policy* (Vancouver: UBC Press, 1997).
55 Wallace, *Geography,* 1-4.
56 Statistics Canada, CANSIM.11, Table 282-0008, 2002, <http://www.statcan.ca/english/Pgdb/labor/obhtm>.
57 Heidi Hartmann, "The Family as the Locus of Gender, Class, and Political Struggle: The Example of Housework," *Signs: Journal of Women in Culture and Society* 6, 3 (1981): 366-94.
58 See Barbara Neis, "In the Eye of the Storm: Research, Activism and Teaching within the Newfoundland Fishery Crisis," *Women's Studies International Forum* 23, 3 (May/June 2000): 287-92; Martha Macdonald, "Lessons and Linkages," *Women and Environments International Magazine* 54/55 (Spring 2002): 19-23.
59 Rees defines carrying capacity as "the maximum rate of resource consumption and waste discharge that can be sustained indefinitely in a given region without progressively impair-

ing the functional integrity and productivity of relevant ecosystems." William E. Rees, "Ecological Footprints and Appropriated Carrying Capacity: What Urban Economics Leaves Out," *Environment and Urbanization* 4 (October 1992): 125.

60 Jacob Songsore and Gordon McGranahan, "The Political Economy of Household Environmental Management: Gender, Environment and Epidemiology," *World Development* 26, 3 (1998): 395-413.

61 M.P. Marchak, S.L. Aycock, and D.M. Herbert, *Falldown: Forest Policy in British Columbia* (Vancouver: David Suzuki Foundation and Ecotrust Canada, 1999).

62 See Hilkka Pietila and Jane Vickers, *Making Women Matter* (London, UK: Zed Books, 1990).

63 See Maria Mies and Vandana Shiva, *Ecofeminism* (London, UK: Zed Press, 1993); Vandana Shiva, *Staying Alive: Women, Ecology and Development* (London, UK: Zed Press 1988).

64 Vandana Shiva, "Development as a New Project of Western Patriarchy," in Diamond and Orenstein, eds., *Reweaving the World,* 189-200.

65 See Aaron Doyle et al., "Framing the Forests: Corporations, the B.C. Forest Alliance, and the Media," in *Organizing Dissent,* edited by W. Carroll, 2nd ed. (Toronto: Garamond, 1997), 240-68.

66 Turner, *Abstract Wild,* 86.

67 Ibid., 87.

68 Greta Gaard, "Ecofeminism and Wilderness," *Environmental Ethics* 19, 1 (1997): 10.

69 Sandilands, *Good Natured.*

70 Green and Paine, "State of the World's," 1.

71 Vance, "Ecofeminism," 9.

72 World Wildlife Fund Canada, "Setting Conservation Priorities."

15
A Vision of Transformation: Ecofeminist Spiritualities in Canada
Heather Eaton

Spirituality is an intriguing aspect of the Canadian environmental and feminist movements. New spiritual sensitivities are emerging due to the number of environmental and women's issues that have arisen and an increased awareness of the magnificence and splendour of life. Bringing forth a spiritual dimension can evoke what is most profound, rousing insightful visions and psychic energies.

Ecofeminist spiritualities are growing and taking many forms. The spiritual dimension of the ecological crisis has been perceived for some time[1] and has been an aspect of ecofeminism from the beginning.[2] There remain questions to be posed concerning the relationship between spirituality and ecology. Spirituality is a potent social force. It can also be an escape or fantasy. Although the intersection of ecofeminism with spirituality opens many new pathways, from historical critiques to an abundance of new expressions, rituals, and activism, there is a vacuum of discussion surrounding what is meant by spirituality. What characteristics must spirituality possess for it to be a socially transformative and political force rather than merely personal comfort? Where is the transformative nexus between spirituality, feminism, and ecology?

This chapter will describe what is occurring in Canada at the nexus of ecology, feminism, and spirituality. A second section addresses the richness and potential of spirituality. The third section is a discussion of how an in-depth understanding of spirituality and socio-political transformation could enhance ecofeminist efforts in Canada.

Spirituality, Ecology, and Feminism in Canada
As there is no conspicuous public force comprising ecofeminist spiritualities in Canada, a first step is to assess the environmental movement in Canada for an integration of spirituality and feminism. The second is to examine the presence of ecological issues and spirituality within Canadian

expressions of feminisms. A third is to estimate the influence of feminism or ecological concerns within Canadian religious organizations.

The Environmental Movement: Feminist and Spiritual Concerns

Twenty years ago (in most places, only ten years ago) ecological concerns did not register much on the social landscape, except by a few prominent individuals such as David Suzuki, Rosalie Bertell, and John Livingston. An absence of ecological concern also existed within social-justice movements, as social and ecological problems were framed as competing needs. Ecological concerns now figure on the cultural landscape, albeit unevenly and within different ecological paradigms. In addition, it would be inaccurate to describe the Canadian environmental movements as cohesive or even like-minded. There are "dozens or more new ecological ideologies, each with its cadre of articulate advocates and ardent followers."[3]

In general, the mainstream environmental movement in Canada, a term used here with some hesitation, has incorporated neither feminist analyses nor spirituality. One can look at the research of Environment Canada or of alternative nongovernmental organizations such as Greenpeace or the Sierra Club of Canada and note the serious and innumerable environmental issues each is tackling. Yet, in general, neither feminism nor spirituality is a pertinent lens through which to examine environmental problems in Canada, although it may be important to individuals. If either is specified, it is at particular moments. There are sporadic references to women's health concerns, some research on women and farming or fisheries, and a mention here and there of indigenous spiritualities conceived in relation to Mother Earth. The Sierra Club of Canada and the David Suzuki Foundation have explicitly connected spirituality to some of their events.[4] Nonetheless, in general, feminism and spirituality are not regularly incorporated by known organizations representing environmental consciousness in Canada.

Canadian Feminisms: Ecological and Spiritual Concerns

Given the difficulty of accurately assessing the extent to which ecological concerns are incorporated into the Canadian feminist agenda, one avenue is to look at some national women's/feminist organizations. Those researched were the Status of Women Canada, the National Action Committee on the Status of Women, the Canadian Research Institute for the Advancement of Women (CRIAW), Match International, the Fédération nationale des femmes canadiennes-françaises, and the National Council of Jewish Women of Canada. It is interesting – disturbing – to note that environmental issues are not on the official agenda of any.[5] Even national events rarely include environmental issues. For example, at a CRIAW conference whose subject was "Feminist Definitions of Caring Communities and Healthy Lifestyles," environmental issues, clearly relevant to the topic, were absent.[6] Although some organizations may list "environment" as an important consideration for women, they rarely articulate more than this.[7]

Perhaps a change is on the horizon. The Fédération nationale des femmes canadiennes-françaises is part of a feminist coalition that sponsored a conference on women's health in 2002 with the Centre for Feminist Research at York University, at which environmental issues were one of three themes. They wrote: "There is an increasing recognition amongst activists that women's health issues need to be examined and addressed from a wider, more integrated perspective that includes the social, cultural and environmental determinants of health. To date a considerable amount of work has been done in each of these areas. However, while sexual and reproductive health issues and the social determinants of health have gained some recognition, environmental issues have not been fully integrated to produce a holistic analysis of health."[8]

Still, one can peruse feminist events[9] or examine the mandates of most known feminist organizations and note that environmental issues are seldom mentioned. The list of distresses upon which these organizations focus is very long, and many issues are complex and global.[10] Nonetheless, the ecological crisis is not of central concern to influential constituents of the feminist movement in Canada.

Another expression of feminism in Canada is within women's environmental organizations. These are usually small, underfunded, and understaffed. One organization, the Women, Environment, Education and Development (WEED) Foundation, notably now defunct, was instrumental in launching a feminist environmental voice in Canada. Out of WEED came the *Women and Environments International Magazine*[11] and the Women's Network on Health and the Environment.[12] There is also the Women's Environmental Network (since 1988)[13] and the environmental section of the Canadian Women's Internet Directory.[14] These groups and the many subgroups and individuals involved are largely responsible for whatever we can call an organized women-environment connection in Canada. They are often the forces that persuade mainstream women's/feminist groups to address environmental issues. The customary intersection point is women's health, and here they are active on many fronts. In general, however, their ecological horizon is narrow. Issues such as species extinction, loss of topsoil, climate change, or the politics of water rights are not on their agendas.

The Canadian women's environmental groups are increasingly linked to international groups and global networks, and their combined influence on national policies and orientations should not be underestimated. Organizations such as the United Nations Division for the Advancement of Women,[15] the United Nations Beijing Declaration and Platform for Action,[16] the World Health Organization,[17] Development Alternatives for Women of a New Era,[18] the People's Decade of Human Rights Education (US),[19] the Women's Environmental Development Organization (US),[20] and many more around the world have explicit environmental commitments and agendas. Thus both intra-Canadian and international exchanges are inserting environmental issues into the Canadian feminist scene.

As for spirituality, occasionally the topic may appear as a workshop option at a conference, usually in terms of women's health. There is significant research on the relationship between spirituality and health, especially breast cancer, and the latter has been linked at times to environmental causes. However, the definition of spirituality is connected to personal comfort rather than to political transformation. Although an appraisal of these organizations reveals a lack of either environmental or spiritual concerns, it is clear that individuals may, and do, make the connections. I am aware from personal experience that spirituality is vital to some of these women and deeply associated with their environmental and feminist worldviews.

Another evaluation criterion is the proliferation of courses linking feminism to ecology in both large and small Canadian universities. Ecofeminism is a known entity in most academic feminist circles. An abundance of related publications has been produced as the core concepts of ecofeminism have been taken into many academic disciplines. Ecofeminist courses exist in departments of women's studies, political science, literature, environmental studies, and/or religious studies. Spirituality is becoming popular in many disciplines, including feminist and environmental studies. Ecospirituality is studied in some places where feminism is less prominent. Occasionally, there are courses linking feminism, ecology, and spirituality, most often within theology or religious studies. How effective university courses are for social transformation is debatable, but the increase in courses indicates some measure of relevance.

Spirituality in Canada: Ecological and Feminist Concerns

Spirituality is popular these days. It is emerging within diverse sectors of society, from corporations to covens, and mainstream religious institutions have experienced a resurgence of spirituality. Often spirituality is linked to something else, such as ethics, business, leisure, health, travel, physical or psychic pain, personal renewal, swimming with dolphins, treks to the astral plane ... you name it. What spirituality actually means in these contexts is as slippery as terms such as "truth," "goodness," "beauty," or even "ecology." Concepts and symbols may be taken from conventional religions. Or they may stand in opposition to known civic religions and be flagged by the popular cliché "I am spiritual but not religious." At times there is a cohesive value system embedded within a specific "spirituality" to which it is accountable. At other times its meaning is sprawling, convoluted, and undefined, accountable only to individual tastes and temperaments.

Within this resurgence of spirituality is ecospirituality: the joining of spirituality and ecological viewpoints. In all major cities in Canada, there are organized ecospirituality efforts reflecting all spiritual persuasions, including Wiccan, Gaian, and interreligious, and rooted in a range of particular traditions, such as those of earth-based groups, deep ecologists, ecofeminists, bioregionalists, and mainstream environmentalists. The groups are large or small, politically active or discursive, and either connected to conventional religions or not. If politically active, they may collaborate with other socially progressive organizations. For example, during the protests at the G8 Summit held in Alberta in June 2002, the Witches of Calgary and Edmonton hosted a Wiccan ecosocial action in conjunction with the Anti-Capitalist Convergence, the Council of Canadians, and the Labour Council.[21] If ecospirituality were measurable by the Internet, it would seem to represent a mainstream reality. But what the Internet represents is indeterminable, except to say that ecospirituality is within the purview of some who use the Internet. Therefore, what can be concluded is that *something* between ecology and spirituality is going on at the level of cultural consciousness and social activity.

Mainstream religious establishments are engaging with the ecological crisis and bringing their resources to bear on mitigating further ecological damage. Although sporadic and uneven, there has been an increase in official religious responses in Canada to the ecological crisis, predominantly Christian. All kinds of avenues are being used, including information sharing, influencing church and public policy, building coalitions with other organizations, and protesting and publishing.[22] Increasingly, formal actions or statements are interreligious. Religious environmental efforts are developing within Canada, although more so elsewhere.[23]

Apart from the United Church of Canada, whose work has been instrumental in climate change negotiations, the religious voices are not adequately addressing ecological concerns. The progressive religious voices in Canada frequently focus on poverty, immigration, indigenous rights, militarism, and other social-justice concerns. It is the peripheral voices of each of these groups that connect to ecological concerns and feminism. Within each religious tradition, there are growing alliances between ecology and spirituality and between gender and spirituality, but few connect all three.

Feminist issues have been taken up by most world religions, at least academically. Feminist spiritualities often dwell outside of religious institutions. At times they are loosely affiliated with known traditions, such as Buddhism or Islam, or are innovative evolutions of such traditions. Other times they are amalgamations and new creations. There are an inestimable number of groups and individuals that connect spirituality with a range of feminist issues and environmental concerns, linking women, spirit, and earth. This connection could be as limited as an honourable, but in passing, mention of Mother Earth or reflect organized political action motivated by various concentrations and combinations of feminism, ecology, and spirituality. Yet mentioning "ecology" or the "sacred earth" reveals little of what these terms mean, how they are used, or whether they are central or peripheral to the scope of a group. Institutionally, looking at the Women's Inter-Church Council of Canada (Christian), one sees only sporadic environmental references, if any.[24] This is equally true of Judaism, Buddhism, Islam, Baha'ism and other mainstream traditions in Canada.

In so far as it is possible to examine the nexus of ecofeminist spirituality in Canada, these three avenues provide an image of what is happening. It is a fragmented and uneven occurrence, with personal force but little political influence. The paradigms, political orientations, issues addressed, types of feminism, and degrees of spiritual depth are wide-ranging, and coherence is neither an actuality nor desirable.

If spirituality were understood in greater depth, it may provide ecofeminism with an invaluable political energy. The next section explores the dimensions of spirituality and its relevance to developing a politically transformative ecofeminist spirituality.[25]

What Is Spirituality?

What, then, is spirituality? As a scholar of religion and a practitioner of spirituality, I increasingly appreciate this rich, primordial, and intimate dimension of human experience. Often spirituality is poorly and uncritically understood and is described with shallow and self-soothing expressions. In order to deepen an appreciation of its power and political influence, several aspects of spirituality will be discussed.

"Spirituality" comes from the Latin word for spirit *(spiritus)*, translated from the Greek word for breath or wind *(pneuma)*, which comes from the Hebrew word for breath, wind, and vitality *(ruah)*. Spirituality is like breathing, as intimate and as vital as breath. It is an integral dimension of human life, meaning that humans are not only intellectual, physical, emotional, and psychic, but also spiritual beings. Spirituality is described as the fire or heart of life, the ground of being. It is dynamic and changing, like the wind, and it is a force, says Teilhard de Chardin, in every molecule in the universe.[26]

Spirituality is often described as "the art of living." It is our stance in the face of existence, how we live our lives. Spirituality refers to the worldviews, ultimate values, and beliefs we hold – often without our awareness or active engagement – about ourselves, others, the world, birth, death, and significant transitions. It is deeply personal, although not individualistic. Within spirituality is an impulse toward transcendence, toward larger and deeper appreciations of existence that shift us from a self-centred existence to a spacious horizon. The great spiritual traditions often speak of "awakening," of awareness, and of knowing levels of reality not immediately apparent.

Some see this spirit of life as connected to divine energy or sacred presence.[27] Others say that spirituality is the ability to experience awe and wonder, to experience reverence in the face of the immensity and elegance of existence. Spirituality fosters an awareness of the goodness and richness of life and a realization that something divine or sacred is at stake within human beings and within all life. The depths of spirituality touch the ineffable, at times described as a profound living mystery at the heart of life and represented by many names: the Beloved, the Logos, the Tao, the Buddha, Enlightenment, Goddess or God, the Christ, the Holy/Sacred, the Other, the Great Being or Spirit, the Self, the Mystery.

Spiritualities are expressed, often in religious language, in countless images derived from various traditions, ranging from the theistic (Christian, Jewish, Islamic, Hindu) to the nontheistic (Buddhist, Jainist, Taoist), indigenous, Goddess-based, earth-based, and contemporary. They are also expressed in art, dance, poetry, and silence. Given that spirituality is experienced within a person in a specific time and place, culture, and set of circumstances, its expressions are context-specific and historically bound. The varieties of spiritual experiences are inestimable.[28] To express spirituality is to use images, symbols, and metaphors, and the choice is unlimited.[29]

Spiritual transformation is a process described by mystics either as a rebirth or as moving from death to life, from sleep to wakefulness, from illusion to enlightenment, from confinement to liberation, from confusion to truth. There are practices that enhance our spiritual growth and others that do not. The capacity for spiritual growth is not dependent upon whether one is single, married, celibate, gay, lesbian, straight, bisexual, or otherwise. It is not dependent upon living in a monastery or the jumble of an inner city. It does, however, have to do with how one attends to life, chooses values, and lives the quest and questions that are fundamentally human.

Those who are spiritually engaged with life are inevitably captivated by its beauty and astonished by its marvelous, exquisite, and extraordinary presence around and within us. In the context of ecofeminist spiritualities, or any authentic spirituality, there has been an awakening to the earth and its wonders. One is then repulsed by the destruction of life. It can be difficult to come to terms with a vision of the fullness and ultimate goodness of life when faced with systems of oppression, intense poverty, relentless suffering, and inherent limitations to change. Authentic spiritual growth moves toward the core of suffering. As there is an indelible connection between the suffering of women and the wreckage of the earth, ecofeminist spiritualities should be those most actively engaged with these issues. Spirituality should not be an appendix to the work of ecofeminists but that which propels it.

Spiritualities are not quick fixes that easily come and go. They are complex systems of symbolic expressions of what communities consider to be profound and sacred. They are a way of life: living traditions that cannot be readily transposed, rearranged, or created. An uncritical embracing of "spirituality," without seeking to clarify what a particular spirituality means and what its political impact might be, can leave the experience and expressions void of liberatory potential. Spirituality can become anything and can thus sprawl into a state of political inadequacy and meaninglessness.

Spirituality is intimately connected to religion. Religions are the skeletal structure of the spiritual life – spirituality being the heart and flesh as it were – giving spirituality a framework, a conscience, and a social or communal context. When religion and spirituality are separate, the former becomes stilted and closed and the latter becomes frivolous, superficial, and uncritical. Religion loses credibility, and rightly so, and spirituality becomes groundless. Both become vulnerable to either fundamentalism, political rigidity, or feebleness. In this era religion and spirituality are often dissociated, and neither are functioning at their deepest and authentic levels.

In the end words fail, as spirituality cannot be taught, only awakened or evoked. There have been many guides, and the wisdom of those who have embarked on this path, on this road less travelled, resides within every culture. John Burroughs eloquently states the cornerstone of religion and spirituality:

> Forms and creeds of religion change,
> But the sentiment of religion – the wonder,
> reverence and love we feel in the presence of the
> inscrutable universe – persists.[30]

Spirituality and Social Transformation

Spirituality can be a potent social force.[31] This is especially true in times of social transition, during which spirituality can develop roots within intense desires for liberation and can be an influential countercultural pressure. Not all spirituality is "political," or oriented toward social transformation. "Prophetic" spiritualities, such as those with overt political and justice commitments, can be distinguished from metaphysical spiritualities. In the first case, the concerns are social and material wellbeing and transformation, and in the second case, the preoccupation is often with the nature of time and being, ontology, or life after death. Political spiritualities have been in dialogue with critical theories, such as Marxism and post-Marxism, the Frankfurt School, social ethics, and liberation theologies, and with the discourses of ideology and utopia.

In the current turbulent era of global transitions, during which the life issues are massive and the political responses inadequate, countercultural movements are growing, as evidenced by antiglobalization/pro-democracy initiatives and demonstrations and world social forums. This is also an era in which spiritual thirst is intense, religious traditions are floundering and regrouping, and there is a dearth of spiritual leaders. The time is ripe for profound spiritual and cultural renewal. Ecofeminism is a part of that renewal, but for it to become a player on a more significant political scale, it needs to be rooted in a political spirituality. To understand how social renewals claim and shape public space, the time-honoured insights of the tensions between ideology and utopia are useful.[32]

Ideology represents the status quo and is a hidden phenomenon. Ideology is a system of interacting symbols that regulates and governs the actions of individuals, institutional frameworks, and political society as a whole.[33] It legitimizes a society and poses as the only rational, universally valid, natural, and true view of reality.[34]

Utopia represents the project of imagining another kind of society, a vision and desire of what could be. In one way or another, utopia reveals the fragility of the existing ideology and "exposes the obfuscating game ideology plays to bolster its credibility."[35] Utopia emerges from an impulse for freedom from constricting conditions. Utopia acts to disrupt the social relations mediated by ideology by juxtaposing an alternative order to that of the hegemonic, injecting new possibilities into the dominant reality. It appears as the counterpart to social ideology: Ideology functions for social integration, and utopia as social subversion. Utopic movements are usually met with fierce resistance from the reigning ideological powers. The interplay of ideology and utopia reveals the two fundamental directions of the social imagination. One cannot work without the other, each has pathological tendencies at the extremes, and the tension between them is insurmountable. They function adequately only within this tension.

It is evident that ecofeminism is a utopic discourse rather than a functioning ideology. It is a public challenge to the dominant system, disputing the legitimacy and systems of authority, exposing the distortions of the governing symbolic system, and envisioning an alternative future. It offers a hypothetical future, proposing a reformation of and improvement upon the present. Ecofeminism is an overt discourse, like all utopic ones, wherein presuppositions are debated in the public domain.

Ecofeminism, regardless of its internal diversity and autocritiques, is a direct confrontation with patriarchal ideology and its legitimation of power. Ecofeminism addresses oppressive modes of social organization. The ecological side confronts the pervasive disregard for earth health and vitality. Thus ecofeminism is injecting into the dominant reality a vision of new possibilities.

Ecofeminist Spiritualities and the Future

Ecofeminism and spirituality in Canada form an inconsistent alliance. Given that much of the environmental movement does not attend to gender, that much of the feminist movement does not address environmental concerns, and that spirituality is not an explicit aspect of either, it is difficult to know where to begin. Ecofeminist efforts in Canada are not sufficiently coherent and active to be considered a utopic force. There is an enormous gap between what is occurring and what could, or even ought to, occur. Many of these troubles have little to do with ecofeminism.

Resistance to change is usually vehement and at times vicious. The current (nonecofeminist) ideology is well entrenched within the worldview of most Canadians. The environmental movement has encountered endless obstacles in moving its agenda forward – likely due to the unconscious anthropocentric values and worldview of Canadians. It is very difficult to bend minds and shift values, hence actions, such that people begin to take earth health seriously. The debate around the Kyoto Protocol is only one example. Advances are being made, but relative to the level of change needed, they are minimal. In general, a similar comment can be made regarding feminism. Many, many developments have occurred over the past fifty years, and there are active, global women's movements. However, it remains to be seen if the legion of violences against women will ever end.

Spirituality has something real and effective to offer to this social mélange. Spirituality can be a powerful force in human lives and social systems, in both ideological and utopic activities. If spirituality is escapist or individualistic, connected to esoteric, inane, or irrational beliefs, or disconnected from the sufferings of the world, then it will be dismissed as apolitical and supportive of or irrelevant to the status quo. However, spirituality arising from the deepest impulses of life can be harnessed as a force for political change. What is needed for spirituality to be a valuable addition to ecofeminism? Four aspects will be discussed.

The first is realizing that a relationship between the natural world and spirituality is as old as human consciousness itself and until recently was an integral aspect of all human cultures. The natural world has been the primary source of religious/spiritual experience for millennia. In all religious traditions, the predominant religious metaphors have been of mountains, deserts, waters, wind, or fire. There have always been those who attribute a holy or sacred dimension to life, to the earth. Surrounded by the complexity, beauty, and mystery of life, they feel a sacred spirit embedded within and animating all life. Meister Eckhart commented that even the tiniest caterpillar is a book about God. Saint Hildegard of Bingen is said to have stated that "God has arranged all things in the world in consideration with everything else." Those who have such experiences are awakened to the great mystery of life. The immensity, order, chaos, sensitivity, creativity, and stunning elegance of life breaks into human consciousness and awakens awareness. For Thomas Berry, religious sensitivities developed *because* of the magnificence of life around us and an engagement with the challenge of life. It is the wind, colours, butterflies, wolves, worms, flowers, and the invigorating challenge of life that shape our religious experiences.[36] Many have expressed these existential insights: Muir, Leopold, Thoreau, Carson, Prigogine, Eiseley, Dillard, and so on. Theirs are testimonies to the possibility of awakening this awareness. Thus the relationship between spirituality and the natural world is not new but rather something that has been lost from modern consciousness. It is latent and can be revitalized.

Second, the Taoists claim that those who contemplate the natural world develop a sense of wonder, awe, and reverence. Contemplation of the earth unveils the magnificence of life and its sacred dimensions, what some call the "soul of the earth." The delicate beauty of plants, the gracefulness of fish and birds, the complex interaction of ecosystems reveal a stunning complexity and elegance at the heart of the world. It is revelatory. The response to these experiences of awe and wonder is reverence, and reverence comes only with habitual contemplation. It becomes a way of seeing, of living.

Third, wonder, awe, and reverence are legitimate ways of knowing. We have become impoverished because we rarely trust that which cannot be compartmentalized, conceptually packaged, or scientifically proven. Yet we can know "beauty," can honour courage, and are moved by reverence. Rabbi Heschel commented that "awe is an intuition for the dignity of all things. Awe is a sense for the transcendence, for the reference everywhere to the mystery in and beyond all things. It enables us to perceive in the world intimations of the divine. What we cannot comprehend by analysis, we become aware of in awe."[37] Awe and reverence reveal truth but a truth that differs from what is recognized in a hard-data-based and product-driven society. Experiences of awe are considered to be romantic, poetic, or charming, even lovely, but not essential for deliberation. Yet to experience awe in the natural world is as old as humanity itself. Thus, when analysis and data fail to persuade, as they often do, awe is influential. At times there is a need to shift from analysis to awe. Awe inspires and creates the possibility of experiencing something as spiritual and sacred. People do not destroy what they experience as sacred. This kind of ecospirituality is a valid dimension of life. If we address ecological issues from the viewpoints of awe, wonder, and reverence as well as from the viewpoints of health, ethics, sustainability, gender, biodiversity, and so on, a dimension is added that is pertinent, powerful, and equally real.

It is important to consider Heschel's statement that "what we cannot comprehend by analysis, we become aware of in awe." Reverence and awe are accurate responses to the majesty of life and open our eyes to dimensions of existence that result in radical amazement. Spiritual mystics such as Heschel have discovered that there is a constant invitation to experience this radical amazement with existence – to experience the great mystery of being alive. It is a journey of fear and wonder and ultimately a response to the infinite mystery that enfolds us and all life. Data on ecological disasters do move some to change and act, but the power of spiritual insights is greater. Herein lies the terrain of genuine new energies, wisdom and understanding, analyses, and awareness. Deeper realities of what it means to be human within the earth community may come forth and provide sufficient energy to make the necessary socio-ecological changes.[38] Still, it remains that wonder and awe cannot be analyzed, only experienced. As Mark Twain remarked, "the researchers and commentators have already thrown much darkness on this subject, and it is possible that, if they continue, we shall soon know nothing at all about it"!

Fourth is the ethical dimension of spiritualities. Throughout any authentic spirituality is an ethic for life. In all religious traditions, those who are "awakened" appreciate the awesome dimension of life and move toward the causes of suffering with compassion and a need for justice. The immense waste of and disregard for life, the overt oppression, and the intense greed for power or wealth at the expense of others, including the earth community, become intolerable. Such abhorrence is expressed with solidarity, compassion for the most vulnerable, and radical socio-political movements for liberation. Spirituality, compassion, and liberation are intimately connected. This confirms, once again, that authentic spirituality cannot be about personal comfort. It propels one into places of great tension and conflict. Injustices cannot be permitted and must be resisted. As Heschel says, "Religion begins with a consciousness that something is asked of us ... Little does contemporary religion ask of man [sic]. It is ready to offer comfort: it has no courage to challenge. It is ready to offer edification: it has no courage to break the idols, to shatter callousness ... To be religious is to be impatient with injustices. A breathless impatience with injustice ... A hysteria about injustices."[39]

There is an indelible affinity between spirituality and justice. Consequently, this connection becomes a necessary element in ecofeminist spiritualities. If spirituality does not move toward justice and socio-political activity, the spirituality is not sufficiently developed. There are fragments of ecofeminist spiritualities evident in Canada, and the connections to justice are evident in some places on some issues. Yet, in order to collect these fragments and infuse ecofeminist spiritualities with a political force, a few concerns must be addressed.

There have been critics of ecofeminist spiritualities, and some concerns are valid. Ecofeminism and its spiritual expressions have, at times, been labelled an apolitical, essentialist, self-nurturing, and unliberatory movement for three reasons.[40] First, the ecological aspect often falls short of a radical environmentalism and is not sufficiently immersed in analyses connected to factual manifestations of ecological issues. Second, from a feminist perspective, ecofeminism has been criticized for ignoring social, cultural, and historical contexts, differences of class and ethnicity among women, or structures of domination, such as industrialism or militarism.[41] Third, it is feared that spiritualities will be ineffective if political transformation is about an individual, more so than a social, change of consciousness. Ecofeminist spiritualities have been denounced for failures to differentiate between naïve, utopic ideals, illusions, and the mythic dimension of spirituality.[42]

Developing a spiritual sensitivity toward the earth can seem a luxurious pastime to those who are working in the trenches. However, there is a reciprocal problem with academics and activists who reject the spiritual dimension. Solipsistic spirituality is inept, politically irrelevant, and dismissible. Yet, when sufficiently and socially harnessed, spirituality is a potent political force with irrevocable and even detrimental impacts. The best of human endeavours, such as civil-rights and antiapartheid movements, have had a spiritual dimension, as have the worst of human actions, such as the attacks on the United States by Muslim terrorists on 11 September 2001 and the abuse of Native students in Canada's Catholic residential schools. Spirituality needs to be conscientiously examined in dialogue with social theories. Its worldview, value system, and potential impact need to be scrutinized. The images and understanding of the sacred are continually in need of evaluation. Spirituality's relationship with ecofeminism should not be abandoned but developed, paying critical attention to the social dimension of spirituality and how it functions.

Conclusion

On the one hand, we live in an era in which it is legitimate to view life as a commodity, to discuss ecological disasters in terms of credits and debits. There is a tendency to see ecologically and spiritually oriented persons as romantic, impractical, or hopelessly unrealistic. Ecological and spiritual sensitivities are trivialized by the realists. Experiencing a forest as a sacred grove is considered incidental or irrelevant. Economics is the measure of ecological health. But beauty, wonder, and sacredness cannot be measured in financial terms. On the other hand, this is an era in which religious institutions do not usually promote wonder, awe, and reverence but rather their own dogmatic formulae in the face of religious plurality. Both religious and economic fundamentalisms are rampant.

Albert Einstein commented that "problems cannot be solved at the level of consciousness at which they were created."[43] Herein lies the spiritual challenge. Ecofeminist spiritualities could be a significant influence for a change of consciousness, and ecofeminist analyses provide astute cultural critiques. The vision is utopic but not unrealistic. Ecofeminist spiritualities could give rise to a wonder, reverence, and sacredness that holds a power far greater than critique and even vision and could be the fuel for a social movement. Another aspect has been evoked: the spiritual and sacred dimension "written in every leaf and tree," as some indigenous traditions teach. It is from this teaching that ecofeminism can learn something invaluable, wise, and formidable, thereby enabling its contribution to socio-political transformation.

Ecofeminist spiritualities in Canada are a disorderly grouping of ideas and activities. Nonetheless, spirituality needs to be on the ecofeminist agenda; it needs to be respected, discussed, debated, and engaged in the context of social theories. Ecofeminist spiritualities must also root themselves in contemplation, in the deep mysteries of life, which are gracefully conveyed by Heschel: "We can never sneer at the stars, mock the dawn or scoff at the totality of being. Sublime grandeur evokes unhesitating, unflinching awe. Away from the immense, cloistered in our own concepts, we may scorn and revile everything. But standing between earth and sky, we are silenced by the sight."[44]

Notes

1 Of hundreds of publications, see Stephen Rockefeller and John Elder, eds., *Spirit and Nature: Why the Environment Is a Religious Issue* (Boston: Beacon, 1992); and David Hallman, *Spiritual Values for Earth Community* (Geneva: WCC Press, 2000).

2 See Rosemary Radford Ruether, *New Woman/New Earth: Sexist Ideologies and Human Liberation* (New York: Seabury Press, 1973); Judith Plant, ed., *Healing the Wounds: The Promise of Ecofeminism* (Toronto: Between the Lines, 1989); Carol Christ and Judith Plaskow, eds., *Weaving the Vision: New Patterns in Feminist Spirituality* (San Francisco: Harper and Row, 1989); Irene Diamond and Gloria Feman Orenstein, eds., *Reweaving the World: The Emergence of Ecofeminism* (San Francisco: Sierra Club Books, 1990); Charlene Spretnak, *States of Grace: The Recovery of Meaning in the Postmodern Age* (San Francisco: Harper, 1991); Carol Adams, ed., *Ecofeminism and the Sacred* (New York: Continuum, 1993).

3 Judith McKenzie, *Environmental Politics in Canada* (Don Mills, ON: Oxford, 2002), 53.

4 In June of 2001, the David Suzuki Foundation asked the Canadian Council of Churches for joint sponsorship on a climate-justice program. In the program, scientific, social-justice, indigenous, ecological, and religious voices from across the country collaborated to persuade the government to sign the Kyoto Protocol. The Sierra Club conference in Kingston, "Planet for the People, 2002," had several workshops on spirituality and faith.

5 Status of Women Canada, <http://www.swc-cfc.gc.ca/direct.html>; National Action Committee on the Status of Women (the NAC is a coalition of more than seven hundred women's/ feminist organizations), <http://www.nac-cca.ca/index_e.htm>; Canadian Research Institute for the Advancement of Women (CRIAW), <http://www.criaw-icref.ca>; Match International, <http://www.web.net/~matchint/en/match.html>; the Fédération nationale des femmes canadiennes-françaises, <http://www.franco.ca/fnfcf/>; National Council of Jewish Women of Canada, <http://www.ncjwc.org/>.

6 The topic headings were: Government Cutbacks and Restraints, Teaching/Learning/ Researching, Feminist Analysis of Employment Trends, Community Awareness, Perceptions of the Body, Women in Isolated Communities, and Defining Women's Health from Diverse Perspectives.

7 Although the National Action Committee on the Status of Women mentions environmental issues on one of their lists of concerns, they do not have an active environmental committee. Nor are environmental issues considered at the level of policy committees, where the bulk of the work is done: on issues affecting economic justice, women of colour, lesbians, Aboriginals, health, immigration, childcare, etc. See <http://www.nac-cca.ca/about/ committee_e.htm>.

8 Some groups are making environmental connections to women's health, as evidenced by their participation in the conference "Rencontre internationale sur les femmes et la santé/

International Women and Health Meeting," York University, August 2002. The groups involved in the conference were the Canadian Research Institute for the Advancement of Women (CRIAW) and the Riverdale Immigrant Women's Centre (RIWC), in collaboration with their key partners: the Canadian Women's Health Network (CWHN) and the Réseau québécois d'action pour la santé des femmes (RQASF). See <http://www.yorku.ca/ycom/stories/08012.html>.

9 See Canadian Women's Health Network, <http://www.cwhn.ca/hot/conferences/default.html>.

10 For example, HIV/AIDS, trafficking in women, refugee and immigrant women, violence and health issues, women with disabilities, international human rights, Aboriginal women, environmental health issues, abortion, mental health, sex workers, the role of global economic institutions in women's lives, global perspectives on sexual and reproductive rights, advocacy and media reporting on women, violence against women of colour or based on sexual orientation, gender perspectives in conflict zones, militarism, poverty, childcare, the girl child, unpaid labour, and on and on.

11 See *Women and Environments International Magazine*, <http://www.weimag.com/>.

12 See Women's Network on Health and the Environment, <http://www.web.net/~wnhe/>.

13 See Women's Environmental Network, <http://www.wen.org.uk/index.htm>.

14 See Canadian Women's Internet, <http://directory.womenspace.ca/Environment/>.

15 See United Nations, <http://www.un.org/womenwatch/daw/index.html>.

16 See United Nations, <http://www.un.org/womenwatch/daw/index.html>.

17 See World Health Organization, <http://www.who.int/health_topics/womens_health/en/>.

18 See Development Alternatives for Women of a New Era, <http://www.dawn.org.fj/>.

19 See People's Decade of Human Rights Education, <http://www.pdhre.org/>.

20 See Women Environment Development Organization, <http://www.wedo.org/>.

21 For a description of the Wiccan action in Calgary written by Starhawk, see Awakened Woman, "A Short Report on the G8 Protests," <http:// www.awakenedwoman.con/star-calgary.htm>. For an overview of Wicca, see the Pagan Federation of Canada on Wicca, <http://www.witchery.ca/wicca/Wiccawhat.htm>.

22 For example, in 2000 several ecumenical coalitions comprising the progressive, politically active wing of the Christian traditions in Canada merged into one organization called Kairos, representing the Canadian Ecumenical Justice Initiatives. Ecological issues are now present throughout their work, including within their specific mandate. In conjunction with the World Council of Churches, Kairos has engaged climate change as a specific concern. Kairos, and the multifaceted issues that it addresses, is both unique and very important to the progressive edges of Christianity in Canada but is little known either among the public, in the pews, or in the theological schools. Yet it is the most politically oriented aspect of the Christian community in Canada, using ecojustice as its principle rubric. See KAIROS, <http://www.kairoscanada.org>.

23 Mary Evelyn Tucker and John Grim, "Overview: The Nature of the Environmental Crisis," introductory paper for the conference series "Religions of the World and Ecology," 6, 7, <http://environment.harvard.edu/religion/publications/book/book_series/cswr/index.html>. This ten-volume series is published by Harvard University Press and comprises edited collections on each of the ten major world religions. Tucker and Grim, with hosts of consultants from numerous disciplines, have created the Forum on Religion and Ecology (FORE) to promote conversation on this issue within educational settings, public policy, research, and outreach. See Forum on Religion and Ecology, <http://environment.harvard.edu/religion>.

24 The Women's Inter-Church Council of Canada is an ecumenical social-justice and women's organization that would be considered progressive from a mainstream Christian viewpoint. There have been a few environmental articles in their publication *Making Waves: An Ecumenical Journal* and at their conferences, but in general environmental issues are absent. See Women's Inter-Church Council of Canada, <http://www.wicc.org>.

25 For an overview and critique of ecofeminist spritualities, see the following: Adams, ed., *Ecofeminism and the Sacred;* Carol Christ, *Rebirth of the Goddess: Finding Meaning in Feminist Spirituality* (London: Routledge, 1998); Diamond and Orenstein, eds., *Reweaving the World;*

Ivone Gebara, *Longing for Running Water: Ecofeminism and Liberation* (Minneapolis: Fortress Press, 1999); Susan Griffin, *Woman and Nature: The Roaring inside Her* (London: Women's Press, 1978); Carolyn Merchant, *The Death of Nature: Women, Ecology, and the Scientific Revolution* (London: Wildwood House, 1980); Plant, *Healing the Wounds;* Anne Primavesi, *From Apocalypse to Genesis: Ecology, Feminism and Christianity* (Minneapolis: Fortress Press, 1991); Eleanor Rae, *Women, the Earth, the Divine* (Maryknoll, NY: Orbis Books, 1994); Rosemary Radford Ruether, ed., *Women Healing Earth: Third World Women on Ecology, Feminism, and Religion* (Maryknoll, NY: Orbis Books, 1996); Rosemary Radford Ruether, *Gaia and God: An Ecofeminist Theory of Earth Healing* (San Francisco: Harper, 1992); Charlene Spretnak, *States of Grace: The Recovery of Meaning in the Postmodern Age* (San Francisco: Harper, 1991); Starhawk, *The Spiral Dance: A Rebirth of the Ancient Religions of the Great Goddess* (San Francisco: Harper and Row, 1979).

26 Pierre Teilhard de Chardin, *The Divine Milieu* (New York: Harper and Rowe, 1960).

27 For numerous definitions of spirituality, see Ronald Rolheiser, *Seeking Spirituality* (London, UK: Hodder and Stoughton, 1998); and *Against an Infinite Horizon* (London, UK: Hodder and Stoughton, 1995).

28 Ninian Smart, *The Religious Experience,* 5th ed. (Upper Saddle River, NJ: Prentice Hall, 1996).

29 Symbols are not the same as signs. In its classic definition, "symbol" refers not to something that points to something else, but to something that actually carries or mediates the other. A symbol mediates an experience that could not be had without the symbol. Symbols, while often understood as divinely ordained, in fact mediate an aspect of reality experienced as sacred (chalices, icons, images, stories, rituals). It is often difficult to separate the symbol from the experience it is mediating. Thus symbols are alive, functioning, and highly powerful and significant, or they are dead and irrelevant.

30 John Burroughs, quoted in Phil Cousineau, ed., *The Soul of the World: A Modern Book of Hours* (San Francisco: Harper, 1993), 26.

31 David Ray Griffin, ed., *Spirituality and Society* (New York: SUNY, 1988), 2.

32 For an in-depth discussion of ecofeminism as a dynamic aspect of the ideology-utopia dialectic, see Heather Eaton, "Ecofeminist Ethics: Utopic Conversations," *Ecotheology* 8 (2000): 45-68.

33 Paul Ricoeur, *Lectures on Ideology and Utopia* (New York: Columbia University Press, 1986); and Ricoeur, "Ideology and Utopia," in *From Text to Action: Essays in Hermeneutics 11,* translated by Kathleen Blamey and John B. Thompson (Evanston, IL: Northwestern University Press, 1991), 308-35.

34 John Van Den Hengel, *The Home of Meaning: The Hermeneutics of the Subject of Paul Ricoeur* (Washington, DC: University Press of America, 1982).

35 Ibid., 180.

36 Thomas Berry, *Dream of the Earth* (San Francisco: Sierra Club Books, 1988), 11.

37 Samuel Dresner, ed., *I Asked for Wonder: A Spiritual Anthology of Abraham Joshua Heschel* (New York: Crossroads, 1997), 3.

38 However, it is possible to have profound experiences of the wonder of existence and still overlook race, class, and gender inequalities. For example, ecofeminists raise questions about some deep-ecology proponents who affirm that radical amazement is crucial for ecological renewal but ignore gender injustices.

39 Dresner, *I Asked for Wonder,* 38-39.

40 For examples, see articles on spirituality in Plant, ed., *Healing the Wounds;* Diamond and Orenstein, eds., *Reweaving the World;* and Adams, ed., *Ecofeminism and the Sacred.* Not all articles can be criticized for these weaknesses. For critiques, see Janet Biehl, *Finding Our Way: Rethinking Ecofeminist Politics* (Montreal: Black Rose Books, 1991); Joni Seager, *Earth Follies: Coming to Feminist Terms with the Environmental Crisis* (New York: Routledge, 1993), 236-52; and Mary Mellor, *Breaking the Boundaries: Towards a Feminist Green Socialism* (London, UK: Virago Press, 1992).

41 Seager, *Earth Follies,* 249.

42 Biehl, *Finding Our Way.*

43 See <http://www.therightside.demon.co.uk/quotes/einstein/>.

44 Dresner, *I Asked for Wonder,* 2.

16
The Listening World: First Nations Women Writers and the Environment
Marian Scholtmeijer

Thanks to the human heart by which we live,
Thanks to its tenderness, its joys, and fears,
To me the meanest flower that blows doth give
Thoughts that do often lie too deep for tears.
                              — William Wordsworth[1]

There's a dandelion on the roadside in Toronto.
Its leaves a dishevelled mix of green and brown.
       A dandelion scraggling 'n' limping along.

            . . . .

My leaves, my face ... my skin ... I feel like
my skin is being scraped off me. There is
       a flower in Toronto. On the roadside.

It takes jackhammers and brutish machines to rip
the concrete from the sidewalks in Toronto
       to beautify the city of blue serge suits

But for this dandy lion, it takes but a seed,
a little acid rain, a whole lot of fight and a
       Black desire to limp along and scraggle forward

   There is a flower.
                              — Lee Maracle (Stó:lo)[2]

William Wordsworth has had a profound influence upon Euro-Western attitudes toward the natural world. As the premier Romantic poet, Wordsworth can be seen as largely responsible for the emergence of a feelingful approach to elements of nature such as his "meanest flower." In this respect, seminal attitudes like those expressed by Wordsworth can illuminate distinctions between Western environmental thought and the environmental thought of First Nations writers. Wordsworth feels tenderness toward the little flower; he experiences joy and compassion when he contemplates it. Typical hierarchic thinking, however, is apparent in Wordsworth's lines: Some things in nature are bigger and more consequential than others. If there can be a "meanest" flower, then some flowers have greater importance. Furthermore, the context for this observation is the wisdom or praiseworthiness of the human heart. The flower is meaningful and a suitable subject for poetry primarily because it provokes deep sentiments in Wordsworth. It is a balm to him; it causes him to reflect upon his own internal state. In this sense, his relationship with the flower is somewhat exploitive, his response somewhat egocentric. Nevertheless, the protectiveness he and others of the Romantic persuasion feel toward "the meanest flower" forms the foundation of environmental thought. Couple that protectiveness with the realization that humankind loses the solace of deeply calm reflection when the natural world is destroyed, and environmental activism follows.

Like Wordsworth, Lee Maracle focuses upon a small and overlooked flower. Unlike Wordsworth, she sees the flower as a fellow being struggling to survive. She admires the hardiness of the dandelion. The flower takes hold in the harshest environment, even on a diet of acid rain. Briefly, Maracle identifies with the dandelion, feeling *with* rather than *for* it (or should I say "her"). Granted, the dandelion illuminates her own struggle, but reciprocally, her own struggle brings her to appreciate the effort, the "black desire," of the dandelion to live. In addition, although subtly and not to a cartoonish extent, she sees the dandelion as an animated being. "Straggle" and "limp" are perfect words for any imagined motion attributed to dandelions, not because they sprawl like morning glories but because they count as weeds in an urban context. Their kind is persecuted. Attempts are made to eradicate them – hence the limping. In contrast to cultivated flowers, they are unloved and unprotected, hence the straggling. But in Lee Maracle's poem, this dandelion is more important than all the "blue serge suits" and "jackhammers" in Toronto.

Maracle's dandelion leads to the first of three observations: One often finds in literary works by Canadian First Nations[3] women writers a sense that the natural world is "peopled"[4] with beings scarcely different from human beings. The perspective is different from both humanization and animism.

The second observation relates to the intended audience for and reception of writing by First Nations women. Much of what appears to be going on in First Nations writing is the invocation of a sense of familiarity. The mother of First Nations writing in Canada, Maria Campbell, launched the field with her memoir *Halfbreed*. The memoir, biography, and life history are staples of First Nations writing. Lee Maracle and Jeannette Armstrong (Okanagan), two of the foremost First Nations women writers, say that they write for their own people. Jeannette Armstrong says, "I do at all times speak to my people when I'm writing. Whenever I waver from that I get lost."[5] Lee Maracle says, "I don't write to and from a culture not my own. I write to and from my own. If I forget that for a minute, if I stray from that for a second, my writing would be useless to all."[6]

Other First Nations women writers seem to be doing the same – or at least the reaction that their work gets from First Nations readers is an instant and joyous recognition of shared experience. In *Honour the Sun*, Ruby Slipperjack (Ojibway) mentions getting powdered milk and vitamin biscuits for lunch at school.[7] First Nations students in my literature class in Wilp Wilx̱o'oskwhl Nisga'a (New Aiyansh, BC) immediately connected with this reference; some of them had suffered the Canadian government biscuits, too. Memories of the biscuits were shared. Likewise, features of the way of life – storytelling, fishing, gathering berries and plants for medicine, setting up camp in the woods – would draw from members of my class their own, similar experiences. In *Talking about Ourselves: The Literary Productions of the Native Women of Canada*, Barbara Godard explains the relationship between oral storytelling and "text-to-life" interaction. "Text-to-life" reading, she says, involves "readers using textual knowledge to make sense of their lives."[8] Whether from their background in oral traditions or from the pleasure of recognition, my students clearly employed the text-to-life approach in their response to First Nations literature. First Nations literature validates life experiences for First Nations readers.

This function is significant for three reasons. First, the life experiences of First Nations people in Canada have been devalued by the dominant culture. When First Nations literature simply speaks about First Nations experiences, it gives life back to First Nations readers. Second, the sharing of memories represents the first step in rebuilding the traditional cultural values that the dominant society sought to destroy. Third – and most important for understanding environmental values – the idea of the familiar in and of itself relates to the lands and the home-places of First Nations people. Materialism and the will to dominance left Europeans estranged from nature, from the places where they lived. As a generalization – and I hope not a stereotype – many First Nations people experience natural environments as home.

This, then, is the second observation: First Nations women writers often re-create the familiarity of natural environments in their writing.

The third observation combines the first two. Led by the work and writing of indigenous peoples themselves, contemporary environmentalism has turned to the wisdom of the Host World to counteract the attitudes of Euro-Western invaders. Contemporary environmentalists seek out traditional ecological knowledge (TEK) and at the same time deplore the destruction of indigenous people's home-spaces. In their most recent writing, First Nations women express a sense of solidarity with other indigenous peoples of the world. In Jeannette Armstrong's novel *Whispering in Shadows*, the protagonist, Penny, comments that "'millions of Indigenous people are being violated and displaced.'" Penny continues: "'I've spent most of my time thinking about technology and its effects on the natural world ... I have even thought about the increase in human violence as an environmental symptom. But in that, I obviously overlooked something right in front of me. I overlooked the communities which are still connected to land in a healthy way as an opposing force to that system. A true natural sustainability. As the only hope for protecting biodiversity!'"[9] It is being recognized that indigenous peoples possess practical wisdom about living with specific environments. Natalia Rybczynski argues that traditional ecological knowledge "is able to form the bases of sustainable resource management practices in part because it is reflexive, but also because it exists within a cosmology of ecological consciousness."[10]

One branch of contemporary environmental thought seeks spiritual wisdom from indigenous people as well. Jim Mason describes what he sees as Native North Americans' spiritual understanding of nature: "Theirs was a living world, teeming with nonhuman spirits, powers, and souls."[11] He goes on to quote Francis Parkman, whom he describes as a "conservative elitist" and who was writing, over a hundred years ago:

> To the Indian ... the material world is sentient and intelligent. Birds, beasts and reptiles have ears for human prayers and are endowed with an influence on human destiny. A mysterious and inexplicable power resides in inanimate things. They, too, can listen to the voice of man, and influence life for evil or for good. Lakes, rivers and waterfalls are sometimes the dwelling-place of spirits; but more frequently they are themselves living beings, to be propitiated by prayers and offerings. The lake has a soul; and so has the river, and the cataract. Each can hear the words of men, and each can be pleased or offended. In the silence of a forest, the gloom of a deep ravine, resides a living mystery, indefinite but redoubtable.[12]

As a broad characterization, both Mason's and Parkman's comments capture an important difference between Euro-Western responses to nature and those of Native North Americans. When it comes to the writing of Canadian First Nations women, however, spiritual powers and mysteries are less apparent in representations of nature than the idea of a peopled world. Trees, lakes, stones, and animals do not have souls as much as they have personalities. The idea of a peopled world puts the conjoint tragedies of environmental destruction and the displacement of indigenous peoples into a unique perspective.

The lands in which displaced indigenous peoples lived were familiar home-places – places they knew intimately, places to which they belonged as much as the trees, plants, animals, stones, and creeks. Because, in First Nations cultures, these trees, plants, animals, stones, and creeks are alive themselves – have hearts, breath, memory, longing, patience, friendliness – the destruction of these places is inseparable from the tragedy of the destruction of indigenous cultures and people. The destruction of an environment is, literally, the destruction of a people, not just because human people occupied the land, but because the land itself is peopled with natural beings. Distinctions drawn between human suffering and environmental depredation, the devotion of energy to one cause at the expense of the other, are wrongheaded because the environment suffers humanly, too. From a First Nations perspective, as a generalization, what the world loses as indigenous people are driven out of their home-places and as environments are destroyed is not only practical and spiritual wisdom, but also a sense of familiarity within nature: a sense of knowing some place in the natural world and of *being known by* that place.

The third observation, then, is that many First Nations women writers reproduce the experience of finding oneself at home in a natural environment that knows and responds to oneself and one's people.

Taken together, these observations reveal that the unique contribution made by First Nations women writers to environmental thought is to articulate and preserve the experience of a natural environment and its human inhabitants as one community, with a shared history, a shared memory, and shared interests. Why First Nations women writers per se? As a matter of observation, it does appear that First Nations women writers re-create the sense of humans and environment as one community more often and more pointedly than do First Nations male writers, perhaps because in general the interactions of First Nations women with the natural environment are less conflicted (hunting and trapping are represented in First Nations writing as predominantly male activities) and gentler than the interactions of First Nations men.[13] In "Equality among Women," First Nations artist Mingwôn Mingwôn (Shirley Bear) endorses the foundational assertion by Native American writer Paula Gunn Allen that "Creation is female. In the beginning was thought, and her name was woman ... to her we owe our lives."[14] Rose Auger, a Cree elder, says of the difference between men's and women's roles that the "women made ceremonies, and she was recognized as being united with the moon, the earth, and all the forces on it."[15] Statements like these, coming from women with insiders' knowledge, suggest the legitimacy of looking for differences between the writing of First Nations men and the writing of First Nations women on the subject of the environment. These statements support the idea, furthermore, that the difference lies in the direction of First Nations women conceiving of humans and natural environments as one integrated community of similar beings.

The Peopled World

That First Nations women writers engage traditional values when they connect with the personhood of natural entities may be gleaned from some Blackfoot charm songs included in the collection *Our Bit of Truth: An Anthology of Canadian Native Literature*. The Otterskin Charm, for example, reads simply "The lake is my lodge." The Owl Charm is "The night is my medicine; / I hoot," and the Jaybird Charm is "The mountains are my lodge; / The woods are my medicine."[16] These charms find correspondences between humans and animals, between the places constructed by humans and the homes of the otter and jaybird, and between the power vested in First Nations medicine and the power drawn from the night by the owl and from the woods by the jaybird. It always bears remembering that someone's home – many beings' homes – is destroyed when a lake is polluted or a mountainside blasted for highways or mining. These traditional charms suggest that creatures have a claim on places in the environment just as humans do. Furthermore, by implication, the lodge built by humans is a part of nature, as is medicine. Analogies between humans and natural beings constitute a starting point for the subtle and telling kinship of which First Nations women write.

Animals are obvious candidates for conception as people. In First Nations traditions, natural elements, too, are human. Leonora Hayden McDowell recalls the tradition of the Cree in her poem "Windsong." "My people talk to the winds," she writes; "And the voices of the winds come back." The winds of the east, west, north, and south each have their own voices and distinctive personas: The East Wind is "a rain-drenched crying child"; while the North Wind is "a strong man, Giant of the North / [who] Drums big talk."[17]

Pauline Johnson (Mohawk) invoked the sense of a living landscape in her poem "Moonset," in which fir trees are dreaming and cedars are "chanting vespers to the sea." Johnson speaks of the "soft responsive voices of the night" and includes not only night birds but the wind, the trees, and the waves.[18] Such sensibilities are not out of reach for other cultures, but it does take a subtle ear to pass beyond the clear voices of night creatures such as frogs or nighthawks to the voices of trees and wind. Johnson's world is alive and speaking.

In Lee Maracle's *Ravensong*, the world is likewise alive and speaking, but few people hear. Celia, the child who does hear, is so enigmatic a character that one wonders for a time if she has died and occupies the spirit world. In *Ravensong*, Raven initiates a plan to counteract the evils brought into the world by white people by bringing an influenza epidemic to the village of First Nations people. Such a catastrophe, Raven argues, is "just birth." Cedar, a tender-hearted spirit, says the plan is "impossibly mean." The novel begins with Raven singing and Wind, Cedar, and Cloud reacting to Raven's song. Maracle deftly integrates the actions and thoughts of these natural beings into her story. One particularly fine instance of integration occurs when Celia sits under a cedar tree watching her sister's efforts to fight the flu: "Cedar brushed Celia's cheek with her lower branch, a soft caress from the smooth side of her needles."[19] In the Euro-Western world, when a human person encounters the branches of a tree, all action is with the human person. There is no thought that the tree might have reached out or that some motive force or feeling might be in the tree herself. The action Maracle describes is subtle yet world-changing. To feel that one is caressed when one encounters a tree branch, or slapped, or brought to attention, or otherwise acted upon rather than acting encapsulates the difference between the Euro-Western view of the environment and that expressed by First Nations women writers. Cedar, in this instance, expresses tender feelings toward the human being she touches.

This sense of a humanly reactive, humanly feeling natural world puts a different cast on instances of identification found in poems by First Nations women. Other beings are not "other," of a different kind than human beings. The devices of analogy or metaphor must yield to the literal. In the poem "Give Me the Spirit of the Eagle," when Leonora Hayden McDowell prays "Keep in my heart a sky-borne vision / Keep my body filled with grace,"[20] she does tribute to the eagle not as a symbol of certain qualities but as a being who literally possesses the qualities she herself seeks. Likewise, in the poem "Where Have the Warriors Gone?" Willow Barton invokes animals to explain her pain in the face of the damage done to her people by priests and educators, and to express the hope that she derives from her own culture. She writes: "i am a running rabbit, a sparrow in flight / frightened by a shadow i cannot comprehend," and "i am a hawk with no place to land." When she speaks of hope at the end of her poem, she writes: "i will dance my dreams upon an eagle's wing / and fly high, higher, higher." The literal eagle's wing and the dance convey the felt, embodied experience of pride and freedom. "Where Have the Warriors Gone?" is not a poem for the eagles, in the same sense that Maracle's "Perseverance" celebrates the spirit of the dandelion, but when Barton writes "i cannot forget that i am cree,"[21] she reaches for eagle's wings to body forth the triumphant return of pride in her heritage.

Identification of human and animal can be very close in First Nations women's writing. In her poem "Grandmother," Louise Bernice Halfe (Cree) blends the figures of a herb-gathering grandmother (Nohkom) and a "shuffling brown bear" so effectively that one cannot tell whether she is honouring the bearlike spirit of the medicine woman or explaining bear behaviour by means of a human analogy.[22] Just as likely, "bear nohkom" is an overarching spirit informing the actions of both bear and grandmother. Either way, the bear's conduct is the conduct of a person in Halfe's poem.

Anishanabe poet Annharte is a master of blending beings. She has a wonderfully ironic sense of humour as well. In her poem "Coyote Trail," she adopts the perspective of a coyote who is tracking a scent and thinking about her trip to town to eat fast food. The poem is in the coyote's words and tones: "like last week I sssll unk into town." The last three lines, however, suggest a wry nod to the poet herself:

I was a writer once
know how to keep track of things
how interdependence works for me[23]

The Coyote figure in First Nations stories possesses an impish sense of humour; she or he is a trickster but at times can be a buffoon, as Thomas King's stories suggest.[24] It would be typical of Coyote to claim to have been a writer. In "Coyote Trail," the word "interdependence" directly relates to the coyote's scavenging in the town. She says that a town dweller is "eager to become me," hence the idea of interdependence. In addition, however, the word "interdependence" points outward to the poet's use of the Coyote figure in her poem. Either seriously, or with a touch of self-mockery, Annharte seems to be indicating how her links with her heritage and the natural world can be capitalized on to produce poetry. Self-mockery would be a highly Coyote-like stance. One way or another, poet and coyote speak simultaneously in the last three lines of "Coyote Trail."

These three lines are an instance of polyphony as Robert Bringhurst explains the term in his article "Singing with the Frogs." Some comments on polyphony from Robert Bringhurst are pertinent to the role of natural beings in writing by First Nations women. Bringhurst himself is a poet, linguist, and translator of myths and legends of West Coast First Nations. Bringhurst describes polyphony as "singing more than one song, playing more than one tune, telling more than one story, at once." He refers to the voices in polyphonic music as "co-equals." He says that "polyphonic literature and music acknowledge and celebrate plurality, simultaneity, the continuing coexistence of independent melodies and rhythms, points of view and trains of thought."[25] Bringhurst's description of polyphony goes to the heart of the phenomenon of a peopled world found in writing by First

Nations women. By this, I do not mean that one often finds actual polyphony in writing by First Nations women but that the philosophical and
metaphysical perspective described by Bringhurst is analogous to relations
between the earth and her beings articulated by First Nations women.

Bringhurst's article is immediately preceded by "partridge song," a poem
by kateri akiwenzie-damm of the Chippewas of the Nawash First Nation. In
"partridge song," akiwenzie-damm renders her voice as a poet indistinguish-
able from the voice of the partridge who is the subject of the poem – or
perhaps who speaks the poem in the first place:

> come to me
> my love
> i am calling
>
> hear my song
> sweet one
> i am drumming
>
> in the reeds
> dear one
> i am waiting
>
> come to me
> my love
> i am calling[26]

Akiwenzie-damm's poem is a perfect illustration of complete polyphony
and an ideal instance of the sense of a peopled world in which natural
beings and human beings interact as co-equals. The speaker in the poem is
simultaneously the partridge and the poet. With its regular, short beats, the
poem sounds like the partridge's song – the swift drumming of his wings to
attract a mate. At the same time, it sounds like the poet calling the partridge, perhaps as part of a ceremonial dance with drums. Akiwenzie-damm
literally gets into the being of the partridge.

That polyphony might have a distinctively female quality in First Nations culture is suggested by a comment from Jovette Marchessault in "Song
One: The Riverside" from *Mother of the Grass*. Marchessault says of the
storytelling Grandmother in "Song One" that "she had the gift of being
able wholly to involve herself in her words, to incarnate herself in flesh
and blood in her subject matter. For example, when she told me about
whales, she became a whale and nothing existed except the whale. She
knew the whale through the movements in her guts, her heart, her kid-
neys, her breasts."[27] In essence, both the whale and the woman speak at
once. Marchessault's Grandmother draws on her experience of her own

being to become the whale, and she can do this because she and the whale share personhood.

The responses of First Nations women to the environment, then, only *appear* to be similar to the Euro-Western phenomena of metaphor, identification, and attribution of human qualities to nonhuman things. The "things" of nature – trees, winds, oceans, eagles, bears, coyotes, partridges – that those in the Euro-Western world see as nonhuman are seen, simply, as other kinds of persons by First Nations women. They are known by consultation with the human being's own state. This means that the second observation I wish to exemplify – familiarity – has a more full-bodied implication in First Nations women's writing than the word "familiarity" by itself connotes.

Familiarity

A pattern of going away from home and returning occurs frequently in stories by First Nations women – especially when the home-place is in nature. In Euro-Western Romanticism and nature writing, discontent with urban life is a persistent theme. The natural world provides tranquility and comfort but is rarely conceived of as home. In stories by First Nations women, urban existence is often not only oppressive, but outright dangerous; people return home to natural environments, and to the elders who know how to live in those environments, for spiritual renewal. This pattern of return for renewal occurs in some of the most important First Nations stories: in *Halfbreed* by Maria Campbell, in *Slash* and *Whispering in Shadows* by Jeanette Armstrong, in the epilogue to *Ravensong*, and in Eden Robinson's prize-winning novel *Monkey Beach*. This pattern of going outward and coming home mimics the pattern of seasonal treks to gather plants for tea or medicine, to pick berries, or to fish. A traditional Tsimshian song says:

> She will gather the sap of young hemlock trees
> in the early spring.
> That is why she was born.
> She will pick strawberries in the early spring,
> That is why she was born[28]

The timeless and time-honoured practice of gathering provisions from nature at seasonal intervals during the year sets up a rhythm for life among First Nations women living traditionally. It is not surprising, then, that this rhythm of return to familiar natural environments should find its way into their stories.

Built on this rhythm, Ruby Slipperjack's *Honour the Sun* possesses an internal, regular pattern based on her mother's morning practice of paying tribute to the rising sun. The mother tells the children, "'When the sun comes over the horizon, he will see you and be very pleased that you're all ready to greet him and he will bless you.'" *Honour the Sun* is composed of journal entries by a young girl called the Owl as she grows from age ten to sixteen, when she leaves home. The tone is nostalgic, although the occasional encounter with adults who are drunk creates disquiet. One of the charming qualities of *Honour the Sun*, however, is the recurrence of loved interactions with nature: blueberry picking, gathering firewood, skating on the frozen lake, camping in the summertime. At the end of the novel, the Owl is preparing to leave for the city, but she will carry rhythms of home with her. Beyond that, she reminds herself that the "'sun will keep coming up till the end of time.'"[29] At the risk of sounding naive, I wish to observe that the regular rising of the sun is a familiar pattern many Euro-Westerners fail to appreciate.

The familiar is often fairly simple. Knowing the land means knowing what to do to survive there. Jeanette Armstrong puts it most succinctly in her novel *Slash* as she contemplates Native North Americans being driven from their lands. Her hero, Tommy, says, "'it must have been terrifying and horrible to be put in a place where you don't even know what plants to eat and medicines to use.'"[30] Tommy returns home to the Okanagan after a long absence during which he participates in complex and dangerous political actions on behalf of Native North Americans. He is a young man full of justified rage at the treatment of his people. Coming home in the wintertime, in the snow, brings him genuine hope and joy:

> I stopped and stretched my arms up toward the soft white flakes that danced around me. I felt the feeling rise inside my head. Like a quiet explosion that spread ripples to all my body. I felt the singing music that the swirling snow danced to. I felt it take hold and I danced to the sound that swirled in white cascades around me, and covered the earth with a promise. A promise that the flowers would bloom again for my people. I knew I was home, really home, and my land welcomed me.[31]

Like *Slash*, Armstrong's *Whispering in Shadows* is built upon social protest in the form of activism for the environment and for indigenous people. The recollected and present-day scenes of return to the Okanagan have the sweet and profound simplicity of the familiar – of the life that needs to be saved. The heart of the novel finds four generations of Okanagan women digging roots in the dry desert hills of their people. The little girl, Penny (her adult life forms the narrative), is in the company of her *tupa* (great-grandmother). Penny's Tupa teaches her that the roots they dig, the berries they gather, wait for them to come.[32] The middle two generations, Penny's mother and grandmother, have learned the same response to nature. Penny's grandmother responds to her daughter's fears about Penny's future: "'We are just to go on doing the best we can. We still have to pick the berries and dig the roots. They will leave us if we don't. So let's get busy. No more talk. The roots are waiting to be dug. Waiting to go home with us to the feast house. Shush now, daughter, it is your loss which speaks. Let's speak only of good things on this day of first roots.'"[33] The continuity of generation-to-generation and season-to-season interaction with the land means that the familiar stretches outward from individual and psychological renewal to the deep, known past and to a hopeful future. The past is not dim, the future not blank, as long as the land abides.

Tradition, Eden Robinson (Haisla-Heiltsuk) says in *Monkey Beach*, is a "human need to express sympathy with tangibles."[34] Her narrator, Lisamarie, has just found her favourite foods in the fridge; the "tangibles" are brownies. Playing cards, too, cross Lisamarie's mind as one of the tangibles. As is apparent, Robinson is a highly conscious writer with a refined sense of humour; she is not about to make humanly intelligible processes arcane. The place calling for Lisamarie's return is Monkey Beach, where Lisamarie's family camps in the summer. Monkey Beach appears first in memory, nostalgically, as the place where her brother Jimmy hoped to get a photograph of a sasquatch and where she herself evidently spotted a great, hairy, brown man with too many teeth. A second sighting of a sasquatch leaves Lisamarie feeling "deeply comforted knowing that magical things were still living in the world."[35]

Monkey Beach is a place to camp and catch crabs and swim and build campfires, like other coastal sites up the channel from Kitamaat, Lisamarie's village. Lisamarie and her family have a comfortable relationship with nature. Monkey Beach is a place "full of power," but it is a power that gives her "a warmth, a tingle,"[36] not feelings of awe or dread.

In First Nations cultures, tradition includes the spirits of the dead. The natural world delivers portents of death, points the way to those who have died. Her brother's favourite crow, Spotty, and voices from the trees give Lisamarie the clues about where to find her brother, who has drowned. At the end of the novel, Lisamarie returns to Monkey Beach to make contact with the dead. Given the context of death and mystery, the return to the place that gives the novel its title leads one to expect profound revelations. Robinson could have pulled out all the stops; her "land of the dead" could have been a fearful place designed to impress upon the reader the dark, inhuman mysteries of nature and the afterlife – like the land of the dead in *Tracks,* by Louise Erdrich (Native American, Chippewa). Granted, Lisamarie has to grapple with a slithery, bloodsucking creature before her dead come to her, but once she gets past that hurdle, the dead she finds are still very much like themselves. Her dead grandmother tells her to "'Go home and make me some grandkids.'" Her dead uncle says, "'You go out there and give 'em hell. Red power!'" As the dead recede, she sees her uncle dancing and showing off by a fire on the beach.[37] Her brother is with them. The special power of Monkey Beach is associated with the dead, but these dead are familiar beings. Even the spirits of the dead do not render places hostile or frightening – or even noticeably hallowed.

I have mentioned the spirits of the dead because the sense that these spirits are abroad in the environment appears to be infused with the same familiarity that characterizes the waiting berries and roots and the welcoming land. In one of the final moments of Armstrong's *Whispering in Shadows*, "the hills wait listening for [the] footfalls [of Penny and her sister] on the path up."[38] If Robinson's genial portrayal is representative, the dead, likewise, watch and listen with friendly expectation. Among the natural beings of the environment are the human relations who have died. This belief reinforces the conception of natural and human beings as belonging to one community.

Even "the Stones Tell Stories"

In her commentary "Ancient Stories, Spiritual Legacies," Louise Profeit-LeBlanc (Tutchone, from the Yukon) says, "I have been nourished by a community that is so vocal, so open, so giving, so rich in oral tradition that we can share stories told from a perspective that is 30,000 years old. Everything from the land exudes stories. Everything. The stones tell stories. If you travel with an elder, they have a story to tell."[39] Profeit-LeBlanc's community includes stones. The community of natural beings, furthermore, includes human beings. Profeit-LeBlanc recalls an archaeological dig where her people lived: "My people hung out there. All the trees there know the story of the people. They suffered with the people when the fish were not plentiful. They rejoiced in the birthing of new babies, the people coming in with meat, the harvesting of the land and the great sharing of stories."[40]

When traditional First Nations people go out into their lands, not only are the places to which they return familiar to the people, but the people, in turn, are familiar to the places, to the stones and the trees who know the stories of the people and have held the stories of those people for millennia. The felt experience that human beings exist in living relationship with all the individual beings in nature redoubles the pain of the destruction of the environment.

At base, communion among human and natural beings arises because all beings come from the same mother. The conception of elements and beings in the natural world as people just like human beings is tied to the traditional First Nations belief that "Creation is female," as Mingwôn Mingwôn affirms.[41] Even seemingly alien substances like cement can, with difficulty, be conceived of as consubstantial with humanity. J.B. Joe's speaker, in her meditation "Cement Woman," begins by rejecting the "cement people" (city dwellers) among whom she finds herself. But a vision of the Mother of All Things brings a healing perspective: "The substances that make up the cement, the fire and the water and the coloured air, are also the substances that make up my own self, the same substances that make up the Mother of All Things. She is in the cement. She is all. She is one. We are one."[42]

The element of motherhood distinguishes a statement like J.B. Joe's from a Buddhist conception of oneness with nature. Instead of impressing upon the human being a serene sense of the nullity of all things, J.B. Joe's revelation leads logically to the conception of a world community of beings who are independently and communally alive.

The poem "recovery" by Marilyn Dumont (Cree/Métis) testifies to the First Nations sense that all things natural are literally born, including trees. "Recovery" begins with the act of entering something, some state:

> you enter by breathing in deep
>   and when you breathe out
>   you're inside
> a tree branching out
>   your palms running up
>   the inside of trunks
> into limbs that reach
>   for spring air and hope,
>   spreading fingers that point
> into leaves
>   blades of grass,
>   now fingers running through
> black
>   moist
>   edible
>   earth
> that you inhale
>   and enter birth[43]

Dumont uses the experiences that trees have all the time to illuminate the healing process for human beings. If trees and humans were completely separate, the idea of inhaling moist earth would be quite uncomfortable. Euro-Western culture reveals instances of horror at the thought of humans or gods being trapped in trees. Because Dumont's tree is a living being with literal limbs, fingers, and lungs – one who was born of the earth as human beings are – human recovery can truly be represented by the union of the human spirit with the spirit of a tree. Here, as before, Lee Maracle's responsive cedar tree from *Ravensong* is illuminating. Trees are tender, receptive beings in the writing of First Nations women; one can conceive of being healed by uniting with the patient, comforting spirit of a tree.

Similarly, in *Whispering in Shadows*, Armstrong has her narrator, Penny, receive comfort from an ancient tree that she and demonstrators are trying to protect from loggers. Like the cedar tree in *Ravensong*, this tree seems to reach out to Penny:

> *"It feels the same as a relative holding me. Soothing me."* The question arises, *"'What do you think people are searching for?'"* and Penny thinks, *"To feel that the tree is alive? Aware? Speaking a language your body knows? Has known for the thousands of years of your various ancestors? That it's as simple as those ravens up there talking about it?"*[44]

With these observations, Armstrong unites the belief that the natural world is humanly responsive with the related beliefs that humans and natural beings share the same essence and that the land knows the people. Trees are intelligent and have memories. They preserve the record of the people's ancestors. When the loggers break past the demonstrators in *Whispering in Shadows*, Penny thinks of the tree: *"It has seen maybe a thousand years and today will be its last."*[45] Obviously, for Penny and for many other First Nations women, the destruction of one-thousand-year-old trees has a deep and painful impact because these trees belong to the community of all beings and know the people who know the trees.

Annharte's poem "Moon Bear" demonstrates that the notion of communality goes beyond service to humanity in writing by First Nations women. To Euro-Western sensibilities, "Moon Bear" is likely to be a confusing poem; the moon, earth, lake, and bears are perplexingly interrelated and reciprocally inform each other's ontology and practice. The poem begins with the line "My moon is a deep lake in mind." The line "She-bears birthing in my winter womb" seems to indicate that the earth is speaking about hibernating bears pregnant with cubs. If the earth is speaking, what is a reader to make of the last lines: "My moon will grow within me to greet / rising bears bringing warm faces to my lips"?[46] Perhaps, in view of the title of the poem, the moon hibernates in the earth. The "rising bears" seem almost to "rise" as the moon does. Clearly, the poem conveys a sense of the cyclical. There may be a key to this poem that I do not possess. I do not think, however, that any key would render all of the natural elements in this poem isolatable. Indeed, the impression is that the moon, lake, earth, bears, winter, cold, and coming spring are all intricately intermingled – and further that there is great tenderness in this intermingling. "Moon Bear" is a wonderful poem. For anyone who loves nature, the felt quality of reciprocal communion among natural beings is pleasurable without analysis. For anyone growing impatient with the chronic Euro-Western appeal to humankind for meaning, the idea contained in "Moon Bear" that the elements of the natural world interact "humanly" brings welcome respite.

To end this section on a less combative note, I turn to Louise Profeit-LeBlanc's sweetly simple poem "The Old Man and the Swans," about an old man sitting by a lake waiting for the swans to return in the spring. He is delighted to see them: "Yes! There they were full of life / Swooping gracefully down upon the ice." More important, the swans are delighted to see him:

"There he is! The old man!
It's his longing and wish that
Brings us here
To the part of the lake
That he holds so dear."[47]

These swans are not unthinking beings who return to the lake out of innate migratory instincts, nor are they mere passive recipients of the old man's gaze. As a critic steeped in Euro-Western beliefs, I am inclined to think, "We should be so lucky." What a lovely world it would be if the creatures and other beings of the natural world truly knew human beings and responded to our kind with pleasure. At a philosophical level, the idea that human beings and natural beings form one community provides a better rationale for environmental protection than managerial and self-interested arguments. The idea that we lose the natural world's friendly, welcoming interest in us when we come into nature as destroyers puts environmental protection on a different footing, having more to do with love and tenderness than with practical considerations. In their writing, First Nations women make it possible and right to conceive of this kind of relationship among human and natural beings.

Conclusion
In "Song One: The Riverside" from *Mothers of the Grass*, Jovette Marchessault delivers a paean to her Grandmother's words and to women's words in general:

Oh, the beauty of these cellular, multidimensional words, this speech which calls up every forgotten and remembered emotion. These words come from all over – from on high as well as from below, from the wet, the thunder-stricken, the swollen, juicy, cloudy. These words cure just as well as thermal, saline springs, as the fountains of youth. These words are red and blue and shellfish green and the rosy pink of tentacles. There is not a shred of religious or political oppression or any other persecution lurking in the depths of these words.[48]

Clearly, Marchessault articulates the ideal. Not incidentally, her praise suggests polyphony: Women's words are thunder words, cloud words, shellfish words, saline-spring words – and dandelion words, coyote words, partridge words, cedar-tree words, eagle words, bear words, swan words, and the words of the stones of the earth. First Nations women put into words – sometimes in plain speech and sometimes structurally – the idea that the natural environment can be a familiar place to humankind, possessing a familiarity felt deep in the body and heart.

Ideally, then, the beings of the natural world speak through First Nations women's writing. At the same time, one gains the sense from this writing that the beings of the natural world are listening to what humankind has to say. Part of responsible and respectful writing is to speak lovingly and truthfully of the natural world. The human heart or mind, then, is not the sole concern when First Nations women write about the natural world. They have the hearts and minds of natural beings to attend to as well. Such an approach might go a long way toward healing human relations with the environment. If everyone thought that nature was full of beings who were taking heed of human actions and words, we might deal a little more gently with the environment and speak with greater care. One begins to wonder what Wordsworth's "meanest" flower thought of Wordsworth.

Notes

1 William Wordsworth, "Ode: Intimations of Immortality," in *English Romantic Writers*, edited by David Perkins (Fort Worth, TX: Harcourt Brace College Publishers, 1995), 334. "Meanest" means "smallest" or "lowliest" in this quotation, and "blows" means "blossoms."
2 Lee Maracle, "Perseverance," in *I Am a Woman* (North Vancouver, BC: Write-On Press, 1988) The Stó:lo are a First Nations people of the Canadian West Coast.
3 The term "First Nations" refers inherently to Aboriginal nations of Canada. "Canadian First Nations" is redundant but is used here for the purposes of orientation.
4 This perspective is not unique to First Nations female writers. Dorothy Wordsworth, "Floating Island at Hawkshead: An Incident in the Schemes of Nature," in *English Romantic Writers*, edited by David Perkins (Fort Worth, TX: Harcourt Brace College Publishers, 1995), 497. Curiously, Wordsworth's sister Dorothy explicitly speaks of a "peopled *world*" (emphasis in the original) in her poem "Floating Island at Hawkshead, an Incident in the Schemes of Nature," in which she writes about the trees, birds, berries, flowers, and insects occupying a "little Island" that has broken from the shore and will eventually sink. Dorothy Wordsworth evidently had a sense of ecology never expressed by her more famous and influential brother.
5 Jeanette Armstrong, "Words," in *Telling It: Women and Language across Cultures,* edited by the Telling It Book Collective (Vancouver: Press Gang, 1990), 23-29.
6 Lee Maracle, "Just Get in Front of a Typewriter and Bleed," in *Telling It: Women and Language across Cultures,* edited by the Telling It Book Collective (Vancouver: Press Gang Publishers, 1990), 40.
7 Ruby Slipperjack, *Honour the Sun* (Winnipeg: Pemmican, 1987), 93.
8 Barbara Godard, *Talking about Ourselves: The Literary Productions of the Native Women of Canada* (Ottawa: Canadian Research Institute for the Advancement of Women, 1985), 3.
9 Jeannette Armstrong, *Whispering in Shadows* (Penticton, BC: Theytus Books, 2000), 146, 147.
10 Natalia Rybczynski, "Predators and Cosmologies," *The Canadian Journal of Native Studies* 17, 1 (1997): 107.

11 Jim Mason, *An Unnatural Order: Uncovering the Roots of Our Domination of Nature and Each Other* (New York: Simon and Schuster, 1993), 51.

12 Ibid., 51-52.

13 One has to grant, however, that if all entities in nature are people in First Nations cultural belief, the use even of plants must create some distress and need for expiation. In *Ravensong*, Lee Maracle's protagonist, Stacey, recalls grating camas root for a feast. She asks her mother, "'Doesn't it hurt?'" Her mother replies, "'Yes, it does ... Camas are here to take care of us. Never forget to be grateful. Don't waste her, remember she sacrifices her life to you. Whisper sweet words to her. Give her courage.'" Lee Maracle, *Ravensong* (Vancouver: Press Gang, 1993), 173.

14 Mingwôn Mingwôn (Shirley Bear), "Equality among Women," in *Native Writers and Canadian Writing*, edited by W.H. New (Vancouver: UBC Press, 1990), 133-36.

15 Rose Auger, quoted in Agnes Grant, "Reclaiming the Lineage House: Canadian Native Women Writers," *Studies in American Indian Literature* 6 (1994): 49.

16 Agnes Grant, ed., *Our Bit of Truth: An Anthology of Canadian Native Literature* (Winnipeg: Pemmican, 1990), 99.

17 Leonora Hayden McDowell, "Windsong," in *Writing the Circle: Native Women of Western Canada*, edited by Jeanne Perreault and Sylvia Vance (Edmonton: NeWest, 1990), 184.

18 Pauline Johnson, "Moonset," in *Pauline Johnson: Her Life and Work*, written and edited by Marcus Van Stern (Toronto: Hodder and Stoughton, 1965), 132.

19 Maracle, *Ravensong*, 14, 44, 62.

20 Leonora Hayden McDowell, "Give Me the Spirit of the Eagle," in Perreault and Vance, eds., *Writing the Circle*, 186.

21 Willow Barton, "Where Have the Warriors Gone?" in Perreault and Vance, eds., *Writing the Circle*, 10, 18.

22 Louise Bernice Halfe, "Grandmother," in Perreault and Vance, eds., *Writing the Circle*, 85-86.

23 Annharte, "Coyote Trail," in *An Anthology of Canadian Native Literature in English*, edited by Daniel David Moses and Terrie Goldie (Toronto: Oxford University Press, 1992), 168-69.

24 Thomas King shows Coyote's buffoonery having world-changing consequences in *Green Grass, Running Water* (Toronto: HarperCollins, 1993) and King, "The One about Coyote Going West," in *One Good Story, That One;* (Toronto: HarperCollins, 1993).

25 Robert Bringhurst, "Singing with the Frogs," *Canadian Literature* 155 (Winter 1997): 114, 118. Bringhurst mentions Inuit throat singing as an example of polyphony but does not draw on his work with First Nations materials for other examples. He does cite observations made by Roy Franklin Barton about the traditional cultural practices of the Ifugao people located in northern Luzon. Barton observed Ifugao priests practising myth recitation. Bringhurst describes how Barton "sometimes met the mythtellers sitting by the streams, talking with the water. Talking with the water, not lecturing the waves, was the favored method for training the voice" (128). I am not aware of any similar practice among Canada's First Nations cultures. It is intriguing, however, to learn that the Cree word for the Cree people is "Nehiyawak," which, according to Emma LaRocque, means "The Exact Speaking People" or, in another dialect, "People of Four Directions." Emma LaRocque, preface to *Writing the Circle: Native Women of Western Canada*, edited by Jeanne Perreault and Sylvia Vance (Edmonton: NeWest, 1990), xv-xxx, xxv-xxvi. I would like to suggest, just as pure speculation, that "exact speaking" might hint at a polyphonic relationship with the earth in oral traditions.

26 kateri akiwenzie-damm, "partridge song," *Canadian Literature* 155 (Winter 1997): 113.

27 Jovette Marchessault, "Song One: The Riverside," translated by Yvonne M. Klein, excerpted from *Mother of the Grass*, in *All My Relations: An Anthology of Contemporary Canadian Native Fiction*, edited by Thomas King (Toronto: McClelland and Stewart, 1990), 175-200.

28 Grant, ed., *Our Bit of Truth*, 113.

29 Slipperjack, *Honour the Sun*, 101, 211.

30 Jeanette Armstrong, *Slash* (Penticton, BC: Theytus Books, 1992), 95-96.

31 Ibid., 206.

32 Armstrong, *Whispering in Shadows*, 275.

33 Ibid., 133.
34 Eden Robinson, *Monkey Beach* (Toronto: Alfred A. Knopf, 2000), 83.
35 Ibid., 315-16.
36 Ibid., 316.
37 Ibid., 373-74.
38 Armstrong, *Whispering in Shadows*, 276.
39 Louise Profeit-LeBlanc, "Ancient Stories, Spiritual Legacies," in the Telling It Book Collective, ed., *Telling It*, 112.
40 Ibid., 113.
41 Mingwôn Mingwôn, "Equality among Women," 133.
42 J.B. Joe, "Cement Woman," in Thomas King, ed., *All My Relations*, 164-70, 169.
43 Marilyn Dumont, "recovery," in Perreault and Vance, eds., *Writing the Circle*, 44.
44 Armstrong, *Whispering in Shadows*, 99, 101, italics in the original.
45 Ibid., 121, italics in the original.
46 Annharte, "Moon Bear," in Moses and Goldie, eds., *An Anthology,* 169-70.
47 Louise Profeit-LeBlanc, "The Old Man and the Swans," in the Telling It Book Collective, ed., *Telling It*, 157-58.
48 Marchessault, "Song One," 189.

Conclusion

This anthology investigates women's experiences in, and critical perspectives on, the Canadian environment, exploring the extensive and varied ways that gendered lives are shaped by a country that is equally extensive and varied. Although Canada remains an "elusive land," it is abundantly clear from the preceding chapters that a gendered lens reveals a more nuanced and interesting environmental narrative than is apparent in the dominant, monolithic one of conquest and garrison. In addition, however, it is also clear that an understanding of gender in Canada is significantly enriched by a conscious attention to questions of nature, landscape, and environment. With these intersecting dimensions in mind, the aim of the collection is to explore a range of women's perspectives on Canadian landscapes in order to better understand the ways that the social and biophysical settings of this landscape were and are integrated in women's lives and also to consider what effects gender has had on the diverse economic, social, cultural, and political conditions that affect Canadians' relations to their natural environments.

Although it is certainly the case that women's experiences have varied historically, geographically, and because of differences in class, race, and sexuality, the authors of this collection significantly address several recurring themes about gender and the Canadian environment. To begin with, the invisibility or marginalization of women in conventional accounts of the Canadian environment is itself deeply problematic. Culturally and historically, the construction of an overarching national narrative of Canadian colonization and settlement in the wilderness that ignores women's significant contributions and perspectives perpetuates an understanding of Canadian nature and nation that privileges the accounts and interests of affluent white men. To the extent to which our national mythologies reify and universalize such a particular understanding of Canada – such a particular intersection of ideas of gender, territory, and nation – other voices find it difficult to claim a legitimate space in which to speak of *their* experiences as important elements in the cultural representation of "Canada." Nature is, by many accounts, part of the Canadian national mythos. Questions posed by this anthology, then, include *whose* nature is privileged in dominant accounts of the nation, and how different might the nation look if viewed through the nature experiences of women who occupy a different range of social positions?

In addition, the marginalization of women in accounts of the Canadian environment has important and ongoing material effects. First, the invisibility of women's labour in nature is part of the means by which gender inequalities are maintained in Canadian society: So long as gardening, canning, botanizing, and other transformative acts in nature are not considered in the economic calculus of the (staple-producing?) nation, women's work will be systematically ignored and undervalued. Even more, a refusal to value these activities as significant elements of a people's livelihood in nature contributes to the continued exploitation of natural resources. In a world in which picking wild blueberries for family or community use does not count as an economically important activity compared to industrial forestry, it is no accident that it is so often women's voices and values that are subordinated. Along with racialized minorities and working-class communities, women have historically found that their environmental needs don't count.

This anthology thus not only questions dominant cultural narratives of nature by including a range of alternative women's accounts of natural environments, but also challenges mainstream economic and political constructions of nature by highlighting the rich textures of women's varied environmental activities. A fuller narrative of the Canadian environment demands such inclusions, and although this anthology by no means exhausts all possibilities, the preceding chapters certainly highlight significant elements of a developing alternative story. In this story, women's "place" is not reduced to the interior space of the household (indeed, many women's places were not in the household at all) but envelops and embraces an extensive biophysical world. It is often, in fact, an active embrace of this biophysical world that enables women to develop empowering modes of knowing and acting; women have found, in natural environments, spaces for personal and collective growth often denied in more socially constricted spaces. Still, different authors demonstrate the *divergent* ways that women integrate the social and biophysical settings of their lives, and these include wild, domestic, and urban environments. The anthology reveals a *range* of women's experience in which gender inspires, mediates, and informs their sense of belonging to and in this country. It emphasizes the ways that a gender-conscious approach contributes to a more inclusive and complete understanding of this environment, but it still recognizes that there is no one size to fit all women or all natures. In this way a fuller picture of women's experiences emerges, one that provides a useful basis for reassessing human relationships to nature in Canada and elsewhere but that still recognizes the elusiveness of the story as a whole.

In these respects, many of the contributions to this anthology echo ecofeminist accounts that insist on the need for the visibility and valuation of women's activities in, and perspectives on, natural environments. In recent ecofeminist literary criticism, for example, women's voices are increasingly recognized as vital to the international canon of writing on nature. Women's activities as naturalists – and, indeed, as authors who incorporate nature into their stories in a wide variety of ways not confined to a single genre – viscerally transcend the narrow sphere of domesticity assigned to women. At the same time, their observations often demonstrate understandings of natural environments that are significantly different from those of their male counterparts. In this rather hybrid space of gender and nature, women both claim and reject gender roles and differences, in addition to the varied racial, class, and sexual dynamics in which such relations are shaped and lived. The more visible the complexities of these relations are in our analyses, the more interesting are the insights about nature apparent in our historical and contemporary literatures.

There is a similar call for visibility in ecofeminist economics and politics. Here, the need actively to consider the important family and community benefits derived from women's subsistence activities suggests a political agenda of democratizing what counts as "significant" nature knowledge. At any given moment and in any given community, there is a variety of values and practices that connect humans with their landscapes and other-than-human animal companions. That the ones associated with women are systematically devalued and ignored is, for ecofeminists, a profound cause of the worldwide ecological crisis in that the quest for profit through commodity extraction and production wreaks havoc with almost all other natural values and uses. In the same way that ecofeminist critics call for a rethinking of the texture of the literary canon to include emphasis on a range of gender-nature relations, ecofeminist economists call for the movement of such nuanced knowledge into the political and policy realm, going so far as to say that the current valuation of commodity over community should be reversed.

Yet it should be pointed out that this anthology also suggests significant disagreements with certain elements of ecofeminism. In the first place, the anthology begins from the premise that women's activities in nature are actively directed by a social construction of gender that organizes women's lives and experiences within a variety of biophysical environments. In the second place, the strong emphasis in this anthology on the diversity apparent among women, *and among landscapes*, suggests a rejection of many of the universalizing tenets of ecofeminist philosophy and politics (e.g., that women's relations to nature are a given in a metanarrative of hierarchical dualism). In particular, the anthology emphasizes, both implicitly and explicitly, that there are significant differences *among* women that make any broad generalization about women's values or voices deeply problematic. While we emphasize that there are significant historical and continuing threads of power and privilege that allow us to draw important insights about the co-imbrication of gender and nature, we also insist that the diversity of women, and the diversity so abundantly apparent in the Canadian environment, makes a complete and universal story both impossible and dangerous.

Given both its agreements with and its departures from these elements of ecofeminist thought, what are some of the specific lessons of this book? First, and most fundamental, women are, and have been, active in experiencing, mediating, interpreting, and living in the biophysical environment. Second, landscape is central, a foreground to women's lives; it infuses, colours, saturates, and hones our lives in ways that are significant but often either taken for granted or forgotten within a cultural context of homogenization. Third, although Canadians live under one national banner, women's experiences may vary significantly from those of men, and of one another. Factors of region, ecology, culture, class, sexuality, and race forge diverse experiences of living in this land. Indeed, while women may identify this land as Canadian, there are significant differences among them. Fourth, the complexity of cultural experience is also revealed by these writings. The interface between culture and ecology is thick with meaning, and we have only begun here to develop a sense of its intricacies. The diversity of experience represented in these accounts indicates that women do not have any "special" or "closer" relationship to nature than do men but rather that their relationships are forged by both the social and physical exigencies of their existences. Fifth, the fabric of the Canadian environment is dynamic, changing both physically and socially, and changing quickly. Our ability to project trajectories for future Canadian environments is informed by the past but limited by knowledge, resources, and hubris. We have only scratched the surface.

We hope that this book generates a sense of curiosity about living in these places that are Canada. Like an archaeological discovery, the anthology asks that we dig deeper, not just into the past, but into additional and emergent sites of experience. One of the issues identified by these contributions as requiring greater attention is that of cultural diversity. The environmental perspectives of minority women, of women in different provinces and regions, of First Nations, francophones, immigrants, gay men and lesbians, and a host of human "others" require further exploration. The perspectives of First Nations women, while acknowledged in ethnobotanical accounts, especially warrant attention given their often-explicit focus on the environment as central to the survival of individuals and culture. Another issue that merits increased exploration is the interface between human society and ecological systems. Attention to the physical environment requires us to attend to the complexity of systems about which we know very little. Ecological objectives should be incorporated into our political and economic policies. Further attention is also required for a better understanding of dynamic and emerging issues, both social and physical. Globalization and the increased integration of the Canadian economy will result in continuing changes to the Canadian environment. Physical changes such as climate change and resource depletion require additional attention as social systems adapt to new regimes.

Finally, we believe that this anthology makes significant contributions to the development of a specifically interdisciplinary scholarly practice. It contributes to our understanding of women's studies through its environmental focus and informs and textures environmental studies with a feminist perspective. Cutting across this already-interdisciplinary terrain of gender-conscious ecology (and vice versa) is an equally important focus on the specifically Canadian dimensions of the intersection. Thus we believe that the anthology also enriches Canadian studies by integrating social and cultural perspectives of the Canadian experience. We believe that the collection not only represents a significant innovation in each of these diverse fields, but, indeed, points to the critical need for interdisciplinary approaches to environmental concerns generally. This field emphasizes the importance of situatedness and specificity in the generation of knowledge and insight about large questions of power, nature, and even ecology; it also insists that there are crucial conversations about the Canadian environment yet to take place among natural science, social science, and the humanities.

Still, we recognize the limitations of our project. In addition to acknowledging the fact that no anthology can possibly include a complete range of gendered perspectives on Canadian nature, we recognize that the representation of certain kinds of voices in these pages repeats and extends some of the historical relations of power with which gender so crucially intersects. Rather than claim to have enumerated women's voices in this text, then, we end by issuing a call to other scholars, activists, and writers to continue to value and search for the richness of nature experiences and perspectives that lies behind racist, classist, and heterosexist formulations of the national landscape. In the process, we also call on readers to recognize and search for the diversity and uniqueness of this *place* we call home; just as our social diversity gives rise to varied experiences of nature, so, too, do the place-specific situations of our lives give rise to a considerable richness of experience. At the end of the day, however, as much as the territory of

Canada situates our belonging, it also defies complete description. We thus hope that the anthology encourages us all to recognize and acknowledge our dependence on the natural environments of this country that is, paradoxically, both an "elusive land" and our home.

Bibliography

Abbey, Edward. *Desert Solitaire: A Season in the Wilderness*. New York, NY: McGraw-Hill, 1968.

Abbott Cone, Cynthia, and Andrea Myhre. "Community Supported Agriculture: A Sustainable Alternative to Industrial Agriculture?" *Human Organization* 59, 2 (2000): 187-97.

Abel, Kerry. "The Northwest and the North." In *Canadian History: A Reader's Guide*, edited by M. Brook Taylor, 325-55. Toronto: University of Toronto Press, 1994.

Aberley, Doug, ed. *Boundaries of Home: Mapping for Local Empowerment*. Gabriola Island, BC: New Society, 1993.

Adams, Carol, ed. *Ecofeminism and the Sacred*. New York: Continuum, 1993.

Aga Khan Rural Support Programme. *Rapid Participatory Rural Appraisal: Frontiers of Research*. London, UK: Aga Khan Foundation, 1991.

Agarwal, Bina. *A Field of One's Own*. Cambridge, UK: Cambridge University Press, 1994.

–. "From Mexico 1975 to Beijing 1995." *Indian Journal of Gender Studies* 3, 1 (1996): 21-35.

–. "A Challenge for Ecofeminism: Gender, Greening, and Community Forestry in India." *Women and Environments International Magazine* 52/53 (Fall 2001): 12-15.

Aggarwal, Ravina. "Trails of Turquoise: Feminist Inquiry and Counter-Development in Ladakh, India." In *Feminist Post-Development Thought: Rethinking Modernity, Postcolonialism and Representation*, edited by Kriemeld Saunders, 69-85. New York: Zed Books, 2002.

Ainley, Marianne. "Science in Canada's Backwoods." In *Natural Eloquence: Women Reinscribe Science*, edited by Barbara Gates and Ann Shteir, 79-97. Madison, WI: University of Wisconsin Press, 1997.

Airhart, Phyllis D. *Serving the Present Age: Revivalism, Progressivism, and the Methodist Tradition in Canada*. Montreal and Kingston: McGill-Queen's University Press, 1992.

akiwenzie-damm, kateri. "partridge song." *Canadian Literature* 155 (Winter 1997): 113.

Alaimo, Stacy. *Undomesticated Ground: Recasting Nature as Feminist Space*. Ithaca, NY: Cornell University Press, 2000.

Alaluusua, S., et al. "Developing Teeth as Biomarker of Dioxin Exposure." *Lancet* 353 (1999): 206.

Alinsky, Saul. "Tactics." In *Rules for Radicals*, 126-48. New York: Vintage Books, 1971.

Allen, David Elliston. *The Naturalist in Britain: A Social History*. London, UK: Allen Lane, 1976.

Allen, Paula, and Eve Ensler. "An Activist Love Story." In *The Feminist Memoir Project: Voices from Women's Liberation*, edited by R.B. DuPlessis and A. Snitow, 413-25. New York: Three Rivers Press, 1998.

Allsopp, Michelle, Ruth Stringer, and Paul Johnston. *Unseen Poisons: Levels of Organochlorine Chemicals in Human Tissues*. Greenpeace International, 1998.

Altmeyer, George. "Three Ideas of Nature in Canada, 1893-1914." In *Consuming Canada: Readings in Environmental History*, edited by Chad Gaffield and Ann Gaffield, 96-118. Toronto: Copp Clark, 1995.

Anderson, Lorraine. *Sisters of the Earth*. New York: Vintage, 1991.

Angeles, Leonora C. "Women Farmers and the Struggle for Sustainable Livelihoods and Organic Farming in a Peri-Urban City in Bukidnon, Philippines." *Urban Agriculture Magazine* (special issue on organic urban agriculture) 4, 1 (2002): 32-33.

–, and Penny Gurstein. "Planning for Participatory Development: Challenges of Participation and North-South Partnerships in Capacity-Building Projects." *Canadian Journal of Development Studies* (special issue on participatory development) 21 (2000): 447-78.

–, and Rebecca Tarbotton. "Local Transformation through Global Connection: Women's Assets and Environmental Activism for Sustainable Agriculture in Ladakh, India." *Women's Studies Quarterly* 29, 1-2 (2001): 99-115.

Angier, Bradford, and Vena Angier. *Wilderness Wife*. Radnor, PA: Chilton, 1976.

Angier, Vena, and Bradford Angier. *At Home in the Woods*. New York: Sheridan House, 1951.

Angus, Ian. *A Border Within: National Identity, Cultural Plurality, and Wilderness*. Montreal and Kingston: McGill-Queen's University Press, 1997.

Annharte. "Coyote Trail." In *An Anthology of Canadian Native Literature in English*, edited by Daniel David Moses and Terrie Goldie. Toronto: Oxford University Press, 1992.

–. "Moon Bear." In *An Anthology of Canadian Native Literature in English*, edited by Daniel David Moses and Terrie Goldie. Toronto: Oxford University Press, 1992.

Archer, S.A., ed. *A Heroine of the North: Memoirs of Charlotte Selina Bompas*. Toronto: Macmillan, 1929.

Armstrong, Jeannette. "Words." In *Telling It: Women and Language across Cultures*, edited by the Telling It Book Collective, 23-29. Vancouver: Press Gang Publishers, 1990.

–. *Slash*. Penticton, BC: Theytus Books, 1992.

–. *Whispering in Shadows*. Penticton, BC: Theytus Books, 2000.

Armstrong, Pat. "The Feminization of the Labour Force: Harmonizing Down in a Global Economy." In *Invisible: Issues in Women's Occupational Health*, edited by K. Messing, B. Neis, and L. Dumais, 368-92. Charlottetown: Gynergy, 1995.

Armstrong, Pat, and Hugh Armstrong. *The Double Ghetto: Canadian Women and Their Segregated Work*. Toronto: McClelland and Stewart, 1994.

Arnstein, Sherry. "A Ladder of Citizen Participation." *Journal of the American Institute of Planners* 35, 4: 216-24.

Arthur, Elizabeth. *Island Sojourn: A Memoir*. 1980. Reprint, Saint Paul: Greywolf Press, 1991.

Ayotte, P., G. Carrier, and E. Dewailly. "Health Risk Assessment for Inuit Newborns Exposed to Dioxin-Like Compounds through Breast Feeding." *Chemosphere* 32 (1996): 531-42.

Bachrach, Peter, and Morton S. Baratz. *Power and Poverty: Theory and Practice*. Toronto: Oxford University Press, 1970.

Ballstadt, Carl, Elizabeth Hopkins, and Michael Peterman, eds. *I Bless You in My Heart: Selected Correspondence of Catharine Parr Traill*. Toronto: University of Toronto Press, 1996.

Barndt, Deborah, ed. *Women Working the NAFTA Chain: Women, Food and Globalization*. Toronto: Second Story Press, 1999.

Barnes, T.J., and R. Hayter, eds. *Troubles in the Rainforest: British Columbia's Forest Economy in Transition*. Canadian Western Geographical Series No. 33. Victoria, BC: Western Geographical Press, 1994.

Barrett, R.J. *Canada's Century: Progress and Resources of the Great Dominion*. London, UK: Financier and Bullionist, 1907.

Barry, John. *Rethinking Green Politics*. London, UK: Sage, 1999.

Barton, Willow. "Where Have the Warriors Gone?" In *Writing the Circle: Native Women of Western Canada*, edited by Jeanne Perreault and Sylvia Vance, 8-18. Edmonton: NeWest, 1990.

Bates, Marston. *The Nature of Natural History*. New York: Charles Scribner's Sons, 1954.

Baumgartner, Frank R., and Bryan D. Jones. *Agendas and Instability in American Politics*. Chicago: University of Chicago Press, 1993.

Baumslag, Naomi, and Dia L. Michels. *Milk, Money, and Madness: The Culture and Politics of Breastfeeding*. Westport, CT: Bergin and Garvey, 1995.

Behar, Ruth, and Deborah Gordon, eds. *Women Writing Culture*. Berkeley: University of California Press, 1995.

Bella, Leslie. *Parks for Profit*. Montreal: Harvest House, 1987.

Bello, Walden. "Fast-Track Capitalism, Geoeconomic Competition and the Sustainable Development Challenge in East Asia." In *Globalization and the South*, edited by Caroline Thomas and Peter Wilkin, 143-62. London, UK: Macmillan, 1997; New York: St. Martin's Press, 1997.

Benham, Lillian. "Shelburne Fishnet Addresses Women's Health Issues." *Coastal Community News Magazine* 5, 1 (1999): n.p.

Berger, Carl. *The Sense of Power: Studies in the Ideas of Canadian Imperialism*. Toronto: University of Toronto Press, 1970.

Berman, Tzeporah. "Standing for Our Lives: Ecofeminism and Lessons from Clayoquot Sound." MA thesis, Faculty of Environmental Studies, York University, 1995.

Berry, Thomas. *Dream of the Earth*. San Francisco: Sierra Club Books, 1988.

Bertell, R. *Planet Earth: The Latest Weapon of War*. Montreal: Black Rose Books, 2001.

Beston, Henry. *The Outermost House: A Year of Life on the Great Beach of Cape Cod*. 1928. Reprint, New York: Penguin, 1988.

Bhabha, Homi. "The Other Question: The Stereotype and Colonial Discourse." *Screen* 24, 6 (1983): 18-36.

–. *The Location of Culture*. London, UK: Routledge, 1994.

Bhatnagar, Bhuvan, and Audrey Williams, eds. *Participatory Development and the World Bank: Potential Directions for Change*. Washington, DC: World Bank, 1992.

Biehl, Janet. *Finding Our Way: Rethinking Ecofeminist Politics*. Montreal: Black Rose Books, 1991.

Binkley, Marion. "Lost Moorings: Offshore Fishing Families Coping with a Fisheries Crisis." *Dalhousie Law Journal* 18, 1 (1995): 84-95.

Birch, Thomas. "The Incarceration of Wildness: Wilderness Areas as Prisons." *Environmental Ethics* 12 (1990): 3-26.

Birkland, Thomas. "Focusing Events, Mobilization, and Agenda Setting." *Journal of Public Policy* 18 (1998): 53-74.

Blumberg, Rae Lesser, Cathy Rakowski, Irene Tinker, and Michael Monteon, eds. *Engendering Wealth and Well-Being: Empowerment for Global Change*. Boulder, CO: Westview Press, 1995.

Boddy, Alexander. *By Ocean, Prairie and Peak: Some Gleanings from an Emigrant Chaplain's Log, On Journeys to British Columbia, Manitoba, and Eastern Canada*. London, UK: Society for Promoting Christian Knowledge, 1896.

Boothroyd, Peter, and Leonora C. Angeles, eds. *Canadian Journal of Development Studies, Special Issue on Canadian Universities and International Development: A Critical Look* 24, 3 (2003).

Bosso, Christopher. "The Contextual Bases of Problem Definition." In *The Politics of Problem Definition: Shaping the Policy Agenda*, edited by David A. Rochefort and Roger W. Cobb, 182-203. Lawrence, KS: University Press of Kansas, 1994.

Bove, Jose, and Francois Dufour. *This World Is Not for Sale: Farmers against Junk Food*. London, UK: Verso, 2001.

Bowering, George. *Bowering's BC: A Swashbuckling History*. Toronto: Viking, 1996.

Boyens, Ingeborg. *Another Season's Promise: Hope and Despair in Canada's Farm Country*. Toronto: Penguin, 2001.

Bradbury, Bettina. "Pigs and Cows and Boarders: Non-Wage Forms of Survival among Montréal Families, 1861-91." In *The Challenge of Modernity: A Reader on Post-Confederation Canada*, edited by Ian McKay, 65-91. Toronto: McGraw-Hill Ryerson, 1992.

Bradley, A.G. *Canada in the Twentieth Century*. London, UK: Archibald Constable, 1905.

Braidotti, Rosi, Ewa Charkiewicz, Sabine Hausler, and Saskia Wieringa. *Women, the Environment and Sustainable Development: Towards a Theoretical Synthesis*. London, UK: Zed Press, 1994.

Brand, Dionne. *In Another Place, Not Here*. Toronto: Alfred A. Knopf, 1996.

Brandth, B., and M. Haugen. "Breaking into a Masculine Discourse: Women and Farm Forestry." *Sociologia Ruralis* 38 (1998): 427-42.

Brant, Beth. *Food and Spirits: Stories*. Vancouver: Press Gang, 1991.

Bringhurst, Robert. "Singing with the Frogs." *Canadian Literature* 155 (Winter 1997): 114-34.

Brodie, Janine. *Politics on the Margins: Restructuring and the Canadian Women's Movement.* Halifax: Fernwood, 1995.

–. "Restructuring and the New Citizenship." In *Rethinking Restructuring: Gender and Change in Canada,* edited by Isabella Bakker, 126-40. Toronto: University of Toronto Press, 1996.

Brody, Julia G., and Ruthann A. Rudel. "Environmental Pollutants and Breast Cancer." In *Environmental Health Perspectives,* Journal of the National Institute of Environmental Health Sciences, 2003. <http://dx.doi.org>.

Brown, Jennifer. *Strangers in Blood: Fur Trade Company Families in Indian Country.* Vancouver: UBC Press, 1980.

Bullard, Robert. *Dumping in Dixie.* Boulder, CO: Westview Press, 1990.

Burns, Robert J., with Mike Schintz. *Guardians of the Wild: A History of the Warden Service of Canada's National Parks.* Calgary: University of Calgary Press, 2000.

Burroughs, John. "Real and Sham Natural History." *Atlantic Monthly* 91 (1903): 298-309.

Buss, Helen. "Women and the Garrison Mentality: Pioneer Women Autobiographers and Their Relation to the Land." In *Re(dis)covering Our Foremothers,* edited by Lorraine McMullen, 123-36. Ottawa: University of Ottawa Press, 1990.

Butala, Sharon. *The Perfection of the Morning: An Apprenticeship in Nature.* Toronto: Harper Collins, 1994.

Butler, W.F. *The Great Lone Land: A Narrative of Travel and Adventure in the North-West of America.* 2nd ed. London, UK: Sampson Low, 1872.

Buttel, Fred. "Theoretical Issues in Global Agri-Food Restructuring." In *Globalization and Agri-Food Restructuring: Perspectives from the Australasia Region,* edited by D. Burch, R. Rickson, and G. Lawrence. Aldershot, UK: Avebury, 1996.

Calahan, James M. *Edward Abbey: A Life.* Tucson, AZ: University of Arizona Press, 2001.

Cameron, Agnes Deans. *The New North: Being Some Account of a Woman's Journey through Canada to the Arctic.* New York: D. Appleton, 1909; reissued as *The New North,* edited by David Richeson. Lincoln: University of Nebraska Press, 1986.

Cameron, Barbara. "From Equal Opportunity to Symbolic Equity: Three Decades of Federal Training Policy for Women." In *Rethinking Restructuring: Gender and Change in Canada,* edited by Isabella Bakker, 55-81. Toronto: University of Toronto Press, 1996.

Campbell, Maria. *Halfbreed.* Toronto: McClelland and Stewart, 1973.

Canada, the Federal, Provincial, Territorial Advisory Committee on Population Health. *Toward a Healthy Future: Second Report on the Health of Canadians.* Ottawa: Ministry of Supply and Services, 1999.

Canadian Paediatric Society and Health Canada. *Nutrition for Healthy Term Infants.* Ottawa: Minister of Public Works, 1988.

Caplan, Pat. "Engendering Knowledge: The Politics of Ethnography." In *Persons and Powers of Women in Diverse Cultures: Essays in Commemoration of Audrey I. Richard, Phyllis Kaberry and Barbara E. Ward,* edited by Shirley Ardener, 65-87. New York: Berg, 1992.

Carroll, M.S. *Community and the Northwestern Logger.* Boulder, CO: University of Colorado Press, 1995.

–, S.E. Daniels, and J. Kusel. "Employment and Displacement among Northwestern Forest Products Workers." *Society and Natural Resources* 13 (2000): 151-56.

Carson, Rachel. *Silent Spring.* Boston, MS: Houghton Mifflin, 1962.

Carter, Sarah. *Capturing Women: The Manipulation of Cultural Images in Canada's Prairie West.* Montreal and Kingston: McGill-Queen's University Press, 1997.

Cartier, A., J.L. Malo, H. Ghezzo, M. McCants, and S.B. Lehrer. "IgE Sensitization in Snow-Crab-Processing Workers." *Journal of Allergy and Clinical Immunology* 78 (1986): 344-48.

Cartier, Jacques. *The Voyages of Jacques Cartier.* Toronto: University of Toronto Press, 1983.

Case, D. Davis. *The Communities Toolbox: The Idea, Methods and Tools for Participatory Assessment, Monitoring and Evaluation in Community Forestry.* Rome: FAO, 1990.

Cather, Willa. *O Pioneers.* New York: Houghton Mifflin, 1913.

–. *Shadows on the Rock.* New York: Alfred A. Knopf, 1931.

–. *A Lost Lady.* Reprint, New York: Vintage Press, 1971 [1923].

–. *One of Ours*. New York, NY: Vintage, 1991 [1922].

Cavanaugh, Catherine, and Jeremy Mouat. "Western Canadian History: A Selected Bibliography." In *Making Western Canada: Essays on European Colonization and Settlement,* edited by Catherine Cavanaugh and Jeremy Mouat, 267-82. Toronto: Garamond, 1996.

–, eds. *Making Western Canada: Essays on European Colonization and Settlement.* Toronto: Garamond, 1996.

Chagnon, Napoleon. *Yanomamo, the Fierce People*. 3rd ed. New York: Holt, Rinehart, and Winston, 1983.

Chambers, Robert. *Whose Reality Counts? Putting the First Last*. London, UK: Intermediate Technology Publications, 1997.

Christ, Carol, and Judith Plaskow, eds. *Weaving the Vision: New Patterns in Feminist Spirituality*. San Francisco: Harper and Row, 1989.

Christiansen-Ruffman, Linda, and Stella Lord. "Under Stress." *Yemaya*, August 2000, 16-17.

Clifford, James, and George Marcus, eds. *Writing Culture: The Poetics and Politics of Ethnography*. Berkeley: University of California Press, 1986.

Coates, Colin M., and Cecilia Morgan. *Heroines and History: Representations of Madeleine de Verchères and Laura Secord*. Toronto: University of Toronto Press, 2002.

Cobb, Roger W., and Charles D. Elder. *Participation in American Politics: The Dynamics of Agenda Building*. Boston: Allyn and Bacon, 1972.

Cobb, Roger W., and Marc Howard Ross. *Cultural Strategies of Agenda Denial: Avoidance, Attack, and Redefinition*. Lawrence, KS: University Press of Kansas, 1997.

Cody, H.A. *An Apostle of the North: Memoirs of the Right Reverend William Carpenter Bompas, D.D.* Toronto: Musson, 1908.

Colborn, Theo, Dianne Dumanoski, and John Peterson Myers. *Our Stolen Future*. New York: Dutton, 1996.

Collins, Jane. "Gender and Cheap Labour in Agriculture." In *Food and Agrarian Orders in the World Economy,* edited by Philip McMichael, 217-32. Westport, CT: Greenwood Press, 1995.

Commission on Resources and Environment (CORE). *Vancouver Island Land Use Plan*. Vol. 1. Victoria, BC: Commission on Resources and Environment, 1994.

Connelly, Pat, and Martha MacDonald. "The Labour Market, the State, and the Reorganization of Work: Policy Impacts." In *Rethinking Restructuring: Gender and Change in Canada,* edited by Isabella Bakker, 82-91. Toronto: University of Toronto Press, 1996.

Cooke, Bill, and Uma Kothari. *Participation: The New Tyranny?* London, UK, and New York: Zed Books, 2001.

Coover, Virginia, Ellen Deacon, Charles Esser, and Christopher Moore. *Resource Manual for a Living Revolution*. Philadelphia: New Society, 1985.

Cormack, Peter. "Using Mapping in Ethiopia." *Footsteps* 17: 8-9.

Cousineau, Phil, ed. *The Soul of the World: A Modern Book of Hours*. San Francisco: Harper, 1993.

Crisler, Lois. *Arctic Wild*. New York, NY: Harper and Row, 1958.

Cronon, William. "The Trouble with Wilderness, or Getting Back to the Wrong Nature." In *Uncommon Ground: Toward Reinventing Nature,* edited by William Cronon, 69-90. New York: Norton, 1995.

–, ed. *Uncommon Ground: Toward Reinventing Nature*. New York: Norton, 1995.

Crosby, Thomas. *Among the An-ko-me-nums, or Flathead Tribes of Indians of the Pacific Coast*. Toronto: William Briggs, 1907.

–. *Up and Down the North Pacific Coast by Canoe and Mission Ship*. Toronto: Missionary Society of the Methodist Church, 1914.

CS/RESORS Consulting Limited. "Women and the Forest Industry." Report to the Policy Development Division, Ministry of Employment and Investment. Victoria, BC: Ministry of Employment and Investment, 1997.

Cuff, David, and Mark Mattson. *Thematic Maps: Their Design and Production*. New York: Methuen, 1982.

Cuomo, Chris J. *Feminism and Ecological Communities: An Ethic of Flourishing*. New York: Routledge, 1998.

Dalal-Clayton, B. *Getting to Grips with Green Plans: National-Level Experience in Industrial Countries.* London, UK: Earthscan, 1996.

Danysk, Cecilia. "'A Bachelor's Paradise': Homesteaders, Hired Hands, and the Construction of Masculinity, 1880-1930." In *Making Western Canada: Essays on European Colonization and Settlement,* edited by Catherine Cavanaugh and Jeremy Mouat, 154-85. Toronto: Garamond, 1996.

Darier, Éric. "Environmental Governmentality: The Case of Canada's Green Plan." *Environmental Politics* 5, 4 (1996): 585-606.

Darnton, Robert. *The Kiss of Lamourette: Reflections in Cultural History.* New York: Norton, 1990.

Davidson, Arnold. *Coyote Country: Fictions of the Canadian West.* Durham: Duke University Press, 1994.

Davidson, Debra, and William R. Freudenburg. "Gender and Environmental Risk Concerns: A Review and Analysis of Available Literature." *Environment and Behaviour* 28 (1996): 302-29.

de Bruijn, Mirjam, Ineke van Halsema, and Heleen van den Hombergh, eds. *Gender and Land Use: Diversity in Environmental Practices.* Amsterdam: Thela, 1997.

Dearden, Philip, and Rick Rollins, eds. *Parks and Protected Areas in Canada: Planning and Management.* Toronto: Oxford University Press, 1993.

DeBruin, A., and A. Dupuis. "Towards a Synthesis of Transaction Cost Economics and a Feminist Oriented Network Analysis: An Application to Women's Street Commerce." *American Journal of Economics and Sociology* 58 (1999): 807-27.

DeGering, Etta B. *Wilderness Wife: The Story of Rebecca Bryan Boone.* New York: McKay, 1966.

DeLind, Laura, and Anne Ferguson. "Is This a Women's Movement? The Relationship of Gender to Community-Supported Agriculture in Michigan." *Human Organization* 58, 2 (1999): 190-200.

Dempsey, Shawna, and Lorri Millan. [Film] *Live Decade: 1989-1999.* Winnipeg: Finger in the Dyke Productions, 1999.

Denzin, Norman. *Interpretive Ethnography.* Thousand Oaks, CA: Sage, 1997.

Devall, Bill, and George Sessions. *Deep Ecology: Living as If Nature Mattered.* Salt Lake City: Peregrine Smith, 1985.

Devitt, Amy J. "Integrating Rhetorical and Literary Theories of Genre." *College English* 62, 6 (2000): 696-718.

Diamond, Irene, and Gloria Feman Orenstein, eds. *Reweaving the World: The Emergence of Ecofeminism.* San Francisco: Sierra Club Books, 1990.

Dickinson, Peter. *Here Is Queer: Nationalisms, Sexualities and the Literatures of Canada.* Toronto: University of Toronto Press, 1999.

difranco, ani. *Revelling/Reckoning* [Sound recording]. Buffalo, NY: righteous babe records/ BMI, 2001.

Dixon, Anne. *Silent Partners: Wives of National Park Wardens.* Pincher Creek, AB: Dixon and Dixon Publishers, 1985.

Doane, Donna L. "Indigenous Knowledge, Technology Blending and Gender Implications." *Gender, Technology and Development* 3, 2 (1999): 235-57.

Doeringer, P., and M. Piore. *Internal Labour Markets and Manpower Analysis.* Lexington: D.C. Heath, 1971.

Domosh, Mona, and Joni Seager. *Putting Women in Place: Feminist Geographers Make Sense of the World.* New York: Guilford Press, 2001.

Donaldson, Laura E. *Decolonizing Feminisms: Race, Gender and Empire Building.* Chapel Hill: University of Northern Carolina Press, 1992.

Douglas, Mary. *Natural Symbols.* London, UK: Barrie and Rockliff, Crest Press, 1970.

–, and Aaron Wildavsky. *Risk and Culture: An Essay on the Selection of Technical and Environmental Dangers.* Berkeley: University of California Press, 1982.

Doyle, Aaron, Brian Elliott, and David Tindall. "Framing the Forests: Corporations, the B.C. Forest Alliance, and the Media." In *Organizing Dissent,* edited by W. Carroll, 240-68. 2nd ed. Toronto: Garamond, 1997.

Dresner, Samuel, ed. *I Asked for Wonder: A Spiritual Anthology of Abraham Joshua Heschel.* New York: Crossroads, 1997.

Drushka, K. *Stumped: The Forest Industry in Transition.* Vancouver: Douglas and McIntyre, 1985.

Dubois, Laurent. "'Man's Darkest Hours': Maleness, Travel and Anthropology." In *Anthropological Theory: An Introductory History,* edited by R. Jon McGee and Richard L. Warms, 307-21. Mountain View, CA: Mayfield Press, 1996.

Duffy, Ann, and Noreen Pupo. *Part-Time Paradox: Connecting Gender, Work and Family.* Toronto: McClelland and Stewart, 1992.

Dumont, Marilyn. "recovery." In *Writing the Circle: Native Women of Western Canada,* edited by Jeanne Perreault and Sylvia Vance. Edmonton: NeWest, 1990.

Dunk, Thomas. *It's a Working Man's Town: Male Working-Class Culture in Northwestern Ontario.* Montreal and Kingston: McGill-Queen's University Press, 1991.

–, Stephen McBride, and Randle Nelsen, eds. *The Training Trap: Ideology, Training, and the Labour Market.* Halifax: Fernwood, 1996.

Dunster, Julian, and Katherine Dunster. *Dictionary of Natural Resource Management.* Vancouver: UBC Press, 1996.

Dunster, Katherine. "Land Stewardship through Community Mapping: The Salish Sea Mapping Project." In *Caring for Our Land and Water: Stewardship and Conservation in Canada.* Conference proceedings, vol. 5, *Traditional Knowledge, Partnerships and Organizations,* edited by S.G. Hilts, L. Milburn, and S. Mulley, 31-37. Guelph: Centre for Land and Water Stewardship, University of Guelph, 2002.

DuPlessis, R.B., and A. Snitow, eds. *The Feminist Memoir Project: Voices from Women's Liberation.* New York: Three Rivers Press, 1998.

Eagles, Paul F.J. "Parks Legislation in Canada." In *Parks and Protected Areas in Canada: Planning and Management,* edited by Philip Dearden and Rick Rollins, 57-74. Toronto: Oxford University Press, 1993.

Eaton, Heather. "Liaison or Liability: Weaving Spirituality into Ecofeminist Politics." *Atlantis* 21, 1 (1997): 109-22.

–. "The Edge of the Sea: The Colonization of Ecofeminist Religious Perspectives." *Critical Review of Books in Religion* 11 (1998): 57-82.

–. "Ecofeminist Ethics: Utopic Conversations." *Ecotheology* 8 (2000): 45-68.

–. "At the Intersection of Ecofeminism and Religion: Directions for Consideration." *Ecotheology* 11/12 (2001): 91-107.

Ecotrust, Pacific GIS, and Conservation International. *The Rainforests of Home: An Atlas of People and Place.* Part 1, *Natural Forests and Native Languages of the Coastal Temperate Rain Forest.* Portland, OR: Ecotrust, Pacific GIS, and Conservation International, 1995.

Egan, B., and S. Klausen. "Female in a Forest Town: The Marginalization of Women in Port Alberni's Economy." *BC Studies* 118 (1998): 5-40.

Eidsvik, Harold. "Canada in a Global Context." In *Endangered Spaces: The Future for Canada's Wilderness,* edited by Monte Hummel, 30-49. Toronto: Key Porter Books, 1989.

Eisenstein, Zillah. *Global Obscenities: Patriarchy, Capitalism and the Lure of Cyberfantasy.* New York and London, UK: New York University Press, 1998.

Eisler, Riane. *The Chalice and the Blade.* San Francisco: Harper Collins, 1987.

Engel-Di Mauro, Salvatore. "Gender Relations, Political Economy, and the Ecological Consequences of State-Socialist Soil Science." *Capitalism, Nature, Socialism* 13, 3 (2002): 92-117.

England, K. "Suburban Pink Collar Ghettos: The Spatial Entrapment of Women?" *Annals of the Association of American Geographers* 83 (1993): 225-42.

Erdrich, Louise. *Tracks.* New York, NY: Harper and Row, 1988.

Ernesti, Johann Augustus. *Elementary Principles of Interpretation.* Andover: Allen, Morrill, and Wardwell, 1842.

Escobar, Arturo. *Encountering Development: The Making and Unmaking of the Third World.* Princeton, NJ: Princeton University Press, 1995.

Estés, Clarissa Pinkola. *Women Who Run with the Wolves: Myths and Stories of the Wild Woman Archetype.* New York: Ballantine Books, 1992.

Ettlinger, N. "Worker Displacement and Corporate Restructuring: A Policy-Conscious Appraisal." *Economic Geography* 66, 1 (1990): 67-82.

Fairbanks, Carol. *Prairie Women: Images in American and Canadian Fiction*. New Haven: Yale University Press, 1986.

Farmer, Fannie Merritt. *The Boston Cooking-School Cookbook*. Boston: Little-Brown, 1896.

Federal Provincial Parks Council. "Protecting a Legacy for Canadians: Overview." <http://www.cd.gov.ab.ca/preserving parks/tppc/>.

Feldman, Shelly, and Rick Welsh. "Feminist Knowledge Claims, Local Knowledge, and Gender Division of Agricultural Labor: Constructing a Successor Science." *Rural Sociology* 60 (1995): 23-43.

Fentress, James, and Chris Wickham. *Social Memory*. Oxford: Blackwell Press, 1992.

Finch, Robert, and John Elder, eds. *The Norton Anthology of Nature Writing*. 1st ed. New York: Norton, 1990.

–, eds. *The Norton Book of Nature Writing*. College edition. New York: Norton, 2002.

Fishery Research Group. "The Social Impact of Technological Change in Newfoundland's Deepsea Fishery." Labour Canada Technology Impact Research Fund Report, 1986.

Fiske, Jo-Anne. "'Ask My Wife': A Feminist Interpretation of Fieldwork Where the Women Are Strong but the Men Are Tough." *Atlantis* 11, 2 (Spring 1986): 59-69.

–, and Caroline Mufford. "Hard Times and Everything Like That: Carrier Women's Tales of Life on the Trapline." In *New Faces of the Fur Trade: Selected Papers of the Seventh North American Fur Trade Conference,* edited by Jo-Anne Fiske, Susan Sleeper Smith, and William Wicken, 13-30. East Lansing: Michigan State University Press, 1998.

–, Susan Sleeper Smith, and William Wicken, eds. *New Faces of the Fur Trade: Selected Papers of the Seventh North American Conference on the Fur Trade*. East Lansing: Michigan State University Press, 1998.

Fitzgibbon, Mary Agnes. *A Trip to Manitoba, or Roughing it on the Line*. Toronto: Rose-Belford, 1880.

Flynn, James, Paul Slovic, and C.K. Mertz. "Gender, Race, and Perception of Environmental Health Risks." *Risk Analysis* 14 (1994): 1101-8.

Forgacs, O. "The British Columbia Forest Industry: Transition or Decline." In *Troubles in the Rainforest: British Columbia's Forest Economy in Transition,* edited by T.J. Barnes and R. Hayter, 167-80. Canadian Western Geographical Series No. 33. Victoria, BC: Western Geographical Press, 1994.

Francis, Daniel. *The Imaginary Indian: The Image of the Indian in Canadian Culture*. Vancouver: Arsenal Pulp Press, 1992.

Francis, Margot. "The Lesbian National Parks and Services: Reading Sex, Race and the Nation in Artistic Performance." *Canadian Woman Studies/les cahiers de la femme* 20, 2 (2000): 131-36.

–. "Wild Kingdom: There's No Life Like It." *Xtra,* 16 May 2002, 6.

Frederickson, Judith A. *As Time Goes By ... Time Use of Canadians: General Social Survey*. Statistics Canada: Housing, Family, and Social Statistics Division. Ottawa: Minister of Industry, 1995.

Freire, Paolo. *Pedagogy of the Oppressed*. New York: Seabury Press, 1970.

Frye, Northrop. *The Bush Garden*. Toronto: House of Anansi, 1971.

Gaard, Greta. "Ecofeminism and Wilderness." *Environmental Ethics* 19, 1 (1997): 5-24.

Gadd, Ben. *Bankhead: The Twenty Year Town*. Banff, AB: Canadian Parks Service, 1989.

Gaffield, Chad, and Ann Gaffield, eds. *Consuming Canada: Readings in Environmental History*. Toronto: Copp Clark, 1995.

Gairdner, William. "Traill and Moodie: The Two Realities." *Journal of Canadian Fiction* 2, 3 (1973): 75-81.

Garcia, Veronica Vasquez. "Taking Gender into Account: Women and Sustainable Development Projects in Rural Mexico." *Women's Studies Quarterly* 29, 1-2 (2001): 85-98.

Gibbs, Lois Marie. *Dying from Dioxin: A Citizen's Guide to Reclaiming Our Health and Rebuilding Democracy*. Boston: South End Press, 1995.

Gibson-Graham, J.K. "Stuffed If I Know! Reflections on Post-Modern Feminist Social Research." *Gender, Place and Culture* 1, 2 (1994): 205-24.

Gilbert, Sandra, and Susan M. Gubar. *The Madwoman in the Attic: The Woman Writer and the Nineteenth-Century Literary Imagination*. New Haven: Yale University Press, 1979.

Glotfelty, Cheryll. "Femininity in the Wilderness: Reading Gender in Women's Guides to Backpacking." *Women's Studies* 25, 5 (September 1996): 439-57.

Godard, Barbara. *Talking about Ourselves: The Literary Productions of the Native Women of Canada*. Ottawa: Canadian Research Institute for the Advancement of Women, 1985.

Goldman, Marlene. "Go North Young Woman: Representations of the Arctic in the Writings of Aritha van Herk." In *Aritha van Herk: Essays on Her Works*, edited by Christl Verduyn, 31-44. Toronto: Guernica, 2001.

Gordon, Charles W. (Ralph Connor). *The Life of James Robertson, D.D.* Toronto: Westminster, 1909.

Government of Canada. *Canadian Environmental Protection Act, Priority Substances List Assessment Report No. 1: Polychlorinated Dibenzodioxins and Polychlorinated Dibenzofurans*. Ottawa: Minister of Supply and Services, 1990.

Granovetter, M. "Economic Action and Social Structure: The Problem of Embeddedness." *American Journal of Sociology* 91 (1985): 481-510.

Grant, Agnes. "Reclaiming the Lineage House: Canadian Native Women Writers." *Studies in American Indian Literature* 6, 1 (1994): 43-62.

–, ed. *Our Bit of Truth: An Anthology of Canadian Native Literature*. Winnipeg: Pemmican, 1990.

Grant, George M. *Ocean to Ocean: Sandford Fleming's Expedition through Canada in 1872*. Revised ed. Toronto: Rose Belford, 1879.

Grass, E. "Employment Changes during Recession: The Case of the British Columbia Forest Products Manufacturing Industries." MA thesis, Simon Fraser University, 1987.

–, and R. Hayter. "Employment Change during Recession: The Experience of Forest Product Manufacturing Plants in British Columbia, 1981-1985." *Canadian Geographer* 33, 3 (1989): 240-52.

Great Lakes Science Advisory Board. *1991 Report to the International Joint Commission*. Windsor: International Joint Commission, 1991.

Green, Michael J.B., and James Paine. "State of the World's Protected Areas at the End of the Twentieth Century." Paper presented at the symposium "Protected Areas in the 21st Century: From Islands to Networks," IUCN World Commission on Protected Areas, Albany, Australia, 24-29 November 1997.

Gregory, Derek. *Writes of Passage: Reading Travel Writing*. New York: Routledge, 1999.

Griffin, David Ray, ed. *Spirituality and Society*. New York: SUNY, 1988.

Griffin, Keith, and A.R. Khan. *Globalization and the Developing World: An Essay on the International Dimensions of Development in the Post-Cold War Era*. Geneva, UNRISD, 1992.

Griffin, Susan. *Woman and Nature: The Roaring Inside Her*. San Francisco: Harper and Row, 1978.

–. *Made from This Earth: Selections from Her Writing*. London, UK: Women's Press, 1982.

Grove, Frederick Philip. *The Turn of the Year*. Toronto: McClelland and Stewart, 1923.

Grzetic, Brenda. "Between Life and Death: Women Fish Harvesters in Newfoundland and Labrador." MA thesis, Memorial University, St. John's, NF, 2002.

–. *Women Fishes These Days*. Halifax: Fernwood Books, 2004.

Guijt, Irene, and Meera Kaul Shah, eds. *The Myth of Community: Gender Issues in Participatory Development*. London, UK: Intermediate Technology Publications, 1998.

Guillet, Edwin. *The Pioneer Farmer and Backwoodsman*. 2 vols. Toronto: University of Toronto Press, 1963.

Gunn, William T. *His Dominion*. Toronto: Canadian Council of the Missionary Education Movement, 1917.

Gusfield, Joseph. "The Literary Rhetoric of Science." *American Sociological Review* 4 (1976): 16-34.

Gustafson, Per E. "Gender Differences in Risk Perception: Theoretical and Methodological Perspectives." *Risk Analysis* 18 (1998): 805-11.

Halfe, Louise Bernice. "Grandmother." In *Writing the Circle: Native Women of Western Canada*, edited by Jeanne Perreault and Sylvia Vance. Edmonton: NeWest, 1990.

Hallman, David. *Spiritual Values for Earth Community.* Geneva: WCC Press, 2000.

Halseth, G. "We Came for the Work: Situating Employment Migration in BC's Small, Resource-Based Communities." *Canadian Geographer* 43 (1999): 363-81.

Hamilton-Temple-Blackwood, Georgina. *My Canadian Journal, 1872-78.* New York: D. Appleton, 1891.

Hanson, S., and I. Johnston. "Gender Differences in Work-Trip Length: Explanation and Implications." *Urban Geography* 6 (1985): 193-219.

Hanson, S., and G. Pratt. *Gender, Work, and Space.* London and New York: Routledge, 1995.

Hapstead, Elisabeth, and Lillian Schlissel. *Women's Diaries of the Westward Journey.* New York: Schocken, 1982.

Haraway, Donna. "Situated Knowledges: The Science Question in Feminism as the Site of Discourse and the Privilege of Partial Perspective." *Feminist Studies* 14, 3 (1988): 575-99.

–. *Primate Visions: Gender, Race, and Nature in the World of Modern Science.* New York: Routledge, 1989.

Harcourt, Wendy, ed. *Feminist Perspectives on Sustainable Development.* London, UK: Zed Press, 1994.

Harding, Lee E., and Emily McCullum. "Protected Areas in British Columbia: Maintaining Natural Diversity." In *Biodiversity in British Columbia: Our Changing Environment,* edited by Lee E. Harding and Emily McCullum, 355-74. Ottawa: Environment Canada and the Canadian Wildlife Service, 1994.

Harrington, Sheila, ed. *Giving the Land a Voice: Mapping Our Home Places.* Saltspring Island, BC: Land Trust Alliance of British Columbia, 1999.

Harrison, Kathryn. "Between Science and Politics: Assessing the Risks of Dioxins in Canada and the United States." *Policy Sciences* 24 (1991): 367-88.

–, and George Hoberg. "Setting the Environmental Agenda in Canada and the United States: The Cases of Dioxin and Radon." *Canadian Journal of Political Science* 24 (1991): 1-27.

–, and George Hoberg. *Risk, Science, and Politics: Regulating Toxic Substances in Canada and the United States.* Montreal and Kingston: McGill-Queen's University Press, 1994.

Hart, E.J. *The Selling of Canada: The CPR and the Beginnings of Canadian Tourism.* Banff, AB: Altitude, 1983.

Hart, R. *Children's Participation: The Theory and Practice of Involving Young Citizens in Community Development and Environmental Care.* London, UK: Earthscan, 1997.

Hartmann, Heidi. "The Family as the Locus of Gender, Class, and Political Struggle: The Example of Housework." *Signs: Journal of Women in Culture and Society* 6, 3 (1981): 366-94.

Hay, E. "Recession and Restructuring in Port Alberni: Corporate, Community and Household Coping Strategies." MA thesis, Simon Fraser University, 1993.

Hayter, R. *Flexible Crossroads: The Restructuring of British Columbia's Forest Economy.* Vancouver: UBC Press, 2000.

–, and T.J. Barnes. "Labour Market Segmentation, Flexibility, and Recession: A British Columbian Case Study." *Environment and Planning* 10 (1992): 333-53.

–, and T.J. Barnes. "The Restructuring of British Columbia's Coastal Forest Sector: Flexibility Perspectives." In *Troubles in the Rainforest: British Columbia's Forest Economy in Transition,* edited by T.J. Barnes and R. Hayter, 181-202. Canadian Western Geographical Series No. 33. Victoria, BC: Western Geographical Press, 1997.

Health Canada. *Towards a Common Understanding: Clarifying the Core Concepts of Population Health.* Ottawa: Ministry of Supply and Services, 2000.

Hedrick, Ulysses P. *The Apples of New York.* 2 vols. New York: Agricultural Experiment Station, 1905.

Hessing, Melody, and Michael Howlett. *Canadian Natural Resource and Environmental Policy: Political Economy and Public Policy.* Vancouver: UBC Press, 1997.

Hodgins, Bruce W., and Margaret Hobbs. *Nastawgan: The Canadian North by Canoe and Snowshoe: A Collection of Historical Essays.* Toronto: Betelgeuse Books, 1985.

Holmes, Len. "E-rules for Radicals? Community Organising in an E-world." Paper prepared for the Ninth International Congress of Asia-Pacific Researchers in Organisation Studies, "Organization Theory in Transition: Transitional Societies, Transitional Theories," Hong Kong, 2001.

Hoover, Helen. *A Place in the Woods*. New York: Knopf, 1969.

Hoover, Sara M. "Exposure to Persistent Organochlorines in Canadian Breast Milk: A Probabilistic Assessment." *Risk Analysis* 4 (1999): 527-45.

Horne, G. *British Columbia Local Area Economic Dependencies and Impact Ratios 1996*. Victoria, BC: Business and Economic Statistics, 1999.

Huffman, N.H. "Charting Other Maps: Cartography and Visual Methods in Feminist Research." In *Thresholds in Feminist Geography: Difference, Methodology, Representation*, edited by J.P. Jones III, H.J. Nast, and S.M. Roberts, 255-83. Lanham, MD: Rowman and Littlefield, 1997.

Huisman, Marcel, et al. "Neurological Condition in 18-Month-Old Children Perinatally Exposed to Polychlorinated Biphenyls and Dioxins." *Early Human Development* 43 (1995): 165-76.

Human Resources Development Canada. *Evaluation of the Atlantic Groundfish Strategy (TAGS): TAGS/HRDC Final Evaluation Report*. Ottawa: Human Resources Development Canada, 1998.

Hummel, Monte, ed. *Endangered Spaces: The Future for Canada's Wilderness*. Toronto: Key Porter, 1989.

Hyndman, Jennifer. *Managing Displacement: Refugees and the Politics of Humanitarianism*. Minneapolis: University of Minnesota Press, 2000.

Ignatieff, Michael. *The Rights Revolution*. Toronto: Anansi, 2000.

Innis, Harold Adams. *Empire and Communications*. Oxford: Clarendon Press, 1950.

International Agency for Research on Cancer (IARC). "Polychlorinated Dibenzo-para-Dioxins and Polychlorinated Dibenzofurans." *IARC Monographs on the Evaluation of Carcinogenic Risks to Humans*. Vol. 69. Lyon: IARC, 1997.

Jackel, David. "Mrs. Moodie and Mrs. Traill, and the Fabrication of a Canadian Tradition." *Compass* 6 (1979): 1-22.

Jacobson, J.L., et al. "Prenatal Exposure to Polychlorinated Biphenyls and Dioxins and Its Effect on Neonatal Neurological Development." *Early Human Development* 41 (1984): 111-27.

Jacobson, J.L., and S.W. Jacobson. "Intellectual Impairment in Children Exposed to Polychlorinated Biphenyls in Utero." *New England Journal of Medicine* 335 (1996): 783-89.

Jameson, Anna. *Winter Studies and Summer Rambles in Canada*. 1838. Reprint, Toronto: McClelland and Stewart, 1923.

Janvrin, Alice J. *Snapshots from the North Pacific: Letters Written by the Right Rev. Bishop Ridley (Late of Caledonia)*. London, UK: Church Missionary Society, 1904.

Jasanoff, Sheila. *Risk Management and Political Culture*. New York: Russell Sage Foundation, 1986.

Jeffrey, Julie. *Frontier Women*. New York: Hill and Wang, 1979; reissued as Jeffrey, Julie Roy. *Frontier Women: "Civilizing" the West? 1840-1880*. New York: Hill and Wang, 1998.

–. *Frontier Women: The Trans-Mississippi West, 1840-1880*. Revised edition. New York, NY: Hill and Wang, 1998.

Jenness, Diamond. *The Indians of Canada*. 6th ed. Ottawa: National Museum of Canada, 1963.

Jenson, Jane. "Part-Time Employment and Women: A Range of Strategies." In *Rethinking Restructuring: Gender and Change in Canada*, edited by Isabella Bakker, 92-110. Toronto: University of Toronto Press, 1996.

Joe, J.B. "Cement Woman." In *All My Relations: An Anthology of Contemporary Canadian Native Fiction*, edited by Thomas King, 164-70. Toronto: McClelland and Stewart, 1990.

Johnson, Osa. *I Married Adventure: The Lives and Adventures of Martin and Osa Johnson*. Garden City, NY: Garden City Publishing Co., 1940.

Johnson, Pauline. "Moonset." In *Pauline Johnson: Her Life and Work*, written and edited by Marcus Van Stern, 132. Toronto: Hodder and Stoughton, 1965.

Jolly, Susie. "'Queering' Development: Exploring the Links between Same-Sex Sexualities, Gender, and Development." *Gender and Development* 8, 1 (2000): 78-87.

Kaplan, Temma. *Crazy for Democracy: Women in Grassroots Movements*. New York: Routledge, 1997.

King, Thomas. *Green Grass, Running Water.* Toronto: HarperCollins, 1993.

–. "The One about Coyote Going West." In *One Good Story, That One.* Toronto: HarperCollins, 1993.

King, Ynestra. "Healing the Wounds: Feminism, Ecology and the Nature/Culture Dualism." In *Reweaving the World: The Emergence of Ecofeminism,* edited by Irene Diamond and Gloria Feman Orenstein, 106-21. San Francisco: Sierra Club Books, 1990.

Kingdon, John. *Agendas, Alternatives, and Public Policies.* Boston: Little-Brown, 1984.

Kirkland, Caroline. *A New Home – Who'll Follow? or Glimpses of Western Life,* by Mrs. Mary Clavers [pseud.]. New York, NY: C.S. Francis, 1839.

Kleymeyer, C.D. "The Uses and Functions of Cultural Expression in Grassroots Development." In *Cultural Development and Grassroots Development,* 17-36. Boulder, CO: Lynne Rienner Publishers, 1994.

Kollin, Susan. *Nature's State: Imagining Alaska as the Last Frontier.* Chapel Hill: University of North Carolina Press, 2001.

Kolodny, Annette. *The Land before Her: Fantasy and Experience of the American Frontiers, 1630-1860.* Chapel Hill: University of North Carolina Press, 1975.

Koopman-Esseboom, Carine, et al. "Effects of Polychlorinated Biphenyl/Dioxin Exposure and Feeding Type on Infants' Mental and Psychomotor Development." *Pediatrics* 97 (1996): 700-6.

Kowalewski, Michael. "Introduction." In *Temperamental Journals: Essays on the Modern Literature of Travel,* 1-15. Athens: University of Georgia Press, 1992.

Kozlowski, S.W.J., G.T. Chao, E.M. Smith, and J. Hedland. "Organizational Downsizing: Strategies, Interventions, and Research Implications." *International Review of Industrial and Organizational Psychology* 8 (1993): 263-332.

Krosenbrink-Gelissen, Lilianne Ernestine. *Sexual Equality as an Aboriginal Right: The Native Women's Association of Canada and the Constitutional Process on Aboriginal Matters, 1982-1987.* Saarbrucken, Germany: Verlag, 1991.

Kwan, Mei-Po. "Feminist Visualization: Re-envisioning GIS as a Method in Feminist Geographic Research." *Annals of the Association of American Geographers* 92, 4 (2002): 645-61.

LaBastille, Anne. *Women and Wilderness.* San Francisco: Sierra Club Books, 1980. Reprint, Berkeley: University of California Press, 1987.

Lachappelle, Dolores. *Earth Wisdom.* Boulder, CO: Guild of Tutors Press, 1978.

Lamb, Gary. "Community Supported Agriculture: Can It Become the Basis of a New Associative Economy?" *Threefold Review* 11 (1994): 39-44.

LaRocque, Emma. "Preface." In *Writing the Circle: Native Women of Western Canada,* edited by Jeanne Perreault and Sylvia Vance, xv-xxx. Edmonton: NeWest, 1990.

Leach, Belinda. "Flexible Work, Precarious Future: Some Lessons from the Canadian Clothing Industry." *Canadian Review of Sociology and Anthropology* 30 (1993): 64-81.

–. "Behind Closed Doors: Homework Policy and Lost Possibilities for Change." In *Rethinking Restructuring: Gender and Change in Canada,* edited by Isabella Bakker, 203-16. Toronto: University of Toronto Press, 1996.

–. "Transforming Rural Livelihoods: Gender, Work, and Restructuring in Three Ontario Communities." In *Restructuring Caring Labour: Discourse, State Practice and Everyday Life,* edited by Sheila M. Neysmith, 209-25. Toronto: Oxford University Press, 2000.

–, and A. Winson. "Bringing Globalization down to Earth: Restructuring and Labour in Rural Communities." *The Canadian Review of Sociology and Anthropology* 32, 3 (1995): 341-64.

Lebowitz, Andrea. *Living in Harmony: Nature Writing by Women in Canada.* Vancouver: Orca Books, 1996.

Lévi-Strauss, Claude. *Structural Anthropology.* Translated by Monique Layton. New York, NY: Basic, 1976.

–. *The Raw and the Cooked.* Translated by John Weightman and Doreen Weightman. New York, NY: Octagon, 1979.

Levy, Caren. "Gender and the Environment: The Challenge of Cross-Cutting Issues in Development Policy and Planning." *Environment and Urbanization* 4, 1 (1992): 134-49.

Liddle, Joanna, and Shirin M. Rai. "Between Feminism and Orientalism." In *Making Connections: Women's Studies, Women's Movements, Women's Lives,* edited by Mary Kennedy, Cathy Lubelska, and Val Walsh, 11-23. Washington, DC: Taylor and Francis, 1993.

Lindstrom, Gunilla. "Polychlorinated Dibenzo-p-Dioxins and Dibenzofurans: Analysis of and Occurrence in Milk." PhD diss., Department of Organic Chemistry, Umea University, Umea, Sweden, 1988.

Lippmann, Walter. *The Phantom Public.* New York: Harcourt Brace, 1925.

Little, J. *Gender and Rural Geography: Identity, Sexuality and Power in the Countryside.* Harlow, Essex: Pearson, 2002.

Littlejohn, Bruce. "Wilderness and the Canadian Psyche." In *Endangered Spaces: The Future for Canada's Wilderness,* edited by Monte Hummel, 12-20. Toronto: Key Porter, 1989.

Lothian, W.F. *A History of Canada's National Parks.* Vol. 1. Ottawa: Parks Canada, 1976.

–. *A Brief History of Canada's National Parks.* Ottawa: Ministry of the Environment, 1987.

Love, Rhoda M. Afterword to *Driftwood Valley: A Woman Naturalist in the Northern Wilderness,* by Theodora C. Stanwell-Fletcher, 332-38. Corvallis, OR: Oregon State University Press, 1999.

Love, Rhonda, L. Jackson, R. Edwards, and A. Pederson, with the Critical Social Science and Health Group. "Gender and Its Inter-Relationship with Other Determinants of Health." Paper presented to the Fifth National Health Promotion Research Conference, "From Research to Policy: Gender and Health Conference," Dalhousie University, Halifax, NS, 4-5 July 1997.

Lutz, Catherine. "The Erasure of Women's Writing in Sociocultural Anthropology." *American Ethnologist* 17 (1990): 611-25.

–. "The Gender of Theory." In *Women Writing Culture,* edited by Ruth Behar and Deborah Gordon, 249-66. Berkeley: University of California Press, 1995.

Luxton, Eleanor. *Banff: Canada's First National Park: A History and a Memory of Rocky Mountains Park.* Banff, AB: Summerthought, 1975.

Luxton, Meg. *More Than a Labour of Love: Three Generations of Women's Work.* Toronto: Women's Press, 1980.

–. "Two Hands for the Clock: Changing Patterns in the Gendered Division of Labour." In *Through the Kitchen Window: The Politics of Home and Family,* edited by M. Luxton, H. Rosenberg, and S. Arat-Koc, 17-36. Toronto: Garamond, 1990.

Lyon, Thomas. *This Incomperable Lande.* Boston: Houghton Mifflin, 1989.

Lyons, Gwynne. *Chemical Trespass: A Toxic Legacy.* Godalming, Surrey, UK: WWF-UK, 1999.

Lyons, Kirsten. "Understanding Organic Farm Practices: Contributions for Ecofeminism." In *Australasian Food and Farming in a Globalised Economy,* edited by D. Burch et al., 57-67. Melbourne: Monash, 1998.

MacBeth, R.G. *Our Task in Canada.* Toronto: Westminster, 1917.

McClintock, Anne. *Imperial Leather: Race, Gender and Sexuality in the Colonial Contest.* New York: Routledge, 1995.

MacDonald, James S. *Annals of the North British Society of Halifax, Nova Scotia, 1768-1893.* Halifax: John Bowes, 1894.

MacDonald, Martha. "Gender and Social Security Policy: Pitfalls and Possibilities." *Feminist Economics* 4, 1 (1998): 1-25.

–. "Lessons and Linkages." *Women and Environments International Magazine* 54/55 (Spring 2002): 19-23.

McDowell, L. "Space, Place and Gender Relations." Part 1, "Feminist Empiricism and the Geography of Social Relations." *Progress in Human Geography* 17 (1993): 157-79.

–. "Space, Place and Gender Relations." Part 2, "Identity, Difference, Feminist Geometries and Geographies." *Progress in Human Geography* 17 (1993): 305-18.

McDowell, Leonora Hayden. "Give Me the Spirit of the Eagle." In *Writing the Circle: Native Women of Western Canada,* edited by Jeanne Perreault and Sylvia Vance, 186. Edmonton: NeWest, 1990.

–. "Windsong." In *Writing the Circle: Native Women of Western Canada,* edited by Jeanne Perreault and Sylvia Vance, 184-85. Edmonton: NeWest, 1990.

MacEwen, Gwendolyn. "The Caravan." In *Modern Canadian Verse*, edited by A.J.M Smith. Toronto: Oxford University Press, 1967.

McGee, R. Jon, and Richard L. Warms. *Anthropological Theory: An Introductory History*. Mountain View, CA: Mayfield Press, 1996.

McGregor, Gaile. *The Wacousta Syndrome: Explorations in the Canadian Landscape*. Toronto: University of Toronto Press, 1985.

McHugh, Sheila J. *Give My Regards to the Beanery. Reflections of a Summer Staff Person at Banff Springs Hotel*. Lethbridge, AB: n.p., 1987.

Macionis, John J., and Linda M. Gerber. *Sociology*. 4th Canadian ed. Toronto: Prentice Hall, 2002.

McKenzie, Judith. *Environmental Politics in Canada*. Don Mills, ON: Oxford, 2002.

Mackenzie, S. "Neglected Spaces in Peripheral Places: Homeworkers and the Creation of a New Economic Center." *Cahiers de Geographie du Quebec* 31, 83 (1987): 247-60.

McLaren, Jean, and Heide Brown, eds. *The Raging Grannies Songbook*. Gabriola Island, BC: New Society, 1993.

McMullen, Lorraine, ed. *Re(dis)covering Our Foremothers*. Ottawa: University of Ottawa Press, 1990.

McNamee, Kevin. "From Wild Places to Endangered Spaces: A History of Canada's National Parks." In *Parks and Protected Areas in Canada: Planning and Management*, edited by Philip Dearden and Rick Rollins, 17-54. Toronto: Oxford University Press, 1993.

McNaughton, Margaret. *Overland to Cariboo*. Toronto: William Briggs, 1896.

MacTavish, W.S., ed. *Missionary Pathfinders: Presbyterian Laborers at Home and Abroad*. Toronto: Musson, 1907.

McWilliams, Margaret. *Manitoba Milestones*. Toronto: J.M. Dent, 1928.

Malo, J.L., P. Chrétien, M. McCants, and S.B. Lehrer. "Detection of Snow-Crab Antigens by Air Sampling of a Snow-Crab Production Plant." *Clinical and Experimental Allergy* 27, 1 (1997): 75-78.

Maracle, Lee. "Just Sit in Front of a Typewriter and Bleed." In *Telling It: Women and Language across Cultures*, edited by the Telling It Book Collective, 37-41. Vancouver: Press Gang Publishers, 1990.

–. *Ravensong*. Vancouver: Press Gang, 1993.

Marchak, M. Patricia. *Green Gold: The Forest Industry in British Columbia*. Vancouver: UBC Press, 1983.

–, S.L. Aycock, and D.M. Herbert. *Falldown: Forest Policy in British Columbia*. Vancouver: David Suzuki Foundation and Ecotrust Canada, 1999.

Marchessault, Jovette. "Song One: The Riverside," translated by Yvonne M. Klein. Excerpted from *Mother of the Grass*, in *All My Relations: An Anthology of Contemporary Canadian Native Fiction*, edited by Thomas King, 175-200. Toronto: McClelland and Stewart, 1990.

Marshall, Barbara. *Reconfiguring Gender: Explorations in Theory and Politics*. Toronto: Broadview Press, 2000.

Marty, Sid. *Men for the Mountains*. Toronto: McClelland and Stewart, 1978.

–. *A Grand and Fabulous Notion: The First Century of Canada's Parks*. Toronto: NC Press and Ministry of Supply and Services, 1984.

Mason, Jim. *An Unnatural Order: Uncovering the Roots of Our Domination of Nature and Each Other*. New York: Simon and Schuster, 1993.

Massey, Dorothy. *Spatial Divisions of Labour: Social Structures and the Geography of Production*. London, UK: Macmillan, 1984.

Mellor, Mary. *Breaking the Boundaries: Towards a Feminist Green Socialism*. London, UK: Virago Press, 1992.

–. *Feminism and Ecology*. New York: New York University Press, 1997.

Melucci, Alberto. "The Global Planet and the Internal Planet: New Frontiers." In *Cultural Politics and Social Movements*, edited by Marcy Darnovsky, Barbara Epstein, and Richard Flacks, 287-98. Philadelphia: Temple University Press, 1995.

Merchant, Carolyn. *The Death of Nature: Women, Ecology and the Scientific Revolution*. London, UK: Harper and Row, 1983.

–. "Ecofeminism and Feminist Theory." In *Reweaving the World: The Emergence of Ecofeminism*, edited by Irene Diamond and Gloria Feman Orenstein, 100-5. San Francisco: Sierra Club Books, 1990.

Mayhew, Claire, Michael Quinlan, and Rande Ferris. "The Effects of Subcontracting/Outsourcing on Occupational Health and Safety: Survey Evidence from Four Australian Industries." *Safety Science* 25, 1 (1997): 163-78.

Messing, Karen. "Don't Use a Wrench to Peel Potatoes: Biological Science Constructed on Male Model Systems Is a Risk to Women Workers." In *Changing Methods: Feminists Transforming Practice*, edited by Sandra Burt and Lorraine Code, 217-63. Scarborough, ON: Broadview Press, 1995.

–. *One-Eyed Science: Occupational Health and Women Workers*. Philadelphia: Temple University Press, 1998.

–, B. Neis, and L. Dumais, eds. *Invisible: Issues in Women's Occupational Health*. Charlottetown: Gynergy, 1995.

Mies, Maria. *Indian Women in Subsistence and Agricultural Labor*. Geneva: International Labor Organization, 1986.

–. *Women, Food and Global Trade: An Ecofeminist Analysis of the World Food Summit*. Bielefeld, Germany: Institute for the Theory and Practice of Subsistence, 1996.

–, and Vandana Shiva. *Ecofeminism*. London, UK: Zed Books, 1993.

Milly, Pascal, and William Leiss. "Mother's Milk: Communicating the Risk of PCBs in Canada and the Far North." In *Mad Cows and Mother's Milk*, edited by Douglas Powell and William Leiss, 182-209. Montreal and Kingston: McGill-Queen's University Press, 1997.

Mingwôn Mingwôn (Shirley Bear). "Equality among Women." In *Native Writers and Canadian Writing*, edited by W.H. New, 133-36. Vancouver: UBC Press, 1990.

Ministry of Environment, Government of Ontario. Environmental Bill of Rights Homepage. <http://www.ene.gov.on.ca/envision/env_reg/ebr/english/>.

Mock, Gregory. "Domesticating the World: Conversion of Natural Ecosystems." In *World Resources 2000-2001: People and Ecosystems: The Fraying Web of Life*. Washington, DC: World Resources Institute, 2000.

Mohanty, Chandra Talpade. "Cartographies of Struggle." In *Third World Women and the Politics of Feminism*, edited by Chandra Talpade Mohanty, Ann Russo, and Lourdes Torres, 1-47. Bloomington: Indiana University Press, 1991.

–. "Under Western Eyes: Feminist Scholarship and Colonial Discourses." In *Third World Women and the Politics of Feminism*, edited by Chandra Talpade Mohanty, Ann Russo, and Lourdes Torres, 51-80. Bloomington: Indiana University Press, 1991.

Mohrbacher, Nancy. "Breastfeeding and Contaminants." *New Beginnings* 2: 128-30. <http://www.lalechleague.org/llleaderweb/LV/LVNBSeptOct86.text>.

Monmonier, Mark, and H.J. DeBlij. *How to Lie with Maps*. 2nd ed. Chicago: University of Chicago Press, 1996.

Moodie, Susanna. *Roughing It in the Bush; or, Forest Life in Canada*. New York, NY: Dodge, 1913.

Morgan, Beatrice. *Random Passage*. St. John's, NF: Breakwater, 1992.

Morgan, D. *Discovering Men*. London, UK: Routledge, 1992.

Morgan, Joan, and Alison Richards. *The Book of Apples*. London, UK: Ebury Press, 1993.

Morris, Alexander. *The Treaties of Canada with the Indians of Manitoba and the North-West Territories, Including the Negotiations on Which They Were Based, and Other Information Relating Thereto*. Toronto: Belfords, Clark and Co., 1880.

–. *Nova Britannia, or Our New Canadian Dominion Foreshadowed*. Toronto: Hunter, Rose and Co., 1884.

Morton, W.L. *The Shield of Achilles: Aspects of Canada in the Victorian Age*. Toronto: McClelland and Stewart, 1968.

Moses, Daniel David, and Terrie Goldie, eds. *An Anthology of Canadian Native Literature in English*. Toronto: Oxford University Press, 1992.

Moss, Pamela, ed. *Feminist Geography in Practice: Research and Methods*. Oxford, UK: Blackwell, 2002.

Mosse, David. "Authority, Gender and Knowledge: Theoretical Reflections on the Practice of Participatory Rural Appraisal." *Development and Change* 25 (1994): 497-526.

Muir, John. *My First Summer in the Sierra*. Boston, MS: Houghton Mifflin, 1911.

Murie, Margaret E. *Two in the Far North*. Anchorage, AL: Alaska Northwest Books, 1997 [1962].

Murphy, Emily. *Seeds of Pine*. London, UK: Hodder and Stoughton, 1914.

Murray, Michael, D. Fitzpatrick, and C. O'Connell. "Fishermen's Blues: Factors Related to Accidents and Safety among Newfoundland Fishermen." *Work and Stress* 11, 3 (1997): 292-97.

Neis, Barbara. "Female Fish Processing Workers: Occupational Health and the Fishery Crises in Newfoundland and Labrador." *Chronic Diseases in Canada* 15, 1 (1994): 12-16.

–. "Can't Get My Breath: Occupational Asthma and Women Snow Crab Processing Workers." In *Invisible: Issues in Women's Occupational Health*, edited K. Messing, B. Neis, and L. Dumais, 3-28. Charlottetown: Gynergy, 1995.

–. "In the Eye of the Storm: Research, Activism and Teaching within the Newfoundland Fishery Crisis." *Women's Studies International Forum* 23, 3 (May/June 2000): 287-92.

–, Brenda Grzetic, and Michelle Pidgeon. "From Fishplant to Nickel Smelter: Health Determinants and the Health of Newfoundland's Women Fish and Shellfish Processors in an Environment of Restructuring." Research report. Toronto: National Network on Environments and Women's Health, 2001.

Nelson, Nici, and Susan Wright, eds. *Power and Participatory Development: Theory and Practice*. London, UK: Intermediate Technology Publications, 1995.

Newfoundland and Labrador, Department of Fisheries and Aquaculture. *The Newfoundland and Labrador Fishery: A Perspective*. St. John's, NF: Fisheries Forum 2000, 14-15 March 2000.

Newton, Judith, and Judith Stacey. "Ms. Representations: Reflections on Studying Academic Men." In *Women Writing Culture*, edited by Ruth Behar and Deborah Gordon, 287-305. Berkeley: University of California Press, 1995.

Neysmith, Sheila M. "Networking across Difference: Connecting Restructuring and Caring Labour." In *Restructuring Caring Labour: Discourse, State Practice, and Everyday Life*, edited by Sheila M. Neysmith, 1-28. Toronto: Oxford University Press, 2000.

Nicholas, David, and Maureen Ritchie. *Literature and Bibliometrics*. London, UK: C. Bingley, 1978.

Norberg-Hodge, Helena. *Ancient Features: Learning from Ladakh*. San Francisco: Sierra Club Books, 1991.

–, Todd Merrifield, and Steven Gorelick. *Bringing the Food Economy Home: Local Alternatives to Global Agribusiness*. London, UK: Zed Books, 2002.

Norwood, Vera. *Made from This Earth: American Women and Nature*. Chapel Hill: University of North Carolina Press, 1993.

Oelhschlaeger, Max. *The Idea of Wilderness*. New Haven: Yale University Press, 1991.

Ontario Ministry of Labour. "The Displaced Workers of Ontario: How Do They Fare?" Unpublished report prepared by Economic and Labour Market Research, Ontario Ministry of Labour, n.d. Reprinted in Commission on Resources and Environment (CORE), *Vancouver Island Land Use Plan*, vol. 2, Appendices. Victoria, BC: Commission on Resources and Environment, 1994.

O'Reilly, Alastair. "Politics, Demographics and the Potential Demise of Newfoundland's Seafood Processing Industry." Paper presented to conference "Stemming the Tide: Keeping Our Workforce Strong," St. John's, NF, 15 November 2001.

Overton, James. "The Politics of Sustainability and Privatization: The Example of Newfoundland's Cod Crisis." Unpublished paper, Department of Sociology, Memorial University, St. John's, NF, 1998.

Owram, Douglas. *Promise of Eden: The Canadian Expansionist Movement and the Idea of the West, 1856-1900*. Toronto: University of Toronto Press, 1980.

Palmer, Gabrielle. *The Politics of Breastfeeding*. London, UK: Pandora Press, 1988.

Pannekoek, F. "'Insidious' Sources and the Historical Interpretation of the Pre-1870 West." In *The Anglican Church and the World of Western Canada, 1820-1870*, edited by Barry Ferguson. Regina: Canadian Plains Research Centre, 1991.

Parkin, D.M., F.L. Bray, and S.S. Devesa. "Cancer Burden in the Year 2000: The Global Picture." *European Journal of Cancer* 37 (2001): S4-S66.

Parr, J. *The Gender of Breadwinners: Women, Men, and Change in Two Industrial Towns, 1880-1950.* Toronto: University of Toronto Press, 1990.

Patandin, Svati, et al. "Effects of Environmental Exposure to Polychlorinated Biphenyls and Dioxins on Birth Size and Growth in Dutch Children." *Pediatric Research* 44 (1998): 538-45.

Patandin, Svati, et al. "Dietary Exposure to Polychlorinated Biphenyls and Dioxins from Infancy until Adulthood: A Comparison between Breast-Feeding, Toddler, and Long-Term Exposure." *Environmental Health Perspectives* 107 (1999): 45-51.

Patandin, Svati, et al. "Effects of Environmental Exposure to Polychlorinated Biphenyls and Dioxins on Cognitive Abilities in Dutch Children at 42 Months of Age." *Journal of Pediatrics* 134 (1999): 33-41.

Pazdro, Roberta J. "Agnes Deans Cameron: Against the Current." In *In Her Own Right: Selected Essays on Women's History in British Columbia,* 101-23. Victoria, BC: Camosun College, 1980.

Peattie, Donald Culross. "They Refused to Go Home." *Saturday Review of Literature,* 21 November 1942, 7.

Perreault, Jeanne, and Sylvia Vance, eds. *Writing the Circle: Native Women of Western Canada.* Edmonton: NeWest, 1990.

Peterman, Michael. "'Splendid Anachronism': The Record of Catharine Parr Traill's Struggles as an Amateur Botanist in Nineteenth-Century Canada." In *Re(Dis)covering Our Foremothers,* edited by Lorraine McMullen, 173-85. Ottawa: University of Ottawa Press, 1990.

Phillipps-Wolley, Clive, and Jane Phillipps-Wolley. *A Sportsman's Eden.* London, UK: Richard Bentley, 1888.

Pietila, Hilkka, and Jane Vickers. *Making Women Matter.* London, UK: Zed Books, 1990.

Pinkerton, Kathrene. *Wilderness Wife.* New York: Carrick and Evans, 1939; reissued as *A Home in the Wilds.* Marlboro, NJ: Taplinger Publishing Co., 1976.

–. *Two Ends to Our Shoestring.* New York: Harcourt Brace, 1941.

Plant, Judith. *Healing the Wounds: The Promise of Ecofeminism.* Toronto: Between the Lines, 1989.

Plummer, J. *Municipalities and Community Participation.* London, UK: Earthscan, 2000.

Plumwood, Val. *Feminism and the Mastery of Nature.* New York: Routledge, 1993.

Pollution Probe. *The Canadian Green Consumer Guide.* Toronto: McClelland and Stewart, 1991.

Poole, Peter. *Indigenous Peoples, Mapping, and Biodiversity Conservation: An Analysis of Current Activities and Opportunities for Applying Geomatics Technologies.* Peoples and Forests Program discussion paper. Washington, DC: Biodiversity Support Program, 1995.

Pothukuchi, Kameshwari, and Jerome Kaufman. "Placing the Food System on the Urban Agenda: The Role of Municipal Institutions in Food System Planning." *Agriculture and Human Values* 16 (1999): 213-24.

Pratt, Annis. "Affairs with Bears: Some Notes towards Feminist Archetypal Hypotheses for Canadian Literature." In *Gynocritics: Feminist Approaches to Writing by Canadian and Quebecoise Women,* edited by Barbara Godard, 157-78. Toronto: ECW Press, 1987.

Pratt, Geraldine. "Feminist Geographies." In *The Dictionary of Human Geography,* edited by R.J. Johnston, D. Gregory, G. Pratt, and M. Watts, 259-62. Oxford: Blackwell, 2000.

Preston, V., D. Rose, G. Norcliffe, and J. Holmes. "Shifts and the Division of Labour in Childcare and Domestic Labour in Three Paper Mill Communities." *Gender, Place and Culture* 7, 1, (2000): 5-19.

Pretty, Jules. *Regenerating Agriculture: Policies and Practices for Sustainability and Self Reliance.* London, UK: Earthscan, 1995.

Prince, Edward E. "Unutilized Fisheries Resources of Canada." In *Conservation of Fish, Birds and Game: Proceedings at a Meeting of the Committee on Fisheries, Game and Fur-Bearing Animals, Commission of Conservation Canada, November 1 and 2, 1915,* edited by James White. Toronto: Methodist Book and Publishing House, 1916.

Profeit-LeBlanc, Louise. "Ancient Stories, Spiritual Legacies." In *Telling It: Women and Language Across Cultures,* edited by the Telling It Book Collective, 111-16. Vancouver: Press Gang, 1990.

–. "The Old Man and the Swans." In *Telling It: Women and Language across Cultures,* edited by the Telling It Book Collective. Vancouver: Press Gang, 1990.

Quinby, Lee. *Anti-Apocalypse: Essays in Genealogical Criticism.* Minneapolis: University of Minnesota Press, 1994.

Rabinow, Paul. "Representations Are Social Facts: Modernity and Post Modernity in Anthropology." In *Writing Culture: The Poetics and Politics of Ethnography,* edited by James Clifford and George Marcus, 234-61. Berkeley: University of California Press, 1986.

Raglon, Rebecca. "Women and the Great Canadian Wilderness: Reconsidering the Wild." *Women's Studies* 25 (1996): 513-31.

Raloff, J. "Dioxin Can Harm Tooth Development." *Science News Online.* 1999. <http://www.sciencenews.org>.

Randall, J.E., and R.G. Ironside. "Communities on the Edge: An Economic Geography of Resource-Dependent Communities in Canada." *The Canadian Geographer* 40 (1996): 17-35.

Ray, Arthur. "Review of *The Fur Trade Revisited: Selected Papers of the Sixth North American Fur Trade Conference.*" *William and Mary Quarterly,* 3rd series, 52, 4 (1995): 740-42.

Rebick, Judy. *Imagine Democracy.* Toronto: Stoddart, 2000.

Reed, Maureen G. "Taking Stands: A Feminist Perspective on 'Other' Women's Activism in Forestry Communities of Northern Vancouver Island." *Gender, Place and Culture* 7, 4 (2000): 363-87.

–. *Taking Stands: Gender and the Sustainability of Rural Communities.* Vancouver: UBC Press, 2003.

Rees, William E. "Ecological Footprints and Appropriated Carrying Capacity: What Urban Economics Leaves Out." *Environment and Urbanization* 4, 2 (October 1992): 121-30.

Reimar, William. "Women as Farm Labor." *Rural Sociology* 15 (1986): 143-55.

Reinharz, S. *Feminist Methods in Social Research.* New York and Oxford: Oxford University Press, 1992.

Reiter, Rayna. *Toward an Anthropology of Women.* New York: Monthly Press, 1975.

Relke, Diana. *Greenwor(l)ds.* Calgary: University of Calgary Press, 1999.

Rich, Louise Dickinson. *We Took to the Woods.* Philadelphia: J.B. Lippincott, 1942.

–. *The Peninsula.* Philadelphia: J.B. Lippincott, 1958.

Richardson, Laurel. "Writing: A Mode of Inquiry." In *Handbook of Qualitative Research,* edited by Norman Denzin and Yvonne Lincoln, 516-19. Thousand Oaks, CA: Sage, 1994.

Ricoeur, Paul. *Lectures on Ideology and Utopia.* New York: Columbia University Press, 1986.

–. "Ideology and Utopia." In *From Text to Action: Essays in Hermeneutics 11,* translated by Kathleen Blamey and John B. Thompson, 308-35. Evanston, IL: Northwestern University Press, 1991.

Robinson, Bart. *Banff Springs: The Story of a Hotel.* Banff, AB: Summerthought, 1973.

Robinson, Eden. *Monkey Beach.* Toronto: Alfred A. Knopf, 2000.

Robinson, M., T. Garvin, and G. Hodgson. *Mapping How We Use Our Land: Using Participatory Action Research.* 3rd ed. Calgary: Arctic Institute of North America, 1994.

Rochefort, David A., and Roger W. Cobb, eds. *The Politics of Problem Definition: Shaping the Policy Agenda.* Lawrence, KS: University Press of Kansas, 1994.

Rockefeller, Stephen, and John Elder, eds. *Spirit and Nature: Why the Environment is a Religious Issue.* Boston: Beacon, 1992.

Rogan, W.J. "Pollutants in Breast Milk." *Archives of Pediatric and Adolescent Medicine* 150 (1996): 981-90.

–, Patricia J. Blanton, Christopher J. Portier, and Eric Stallard. "Should the Presence of Carcinogens in Breast Milk Discourage Breast Feeding?" *Regulatory Toxicology and Pharmacology* 13 (1991): 228-40.

–, and B.C. Gladen. "PCBs, DDE, and Child Development at 18 and 24 Months." *Annals of Epidemiology* 1 (1991): 407-13.

–, and B.C. Gladen. "Breast-Feeding and Cognitive Development." *Early Human Development* 31 (1993): 181-93.

Rolheiser, Ronald. *Against an Infinite Horizon*. London, UK: Hodder and Stoughton, 1995.

–. *Seeking Spirituality*. London, UK: Hodder and Stoughton, 1998.

Room, Adrian. *Brewer's Dictionary of Phrase and Fable*. London, UK: Cassell and Co., 1999 [1870].

Roorda, Randall. *Dramas of Solitude: Narratives of Retreat in American Nature Writing*. Albany: State University of New York Press, 1998.

Rosaldo, Michelle Zimbalist, and Louise Lamphere. *Woman Culture and Society*. Stanford: Stanford University Press, 1974.

Rose, Phyllis. Introduction to *The Norton Book of Women's Lives*, edited by Phyllis Rose, 11-37. New York: Norton, 1993.

Rosowski, Susan. *Birthing a Nation: Gender, Creativity, and the West in American Literature*. Lincoln: University of Nebraska Press, 1999.

Ross, Catherine, and Marieke Van Willigen. "Education and the Subjective Quality of Life." *Journal of Health and Social Behaviour* 38 (September 1997): 275-97.

Rothenberg, David, ed. *Wild Ideas*. Minneapolis: University of Minnesota Press, 1995.

–, and Marta Ulvaeus, eds. *The World and the Wild*. Tucson: University of Arizona Press, 2001.

Rowe Consulting Economists. *Effect of the Crisis in the Newfoundland Fishery on Women Who Work in the Industry*. St. John's, NF: Women's Policy Office, Government of Newfoundland and Labrador, 1991.

Rowe, J. Stan. *Home Place*. Edmonton: NeWest, 1990.

Royal Commission on the Regeneration of Toronto's Waterfront. *Regeneration: Toronto's Waterfront and the Sustainable City: Final Report*. Honourable David Crombie, commissioner. Toronto: Minister of Supply and Services, 1992.

Ruether, Rosemary Radford. *New Woman/New Earth: Sexist Ideologies and Human Liberation*. New York: Seabury Press, 1973.

Rybczynski, Natalia. "Predators and Cosmologies." *The Canadian Journal of Native Studies* 17, 1 (1997): 103-13.

Saad, Layla. "Cultivating Citizenship through Culture: The Use of Participatory Planning Approaches in Community-Based Watershed Management in Santo Andre, Brazil." MSc thesis, University of British Columbia, 2002.

Sachs, C. *Gendered Fields: Rural Women, Agriculture and Environment*. Boulder, CO: Westview Press, 1996.

Salter, Liora. *Mandated Science: Science and Scientists in the Making of Standards*. Boston: Kluwer Academic Publishers, 1988.

Sanders, Rosanne. *The English Apple*. London, UK: Phaidon Press, 1988.

Sandilands, Catriona. "On 'Green Consumerism': Environmental Privatization and 'Family Values.'" *Canadian Women's Studies/Les Cahiers de la Femme* 13, 3 (Spring 1993): 45-47.

–. *The Good Natured Feminist: Ecofeminism and the Quest for Democracy*. Minneapolis: University of Minnesota Press, 1999.

–. "Desiring Nature, Queering Ethics: Adventures in Erotogenic Environments." *Environmental Ethics* 23, 2 (2001): 169-88.

–. "From Unnatural Passion to Queer Nature." *Alternatives Journal* 27, 3 (2001): 30-34.

–. "Cross-Border Natures: Nationalism and Tourism in Waterton-Glacier International Peace Park." In *The American and Canadian Wests: Essays on the History of the Borderlands of the Western United States and Canada*, edited by Sterling Evans. Albuquerque, NM: University of New Mexico Press, forthcoming.

Saul, John Ralston. *The Unconscious Civilization*. Concord, ON: Anansi, 1995.

Schlosser, Eric. *Fast Food Nation: The Dark Side of the All-American Meal*. Boston and New York: Houghton Mifflin, 2001.

Schmitt, Peter J. *Back to Nature: The Arcadian Myth in Urban America*. 1969. Reprint, Baltimore: Johns Hopkins University Press, 1990.

Schneider, Anne, and Helen Ingram. "The Social Construction of Target Populations: Implications for Politics and Policy." *American Political Science Review* 87 (1993): 334-47.

Schueler, Don. *A Handmade Wilderness*. New York: Houghton Mifflin, 1996.

Schultz, Irmgaard. "Women and Waste." *Capitalism, Nature, Socialism* 4, 2 (1993): 51-63.

Seager, Joni. *Earth Follies: Coming to Feminist Terms with the Environmental Crisis*. New York: Routledge, 1993.

Searle, Rick. *Phantom Parks: The Struggle to Save Canada's National Parks*. Toronto: Key Porter, 2000.

Semple, Neil. *The Lord's Dominion*. Montreal and Kingston: McGill-Queen's University Press, 1996.

Shankland, Alex. "Analyzing Policy for Sustainable Livelihoods." In *IDS Research Report 49*. Sussex: Institute for Development Studies, September 2000.

Shapiro, Harry. *Man, Culture and Society*. London, UK: Oxford University Press, 1971.

Shaw, Randy. *The Activist's Handbook: A Primer for the 1990s and Beyond*. Berkeley: University of California Press, 1996.

Shecter, Arnold, John Jake Ryan, and Olaf Papke. "Decrease in Levels and Body Burden of Dioxins, Dibenzofurans, PCBs, DDE, and HCB in Blood and Milk in a Mother Nursing Twins over a Thirty-Eight Month Period." *Chemosphere* 37 (1998): 1807-16.

Shields, Carol. *Voice and Vision*. Ottawa: Borealis Press, 1977.

Shields, Robert. *Places on the Margin: Alternative Geographies of Modernity*. London, UK: Routledge, 1991.

Shiva, Vandana. *Staying Alive: Women, Ecology and Development*. London, UK: Zed Press, 1988.

–. "Development as a New Project of Western Patriarchy." In *Reweaving the World: The Emergence of Ecofeminism*, edited by Irene Diamond and Gloria Feman Orenstein, 189-200. San Francisco: Sierra Club Books, 1990.

–. *The Violence of the Green Revolution: Third World Agriculture, Ecology and Politics*. Atlantic Highlands, NJ: Zed Press; Penang, Malaysia: Third World Network, 1991.

–. *Biopiracy: The Plunder of Nature and Knowledge*. Boston: South End Press, 1997.

–. "Golden Rice and Neem: Biopatents and the Appropriation of Women's Environmental Knowledge." *Women's Studies Quarterly* 29, 1-2 (2001): 12-23.

–, ed. *Close to Home: Women Reconnect Ecology, Health and Development Worldwide*. Philadelphia and Gabriola Island, BC: New Society Publishers, 1994.

Silent Spring Institute. *The Cape Cod Breast Cancer and Environment Study: Results of the First Three Years of Study*. Newton, MA: Silent Spring Institute, 1998. <http://www.silentspring.org/newweb/publications/SilentSpring97report.pdf>.

–. *Cape Cod Breast Cancer and Environment Atlas*. Newton, MA: Silent Spring Institute, 2000. <http://www.silentspring.org/newweb/atlas/index.html>.

Sime, J.A., and D.E. Schuler. "The Park Warden Function in the National Parks Service." Hull, QC: Parks Canada, National Parks Documentation Centre, 1968.

Slipperjack, Ruby. *Honour the Sun*. Winnipeg: Pemmican, 1987.

Slocum, Sally. "Woman the Gatherer: Male Bias in Anthropology." In *Toward an Anthropology of Women,* edited by Rayna Reiter, 36-50. New York: Monthly Press, 1975.

Slovic, Paul, Baruch Fischoff, and Sarah Lichtenstein. "Rating the Risks." *Environment* 21 (1979): 14-20, 36-39.

Smallwood, William Martin. *Natural History and the American Mind*. New York: Columbia University Press, 1941.

Smart, Ninian. *The Religious Experience*. 5th ed. Upper Saddle River, NJ: Prentice Hall, 1996.

Smith, Dorothy. "A Peculiar Eclipsing: Women's Exclusion from Men's Culture." *Women's Studies International Quarterly* 1, 4 (1978): 281-95.

–. *The Everyday World as Problematic: A Feminist Sociology*. Boston: Northeastern University Press, 1997.

Smith, Muriel W.G. *National Apple Register of the United Kingdom*. London, UK: Ministry of Agriculture, Fisheries and Food, 1971.

Smith, Y. "The Household, Women's Employment and Social Exclusion." *Urban Studies* 34, 8 (1997): 1159-78.

Snyder, Gary. *The Practice of the Wild*. San Francisco: North Point Press, 1990.

Songsore, Jacob, and Gordon McGranahan. "The Political Economy of Household Environmental Management: Gender, Environment and Epidemiology." *World Development* 26, 3 (1998): 395-413.

Sontag, Susan. "The Anthropologist as Hero." In *Against Interpretation and Other Essays*, 69-81. New York: Dell, 1969.

Spretnak, Charlene. *States of Grace: The Recovery of Meaning in the Postmodern Age*. San Francisco: Harper, 1991.

Stanton, M. "Social and Economic Restructuring in the Forest Products Industry: A Case Study of Chemainus." MA thesis, University of British Columbia, 1989.

Stanwell-Fletcher, Theodora C. *Driftwood Valley*. 1946. Reprinted as *Driftwood Valley: A Woman Naturalist in the Far North*. New York: Penguin, 1989.

–. *This Tundra World*. Boston: Little-Brown, 1952.

Statistics Canada. *Profile of Census Divisions and Subdivisions*. 1996 Census of Canada, Catalogue number 95-191-XPB. Ottawa: Industry Canada, 1999.

–. *Women in Canada 2000: A Gender-Based Statistical Report*. Ottawa: Ministry of Industry, 2000.

Stone, Deborah A. "Causal Stories and the Formation of Policy Agendas." *Political Science Quarterly* 104 (1988): 281-300.

–. *Policy Paradox: The Art of Political Decision Making*. New York: Norton, 1997.

Struzik, Ed. "Blackrobes: Across the Tundra and Forest, the Oblates Have Left a Quixotic Legacy." *Equinox* 9, 51 (June 1990): 42-55.

Sturgeon, Noël. "Theorizing Movements: Direct Action and Direct Theory." In *Cultural Politics and Social Movements*, edited by Marcy Darnovsky, Barbara Epstein, and Richard Flacks, 35-51. Philadelphia: Temple University Press, 1995.

–. *Ecofeminist Natures: Race, Gender, Feminist Theory and Political Action*. New York: Routledge, 1997.

Sullivan, M.J., S.R. Custance, and C.J. Miller. "Infant Exposure to Dioxin in Mother's Milk Resulting from Maternal Ingestion of Contaminated Fish." *Chemosphere* 23 (1991): 1387-96.

Tarbotton, Rebecca. "Global Connections, Local Transformation: Women, Agriculture and Activism in Ladakh, India." MA thesis, University of British Columbia, 2000.

Telling It Book Collective, ed. *Telling It: Women and Language across Cultures*. Vancouver: Press Gang, 1990.

Teske, E., and B. Beedle. "Journey to the Top: Breaking through the Canopy: Canadian Experiences." Unpublished report for the Canadian Forest Service and British Columbia Ministry of Forests, 2001.

Theberge, John B. "Ecology, Conservation, and Protected Areas in Canada." In *Parks and Protected Areas in Canada: Planning and Management*, edited by Philip Dearden and Rick Rollins, 137-53. Toronto: Oxford University Press, 1993.

Thomas, Clara. "Journeys to Freedom," *Canadian Literature* 51 (1972): 19-26.

Thompson, Elizabeth. *The Pioneer Woman: A Canadian Character Type*. Montreal and Kingston: McGill-Queen's University Press, 1991.

Thompson, Kimberly M., and John D. Graham. "Producing Paper without Dioxin Pollution." In *The Greening of Industry: A Risk Management Approach*, edited by John D. Graham and Jennifer Kassalow Hartwell, 203-68. Cambridge, MA: Harvard University Press, 1997.

Thoreau, Henry David. *Walden*. 1854. Reprint, Princeton. NJ: Princeton University Press, 1971.

–. "Walking." In *The Natural History Essays*. Salt Lake City: Peregrine Smith Books, 1980.

Thurston, John. *The Work of Words: The Writing of Susanna Strickland Moodie*. Montreal and Kingston: McGill-Queen's University Press, 1996.

Tigges, L.M., A. Ziebarth, and J. Farnham. "Social Relationships in Locality and Livelihood: The Embeddedness of Rural Economic Restructuring." *Journal of Rural Studies* 14 (1998): 203-19.

Tovey, Hilary. "Food, Environment and Rural Sociology: The Organic Farming Movement in Ireland." *Sociologica Ruralis* 37, 1 (1997): 21-37.

Traill, Catharine Parr. *Canadian Wildflowers*. Illustrated by Agnes Chamberlain. Montreal: J. Lovell, 1869.

–. *Studies of Plant Life in Canada*. Ottawa: A.S. Woodburn, 1885.

–. *The Canadian Crusoes*. Toronto: McClelland and Stewart, 1923.

–. *The Backwoods of Canada*. Edited by Michael Peterman. Ottawa: Carleton University Press, 1997.

–. *Pearls and Pebbles*. Edited by Elizabeth Thompson. Toronto: Natural Heritage Books, 1999.

Tripp-Knowles, P. "The Feminine Face of Forestry in Canada." In *Challenging Professions: Historical and Contemporary Perspectives on Women's Work*, edited by E. Smyth, E. Acker, and P. Bourne, 194-211. Toronto: University of Toronto Press, 1999.

Trower, P. *Chainsaws in the Cathedral: Collected Woods Poems, 1964-1998*. Victoria, BC: Ekstasis Editions Canada, 1999.

Trumpener, Katie. *Bardic Nationalism: The Romantic Novel and the British Empire*. Princeton, NJ: Princeton University Press, 1997.

Tucker, L. Norman. *Western Canada: Handbooks of English Church Expansion*. London, UK: A.R. Mowbray, 1908.

Turnbull, Colin. *The Mountain People*. New York: Simon and Schuster, 1972.

Turner, Jack. *The Abstract Wild*. Tucson: University of Arizona Press, 1996.

Tuttle, Charles R. *Our North Land: Being a Full Account of the Canadian North-West and Hudson's Bay Route, together with a Narrative of the Experiences of the Hudson's Bay Expedition of 1884*. Toronto: C. Blackett Robinson, 1885.

Tyrrell, J.W. *Across the Sun-Arctics of Canada: A Journey of 3,200 Miles by Canoe and Snowshoe through the Barren Lands*. Toronto: William Briggs, 1897.

United States Environmental Protection Agency (EPA). *Health Assessment Document for 2,3,7,8-Tetrachlorodibenzo-p-dioxin (TCDD) and Related Compounds*. External review draft, 1994.

–. *Estimating Exposure to Dioxin-Like Compounds*. Vol. 1, *Executive Summary*. External review draft, 1994.

Valaskakis, Gail Guthrie. "Postcards of My Past: Indians and Academics." In *Between Views*, edited by Daina Augaitis and Sylvie Gilbert, 31-35. Banff, AB: Banff Centre for the Arts, 1991.

Van Den Hengel, John. *The Home of Meaning: The Hermeneutics of the Subject of Paul Ricoeur*. Washington, DC: University Press of America, 1982.

van den Hombergh, Heleen. *Gender, Environment and Development: A Guide to the Literature*. Utrecht, Netherlands: International Books, 1993.

van Herk, Aritha. *Judith*. Toronto: McClelland and Stewart, 1978.

–. *The Tent Peg*. Toronto: McClelland and Stewart, 1981.

–. *No Fixed Address: An Amorous Journey*. Red Deer, AB: Red Deer College Press, 1986.

–. "Cather in Ecstasy." Paper presented at the International Cather Seminar, Quebec City, Quebec, June 1995.

Van Kirk, Sylvia. *"Many Tender Ties": Women in Fur Trade Society in Western Canada, 1670-1870*. Winnipeg: Watson and Dwyer, 1980; reissued as *Many Tender Ties*. Norman, OK: University of Oklahoma Press, 1983.

Van Strum, Carol, and Paul Merrell. *No Margin of Safety: A Preliminary Report on Dioxin Pollution and the Need for Emergency Action in the Pulp and Paper Industry*. Greenpeace, US, 1987.

Vance, Linda. "Ecofeminism and Wilderness." *National Women's Studies Association Journal* 9, 3 (1997): 60-77.

Verduyn, Christl. "The Grace of Living and Writing: An Interview with Aritha van Herk." In *Aritha van Herk: Essays on Her Works*, edited by Christl Verduyn, 31-44. Toronto: Guernica, 2001.

–, ed. *Aritha van Herk: Essays on Her Works*. Toronto: Guernica, 2001.

Visweswaran, Kamala. *Fictions of Feminist Ethnography*. Minneapolis: University of Minnesota Press, 1994.

Wadland, John. "Wilderness and Culture." In *Consuming Canada: Readings in Environmental History*, edited by Chad Gaffield and Ann Gaffield, 12-15. Toronto: Copp Clark, 1995.

Wallace, Archer. *Blazing New Trails*. Toronto: Musson, 1928.

Wallace, Iain. *A Geography of the Canadian Economy*. Toronto: Oxford University Press, 2002.

Wallace, W. Stewart. *The Growth of Canadian National Feeling*. Toronto: Macmillan, 1927.

War Resisters League. *Reviving Resistance: Tools for Anti-Nuclear Organizing in the Age of Terror*. New York: War Resisters League, 2002. <http://www.warresisters.org>.

Warkentin, Germaine. *Canadian Exploration Literature: An Anthology: 1660-1860*. Toronto: Oxford University Press, 1993.

Weaver, Emily P. *Canada and the British Immigrant*. London, UK: Religious Tract Society, 1914.

Weytjens, K.A., A. Cartier, J.L. Malo, P. Chrétien, F. Essiembre, S.B. Lehrer, et al. "Aerosolized Snow-Crab Allergens in a Processing Facility." *Allergy* 54, 8 (1999): 892-93.

Whatmore, S. *Farming Women: Gender, Work and Family Enterprise*. London, UK: Macmillan, 1991.

–, R. Marsden, and P. Lowe. "Feminist Perspectives in Rural Studies." In *Gender and Rurality*, edited by S. Whatmore, T. Marsden, and P. Lowe, 1-10. London, UK: David Fulton, 1994.

White, Gilbert. *The Natural History of Selborne*. Edited by Richard Mabey. Harmondsworth: Penguin Books, 1977.

White, James, ed. *Conservation of Fish, Birds and Game: Proceedings at a Meeting of the Committee on Fisheries, Game and Fur-Bearing Animals, Commission of Conservation Canada, November 1 and 2, 1915*. Toronto: Methodist Book and Publishing House, 1916.

Williams, Raymond. *The Country and the City*. London, UK: Hogarth Press, 1985.

Williams, Susan. *Our Lives Are at Stake: Women and the Fishery Crisis in Newfoundland and Labrador*. ISER Report No. 11. St. John's, NF: Institute of Social and Economic Research, Memorial University, 1996.

–. "What's Happening with Youth? The Impact of Economic Change on Young People in Newfoundland and Labrador." Report prepared for Health Canada Health Promotion and Programs Branch, Atlantic Region, by the Canadian Mental Health Association, Newfoundland and Labrador Division, St. John's, NF, 1998.

–, and Barbara Neis. *Stress, Repetitive Strain Injuries and Fishplant Workers in Newfoundland*. St. John's, NF: Institute of Social and Economic Research, Memorial University, 1993.

Wood, Dennis, and John Fels. *The Power of Maps*. New York: Guilford Press, 1992.

Woodsworth, James. *Thirty Years in the Canadian North-West*. Toronto: McClelland, Goodchild, and Stewart, 1917.

Wordsworth, Dorothy. "Floating Island at Hawkhead: An Incident in the Schemes of Nature." In *English Romantic Writers*, edited by David Perkins. Fort Worth, TX: Harcourt Brace College Publishers, 1995.

Wordsworth, William. "Ode: Intimations of Immortality from Recollections of Early Childhood." In *English Romantic Writers*, edited by David Perkins, 329-34. Fort Worth, TX: Harcourt Brace College Publishers, 1995.

World Commission on Environment and Development (WCED). *Our Common Future*. New York: Oxford University Press, 1987.

World Conservation Monitoring Centre (WCMC). *Protected Areas Database*. Cambridge, UK: WCMC, May 1999.

World Health Organization (WHO). *Assessment of Health Risks in Infants Associated with Exposure to PCBs, PCDDs and PCDFs in Breast Milk*. Copenhagen: WHO, 1988.

–, European Centre for Environment and Health. "Contamination with Dioxin of Some Belgian Food Products." 1999. <http://www.who.dk/envhlth/dioxin/dioxin.htm>.

World Resources Institute. *World Resources 1992-93*. New York: Oxford University Press, 1992.

World Wildlife Fund Canada. "Setting Conservation Priorities in the Twenty-First Century." In *The Nature Audit: Report No. 1-2003*. Toronto: World Wildlife Fund Canada, 2003, <http://www.wwf.ca/About-WWF/WhatWeDo/TheNatureAudit.asp?page=0.1>.

Worster, Donald. *Nature's Economy: A History of Ecological Ideas*. Cambridge: Cambridge University Press, 1985.

Wright, Billie. *Four Seasons North: A Journal of Life in the Alaskan Wilderness*. New York: Harper Collins, 1973.

Wright, M. "Women in the Newfoundland Fishery." In *Framing Our Past: Canadian Women's History in the Twentieth Century,* edited by S.A. Cook, L.R. McLean, and K. O'Rourke, 343-46. Toronto: Oxford University Press, 2001.

Yalom, Marilyn. *A History of the Breast.* New York: Ballantyne, 1997.

Yepsen, Roger. *Apples.* New York: Norton, 1994.

Youmans, Letitia. *Campaign Echoes: The Autobiography of Mrs. Letitia Youmans, the Pioneer of the White Ribbon Movement in Canada, Written by the Request of the Provincial Woman's Christian Temperance Union of Ontario.* 3rd ed. Toronto: William Briggs, 1893.

Young, Egerton Ryerson. *By Canoe and Dog-Train among the Cree and Salteaux Indians.* London, UK: Charles H. Kelly, 1903.

Young, Iris Marion. *Justice and the Politics of Difference.* Princeton, NJ: Princeton University Press, 1990.

Zeller, Suzanne. *Inventing Canada: Early Victorian Science and the Idea of a Transcontinental Nation.* Toronto: University of Toronto Press, 1987.

Contributors

Leonora C. Angeles (PhD) is an assistant professor at the University of British Columbia.

Katherine Dunster is a consulting conservation ecologist and landscape architect working on the West Coast of Canada. She holds a PhD in geography from the University of Toronto and an MLArch in landscape architecture from the University of Guelph.

Heather Eaton is a professor at St. Paul's University, Ottawa. Her areas of research and teaching include religion, feminism, ecology, and transformative social movements.

Jo-Anne Fiske (PhD) is a professor and co-ordinator of Women's Studies at the University of Lethbridge.

Brenda Grzetic is a PhD student at Memorial University of Newfoundland.

Kathryn Harrison (PhD) is an associate professor in the Department of Political Science at the University of British Columbia.

Melody Hessing (PhD) is a faculty member in the Department of Sociology and Anthropology at Douglas College, New Westminster, BC, an adjunct professor at Simon Fraser University, and a research associate at the University of British Columbia.

Anne L. Kaufman (PhD) specializes in Western American and Canadian women writers. She teaches at Milton Academy.

Sherilyn MacGregor (PhD) currently holds a SSHRC postdoctoral fellowship in the Centre for the Study of Environmental Change at Lancaster University.

Martha McMahon (PhD) is an associate professor in the Department of Sociology at the University of Victoria, BC.

Barbara Neis (PhD) is a professor in the Department of Sociology at Memorial University, NF.

Daniel O'Leary (PhD) specializes in the study of Victorian Canadian and Victorian literature and intellectual culture. He teaches in the Department of English at the University of British Columbia.

Rebecca Raglon (PhD) teaches in the Department of English and the Foundations Program at the University of British Columbia.

Maureen G. Reed (PhD) is a professor in the Department of Geography at the University of Saskatchewan. Her areas of study include environmental policy, women, and issues in environmental management.

Randall Roorda (PhD) is an associate professor in the Department of English at the University of Kentucky and author of *Dramas of Solitude: Narratives of Retreat in American Nature Writing*.

Layla Saad recently completed her MA in the School of Community and Regional Planning, University of British Columbia.

Catriona Sandilands (PhD) is an associate professor in the Faculty of Environmental Studies at York University and Canada Research Chair in Sustainability and Culture.

Marian Scholtmeijer (PhD, LLB) teaches at the University of Northern British Columbia.

Rebecca Tarbotton recently completed her MA in the School of Community and Regional Planning, University of British Columbia.

Index

Note: The letter "t" after a page number refers to a table.

Printed and bound in Canada by Friesens

Set in Stone by Artegraphica Design Co. Ltd.

Copy editor: Robert Lewis

Proofreader: Deborah Kerr

Indexer: Noeline Bridge